Essays on the Ancient Near East

JACOB J. FINKELSTEIN
(1922-1974)

Memoirs of the

Connecticut Academy of Arts & Sciences

December *Volume XIX* *1977*

Essays on the Ancient Near East

in Memory of Jacob Joel Finkelstein

EDITED BY

MARIA DE JONG ELLIS

Published for the Academy

by

ARCHON BOOKS

HAMDEN, CONNECTICUT

First published 1977 for the Academy by Archon Books,
Hamden, Connecticut.
Printed in the United States of America

Library of Congress Cataloging in Publication Data

Main entry under title:

Essays on the ancient Near East in memory of
Jacob Joel Finkelstein.

(Memoirs of the Connecticut Academy of Arts and Sciences ; v. 19)
"Bibliography of Jacob J. Finkelstein," by P. Machinist and N. Yoffee: p.
Includes index.
1. Assyro-Babylonian philology—Addresses, essays, lectures. 2. Near East—Civilization—Addresses, essays, lectures. 3. Finkelstein, Jacob J., 1922–1974—Addresses, essays, lectures. I. Finkelstein, Jacob J., 1922–1974. II. Ellis, Maria deJ. III. Series: Connecticut Academy of Arts and Sciences, New Haven. Memoirs ; v. 19.
Q11.C85 vol. 19 [PJ3189] 492'.1 77-14136
ISBN 0-208-01714-3

TABLE OF CONTENTS

FOREWORD

Jacob Joel Finkelstein came to Yale University in 1965 as the William M. Laffan Professor of Assyriology and Babylonian Literature. The very next year he convened, with characteristic vigour and enthusiasm, an Assyriological Colloquium at Yale. This was the first of what became a series of informal, pleasant, and fruitful gatherings of cuneiformists from the Northeastern states, held every December in New Haven. He had arranged the meeting of 1974 when he was stricken and died, suddenly and unexpectedly, on Thanksgiving Day, the 28th of November.

The idea of a memorial collection of essays grew out of the Assyriological Colloquium, and when questions arose about a proper place of publication, the publications committee of the Connecticut Academy of Arts and Sciences found it very natural to offer a volume of the Academy's Memoirs for the purpose. Indeed, Jack Finkelstein was a valued and active member of the Academy, as are many of the contributors to this volume.

Two particular acknowledgments of indebtedness are in order: to Dr. Maria deJong Ellis who not only performed all the usual thankless tasks of an editor, but also supervised the composition of the text at the Babylonian Section of the University Museum in Philadelphia and actually did much of it herself; and to Professor Philip Finkelstein, Jack's younger brother, whose generosity helped us produce this volume at a reasonable price without sacrifice of quality or appearance.

Finally a more personal remark. It is now nearly three years since Jack died, but I have yet to realise fully that he is gone forever. Quite often when, say, I discover a nice new tobacco, or hear a singularly clever—or stupid—remark, I find myself thinking that this I must share with Jack, only to be brought up short. Indeed, he seems so very ill-suited to be dead for those who knew him well. To those who did not I hope that this volume will convey at the very least a sense of the deep affection he kindled in those who knew him, and who shared his concerns and commitments.

Asger Aaboe
Academiae Praeses

New Haven, July 1977

Editorial Remarks

When the Assyriological Colloquium met in New Haven soon after Jack Finkelstein's unexpected and untimely death, it was decided to produce a volume of studies honoring his memory—and expressing his colleagues' appreciation for the contributions to Assyriology he made. Implicit in this appreciation, of course, is the acknowledgment that much that he intended to do now may never be done. Jack was moving into new and different fields; having long had an interest in theoretical aspects of legal systems and their development, he published *The Goring Ox: Some Historical Perspectives on Deodands, Forfeitures, Wrongful Death and the Western Notion of Sovereignty* in 1973. This was to have been the third and final section of a much longer work, *The Ox that Gores*. He finished a complete draft of that study shortly before his death; it is hoped that the work still may be published in some form.

The volume of studies presented here includes contributions by those colleagues whom Jack drew together every year in the Yale Assyriological Colloquium (see p. 103 of this volume for a list of meeting topics), and by former students of his, as well as by several colleagues from elsewhere. Considerations of size unfortunately forced us to limit contributions in the latter category.

The scholars who participated in this endeavor are all active in various aspects of Near Eastern studies. We felt, however, that it would be appropriate to cast some light on Jack's activities in the area of the theory of law also, and we therefore asked Professor Leon Lipson of the Yale Law School if we could include in this volume the text of the memorial tribute which he read at the service held in Jack's memory at Yale on December 17, 1974.

The editorial committee for this volume consisted of Jerrold S. Cooper, Norman Yoffee, and myself. I would like to thank the other members of the committee, and Martha Roth, for their assistance in the preparation of this book.

Maria deJ. Ellis

Philadelphia, August 1977

LIST OF ABBREVIATIONS

AAA	Liverpool Annals of Archaeology and Anthropology
AASF	Annales Academiae Scientiarum Fennicae
"AB"	tablets in the collection of the Bodleian Library, Oxford; now housed in the Ashmolean Museum
ABAW	Abhandlungen der Bayerischen Akademie der Wissenschaften
AbB	Altbabylonische Briefe in Umschrift und Übersetzung
AbKM	Deutsche Morgenländische Gesellschaft, Abhandlungen für die Kunde des Morgenlandes
ABL	R. F. Harper, Assyrian and Babylonian Letters
ACT	O. Neugebauer, Astronomical Cuneiform Texts
AD	G. R. Driver, Aramaic Documents from the 5th Century B.C.
ADD	C. H. W. Johns, Assyrian Deeds and Documents
AfK	Archiv für Keilschriftforschung
AfO	Archiv für Orientforschung
AGE	K. Tallqvist, Akkadische Götterepitheta (ASSF 43/1)
AHw	W. von Soden, Akkadisches Handwörterbuch
AJSL	American Journal of Semitic Languages and Literatures
AKA	E. A. W. Budge and L. W. King, The Annales of the Kings of Assyria
AMT	R. Campbell Thompson, Assyrian Medical Texts . . .
An	lexical series An=*Anum*
AnBi	Analecta Biblica
ANES	Journal of the Ancient Near Eastern Society of Columbia University
ANET	J. B. Pritchard, Ancient Near Eastern Texts Relating to the Old Testament
Annuaire	Annuaire de l'École Pratique des Hautes Études, IVe Section
AnOr	Analecta Orientalia
AnSt	Anatolian Studies
AO	tablets and objects in the collections of the Musée du Louvre
AOAT(S)	Alter Orient und Altes Testament (Supplement)
AOS	American Oriental Series
AP	A. E. Cowley, Aramaic Papyri from the 5th Century B.C.
APAW	Abhandlungen der Preußischen Akademie der Wissenschaften
ARM	Archives royales de Mari (=TCL 22—)
ARMT	Archives royales de Mari, Textes
ArOr	Archiv Orientální
ARU	J. Kohler and A. Ungnad, Assyrische Rechtsurkunden
AS	Assyriological Studies (Chicago)
ASSF	Acta Societatis Scientiarum Fennicae
Ass.	field numbers of tablets and objects excavated at Assur
Assur	M. Lidzbarski, Altaramäische Urkunden aus Assur
BA	Beiträge zur Assyriologie . . .
Bab.	Babyloniaca
Bagh.Mitt.	Baghdader Mitteilungen
Balkan, Schenkungsurkunde	K. Balkan, Eine Schenkungsurkunde aus der althethitischen Zeit, Gefunden in Inandık 1966

Barnett-Falkner, Sculptures	R. D. Barnett and M. Falkner, The Sculptures of Assur-naṣir-apli II (883-859 B.C.), Tiglath-pileser III (745-727 B.C.), Esarhaddon (681-669 B.C.) from the Central and South-west Palaces at Nimrud
Barrelet, Figurines	M.-T. Barrelet, Figurines et reliefs en terre cuite de la Mésopotamie antique, 1
BASOR	Bulletin of the American Schools of Oriental Research
BBSt	L. W. King, Babylonian Boundary Stones
BE	Babylonian Expedition of the University of Pennsylvania, Series A: Cuneiform Texts
Ben-Yehuda, Thesaurus	Eliezer Ben Yehuda, Thesaurus Totius Hebraitatis (A Complete Dictionary of Ancient and Modern Hebrew)
Berger, Königsinschriften	Die neubabylonischen Königsinschriften (AOAT 4/1)
BiAr	The Biblical Archaeologist
Bib.	Biblica
Biggs, Šaziga	R. D. Biggs, ŠÀ.ZI.GA: Ancient Mesopotamian Potency Incations (TCS 2)
BiOr	Bibliotheca Orientalis
Birot, Tablettes	M. Birot, Tablettes économiques et administratives d'époque babylonienne ancienne conservée au Musée d'Art et d'Histoire de Genève
BM	tablets in the collections of the British Museum
BMS	L. W. King, Babylonian Magic and Sorcery
Bo.	museum numbers of unpublished tablets excavated at Boghazköi
Boissier, Choix	A. Boissier, Choix de textes relatifs à la divination assyro-babylonienne
Boissier, DA	A. Boissier, Documents assyriens relatifs au présages
Borger, Einleitung	R. Borger, Einleitung in die assyrischen Königsinschriften, 1
Borger, Esarh.	R. Borger, Die Inschriften Asarhaddons, Königs von Assyrien (AfO Beiheft 9)
Borger, HKL	R. Borger, Handbuch der Keilschriftliteratur
Brinkman, Political History	J. A. Brinkman, A Political History of Post-Kassite Babylonia, 1158-722 B.C. (AnOr 43)
BRM	Babylonian Records in the Library of J. Pierpont Morgan
BSGW	Berichte über die Verhandlungen der Königlichen Sächsischen Gesellschaft der Wissenschaften zu Leipzig
BSOAS	Bulletin of the School of Oriental and African Studies
Budge, Assyrian Sculptures	E. A. W. Budge, Assyrian Sculptures in the British Museum: Reign of Ashurnaṣir-pal 885-860 B.C.
CAD	The Assyrian Dictionary of the Oriental Institute of the University of Chicago
Cagni, Erra	L. Cagni, L'epopea di Erra
CAH	The Cambridge Ancient History
CBQ	Catholic Biblical Quarterly
CBS	tablets in the collections of the University Museum of the University of Pennsylvania, Philadelphia
CCNA	F. M. Fales, Censimenti e catasti di epoca Neo-Assira
Craig, ABRT	J. A. Craig, Assyrian and Babylonian Religious Texts
CRRA	Compte rendu, Rencontre Assyriologique Internationale
CT	Cuneiform Texts from Babylonian Tablets in the British Museum
CUA	tablets in the collections of the Catholic University of America
DEA	L. Delaporte, Épigraphes araméens

Diri	lexical series diri DI *siāku*=(*w*)*atru*
DISO	C.-F. Jean and J. Hoftijzer, Dictionnaire des inscriptions sémitiques de l'ouest
Dream-book	A. L. Oppenheim, The Interpretation of Dreams in the Ancient Near East (Transact. of the American Philosophical Society, 46/3)
D.T.	tablets in the collections of the British Museum
Ea	lexical series ea A=*nâqu*
Ebeling, Handerhebung	E. Ebeling, Die akkadische Gebetsserie Šu-ila "Handerhebung" (VIO 20)
Edzard, Gesellschaftsklassen	D. O. Edzard (ed.), Gesellschaftsklassen im alten Zweistromland, 18 RAI
Edzard, Zweite Zwischenzeit	D. O. Edzard, Die "Zweite Zwischenzeit" Babyloniens
Ellis, Agriculture	M. deJ. Ellis, Agriculture and the State in Ancient Mesopotamia
Ellis, Domestic Spirits	R. S. Ellis, Domestic Spirits: Apotropaic Figurines in Mesopotamian Buildings
Ellis, Taxation	M. deJ. Ellis, "Taxation in Ancient Mesopotamia: The History of the Term *miksu*," JCS 26 (1974) 211-50
En.el.	*Enūma eliš*
ERE	encyclopedia of Religion and Ethics
Erimḫuš	lexical series erimḫuš=*anantu*
Falkenstein, ATU	A. Falkenstein, Archaische Texte aus Uruk
Fish, Letters	T. Fish, Letters of the First Babylonian Dynasty in the John Rylands Library, Manchester
FLP	tablets in the John Frederick Lewis Collection of the Free Library of Philadelphia
Frank, Beschwörungsreliefs	C. Frank, Babylonische Beschwörungsreliefs (LSS 3/3)
Frankfort, Cylinder Seals	H. Frankfort, Cylinder Seals: A Documentary Essay on the Art and Religion of the Ancient Near East
FuB	Forschungen und Berichte (Berlin)
Gadd, Teachers	C. J. Gadd, Teachers and Students in the Oldest Schools
Garelli, Gilg.	P. Garelli, Gilgameš et sa légende: Études reçueillies par Paul Garelli à l'occasion de VIIe RAI
Geiger, Urschrift	Abraham Geiger, Urschrift und Übersetzungen der Bibel in ihrer Anhängigkeit von der Innern Entwicklung des Judentums
Genouillac, Kich	H. de Genouillac, Premières recherches archéologiques à Kich
Gesenius-Buhl, Handwb.	Gesenius-Buhl, Hebräisches und aramäisches Handwörterbuch über das Alte Testament
Gibson, Kish	A. McGuire Gibson, The City and Area of Kish
Gilg.	Gilgāmeš epic, cited from Thompson Gilg. (M.=Meissner Fragment, OB Version of Tablet X, P.=Pennsylvania Tablet, OB Version of Tablet II, Y.=Yale Tablet, OB Version of Tablet III)
Goetze, AM	A. Götze, Die Annalen des Muršiliš (MVAG 38)
Goetze, Kleinasien	A. Götze, Kleinasien zur Hethiterzeit: Eine geographische Untersuchung
Goldziher, Philologie	I. Goldziher, Abhandlungen zur arabischen Philologie
Gössmann, Era	F. Gössman, Das Era-Epos
Grayson, Chronicles	A. K. Grayson, Assyrian and Babylonian Chronicles (TCS 5)
Grayson, Royal Inscriptions	A. K. Grayson, Assyrian Royal Inscriptions (Records of the Ancient Near East, 1-2)
Green, Eridu	Eridu in Sumerian Literature (University of Chicago dissertation, 1975)
Groneberg, Dialekt	B. Groneberg, Untersuchungen zum hymnisch-epischen Dialekt de-

	altbabylonischen literarischen Texte (Munster dissertation, 1971)
Güterbock, Kumarbi	H. G. Güterbock, Kumarbi: Mythen vom churritischen Kronos (Istanbuler Schriften 16)
Güterbock, Siegel	H. G. Güterbock, Siegel aus Boğazköy (AfO Beiheft 5, 7)
Hallo and van Dijk, Exaltation of Inanna	W. W. Hallo and J. van Dijk, The Exaltation of Inanna (YNER 3)
Hatt.	Annals of Hattušili, cited after A. Götze, Ḫattušiliš (MVAG 29/3)
Heuzey, Figurines antiques	L. Heuzey, Les figurines antiques de terre cuite du Musée du Louvre
Ḫḫ	lexical series ḪAR.ra=*ḫubullu*
Hoffner, Al.Heth.	H. A. Hoffner, Jr., Alimenta Hethaeorum (AOS 55)
HSS	Harvard Semitic Series
HTR	Harvard Theological Review
HUCA	Hebrew Union College Annual
HWb (Erg.)	J. Friedrich, Hethitisches Wörterbuch (Ergänzungsheft)
IBoT	Istanbul Arkeoloji Müzelerinde bulunan Boğazköy tabletleri(nden seçme metinler) 1-2
Idu	lexical series Á=*idu*
IEJ	Israel Exploration Journal
IM	tablets and objects in the Iraq Museum
Image of Tammuz	T. Jacobsen, The Image of Tammuz and Other Essays (W. L. Moran, ed.)
Ist.Mitt.	Istanbuler Mitteilungen
JAOS	Journal of the American Oriental Society
JBL	Journal of Biblical Literature
JCS	Journal of Cuneiform Studies
JNES	Journal of Near Eastern Studies
JRAS	Journal of the Royal Asiatic Society
JTVI	Journal of the Transactions of the Victoria Institute
K.	tablets in the Kouyunjik collection of the British Museum
KAH	Keilschrifttexte aus Assur historischen Inhalts
KAI	H. Donner and W. Röllig, Kanaanäische und aramäische Inschriften
Kammenhuber, HW^2	J. Friedrich and A. Kammenhuber, Hethitisches Handwörterbuch (2nd rev. ed.)
KAR	Keilschrifttexte aus Assur religiösen Inhalts
Kaufman, Influences	S. A. Kaufman, The Akkadian Influences on Aramaic (AS 19)
KB	Keilinschriftliche Bibliothek
KBo	Keilschrifttexte aus Boghazköi
Ki(sh)	tablets excavated at Kish in the Ashmolean Museum, Oxford
Knudtzon, Gebete	J. A. Knudtzon, Assyrische Gebete an den Sonnengott
Koehler, Lexikon	L. Koehler and W. Baumgartner, Hebräisches und aramäisches Lexikon zum alten Testament
Kraus, Texte	F. R. Kraus, Texte zur babylonischen Physiognomatik (AfO Beiheft 3)
Krecher, Kultlyrik	J. Krecher, Sumerische Kultlyrik
KUB	Keilschrifturkunden aus Boghazköi
Kupper, Les Nomades	J.-R. Kupper, Les Nomades en Mésopotamie au temps des rois de Mari
Labat, Manuel	R. Labat, Manuel d'épigraphie accadienne
Lambert, BWL	W. G. Lambert, Babylonian Wisdom Literature

Lambert-Millard, Atra-ḫasīs	W. G. Lambert and A. R. Millard, Atra-ḫasīs: The Babylonian Story of the Flood
Landsberger, Date Palm	B. Landsberger, The Date-Palm and Its By-Products According to the Cuneiform Sources (AfO Beiheft 17)
Langdon, Exc. Kish	S. Langdon, Excavations at Kish
Laroche, DDL	E. Laroche, Dictionnaire de la langue louvite
Lenormant, Choix	F. Lenormant, Choix de textes cunéiformes inédits ou incomplètement publiés jusqu'à ce jour
LIH	L. W. King, The Letters and Inscriptions of Ḫammurabi
Lipiński, Studies	E. Lipiński, Studies in Aramaic Inscriptions and Onomastics, 1
LKA	E. Ebeling, Literarische Keilschrifttexte aus Assur
LKU	A. Falkenstein, Literarische Keilschrifttexte aus Uruk
LSS	Leipziger Semitistische Studien
LTBA	Die lexikalischen Tafelserien der Babylonier und Assyrer in den Berliner Museen
Luckenbill, ARAB	D. D. Luckenbill, Ancient Records of Assyria and Babylonia
LXX	The Septuagint
MAD	Materials for the Assyrian Dictionary
Madhloom, Chronology	T. Madhloom, The Chronology of Neo-Assyrian Art
MAH	tablets in the collections of the Musée d'Art et d'Histoire, Geneva
Malku	synonym list *malku=šarru*
MAOG	Mitteilungen der Altorientalischen Gesellschaft
MDOG	Mitteilungen der Deutschen Orient-Gesellschaft
MDP	Mémoires de la Délégation en Perse
Meier, Maqlu	G. Meier, Die assyrischen Beschwörungssammlung Maqlû (AfO Beiheft 2)
MIO	Mitteilungen des Instituts für Orientforschung, Berlin
MLC	tablets in the collections of the J. Pierpont Morgan Library; now housed in the Yale University Babylonian Collection
MSL	Materialien zum sumerischen Lexikon
Muffs, Elephantine	Y. Muffs, Studies in the Aramaic Legal Papyri from Elephantine (SD 8)
MVAG	Mitteilungen der Vorderasiatisch-Aegyptischen Gesellschaft
N	tablets from Nippur in the collections of the University Museum of the University of Pennsylvania, Philadelphia
N-T	field numbers of tablets excavated at Nippur by the Oriental Institute and other institutions
NA	Neo-Assyrian
Nabnitu	lexical series SIG_7+ALAM=*nabnītu*
NBC	tablets in the Babylonian Collection, Yale University
ND	field numbers of tablets and objects excavated at Nimrud (Kalḫu)
Ni	tablets excavated at Nippur, in the collections of the Archaeological Museum, Istanbul
Nigga	lexical series nigga=*makkūru* (published MSL 13 91-124)
Noth, IPN	M. Noth, Die israelitische Personnamen
NRVU	M. San Nicolò and A. Ungnad, Neubabylonische Rechts- und Verwaltungs-urkunden
OAkk	Old Akkadian

OB	Old Babylonian
OBGT	Old Babylonian Grammatical Texts (published MSL 4 47-128)
OECT	Oxford Editions of Cuneiform Texts
OLZ	Orientalistische Literaturzeitung
Or. (NS)	Orientalia (Nova Series)
OrAnt	Oriens Antiquus
PAPS	Proceedings of the American Philosophical Society
PBS	Publications of the Babylonian Section, University Museum of the University of Pennsylvania, Philadelphia
PN	personal name
Postgate, Royal Grants	J. N. Postgate, Neo-Assyrian Royal Grants and Decrees (Studia Pohl series maior 1)
Proto-Ea	see Ea (published MSL 2 35-94)
Proto-Izi	lexical series (published MSL 13 7-59)
Proto-Kagal	lexical series (published MSL 13 63-88)
PRT	E. Klauber, Politisch-religiöse Texte aus der Sargonidenzeit
PRU	Palais royale d'Ugarit
PSBA	Proceedings of the Society of Biblical Archaeology
PUL	tablets in the collections of the Université de Liège
R	H. C. Rawlinson, The Cuneiform Inscriptions of Western Asia
RA	Revue d'assyriologie et d'archéologie orientale
RAcc	F. Thureau-Dangin, Rituels accadiens
RAI	Rencontre Assyriologique Internationale
Rép.Géog.	Répertoire géographique des textes cunéiformes
RHA	Revue hittite et asianique (f.=fascicle number follows, not volume number)
Riemschneider, Landschenkungsurkunden	K. K. Riemschneider, "Die hethitischen Landschenkungsurkunden," MIO 6 (1958) 321-81
RLA	Reallexikon der Assyriologie
RLV	Reallexikon der Vor- und Frühgeschichte
Rm.	tablets in the collections of the British Museum
Roberts, Pantheon	J. J. M. Roberts, The Earliest Semitic Pantheon
Römer, Königshymnen	W. H. Ph. Römer, Sumerische 'Königshymnen' der Isin-Zeit
RS	field numbers of tablets excavated at Ras Shamra
RSP	L. Fisher, Ras Shamra Parallels
RSV	Revised Standard Version of the Bible
Sa	lexical series Syllabary A (published MSL 3 3-45)
SAI	B. Meissner, Seltene assyrische Ideogramme
SAKI	F. Thureau-Dangin, Die sumerischen und akkadischen Königsinschriften (VAB 1)
Salonen, Hippologica	A. Salonen, Hippologica Accadica (AASF 100)
Salonen, Türen	A. Salonen, Die Türen des alten Mesopotamien (AASF 124)
Sb	lexical series Syllabary B (published MSL 3 96-128, 132-53)
SB	Standard Babylonian
SBAW	Sitzungsberichte der Bayerischen Akademie der Wissenschaften
Schramm, Einleitung	W. Schramm, Einleitung in die assyrischen Königsinschriften, 2

v. Schuler, Dienstanw.	E. von Schuler, Hethitische Dienstanweisungen für höhere Hof- und Staatsbeamte (AfO Beiheft 10)
Seux, Épithètes	M.-J. Seux, Épithètes royales akkadiennes et sumériennes
Sjöberg, Temple Hymns	Å W. Sjöberg and E. Bergmann, The Collection of Sumerian Temple Hymns (TCS 3)
SLOB	S. J. Lieberman, Sumerian Loanwords in Old Babylonian Akkadian (HSS 21)
ŠL	A. Deimel, Šumerisches Lexikon
von Soden, GAG	W. von Soden, Grundriß der akkadischen Grammatik (AnOr 33)
von Soden, Syllabar²	W. von Soden, Das akkadische Syllabar (AnOr 42)
Sollberger, Corpus	E. Sollberger, Corpus des inscriptions "royales" présargoniques de Lagaš
SPAW	Sitzungsberichte der Preußischen Akademie der Wissenschaften
Speleers, Reçueil	L. Speleers, Reçueil des inscriptions de l'Asie antérieure des Musées Royaux du Cinquantenaire à Bruxelles
SRT	E. Chiera, Sumerian Religious Texts
Stark, Names	J. K. Stark, Personal Names in Palmyrene Inscriptions
StBoT	Studien zu den Boğazköy-Texten
STC	L. W. King, The Seven Tablets of Creation
StOr	Studia Orientalia, Helsinki
STT	O. R. Gurney, J. J. Finkelstein, and P. Hulin, The Sultantepe Tablets
Studia Orientalia Pedersen	Studia orientalia Ioanni Pedersen dicata
Studies Landsberger	H. G. Güterbock and T. Jacobsen, eds., Studies in Honor of Benno Landsberger on His 75th Birthday, April 21, 1965 (AS 16)
S.U.	tablets excavated at Sultantepe-Urfa
Symbolae Bohl	M. A. Beek, A. A. Kampman, C. Nijland and J. Ryckmans, eds., Symbolae Biblicae et Mesopotamicae Francisco Mario Theodoro de Liagre Böhl dedicatae
Symbolae David	J. A. Ankum, R. Feenstra, W. F. Leemans, eds., Symbolae Iuridicae et historicae Martino David dedicatae. Tomus alter: Iura Orientis antiqui
Szlechter, TJA	E. Szlechter, Tablettes juridiques et administratives de la IIIe Dynastie d'Ur et de la Ire Dynastie de Babylone
Szlechter, Tablettes	E. Szlechter, Tablettes juridiques de la 1re Dynastie de Babylone
Tallqvist, APN	K. Tallqvist, Assyrian Personal Names (ASSF 43/1)
Tallqvist, Götterepitheta	K. Tallqvist, Akkadische Götterepitheta (StOr 7)
Tallqvist, NBN	K. Tallqvist, Neubabylonisches Namenbuch (ASSF 32/2)
Tammuz	see Image of Tammuz
TCL	Textes cunéiformes du Louvre
TCS	Texts from Cuneiform Sources
TDOT	Theological Dictionary of the Old Testament
Tell Halaf	J. Friedrich et al, Die Inschriften vom Tell Halaf (AfO Beiheft 6)
Thompson, Devils	R. Campbell Thompson, Devils and Evil Spirits of Babylonia and Assyria
Thompson, Gilg.	R. Campbell Thompson, The Epic of Gilgamish
TSBA	Transactions of the Society of Biblical Archaeology
TuL	E. Ebeling, Tod und Leben nach den Vorstellungen der Babylonier
TuM	Texte und Materialien der Frau Professor Hilprecht Collection of Babylonian Antiquities im Eigentum der Universität Jena
U.	field numbers of tablets and objects excavated at Ur

UCP	University of California Publications in Semitic Philology
UE	Ur Excavations
UET	Ur Excavations, Texts
UVB	Vorläufiger Bericht über die Ausgrabungen im Uruk-Warka
VA Ass.	objects from Assur in the collections of the Vorderasiatische Museen, Berlin
VAB	Vorderasiatische Bibliothek
Van Buren, Clay Figurines	E. Douglas Van Buren, Clay Figurines of Ancient Mesopotamia
Van Buren, Foundation Figurines	E. Douglas Van Buren, Foundation Figurines and Offerings
VAS	Vorderasiatische Schriftdenkmäler
VAT	tablets in the collections of the Staatliche Museen, Berlin
VBoT	A. Götze, Verstreute Boghazköi-Texte
VIO	Veröffentlichungen des Instituts für Orientforschung, Berlin
VT	Vetus Testamentum
W.	field numbers of tablets and objects excavated at Uruk/Warka
Waterman, Royal Correspondence	L. Waterman, Royal Correspondence of the Assyrian Empire
Weidner, Reliefs	E. Weidner, Die Reliefs der assyrischen Könige, 1: Die Reliefs in England, in der Vatikan-Stadt und in Italien (AfO Beiheft 4)
Wilcke, Lugalbanda	C. Wilcke, Das Lugalbandaepos
Wiseman, Treaties	D. J. Wiseman, The Vassal Treaties of Esarhaddon (Iraq 20/1)
WO	Die Welt des Orients
WVDOG	Wissenschaftliche Veröffentlichungen der Deutschen Orient-Gesellschaft
WZJ	Wissenschaftliche Zeitschrift der Friedrich-Schiller-Universität Jena
WZKM	Wiener Zeitschrift für die Kunde des Morgenlandes
YBC	tablets in the Babylonian Collection, Yale University Library
YNER	Yale Near Eastern Researches
YOR	Yale Oriental Series, Researches
YOS	Yale Oriental Series, Babylonian Tablets
ZA	Zeitschrift für Assyriologie
ZAW	Zeitschrift für alttestamentliche Wissenschaft
ZDMG	Zeitschrift der Deutschen Morgenländischen Gesellschaft
Zimmern, Fremdw.	H. Zimmern, Akkadische Fremdwörter . . ., 2nd. ed.
Zimmern, Ištar und Ṣaltu	H. Zimmern, Ištar und Ṣaltu: Ein akkadisches Lied (BSGW, phil.-hist. Kl. 68/1)
Zimolong, Vokabular	B. Zimolong, Das sumerisch-assyrische Vokabular Ass. 523, herausgegeben mit Umschrift und Kommentar (Leipzig dissertation, 1922)

A TEXT CONCERNING SUBDIVISION OF THE SYNODIC MOTION OF VENUS FROM BABYLON: BM 37151

Asger Aaboe
Yale University

Peter J. Huber
Swiss Federal Institute of Technology

We dedicate this short paper to the memory of Jacob Finkelstein, our good friend and colleague, in the fond belief that he would have received it, as he did our other work, with fiercely defiant protestations of his inability to understand *one single* word of it.

Introduction

Among the Babylonian planetary theories,[1] that for Venus is by far the worst documented, and the need for new texts concerning this planet is obvious. It is therefore disappointing that the present text—the only Venus text but one[2] to come to light since the publication of ACT—rather seems to introduce new problems instead of helping us toward solutions of the old.

The concern of the Venus theory in the ACT material is with six characteristic synodic phenomena which are (as for Mercury)

Ξ :	(*ina* šú . . . igi)	= first visibility	in the West (evening)
Ψ :	(*ina* šú . . . uš)	= stationary point	
Ω :	(*ina* šú . . . šú)	= last visibility	
Γ :	(*ina* nim . . . igi)	= first visibility	in the East (morning)
Φ :	(*ina* nim . . . uš)	= stationary point	
Σ :	(*ina* nim . . . šú)	= last visibility	

in the terminology of ACT.

Times and longitudes for a sequence of one of these phenomena are computed according to methods which we understand imperfectly. It is clear, however, that unlike all other planetary schemes, the procedures for Venus belong to neither of the two major systems of mathematical astronomy, System A and System B.[3]

The basic feature of the Venus schemes is the relation that five consecutive synodic phenomena of the same kind (e.g., five consecutive stationary points Φ) correspond to a progress in longitude of eight full revolutions in the ecliptic less 2;30°. In respect of date, five such phenomena lead to an advance of 99 synodic months less four days. In the lunar calendar this time interval is either eight years less four days, or eight years plus one month less four days, depending on where in the intercalary cycle the phenomena fit. This part of the Venus theory is, of course, well understood, and it is based on excellent values of mean synodic arc and mean synodic time.

What is not under control is the principle according to which the five phenomena are distributed, in longitude and time, within one eight-year cycle. A comparison of the preserved Venus longitudes and dates with modern tables[4] shows, on the whole, very good agreement. It may well be that the Venus texts are closer in character to the Goal-Year texts, as Sachs[5] calls them, than to standard ephemerides of the ACT type, and that the excellence of the eight-year period and the regular behavior of Venus prevented the development of more sophisticated theories for this planet by making it unnecessary.

The present text, we repeat, throws no new light on these problems. It introduces us to a subdivision of the

1. For details consult O. Neugebauer, Astronomical Cuneiform Texts (3 vols., London, 1955) and A History of Ancient Mathematical Astronomy, Studies in the History of Mathematics and the Physical Sciences 1 (in 3 parts) (Berlin-Heidelberg-New York, Springer, 1975).
2. O. Neugebauer and A. Sachs, "Some Atypical Astronomical Cuneiform Texts I," JCS 21 (1967) 183-218, Text C ii.
3. Asger Aaboe, "On Period Relations in Babylonian Astronomy," Centaurus 10 (1964) 213-31.
4. Brian Tuckerman, Planetary, Lunar, and Solar Positions 601 B.C. to A.D. 1, American Philosophical Society (1962).
5. A. Sachs, "A Classification of the Babylonian Astronomical Tablets of the Seleucid Period," JCS 2 (1948) 271-90, and "Babylonian Observational Astronomy," Phil. Trans. Royal Soc. London, Ser. A276 (1974) 43-50.

Ancient Near Eastern Studies in Memory of J. J. Finkelstein
Connecticut Academy of Arts and Sciences, Memoir 19

synodic motion of Venus into parts within each of which the daily progress of Venus is considered constant, if our tentative reconstruction is correct, in analogy to well documented procedures for other planets.[6]

Text: BM 37151 (80-6-17, 901)=37249 (80-6-17, 1003)[7]
Contents: Venus for 8 years
Provenance: Babylon (based on BM number)
Date: S.E. 181-199 (?)
Transcription: Figure 1

Obverse 1.	[ina šú	10	absin	igi]
	[	]19	má[š	]
	[ ]	2	múl-múl [	]
	[ ]	24	múl-múl [	]
5.	[ ]	25;20	múl-múl	uš[ ]
	[ina šú]	18;40	múl-múl	šú[ ]
	[ina ni]m	15;20	múl-múl	igi[ ]
	[ ]	7?;40?	múl-múl	uš[ ]
	[ ]	2?;40?	maš-maš	ta 15?[ ]
10.	[ ]	2[9;20?	a]	ta 1 en 1[ ]
	[ina] nim	28[	máš	šú] ta? 12 en?[ ]
	[ina] šú	1[0+x	ḫun	igi]
	[ ]	2[0+x	ă	]
	[ ]	[		]
15.	[ ]	[		]
	[ ]	[		uš]
	[ ]8 ina šú	[		šú]
	[ ]9 ina nim	[		igi]
	[ ]	[		uš]
20.	[ ]	[		]
	[ ]	11[...	hun	]
	[ ]4? ina nim	10 [	ăbsin	šú]
	[ ]1? ina šú	22 [	gír	igi]
	[ ]	29;30 [	zib	]
25.	[ ]	11;30 [	$alla_x$	]
26-30 destroyed				
31-39 destroyed				
Reverse 1'=40.	[ ]4? ina nim			igi]
	[ ]5?	24[	gu	uš]
	[ ]5?	19? [	zib	]
	[ ]5?	15?;40? [	maš-maš	]
	[ ] ina nim	17	g[ír	šú]
6'=45	[ ]10 ina šú	2	gu [	igi]
	[ ]2?	9;30	maš-[maš	]
	[ ]1?	21;30	absin[	]
	[	13	rín [	]
	[	14;40	rín	uš[ ]
11'=50	[ ]2? ina šú	10;40	rín	šú[ ]
	[ ] ina nim	5;20	rín	igi[ ]
	[ ]	28;20	absin	uš[ ]
	[ ]	23;20	rín	[ ]
	[ ]	20	máš	[ ]
16'=55	[ ]7? ina nim	26;30	maš	šú[ ]
	[ ] ina šú	7;30	absin	i[gi]
	[ ] 2,30 ki	[		]
	[ ] šá 8 aná 8?[mu?			]
Rest destroyed				

Fig. 1: BM 37151

6. See Neugebauer, ACT and P. Huber, "Zur täglichen Bewegung des Jupiter nach babylonischen Texten," ZA 52 (1957) 265-303.

7. The text is published through the courtesy of the Trustees of the British Museum. A. Aaboe's visits to the British Museum were supported by a Guggenheim Fellowship and by various grants from the National Science Foundation.

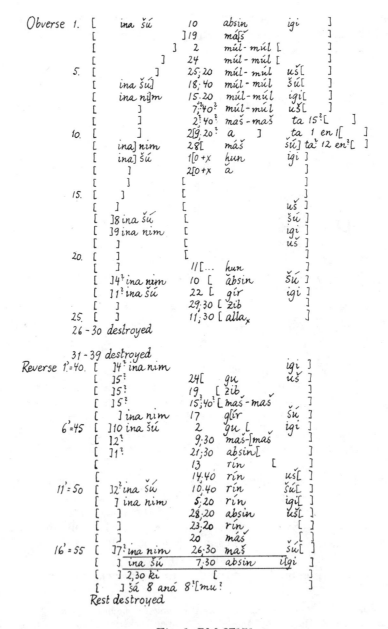

Description of Text

The text consists of two fragments which we rejoined, and it is now ca. 3½″ high and 1½″ wide. No edges are preserved. There is a catch line, between horizontal rulings, and a colophon at the bottom of its reverse, and we believe that only one line is missing at the beginning of the obverse. If this is so, the text covers precisely one eight-year cycle, beginning and ending, counting the catch line, with first visibility in the evening (Ξ).

The surface of the obverse is crumbling badly (salt), but the writing on the reverse is small, sharp, and neat. The text employs exclusively the three-wedge, cursive form of "9." In the transcription we follow A. Sachs in using $alla_x$ (KUŠÚ) for the zodiacal sign Cancer.

In Obverse, line 18′, the colophon has [ ] 2,30 ki, i.e., 2;30° in longitude, and in the next line we read *šá* 8 *aná* 8 (?) [mu] or, freely rendered, by eight-year intervals. These two statements alone would serve to identify our fragment as a Venus text.

Commentary

The text gives dates and longitudes of a sequence of phenomena for Venus. Of the dates, no years, no months, but only a few badly preserved day numbers remain and the longitudes alone do not allow us to date it securely. It is reasonable to assume that it belongs to the Seleucid period, and if so it must refer to 8 years near S.E. 191 (= -120); the next earlier possible date would be near -371. If we compare our text to other Babylonian texts (ACT Nos. 400 and 420) and to modern tables we find that its longitudes would fit best if it began in -128, and slightly worse if in -120. The traces of dates, particularly in lines 17 and 18 which suggest an interval of invisibility of only one day, agree better with a beginning in -120. We tend to prefer this later date since the agreement in longitudes is none too good in either case. Thus modern tables give stationary points for Venus on -122 March 16 at $\lambda = 329.9°$ and on -121 September 5 at 187.8°.[8] The differences to the longitudes of our text's lines 41 and 49 are, then, 0.1° and 6.9°, respectively, whereas we for that epoch would expect a systematic difference of some 4.7° due to the difference between Babylonian and modern conventions of counting longitudes.

The unique feature of our text is that it considers five new events in addition to the six standard synodic phenomena, three of them between Ξ and Ψ, and two between Φ and Σ. We are not aware of any particular situations of Venus that are both astronomically significant and occur regularly in the required number. Thus this subdivision of Venus's synodic travel was very likely introduced for computational purposes, and, we believe, consists in a partition of the synodic period into intervals during each of which the planet was taken to move with constant speed. All eleven phenomena—new and old—would then mark points of discontinuity of Venus's velocity, quite in analogy to the Babylonian theory for Jupiter's daily progress.[9] Indeed, the phrases "ta . . . en" (= "from . . . to") at the ends of line 9-11 are reminiscent of procedure texts for the daily motion of Jupiter (e.g., ACT No. 810).

Since the dates are largely destroyed, it is not possible to reconstruct the details of the scheme with any degree of certainty. Some synodic arcs (Ξ to Ξ) seem to agree very closely (within 1°) with their mean value 575;30°. Some (Σ to Σ) oscillate by about 4° around it. Further, the different lengths of the retrograde stretches (lines 5ff.: 6;40 + 3;20 + 7;40 = 17;40, and lines 49ff.: 4 + 5;20 + 7 = 16;20) suggest that the planet is assumed to behave differently on different parts of the ecliptic. One could reproduce such a differentiated behavior either (i) by letting both velocities and durations of the stretches of uniform motion depend on the position in the ecliptic, or (ii) by changing only the durations while keeping the velocities fixed.

The Jupiter schemes employ the former device (i). The present text could in principle be explained by (ii), if one is willing to assume at least two scribal errors (19 for 20 in line 2, and 26;30 for 27;30 in line 55) and one rounding to the nearest integer (in line 44, 16;55 rounded to 17). Then, a possible scheme would be the following where the unbracketed time intervals correspond to lines 1-12, those in parentheses to lines 45-56:

after Ξ :	104	(102)	days with		1;15	degrees per	day
	90	(90)	"	"	1; 8	" "	"
	44	(43)	"	"	0;30	" "	"
to Ψ :	4	(5)	"	"	0;20	" "	"
Ψ to Ω :	20	(12)	"	"	-0;20	" "	"

8. Tuckerman, op. cit.

9. Huber, ZA 52 (1957) 265-303.

Ω to Γ :	10	(16)	"	"	-0;20	"	"	"
Γ to Φ :	23	(21)	"	"	-0;20	"	"	"
after Φ :	30	(30)	"	"	0;50	"	"	"
	80	(80)	"	"	1; 5	"	"	"
to Σ :	119	(126)	"	"	1;15	"	"	"
Σ to Ξ :	62?	(56)	"	"	1;15	"	"	"

We used days as units of time in analogy to the Jupiter schemes, though the employment of *tithis* (1 synodic month = 30 *tithis*) is not excluded. The velocity 1;15 occurs elsewhere in ACT No. 1013, a text of otherwise unknown significance. The total motion over the entire eleven phenomena would be 575;35° in 586 days (575;30° in 581 days).

The details of the reconstructed scheme are, of necessity, advanced with all sorts of reservations, but the fact of the subdivision of the synodic motion of Venus into eleven parts in this text remains beyond doubt.

LES NOMS DE MARDUK, L'ÉCRITURE ET LA "LOGIQUE" EN MÉSOPOTAMIE ANCIENNE

J. Bottéro
École Pratique des Hautes Études, Paris

> In our approach towards any aspect of non-Western civilization we commonly expose ourselves to the hazard of applying Western categories to phenomena completely alien to us . . .
>
> J. J. Finkelstein, "Mesopotamian Historiography," Proceedings of the American Philosophical Society 107/6 (1963) 461a.

1. Depuis que L. W. King les a publiées, en 1902, dans STC 2 51-60, on n'a quasiment rien ajouté aux deux tablettes retrouvées en fragments incomplets et dispersés, parmi la Bibliothèque d'Assurbanipal, et qui représentent apparemment, en deux exemplaires, à peu près la moitié d'un seul et même texte.

Du premier (**A**), recomposé de Sm 11+980 (STC 2 51-53) +Sm 1416 (pl. 55) +K.4406 (pl. 54s) +82-3-23,151 (pl. 54), à quoi il faut ajouter K.13614 (CT 19 6) +K.11168 (RA 17 [1920] 169), nous avons le début; de l'autre (**B**), qui regroupe Rm 366+80-7-19, 288+293 (pl. 56-58) +K.2053 (pl. 59s) +K.8299 (pl. 60), la fin.

Il semble bien, du reste, qu'on ne se soit guère intéressé, depuis, à cette oeuvre, et que nul n'ait éprouvé le besoin de pousser l'analyse sommaire que King en avait donnée dans STC 1 157ss. L'étrange prétention de S. Langdon, qui voulait y retrouver "un texte sumérien de la VIIme tablette du Poème de la Création" (PSBA [1910] 115ss et 159ss), a été proprement exécutée par A. Ungnad (ZA 31 [1915s] 153ss), démontrant qu'il n'y avait là rien d'autre qu'une sorte de "commentaire"[1] pour expliquer, à sa façon, ces Noms de Marduk dont l'énumération paraphrasée termine l'*En.el.*: aussi F. M. Th. Böhl, par exemple, en a t'il tenu compte dans son étude: "Die fünfzig Namen des Marduk" (AfO 11 [1936s] 191s). Mais personne n'est allé plus loin, ni ne s'est posé la moindre question sur le *comment* et le *pourquoi* d'un tel type d'explication, et encore moins sur le mode de vision des choses qu'il implique.

2. Pour en discuter ici, même compendieusement, il sera plus commode de placer d'emblée sous les yeux du lecteur la transcription de ce qu'il nous reste dudit "commentaire,"[2] remis dans l'ordre de l'*En.el.*,[3] dont le texte, pour plus de clarté, sera reproduit, en parallèle.

En.el. VII 1.	**^{d}ASARI(RI)**	**(A) Sm 11+: f. i**	**[^{d}AS]ARI**		**(RI)** *šá-rik*
	šarik			RU	*šá-ra-ku*
	mêrešti			SAR	*me-reš-tu*
	šâ				
	eṣrata		SI	A	*eṣ-ra-tu*
	ukinnu			RÁ	*ka-a-nu*

4

1. Le colophon de (**B**) (fin du §2) lui donne au moins le titre de *ṣâtu* (U_4.UL.DÙ.A), c'est-à-dire (CAD Ṣ 119a; AHw. 2 1097a) une sorte de "liste de mots extraits du texte et expliqués," définition qui, on le verra (notamment §4 et n. 34), ne s'applique que d'une façon assez particulière à notre document, lequel, par ailleurs, diffère notablement des textes que nous qualifions couramment, entre nous, de "commentaires." C'est donc par approximation que nous lui garderons ce nom. On sait, d'ailleurs, que nul assyriologue n'a encore entrepris de préciser, *en historien*, la typologie et la nomenclature des ouvrages rédigés ou compilés par les vieux "philologues" de Babylone, lexicographes, grammairiens, annotateurs ou commentateurs (comp. M. Civil en JNES 33 [1974] 329; voir encore la n. 62 et W. G. Lambert en AfO 17 [1954] 320).

2. Une édition critique, qui aurait exigé au moins le réexamen des originaux, sinon la recherche d'éventuels duplicats, m'a paru inutile pour mon présent dessein. La transcription qu'on aura sous les yeux a seulement tenu compte du caractère particulier, du but et de l'esprit du document, non moins que des règles qui le commandent, expliqués plus loin (§§3s) tout du long: c'est là qu'on trouvera justifiées un certain nombre de lectures peut-être d'abord inattendues ou de restitutions apparemment téméraires. Chaque morceau subsistant du "commentaire" est précédé de l'indication des fragments de tablettes qui en préservent le texte (le §1 fournit les références à leur autographie dans STC 2, ou ailleurs). Les Noms respectifs de Marduk, qui introduisent chaque "couplet" de la Liste, vu leur importance, sont imprimés partout en capitales, ce qui vaut également pour le texte entier du présent article où, au surplus, *Nom* (avec majuscule) renvoie toujours à l'un d'eux. Lorsque, dans la suite du "commentaire," un de ces Noms est dérobé par quelque lacune, on le trouve, entre parenthèses, en tête du fragment, ou du groupe de fragments qu'il intéresse, dans la colonne réservée au texte de l'*En.el.* (voir par exemple 15; 35, etc; avant 135, ^{d}**NÊBIRU** n'est pas répété, parce que c'est toujours lui, depuis 126, qui commande ce verset).

3. Texte ("reçu") de W. G. Lambert-S. B. Parker, Enuma eliš (1966).

Ancient Near Eastern Studies in Memory of J. J. Finkelstein
Connecticut Academy of Arts and Sciences, Memoir 19

2.	*banû*	RU	RÚ	*ba-nu-u* [4]
	še'am		SAR	*še-em*
	u			
	qê	MA	SAR	*qu-ú*
	mušêṣû		MA$_4$	*a-ṣu-ú*
	urqît[i]		SAR	*ár-qu*
3.	^{d}**ASAR.ALIM**	^{d}**ASAR**		**ALIM**
	šâ			
	ina			
	bît	[?]	SA	*bi-i-tú*
	milki		SÁ	*mil-ku*
	kabt[u]		ALIM	*kab-tu*
	šûturu		SA	*at-ru*
	milik-šu		SÁ	*mil-ku*
4.	*ilû*		DINGIR	*i-lu*$_4$
	utaqqû<-šu>	[S]À?	SA	*ú-qu-u*
	adir		SA$_5$	*a-da-ru*
	lâ	[S]À?		
	aḫzu		SA$_5$	*a-ḫa-zu*
5.	^{d}**ASAR.ALIM.NUN.NA**	[^{d}**ASA]R̊**	.	**ALIM.NUN.NA**
	karûbu	[		*k]a-[r]u-b[u]*
	.....		.....	.....
9.	^{d}**TU.TU**	(B) Rm 366+: f. i [^{d}**T]U.TU**		*ba-nu-ú*
	bân		TU	*ba-nu-u*
	têdišti-šunu		TU	*e-de-šú*
	š[û]-ma		DA	*šu-ú*
10.	*lillil*	[?]	TU$_9$	*el-lu*$_4$
	sagî-šunu-ma	[?]	DÙ	*sa-gu-ú*
	šunu	[?]	[D]A	*šu-ú*
	lû	[?]	[DA?]	*lu-ú*
	[p]a[š]ḫu		[DU$_6$.D]U?	*pa-šá-ḫu*
11.	*libnî-ma*		TU	*[ba-nu]-ú*
	šipta		TU$_6$	*šip-[t]u*$_4$
	ilî		DINGIR	*i-l[u*$_4$*]*
	linûḫû		TI	*na-a-ḫu*
12.	*aggiš*		TU$_4$	*a-ga-gu*
	lû		DA [5]	*lu-ú*
	tebû		TU$_4$	*te-bu-ú*
	linê'û		TU	*na-'-ú*
	[irat-s]un		DU$_8$	*ir-tu*
13.	*lû*		DA	*lu-ú*

4. Ligne de séparation omise, comme en 10, 84, 103, 121.

5. Ecrit ŠA; mais comp. début de 13, et contexte.

šušqû-ma		DA	*šá-qu-ú*
ina	MU	TA	*i-n[a]*
puḫur		TU$_6$	*p[u-uḫ-ru]*
ilī		DINGIR	*[i-lu$_4$]*
[abbê]-šu		D[INGIR	*a-bu]*
. . . . .		. . . . .	. . . . .

{ }[6]

(15. ^{d}**TU.TU.**^{d}**ZI.UKKIN.NA**) (B) K.2053: f. + (A) Sm.11+: f. ii

17. *alkat-sun*		ZI	*[a-la-ku?]*
iṣbatu-ma		ZI	*[ṣa-ba-tu?]*
u'addû		ZU	*[e-du-u]*
[manzas-sun]		NA	*ma[n-za-zu]*
18. *ai*		TA	*a-[a]*
immaši		TU$_9$/ZÌ	*b[a-]/z[u]*[7]
ina		TA	*i!*[8]*-[na]?*
apâti		UKKIN	*a-p[a-(a)-tu?]*
epšêta-[šu]		TU	*ep-še-[tu]*
[likillâ]		DU$_8$	*ku-u[l-lu]*
19. ^{d}**TU.TU.**^{d}**ZI.KÙ**	^{d}**KIMIN.AN.NA.**		**ZI.KÙ.GA**[10]
šalšiš[10]			
imbû		DÙ	*ba-nu-⌜ú⌝*
mukîl		DÙ	*na!*[10]*-bu-ú*
têlilti		ZI	*ka-a-nu*
		KÙ	*el-lu$_4$*
		KÙ	*te-lil-tu$_4$*
20. *il*	TU	DINGIR	*i-lu$_4$*
šâri	DU	TU$_{15}$	*šá-a-ri*
ṭâbi		DU$_{10}$	*ṭa-a-bu*
bêlu		DINGIR	*be-lu$_4$*
tašmê		ZI	*še-mu-ú*
u			
magâri		ZI	*ma-ga-rù*
21. *mušabši*		ZI	*ba-šu-ú*
ṣimri		KÙ	*ṣi-im-ru*
u			
kubuttê		KU$_6$	*ku-bu-ut-te-e*
mukîn		ZI	*ka-a-n[u]*
ḫegalli	[	]	*ḫé-g[ál-lu?]*
. . . . .		. . . . .	. . . . .

{ }[9]

6. Ligne de séparation marquée ici par erreur, comme en 18.

7. Si l'on en juge à ce qu'il subsiste de son premier signe, seul conservé, le terme accadien n'est sûrement pas le *mašû* du texte "reçu": variante.

8. Ecrit A[B], au moins d'après la copie de King.

9. Voir n. 6.

10. Noter la double variante, dont la seconde est peut-être seulement graphique, dans le Nom de Marduk. Autre variante: *mukîn*, au lieu du *mukil* du texte "reçu." Le "commentateur" semble avoir oublié, ou omis, *šalšiš*, en tête (voir encore n. 57), et il a écrit, par erreur, NI-*bu-u* au lieu de NA-*bu-u*.

(35. ^{d}ŠÀ.ZU)	(B) K.8299: f. + (A) Sm.11+: f. iii			
37. *mukîn*		[	ZI?	*ka-a-nu?]*
puḫri		[	ŠÀ?	*pu-u]ḫ-rù*
šâ				
ilī		[	DINGIR	*i]-lu*$_4$
muṭîb		[	ŠA$_6$?	*ṭa-a]-bu*
libbi-šun		[	ŠÀ	*lib]-bi*
38. *mukanniš*			Z[I?	*ka-n]a-šú*
lâ				
mâgiri			ZI	*[ma]-gi-ri*
ṣ[ulû]l-šun			ZU	*[ṣu-l]u-lu*
rapšu			ZU	*ra-pa-šú*
(39.)			omis	
40. *šâ*				
sarti			ZU	*sar-tu*$_4$
u				
k[it]tu			ZI	*k[a]-a-n[u]*
umtassâ			ZU	*m[u-u]s!-su-u*
ašruš-šu			ZI	*[aš]-rù*
. . . . .			. . . . .	. . . . .
82. ^{d}**A.GILIM.MA**	(A) K.4406: r. i	^{d}<A?>	**.GILIM.**	**MA**
šaqû			ÍL	*šá-qu-[u]*
nasiḫ			MA	*na-sa-[ḫu]*
agî			GIL(ĬM)	*a-gu-[u]*
ašir			GIL(IM)	*a-šá-[ru]*
šal[g]i			GIL(IM)	*šal-g[u]*
			šar a-gi-i	*šar-ra-[ḫu?]*
83. *banû*			MA	*ba-nu-u*
erṣeti			IM	*er-ṣ[e-tu]*
eliš			DINGIR	*e-[lu-u?]*
mê			MU$_9$	*mu-[u]*
mukîn			GI	*ka-[a-nu]*
elâti			DINGIR	*e-[lu-u?]*
84. ^{d}**ZU.LUM**			^{d}**ZU.**	**[LUM]**
mu'addi			ZU	*[e-du-u?]*
qerbîti		UL	ÙL	*[qer-bi-tu]*
ana			DINGIR	*[a-na?]*
ilī			DINGIR	*[i-lu*$_4$*]*
palik			Z[U	*pa-la-ku?]*
binûti			UL	*[bi-nu-tu?]* [11]
85. *nadin*			M[U?	*na-da-nu?]*
isqi			Z[U	*is-qu?]*
u				

11. Voir n. 4.

nindabê		ZI	ZÌ	[*nin-da-bu-u*?]
pâqidu			DING[IR	*pa-qa-du*?]
ešrêti			Z[Í?	*e-šir-tu*?]
86. *ilu*			U[L?	?]
mummu		*mu-um-m*[*u*		?]
			DIN[GIR	?]
		mu-um-m[*u*		?]
. . . . .		. . . . .		. . . . .
91. **^{d}LUGAL.ÁB.DUBÚR**	(A) K.11169	[**^{d}LUGAL**		**ÁB.DUBÚR**?]
šarru			[LUGAL	*šarru*]
sapiḫ		DU	B[ÍR	*sa-pa-ḫu*?]
epšêt			DÙ	*e*[*p-še-tu*]
Tiamat			AB	*tam-tim*
nasiḫu		DU	BU	*na-sa-ḫu*
kakki-[*šá*]			DÙ	*kak*-[*ku*]
92. *šâ*			LÚ	[*šá-a*]
ina				
rêši			DIN[GIR	*re-e-šu*?]
. . . . .			. . . . .	. . . . .
(93. **^{d}PA$_4$.GAL.GÚ.EN.NA**)	(A) K.4406: r. ii			
94. *šâ*		[		]
ina		[		*i*]-*na*
ilî			[DINGIR]	*i-lu*$_4$
aḫḫê-šu			[PA$_4$?]	*a-ḫu*
šurbû			[GAL?]	*šu-ur*!-*bu-u*[12]
			[GAL?]	*ra-bu-u*
etel				*e-tel-lum*
napḫar-šun			[GÚ]	*nap-ḫa-rù*
95. **^{d}LUGAL.DUR.MAḪ**		[^{d}]**LUGAL.**		**DÚR.MAḪ**[13]
šarru			LUGAL	*šar-ru*
markas			DÚR	*mar-ka-su*
ilî			DINGIR	*i-lu*$_4$
bêl			LUGAL	*be-lu*$_4$
Durmaḫi			DÚR.MAḪ	*dur-ma-ḫu*
96. *šâ*			LÚ	*šá-a*
ina			DÚR	*i-na*
šubat			DÚR	*šub-tu*$_4$
šarrûti			LUGAL	*šar-ru*
šurbûti			MAḪ	*ru-bu-u*
an			DÚR	*a-na*
ilî			DINGIR	*i-lu*$_4$
maʾdiš			MAḪ	*ma-ʾ-du*
ṣîru			MAḪ	*ṣi-i-ri*

12. Ecrit RU.

13. Variante graphique DÚR/DUR dans le Nom.

97. **^{d}A.RÁ.NUN.NA**		**^{d}A.RÁ.**	**NUN.NA**
mâlik		A.RÁ	*mil-ku*
^{d}Éa	RU	NUN	*^{d}É-a*
bân		RÚ	*ba-nu-u*
ilī		DINGIR	*i-lu$_4$*
abbê-[*šu*]		A	*a-bu*
98. *šâ*		RA	*šá-a*
ana		RA	*a-na*
alakti		A.[R]Á	*a-lak-tu*
rubûti-šu		N[UN]	[*r*]*u*?!*-bu-u*
lâ		NU	[*l*]*a-a*
umaššalu		RÚ	[*ma-šá-lu*?]
ilu		DIN[GIR	*i-lu$_4$*]
aiium-ma	[		*a-a-um-ma*?]
[			]
. . . . .		. . . . .	. . . . .

(101. **^{d}LUGAL.ŠU!.AN.NA**) (A) K. 13614

102.	. . . .	. . . . .
nibût	[	*n*]*i*?*-b*[*u*?]
Anšar	[ ]	*An-*[*šar*?]
103. **^{d}IR.UG$_5$.GA**	[^{d}]**IR.**	**Ú.G[A]**[14]
šalil	[ ] IR	*šá-la-l*[*u$_4$*]
gimri-šunu	[G]Ú	*gim-ri*
qerbiš	[IR$_5$?]	*qé-re-bu*
Tiamat	[ ]	*tam-tim*
	←→	←→ [15]
104. *šâ*		
napḫar	[GÚ?]	*nap-ḫa-ru*
uzni	[GE$_{14}$?]	*uz-nu*
iḫmumu	[UR$_4$?	*ḫa-ma*]*-mu*
ḫasîsa	[GI?	*ḫa-si-su*?]
palki	[GI?	*pal-ku*]
	[	]

(107. **^{d}KIN.MA**) (A) K.4406: r. iii

108. *šâ*	[	]
ana	[	]
šume-šu	[MU?	*šu-mu*?]
ilû	[DINGIR	*i-l*]*u*?
kîma	[	*ki-m*]*a*?
meḫê	[IM?	*me-ḫu*]*-u*
	[*me-ḫu-u*	*ša-a*]*-ru*
išubbû	[	*ša*]*-a-bu*
palḫiš	[ ]	*p*[*al*]*-ḫiš*
	[ ]	MIN?
109. **^{d}É.SISKUR$_x$**	[**^{d}É.**]	**SISKUR$_x$**
šaqîš	[ ] IL	*šá-qu-u*
ina	[ ] RA	*i-na*
bît	[ ] É	*bi-i-tú*

14. Variante graphique UG$_5$/Ú.GA dans le Nom.

15. Voir n. 4.

ikribi	SISKUR$_x$	*ik-ri-bu*
	RA	*ra-mu-u*
lišîb-ma	RA	*a-šá-bu*
110. *ilû*	DINGIR	*i-lu$_4$*
maḫri-šu	[S]I$_{17}$	*maḫ-ru*
lišêribu	[GU]R$_8$?[16]	*e-re-bu*
kadrâ-šun	[SISKUR$_x$?]	*kàd-ru-u*
111. *a-di*	[	*a*]-*di*
irib-šunu	[SISKUR$_x$?	*ir*]-*b*[*u*]
. . . . .	. . . .	. . . . .

(B) K.2053: r. ii + (A) Sm 11+: r. i

112.		
mamman	[	]
ina	RA [	]
bali-šu	[	]
lâ	RU	
ibannâ	RU RÚ	[*ba-nu-u*?]
niklâte	RÚ	[*na-ka-lu*?]
113.	[I]S$_5$?	[ ][17]
erba	*er-bu*	[ ]
ṣalmat qaqqadi	RI	[*ṣalmat qaqqadi*?
binâtuš-šu	RU R[Ú]	*ba-nu-ú*?]
114. *ela*	E[$_{11}$	*e-lu-u*?]
šâšu	RA	[*šu-ú*?]
ṭême	KU[18]	[*ṭe-e-mu*?]
ûmê-šina	U$_4$	[*u-mu*]
lâ	RA	[*la-a*]
i'adda	ZU	[*e-du-u*]
ilu	DINGIR	[*i-lu$_4$*]
mamman	ZU	[*mam-man*?]
115. **^{d}GIBIL**	**^{d}GI[BIL**	*mu-ki-in*?]
mukîn	GI	[*ka-a-nu*]
aṣât	RU R[Ú!	*a-ṣu-u*?]
kakkî	[	*kakku*?]
116. *šâ*	L[Ú	*šá-a*]
ina	RA	[*i-na*]
tâḫazi	IR	[*ta-ḫa-zu*?]
Tiamat	RÚM(MA)	*t*[*am-tim*]
ibannâ	RU RÚ	[*ba-nu-u*]
niklâti	RU RÚ	*n*[*a-ka-lu*?]
117. *palka*	GI	*p*[*al-ku*]
uzni	GI	*u*[*z-nu*]
itpêša	RU RÚ	*e*-[*pe-šu*?]

16. Une autre lecture que [GUR]$_8$(=TU) est possible, notamment É: voir §21s.

17. J'ignore à quoi peut bien répondre cette ligne.

18. Ou KU! Dans sa copie de (A), King paraît avoir pensé à L[U], ici hors de question.

		Left column		Right column
ḫasîsa			GI	*ḫ*[*a-si-su*]
118. *libbu*		IR	I[R$_5$	*li-ib-bu*]
rûqu		IR	[IR$_5$?	*ru-u-qu*]
šâ			RA	[*šá-a*]
lâ			RA	[*la-a*]
ilammadu		IR![19]	[IR$_5$?	*la-ma-du*?]
ilu			[DINGIR	*i-lu*$_4$]
gimras-sun			[GÚ?	*gim-ru*?]
. . . . .		. . . .		. . . . .
121.	(A) 82-3-23,151			
mummu		[	*mu*] -	*um-mu*[20]
erpêti		[	]	*er-pe-e-tú*
		[	]	*ma-lu-u*[21]
lištakṣibam-ma		[	]	*ka-ṣi-bu* [22]
122. *šapliš*				
ana				
nišê		[	]	*ni-ši*
te'ûta		[	]	*te-'-u-tú*
liddin		[	]	*na-da-na*
123. ^{d}**A.ŠÁ.RU**		[^{d}**A.**		**Š]Á.RU**
šâ		[	RA?	*š*]*á-a*
kîma		[		*k*]*i-ma*
. . . . .		. . . .		. . . . .
126.	(A) Sm 11+: r. iii + (B) K.1053: r. ii			
^{d}**NÉ.BI.RU**		[^{d}**NÉ.**		**BI].R[U]**
kakkab-šu			[DINGIR]	*k*[*a*]*k-k*[*a-b*]*u*
šâ			[R]A	*šá-*[*a*]
ina			RA	*i-na*
šamê			DINGIR	*šá-me-e*
ušâpû			E$_{11}$	*šu-pu-u*
127. *lû*			RA	*lu-ú*
ṣabit			RA	*ṣa-ba-tú*
kunsaggi			KUN.SAG.GÁ	*re-e-šu ár-kàt*
			DINGIR	*re-e-šu*
			RU	*ár-kàt*
šunu				
šâšu		[RA]	*šá-a*	[23]

19. Ecrit NI.

20. En tête de la case, [MU?].UM.MU serait écrit sur les deux colonnes, comme si les auteurs l'avaient pris pour un Nom de Marduk. On peut cependant supposer autre chose, par exemple: [*mu-um-mu*]//*um-mu*; mais une telle équivalence, sans autre appui, ne saurait être prise en considération, malgré la lumière qu'elle apporterait à l'intelligence de *En.el.* I 4: voir Annuaire 1975-76 de l'Ecole Pratique des Hautes Etudes, IVe Section (cité ici: Annuaire 1975-76) p. 81 n. 4.

21. *Malû*, dont il y a peu de chances qu'il compose avec *ka-ṣi-bu* un "doublet explicatif" (voir n. 34), suppose une addition au texte reçu. Noter cependant dans l'idéogramme traditionnel de *erpetu* voisin, IM.DIRI, la présence de DIRI, qui (lu SI.A) répond normalement à *malû*.

22. Voir n. 4.

23. [RA]: *ša-a* et RU: *pa-la-su* (avec, entre ces deux derniers, au moins, le double clou oblique de séparation), sont écrits, faute de place apparemment, sur une seule ligne: la première couple dans la colonne de gauche, l'autre dans celle de droite.

	lû				
	palsu-šu				RU :*pa-la-su*
128.	*mâ*			MA	*ma-a*
				MA	*ma-ru*[24]
	šâ			RA	*šá-a*
	qerbiš		IR	RA	*i-na*
				IR$_5$	*qer-bu*
	Tiamat			RÚM	*tam-tim*
	itebbiru			BU	*e-be-ru*
	lâ			RA	*la-a*
	nâḫiš			BÍ/NE	*na-a-ḫ*[*u*]
129.	*šum-šu*			BÍ	*šu-uš-šú*
	lû			RA	*lu-ú*
	^{d}*Nêbiru*			NÉ.BI.RU	*Né-bi-ru*
	âḫizu		IR	RA	*a-ḫa-zu*
	qerbi-šu			IR$_5$	*qer-bu*
130.	*šâ*			RA	*šá-a*
	kakkabê			DINGIR	*kak-ka-bu*
	šamâmi			DINGIR	{ (A) *šamê(e)* (B) *šá-me-e*
	al-kat-sunu		RA	RÁ	*a-la-ku*
	likîn-ma		MIN	RÁ	*ka-a-nu*
131.	*kîma*			IR$_5$	*ki-ma*
	ṣêni			RI	*ṣe-e-nu*
	lirʾâ			RI	*re-ʾ-u*
	ilû			DINGIR	*i-lu*$_4$
				IR$_5$	*lìb-bi*
				ŠÀ	*lìb-bi*
	gimra-šun			ŠÀ	*pu-uḫ-ru*[25]
132.	*likmî*			IR	*ka-mu-u*
	Tiamat			RÚM	*tam-tim*
				IR	ŠI x[ ]
	napišta-šu			ŠI	*na-p*[*iš-tú*?]
	lisîq			RIM	*sa-*[*a-qu*]
	u				
	likrî			RIM	*k*[*u-ru-u*?]
	. . . . .		. . . .		. . . . .
135.		(B) Rm 366+: r. ii			
	aššu			IR	*šu-ú*
	ašri			DINGIR	*áš-rù*
			RU	*áš-ru*	*šá-mu-ú*
	ibnâ			RÚ	*ba-nu-u*
	iptiqa			RÚ	*pa-ta-qu*

24. *Mâru*, inconnu du texte "reçu," en suppose-t'il une variante? Ou bien aurions-nous affaire, dans les deux premières lignes de la case, à l'un de ces "raisonnements" par analogie (§27) pour démontrer que MA=*ma-a* comme/parce que MA=*mâru* (pour cette dernière équivalence, voir §26; pour la première: §24).

25. Variante du texte "reçu": *puḫra-šun* au lieu de *gimra-šun*; cf. du reste VAT 14511, dans LKU p. 13 (et pl. 13) no. 38 Rs. 1.

	dannina	RU *dan-ni-nu*	*dan-ni-ni* *erṣeti(tì)*
136.	**ᵈEN.KUR.KUR** *šum-šu* *ittabi* *abu* ᵈ*Enlil*	**<ᵈ>EN.KUR.KUR**[26] MA MA A EN.KUR.KUR	*šum-šu* *šu-mu* *na-bu-u* *a-bu* ᵈ*En-líl*
137.	*zikri* ᵈ*Igigi* *imnû* *nagab-šun*	MA DINGIR MA GÚ![28]	*zik-ri* ᵈ*Í-gì-gi* *ni-bu*[27] *nag-bu*
138.	*išmê-ma* ᵈ*Éa* *kabatta-šu* *ittangi*	[ ] [ ] [ ]x LI LI LI	*še-mu-u* ᵈ[*É-a?*] *k[a-bat-tu]* *ra-[a-šú]* *na-g[u-u]* *ḫi-d[u-tu]*
139.	*mâ* *šâ* *abbê-šu* *ušarriḫu* *zikir-šu*	MA A MA MA	*ma-[a]* *a-[bu]* *šur-r[u?]-ḫ[u?]* *zik-ru*[29]

140[30]	*šu-ú ki-ma ia-a-ti-ma* ᵈ[*É-a lû šum-šu*]
141	*ri-kis par-ṣi-ia ka-li-[šu-nu li-bil-ma]*
142a	*ù gim-ri te-[re-e-ti-ia]*
142b	*šu-ú lit-[tab-bal]*
143	*ina zi-kir ḫanšâ il[û.MEŠ rabûtu.MEŠ]*
144a	*ḫanšâ šumê.MEŠ-šú i[m-bu-u]*
144b	*ú-šá-te-ru al-[kàt-su]*

Colophon:	*an-nu-ú ṣâtu*(U₄.UL.DÙ.A) *ù* [*šu-ut pî?*] *šá* L+I *šumê.*MEŠ *š*[*á* ᵈ*Marduk*] *šá ina lìb-bi* ᵈASARI(RI) x[ ]
	[*ek*]*al* ᵐᵈ*Aššur-*[*bani-apal*] [*šàr*] *kiššati šà*[*r mât* ᵈ*Aššur.*KI] [. . .] . . .

26. La présence de DINGIR parmi les sumérogrammes, un peu plus loin, en 137, suppose (voir §8) que le déterminatif DINGIR a été omis par erreur devant EN.KUR.KUR. Même omission, cependant, à la fin de la case 136, ainsi que pour NÊBIRU en 129.

27. Variante *nabû*: "nommer," au lieu de *manû* "énumérer, épeler," du texte "reçu."

28. Ecrit UZU.

29. On sait (voir Annuaire 1975-76 p. 107s) qu'aux cinquante Noms (de ᵈ**MARDUK**: VI 123a, à ᵈ**NÊBIRU**: VII 126) d'un état antérieur de la Liste, deux autres ont été ajoutés, conférés, le premier par Enlil (<ᵈ>**EN.KUR.KUR**: VII 136), le second par Éa (ᵈ**Éa**: 140). La disposition du "commentaire" laisse entendre que ses auteurs ont pris ici en compte le seul premier (dont ils ont étendu indûment le développement jusqu'à 137-39, qui font partie de la présentation du deuxième Nom supplémentaire). Leurs raisons nous échappent, mais leur choix pourrait expliquer que dans le Colophon (fin du §2), et en dépit du chiffre de "*Cinquante*" répété deux fois aux vers 143s, il soit fait allusion aux "*Cinquante et un Noms d[e Marduk*]".

30. A la fin, notre document se contente de reproduire, en les coupant un peu autrement, çà et là, que le texte reçu, les cinq derniers vers de la Liste, sans "commenter" au moins 140-42, qui, dans *En.el.* sont rattachés au dernier Nom donné à Marduk par Éa (voir la note précédente).

3. Il s'agit donc ici de la Liste des "Cinquante Noms" de Marduk, qui termine l'*En.el.*, et plus précisément de la seconde partie de cette Liste: VII 1-137.[31] On sait que dans cette conclusion du Poème, les diverses dénominations, à peu près toutes sumériennes,[32] données à Marduk, pour définir son "destin," par les dieux devenus ses sujets,[33] sont énumérées, chacune à la tête d'une façon de strophe de longueur variable, qui le prend pour thème d'une paraphrase dans le registre panégyrique. Le "commentaire" suit mot pour mot la teneur de ces couplets, reproduisant chaque fois, en tête du groupe de cases qu'il consacre à chacun, l'amorce du premier vers, c'est-à-dire d'abord le Nom qui le commande et qui l'introduit régulièrement dans le texte de l'*En.el.*

4. Une première lecture suffit pour s'aviser que les auteurs de notre document n'ont pas entendu le moins du monde "commenter," à proprement parler, ces Noms,[34] lesquels se trouvaient déja dûment expliqués chacun dans la strophe correspondante du Poème. Ils voulaient seulement démontrer que ces *explications* n'étaient, en somme, que l'*explicitation* des Noms eux-mêmes, dans lesquels elles se trouvaient encloses, comme les parties dans le tout, et d'où il avait donc suffi de les extraire. Pour montrer comment, ils ont pris pour modèle et pour cadre ce qui constituait à la fois le produit spécifique et l'instrument par excellence de leur formation *bilingue*, c'est-à-savoir la *Liste* parallèle de termes sumériens, d'une part, et de leurs équivalents accadiens, de l'autre. Dans cette culture, comme qui dirait diplopique, essentiellement enracinée dans le monde sumérien et épanouie dans l'univers accadien, de telles Listes ne formaient pas seulement l'armature de la lexicographie, mais, pour les lettrés au moins, la propre assise de la pensée. Et, en particulier, un certain nombre de textes traduits et de commentaires explicatifs en avaient adopté le principe et la présentation. C'est le cas du nôtre: en sa disposition il offre, sur ses deux colonnes, toutes les caractéristiques de la liste bilingue; et, si l'interprétation ici avancée en est admise, on y reconnaîtra une démonstration

31. Voir à ce sujet la discussion dans Annuaire 1975-76 pp. 106ss.

32. Ou prises comme telles. Car, sans parler de ^{d}**MARDUK** (VI 123a), de ^{d}**MÂR(U) ŠAMŠI** (127), de ^{d}**MARUKKA** (133), de ^{d}**MARUTUKKU** (135), d'une part, et, de l'autre, de ^{d}**GIBIL**, peut-être (VII 115), lequel a pu idéographier ^{d}**GIRRU** (voir §14), et de ^{d}**ADDU** (119), ^{d}**AŠARU** (123) au moins, et ^{d}**NÊBIRU** (125) sont bel et bien accadiens. Mais les "commentateurs" les traitent manifestement comme les autres, les découpant comme eux en sumérogrammes. Déjà en I 101s., les auteurs de l'*En.el.* se sont comportés de même, refusant de distinguer une langue de l'autre, quand ils ont interprété tacitement le nom de ^{d}**MARDUK** par **MÂR** ("Fils"), mot accadien, et **UTU** ("Soleil"), sumérien—exégèse reprise en VI 127s. Comme on le comprendra mieux plus loin (§32ss), ce qui compte, c'est le Nom, le mot, référé directement à la chose et traité comme elle, significatif et gros de connaissances par lui-même: ses accointances linguistiques sont, de ce point de vue, parfaitement insignifiantes, et nos "commentateurs" ne sont pas des linguistes.

33. Voir Annuaire 1975-76 pp. 106, 113.

34. En dehors des équivalences propres au but et à l'esprit du présent "commentaire," tels qu'ils sont résumés ici, on n'y trouve qu'un très petit nombre de passages qui rappellent les procédés explicatifs des commentaires "classiques." Ainsi, en 135, où *danninu*, mot rare et peut-être obscur, une fois équiparé au sumérogramme RU, du Nom de ^{d}**NÊBIRU**, est éclairé par son synonyme *erṣetu* (comp. LTBA 2 11: i 2); peut-être aussi en 82 où—on ne voit guère pourquoi—*šar agî*, qui ne figure pas dans le texte, mais est peut-être évoqué par *agû*, voire par l'assonance *šalgu*(?!), qui y figurent, est expliqué par *šar-ra*-[?] (à lire sans doute *šar-ra-ḫu*, "glorieux," "éclatant" AHw 2 1187b; *šar agî* se dit de Sîn dans WO 1 456 i 4 et 2 28 I 7; et comp. aussi *agû tašriḫti*—mot à mot: "la couronne de gloire="la pleine lune" CAD A/1 156b:2'; le commentateur veut-il suggérer que mettre Marduk en relations avec la "couronne," c'est lui attribuer l'éclat et la splendeur de la pleine Lune?). Autre type d'explication "philologique," par répétition du sumérogramme devant deux mots accadiens, à la suite, dont l'un est dans le texte et l'autre représente, soit un vocable de même "racine"(19: KÙ=*ellu* et *têliltu*; 94: [GAL?]=*šurbû* et *rabû*), soit de même sens (109: RA=*ramû* et *ašâbu*; 19: DÙ=*banû* et *nabû*; voir aussi la note 20, plus haut?), cité peut-être ici parce qu'il figurait seul dans les ouvrages de référence consultés et transcrits par le "commentateur," lequel leur aurait ajouté, pour souligner leur identité de sens, ceux qui figuraient réellement dans le texte de l'*En.el.* (*têliltu; šurbû; ašâbu; nabû*, etc). En 86, vu le mauvais état du texte, nous ignorons de quoi il retourne (comp. aussi n. 20), tandis qu'en 108 semblent avoir été équiparés au même mot accadien *palḫiš*, deux sumérogrammes, dont l'un au moins, les deux peut-être, tiré(s) du Nom ^{d}**KIN.MA**. Pour 131, 138 et 132, véritables schémas de raisonnements, voir §27. D'un extrême intérêt et à souligner absolument, est 127, où le "commentateur," agissant d'abord comme aurait fait un pur "philologue," traduit en accadien le mot rare et savant KUN.SAG.GÁ en montrant qu'il se rend parfaitement compte de sa composition à partir de deux mots sumériens, dont l'un (SAG) marque "la tête," "la partie antérieure," l'autre (KUN), "la queue," "la partie postérieure": il s'agirait du point extrême d'une droite, de son extrémité où, ne pouvant aller plus loin, qui la suit doit "faire tête-queue" et retourner sur ses pas: sens qui convient parfaitement au contexte. Mais après ce travail proprement "philologique," notre auteur revient à son propos, qui est de trouver ce contenu de KUN.SAG.GA, à savoir *rêšu arkat*, non dans ses élément effectifs de composition, KUN et SAG, mais dans des sumérogrammes tirés du Nom de Marduk (^{d}**NÊBIRU**); il juxtapose donc: à *rêšu*: DINGIR (pour cette équivalence, inconnue ailleurs et "déduite," voir §25), au lieu de SAG, et à *arkatu*: RU (équivalence inconnue et dont nous ignorons comment on y était parvenu), au lieu de KUN (lequel, du reste, n'équivaut à *arkatu* que *ad sensum*, et par "déduction," son répondant traditionnel étant *zibbatu*). C'est peut-être ici le passage qui montre le mieux à quel point notre "commentaire" entend se démarquer, pour suivre son propre chemin, des procédés purement "philologiques," et recourir à un tout autre type d'explication.

typique de cette forme de pensée pour ainsi dire amphibie: suméro-accadienne, caractéristique de la civilisation ancienne de Mésopotamie.[35]

5. *La colonne sumérienne*, à gauche, n'est constituée, ni par le mot à mot d'un texte suivi à traduire,[36] ni par un choix de termes difficiles ou obsolètes à expliquer:[37] tous les vocables sumériens qu'elle enregistre sont tirés du Nom de Marduk mis en exergue à la strophe correspondante de l'*En.el.*, chacun fournissant un morceau du texte de cette strophe, et leur suite permettant ainsi d'en reproduire la teneur au complet, comme on a pu s'en rendre compte (§ 2).

Or, et c'est une première constatation d'une grande portée, dans le but d'obtenir, en partant du Nom, autant de sumérogrammes qu'il leur était nécessaire pour retrouver l'intégralité du texte de l'*En.el.*, les auteurs de notre pièce ont traité ledit Nom en procédant suivant les règles de leur propre *écriture*.

6. Celle-ci, on le sait, transcrivait un mot, soit par son idéogramme—c'est-à-dire le signe, ou le groupe de signes, qui le définissait comme objet, abstraction faite de sa prononciation exacte dans le langage parlé—, soit en le décomposant en ses éléments phonétiques, lesquels, vu l'origine et l'histoire de l'écriture cunéiforme,[38] n'étaient, en somme, que des idéogrammes dépouillés de leur sens matériel et objectif, à l'avantage de leur seule présentation phonétique: naturellement en sumérien, avant tout, puisque l'écriture avait été mise au point d'abord pour cette langue. Ainsi nos auteurs ont-ils découpé les divers Noms de Marduk en sumérogrammes: en mots sumériens.

Comme dans l'orthographe courante, ces derniers sont parfois polysyllabiques: ALIM (3); UKKIN (18); LUGAL (95,bis; 96); A.RÁ (97); [DU$_6$.D]U (10); EN.KUR.KUR (136), etc.; mais, beaucoup plus souvent, d'une seule syllable. Le type CVC n'est pas très fréquent: B[ÍR] (91); GAL (94,ter); GIL (82,ter:?); DÚR (95; 96,ter), etc.; ni le type VC: AB (91); UL (84; 86); ÍL (82; 109), etc. C'est le groupe CV qui l'emporte largement en nombre: BU (128); BÍ (129); DA (9ss); DU$_8$ (12), etc.

7. Un certain nombre de ces sumérogrammes tirés des Noms, y figuraient déjà à titre de composantes *actuelles*: ALIM dans ^{d}**ASAR.ALIM** (3); LUGAL.DÚR et MAḪ dans ^{d}**LUGAL.DÚR.MAḪ** (95s); SISKUR$_x$ dans ^{d}**É.SISKUR$_x$** (109); ZU dans ^{d}**ZU.LUM** (84s), etc. Mais d'autres ne s'y trouvaient que *virtuellement*: on ne les y reconnaît point du premier coup, mais il a fallu, pour ainsi dire, les découper du continu phonétique que forment les divers Noms. Par exemple LÚ sorti de LUGAL en 96; GI, ÍL et IM, de GILIM en 82ss; A, SAR et RU (pour RÁ, voir § 12), de ASARI en 1s; KU et U$_4$ de SISKUR$_x$ en 114, etc. Un tel procédé est pareillement régulier dans la pratique de l'écriture cunéiforme, laquelle, lorsqu'elle phonétise un mot, le tronçonne, théoriquement avec une assez grande liberté, soit en groupes CVC, soit en CV et VC, alternés ou non. En tirant de ASARI(1ss) les sumérogrammes A, SAR et RU/RÁ, ou KU et U$_4$ de SISKUR$_x$ (109ss), les auteurs de notre document ont donc procédé à partir de ces mots, non point prononcés, mais *écrits* (ou, ce qui revient au même, pouvant l'être), et écrits selon les possibilités de leur orthographie: A-SAR-RU/RÁ; SIS/SI-IS-KU-U-UR, etc.

8. Ce n'est pas la seule des conventions propres au cunéiforme que l'on trouve ici appliquées pour réglementer l'extraction des sumérogrammes à partir des Noms de Marduk. Ces derniers, dans le texte de l'*En.el.*, sont tous précédés, comme il est d'usage, par le signe, *écrit mais non prononcé*, qui les caractérise comme appartenant à un être de la classe des dieux: le "déterminatif" DINGIR. Voilà pourquoi l'on trouve si souvent DINGIR parmi les mots sumériens de la première colonne (4; 11; 13,bis; 20,bis; [37]; 83,bis; etc.): il n'y serait pas apparu si l'on était parti d'un Nom seulement prononcé. Voir aussi la fin du §14.

9. L'usage fréquent des homophones, caractéristique du système cunéiforme, se trouve largement appliqué ici. Par exemple, en 9ss, pour marquer le phonème TU, du Nom ^{d}**TU.TU**, on a successivement: TU (9; 11s); TU$_4$ (12,bis); TU$_6$ (11); TU$_9$ (10; 18); et TU$_{15}$ (20). De même encore DÙ (10; 19,bis; 91,bis), DU$_8$ (12;

35. L'excellente mise au point de W. von Soden, Zweisprachigkeit in der geistigen Kultur Babyloniens (Sitzungsberichte der Österreichischen Akademie der Wissenschaften, Sph 235/1 [1960]) est ici à relire et à méditer: elle est fondamentale sur le chapitre où nous place notre document.

36. Je ne connais pas de traduction suméro-accadienne faite en colonnes et mot pour mot; mais il y en a par parcelles de phrases, comprenant chacune quelques mots, et rangées en parallèles face à leur traduction: ainsi RA 17 (1920) 122s=Lambert, BWL 226ss. Le dispositif le plus souvent adopté est la succession: phrase sumérienne — traduction en accadien, et, très souvent, en alternance d'une ligne à l'autre.

37. On peut citer au moins STT 2 272 no. 402, comme exemple.

38. Voir encore plus loin §33s. Le système et le fonctionnement de cette écriture sont supposés ici connus du lecteur: il m'a semblé superflu de renvoyer *toties quoties* aux exposés classiques de R. Labat en son Manuel et de W. von Soden dans son Syllabar^2.

18) et DU_{10} (20); É (109), È (110?) et E_{11} (114; 126); UL (84; 86) et ÙL (84), etc.

10. Quant le signe est polyvalent, phénomène courant en cunéiforme, il arrive que la valeur phonétique choisie pour s'accorder au Nom, et d'autant plus volontiers que cette valeur est plus rare, soit précisée par une de ces gloses dont les copistes, conscients de l'ambiguité possible de leur système dans tels ou tels cas, faisaient épisodiquement usage[39]. Ici, les gloses précèdent les mot dont elles définissent la prononciation[40]. Ainsi trouvons-nous DU devant ḪI pour orienter vers la lecture DU_{10} (20); UL devant KIB, pour ÙL (84); ZI devant KU, pour ZÌ (85); IR devant ḪAR, pour IR_5 (118,bis; 128s; mais non 131); MA devant SAR, pour MA_4 (2); RA devant DU, pour RÁ (130,bis; la seconde fois RA est remplacé par MIN: "item"); TU devant IM, pour TU_{15} (20), etc.; et, devant KAK, tantôt DU pour DÙ (91,bis; mais non 10, et 19,bis); tantôt RU, pour RÚ (2; 97; 113; 115; 116,bis; 117; 135a; mais non 98; en 135b, peut-être parce qu'il suit immédiatement 135a, la glose ne figure pas non plus). La répétition de la même glose, deux et jusqu'à trois fois à peu de lignes de distance, voire à la suite (4?; 112; 116; 118; 130), non moins que son omission dans certains cas où on l'aurait attendue (comme pour les valeurs rares KU_6 de ḪA en 21; TU_9 de KU en 10, et surtout en 18, où l'on peut hésiter entre TU_9 et ZÌ; cf. aussi 128: BÍ ou NE?), font partie de ces inconséquences trop fréquentes dans la pratique des scribes et la tradition manuscrite, pour qu'il vaille la peine de s'y attarder ici.

On notera du moins un autre type possible de glose, ou, si l'on veut, d'indicatif phonétique, en 116: RÚM y est suivi d'un MA (lequel ne se voit plus, pour la même valeur, après le même signe, en 128 et 132) qui, en précisant par un artifice connu ailleurs, la consonne dernière du phonème, à savoir M, semble avoir eu pour but d'éviter la lecture séparée des deux signes qui composent RÚM: NE et RU.

11. Si l'on juxtapose les sumérogrammes de la première colonne du texte aux éléments actuels ou virtuels du Nom dont ils sont tirés, on constate plus d'une fois un certain flottement phonétique. On aura, notamment, une sonore au lieu d'une sourde: DÙ, DU_8, et DU_{10}, alors que, le Nom étant ^d^**TU.TU**, on attendait TU (9ss; 18-20); GÚ, au lieu du KU qu'aurait demandé <^d^>**EN.KUR.KUR** (137), et, pareillement peut-être [GU]R_8 à la place du KUR réclamé par ^d^**É.SISKUR$_x$** (110).[41] Un tel procédé est courant, en particulier à l'époque ancienne, où l'on sait que le système écrit avait souvent renoncé à distinguer régulièrement, même à l'initiale, entre sourde, sonore et emphatique, un seul et même signe servant à marquer BI et PÍ, KU et QU, DU et ṬU, etc. Il y a gros à parier que cet usage aura donné naissance à un certain sentiment de l'équivalence *écrite* de ces phonèmes voisins, lequel se trahit ici par de tels à-peu-près.

12. Chacun sait aussi qu'à partir de la fin du IIe millénaire tout au moins, la chute, dans le langage parlé, des voyelles finales brèves, a en quelque sorte transformé en façons de *šewâ* les éléments vocaliques des groupes CV. Voilà sans doute qui rend compte d'un autre avatar ici constatable: nous voyons, en effet, certains sumérogrammes du type CV garder, certes (telle quelle, ou avec passage éventuel à la sonore, etc., correspondante: voir §11), leur consonne, mais avec une variation surprenante des voyelles. Ainsi lisons-nous GÚ, et peut-être [GE_{14}?] et [GI?], au lieu du GA réclamé par ^d^**IR.UG$_7$/Ú.GA** (103s); MU_9 au lieu de MA pour ^d^**A.GILIM.MA** (83); RA/RÁ au lieu de RU pour ^d^**A.ŠA.RU** et ^d^**NÉ.BI.RU** (123 et 126s); TA et TI, au lieu de TU, pour ^d^**TU.TU** (11; 13; 18), et, avec passage à la sonore, DA, au lieu de TU pour le même Nom (9s; 12; 13, bis); ZÍ/ZÌ pour ZU dans ^d^**ZU.LUM** (85), et ZU pour SI dans ^d^**É.SISKUR$_x$** (114,bis), etc. La quiescence de la

39. Ce sont des manières d'*Aussprachеglosse*, pour utiliser la nomenclature de J. Krecher dans RLA 3 433s. La copie de King ne permettant pas toujours de discerner si la glose a bien été, comme souvent, écrite, ou non, en plus petit corps et légèrement au dessus de la ligne d'écriture (RLA 3 431s.), j'ai pris le parti de la surélever, seulement, pour qu'on la distingue, dans la partie gauche de la colonne sumérienne.

40. Deux, du moins, semblent échapper à ce rôle, sans qu'on en voie clairement un autre à leur attribuer: en 1 et 13, comment SI, devant DU (à lire RÁ, ou RI_6, dans le contexte), d'une part, et MU devant TU_6, de l'autre, pouvaient-ils préciser la valeur phonétique du signe qui les suit? Pour 13, on se demandera si, pour une fois, le glossateur n'a pas eu une autre idée derrière la tête: il est de fait, et que le signe KA×LI, lu ici TU_6, a une valeur phonétique MU, à savoir MU_6 (MSL 8/1 21:158 et n.), et que *puḫru*, ici juxtaposé à TU_6, pouvait avoir pour idéogramme ME (MSL 9 126:51). Dans ces conditions la glose MU pourrait indiquer (approximativement: MU pour ME; mais nous savons que de tels à-peu-près n'ont ici rien de scandaleux: voir §§9, 11-13), non pas comment il fallait prononcer le signe KA×LI dans ce contexte, qui de toute façon réclamait TU_6, mais comment il se prononçait (à peu près) lorsqu'il devait signifier *puḫru*. En d'autres termes, le glossateur aurait insisté ici sur ce que son choix de TU_6 était bien arrêté, vu le contexte, et en dépit du fait qu'il eût fallu, vu le sens, lire MU_6. Pour 1, je me demande si l'auteur n'aurait pas accouplé deux valeurs phonétiques, également en accord (approximatif: voir §§9ss) avec le Nom ^d^**ASARI**, et pouvant toutes deux répondre plus ou moins à *kânu*; d'une part SI représentant ZI=*kânu* (Idu I 33, cité dans CAD K 159b), pour SA, et de l'autre RÁ (ou RI_6), une des valeurs du signe (DU), qui sous le lecture GIN signifie également *kânu* (Idu II 332, cité ibid.). SI ne serait donc pas une glose, mais un doublet de RÁ.

41. En 110, faut-il lire, au lieu de S]I_{17} simplement ŠI en supposant le passage de la sifflante simple à la chuintante?

voyelle finale saute aux yeux dans des cas comme MU pour ^{d}**ZU.LUM** (85); RÚ/RI/RA pour ^{d}**É.SISKUR**$_x$ (109ss); LÚ pour ^{d}**GIBIL** (116) et LI pour ^{d}**BÊL MÂTÂTI** (138,ter; voir § 14). A travers les exemples cités plus haut et la pratique orthographique au Ier millénaire, serait-on arrivé, dans le pays, à une sorte de dépréciation des voyelles, en général, au profit des consonnes, comme des Sémites pouvaient, du reste, y incliner, vu le caractère général de leur idiome? Il ne faut pas oublier qu'à l'époque, pour les langues sémitiques du Nord-Ouest tout au moins, l'écriture "alphabétique" était en usage depuis plusieurs siècles, laquelle ne tenait justement à peu près nul compte du vocalisme.

Quoi qu'il en soit, il y a au moins un cas, ici, où une telle indifférence vocalique a touché l'interconsonantique: B[ÍR], au lieu de BUR dans ^{d}**LUGAL.ÁB.DUBÚR** (91). Peut-être faut-il rappeler, entre les conventions de l'orthographe propres à justifier une telle licence, que, pour plus d'un groupe CVC, la mutation de la voyelle, évidemment provoquée, en dernière analyse, par une certaine indifférence à son timbre, a joué un rôle dans la production de nombre de valeurs nouvelles: on trouve couramment, dans le syllabaire, des valeurs CVC où V représente, non seulement la voyelle originelle, mais une ou deux autres: NAG et NIK$_5$ (von Soden Syllabar[2] p. 5:21); ŠAḪ, ŠIḪ, et ŠÚḪ (p. 5s:26); TIM, TÀM, et TUM$_8$ (p. 13:68), etc.

13. Un autre phénomène linguistique encore a contribué à la modification du syllabaire: c'est la chute de la mimmation qui, à partir de la seconde moitié du IIe millénaire, a raccourci nombre de valeurs CVC dont la dernière consonne était un M: TUM→TU$_4$; RUM→RÙ; LIM→LÌ; ṢUM→ṢU, etc. Une pareille évolution a pu semblablement faire naître ce sentiment du caractère pour ainsi parler "virtuel" du M final, qui justifierait ici une variante comme RÚM, au lieu de RU, pour ^{d}**NÉ.BI.RU** (128; 132). Par parenthèse, c'est à partir de ce RÚM, et compte tenu de ce qui a été noté au paragraphe précédent, que l'on peut expliquer le double MA de 128.

14. Enfin, considéré la bipolarité radicale de l'écriture cunéiforme, au moins à partir de la fin du IIIe millénaire, avec cette constante *possibilité* d'une double valeur et d'une double lecture: en sumérien et en accadien, on ne sera point surpris de constater ici que le "découpement" de deux Noms, au moins, celui de ^{d}**GIBIL** (115ss) et celui de <^{d}>**EN.KUR.KUR** (136ss), s'est manifestement opéré *à la fois* sur leur teneur sumérienne (d'où, pour le premier, l'élément LÚ, en 116, et, pour le second, GÚ et EN.KUR.KUR, en 136s), mais aussi sur leur équivalence en accadien, c'est-à-savoir, pour le premier: **GIRRU**, qui explique IR/IR$_5$, RÚ et RA en 115ss, et **BÊL MÂTÂTI** pour le second, ce qui rend compte de MA, A et LI en 136ss. C'est cette même bipolarité qui explique la mise en avant, en 109—comp. 82—, de ÌL (our *šaqû*), évidemment tiré du ÌL, répondant accadien du déterminatif DINGIR (voir le §8).

15. De tout ce qui précède, on conclura qu'une telle désintégration des Noms, dont le résultat a fourni de ses sumérogrammes la première colonne du "commentaire," n'a pu s'accomplir qu'en fonction d'une certaine vision *graphique* des mots: ce ne sont pas les Noms *prononcés* qui ont fourni la matière du monnayage en sumérogrammes, mais les Noms *écrits*, et écrits suivant les divers usages, conventions et licences du système propre au pays.

16. D'un autre point de vue, qui n'a pas moins d'importance, sur un plan différent, on se sera avisé que rien, apparemment, n'obligeait à faire figurer dans la première colonne, et quel qu'ait été le mode de découpement de chaque Nom, *toutes* ses composantes, et encore moins de les aligner *dans l'ordre* même dans lequel elles pouvaient former le Nom. C'est ainsi que pour ^{d}**ASARI** (1s), nous trouvons à la suite RU (pour RI: §12), puis SAR, puis deux fois A, puis RÁ et RÚ (également pour RI), et quatre fois SAR; et que pour <^{d}>**EN.KUR.KUR/BÊL MÂTÂTI**, en 136ss, nous avons MA, MA, A, EN.KUR.KUR, MA, DINGIR, MA, GÚ, [x, x, x], LI, LI, LI, MA, A, MA, et MA, dans le plus parfait désordre et sans la moindre trace de BE, TA, TI et EN. Pour expliquer cette double liberté, il faut d'abord se souvenir que le propos des auteurs étant de reconstituer en bon ordre, dans la colonne accadienne, comme on va le voir, le texte correspondant de l'*En.el.*, il n'était guère possible, en pratique, et en dépit des nombreuses facilités offertes pour le sectionnement du Nom, de trouver dans les éléments de ce dernier de quoi répondre mot pour mot à ce texte: il fallait donc partir du texte et ne chercher dans le Nom, pour les en tirer, que les répondants sumériens propres à s'adapter à la suite du texte, quels que fussent la place qu'il occupaient dans le Nom et le nombre de fois qu'il serait nécessaire de les répéter. D'autre part, la conception du Nom et de ses vertus, aux yeux de nos auteurs, était manifestement telle (voir §32) que l'important n'était pas de le voir figurer en entier et en ordre dans les sumérogrammes de la première colonne, mais de n'y rien faire paraître qui, d'une manière ou d'une autre, n'avait été tiré de lui. Le Nom, en somme, était traité à la façon d'une substance simple, dont toutes les propriétés se retrouvent intégralement en chacune de ses parcelles.

17. *La deuxième colonne*, on l'a dit, contient donc, sous la forme des mots accadiens traduisant les sumérogrammes de la première, les éléments du texte entier, et en ordre, des vers qui paraphrasent les Noms correspondants.

Ces mots n'y apparaissent que rarement dans la propre forme qu'ils ont revêtue dans le texte (*šá-a-ri*: 20; *ku-bu-ut-te-e*: 21; [*lib*]-*bi*: 37; *ni-ši*: 122; *pal-ḫiš*: 108, etc.), et encore, plus d'une fois peut-on supposer que c'est par accident: par l'effet des habitudes graphiques du temps, avec les voyelles finales brèves quiescentes et indifférenciées (§ 12), ce qui explique, par exemple, le *-i* grammaticalement injustifiable de *ṣi-i-ri* (96), et de *dan-ni-ni* (135).

Normalement, et comme c'est à peu près la règle dans les listes lexicographiques et les commentaires proprement dits, les noms, adjectifs, et pronoms[42] sont réduits au nominatif (masculin) singulier (*me-reš-tu*: 1; *kab-tu*: 3; etc.), et les verbes à l'infinitif G (*ša-ra-ku* et *a-ṣu-ú*: 1s, etc.; le participe *ka-ṣi-bu*, en 121, est surprenant), même quand cette forme ne *nous* paraît point, comme telle, en usage (*ú-qu-u*: 4). On trouve, comme ailleurs, des exceptions, qu'il ne vaut guère la peine de recenser ou discuter ici: la forme verbale du texte est parfois respectée (*šur-r*[*u*]-[*ḫ*]*u*: 139); un substantif ou adjectif de même racine peut être substitué à un verbe (*el-lu*$_4$ pour *elêlu*: 10; *at-ru* pour *šûturu*: 3; etc.), ou vice-versa (*e-de-šu* pour *têdištu*: 9; *še-mu-u* pour *tašmû*: 20; etc.); ou alors des termes de même racine, mais thématiquement différents (*šar-ru* pour *šarrûtu*: 96; *mil-ku* pour *mâliku*: 97; etc.). Si les suffixes-terminatifs *-iš* et *-u*(*m*) ont normalement disparu, comme tous les éléments flexionnels du mot ou incorporés à lui (*ma-*ʾ*-du* pour *mâ*ʾ*diš*: 96; [*aš*]-*rù* pour *ašruššu*: 40), *p*[*al*]-*ḫiš* a subsisté, en 108, et l'on trouve, une fois (128; mais non 103), *qerbiš* analysé en *ina*, suivi de *qerbu* (à moins que cette transcription ne suppose une variante textuelle: *ina qereb*?).

18. Sauf oubli (voir n. 44), ne figurent sans exception dans la colonne accadienne que les représentants des "mots-pleins" du texte, ceux qui expriment des notions objectives et indépendantes. Parmi les "mots-creux," purement directionnels et par là assimilables aux éléments flexionnels incorporés dans les mots-pleins, certains n'apparaissent jamais: telles les notes de coordination: *u* (2; 20s; 41; 132; 134) et *-ma* (9; 11; 13; 17; [98]; 109; 121; 130; 138), ainsi que *lu-* précatif ou assertif, *lorsqu'il est joint au verbe* (10; 11, bis; 12; 18; 109s; 121s; 130s; 132,ter); par contre il est régulièrement pris en compte (sauf 127b: répétition de 127a) lorsqu'il est isolé du mot qu'il commande (10b et 12s: DA; 127a et 129: RA). Sans parler de *a-di* ([111]); *e-la* (114: E$_{11}$), *ai* (18: TA) et *mâ* (128 et 139: MA), *hapax*, ou à peu près, dans la colonne accadienne, on y trouve les autres mots-creux le plus souvent, mais non toujours.[43] Ainsi la note relative *šâ* ([94], et [108]; 92, 96 et 116: LÚ; 98, 118, 123, 126, 128 et 130: RA), laissée de côté en 1; 3; 37; 40; 104; 139; la négation *lâ*, omise en 4 et 38, mais "traduite" partout ailleurs (98: NU; 114, 118 et 128: RA); et les prépositions *ina* (13 et 18: TA; [94]:?; 96: DÚR; 109, 112, 116, 126 et 128: RA; en 112, à cause de l'état du texte, on ne sait si l'expression *ina bali-šu* était rendue *ina*+*bali*(*-šu*), *ina bali*+*šu*, ou *ina*+*bali*+*šu*, le *lâ* qui suit se trouvant escamoté) et *ana* (84: DINGIR; 96: DÚR; 98: RA; [108]:?), rarement laissées pour compte (*ina* en 3 et 92; *ana* en 122[44] et 135, où *aššu* est représenté seulement par *šû*—voir la n. 42). Il n'est pas nécessaire, et il serait beaucoup trop long de discuter ces inconséquences; mais personne ne niera que le présent chapitre soit d'un réel intérêt pour quiconque se préoccuperait d'y chercher les vestiges d'une certaine vision *indigène* de la grammaire, domaine de recherche encore malheureusement bien trop peu exploré . . .

19. Grâce au monnayage des Noms dans les sumérogrammes de la première colonne, et à la traduction accadienne de chacun de leurs éléments, reconstituant dans la deuxième colonne le texte pratiquement entier, et dans l'ordre, de l'*En.el.*, il devait sauter aux yeux de tout lecteur—et c'est précisément la conviction

42. Les pronoms personnels proprement dits (pour la "particule relative" *šâ*, voir § 18) sont rendus *šu-ú* (DA en 9 et 10; IR en 135, où il ne s'agit en fait que du suffixe de *aššu*, dont le *ana* est escamoté—comp. § 18: *ana*) et *šá-a* ([RA] en 127, pour deux pronoms: *šunu* et *šâšu*, qui se suivent dans le texte et dont nous ignorons lequel était visé; comp. aussi 114).

43. Lexicographiquement le plus souvent étrange, sinon aberrant (par exemple ce RA protéiforme et "traduit" aussi bien par *lû*, *šâ*, *lâ*, *ina* et *ana*!), le rendu varié des "mots-creux" illustre surtout le souci principial des auteurs de ne choisir leurs sumérogrammes qu'en accord avec la composition du Nom intéressé.

44. Il est possible, ici, qu'après avoir oublié la ligne de séparation entre 121 et 122 (voir plus haut, n. 22), le copiste, distrait, ait également sauté les deux premiers mots de 122: *šapliš* et *ana*.

que lui voulaient inculquer les auteurs du "commentaire"—que tout ce que la plus ou moins longue paraphrase de chaque Nom expliquait de ce dernier, s'y trouvait inclus et déductible. Autrement dit, si l'on partait du Nom, en suivant les règles de l'écriture et de sa bivalence suméro-accadienne, on pouvait donc arriver à savoir tout ce qu'il contenait: les prérogatives, les prouesses, les qualités, les vertus du porteur de ce Nom. De celui-ci à celles-là, il y avait *explicitation*, et *progrès dans la connaissance*: on en savait davantage lorsque, après avoir lu le nom de ^{d}**ASARI**, on en concluait, au terme des opérations mentales appropriées, qu'en tant que tel, Marduk, sujet de ce nom, était "Donateur de l'agriculture, Fondateur du cadastre-des-terres, Créateur des céréales et des fibres et Producteur de tout-ce-qui-verdoie" (*šarik mērešti šâ eṣrata ukinnu / banû šeʾam u qê mušēṣû urqīti*). Une telle analyse du nom constituait ainsi un instrument du savoir, une clé pour apprendre, une règle de la logique, c'est-à-dire des normes de la connaissance et de l'acquisition de la vérité. C'est la leçon la plus claire et la plus remarquable qui ressort premièrement de l'étude de notre texte, lequel, sous sa mise en forme de Liste bilingue, agrémentée d'un petit nombre "d'explications,"[45] et sous sa désignation de "commentaire" (*ṣâtu*, voir n. 1), est en fait un véritable traité de science théologique *de divinis nominibus*.

20. Il vaut la peine, à présent, d'examiner d'un peu plus près ce qui fondait et cautionnait un tel progrès dans la connaissance, tirant et concluant d'un Nom à la nature de son sujet. Le moyen-terme de ce passage, ce qui contenait à la fois le point de départ et le point d'arrivée, était fourni essentiellement par le système d'équivalences entre sumérogrammes de la première colonne et leurs répondants accadiens dans la seconde. Un certain nombre de ces équipollences sont parfaitement connues et pour ainsi dire classiques en lexicographie suméro-accadienne, où chaque mot de cette dernière langue possède traditionnellement dans la première un répondant, parfois deux ou trois, que l'on appelle volontiers son "idéogramme." C'est le rôle que jouent ici nombre de sumérogrammes en question. Aussi, dans la liste qui suit, est-il bien inutile de documenter ces "valeurs" par des références que tous les assyriologues connaissent ou peuvent dénicher en un tournemain. On trouve donc: A=*abu* (136); A.RÁ=*alaktu* (98; mais non 17, où le sumérogramme est ZI: voir § 23); GAL=*rabû*, et son "superlatif" *šurbû* (94: voir note 34); GÙ=*napḫaru* (94; 104?); GI=*kânu* (83; 115; mais ZI en 21; 37: voir ci-dessous; et SI/RÁ—voir n. 40—en 1); DÙ=*banû* (19; lu RÚ en 2; 97; 116; 135: voir § 10; en 83, le sumérogramme est MA: voir § 22); DÙ =*epištu* (91; en 18, le sumérogramme TU est un homophone de DÙ: voir § 9); DU_8=*irtu* (12); DU_{10}=*ṭâbu* (20; en 37, l'équivalent devrait être [$ŠA_6$]: voir plus bas); DINGIR=*ilu* (passim); É=*bîtu* (109; mais SA en 3: voir n. 48); U_4=*ûmu* (114); ZU=*edû* (17; 84; 114); ZI=*kânu* (21; 37; représenté par GI en 83; 115: voir ci-dessus); KÙ=*ellu*, *têliltu* (19: voir note 34); LÚ=*šâ* (92; 96); LUGAL=*šarru* (95), et *bêlu* (ibid.; représenté par DINGIR en 20: voir § 25); MAḪ=*ṣîru* (96); NU=*lâ* (98); NUN=*rubûtu* (98); RU=*šarâku* (1); SAR=*arqu* (2; pour *urqîtu*); $SISKUR_x$=*ikribu* (109); [ŠÀ]=*libbu* (37); [$ŠA_6$]=*ṭâbu* (37; voir aussi DU_{10}, ci-dessus); TU_6=*šiptu* (11); TU_{15}=*šâru* (20); sans compter les équations DÚR.MAḪ =*durmaḫu* (mot sumérien accadisé) en 95 et NÉ.BI.RU =*Nêbiru* (mot accadien pris pour pseudo-idéogramme) en 126 et 129.

21. Il arrive que ces équivalences courantes soient obtenues ici moyennant une autre lecture du mot sumérien que celle que l'usage, les vocabulaires du cru et nos dictionnaires, mettent en avant comme la valeur propre et première du signe utilisé dans le sens en question. Par exemple, en tenant compte du phonétisme des Noms intéressés, c'est bien DINGIR que nous avons ici, au lieu de AN, pour *elû* en 83 (bis), et pour *šamû* en 126 et 130; [GU]R_8 au lieu de [T]U pour *erêbu*, en 110 (?; on peut lire aussi [È]: voir § 22); DÚR, au lieu de ÈŠ/ŠÈ, pour *ana*, en 96; KU, au lieu de UMUŠ/$UŠ_4$, pour *ṭêmu*, en 114; MA_4 au lieu de SAR pour *aṣû*, en 2; [S]I_{17} au lieu de IGI pour *maḫar* en 110; SA au lieu de SA_5=DIRI, pour *atru*, en 3; SA_5 au lieu de DIRI pour *adâru*, en 4; RÚ, à la place de DÙ pour *banû* (2; 97; 116; 135: voir § 20); RIM au lieu de LAGAB pour *kârû*, en 132; TU_4 au lieu de ÍB pour *agâgu* en 12.

Le choix de ces valeurs, la plupart rares et inusuelles, était évidemment commandé par la constitution phonétique du Nom dont on tirait ces sumérogrammes; mais il suppose aussi, et surtout, que *l'on tenait pour sémantiquement équivalentes toutes les valeurs sumérographiques d'un seul et même signe*, comme on les estimait d'autre part (§ 9) phonétiquement interchangeables. Ce qui fondait leur unité réelle, leur identité profonde, c'était donc *le signe lui même* qu'elles affectaient, les unes comme les autres. Le signe cunéiforme de "l'étoile" pouvait être lu aussi bien DINGIR que AN, et entendu sémantiquement aussi bien du "dieu," du "ciel," de "ce qui est en haut," "supérieur," "dominant," etc.: c'est parce que chacune de ces lectures et

45. Voir la note 34, ci-dessus.

chacune de ces traductions appartenait *au même signe* qu'elles étaient permutables et que l'on pouvait légitimement passer de l'une à l'autre. Une telle maxime n'étonnera que ceux, parmi nous, qui, habitués aux transcriptions du cunéiforme en nos caractères, oublient qu'*aux yeux des usagers de cette écriture, seuls existaient les signes cunéiformes, avec toutes leurs virtualités de lecture et de sens.*

22. Sans parler de la fantaisie qui semble présider au rendu "sumérien" de plus d'un "mot-creux" (voir §18), parfois bien faite pour laisser perplexe un sumérologue,[46] enregistrons encore un certain nombre d'équivalences qui, pour attestées qu'elles soient en quelque recoin de notre lexicographie, n'en demeurent pas moins rares et exceptionnelles; et c'est pourquoi il est utile ici de les documenter. Par exemple ALIM=*kabtu* (MSL 3 99:46 et CAD K 25a) en 3; BU=*nasâḫu* (MSL 3 106:120b) en 82; [GE_{14}]=*uznu* (A II/4 dans CT 12 1 i 12), en 104—en 117 on trouve l'homophone GI; voir §25; DINGIR=*bêlu* (A II/6 ii 8s, cité dans CAD B 192a), en 20; DÚR=*markasu* (2 R 47 18:21ef), en 95; [È? (au lieu de [$GUR]_8$; voir §22)]=*erêbu* (Diri I 150, cité dans CAD E 259b), en 110; EN.KUR.KUR=*Enlil* (comp. CT 16 1:27; autres réff. dans Tallqvist, Götterepitheta 48), en 136; [UR_4]=*ḫamâmu* (MSL 3 146:269), en 104; IR=*šalâlu* (MSL 9 130:330), 103; IM=*erṣetu* (Idu II 340s, cité dans CAD E 308b), en 83; ÍL=*šaqû* (4 R^2 26 3:33s), en 82 et 109; MA=*banû* (Comment. Théodicée 53, dans Lambert, BWL 74), en 83; MAḪ=*maʾdu* (MSL 2 139:21), en 96; MU=*nadânu* (A III/4, dans CT 12 8 i 27), en 85; NA=*manzazu* (MSL 3 120:276), en 17; NUN=*Éa* (SAI 1722 et Tallqvist, Götterepitheta 431), en 97; PA_4=*aḫu* (MSL 3 104:101 et CAD A/1 195b), en 94; RU=*šarâku* (MSL 3 112:179), en 1; SÁ=*milku* (cf. AHw 2 652a), en 3; TU=*banû* (CAD B 84a; homophone de DÙ, ou associé à *alâdu*?), en 9, 11. Il n'est pas dit que certaines au moins de ces équivalences ne soient pas à traiter comme celles que nous allons étudier aux paragraphes suivants, avec la seule différence que, par hasard sans doute, elles nous sont attestées.

23. Car tout le reste des équations suméro-accadiennes portées dans notre document, semble inconnu de nos sources lexicographiques et de nos dictionnaires. Du moins ai-je été incapable, en dépit de tous mes efforts, de documenter les équivalences suivantes: A=*eṣratu* (1); BU=*ebêru* (128); BÌ=*šum-šu*, écrit *šuššu* en (A), (129)[47]; GIL(IM)=*agû* (82), *ašâru* (82), et *šalgu* (82): voir §25, sub RIM; IR_5=[*rûqu*] et [*lamâdu*] (118); IR_5=*kîma* (131), voir aussi §25; KÙ=*ṣimru* (21); MA=*šurruḫu* (139); RI=[*ṣalmat qaqqadi*] (113); RU=*palâsu* (127), et *arkatu* (127); RÚ=[*mašâlu*] (98); SA=*uqqû* (4); TU=*edêšu* (9); TU_4=*tebû* (12); ZI=[*alâku*] et [*ṣabâtu*] (17), et aussi *šemû* (20; mais non, sans doute [138]), ainsi que *magâru* (20; 38), *bašû* (21), et *ašru* (40); ZU=*ṣulûli* (38), *rapâšu* (38), *sartu* (40), et *mussû* (40).

En présence de ces juxtapositions, et quand on voit, par exemple, GIL(IM) recevoir trois valeurs accadiennes différentes et sans le moindre lien apparent entre elles, dans la même case du "commentaire"; et ZI, d'une part, ZU, de l'autre, s'en voir attribuer respectivement cinq ou six, sans compter leurs répondants traditionnels (voir §20), on est comme contraint de penser que les auteurs du document ont dû pratiquer une étonnante érudition, voire une véritable virtuosité lexicographique, non certes dans le pur arbitraire, mais en suivant certaines règles et se conformant à certains procédés.

24. De fait, si l'on examine de près quelques unes de telles équivalences, un peu moins hermétiques ou aberrantes, il est par aventure possible de conjecturer l'une ou l'autre, au moins, des principales opérations de l'esprit qui y ont abouti, voire des "lois" qui ont dû commander ce système. Il s'agit essentiellement, on va le comprendre, de rapprochements, d'associations, peut-être phonétiques, mais surtout sémantiques, grâce auxquels se justifie la juxtaposition, d'abord inattendue.[48]

Des *associations phonétiques*, plus rares, paraissent çà et là imaginables, dans la mesure où le recours à une prononciation identique, ou voisine, pourrait rendre raison à lui seul du passage du sumérogramme à sa "traduction" accadienne. Par exemple MA pour *ma-a* (128; 139); MU_9 pour *mu-ú* (83); RI/RE pour *reʾû* (131; et de là, par association sémantique—§25—l'équivalence avec *ṣênu*, ibid., le "menu bétail" constituant le

46. Voir la note 43, ci-dessus.

47. P. Jensen (KB 6/1 357:12) avait déjà tiqué sur cette prétention de "rendre un double terme accadien (*šum-šu*) par un mot sumérien unique." En fait, il est à présumer que l'auteur de cette équivalence, à la recherche d'un ensemble phonétique accordable avec la présentation du Nom qu'il expliquait (^{d}**NÊBIRU**), s'est arrêté, devant le complexe sumérien MU.BÌ, au second élément (en réalité le seul suffixe possessif), persuadé que *šum-šu*, comme MU.BÌ, formaient chacun un tout sémantique dont les parties possédaient toute la vertu de l'ensemble (comp. §§16; 19; 24; 28; 32s): pour nous, mais pour nous seulement, c'est de la "mauvaise philologie" (Jensen).

48. On peut se demander si certaines *équivalences* purement *graphiques* n'ont pas également joué. Dans 3, comme on n'a, de près ou de loin, rien qui rapproche SA de *bîtu*, faudrait-il donc recourir à la quasi-identité bien connue du dessin de SA et du dessin de É, au moins à l'époque ancienne?

propre objet essentiel du "pâturage"). Et encore, peut-être, DINGIR, prononçable AN=*ana* (84). Voir encore §25, sub DÙ.

Sur le même plan, on peut se demander si les équations KU_6=*kubbuttû* (21); MA=*nasâḫu* (82); RA(<RI)=*aḫâzu* (129); TI=*nâḫu* (11); TU=*nê'u* (12), ainsi qu DU_8=*kullu* (18), n'auraient pas été tirées, par abréviation, des mots sumériens qui correspondent traditionnellement à ces termes accadiens, à savoir: KUL, MAR, DIRI, TIR, TUL, et ŠU.DU_8; tandis que pour AB=*tâmtu* (91; ailleurs RÚM: voir §25), on aurait dégagé le seul élément central de A.AB.BA, "idéogramme" usuel de *tâmtu* (comp. du reste ŠL 128:5). Après tout, ce ne serait pas la première fois que nous rencontrons, ici au moins, un mot traité comme une substance dont chaque parcelle renferme toutes les propriétés: pourquoi, non pas assurément à *nos* yeux, mais à ceux des "philologues" auteurs de notre document et de leurs contemporains lettrés, RA, équivalent à RI, extrait de DIRI, n'aurait-il pas eu la même valeur d'évocation, le même sens, que DIRI?

25. Beaucoup plus nombreuses et, semble-t'il, moins discutables, sont les *associations sémantiques*: non certes directement entre le mot sumérien et son correspondant en la colonne accadienne, mais, obliquement, entre ce dernier et un terme, plus ou moins synonyme, que traduit régulièrement ledit mot sumérien. En voici quelques exemples.

A.RÁ, qui peut signifier *ṭêmu* (MSL 13 84:16), touche donc à *milku* (97), dont le sens est voisin, les deux vocables se trouvant fréquemment rapprochés (La voix de l'opposition en Mésopotamie [1973] p. 146s).

GAL: *rabû* (comp. 94), implique la supériorité, et par conséquent l'autorité que marque *etellu* (ibid.).

Sous GI (homophone approximatif—§ 9—de [GE_{14}]: cf. § 22) nous trouvons ici trois mots: *palku*, *uznu* et *ḫasîsu* (117), que traduisent tous cette idée, traditionnelle en Mésopotamie ancienne, de "l'intelligence" fondée d'abord sur la docilité à l'enseignement des anciens et des sages (H. Holma, Körperteile p. 29s; P. Dhorme, Emploi métaphorique p. 89s).

DINGIR qui, par lui-même et par son homographe AN, marque à la fois le ciel (*šamû*/*šamâmu*: 126; 130) et le divin (*ilu*: passim), c'est-à-dire tout ce qui est "en-haut," "supérieur," "dominateur," peut donc s'étendre jusqu'aux concepts de "seigneur" (*bêlu*: 20), de "gouvernement" (*pâqidu*: 85), de "tête" (*rêšu*: 92), "d'étoile" (*kakkabu*: 130; le pictogramme primitif représentait du reste une étoile: Falkenstein ATU, Liste, p. 51s:192s, et p. 35; et comp. plus haut § 21 et plus loin § 34), voire de cette dénomination globale des dieux que représente le collectif ᵈ*Igigi* (137). Même l'idée de "paternité" ([*abu*]: 13) y est aisément réductible.

DÙ (lu aussi bien DÙ que RÚ: § 10) répond à une notion fort ample: celle de "facture," "fabrication," "création" (*epêšu*: 91—en 18: TU; *banû*: 2, 97, 116, 135— comp. aussi 9 et 11 où le sumérogramme est TU, pour DÙ: voir §11), sous laquelle entrent aussi bien *patâqu*, lequel signifie également, en gros, "fabriquer" (135), que *nabû* (19), mot à mot "nommer/nomination," terme qui, dans la vision mésopotamienne des choses, équivalait à "faire exister selon les qualités exprimées par le nom que l'on énonce."[49] D'autre part, y entrent aussi *itpêšu*: "habile-à-fabriquer" (117), du reste étymologiquement rattachable à *epêšu*, et même toute "oeuvre" comme telle, y compris "l'oeuvre-faite-avec-art" (*nikiltu*<*nakâlu*: comp. 116). En 91, l'équivalence avec *kakku* "arme" serait-elle phonétique (§24): le signe DÙ a également la lecture KAK.

IR, qui s'entend *šalâlu* "prendre en butin" (103), fait naturellement penser au "combat" ([*tâḫazu*]: 116), et à la "victoire" (*kamû*: 132).

IR_5, sumérogramme traditionnel du "poumon," puis, plus généralement, de "l'intérieur-du-corps": des "entrailles" (*ḫašû*), est donc parallèle, pour le sens général, à *libbu*: "le coeur" (131), et à *qerbu*: "l'intérieur" ([103]; 128s).

IM signifie, d'une part, la "glèbe," le "sol argileux" (ṭîṭu), ce qui touche à la "terre" (*erṣetu*: 83); d'autre part, sous la lecture TU_{15}, le "vent" (*šâru*: 20), et donc aussi ce vent violent et dévastateur qu'est la "tempête" (*meḫû*: 108?).

MAḪ, parce qu'il note tout ce qui est "surélevé," "suréminent," "sublime." *ṣîru* (96), se rapproche de *rabû*, qui signifie "grand" (comp. du reste MSL 3 150: 335), et peut donc aller jusqu'au "Prince," mot à mot au "Grand" (*rubû*: 96; en 98 on trouve de ce mot l'idéogramme traditionnel, NUN); dans une autre direction, il suggère la multitude imposante, la grande quantité, le "nombreux" (*ma'du*: 96).

ramû: "jeter," mais aussi "fonder-une-maison" et "s'y installer" (AHw 2 952s), a ici pour sumérogramme

49. Rappelons au moins (ci-dessus, n. 34) l'équivalence explicative éloquente *banû-nabû* ("créer/nommer") de 19; et plus loin, §25, sub DÙ, et §32. Il n'est pas impossible, soit dit en passant, que l'alternance phonétique de ces deux mots (B+N//N+B) ait poussé aussi à les juxtaposer.

RA (109; en réalité: RI; comp. § 12, et § 24 pour *aḫâzu*): il est donc aisé de conférer à RA la valeur, voisine, de "l'habitation," de "l'installation-à-demeure" (*ašâbu*: ibid).

RIM (sous la lecture NIGIN) marque couramment l'action "d'entourer," "encercler" (*lamû*): on peut donc lui donner (sous son autre lecture GIL(IM), voir § 21) la valeur de "couronne," "diadème" (*agû*: 82), qui "encercle la tête"; et, d'autre part, de "surveillance" (*ašâru*: ibid), qui "entoure d'attention" son objet.[50]

A RÚM (RÌM<ERÌM) répond couramment, en accadien, "l'ennemi": *aiâbu*; il peut donc désigner l'être qui, dans l'*En.el.*, est l'Ennemie par antonomase, à savoir *Tiamat* (128; 132).

SAR se réfère, en général, à la "classe" des légumineuses, des plantes du jardin potager, dont il est le "déterminatif" (voir encore § 34). Rien de surprenant que lui soient attribuées ici diverses valeurs, toutes relatives à la "culture des plantes" (*mêreštu*: 1), à la "verdure" (*arqu*, pour *urqîtu*: 2), au "croît" (mot à mot, la "sortie": *aṣû* ibid.) des végétaux, voire à ces deux plantes cultivées essentielles qu'étaient, dans le régime local, les "céréales" (*šêʾu*: ibid.) pour se nourrir, et les "fibres végétales," le "lin" (*qû*: ibid.) pour s'habiller.

SISKUR$_x$ nom, sumérien du "sacrifice": *nîqu*, par effusion (*nâqu*) de la libation ou du sang de la victime, peut donc s'entendre également de ces autres types d'offrandes liturgiques que désignent, d'une part [*kadrû*] (110), et de l'autre, [*irbu*] (111).

Du fait que la valeur courante de UKKIN est "rassemblemment," "réunion plénière" de personnes (*puḫru*—comp. *En.el.* I 132, 153, etc., ainsi que VII 13, 37, etc.; ici, ce mot, en 131 et [37?] est rendu ŠÀ—voir § 27—et TU$_6$, en 13—voir §§9, 20), on peut donc y voir ce fourmillement qu'évoquent les "populations" (*apâtu*: 18).

26. Dans tous ces cas, peut-être à nos yeux plus transparents, le passage du sumérogramme au mot accadien qui lui est juxtaposé en la deuxième colonne, s'est donc opéré de manière oblique, indirecte, moyennant un véritable *raisonnement*, au moins implicite, et par recours à un *moyen terme*. Prises une par une, les hypothèses formulées au § précédent pour repérer ces moyens termes et restituer ces opérations discursives, sont toutes fragiles et pourraient s'imputer à quelque imagination débridée. Mais leur multiplication, leur mise ensemble, la concordance des cheminements de l'esprit qu'elles supposent, renforcent, pour ainsi parler, en proportion géométrique leur crédibilité. D'autant que la juxtaposition assez fréquente, dans la même case, ou pas loin, de plusieurs de ces équivalences ainsi obtenues, pour le même sumérogramme (comp. SAR: 1s; GIL(IM): 82; MAḪ: 96; [SISKUR$_x$]: 110s; GI: 117, etc.), laisse entendre qu'elles ont pu l'être par une même dialectique. Parfois, cette dernière est comme transparente. Par exemple, si l'on a donné ici (128) l'équivalence *mâru* à MA, c'est visiblement par substitution de MA à PÈŠ (deux valeurs différentes du même signe), lequel est un homophone de PEŠ, désignation du "fils" dans certaines graphies rares et érudites, comme dans les Colophons (H. Hunger, Kolophone, 167b; et AHw 1 615b:1f); du sens ainsi obtenu, on pouvait passer sans effort, pour le même MA, à celui de *šumu* (136), lequel désigne la "descendance" en même temps que le "nom" (Stamm, Namengebung, p. 40), et de là à *zikru* (139) et à *nabû/nîbu* (136s), qui marquent eux aussi la "dénomination."

27. S'il fallait faire toucher du doigt la vraisemblance d'opérations mentales plus compliquées encore, pour aboutir à telle ou telle équation lexicographique ici attestée, on en trouverait des reflets non-équivoques dans notre "commentaire" lui-même. Par exemple, en 138, en vue d'obtenir la parité, inconnue par ailleurs, de LI avec *nagû* "jubiler," l'auteur rappelle d'abord, sur une première ligne, purement explicative puisqu'elle ne répond à rien du texte de l'*En.el.*, que LI équivaut notoirement à *râ*[*šu*]: "être en joie" (comp. MSL 3 114:203); après quoi, tout le monde sachant que *nagû* s'avoisine, par le sens, de *râšu*, il peut donc conclure que LI est également juxtaposable à *nagû*; et même, *ad complementum doctrinae*, il prend soin de souligner en conclusion la valeur générale de "joie" attribuable à LI, par une troisième équivalence, également connue: LI=*ḫidû*[*tu*] (comp. RA 16 [1919] 167:III 18s, où l'on a LI: *ḫadû*, et LI.LI: *ḫidiâtu* et *rîšâtu*). Ces trois lignes résument donc tout un discours, par rapprochement de synonymes; par passage d'un sens à un autre, voisin; par recoupements sémantiques.

Cheminement analogue de la pensée en 135. Le "commentateur" se propose de conférer à AN, lu DINGIR (§ 21), la valeur accadienne *ašru* "lieu." Il recourt donc, sans doute, à ses autorités lexicographiques (peut-être Malku II 100, cité dans CAD A/2 456b) pour poser que *ašru* est synonyne de *šamû*: "ciel," lui-même, on le sait, traduction accadienne de AN.

En 131, la dialectique est quelque peu différente, mais aussi méandreuse et progressant toujours d'un

50. J'ignore comment on a pu passer de GIL(IM) à *šalgu*, ibid.

"synonyme" à l'autre, d'un sens voisin à l'autre. Il s'agit de démontrer, si l'on peut ainsi parler, l'équation IR_5=*puḫru*. On pose d'abord que IR_5 équivaut à *libbu* (équivalence sémantique: § 25); puis, ce que tout le monde savait, que ŠÀ se traduit aussi par *libbu*; enfin, ce que *nous* ignorons, que ce même ŠÀ s'entendait également de *puḫru*: si ŠÀ a pour équivalents *libbu* et *puḫru*, IR_5, qui répond au premier, doit répondre de même à l'autre: C.Q.F.D.[51]

28. Ainsi pouvons-nous donc avancer que toutes les équivalences rares, inusuelles, inconnues, entre sumérogrammes de la première colonne et mots accadiens de la seconde, ont été en quelque sorte démontrées et acquises, disons conquises, soit par nos propres auteurs, soit, avant eux, par leurs garants lexicographiques,[52] au moyen de véritables "raisonnements," qui recouraient, pour l'essentiel, au procédé de l'analogie et des équations successives d'un terme á l'autre, pour aboutir à mettre en rapports d'équivalence le premier et le dernier de la série: si A=B et si B=C, donc A=C. Voilà les procédures au moyen desquelles nos "commentateurs" sont parvenus à tirer des divers Noms de Marduk l'intégralité du texte consacré par l'*En.el.* à leur paraphrase, démontrant de la sorte que chacun de ces Noms—comme l'universel renferme le particulier—*contient* la totalité des attributs, des qualités, des mérites et des hauts-faits de ce dieu: bref, de sa *Nature* telle que le Poème la détaille.

29. Or, ces opérations, que *nous* serions tentés d'interpréter au mieux comme ludiques, n'étaient pas le moins du monde, aux yeux de leurs usagers, des "jeux de mots," ni des jeux tout court. Le sérieux de leur sujet écarte d'emblée une pareille explication: notre document est un traité de théologie (voir §19), et il porte sur une des oeuvres les plus vénérables et "sacrées" de la littérature religieuse du pays.[53]

Les mêmes procédés d'herméneutique et d'analyse exégétique se retrouvent du reste ailleurs, parmi cette littérature, et peut-être plus volontiers lorsqu'il s'agit de réalités surnaturelles. Un des documents qui, disposition matérielle mise à part, ressemble le plus au nôtre et pourrait aisément lui être confronté, est cette tablette néo-babylonienne (VAT 17115), publiée par Fr. Köcher (AfO 17 [1954s] 131s), qui porte une "explication des Noms[54] de l'Esagil," le temple de Marduk à Babylone. Mais on peut également renvoyer, çà et là, à plus d'un trait de la même veine: tels, parmi le commentaire (tout ce qu'il y a, par ailleurs, de plus "philologique") de la "Théodicée," ces interprétations des Noms divins de ^{d}*Mami* (Lambert, BWL 74:53), ou de ^{d}*Zulummar* (ibid, 88:277), et cette explication de la "fosse préparée au lion pour ses crimes" comme l'Enfer (ibid, 75:62), ou encore, dans le commentaire Rm 2, 127, rev. 8s (AfO 24 [1973] 102), le sens donné au XIIe mois; et, dans un contexte "profane," citons au moins JNES 33 (1974) 332 lignes 46ss.

30. Une pareille dialectique, il ne faudrait du reste pas l'imaginer réservée aux seuls exégètes et commentateurs de basse-époque: elle a certainement joué, et beaucoup plus que nous le croirions sans doute, dans la composition même de mainte oeuvre, religieuse ou mythologique en particulier. Le prologue du Poème d'Erra, par exemple, ne se comprend guère si, à travers les épithètes conférées notamment à Īšum, on n'entrevoit toute une herméneutique bilingue du même type que celle a laquelle notre "commentaire" nous a accommodés.[55]

Et même, sans chercher plus loin d'autres témoignages—du reste pas toujours faciles à débusquer, vu notre peu de familiarité avec un tel code, et le danger qu'on court à se lancer sans munitions solides à un pareil pourchas, au cours duquel il est difficile de se garder de l'imaginaire et de l'arbitraire—il existe en tout cas un monument éclatant de l'importance prise par cette façon de philologie sacrée, et cela, dès au moins la fin du second millénaire, parmi les lettrés et les théologiens de Babylone: c'est la propre Liste des Noms de Marduk, à la fin de l'*En.el.*, autour de laquelle tourne notre "commentaire." On aurait tort de penser que ce dernier est

51. En 132 doit se cacher quelque procédure analogue, pour "démontrer" une valeur *napištu* de IR, par un intermédiaire qui pourrait être ŠI; mais une cassure intempestive ne nous permet pas de l'affirmer. Or ŠI est le répondant emesal de ZI, qui signifie *napištu* (MSL 4 25:189). Voir encore la note 34, ci-dessus.

52. On a cité plus haut (notamment §22), à plusieurs reprises quelques séries lexicographiques, en particulier Sb (dans MSL 3), qui cautionnent plus d'une valeur rare et inusuelle, attestée également ici. Seule une étude approfondie, et sur le plan *historique*, comme je l'ai dit (voir n. 1), de toutes ces séries, permettra de discerner dans quelle mesure leurs auteurs ont pu et dû recourir, pour fonder leurs équivalences, entre autres aux procédés mis en lumière par notre "commentaire." Voir encore la n. 62.

53. Comp. Annuaire 1975-76 p. 77s.

54. Il y en a 18 en tout.

55. Par exemple Īšum: *ṭâbiḫu* (ŠUM: ŠL 126 17) *nâ'du* (I: MSL 3 132:20), au vers I 4; *diparum, diparu=išatu*, dans LTBA 2 2 iv 22), au vers 10, et *namṣarum* au vers 12 (ce nom du "poignard" a pour idéogramme à la fois GÍR—CT 12 13 iv 8—élément essentiel de Girru, autre nom du Feu, et U-GUR—MSL 3 143:208—un des idéogrammes de Nergal, c'est à dire d'Erra, dont Īšum est l'auxiliaire). Comp. aussi, au vers 21, *bêlu muttallik muši*, qui est la traduction accadienne de EN.GI_6.DU.DU, ibid., etc.

une construction secondaire, surajoutée, élucubrée à part et étrangère au moins à l'esprit du Poème.[56] Il est impossible d'étudier sérieusement ce texte en lui-même sans voir clair comme le jour qu'il a été conçu sur les mêmes principes, au moyen des mêmes rapprochements et raisonnements que son "commentaire," et que ce dernier n'a donc rien inventé, rien ajouté d'essentiel à l'original, mais s'est contenté d'en démonter le mécanisme et de le mettre à la fois en forme et en valeur. Autrement dit, les propres auteurs de la fin de l'*En.el.*, avaient déjà, pour leur compte et selon les méthodes explicitées plus tard par leurs "commentateurs,"[57] tiré leur paraphrase de chaque Nom des éléments de ce dernier.

31. On le perçoit d'emblée à lire certains vers qui sont, au bout du compte, de pures et simples traductions, en accadien, du Nom sumérien correspondant, des variations, par synonymes et idées voisines, du thème qui lui est propre. Ainsi, ^{d}**MER.ŠÀ.KÚŠ.Ù**, dans le distique qui lui est consacré (VI 137s), est-il, en somme, traduit trois fois, d'abord par les équivalents accadiens propres de MER (*ezzu*: comp. SBH 141 no. IV 215s, ME.ER.RA.AŠ=*e-ze-zi-šú*) et de ŠÀ.KÚŠ.Ù(*muštâlu*: comp. J. Krecher, Kultlyrik 135s Anm. 404), puis par d'autres, un peu plus lointains et que nos dictionnaires n'enregistrent pas comme des valeurs propres de ces sumérogrammes, mais dont le sens *réel* est voisin. A la suite (VI 139ss), ^{d}**LUGAL.DÍM.ME.ER.AN.KI.A** est également rendu mot pour mot en 141: ***bêl ilī ša šamê u erṣeti***, et l'on trouve en 140 et 142 des équivalents de LUGAL (*šarru*), de DINGIR (*ilu* et *abu*)[58] et de AN.KI.A (*eliš u šapliš*): nous pourrions certainement en découvrir d'autres, si nous avions à notre disposition, sinon les connaissances et la forme d'esprit, au moins les ouvrages de référence des auteurs de la Liste. Et cela vaut pour le texte entier de cette dernière.

Il suffit, du reste, pour se rendre compte à quel point leur composition est calculée et savante, ne laissant qu'une part exiguë au lyrisme et à la liberté de l'inspiration, d'examiner leur vocabulaire: quantité de mots ou d'expressions sont répétés, parfois d'un vers à l'autre, en réponse, manifestement, aux mêmes éléments du Nom correspondant. Par exemple, dans le premier groupe de dénominations, à la suite et autour de ^{d}**MARDUK** (VI 123a-44),[59] on trouve *šakin* en 124 et, de la même racine, *šikittu* en 129 (pour *šakânu*: MAR, comp. MSL 3 146:279); *banû* (DÙ: voir §25) en 129, 131, 133; *nišû* (UKU: MSL 3 145:244) en 129; 135s. Dans le groupe de ^{d}**EN.BI.LU.LU** (VII 57-69) reviennent ***bêlu*** (EN) en 57, 61 et 54; *mudeššû* (LU=*dešû*: MSL 2 151:40) en 57 et 69; *šâkinu* (LÁ=*šakânu*: MSL 9 127:119) en 58 et 66; *šutêšuru* (UL_4=*ešêru*: A VIII/2 251, cité dans CAD E 352b) en 59 et 63, etc. Même si nous n'arrivons pas toujours à repérer les équivalents sumérographiques de nombre de ces termes, leur seule prolifération nous laisse assez entendre que le texte entier a été véritablement composé, étudié et construit selon les propres règles et l'optique même que notre "commentaire" nous a permis de mieux isoler et entendre: en tirant tout ce qui est dit de Marduk à l'occasion d'un de ses Noms, des éléments de ce Nom, traités comme des sumérogrammes et affectés de leurs valeurs accadiennes, que ces dernières soient triviales ou qu'il ait fallu les poser en conclusion de raisonnements et de rapprochements analogiques plus ou moins indirects. C'est du reste pourquoi chaque "strophe" se présente, non comme un panégyrique libre de Marduk, mais comme la simple apposition au Nom des qualificatifs qu'on lui reconnaît, évidemment à travers ce Nom: "^{d}**ASAL.LÚ.ḪI.**^{d}**NAM.TI.LA**, (c'est) le dieu vivificateur . . ." (VI 151); "^{d}**TU.TU**, c'est l'auteur de Leur rénovation . . ." (VII 9); "^{d}**ASAR.ALIM**, (c'est) celui dont l'avis prédomine en la Salle-du-Conseil . . ." (VII 12). Partout "l'explication" n'est, grammaticalement aussi bien

56. Voir déjà, ci-dessus, n. 32, l'explication du Nom de ^{d}**MARDUK** en I 101s (et VI 127s), tout à fait dans le même esprit que notre "commentaire."

57. Les analyses des auteurs du "commentaire" ont-elles coïncidé pas à pas avec celles des auteurs de la Liste? Il est au moins probable que ceux-là sont allés plus loin que ceux-ci dans le système, quand, par exemple, ils ont voulu inclure dans la paraphrase du Nom de Marduk la formule qui, dans la Liste, ne fait que présenter la collation de ce Nom, sans entrer le moins du monde en son explication et sans avoir, par conséquent, le moindre lien interne avec lui. On a une trace de cet excès en 19, où, de la formule: ^{d}**TU.TU.**^{d}**ZI.KÙ** ***šalšiš imbû***: "^{d}**TU.TU**, ils (le) nommèrent en troisième lieu ^{d}**ZI.KÙ**," il subsiste au moins le verbe ***nabû***, ***šalšiš*** semblant avoir été laissé pour compte (voir n. 10). Mais c'est surtout à propos de 136ss que les "commentateurs" montrent le bout de leur oreille. Ce passage, qui n'appartient pas à la Liste proprement dite (voir Annuaire 1975-76 p. 107, et plus haut, n. 29), n'est évidemment pas construit comme elle: le texte n'en est point une paraphrase du Nom, apposée à lui et "graphiquement" rattachée à lui pour démontrer qu'elle n'en est que l'explicitation. Pourtant, nos "commentateurs" ont poursuivi bravement à son propos une analyse qui est sans doute de leur seul cru. On pensera donc que dans le reste de leur oeuvre, s'ils ont travaillé selon le même esprit que les auteurs de la Liste, et peut-être, souvent, avec les mêmes éléments, les mêmes raisonnements et les mêmes équivalences—par la force des choses!—ils y ont certainement mis du leur, et leur "commentaire" n'est point la simple rédaction, en détail et en forme, de tout le travail de "philologie sacrée" qui avait précédé et préparé la composition de la Liste par ses propres auteurs, quelques siècles, sans doute, auparavant. (Nous ignorons le temps où notre "commentaire" a vu le jour.)

58. Pour l'équivalence DINGIR=*abu*, voir déjà ci-dessus, §25: DINGIR.

59. Annuaire 1975-76 p. 110.

que *in re* que le prédicat du Nom qu'elle explique, comme pour mieux souligner leur totale identité.

32. Il semble donc que cette herméneutique, cette procédure qui consiste à *analyser les mots pour avancer dans la connaissance des choses*, et dont le mécanisme est si bien démonté par notre "commentaire," a pu et dû jouer un rôle important dans la pensée et la production intellectuelle des vieux Mésopotamiens. Pourquoi?

Si l'on y réfléchit, une pareille "logique," tellement loin de la nôtre, implique un double postulat, également éloigné de notre propre optique: *une conception réaliste*, et *du nom*, c'est-à-dire du mot en tant qu'il dénomme et désigne, et *de l'écrit*.

Le premier point est connu de tous ceux qui ont eu affaire à la civilisation ancienne de Mésopotamie. On sait de longue date que le nom n'y était point, comme à nos propres yeux, un épiphénomène, un pur accident extrinsèque de la chose, un *flatus vocis*, simple conjonction arbitraire d'une relation de signification avec un groupement de phonèmes. Tout au contraire, ces vieilles gens s'étaient persuadés que le nom a sa source, non dans l'individu qui nomme, mais dans la chose nommée, qu'il en est une émanation inséparable, comme l'ombre portée, le calque, la traduction de sa nature: si bien qu'à leurs yeux "recevoir un nom" et exister (évidemment: selon les qualités et la présentation mises en avant par ce nom), c'était tout un.[60] Les premiers vers de l'*En.el.*, que l'on cite volontiers pour illustrer cette façon de voir, ne sont qu'une pièce d'un immense dossier, qu'il paraît inutile de déployer ici. Du moins cette conception réaliste de l'onomastique, du vocabulaire, éclate-t'elle, plus nettement peut-être que n'importe où ailleurs, dans notre "commentaire": on y a vu que chaque Nom de Marduk, contient, réellement et matériellement, tous les pouvoirs, les mérites, les prérogatives, les qualifications qu'il définit de ce dieu et que leur total fabuleux de Cinquante pour lui tout seul nous permet ainsi, non seulement de reconnaître en lui une "personnalité extraordinaire" (VII 144), même sur le plan divin, mais d'acquérir de cette personnalité une connaissance approfondie.[61]

Le contexte de la Liste des Noms laisse également mieux percevoir à quoi, en définitive, chacun doit sa valeur: c'est que chacun exprime une volonté et une décision particulière des dieux concernant celui qui en est le sujet: chacun *définit son destin*. Et ce qui est vrai de Marduk, ici, l'est également partout de toute chose: son nom et son destin se confondent; son nom ne fait que matérialiser et préciser son destin. Si le nom a sa source dans la chose nommée, c'est qu'il y a été déposé, en même temps que sa nature, qu'il programme, par les dieux disposant de son *destin*: autrement dit de *ce qu'il doit être*, Or—et sans doute est-ce une raison pour laquelle, dans la mythologie locale, les Destins sont le plus souvent présentés comme consignés sur une Tablette fameuse—le nom, le mot, n'a sa pleine valeur, sur ce plan réaliste, qu'en tant qu'il est *mis par écrit*.

33. Cet autre postulat de la "logique" mésopotamienne, on en a moins parlé; peut-être même l'a-t'on jusqu'ici méconnu ou méjugé: mais il est tout aussi capital, et il ne ressort pas avec moins d'évidence de l'examen détaillé auquel s'est trouvé soumis notre "commentaire."

Pour nous, l'écriture, totalement alphabétisée, c'est-à-dire fondée sur l'analyse phonétique du mot, qu'elle pousse jusqu'à ses éléments irréductibles, a pour fonction première de *fixer* matériellement ce qui, comme mot prononçable, n'a qu'une existence transitoire, et, comme concept signifié, qu'une réalité intramentale et incorporelle. L'écriture nous sert donc seulement à conférer une existence objective, indépendante et durable à la parole, laquelle traduit notre pensée, notre façon de voir les choses. Elle s'efface devant la parole et ce que représente la parole: elle n'est rien sans elle, et elle ne lui ajoute rien, si ce n'est la matérialité et la durée.

Il n'en était pas du tout ainsi pour les vieux Mésopotamiens. On ne doit pas oublier, en effet, que non seulement ils ont créé leur écriture (et probablement, du même coup, l'Ecriture), mais que le premier stade de cette dernière, la première forme qu'elle a prise en venant au jour, c'est ce que l'on appelle, au moins en son étape originelle, la *pictographie*. Or, la pictographie n'est pas une écriture de mots, puisqu'elle ignore, comme telle, tout phonétisme, mais une *écriture de choses*. Elle transcrit directement ces dernières par des croquis, qui sont aussi des choses, puisque des objets matériels y sont encore reconnaissables. Même après l'invention du phonétisme, c'est-à-dire de la possibilité de dépouiller ces croquis de leur signification objective pour les arrêter au seul groupement de phonèmes qui constitue le prononcé de la chose dans la langue courante, le système cunéiforme n'a jamais abandonné ses habitudes originelles et foncières de référence immédiate aux choses; et même ses phonogrammes, il n'a jamais perdu de vue qu'ils n'étaient, au bout du compte, que des pictogrammes dépouillés, au profit de leur seule valeur linguistique, de leur

60. Voir ci-dessus, la n. 49.

61. Voir Annuaire 1975-76 pp. 108, 113.

contenu objectif (comp. déjà § 6), qu'ils pouvaient, du reste, retrouver à tout instant, comme l'a amplement démontré notre "commentaire."

Voilà pourquoi, au regard de ces vieilles gens, l'écriture était radicalement *concrète et réaliste*: ce qui était écrit, ce n'était point d'abord le mot, le nom prononcé de la chose, mais la chose, munie d'un nom, certes, mais inséparable d'elle, confondu avec elle, comme on l'a rappelé à l'instant (§ 32). Et ce nom écrit, pareil à la chose elle-même, constituait une donnée matérielle, concrète, massive, comparable à une substance dont chaque portion, fût-ce la plus petite, contenait toutes les vertus de l'ensemble. Aussi pouvait-on l'exploiter, tout autant que la chose elle-même: le scruter, comme elle, l'analyser, le réduire en ses éléments et en faire ainsi comme sortir tout ce qu'il contenait de réalités et d'intelligibilité de la chose.

34. Les opérations de l'esprit grâce auxquelles s'effectuaient ces analyses, ces examens, ces avancées dans le savoir, ces "raisonnements," comme on peut les appeler, "par moyens termes," permettant de passer pour le même sumérogramme *écrit* à divers sens voisins dont le cumul enrichissait la connaissance du sujet du nom, on ne peut également les comprendre, les juger non-absurdes, en percevoir la rationalité, que si l'on se place dans une même vision réaliste de l'écriture. La polysémie de chaque signe (§§ 20ss, surtout 25) remonte, en effet, à la pictographie originelle. Dans un pareil état de l'écriture, où une chose, pour être écrite, devait être dessinée, au moins silhouettée, *c'est-à-dire demeurant elle-même, mais transposée*, il était forcément impossible de tout écrire: non seulement parce qu'il eût fallu un nombre quasiment infini de signes, mais aussi parce que quantité de réalités appréhendées par l'esprit, telles les actions, les mutations, les notions générales, échappent à toute représentation ponctuelle. Pour rendre l'écriture utilisable, il fallait donc amplifier au maximum la richesse sémantique d'un nombre suffisamment réduit de pictogrammes, en faisant de ces derniers des idéogrammes, c'est-à-dire en mettant en relations la chose que chacun d'eux, originellement et essentiellement, incarnait et représentait, avec un certain nombre d'autres: objets, activités ou abstractions, rattachés à elle, dans le monde réel, par un quelconque lien, perçu ou imaginé, de causalité, de ressemblance, de substitution, d'accompagnement, voire de pur symbolisme. C'est ainsi que le signe de "l'étoile" (§ 25, sous DINGIR) a pu marquer tout ce qui est au ciel, et par conséquent en haut, supérieur et dominateur; et que tout le domaine sémantique de la culture des plantes avec ses résultats et ses produits, s'est trouvé, au moins virtuellement, associé au pictogramme qui représentait la "plante arrosée" (A. Falkenstein ATU, Liste p. 34:115), c'est-à-dire cultivée.

L'écriture, en son état natif, avait donc regroupé et relié les choses en des manières de *constellations sémantiques*, autour d'un centre: d'une notion, généralement tirée de l'objet représenté d'abord par le pictogramme, grâce à laquelle on pouvait légitimement passer de l'une à l'autre. Certes, plus tard, avec la mise au point du phonétisme, ce stade originel a pu se dépasser et l'écriture, désormais axée, non plus sur les choses, mais sur la langue, gagner en clarté, en précision, en universalité, rendant pratiquement inutiles ces recours aux "constellations sémantiques," seule ressource de la pictographie. Aussi la signification de "l'étoile" a-t'elle été réduite, pratiquement, au ciel et au monde divin; et celle de la "plante cultivée," à la notion générale de légumineuse, de plante potagère. Mais *à ses usagers lettrés*, il est toujours resté de l'écriture cunéiforme cette vision archaïque: concrète, réaliste, polysémique, et qui, à travers un seul et même signe, permettait ainsi de passer d'une chose à l'autre, de tirer une réalité de l'autre, et d'enrichir de la sorte la connaissance d'un objet donné, par la seule analyse de son nom écrit, comme nous l'avons suffisamment vu pratiquer aux auteurs de notre "commentaire."

---

35. On pensera peut-être, si l'on a eu le courage de lire cette discussion jusqu'au bout, que c'est ici bien du travail pour peu de chose. Mais d'abord, pour un historien aussi conscient des exigences de son métier que l'était notre ami trop vite disparu, que nous honorons ici et auquel j'ai repensé tout le temps en écrivant ces lignes, il vaut toujours la peine de se garder, à n'importe quel prix, du "danger d'appliquer nos propres catégories à des phénomènes qui nous sont totalement étrangers": et, pour peu que l'on y réfléchisse, l'écriture est l'un de ces phénomènes. D'autre part, vu l'importance de cette écriture dans toute la civilisation mésopotamienne ancienne—importance à mon sens encore sous-estimée—n'est-il pas indispensable de s'en faire une idée plus claire et d'en mieux percevoir tout ce que ses usagers y voyaient et tout ce qu'ils en pouvaient tirer? Non seulement notre intelligence de leur littérature lexicographique,[62] toujours si mal

62. Voir déjà la n. 52, ci-dessus. L'importance donnée, dans ces listes, aux synonymes (notamment: Malku), homonymes (notamment: Nabnîtu), voire antonymes (par ex.: Erimḫuš) est significative, puisque toutes ces corrélations, non seulement

connue, en dépend, mais même notre possibilité de comprendre ce qui, *à nos yeux* occupation naïve et frivole, était *pour eux* spéculation rationnelle et "scientifique." Pour ne citer qu'un exemple de poids: une grande partie de la déduction divinatoire relève de cette même conception du mot-chose, de l'écrit-réalité, et de la possibilité d'en disséquer le contenu pour en faire avancer la connaissance.[63] Et qui niera l'importance de la déduction divinatoire, non seulement pour l'histoire de la pensée mésopotamienne, mais pour la préhistoire de la nôtre?

---

tournent autour des *mots*, mais permettent de passer de l'un à l'autre par rassemblance ou par opposition et de reconstituer de ces "constellations sémantiques" qui paraissent avoir occupé une place centrale dans le système de pensée et de mise en ordre du monde par l'écriture, propre à nos vieux Mésopotamiens. La thèse de A. Cavigneaux, Die sumerisch-akkadischen Zeichenlisten. Überlieferungsprobleme (München, 1976), premier travail systématique important sur ce riche domaine, éclaire grandement les problèmes ici contemplés.

63. Voir J. P. Vernant et al., Divination et rationalité (1974), notamment pp. 162ss.

LE DROIT ET LE TORDU

Elena Cassin
Centre Nationale de la Recherche Scientifique, Paris

Les quelques réflexions qui font l'object de cet article ont pour point de départ une analyse de certains aspects de la notion de légitimité dont témoignent, entre autres, des passages du deuxième livre de Samuel.

Il m'a semblé que Jack Finkelstein qui avait une intelligence si aigue des questions touchant au droit et à la société, aurait trouvé quelque intérêt á les lire.

Voici les faits.

Au moment où David devient effectivement roi de Juda (II Sam. 2:4), sur une portion réduite du royaume d'Israel règne Išbaᶜal, le dernier fils survivant de Saul, si on excepte les deux fils que celui-ci a eu de Rispah qui, toutefois, n'était que sa concubine et non une de ses épouses.

Après la mort d'Abner, lorsque Išbaᶜal meurt assassiné, la maison de Saul possède encore un rejeton légitime: Meppibaᶜal ou Meribaᶜal,[1] le fils de Jonathan, qui n'était qu'un enfant en bas-âge lorsque son père et son grand père périssent à Guilboa. A la suite de ces événements tragiques, la nourrice qui a la garde de l'enfant se sauve du palais en emportant dans les bras le petit Meribaᶜal.[2] Mais, dans sa hâte à s'enfuir, elle laisse choir l'enfant qui, à la suite de cette chute, ne recouvre plus l'usage normal de ses jambes; il reste estropié et boitera toute sa vie.[3]

L'attitude de David envers ce rejeton direct et légitime de Saul est très complexe. D'une part, il semble même ignorer son existence jusqu'à une date tardive et cherche à en être informé seulement une fois l'ensemble de tribus formant le royaume d'Israel réuni à nouveau entre ses mains. A ce moment, il fait preuve de magnanimité envers Meribaᶜal. Toutefois, le texte le précise, il est mû en agissant ainsi par un sentiment de miséricorde[4] envers la mémoire de Jonathan auquel tant de liens l'unissaient. Lorsque Meribaᶜal apparait devant lui, David l'encourage à ne pas avoir peur puisqu'il veut, en souvenir de son père, user à son égard de miséricorde. On peut se demander pour quelle raison Meribaᶜal devrait avoir peur de David contre lequel il n'a jamais combattu ni manifesté aucune hostilité.[5] Mais tout le passage est articulé de façon à montrer que David n'agit pas par calcul politique, mais seulement par bonté et pitié, ce qui exclut toute arrière pensée chez David dans ses rapports avec le fils de Jonathan.

La générosité royale se traduit par un geste précis: David rendra à Meribaᶜal la totalité des biens immobiliers de Saul à la condition expresse qu'un ancien homme lige de Saul, Siba[6] gère les biens pour le compte de Meribaᶜal. Quant à celui-ci, David préfère le garder dans son entourage immédiat et, sans lui confier de fonction précise à la cour, il en fait son convive. Cet arrangement, bien qu'il ait toute l'apparence d'un acte gratuit, poursuit en réalité, un but intéressé: neutraliser conplètement Meribaᶜal en tant qu'héritier présomptif au trône. A partir de ce moment, Meribaᶜal est économiquement dépendant de Siba et la suite du récit le démontrera. En outre, en le faisant asseoir à sa table, David inclut Meribaᶜal parmi les gens de sa maison et marque ainsi la situation d'infériorité où l'héritier légitime se trouve par rapport à lui.

En d'autres occasions la conduite de David envers les descendants de Saul est empreinte de la même

1. Sauf dans I Chr. 8:34 et 9:40 où on trouve: *mᵊriḇ-baᶜal*, dans tous les autres passages le nom est: *mᵊp̱î-baᶜal, baᶜal* étant vocalisé *bošeṯ*. Sur une dérivation egyptienne du nom *Merri-baᶜal*, voir Humbert, ZAW 38 (1919-30) 86: Aimé (*mry*) de Baᶜal, et Spiegelberg, ZAW 38 (1919-20) 172, qui est d'opinion contraire. Pour J. Pedersen, Israel 3/4 514, *Mᵊrîbaᶜal* signifie: Homme de Baᶜal, quant à M. Noth, IPN p. 143 n. 2, avec Meribaᶜal on aurait exemple intéressant de mélange d'éléments araméens et cananéens dans un nom israélite. E. Dhorme, La Bible 1 (La Pleiade, 1971) 938 n. 4, lit *Mippibaᶜal*, d'après la Septante "ce qui donne comme sens: de la bouche de Baᶜal," plutôt que *Mᵊp̱îbaᶜal* (*bošeṯ*) du texte hébreu. La lecture *Mᵊrîbaᶜal* me parait préférable puisqu'elle est celle donnée par le livre des Chroniques qui en plusieures occasions semble avoir conservé avec plus de fidélité les noms hébreux tels quels.

2. II Sam. 4:4.

3. Meribaᶜal est dit: frappé des deux pieds, *nᵊḵēh ragᵊlayim* (II Sam. 4:4a; 9:3b); (boiteux, *pissēaḥ* (II Sam. 19:27); boiteux des deux pieds, *pissēaḥ šᵊtê ragᵊlā(y)w* (II Sam. 9:13). En outre, le passage de II Sam. 4:4b a: il tomba et devint boiteux: *wayyipāsēaḥ*.

4. II Sam. 9:3a: *ḥesed ʾĕlōhîm*.

5. Lorsque Meribaᶜal dit plus tard (II Sam. 19:29) "qu'il n'y avait dans la maison de mon père que des hommes dignes de mort," il fait peut être allusion aux nobles de la tribu de Benjamin avec à leur tête Šimei, fils de Gera. Quant à lui-même quelsqu'aient été les desseins des anciens serviteurs de Saul à son égard, il a vécu jusqu'au jour où le roi l'a fait venir, dans la maison the Machir à Lodebar.

6. Le personnage est intéressant. Dans ce passage (II Sam. 9:2) il est désigné comme "un serviteur de la maison de Saul" et plus loin, verset 9, comme "le serviteur de Saul." Dans II Sam. 19:18 Siba, "serviteur de Saul," avec ses quinze fils, ses vingt serviteurs, fait partie des nobles de Benjamin accourus au devant de David qui s'apprête à traverser le Jourdain pour rentrer à Jerusalem.

Ancient Near Eastern Studies in Memory of J. J. Finkelstein
Connecticut Academy of Arts and Sciences, Memoir 19

ambivalence. Par exemple, lorsqu'il exige de Išbaᶜal que Mical lui soit rendue,[7] il semble agir par intérêt parce que la présence d'une fille de Saul à côté de lui, en tant qu'épouse, en affirmant sa qualité de beau-fils de Saul, lui confère un droit supplémentaire à la royauté sur l'ensemble d'Israel. Du reste, il n'hésitera pas à punir Mical, en ne s'approchant jamais plus d'elle, lorsqu'elle le tancera de manquer de manières royales.

La réponse de David est d'ailleurs significative: "c'est Yahwe qui m'a choisi de préférence à ton père et à toute sa famille pour m'instituer chef sur son peuple."[8] De même, il n'hésite pas à frapper les assassins d'Išbaᶜal[9] ou l'Amalécite qui vient lui annoncer la mort de Saul à laquelle il avoue n'être pas étranger,[10] mais il permettra, sans l'ombre d'un regret, que la vengeance par le sang des Gabaonites[11] s'assouvisse sur tout ce qui reste de la descendance de Saul, sauf Meribaᶜal. Vis-à-vis de ce dernier, le comportement de David apparait étrangement inconséquent. Généreux en apparence—David le tire de sa retraite où il se tenait cantonné et lui rend les biens de son grand-père—il n'hésite pas à tout lui reprendre quelque temps après, prêtant foi aux propos mensongers de Siba. Lorsqu'il s'avère que ce dernier a accusé injustement son maître, il ne punira pas le calomniateur, ainsi que l'on s'y attendrait; mais au contraire, il fait la part égale entre calomnié et calomniateur en divisant les biens de Saul entre les deux. En agissant ainsi, il se comporte comme si les allégations de Siba, même si elles se sont avérées fausses et destinées uniquement à susciter la colère de David envers Meribaᶜal, avaient fait naître, dans l'esprit du roi, une méfiance envers l'innocent, une suspicion sur ses intentions véritables telle que rien désormais n'est en mesure de le disculper entièrement.

Si on prend la peine d'examiner les passages de II Samuel qui concernent les relations entre David et Meribaᶜal, un ensemble d'éléments nous permet d'éclairer ce que nous venons tout juste de suggérer.

Les faits, auxquels je viens de faire allusion, se situent au moment de la révolte d'Absalom. Siba[12] accourt à la rencontre de David qui s'est enfui précipitamment de Jérusalem, à pied, suivi de ceux parmi ses serviteurs qui lui sont restés fidèles. Siba se présente au roi avec deux ânes chargés de ravitaillement. Au roi qui lui demande: "Que vas-tu faire de ces choses?," Siba répond: "Les ânes serviront de monture à la maison du roi.[13] Quant à la cargaison de fruits, de raisins secs et de pains ce sera pour nourrir les jeunes gens, et le vin pour la boisson de ceux qui sont fatigués." La monture, l'âne, joue dans tous les récits un rôle singulier: tantôt par son absence—c'est parce qu'il manque d'âne, que Meribaᶜal ne pourra pas rendre hommage à David en fuite—,tantôt par sa présence—l'âne porteur de dons en nature sert à créer l'allégeance entre Siba et David[14] et deviendra ensuite monture pour le roi. Lorsque le roi demande pour quelle raison Meribaᶜal n'est pas venu, lui aussi, à sa rencontre, Siba répond perfidement: "mon maître est resté à Jérusalem car il s'est dit: 'aujourd'hui la maison d'Israël me rendra la royauté de mon père'." En réalité les choses se sont passées tout différement et David n'apprendra que plus tard, lorsque tout sera rentré dans l'ordre, la véritable version des faits.[15] C'est l'invalidité dont est atteint Meribaᶜal, et plus encore la duplicité de Siba qui ont empêché le fils de Jonathan de venir à la rencontre du roi, comme il l'aurait voulu. Meribaᶜal ne pouvant marcher voulait qu'on lui selle un âne[16] pour pouvoir se rendre au devant de David. Siba prépare effectivement deux ânes, mais au lieu de les mettre à la disposition de son maître, il les charge de pains et de fruits qu'il offre au roi et à ses serviteurs. Il parvient ainsi à empêcher qui Meribaᶜal montre sa dévotion à David, à un moment particulièrement critique où celui-ci compte ses vrais amis. De plus, il éveille par ses paroles la méfiance du roi envers Meribaᶜal en l'accusant de vouloir profiter de la situation pour

7. II Sam. 3:13-14: le retour de Mical est la condition posée par David à Abner et, ensuite, à Išbaᶜal pour commencer des tractations de paix.

8. II Sam. 6:20sq.

9. II Sam. 4:12.

10. Selon le récit de la mort de Saul conservé dans II Sam. 1:9sq., l'Amalécite, se tenant serré contre le roi, l'aide, en quelque sorte, à se tuer. Cette version est différente de celle transmise par I Sam. 31:4sq., selon laquelle Saul, après le refus de son porteur d'armes de le transpercer de son épée, se serait donné lui-même la mort en se jétant sur sa propre épée.

11. II Sam. 21:8.

12. II Sam. 16:1: Siba est désigné ici comme le serviteur de Meribaᶜal

13. II Sam. 16:2.

14. La tromperie de Siba poursuit un double but: d'une part dissocier Meribaᶜal de David, d'autre part créer une communication entre le roi et lui-même. La demarche de Siba est de ce fait, dans un sens, parallèle, toute proportion gardée, à celle d'Abigail, la femme de Nabal (II Sam. 13:30sq.). L'un et l'autre accourent au devant de David avec des ânes chargés à peu près des mêmes denrées; l'un et l'autre cherchent par ces dons de nourriture à interrompre à leur profit une relation qui s'était nouée entre deux personnes, rélation négative, faite d'hostilité, dans le cas de Nabal, positive et bâtie sur la commensalité, dans le cas de Meribaᶜal. L'une, Abigail, parvient ainsi à écarter le Fou du chemin de l'oint de Yahwe, tandis que l'autre, Siba, reussit par la calomnie à supplanter le Boiteux.

15. II Sam. 19:27sq.

16. II Sam. 19:27sq.; Meribaᶜal dit: "Je vais me seller une ânesse."

s'emparer du trône. Bien que l'accusation fut absurde—même si Absalom sortait vainqueur de la lutte qui l'opposait à son père, il n'y aurait aucune chance pour que Meribaᶜal puisse accéder au trône, qui aurait été acquis dans ce cas à Absalom—elle était de nature à troubler profondément David. En effet, le propos tenu par Siba, tout en étant mensonger dans la lettre, faisait allusion à une situation réelle. Meribaᶜal est, en effet, l'héritier légitime de Saul. A cause de celà, David prête foi au discours absurde de Siba, dépouille le malheureux Meribaᶜal de tout ce qu'il lui avait rendu quelque temps auparavant et même, lorsque sa bonne foi ne peut plus être mise en doute, ne punit pas le coupable mais au contraire, le met sur un pied d'égalité avec sa victime innocente.[17]

Avant d'aller plus loin, dans l'analyse de l'épisode de Meribaᶜal, il nous faut considérer la signification que la boiterie a dans ce contexte.

En général, dans la Bible, le fait d'être boiteux[18] figure parmi les infirmités qui interdisent l'exercice de la prêtrise[19] à celui qui en est atteint. Les autres infirmités qui sont visées dans Lév. 21:20, sont la cécité totale ou partielle (celui qui a une tâche dans l'oeil), la fracture d'une main ou d'un pied, le fait d'être bossu ou trop maigre,[20] la difformité des traits du visage, le fait d'avoir un testicule écrasé, et, enfin, la gale et une autre maladie de la peau difficile à identifier.[21]

Entre ces deux entités en présence: Yahwe, qui est par essence parfait, et le peuple qui peut atteindre un type de perfection—*gôy qādôš*, "une nation sainte"[22]—dans la mesure où il accepte pleinement la *bᵊrîṯ* qu'il a conclue avec Dieu, aussi bien l'agent médiateur, le prêtre sacrificateur, que l'animal grâce auquel la médiation a pu avoir lieu, ne doivent présenter aucun défaut.

Ainsi, on ne pourra sacrifier à Yahwe aucun animal, qu'il s'agisse de gros ou de petit bétail qui ne soit parfait à savoir, tout animal qui présente une tare,[23] qu'il soit aveugle, estropié,[24] mutilé ou qu'il ait une maladie de peau.[25] Dans Deut. 15:20-21, il est en outre prescrit qu'on n'offrira pas en sacrifice un *bᵊḵôr*, de gros ou de petit bétail qui soit "boiteux[26] ou aveugle ou qui ait quelque tare mauvaise." Cette bête doit être mangée en famille (dans tes portes), comme on mange de la gazelle et du cerf.

En définitive, si on réfléchit sur les anormalités qui sont prises en considération à propos du prêtre dans Lév. 21:18-20, et à propos de l'animal à sacrifier dans Lév. 21:19-22, il résulte qu'elles peuvent être réduites à trois et même à deux catégories.

La première comprend la boiterie et la cécité qui sont d'ailleurs mentionnées les premières dans Lév. 21:18. Ces deux infirmités concernent, toutes les deux, l'équilibre du corps. Chez l'homme, tout mal qui affecte un point quelconque des deux axes qui soutiennent le torse, produit une instabilité de tout le corps. De même, chez les quadrupèdes, une patte infirme, brisée ou coupée, détruit la stabilité de son assise en l'obligeant à sautiller au lieu de marcher.[27]

Quant à l'aveugle, son comportement se caractérise par une allure incertaine et déconnectée au niveau des mains qui cherchent un appui et des pieds qui trébuchent à tout dénivellement du sol, de sorte que son équilibre est bouleversé. A partir de ces deux infirmités, boiterie et cécité, qui constituent en un sens les deux pôles extrêmes du déséquilibre, on peut regrouper les difformités et mutilations qui sont mentionnées dans le verset suivant:[28] fracture de la jambe ou de la main (unijambiste ou manchot?), tâche dans l'oeil (borgne), un testicule écrasé gibbosité, atrophie ou maigreur excessive, difformité ou mutilation du visage. Toutes ces

17. II Sam. 19:30: David décide: "J'ai dit: toi et Siba vois partagerez les terres."

18. Lév. 21:18: *pissᵊaḥ*; II Sam. 5:6b: *pissᵊḥîm*.

19. L'homme de la descendance d'Aaron qui présente sur son corps une tare ne pourra offrir son aliment à Yahwe, mais il pourra toutefois manger comme ses frères de l'aliment de son dieu (Lév. 21:22). L'explication donnée, entre autres, par E. Dhorme, que les prescriptions sur la perfection physique des prêtres sont des survivances de l'époque où le prêtre se présentait nu devant son dieu, n'est guère soutenable. Comment une religion dont un des fondements essentiels est l'idée de totalité et d'intégrité aurait-elle pu tolérer qu'on offre à la divinité quelque chose d'imparfait et que l'officiant du sacrifice, nu ou habillé peu importe, porte sur son corps les stigmates d'un état qui est le contraire de la sainteté? Cf. J. Pedersen, Israel 3/4 274sq.; M. Douglas, De la souillure p. 71sq., qui reprend sur ce point en grande partie les idées de Pedersen en leur conférant une dimension plus anthropologique.

20. Lév. 21:20: la traduction du terme *daq* semble bien être "maigre" dans ce contexte plutôt que "atrophié."

21. Voir plus loin et note 29.

22. Ex. 19:6a.

23. Le terme que l'on traduit communément par tare dans Lév. 22:20-21 ainsi que dans d'autres passages, entre autre Lév. 21:17, signifie en réalité "quoique ce soit," comme la forme apparentée *mᵊûmāh*. Cf. H. Zimmern, Fremdw. p. 20. Toute la notion d'impureté est dans ce terme. L'homme, l'animal ou l'objet qui a "quelque chose," est différent, sort de ce fait de la norme et est impur.

24. Lév. 22:22: "qui a une fracture"; *šābûr*.

25. Voir plus loin n. 29.

26. *pisseḥa*.

27. Il en est de même si il s'agit d'un animal qui nait avec cinq pattes out trois, selon la Mischna, Bekhorot 6, il est *trefa*.

28. Lév. 21:19-20.

tares relèvent d'un défaut d'équilibre ou de symétrie, deux notions qui sont pour nous voisines et qui l'étaient encore plus pour les Hébreux.

La dernière catégorie concerne uniquement les maladies de la peau et du cuir chevelu, gale (*gereḇ*)[29] et teigne (*yalleḇeṯ*),[30] défauts qui sont également considérées comme un motif pour écarter du sacrifice l'animal qui en est atteint. Ces maladies quelle que soit leur nature exacte provoquaient des anomalies de la pigmentation de la peau qui présentait, de ce fait, des tâches plus claires ou plus obscures comme c'est le cas pour le vitaligo. De même, les alopécies du cuir chevelu produisaient dans la chevelure des zones plus claires.[31]

On peut se demander quel lien relie entre elles ces trois catégories d'infirmité qui sont en rapport respectivement avec le déséquilibre, l'asymétrie et la polychromie. Un élément dont on doit tenir compte est, qu'aussi bien le boiteux et l'aveugle, que le malade atteint d'une maladie de l'épiderme s'écartent de la voie qui leur a été assignée par Yahwe. Tandis que les deux premiers n'obéissent plus à la règle de leur nature qui est de se tenir fermement sur leur assise et de poser avec assurance le pied sur le sol—mais ils trébuchent et tatonnent pour trouver leur chemin et sont même obligés de se servir d'une béquille ou d'un bâton[32] comme d'une troisième jambe—l'autre, le galeux ou le teigneux, devenant tacheté ou multicolore, ou offrant aux regards un crâne, par endroits dénudé, s'écarte lui aussi de sa voie normale qui est d'avoir une peau uniforme. Chacun sa nature, comme dit le prophète: "Un Choushite peut-il changer sa peau et un léopard ses rayures?"[33]

D'autres passages bibliques donnent, à la boiterie et à la cécité un relief particulier.

Pour Malachie 1:8 et 13, l'animal volé,[34] boiteux,[35] aveugle ou malade qu'on sacrifie à Yahwe contrairement à la loi, devient l'image même du laisser-aller et de l'attitude négligente que le peuple témoigne à l'égard de son dieu. Immoler un animal malade, c'est offrir à Yahwe un présent indigne, insultant même, dont on n'oserait pas faire cadeau à un gouverneur pour sa table. La brebis boiteuse deviendra ainsi, d'une part l'objet que l'on offre par dérision à Dieu, et d'autre part, l'image de l'homme, voire du peuple rejete, exclu, exilé: "En ce jour là, oracle de Yahwe, je recueillerai la (brebis) boiteuse et je ramasserai la pourchassée, ainsi que celle que j'avais maltraitée."[36] La même image revient chez Sophonie: "En ce temps-là, je sauverai la (brebis) boiteuse et je ramasserai la pourchassée."[37]

La pensée des prophètes joue tout le temps sur cette double signification de la boiterie. D'une part celui qui trébuche et tombe est l'homme qui n'a pas obéi à l'enseignement de son dieu, qui s'est montré indocile ou infidèle, sous les pieds duquel le sol s'est dérobé. "Leurs pieds courent au mal. Ils rendent tortueux leurs chemins, celui qui y marche ne connait pas la paix,"[38] et plus loin "Nous tâtonnons[39] comme des aveugles le long d'un mur, nous tâtonnons comme ceux qui n'ont plus d'yeux, nous trébuchons[40] en plein midi comme au crépuscle." La relation entre celui qui marche et l'espace sur lequel il se meut apparait inversée. Ce n'est pas à cause des aspérités du sol que le pied du pécheur chavire, c'est à cause de ses actions que sa voie est pleine d'embûches. De même, entre le fait de ne pas voir et la clarté du jour il y a la même relation: celui qui tâtonne en plein jour est comme un aveugle pour qui il est indifférent que le jour succède à la nuit. "Yahwe te frappera de folie, de cécité, de confusion."[41] On trouve la même idée dans Deut. 28:29: "Tu seras tâtonnant en plein midi, comme tâtonne l'aveugle (qui est toujours) dans l'obscurité." Des verbes comme tâtonner, *gāšaš* et

29. Selon De. 28:27, *gereḇ* est certainement une affection grave de la peau, qu'on peut rapprocher entre autres de l'accadien *garābu*—sorte d'éruption scabieuse dont peuvent être également atteints les moutons—qui se manifeste par l'apparition de tâches blanches (AMT 84 4 iii 9). *Garābu* est donné par les vocabulaires comme un mal identique à *saḫaršubb/ppû* qui apparait parmi les malédictions des *adē* d'Asarhaddon (Wiseman, Treaties lignes 419-21); celui qui en souffre, ira errant dans le désert comme l'onagre et la gazelle.

30. Dhorme, La Bible, traduit ce terme par "dartreux"; L. Koehler, Lexikon p. 383a, "herpès." *yalleḇeṯ*, qui apparait seulement dans Lév. 21: 20 et 22, est traduit dans la Vulgate par *impetigo*.

31. Les prescriptions de Lév. 13:40sq. au sujet de la calvitie sont formelles. Si la calvitie est totale, l'homme est pur; si le cuir chevelu est dégarni en partant du front, il est pur également. La calvitie ne rend pas impur et peut être considérée comme un phénomène normal lorsqu'elle se situe en continuation de la peau soit que le crâne soit complètement glabre—comme était Elie—soit que le front soit dégarni.

32. Voir le passage de II Sam. 3:29 où "l'homme maniant le fuseau" (*pelekh*) est devenu dans la LXX: "l'homme qui se sert d'un bâton" (skutále), c'est à dire le boiteux ou l'aveugle.

33. Jé. 13:25.

34. Seulement dans 1:13b: *gazul*: une bête volée, prise sans donner de contrepartie, objet de ce fait d'une action déséquilibrée, boiteuse, ne peut pas être offerte à Yahwe.

35. *pisséaḥ*.

36. Mi. 4:6. La boiteuse est ici *ṣōlēᶜāh*.

37. So. 3:19: *ṣōlēᶜāh*.

38. Is. 59:7.

39. Verset 10: *nᵊgašᵊšāh*.

40. Verset 10: *kāšalᵊnû*.

41. Les mêmes termes se retrouvent dans Za. 12:4: "en ce jou là, oracle de Yahwe, je frapperai tout cheval de confusion et son cavalier de folie, je frapperai tous . . . les peuples de cécité."

kāšal, trébucher, qui reviennent avec fréquence dans ce contexte désignent la démarche incertaine qui est aussi bien celle de l'aveugle, lorsqu'en cherchant sa voie il essaie de pallier par le toucher à son infirmité, que celle du boiteux ou de l'homme que la faiblesse de ses membres inférieurs oblige à poser le pied avec précaution, quelque soit le chemin qu'il parcourt.

D'autre part, toujours chez les prophètes, le boiteux et l'aveugle symbolisent le peuple d'Israël qui a été précipité à cause de ses infidélités dans le malheur de l'exil: "Voici que moi, je l'ai fait venir du pays du Nord et je les rassemble des confins de la terre. Parmi eux l'aveugle et le boiteux,[42] celle qui a conçu et celle qui a enfante"; et plus loin la même image continue: "Je les dirigerai . . . par le droit chemin où ils ne trébucheront pas."[43] Les exclus, les marginaux que sont le boiteux et l'aveugle retrouvent, grâce à Yahwe un chemin sans embuche. Et Isaie: "Je ferai aller les aveugles par une route qu'ils ne connaissent pas. Je les ménerai par des chemins qu'ils ne connaissent pas. Je rendrai devant eux les ténèbres lumineuses et les lieux accidentés, unis."[44]

De ces exemples que l'on pourrait aisément multiplier, il apparait que la boiterie et la cécité sont senties par les prophètes comme des infirmités aux multiples résonnances socio-religieuses. L'homme qui avance en boitant, comme l'aveugle qui hésite et tâtonne pour trouver son chemin, ne sont pas seulement des infirmes. Ils sont aussi des individus exclus, déchus, ou non intégrés: leur allure tâtonnante, incertaine, les désigne comme des êtres au ban de la société.

Deux passages des livres historiques sont significatifs à ce propos. Lorsque David s'apprête à conquérir Jérusalem, après avoir reçu l'onction des anciens d'Israël à Hébron, le Jébusite qui tient la ville lui fait transmettre ce message: "Tu n'entreras pas ici puisque les aveugles et les boiteux te repousseront."[45] Après que David se fut emparé de la forteresse de Sion, le texte fait à nouveau allusion à l'inimitié de ces deux catégories d'infirmes. Avant de se rendre maître de la citadelle, David aurait dit: "Quiconque veut battre le Jébusite, qu'il atteigne par le canal les boiteux et les aveugles qui haïssent la personne de David."[46]

Quel est le sens de l'hostilité que ces deux catégories d'invalides paraissent avoir voué à l'oint de Yahwe? En général, on considère que l'expression "les aveugles et les boiteux"[47] est employée comme qualification méprisante et ironique de ceux qui sont opposés à David. Bien que cette explication puisse paraître partiellement juste, il est difficile de ne pas considérer que, dans l'opposition affirmée à deux reprises entre David, d'une part et les boiteux-aveugles d'autre part, il y a des éléments plus précis et concrets, et qu'en qualifiant les ennemis de David d'aveugles et de boiteux, le texte ne cherche pas seulement à les abaisser ou à les ridiculiser. Quant au fait, que II Sam. 5:8b prétende justifier par leur attitude hostile à David la défense qui est faite aux même catégories d'infirmes de servir comme prêtres, cela aussi demande à être analysé.

Il est évident que tout un arrière plan historique du personnage de David, et à travers lui, de l'accession au pouvoir royal de la tribu de Juda nous échappe. Mais il me semble qu'entre l'histoire des vicissitudes de Meribaᶜal et l'inimitié des boiteux—et des aveugles—envers David, il y a probablement un lien.

Dans un cas, comme dans l'autre, il s'agit d'une relation entre David d'une part, et les boiteux—et les aveugles—d'autre part. Dans cette relation, les deux termes se valorisent l'un par l'autre, de sorte qu'en étudiant leurs aspects opposés, ils peuvent nous devenir en quelque sorte plus accessibles.

Le lien qui se noue entre David et le dieu d'Israël est complexe. David apparait à l'origine comme appartenant à un monde socialement différent de celui d'où est sorti le premier oint de Yahwe. Contrairement à Saul qui possède des ânesses,[48] David est un berger de petit bétail[49] et un chasseur. Il porte sur sa personne les stigmates de sa condition sociale. Il est rouquin, comme Esau et, selon une version de sa légende, habitué à chasser les fauves, lions et ours, et même à se battre contre eux en corps à corps.[50] Ce trait héroique (Samson), élément important parmi les composantes de la personne du roi assyrien, est par contre unique en Israël. Les armes de David, la fronde, ne sont pas celles d'un guerrier, d'un *gibbōr ḥayl*.[51] Lorsque le grand et fort Saul veut lui faire endosser son armure, ce qui équivaut à une véritable investiture de guerrier, David est obligé de refuser.[52] Cet armement ne convient ni à sa petite taille, ni à sa condition

42. Jé. 31:8: *ʾiwwēr ûpssēaḥ*.
43. Jé. 31:9b: *lōʾ yikkāšᵊlu*.
44. Is. 42:16.
45. II Sam. 5:6b; les aveugles et les boiteux: *haᶜiwᵊrîm wᵊhappisᵊḥîm*.
46. II Sam. 5:8.
47. Cf., par exemple, E. Dhorme, La Bible 1 941 n. 6: "les aveugles et les boiteux . . . semblent une défense suffisante. Reflexion ironiqué."
48. I Sam. 9:3sq.
49. I Sam. 16:11; 17:15, 20, 34; II Sam. 7:8; I Chr. 17:7b.
50. I Sam. 17:35.
51. La version de la légende de David conservée dans I Sam. 16, fait de lui un musicien qui est, en outre, un *gibbōr ḥayil*, verset 18.
52. I Sam. 17:38-39.

sociale. Les cinq pierres plates qu'il ramasse dans le torrent lui suffiront pour armer sa fronde. Il est clair que tous ces éléments font partie de la légende, dans la mesure où ils servent à mettre en évidence l'efficacité de la bénédiction de Yahwe qui permet à celui qui la reçoit de vaincre, armé d'une arme de berger, un guerrier redoutable comme Goliath.

Toutefois, quelque soit le poids de son origine, ses traits d'outsider auraient plutôt tendance à s'effacer à travers la multiplicité d'épreuves réussies qui l'habilitent à l'exercice de la royauté.

David, vainqueur des lions, mais aussi de cet autre lion[53] flamboyant qu'est Goliath, s'intègre progressivement à la famille de Saul. Avant tout en s'identifiant au fils héritier de Saul, Jonathan, en nouant avec lui une *b^{ə}rît* qui est en même temps une adoption en fraternité: Jonathan lui donne ses armes et le couvre de son manteau.[54] Investiture cette fois-ci réussie à l'opposé de ce qui s'était passé avec Saul. En deuxième lieu par son mariage avec la fille cadette de Saul, Mical, après avoir été fiancé à l'aînée, Merab.[55] Et enfin à la mort de Saul en recevant "dans son sein" les femmes de Saul[56] David régularise définitivement sa succession.

L'onction des anciens d'Israël à Hébron,[57] viendra couronner cette ascension prestigieuse qui s'achève avec la conquête de Jérusalem. De sorte que lorsque David s'intéresse enfin au "reste" de la maison de Saul,[58] il est déjà légitimé, sinon légitime.

Meribaᶜal par contre suit le chemin inverse. Fils de Jonathan, héritier légitime au trône après la mort de son grand père, de son père et de son oncle, la régularité de sa naissance de porphyrogénète est mise en relief par les deux jambes parfaitement égales qu'il a à sa naissance. C'est seulement par un accident qu'il devient *pissēaḥ*, boiteux. Il y a là un élément très significatif. En effet, tandis que pour David le processus d'intégration s'accélère après la mort de Saul, pour Meribaᶜal, en sens inverse, la dégradation se confirme. Confiné loin de la cour, il est supplanté par David d'abord et ensuite par un ancien serviteur de son grand père. Invalide, ses jambes inégales ont interrompu toute communication avec les gens de son ancien milieu, les chefs du peuple d'Israël. Dans ce contexte, la calomnie[59] de Siba sur Meribaᶜal acquiért toute sa valeur. En attribuant à Meribaᶜal des visées sur le trône qui, bien qu'absurdes peuvent trouver dans l'esprit de David une certaine crédibilité, Siba coupe à son propre profit la relation qui s'était établie peu de temps auparavant entre le roi et le fils de Jonathan. Le propre de la calomnie est d'entamer l'intégrité de celui qu'elle atteint, de sorte que le calomnié ne peut redevenir entier, normal, que si le discours qu'on a tenu sur lui revient comme un boomerang à son point de départ et frappe le calomniateur, entrainant dans son sillage un châtiment de même type et gravité que celui qui aurait puni son innocente victime. Or, dans le cas de Siba, rien de tel n'a lieu. David ne rétablit pas completement Meribaᶜal dans sa situation antérieure—tout en lui faisant une concession—et ne punit pas Siba tout en ayant l'air de le punir par la privation de la moitié des terres que sa calomnie lui avait valu. Etrange jugement, boiteux, sur le caractère duquel les rabbins ne se tromperont pas puisqu'ils verront dans cette décision du roi la préfiguration de ce qui aura lieu deux générations plus tard, à l'époque de Roboam, fils de Salomon, avec l'éclatement du royaume d'Israel en deux tronçons.[60] Dans cette perspective, la partie des biens de Saul dont Meribaᶜal est définitivement écarté par la décision de David, représente symboliquement cette partie du royaume qui dans l'avenir échappera à la maison de David et formera un état séparé.

53. Goliath, I Sam. 17:43a, se compare à un chien lorsqu'il voit avancer vers lui David avec son bâton (*maqēl*); en réalité son aspect rutilant de bronze, du casque aux jambières est typiquement léonin. D'ailleurs, I Sam. 17:35 identifie Goliath à un lion ou à un ours.

54. I Sam. 18:33: "Jonathan enleva le manteau qu'il avait sur lui et le donna à David et ses vêtements et même son épée jusqu'à son arc et à sa ceinture." Le minutieux énoncé des effets dont Jonathan se dépouille pour en revêtir David nous fait participer au déroulement du rite d'investiture. C'est Jonathan, le prince, qui agit seul. En même temps, comme J. Pedersen l'avait très bien senti (cf. Israel 1/2 279sq.), le transfert des vêtements de Jonathan à son ami est l'accomplissement de ce qui a déjà eu lieu au verset 1 lorsque "l'âme (*nepeš*) de Jonathan fut liée à l'âme de David, et Jonathan l'aima comme son âme."

55. I Sam. 18:17-21.

56. II Sam. 12:8; Yahwe parle à David par la bouche du prophête Nathan: "Je t'ai donné la maison de ton seigneur (c'est à dire, Saul) et les femmes de ton seigneur dans ton giron." Sur la signification que prend dans un contexte dynastique la possession des femmes du roi défunt, voir mon article dans RA 63 (1969) 144sq.

57. II Sam. 5:3.

58. II Sam. 9:1sq.

59. Ce n'est peut être pas le fait du seul hasard si dans II Sam. 19:28 Meribaᶜal pour dire que Siba l'a calomnie auprès du roi, emploie le verbe *ragal*, qui signifie "marcher sur les talons de quelqu'un" (italien "pedinare") "surveiller," "espionner" et enfin, comme ici, "rapporter des informations fausses à quelqu'un sur quelqu'un d'autre."

60. Lorsque David (II Sam. 19:29) décide le partage des terre de Saul entre Meribaᶜal et Siba, une voix du ciel prophétise la division future du royaume; cf. L. Ginzberg, Legends of the Jews 4 77; 6 244 ligne 2. Selon une source le temple aurait été détruit parce que David a écouté Siba.

L'interprétation que les rabbins donnent d'un acte moralement injuste, mais sans incidence réelle sur les affaires de l'Etat, éclaire la conception qu'ils ont de la personne de Meribaᶜal.[61] Dans leur esprit, celui-ci continue à incarner la légitimité monarchique, de sorte que tout ce qui le touche se répercute sur les affaires de l'Etat. Meribaᶜal écarté du trône de Saul, reste quand même lié aux avatars du pouvoir. Sa faiblesse toutefois le laisse complètement à la merci de David. Celui-ci non plus n'est pas libre de disposer à son gré du dernier rejeton de la famille de Saul, lié comme il est par le serment qu'il a prêté jadis, de ne jamais retrancher sa bienveillance de la descendance de Jonathan. La situation dans laquelle ils se trouvent, l'un vis-à-vis de l'autre, est ambiguë.

Devenu un obscur sujet de David, ignoré de la plupart, prêt à formuler sa dévotion dans les termes les plus humbles à celui qui s'est installé, à la force du poignet, sur le trône qui lui était destiné, Meribaᶜal n'en est pas moins un déclassé, "un chien mort," comme il se qualifie lui-même. De sorte que, lorsque ses lèvres prononcent des paroles apaisantes qui affirment sa bonne foi, son dévouement et sa parfaite loyauté à la personne de l'oint de Yahwe, ses pieds tordus disent autre chose. Dans le dialogue qui se lie entre David et lui il y a dissonance. Ce que Meribaᶜal dit, et que les oreilles de David entendent est en contradiction avec l'homme que le roi voit devant lui. Tout le problème est là.

Le boiteux apparait comme un homme dangereux pour le pouvoir établi. Celà pour plusieurs raisons: avant tout sa démarche ressemble à celle d'un homme qui tout en ayant deux jambes parfaitement saines s'avance sur un chemin accidenté, glissant et tortueux. On a déja fait allusion aux significations multiples, toutes négatives qu'a le fait de trébucher et tatonner. On peut ajouter maintenant un autre élément au dossier. Le boiteux qui avance clopin, clopant, en allant deci-delà, peut être assimilé à celui qui hésite continuellement entre deux directions à prendre. Ainsi, lorsque le prophète Elie tourne en dérision les prophètes de Baᶜal qui exécutent près de l'autel de leur dieu une danse de claudication,[62] il fustige en même temps le peuple d'Israël qui ne cesse de clocher de deux côtés. "Jusqu'à quand clocherez-vous des deux pieds,[63] tantôt du côté de Yahwe, tantôt du côté de Baᶜal?" Vue sous cet aspect, la boiterie apparait comme synonyme d'idolatrie. Le boiteux est, de ce fait, un être dangereux dont la place se situe à l'extremité opposée de celle occupée par l'homme qui suit les préceptes de Yahwe. Dans cette optique la haine qui existe entre l'oint de Yahwe, d'une part, et les boiteux et les aveugles,[64] d'autre part, devient compréhensible dans la mesure où David, malgré ses imperfections et ses péchés, ne cesse pas un seul instant de "marcher droit," c'est-à-dire de montrer une inlassable fidélité à Yahwe.

Toutefois, le rapport entre David et le fils de Jonathan est plus complexe. Pour comprendre sa situation, il est nécessaire de faire appel à d'autres notions qu'à celle de pluralisme religieux.

La trace inégale que les pieds invalides du boiteux laissent sur le sol nous invite à tourner nos regards vers des aspects de déséquilibre physique, soit congénital, soit accidentel comme celui du borgne, du bigle, du manchot et également vers les anomalies vestimentaires en comprenant sous cette étiquette également les diverses façons de se coiffer ou de raser la barbe.

En effet, toute rupture de l'équilibre physique place celui qui la subit, soit qu'on la lui impose, soit qu'il la choisisse délibérément, dans une situation d'anormalité qui peut aller de la simple originalité jusqu'à la degradation sociale et à la mise au ban.

Un des exemples le plus célèbre est celui des messagers que David envoie apporter ses condoléances à Hanoun, roi des Ammonites, après la mort de son père.[65] Les soupconnant d'être des espions, Hanoun les

61. Selon Berakhot 4a, David aurait gardé Meribaᶜal auprès de lui afin qu'il le conseille sur la façon de se comporter en toute situation. Il était son maître dans la Halakha.

62. I Rois 18:26-27: "Ils invoquèrent le nom de Baᶜal, du matin jusqu'a midi, en disant: 'O Baᶜal, réponds-nous.' Mais pas de voix, pas de réponse, et ils clochaient des pieds auprès de l'autel qu'on avait fait" (*wayᵊpassᵊḥû ᶜal-hammizbēaḥ*). E. Dhorme, La Bible p. 1111 n. 26, rapproche le comportement des prophètes de Baᶜal, qui est un rite de circombulation autour de la *maṣṣēbāh* en boitillant, à la danse qu'exécutent des marchands tyriens (Héliodore, Ethiopiques 4 17) après avoir offert un banquet en l'honneur d'Heraclès Tyrien. Cette danse qui consistait successivement à sauter en l'air, puis à s'accroupir près du sol en pliant les genoux et "en tournant sur soi-même comme des possédés," est plutôt une danse du type du *kordax*, danse de fin de repas, qui s'exécutait à genoux pliés; cf. Ch. Picard, Rev.Arch. 20 (1942-43) 96-124.

63. Elie demande au peuple (verset 21): "Jusqu'à quand clocherez-vous de deux côtés (*ʾattem pôsᵊḥîm ᶜal-šᵊtê hassᵊippîm*)? Si Yahwe est dieu, allez à sa suite, si c'est Baᶜal, suivez-le."

64. Dans II Sam. 5:6, 8, les boiteux et les aveugles apparaissent comme les alliés des Jébusites, donc les ennemis de David. Il n'est pas sans intérèt de rappeler que les Jébusites ainsi que d'autres peuples jadis ennemis des Hébreux (Ge. 15:20) résurgissent beaucoup plus tard dans les exorcismes juifs sous forme de démons; cf. S. Eitrem, Notes on Demonology in the New Testament, Symbolae Osloenses, fasc. suppl. 12 (1950) 17.

65. II Sam. 10:4-5.

renvoie à David après leur avoir rasé la barbe à moitié et avoir coupé la moitié de leur vêtement. Ainsi attifés, les messagers n'osent pas se montrer en Israël et David leur enjoint d'attendre dans la première ville frontière entre le pays des Ammonites et Israël, à Jericho, que leur barbe ait repoussé. La barbe et les vêtements étant des véhicules particulièrement sensibles de la personnalité, il ne fallait pas pour leur honneur, et pour celui du roi qu'ils représentaient, qu'ils soient vus, traités de cette façon particulièrement ignominieuse.

Parfois un accoutrement inusité, choquant même, peut être le signe, chez celui qui l'adopte à un moment donné, d'une marginalité volontaire. Ainsi, les poètes arabes, au moment de lancer l'*hidja*, s'exibent, une épaule nue, la moitié de la chevelure ointe et un seul pied chaussé de sandale.[66] En s'attifant de la sorte, ils s'affichent comme des être à part, menacants pour ceux qui sont la cible de leur malédiction. Ils savent que cette attitude de défi, est nécessaire pour rendre leur *carmen* plus efficace. Dans l'aspect extérieur du poète satirique, c'est la chaussure unique qui apparait comme particulièrement choquante.[67] Pour les Arabes, un pied nu, l'autre chaussé, c'est en effet la façon d'être de Satan, le boiteux par excellence.[68] On voit à quel point monocrépidisme[69] et boiterie s'entrelacent dans la pensée arabe.[70] En effet, autant l'habitude d'aller les pieds nus est considérée comme une preuve d'ascétisme, autant il est recommandé par le prophète lui-même, lorsqu'une lanière d'une sandale se déchire, d'éviter de marcher chaussé seulement d'un pied.[71]

Celui qui chemine dans ces conditions, se trouve dans une relation particulière avec l'espace sur lequel il procède: les deux traces que ses pieds impriment sur le sol sont aussi inégales que s'il avait deux pieds différents. De sorte que l'homme qui a un seul pied chaussé est, à sa façon, boiteux. Dès lors, nous nous trouvons confronté, à propos du monocrépide au même type de problèmes qu'avait soulevé la boiterie. La démarche de l'homme chaussé d'un seul pied est aussi ambiguë que celle du boiteux et, au moins d'un certain point de vue, elle rentre dans le même schème.

A ce propos, un examen même rapide du passage de Deut. 25:5sq., peut être instructif. Il y est question de la situation où vient à se trouver une veuve sans enfant, vivant avec son beau-frère[72] lorsque celui-ci refuse de la prendre comme femme, ainsi que la coutume le lui prescrit. Selon Deut. 25:6, la femme doit obliger son beau-frère à se présenter à la Porte, devant les anciens, qui lui demandent s'il est disposé à épouser sa belle-soeur. Au cas d'un nouveau refus—qu'il prononce en se tenant debout devant les Anciens[73]—la belle-soeur doit lui enlever une chaussure et cracher devant lui[74] en disant: "ainsi fait-on à celui qui renonce à relever la maison de son frère." Le texte ajoute qu'à partir de ce moment, on appellera cet homme et les siens, la "maison du déchaussé."[75] Dans le judaïsme post-biblique, la cérémonie tout entière tirera son nom, *ḥalizah*, de l'acte du déchaussement, à preuve qu'il s'agissait là du moment culminant de l'entière procédure. Les rabbins discuteront si c'est le pied droit ou le gauche que le beau-frère devait tendre vers la belle-soeur afin qu'elle le déchausse, sur le genre de sandale qui pouvait être valablement utilisée pour la *ḥalizah*.[76]

En déchaussant son beau-frère devant les anciens, la veuve négligée de Deut. 25:5-10 montre, avec toute la publicité voulue qu'à partir de ce moment les droits, que même en ne s'en prévalant pas son beau-frère conservait sur elle, sont définitivement caducs.[77] Cette rupture avec le passé qui est encore accentuée par l'acte de cracher dans la mesure où il signifie le rejet d'une situation antérieure, laisse la femme libre de

66. Malgré les nombreuses et importantes études parues depuis, cf. les références données dans l'Encyclopedie de l'Islam² 3 363, à l'article *Hidjā* (Ch. Pellat), je renvoie à I. Goldziher, Abhandlungen zur arabischen Philologie 1 46, qui a été le premier à souligner l'importance qu'a dans ce contexte le formalisme cérémoniel.

67. Cf. Goldziher, Philologie p. 50.

68. Cf. Goldziher, Philologie p. 50.

69. Cf. les très nombreuses références que donne à ce sujet A. J. Wensinck, A Handbook of Early Muhammedan Tradition p. 213. Je reviendrai sur la question du monocrépidisme dans un prochain article.

70. A ce sujet, le commentaire que Aḥmed al-Abšiḥi, al-Muštaṭraf, donne de la malédiction: "Que dieu éteigne sa lumière et lui enlève la sandale" comme signifiant: que dieu le rende aveugle et boiteux," me semble particulièrement suggestif. Cf. J. Pedersen, Der Eid p. 97.

71. Goldziher, Philologie p. 49: "S'il arrive à l'un d'entre vous que la lanière d'une sandale se déchire, jusqu'à ce qu'il ne l'ait reparée, qu'il ne garde pas l'autre au pied."

72. Le texte précise qu'il s'agit de deux frères habitant ensemble, ce qui signifie: dans l'indivision.

73. Dans le cas de Ruth 4:8 le *goʾel* en titre ôte sa sandale et la transmet à Boaz devant les Anciens à la Porte.

74. Sur la signification de cracher devant le beau-frère défaillant, voir ma note dans "La contestation dans le monde divin" dans La voix de l'opposition en Mésopotamie" (Bruxelles, 1973) p. 96 n. 24. Je traduis (verset 9a) "elle crachera devant lui," plutôt que "elle lui crachera à la face," parce que, entre autres, encore au IIIe siècle, telle était la pratique parmi les Juifs de Babylone; cf. J. Neusner, A History of the Jews in Babylonia 3 277-78.

75. Verset 10: *bêṯ ḥalûṣ hannaʿal*.

76. J. Neusner, History of the Jews 2 204.

77. Le verset 5 mentionne clairement le fait que la veuve "ne paut appartenir au-dehors à un homme étranger."

disposer d'elle-même. Inversement, le déchaussé, en renonçant publiquement à remplir les obligations qui découlent de sa situation de frère du mort, n'est plus à la place qu'il occupait précédemment sur l'échiquier familial: il déchoit et s'abaisse socialement. Le déchaussement assume dans son cas la fonction d'une désinvestiture et il serait ici nécessaire de faire appel aux témoignages qui nous sont fournis avec largesse par les anciennes civilisations proche-orientales.[78] Il nous indiffère de savoir que la *ḥalizah* était devenue, dans le monde post-biblique, une procédure commode pour permettre à une veuve de se remarier avec l'époux de son choix. Ce qui importe est de comprendre la fonction qu'avaient le renoncement public et le déchaussement à une époque plus ancienne et dans quel ensemble de relations ils s'inséraient.

Celui qui refuse de faire des enfants à la veuve de son frère, plonge le nom du mort dans l'oubli, mais lui-même ne s'en tire pas à bon compte. Désormais, une étiquette sera accrochée à sa famille, "déchaussé."

D'une part, oubli, c'est-à-dire effacement total d'un homme et de sa descendance virtuelle; de l'autre, déséquilibre, c'est-à-dire une forme de boiterie envisagée également comme tare héréditaire puisqu'elle deviendra l'appellation de ses descendants.

Si maintenant on compare le cas du déchaussé de Deut. 25 et celui du boiteux Meribaᶜal, on s'aperçoit qu'ils ont quelques points communs.

Avant tout, dans un cas comme dans l'autre, il s'agit de personnes qui sont dépossédées d'un droit. Pour le premier le déchaussement représente la perte acceptée—de bon ou mauvais gré—d'un droit qu'il détenait; pour le second, la boiterie est le signe de la revendication d'un droit dont il a été frustré.

Le déchaussement est la sanction d'un changement d'état—d'une déchéance—qui est définitif, tandis que la boiterie est le témoignage de la perte d'un droit que peut ne pas être définitive.

Meribaᶜal se trouve tour à tour dans deux états en quelque sorte contradictoires: oublié de tout le monde, il vit confiné dans une retraite qui ressemble à un exil; il est tiré de son isolement pour tomber aussitôt dans la situation opposée: celle du calomnié, c'est-à-dire de quelqu'un dont on parle trop et mal.

Oublié ou calomnié, il apparait aux autres sous un double aspect; d'une part, sa boiterie (de même que d'autres infirmités: cécité, surdité, folie) le situe, en dehors de la societé, parmi les déchus et les marginaux; d'autre part, elle le désigne comme revendiquant le pouvoir royal auquel il peut légitimement prétendre.

Ainsi lorsque Meribaᶜal se présente une dernière fois devant le roi,[79] les pieds non faits, la barbe en désordre, les vêtements sales, dans une tenue de pénitent et qu'il cherche à se disculper en soulignant à nouveau que, boiteux *pissēaḥ*, et privé de monture, il n'a pas pu suivre le roi, celui-ci, ne voyant en lui que "le boiteux," c'est-à-dire le descendant de Saul, lui répond, irrité: "Pourquoi dis-tu encore tant de paroles? J'ai dit: Toi et Siba, vous partagerez les terres."

Des faits réunis dans les pages qui précèdent et des réflexions qu'ils ont suscitées, une constatation générale me semble découler: les mythes ou l'histoire légendaire ou semi-légendaire nous tiennent un discours dont chaque élément ne peut se comprendre qu'en fonction de sa relation avec les autres. Ainsi en est-il du boiteux autour duquel a été centrée notre analyse. Loin d'avoir un rôle à peu près fixé à l'avance comme un masque de "la commedia dell'arte," nous l'avons vu assumer une signification différente selon la situation dans laquelle il évoluait.

Revendiquant dans un contexte dynastique (Meribaᶜal), déchu définitif dans un contexte familial (levir), la bancal devient idolâtre, pluraliste, infidèle aux préceptes divins, dans sa relation avec Yahwe. Comme dit le psalmiste: "Yahwe tord le chemin des méchants."[80]

Dans l'éventail des combinaisons où il peut apparaître nous avons ici privilégié un certain type de discours, tout en étant conscients que d'autre discours nous présentent une version du boiteux opposée. Ainsi en est-il de Jacob, "le seul et veritable supplantateur," dont la cuisse boiteuse devient le signe emblèmatique de sa victoire sur Elohim, ou du bégaiement—autre forme de boiterie—de Moise qui fut pourtant l'agent de communication par excellence entre Yahwe et son peuple. Pour l'un comme pour l'autre, l'infirmité est indissociable de leur éléction.

78. Cf. J. Pedersen, Der Eid p. 176.
79. II Sam. 19:30.
80. Ps. 146:9.

GILGAMESH DREAMS OF ENKIDU: THE EVOLUTION AND DILUTION OF NARRATIVE

Jerrold S. Cooper
The Johns Hopkins University

I really became hooked on Assyriology when, as an impressionable sophomore at Berkeley, I attended Jack Finkelstein's class on the "Religion and Cosmology of Ancient Mesopotamia." The high point of that semester was the several sessions devoted to the Gilgamesh Epic, which took the form of a rambling section-by-section explication of the text. Eyes sparkling, hands gesticulating to underline every point, and voice ranging excitedly over several octaves (or so it seemed), Jack's enthusiasm and even love for the text proved contagious. I remember very clearly asking him then whether he ever planned to write about Gilgamesh. He answered no, he was too busy with his work on cuneiform law, but he hoped that "one of you guys" would eventually develop some of the ideas he had about the text.

One prejudice that I have maintained from those years is Jack's preference, from an esthetic standpoint, for the Old Babylonian Gilgamesh texts over the Standard Babylonian version. The word he chose to describe the latter, "prolix," sent me scurrying to the dictionary. Esthetic judgements themselves, however, have little value unless they are justified by a careful reading of the texts in question. Can the freshness and immediacy of the Old Babylonian Gilgamesh that I, under Jack's influence, have always admired, be convincingly documented, or is this admiration either a misconception—unconsciously nurtured by the knowledge that the Old Babylonian versions are older—or perhaps just a preference for poetry less sophisticated and ornate? Without denying the virtues of the Standard Babylonian Gilgamesh,[1] I think I can show that where discrepancies appear when corresponding portions of both versions are compared (where both are preserved), the Old Babylonian text is generally the better one. I am not referring here to the use of different epithets and formulas, the substitution of one synonym or synonymous phrase for another,[2] or the elaboration or simplification of a passage as such, but rather actual differences in the narrative that affect the sense of the composition. In subsequent studies,[3] I will try to demonstrate that the superiority of the Old Babylonian text can be perceived not only for Gilgamesh, but for all other Akkadian "epic" compositions that are extant in both Old Babylonian and Standard Babylonian versions (Atraḫasis, Anzu, Etana, Naram-Sin). Here, however, I would like to focus on the two dreams of Gilgamesh foretelling the coming of Enkidu.

Two major causes of discrepancies between the Old Babylonian and Standard Babylonian versions of an Akkadian composition are the Standard Babylonian tendency toward verbatim repetition of passages unique in the Old Babylonian text, and the homogenization of originally different events in a series. The Old Babylonian and Standard Babylonian versions of Gilgamesh's two dreams illustrate these tendencies nicely.[4] In both versions of the first dream, Gilgamesh sees a meteorite fall from the starry sky. Attempting to move it, he fails, and the populace gathers around the object and kisses its feet. Here the two versions diverge: in the Old Babylonian recounting, he manages to move the meteorite with the people's help and brings it to his mother. In the Standard Babylonian story, he made love to it "as to a wife" and set it before his mother, and she "made it equal" with him. In the second dream, an ax has fallen in the middle of Uruk, and the people again are gathered around. In the Old Babylonian version, the ax is described as having a strange appearance, but Gilgamesh is overjoyed to see it and makes love to it "as to a wife." Then he takes it up and sets it at his side. In the Standard Babylonian version, Gilgamesh first sets the ax before his mother, *then* makes loves to it, and, as in the first dream, the mother "makes it equal" with him.

1. The poetry of the SB version, which demands monographic attention, has peerless moments, but judgements such as Landsberger, Garelli Gilg. 34 ("die Intentionen des älteren Dichters allerseits gewahrt blieben, die Behandlung des Stoffes jedoch bereichert und verfeinert wurde"), and Hallo, IEJ 12 18f. ("the far-reaching changes which we can trace precisely in this composition in the passages where both the Old Babylonian and the Neo-Assyrian versions are preserved show that the adaptation was at the same time the work of a creative genius whose name was worthy of being remembered"), must certainly be modified.

2. While changing literary tastes and conventions may account for some substitutions, most remain mysterious. The change, in the texts treated here, of *nuššu* (OB Gilg. P i 9) to *šubalkutu* (SB v 30), for example, might be explained as the SB redactor's desire to avoid using *nuššu* twice in the same line. But why would a scribe be moved to change *iktabit elija* to *dān elija* (OB Gilg. P i 8 and SB v 29)? Many, but not nearly all, of the differences between OB and SB literary style have been discussed by Hecker, AOATS 8 196ff.

3. One is to appear in a future JAOS.

4. The texts, with translations, are appended for the reader's convenience.

Ancient Near Eastern Studies in Memory of J. J. Finkelstein
Connecticut Academy of Arts and Sciences, Memoir 19

The Old Babylonian text carefully relegates the combative aspect of the Gilgamesh-Enkidu relationship—with Gilgamesh's ultimate victory (moving the meteorite)—to the first dream, and the loving and helpful aspects to the second; the Standard Babylonian redactor has made the two dreams virtually identical from the moment the citizens of Uruk assemble around the fallen object. Only the foot-kissing of the first dream is omitted in the narrative of the second; otherwise, the love-making, from the second Old Babylonian dream, the bringing of the object to the mother, from the first Old Babylonian dream, and her "making it equal"[5] are in both Standard Babylonian dreams. The clumsiness of the conflation is underscored by the inverse order of events in the second dream, where we are asked to imagine Gilgamesh making love to an ax in his mother's presence! More seriously, the Standard Babylonian conflation robs the dreams of their most powerful imagery: Gilgamesh, in the first Old Babylonian dream, moving the massive object with his men's assistance, and, in the second Old Babylonian dream, picking up the newly loved ax and placing it at his side, where the pun "side/brother" (both=Akkadian *aḫu*) foreshadows his future relationship with Enkidu.[6]

The Standard Babylonian penchant for symmetry and repetition also expresses itself—this time without disturbing the narrative—in the description of the assembled people of Uruk. In the first dream, the Old Babylonian *Uruk mātum paḫir elišu* is expanded to three lines in SB v 31ff.[7] In the second dream, the elliptical Old Babylonian *elišu paḫru* is found at the end of SB vi 9, but is then followed there by the same three lines used to describe the gathering in the first dream.

Turning to the dreams' interpretations by Ninsun, the mother of Gilgamesh, the same processes can be observed. In the Old Babylonian interpretation of the first dream, all that is really repeated from the dream itself is the description of the men kissing the object's feet; even the verbs used to describe Gilgamesh bringing it/him to his mother differ in the dream and in the interpretation.[8] Rather than looking back to the dream being explicated, there is a direct foreshadowing of the dream to come in OB P i 20 ~ 32, and less directly in P i 22 (cf. 33f.). The Standard Babylonian interpretation is preceded by a recapitulation of the dream (v 41-44 ~ 27-30; 45-48 ~ 36-39),[9] and the interpretation itself refers back to the meteorite (vi 3).[10] The foreshadowing of the second dream which occurs in the Old Babylonian interpretation is perhaps reflected by the second, rather clumsy, recapitulation of the love-making in SB vi 4. The meat of both Standard Babylonian dream interpretations is the "rescuing friend" motif of vi 1 = 20, which is absent in the Old Babylonian interpretation of the first dream, but possibly was present in the short, broken, second Old Babylonian interpretation, and essentially foreshadows the second speech of the elders to Gilgamesh in SB III i~OB Y vi 19ff. It must be noted here, with Oppenheim,[11] that neither version, oddly enough, interprets Gilgamesh's initially unsuccessful efforts to move the meteorite, the very incident which foretells his combat with Enkidu.

The second dream interpretation is no more than three lines long in the Old Babylonian version, and only the final line is preserved. The Standard Babylonian interpretation, with the exception of the initial line, is constructed entirely of lines utilized in the first interpretation: vi 19=v 47, vi 20=v 46, vi 21ff.=vi 1ff. Judging from the single preserved line of the Old Babylonian text, this was hardly the case there. That single preserved line, *aššum uštamaḫḫaru ittika* "because I shall 'make him equal' with you," seems to be the inspiration for the recurrent Standard Babylonian line *atti/anāku tultamaḫ(ḫa)rišu/ultamaḫḫaršu ittīja/ittika* (v 39, 46; vi 15, 20). Because Gilgamesh, in his dream, loved the ax (= Enkidu) and placed it at his side (or made it his brother; see above), the preceding lost lines of the second Old Babylonian dream interpretation must refer to the future relationship between Gilgamesh and Enkidu, as did the Old Babylonian interpretation of the first dream. It then follows that *šutamḫuru* here must mean that Ninsun plans to treat Enkidu as a son or put him on a par with Gilgamesh, and this actually seems to occur later in the epic.[12] For

5. For this phrase, see below.

6. Cf. Schott, ZA 42 (1934) 103. Note also Gilgamesh's description of Enkidu in SB VIII ii 4 as *ḫaṣṣin aḫija*, "the ax at my side."

7. These lines and the two that follow are repeated verbatim in SB II ii 35ff.

8. The difference in verbs in the OB version is appropriate to the difference in objects (*tabālu* for the meteorite, *tarû* for a human being). SB *nadû* seems inappropriate when applied to a beloved person.

9. The love-making here again seems to be in front of the mother!

10. This description of Enkidu in SB vi 2f. as "strongest in the land, he is mighty, his might is as strong as a meteorite," is used both earlier and later in the SB version (I iii 3f.=30f.; ZA 62 [1972] 224:117f.; II iii 43f.).

11. Dream-book 215.

12. The difficult passage SB III iv 16ff. cannot be discussed anew here, but it is perhaps sufficient to note Gilgamesh's constant reference to Enkidu as his "brother," which, whether it denotes a

this reason, Landsberger's lumping together of *šutamḫuru* in these passages with *šumḫuru*, as a technical expression for dream interpretation should be rejected.[13] That the word has insinuated itself into the Standard Babylonian text at every possible opportunity must be viewed in the same light as the constant recurrence there of the love-making phrase, which also occurs only once in the Old Babylonian version.

Two quite different Old Babylonian dream reports and their interpretations have been transformed into very similar dreams with nearly identical interpretations in the Standard Babylonian recension, losing thereby much of their vitality and even meaning. Ironically, this scribal distortion of the text was accomplished by using the very formulaic phrases and repetitions that we associate with the oral poet. The grossly inappropriate imposition of these phenomena by the Standard Babylonian redactors on a prior text[14] ultimately calls into question the status of all Standard Babylonian versions of earlier compositions, a matter which will be pursued elsewhere.

APPENDIX

The Dreams of Gilgamesh in their OB and SB Versions[15]

The First Dream

SB I col. v	OB P col. i
itbīma Gilgameš šunāta ipaššar izakkara	*itbēma Gilgameš šunātam ipaššar*
ana ummišu	*izzakkaram ana ummišu*
ummi šunat aṭṭula mušītija	*ummi ina šāt mušītija*
	šamḫākuma attanallak / ina birīt eṭlūtim
ibšûnimma kakkabū šamê	⌜*ibbašû*⌝*nimma*[16] *kakkabū šamā'ī*
kīma kiṣru ša Anim imtanaqqut eli ṣērija	⌜*kiṣ*⌝*rum*[17] *ša Anim imqut ana ṣērija*
aššīšuma dān elija	*aššīšuma iktabit elija*
ultablakkissu ul eleʾa nussu	*unīššuma nuššašu ul elteʾi*
Uruk mātum izzaz elišu	*Uruk mātum paḫir elišu*
[*mātum puḫḫurat*] *ina* [*muḫḫišu*]	
[*idappir umm*]*ānu e*[*li ṣērišu*]	
[*eṭlūtu uk*]*tammaru elišu*	
[*kī šerri la*]*ʾi unaššaqu šēpēšu*	*eṭlūtum unaššaqu šēpēšu*
[*arāmšuma kīm*]*a aššate elišu aḫbub*	*ummidma pūti / īmidu jâti*
[*u a*]*ttadīšu ina šapliki*	*aššiašuma atbalaššu ana ṣēriki*
[*atti tult*]*amaḫrišu ittija*	
[*ummi Gilgameš emqet mū*]*dât kalāma īdi*	*ummi Gilgameš mūdiat kalāma*
izakkar ana bēliša	*izzakkaram ana Gilgameš*
[*sinnišat rīmat Ninsun*] *emqet mūdât kalāma*	
īdi izakkar ana Gilgameš	
[*ibšûnik*]*ku*? *kakkabū šamê*	
[*kīma kiṣir A*]*nim ša imtanaqqutu eli ṣērika*	

family relationship or simply close friendship and social equality, supports my point.

13. RA 62 (1968) 118 n. 73. Another reference for *šumḫuru* in this context is LKA 14 r. i 4=23 (dreams of Etana). The occurrence of *šutamḫuru* at the very end of the OB dream interpretation, and in the present-future tense, also makes Landsberger's interpretation improbable.

14. I am not necessarily assuming that the SB version was redacted directly from the extant OB version; that may or may not be the case. But whether the changes I find so disturbing occurred simultaneously or serially is irrelevant. I am also not disregarding the fact that the OB text has its own problems, one of which is the peculiar interpretation of the first dream, mentioned above.

15. For bibliography see Borger, HKL 1 and 2, under Thompson EG and Langdon PBS 10/3. I have tried to keep philological notes to a minimum. OB Gilg. P has been collated from the original, and studied with constant reference to the excellent photos by David I. Owen (the reproduction of the obverse in Horizon 15 114 is a bit small, but can still be used profitably).

16. *-ba-šu-*, upon collation, is much more probable than *-taḫ-ru-* (von Soden, OLZ 1955 514).

17. Collation neither confirms nor denies an initial *ki-iṣ-* as opposed to von Soden's suggested *ši-ip-* (OLZ 1955 514). *kiṣrum* has been retained here because there is no reason to assume that the OB and SB texts are not in agreement on the object of the first dream, since they clearly do agree on the object of the second (*ḫaṣṣinnu*).

[taššīšuma d]ān elika
[tultablakkissu ul] tele'a nussu
[atta tadd]īšu ina šapliya
[u anāku ultamaḫ]ḫaršu ittika
[tarāmšuma kīma aššate] elišu taḫ[bub]

col. vi

[illakakkumma dannu tap]pû mušēzib [ibri]
[ina māti dān] emūqi ī[šu]
[kīma kiṣru ša Anim] dunnuna emū[qāšu]
[tarāmšuma kīma aššate] elišu taḫbub
[u šû ušte]nezzibka kâša
[damqat šūqu]rat šunatka

mindē Gilgameš ša kīma kâti
ina ṣēri iwwalidma / urabbišu šadû
tammaršuma taḫaddu atta
eṭlūtum unaššaqu šēpēšu
teddira⌜x x (x)⌝-ú-ma[18]
⌜ta⌝tarrâššu ⌜ana⌝ ṣē⌜ri⌝ja

The Second Dream

[Gilgameš šanîš izakkar] ana ummišu

[ummi āt]amar šanīta šutta
[ina Uruk supūr]i ḫaṣṣinnu nadīma elišu paḫru
[Uruk mā]tum izzaz elišu
[mātum puḫḫur]at ina muḫḫišu
[idappir ummā]nu eli ṣērišu
[anāku] attadīšu ina šapliki
[arāmsum]a kī aššate elišu aḫbub
[u atti t]ultamaḫḫarišu ittija
[ummi Gilgameš] emqet mūdât kalāma īdi
izakkara ana mārīša
[sin]nišat rīmat Ninsun emqet mūdât kalāma īdi
izakkara ana Gilgameš
ḫaṣṣinnu ša tāmuru amēlu
tarāmšuma kīma aššate taḫabbub elišu
u anāku ultamaḫḫaršu ittika
illakakkumma dannu tappû mušēzib ibri
ina māti dān emūqi īšu
kīma kiṣru ša Anim dunnuna emūqāšu

⌜i⌝ttilamma ītamar šanītam
⌜it⌝bi[19] *ītawâm ana ummišu*
[um]⌜mi āt⌝amar šanītam
[ ]x[20] *e-mi-a ina sūqim*
[ša Uru]k ribītim / ḫaṣṣinnu nadīma
elišu paḫru
āmuršuma aḫtadu anāku
arāmšuma kīma aššatim / aḫabbub elišu
elqēšuma aštakanšu / ana aḫija
⌜ummi⌝ Gilgameš mūdât ⌜kalā⌝ma
[izzakkaram ana Gilgameš]

[two lines not preserved]

col. ii

aššum uš[ta]maḫḫaru ittika

The First Dream

Gilgamesh arose, explaining his dream,
speaking to his mother:
"Mother, my dream which I saw this night:

"The stars in the sky appeared to me,
"And something like a meteorite fell near me.

Gilgamesh arose, explaining his dream,
Speaking to his mother:
"Mother, in my (dream) this night,
"Feeling luxuriant, I was strolling
"Among the men,
"The stars in the sky appeared to me,
"And a meteorite[21] fell near me.

18. There are probably three, perhaps only two, signs between RA and Ú. The traces of the last two do not exclude *-aš-šu-* (cf. von Soden, OLZ 1955 514), but the wedge corresponding to the proposed AŠ is preceded by traces of another sign, which cannot be simply A. Thus, a reading *te-ed-di-ra-(a-)aš-šu-ú-ma* seems to be ruled out.

19. The sign before I of *i-ta-wa-a-am* is BI, not TA, and the traces preceding it (ending in a vertical wedge) could be ⌜ID⌝. The absence of the enclitic copula, however, casts some doubt on the restoration.

20. [G]AL (von Soden, ZA 53 [1959] 210) for the first visible sign is by no means certain, and the next three signs are, unfortunately, as copied.

21. See n. 17, above.

"I tried to lift it, but it was too strong
for me,
"I tried shoving it, but couldn't move it,
"The land of Uruk was standing over it,
"The land was assembled around it,
"The people were jostling about it,
"Then the men gathered around it,
"And were kissing its feet as if it were
a little baby;
"I loved it, and embraced it[22] as a wife,
"And then I set before you (and)
"You 'made it equal'[23] with me."
The mother of Gilgamesh, wise, knowing, who knows
all, said to her master,
The woman, wild cow Ninsun, wise, knowing,
who knows all, said to Gilgamesh:
"The stars in the sky appeared to you,
"That which fell near you was something like
a meteorite,
"You tried to lift it, but it was too strong for you,
"You tried shoving it, but couldn't move it,
"You set it before me,
"And I 'made it equal' with you,
"You loved it, and embraced it as a wife,
(this means):
"A strong companion will come to you,
who rescues his friend,
"Strongest in the land, he is mighty,
"His might is as strong as a meteorite.
"You loved him and embraced him as a wife,
"And he will constantly rescue you.
"Your dream is favorable and precious."

"I tried to lift it, but it was too
heavy for me,
"I tried moving it, but couldn't move it.
"The land of Uruk was assembed around it.

"The men were kissing its feet;

"I *pushed against it with* my forehead,
and *they pushed with* me, (and)
"I lifted it and brought it to you."
The mother of Gilgamesh, who knows all,
Said to Gilgamesh:

"Indeed, Gilgamesh, one like you
"Has been born on the plain, the
hills have raised him.

"You will see him and be glad,
"The men will kiss his feet,
"You will hug him . . . and
"You will bring him to me."

The Second Dream

Gilgamesh spoke again to his mother:

"Mother, I've seen a second dream:
"In *enclosed* Uruk an ax had fallen, and
they were assembled around it,
"The land of Uruk was standing over it,
"The land was assembled around it,
"The people were jostling about it.
"I set it before you,
"Loved it, and embraced it as a wife,
"And then you 'made it equal' with me."

The mother of Gilgamesh, wise, knowing,
who knows all, said to her son,

He lay down and saw a second (dream),
He arose, telling it to his mother:
"Mother, I've seen a second (dream):
". . . in the streets of downtown Uruk,
"An ax had fallen, and / they were
assembled around it.

"I saw it and was glad,
"I loved it, and as a wife / I embraced it,
"(Then) I took it and placed it at my side."[24]
The mother of Gilgamesh, who knows all,
Said to Gilgamesh:

22. The translation of *ḫabābu* follows Moran, Biblica 50 (1969) 31 n. 3. In our references, and those in Biggs Šaziga 31:46 and 33:8 (parallel with *ritkubu* and *râmu*), the word is most certainly a euphemism for sexual intercourse.

23. For this phrase, see the discussion above.

24. For the pun here, see the discussion above, with n. 5.

The woman, wild cow Ninsun, wise, knowing,
who knows all, said to Gilgamesh:
"The ax which you saw, oh man—[25]
"You loved it, and embraced it as a wife,
"And then I 'made it equal' with you—
(this means):
"A strong companion will come to you,
who rescues his friend,
"Strongest in the land, he is mighty,
"His might is strong as a meteorite."

[two lines destroyed]

"Because I will 'make him equal' with you."

25. Translating with Landsberger, RA 63 (1969) 117 n. 71 line 18.

ANOTHER LOOK AT THE NUZI SISTERSHIP CONTRACTS

B. L. Eichler
University of Pennsylvania

Within the Nuzi documents relating to family law, there is a set of documents in which females are acquired for purposes of marriage. These documents may be divided into two groups. The first group comprises marriage contracts by which the woman immediately assumes the status of wife. These contracts, which usually bear the superscription *ṭuppi riksi*, "document of (marriage-)contract,"[1] record the payment of the marriage price and contain various stipulations concerning the woman's status and the property rights of her children to the estate of her husband.[2] The second group comprises contracts of adoption for purposes of matrimony[3] in which the woman assumes a status other than wife prior to her marriage. Her status may be either that of a "daughter or daughter-in-law" or that of a "sister." In contracts bearing the superscription *ṭuppi mārtūti u kallatūti*, "document of daughter or daughter-in-lawship,"[4] the adopted female is to be taken as wife either by the adopter, his son, his slave or by any unnamed third party according to varying stipulations. In contracts bearing the superscription *ṭuppi aḫātūti*—"document of sistership" the adopted female is to be given in marriage by her adoptive brother. This article will focus upon the sub-set of Nuzi

1. P. Koschaker, Neue keilschriftliche Rechtsurkunden aus der El-Amarna-Zeit (Leipzig, 1928) p. 85. Although in Nuzi the term *riksu* "binding arrangement" may refer to agreements of land transfer resulting from exchange (JEN 361:37) or sale-adoption (JEN 383:46), the superscription *ṭuppi riksi* is used almost exclusively for marriage contracts. Note, however, the use of *ṭuppi riksi* with reference to land transfer contracts in JEN 439:1 and 385:36. Cf. C. H. Gordon, "The Status of Woman Reflected in the Nuzi Tablets," ZA 43 (1936) 158 n. 3.

2. Most of the Nuzi *ṭuppi riksi* documents describe the marriage of a woman to a free man and contain stipulations concerning her status as chief wife and the inheritance rights of her children. Other documents, bearing the same superscription, describe the marriage of a woman to a slave. These contracts usually stipulate that the woman is bound to the household of the slave's owner and that at least some of her children will become slaves. A thorough collection of the various groups of marriage-related texts from Nuzi may be found in J. Breneman, Nuzi Marriage Tablets (unpubl. Ph.D. diss., Brandeis University, 1971).

3. The characterization of these documents as adoptiones in matrimonium was introduced by P. Koschaker (NRUA p. 84, with a subsequent shift of emphasis in "Fratriarchat, Hausgemeinschaft und Mutterrecht in Keilschriftrechten," ZA 41 [1933] 20ff.) and accepted by E.-M. Cassin (L'Adoption à Nuzi [Paris, 1938] pp. 42ff.). A. Van Praag used the designation adoption matrimoniale (Le droit matrimonial assyro-babylonien [Amsterdam, 1945] pp. 79ff.), while G. Cardascia prefers the designation adoptio ad maritandam ("L'Adoption matrimonale à Babylon et à Nuzi," Revue historique de droit français et étranger 37 [1959] 2 n. 1).

A few scholars have offered hypotheses which explore possible motivations prompting such adoptions. Koschaker compared the texts to the modern Greek practice in which childless couples adopt a ψυχοκόρι who serves them without pay for several years after which they arrange for her marriage (ZA 41 [1933] 22f.). Van Praag stressed an economic motive by which the natural father or brother, in immediate need of the girl's bride-price, could arrange for her adoption without waiting until she became full grown to arrange for her marriage (Droit matrimonial p. 81). Cardascia criticized both of these hypotheses (Revue historique de droit 37 [1959] 8 n. 33 and pp. 9f). In their stead, he proposed that these adoptions reflected a type of prenuptial levirate creating a familial alliance (ibid. pp. 12ff). To be sure, varying motives must have prompted these adoptions. The general impression left by many of the texts, however, is that the adopter seems to have considered these adoptions more of a business investment rather than a matter of family law.

4. The superscriptions found in this group of contracts vary. Of the approximately forty attested contracts, about 40% contain the full superscription *ṭuppi mārtūti u kallatūti* (variant: *kallūti*), while 50% bear the superscription *ṭuppi mārtūti* and 10%, *ṭuppi kallatūti* (variant: *kallūti*). On the basis of clausal analysis, it is still impossible to discern any difference between these contracts stemming from the varying superscriptions (cf. C. Gordon, ZA 43 [1936] 153). Therefore most scholars have considered the superscriptions to reflect full and abbreviated formulas and the texts to be representative of the same institution (E. A. Speiser, "New Kirkuk Documents Relating to Family Laws," AASOR 10 [1928-29] 25; I. Mendelsohn, "The Conditional Sale into Slavery of Free-born Daughters in Nuzi and the Law of Ex. 21:7-11," JAOS 55 [1935] 191 n. 4; A. Skaist, "The Authority of the Brother at Arrapḫa and Nuzi," JAOS 89 [1969] 11 n. 5; but cf. A. Van Praag, Droit matrimonial pp. 82f. and Cardascia, Revue historique de droit 37 [1959] 4f.). Nevertheless, the clausal analysis does reveal differences in this group of contracts which are not distinguishable by the varying superscriptions. One sub-group states that the adopted female is to be married to whomever the adoptive father wishes, sometimes limited to members of the adoptive family and at times including outsiders. The other sub-group states that the adopted female shall be married to a slave. This latter sub-group of contracts indicates that she remains bound to the household of her adoptive father. Upon the death of her slave-husband, her adoptive father shall marry her to yet another slave. Her children and her estate also belong to her adoptive father. These two sub-groups have been described as representing adoptiones in matrimonium conjugale and adoptiones in matrimonium servile (E.-M. Cassin, L'Adoption à Nuzi pp. 42ff.).

The translation of the superscription remains uncertain. CAD, following Koschaker (ZA 41 [1933] 22), interprets the superscription to mean a document of adoption into the status of a dependent woman (sub *kallūtu*, CAD K 86a). The superscription may also mean a document of adoption into a filial or affinal relationship.

Ancient Near Eastern Studies in Memory of J. J. Finkelstein
Connecticut Academy of Arts and Sciences, Memoir 19

sistership documents in an attempt to elucidate the transaction and its relationship to the set as a whole.

The first published Nuzi sistership contracts were presented in transliteration and translation by P. Koschaker[5] in 1928 and by E. A. Speiser[6] in 1930. The corpus of marriage-related documents treated by Speiser contains two texts which have remained central to the interpretation of the Nuzi sistership transaction. The same parties are involved in both texts. The first, HSS 5 69, bears the superscription *ṭuppi aḫāti*,[7] "document of sistership," and states that Akkul-enni has given his sister, Bēlt-akkadi-ummi, to Ḫurazzi. The second, HSS 5 80, bears the superscription *ṭuppi riksi*, "document of (marriage-)contract" and states that Akkul-enni is to give his sister, Bēlt-akkadi-ummi in marriage to Ḫurazzi. Speiser remarked in his preliminary observations on these two texts that the choice of superscription is sometimes influenced by the party commissioning the writing of the document. Thus he concluded that HSS 5 69 is called a "document of sistership of Akkul-enni" because it is his sister whom he is giving to Ḫurazzi. He further argued that this superscription cannot reflect on the nature of his sister's arrangement with Ḫurazzi since according to HSS 5 80 the girl is acquired by Ḫurazzi as wife and not as sister.[8]

A careful reading of the two texts indicates, however, that the difficulty does not lie in the different superscriptions alone. In contrast to HSS 5 80 in which Bēlt-akkadi-ummi is given to Ḫurazzi in wifehood (*ana aššūti*) by her brother, HSS 5 69 clearly states that she had been given to him in sistership (*ana aḫāti*). On the basis of this datum, Koschaker, assuming that both texts undoubtedly reflect the same transaction, concluded that in Nuzi society the terms sistership and wifehood could be equated.[9] According to Koschaker, this equation reflects a fratriarchal family structure in which the oldest brother exercises final authority and all male-female relationships including that of husband and wife were described terminologically as brother and sister. Although by the middle of the second millennium B.C., partriarchy had superceded this fratriarchal structure in Nuzi, the authority of the brother was nevertheless only suppressed during the lifetime of the father. Upon his death, the authority of the brother once again emerged. This fraternal authority, Koschaker argued, cannot be derived from that of the father, since the need for the woman's consent to the arrangement evident in Nuzi sistership contracts signifies that her brother did not exercise the same authority over her as did her father. Koschaker therefore maintained that the brother's authority must have stemmed from a fratriarchal family system. Thus, to Koschaker, the Nuzi socio-legal traditions reflected two different family structures. On the one hand, when a brother gave his fatherless sister in adoption *ana mārtūti u kallatūti*, the terminology reflected his role as successor to the father's authority in a patriarchal structure. On the other hand, when he gave her in marriage *ana aḫātūti*, the terminology reflected his role in a fratriarchal structure. Thus Koschaker concluded that the terms *ana aššūti*, *ana aḫātūti*, and *ana mārtūti u kallatūti* represented equivalent institutions, and that the interchangeability of the term *ana aḫātūti* with *ana aššūti* represented a vestige of an earlier era of fratriarchal family structure in which a woman was both wife and sister to her husband.[10]

Both C. Gordon and H. Lewy rejected Koschaker's basic assumption that the two texts, HSS 5 69 and 80, record the same transaction. Hence, in their opinions, sistership and wifehood could not be equated. Gordon postulated that the woman's status as sister must have been terminated by an *andurāru*, "release proclamation," thus making it possible for her brother to assign her later to the same man with the status of wife.[11] In attempting to distinguish the sistership transaction from that of daughtership or daughter-in-lawship, Gordon maintained that unlike the *mārtūtu u kallatūtu* transaction in which the father ceded all parental rights to the adopter, the natural brother in an *aḫātūtu* transaction shared his rights with the adoptive brother.[12]

H. Lewy, on the basis of her analysis of the newly published text JEN 636, concluded that Nuzi sistership transactions represented a type of concubinage.[13] According to her, in this text an adoptive brother declares before witnesses that he has returned his adopted sister, who bore him two children, to her natural brother. Lewy therefore deduced that "a woman adopted by a man as his sister lived in the man's house as his concubine, i.e. she had intercourse with him without being his legal wife (*aššatu*)" and furthermore that

5. NRUA pp. 173f., with a discussion of the texts on pp. 90f.

6. AASOR 10 (1928-29 [1930]) no. 27 pp. 60f., and no. 29 pp. 62ff., with discussions of the texts on pp. 21ff.

7. *aḫāti/aḫatūti*. For other examples in which nouns and their abstract derivatives are interchanged, see C. Gordon, Or. NS 7 (1938) 49.

8. AASOR 10 (1928-29 [1930]) pp. 21f.

9. ZA 41 (1933) 14.

10. ZA 41 (1933) 29ff.

11. ZA 43 (1936) 154 n. 1.

12. ZA 43 (1936) 156. Gordon based this primarily upon a deduction from the family situation in which a woman may have many brothers but only one father.

13. "Gleanings from a New Volume of Nuzi Texts," Or. NS 10 (1941) 210-14.

"there can be no doubt that in Nuzi a brother had *ipso facto* the right to live in concubinage with his sister."[14] Lewy further sought support for her position in the fact that some of the Nuzi depositions recording the declarations of women adopted into sistership contain the expression *lalâšu nadānu*, which she translated as "to offer her charm" to her adoptive brother.[15] As for the relationship between the two contracts HSS 5 69 and 80, Lewy reasoned that in HSS 5 69 (*ṭuppi aḫāti*) Bēlt-akkadi-ummi was first adopted into sistership by Ḫurazzi as his concubine for a kind of tentative or trial marriage. Only at a later time did Ḫurazzi transform this concubinage into a formal legal marriage, documented in the *ṭuppi riksi*, HSS 5 80.[16]

In his most recent study of Nuzi sistership, Speiser, like Gordon and H. Lewy, did not accept Koschaker's equation of texts HSS 5 69 and 80 as recording the same transaction.[17] He did, however, espouse Koschaker's position that these two texts indicate that a woman could have the concurrent status of wife and sister in Nuzi society, based upon its presumed original fratriarchal family structure. Thus in Nuzi, a husband could acquire fratriarchal rights and obligations to his wife from her natural brother. Accordingly, Speiser maintained that the Nuzi sistership documents reflect an underlying concept under which "a woman given in marriage by her brother, either natural or adoptive, became legally her husband's sister."[18] Speiser further asserted that this status of wife-sister, to which the woman's consent was prerequisite, afforded the woman an "exceptional socioreligious solicitude and protection which was not enjoyed by ordinary wives" and "was evidently a mark of superior status."[19]

Within recent years, the theoretical basis for Speiser's interpretation has been weakened by A. Skaist's cogent critique of Koschaker's hypothesis of an original fratriarchal family structure in Nuzi society.[20] Skaist argues that on the basis of current anthropological research and theory, there is no evidence to support Koschaker's position. Furthermore, he maintains that the need for such a hypothesis arose from Koschaker's fallacious assumption that in a patriarchal family there must be patrilineal succession to the father's authority. According to Skaist, the fact that the woman's consent was prerequisite to the arrangement transacted for her by her brother does not necessitate the derivation of the brother's authority from a non-patriarchal family structure. To him, the Nuzi family type seems to have been "the patrilocal extended family, patripotestal in authority and patrilineal in inheritance and descent" although there is "no patrilineal succession to the father's power over female children."[21] Thus the situation at Nuzi would be analogous to the early Roman family structure in which the female orphan in Rome was *sui juris* but nevertheless in need of a guardian. The authority of the brother at Nuzi, Skaist suggested, was that of a guardian whose authority over her would be less than that of her father.[22]

While vitiating the argument for wife-sister marriage at Nuzi, this proffered explanation of the brother's authority does not shed light on the nature of the Nuzi sistership transactions. Since the adopter-adoptee relationship should remain the same whether a girl's father or brother negotiates the arrangement on her behalf, Skaist readily admits the problem in explaining the origin of the term *aḫātūtu* to describe adoptions for purposes of matrimony when the term *mārtūtu u kallatūtu* is so employed. In an attempt to resolve this problem, Skaist posits two types of sistership documents—one reflecting real sistership agreements and the other reflecting a fusion of elements from real sistership agreements with adoption transactions for purposes of matrimony.[23]

14. Or. NS 10 (1941) 210f. Critical remarks concerning this interpretation have been expressed by Van Praag, Droit matrimonial p. 82 n. 7; Cardascia, Revue historique de droit 37 (1959) 3 n. 7; and V. Korošec, "Keilschriftrecht," Orientalisches Recht (Leiden, 1964) p. 172 n. 9.

15. Or. NS 10 (1941) 211. Also cf. Koschaker, ZA 41 (1933) 28 n. 3.

16. Or. NS 10 (1941) 210. For her discussion of the juridical details concerning these two contracts, see ibid. p. 213.

17. In "The Wife-Sister Motif in the Patriarchal Narratives," Oriental and Biblical Studies: Collected Writings of E. A. Speiser, ed. by J. J. Finkelstein and M. Greenberg (Philadelphia, 1967) p. 68, Speiser refers to them as parallel documents, deemed necessary in addition to the usual marriage contract. Originally, however, Speiser had fully accepted Koschaker's position ("Nuzi Marginalia," Or. NS 25 [1956] 12f.).

18. Oriental and Biblical Studies p. 75.

19. Oriental and Biblical Studies p. 75. Because of Speiser's attempt to relate the Nuzi data to the wife-sister motif found in the patriarchal narratives of the Bible, his interpretation of the nature of the Nuzi sistership transaction has gained widespread popularity. Critical remarks questioning the validity of Speiser's position have been offered, however, by D. Freedman, "A New Approach to the Nuzi Sistership Contracts," JANES 2 (1969) 77-85; C. J. Mullo Weir, "The Alleged Hurrian Wife-Sister Motif in Genesis," Transactions of the Glasgow University Oriental Society 22 (1967-68 [1970]) 14-25; and J. Van Seters, Abraham in History and Tradition (New Haven, 1975) 71-76. [S. Greengus, "Sisterhood Adoption at Nuzi and the 'Wife-Sister' in Genesis," HUCA 46 (1975 [1976]) appeared when the present work was in proof.]

20. JAOS 89 (1969) 10-17, especially pp. 13ff.

21. JAOS 89 (1969) 16.

22. JAOS 89 (1969) 16.

23. JAOS 89 (1969) 16f.

In light of this review of previously advanced interpretations of the nature of Nuzi sistership transactions it is evident that a re-examination of the data for the clarification of issues would be useful, even if solutions may not be readily apparent. Before proceeding to a detailed analysis of the corpus of Nuzi sistership transactions, it should be noted that there is one basic premise common to the interpretations proffered by Koschaker, H. Lewy, and Speiser. This premise, simply stated, is that the adoptive brother acquires conjugal rights to his adopted sister.[24] Koschaker deduced this by equating the term sistership with wifehood on the assumption that texts HSS 5 69 and 80 recorded the same transaction. Hence the term husband is synonymous with that of (adoptive) brother. As mentioned above, this assumed equation has not been unanimously accepted, nor is there circumstantial evidence to support it.[25] H. Lewy seemed to offer new evidence for the validity of this premise by contending that JEN 636 records the fact that a woman taken into sistership had borne her adoptive brother children.[26] A re-examination of this text is offered below:

JEN 636

[EM]E-*šu ša* ^{m}*I-in-ni* DUMU *En*-[ ]
a-na pa-ni LÚ.MEŠ *ši-bu-ti*
an-nu-tu_4 *ki-na-*[*an*]*-na iq-ta-*[*bi*]
^{f}*Ḫi-in-zu-ri a-ḫa-as-sú*
š[*a* ^{m}]*Zi-ki-ba* DUMU *Eḫ-el-t*[*e-šub*] *ù*
a-na [x-x]*-ti a-na ya-ši at-ta-din*
ù [*i-na*]*-an-na a-n*[*a-k*]*u a-na a-ḫa-t*[*i-šu*]
a-na ^{m}*Zi-ki-pa um-te-eš-ši-ir*
ù [^{m}]*Zi-ki-pa* 1 TÚG *a-na*
^{m}*I-in-ni at-ta-dì-in-mi*
ù ^{m}*I-in-ni qa-an-na-šu*
a-n[*a*] *pa-ni* IGI.M[EŠ] *im-ta-šar*
um-ma ^{m}*Zi-ki-pa-ma a-na-ku*
^{f}*Ḫi-in-zu-ri a-ḫa-ti-ya*
a-šar ^{m}*I-in-ni a-ku-*ka_4*-ru-um-ma* DÙ-*šu*
um-ma ^{m}*I-in-ni-ma še-er-ri-šu*
[*š*]*a* ^{f}*Ḫi-in-zu-ri* [x x]*-mi-il-du*
[*a-na-ku*] *el-te-qè-*[*m*]*i u* ^{f}*Zi-ge*
[*a-na* ^{m}]*Zi-ki-pa-ma um-te-eš-ši-ir*
[*ma*]*-an-nu-um-me-e i-na be-ri-šu-nu*
[*i*]*š-tu a-wa-ti ša id-bu-bu*
KI.KAT.BAL (for KI.BAL-*kat*) [1] MA.NA KÙ.BABBAR
[1] MA.NA GUŠ[KIN] *ú-ma-al-la*
[*ṭu*]*p-pí ina* EGIR-*ki šu-du-ti*
[*i-na b*]*a-ab* É.GAL-*lim*
[*ša-ṭì*]*-ir*
IGI [. . . DUMU] *Ki-pa-a-a*
IGI [*Ut-ḫáp-ta*]*-e* DUMU *En-na-ma-ti*
[IGI] *Wa-an-ti-iš-še* DUMU [. . . *ḫ*]*i-ya*
[IGI] *Eḫ-el-t*[*e*]*-šup*
[DUMU] *Ge-el-*[*t*]*e-e-a*
[IGI *Ú*]*-nap-ta-e* DUMU *El-ḫi-ip-*LUGAL
[IGI *Ḫ*]*u-ti-ya* DUMU *E-ge-*[*g*]*e*
IGI *Te-ḫi-ip-zi-iz-za* DUMU *Ar-nu-zu*
IGI *Ḫa-ni-a* DUMU ^{f}*Túl-pu*

24. Cf. P. Koschaker, ZA 41 (1933) 28; H. Lewy, Or. NS 10 (1941) 210f.; Speiser, Oriental and Biblical Studies p. 69. According to Lewy, the adoptive brother immediately gains sexual rights to his adopted sister who assumes the status of concubine rather than legal wife. According to Speiser, these rights are gained only after the adoptive brother marries his adopted sister who thus becomes his legal wife.

25. For the nature of the circumstantial evidence, see below n. 92.

26. Or. NS 10 (1941) 210.

ŠU ᵐ*A-kip-ta-še-en-ni* DUB.SAR-*rù*
DUMU *Ḫu-i-til-la*

seal impressions

[NA$_4$] *Ut-ḫáp-ta-e*	NA$_4$ Z[*i*(?) . . .][27]
[NA$_4$ DUB].SAR-*rù*	NA$_4$ *Wa-*[*an-ti-iš-še*]
[NA$_4$ . . .][28]	NA$_4$ *T*[*e-ḫi-i*]*p-*[*z*]*i-iz-za*(!)
[NA$_4$] *Ú-*[*nap*]*-ta-e*	[NA$_4$ *Eḫ-el-t*]*e-šup*

(1) The tongue of Inni, son of En. . ., he has declared in the presence of these witnesses thusly:
(4) "As for Ḫinzuri, the sister of Zikipa son of Eḫel-tešup, (6) whom he had given[29] to me in . . .-ship, I have now released her to [her brot]her[30] to Zikipa."

(9) Accordingly, Zikipa has given one garment to Inni and Inni has pressed the hem of his garment[31] in the presence of witnesses.

(13) Thus (declares) Zikipa: "I have redeemed Ḫinzuri, my sister."

(16) Thus (declares) Inni: "Ḫinzuri's brood . . .[32] I have taken, but I have released Zige to Zikipa."

(20) Whoever between them violates any of the matters agreed to, shall pay a fine of [one] mina of silver and [one] mina of gold. (24) The document was written after a *šūdūtu*-proclamation at the palace gate.[33]

(27-35) eight witnesses

(36) Akip-tašenni son of Ḫui-tilla, the scribe.

(38-41) eight seals

Crucial to H. Lewy's interpretation of this text as recording the redemption of a woman from a sistership arrangement during which she bore her adoptive brother children is Lewy's restoration of line 6 to read *a-na* [*a-ḫa-t*]*u-ti*—"in sistership."[34] Lewy argued that the restoration *a-na* [*aš-š*]*u-ti*, "in wifehood" is precluded by the use of the term *šerru*, "brood" to designate Ḫinzuri's children born to Inni.[35] The choice of restorations is not limited, however, to only *aḫātūti* or *aššūti*. There are two other possible restorations which are to be preferred to *aḫātūti*. The first is *a-na* [GEMÉ]*-ti*,[36] "into status of female slave"; under such circumstances Inni would be Ḫinzuri's master rather than her adoptive brother. One could demur, however, that according to this restoration JEN 636 would be the only attestation of a woman being sold into such servitude by her brother rather than by her father. The second possible restoration is *a-na* [*kal-lu*]*-ti*, "into daughter-in-

27. The seal is probably that of the son of Kipaya in line 37 rather than that of Zikipa.

28. The seal may be that of Ḫutiya in line 33, or that of Ḫaniu in line 35.

29. *attadin/ittadin*. Note the same confusion of first and third person singular in line 10. For other examples of the apparent difficulty with which the Nuzi scribes handled the pronominal verbal prefixes, see C. Gordon, Or. NS 7 (1938) 220. As for the construction with the "resumptive" *u* preceded by the genitival *ša*, cf. G. Wilhelm, Untersuchungen zum Hurro-akkadischen von Nuzi (Neukirchen-Vluyn, 1970) p. 55.

30. *aḫātu/aḫu*. For other examples, see AASOR 16 no. 54:11, HSS 19 67:10, 68:12, 69:14, and 80:9.

31. For the meaning of the expression *qannam mašāru* "to press the hem" (presumably upon the tablet), see Koschaker, NRUA p. 20 and Cassin, L'Adoption à Nuzi pp. 199f., contra Speiser, AASOR 16 p. 90. It is clear from texts in which one of the contracting parties is represented by a single person and the other party by more than one person that the contracting party who makes the payment impresses his own hem in the presence of witnesses (e.g., RA 23 [1926] 144 no. 10:44). It should be noted that JEN 636 is the only text in which this gesture is not made by the payer. This perhaps could be explained by the fact that it is the only text in the corpus which records a redemption rather than purchase transaction. The exact import of this symbolic gesture which is attested in land transfers (e.g., JEN 68, 112), purchases of male and female slaves (e.g., HSS 19 113, 123), and payments of bride-price (e.g., JEN 186), is unknown. To Gordon, it represented an act of good faith ("Nuzi Tablets Relating to Women," Le Muséon 48 [1935] 122). To Cassin, it is a public attestation that full payment has been made (L'Adoption à Nuzi p. 200). Cf. H. Petschow, "Gewand(saum) im Recht," RLA 3 321.

32. H. Lewy would see in this break the personal name of a male child (Or. NS 10 [1941] 210). Another possible restoration may be [*ana ya-ši*]*-mi il-du* for *ana yâšimi uldu* "whom she bore for me."

33. *ṭuppi/ṭuppu*. For a review of the literature discussing the nature of the *šūdūtu*-proclamation clause, see B. Eichler, Indenture at Nuzi (New Haven, 1973) pp. 32f. To the cited bibliography should be added M. Müller, "Sozial- und wirtschaftspolitische Rechtserlässe im Lande Arrapḫa," Schriften zur Geschichte und Kultur des alten Orients 1 (1971) 56ff. This reference was furnished by G. Wilhelm, JAOS 96 (1976) 278 n. 4.

34. Or. NS 10 (1941) 209. Note that the copy does not seem to show definite traces of the *tu* sign.

35. Or. NS 10 (1941) 209 n. 3. Although, as stated by Lewy, the term *šerru* in Nuzi refers either to the offspring of slave girls or to progeny expected from marriage to a free woman, the term may exceptionally be used to describe children already borne by one's legal wife (HSS 19 19:52).

36. Cf. RA 23 (1926) 155 no. 52:7, AASOR 16 no. 34:5, and JEN 452:3. In HSS 19 117:5, the term is written GEMÉ-*tu*$_4$*-ti* while it occurs syllabically as *a-mu-ti* in JEN 456:26.

lawship." In this case, the circumstances recorded in JEN 636 would be paralleled by data from other Nuzi texts. According to JEN 430, a girl given by her father *ana kallatūti* is designated as the wife of a slave and is bound to the household of her adoptive father for the rest of her life. Although the *kallatūtu* arrangement is usually negotiated by the girl's father, there are texts which attest to such negotiations conducted by her brother.[37] Furthermore, on the assumption that *mārtūtu u kallatūtu* arrangements are similar or even identical with *kallatūtu* arrangements, there is the additional data that the woman's children, who become slaves of her adoptive father, are designated as *šerru*,[38] and that the woman may be released from such a status.[39] Accordingly, JEN 636 would record a brother's redemption of his sister from a *kallūtu* arrangement during which time she had produced children for the household of her adoptive father.[40]

With the exclusion of this text from the sphere of Nuzi sistership transactions, the remaining evidence marshalled by H. Lewy to confirm her position is significantly weakened. Lewy argued that the Nuzi sistership depositions in which the woman declared that she had given her *lalû*, "charms" to her adoptive brother support her contention that the adoptive brother gained sexual rights to his adopted sister. While the term *lalû* often bears the connotation of sexual charm and allure, it is also attested in non-sexual contexts connoting willingness and desire.[41] Without the weight of the evidence from JEN 636, there is no compelling reason to prefer the sexual to the non-sexual meaning of the term in the context of the sistership depositions. Thus there is no evidence to substantiate the premise that the Nuzi sistership transaction bestowed upon an adoptive brother sexual rights to his adopted sister.

In considering the corpus of Nuzi sistership documents, one is dismayed by the disparate nature of the data, which defy a comprehensive interpretation of the transaction. The relatively small corpus of eleven texts represents approximately one-seventh of the marriage-related documents in the Nuzi texts. Eight of the texts are depositions concerning sistership adoptions; the remaining are contracts bearing the superscription *ṭuppi aḫātūti*, "document of sistership."[42] The documents are summarized individually below.

I. SISTERSHIP DEPOSITIONS

A. *Depositions made by the brother*

1. HSS 19 68: Zike son of Kula-ḫupi declares that he has given his sister Azena into sistership to Teḫip-šarri son of Itti-šarri, who shall give her in marriage to whomever he wishes and receive her marriage price from her future husband. Zike, who bears the responsibility to clear his sister from any prior claims, has received two homers and twenty *qa* of barley as his *qištu*-gift[43] from Teḫip-šarri. Azena then declares that she has been given into sistership with her consent.[44] The penalty for breach of contract is two oxen. The document, written in Nuzi, concludes with a *šūdūtu*-clause.

2. HSS 19 69: Erwi-ḫuta[45] declares the giving of his sister Wurunnaya in sistership to Teḫip-šarri son of

37. Cf. JEN 437 and HSS 5 79, in which a brother gives his sister *ana kallūti*. In JEN 429 and HSS 19 87, he gives her *ana mārtūti u kallūti*.

38. Cf. JEN 432 and 433.

39. Cf. JEN 638. This text forms a unit with JEN 440 and 649 which is parallel to JEN 113. This unit has been discussed by J. Lewy, "A New Volume of Nuzi Texts," BASOR 79 (1940) 30 n. 2; H. Lewy, Or. NS 10 (1941) 216f.; P. Koschaker in his review of E. R. Lacheman, JEN 6, published in OLZ 47 (1944) 100; and E.-M. Cassin, "Symboles de cession immobilières dans l'ancien droit mésopotamien," L'Année Sociologique 5 (1952 [1955]) 117 n. 1.

40. This redemption may have taken place upon the death of her designated husband who was probably Inni's slave. According to the *mārtūtu u kallatūtu* transactions in which the woman is given to a slave-husband, the adopted woman is permanently attached to her adoptive father's household, to be given to another slave-husband upon the death of her former husband (e.g., JEN 437, and AASOR 16 no. 30).

41. Cf. CAD L 49ff. and AHw 1 530 sub *lalû*. AHw, unlike CAD, lists these Nuzi references under the meaning of sexual allure.

42. The most recent transliteration and translation of these texts appear in Breneman, Nuzi Marriage Tablets pp. 160ff. I have relied only upon his transliteration of the unpublished text "Yale 12," which is to be published by E. R. Lacheman.

Note that HSS 13 15 is not a sistership transaction (contra CAD A 173a sub *aḫātu* A 2b), but rather an adoption into daughtership in which a father gave his daughter to his sister. Cf. HSS 5 7, 70, and 74, which form a unit together with the above-mentioned text.

43. *kīma* NÍG.BA-*šu*. The Akkadian reading of the logogram occurs in JEN 439:8 as *qi-iš-ti-i-šu*. The term *qištu* in the Nuzi tablets is usually used to describe the disguised sale price paid for land transferred in sale-adoption contracts (cf. F. R. Steele, Nuzi Real Estate Transactions [New Haven, 1943] 17f., 30). The term, however, also describes payment made in exchange for a sister given *ana mārtūti* (HSS 14 543) and in exchange for *mulūgu*-property (HSS 5 76; and HSS 19 79).

44. *ramāniya* KA-*ya*. This phraseology connoting consent seems to be a composite of the two more commonly occurring expressions for consent in Nuzi, namely *ramāniya* (cf. HSS 5 25:18) and *pîšu u lišanšu* (JEN 455:1). This composite expression also occurs in the following text HSS 19 69:13.

45. Erwi-ḫuta is described in the text as LÚ *ú-tù-*[*lu*(?)] "herdsman."

Itti-šarri, who shall give her in marriage to whomever he wishes and receive her marriage price. Erwi-ḫuta, who bears the responsibility to clear his sister from any prior claim, has received one homer of barley and one *tal* of oil as his *qištu*-gift from Teḫip-šarri. Wurunnaya then declares that she has been given into sistership with her consent. The penalty for breach of contract is two slave girls. The document, written in Nuzi, concludes with a *šūdūtu*-clause.

Both of these depositions, written by the same scribe, record the giving of two women by their respective brothers to the same Teḫip-šarri in sistership. The consent of the woman is noted in each case. In each transaction, Teḫip-šarri gives the brother a relatively small *qištu*-gift,[46] thereby gaining the sole right to the marriage price which the woman will eventually fetch. The fact that the brothers accepted the *qištu*-gift in lieu of their sisters' future marriage price seems to indicate that they were economically hard pressed when the agreement was contracted. It is also possible that these transactions may have entailed the settling of a prior indebtedness to Teḫip-šarri by the women's brothers, with the *qištu*-gift representing the difference between the woman's price and the debt owed.

B. *Depositions made by the sister*

3. AASOR 16 No. 54: Kuni-ašu, daughter of Ḫut-tešup, had been given into marriage by Akam-mušni for forty shekels of silver. Now, subsequent to the death of her husband and Akam-mušni, she enters into a sistership agreement[47] with her natural brother, Akiya, son of Ḫut-tešup. Accordingly, Akiya is to give her in marriage and receive 10 shekels of silver from her husband. The penalty for breach of contract is one mina of gold.

In this text, the sistership transaction is the vehicle by which a natural brother acquires rights to at least part of his widowed sister's future marriage price. The necessity for such an arrangement seems to indicate that a married sister was free from the authority that her natural brother may have previously excercised over her. It should be noted, however, that Kuni-ašu had been given in marriage by Akam-mušni. Although the relationship between them is not stated, Akam-mušni probably adopted her for purposes of matrimony from her father or brother. Hence any assumed authority of her brother over her may have been terminated even prior to her initial marriage in this particular case.

4. HSS 5 26: Zi. . . declares her desire[48] to be adopted into sistership by Akawa-til, son of Elli, who will ward off her attackers and protect her possessions(?),[49] treat her as a sister and come to her assistance. In return, upon her marriage he is to receive twenty shekels of silver and her (natural) brother Elḫin-namar shall receive twenty shekels. The penalty for breach of contract is one slave girl. The document, written in Nuzi, concludes with a *šūdūtu*-clause.

This text vividly records the benefits which sistership adoption afforded the woman. It thus explains why in the text above, cited as No. 3, a woman free from her brother's authority would seek a sistership arrangement despite the resultant monetary loss to her of her own marriage price had she herself contracted her future marriage.[50] The adoptive brother would agree to these obligations vis-à-vis his adopted sister for

46. According to the relative value of commodities in the Nuzi texts (cf. Eichler, Indenture at Nuzi pp. 15f.), one homer of barley is equivalent to approximately 1.5 shekels of silver, while the relative value of oil remains unknown. Even at pre-harvest rates, when one homer of barley might be as high as 4 shekels of silver (Cross, Movable Property in the Nuzi Documents [New Haven, 1937] p. 36 n. 81), the gifts are relatively small in proportion to the average Nuzi bride-price (cf. Koschaker, ZA 41 [1933] 16) or the purchase price of a female slave (cf. Eichler, Indenture at Nuzi p. 16 with n. 35).

47. The initiating action is described as *ina sūqi* PN *ṣabātu u ana aḫātūti epēšu* "to seize PN in the street and to appoint into sistership" (lines 10-14). Due to the scribal confusion in Nuzi of first and third pronominal verbal prefixes, it is not clear whether Kuni-ašu or her brother Akuya initiated this transaction. Cf. Speiser, AASOR 16 pp. 104f. For the implication of the phrase *ina sūqi* "in the street," see below n. 48.

48. The expression used is *lalûya*(!) *nadānu*, which is modified by the phrase *ištu sūqi* "from the street." According to Speiser, this phrase alternates with the phrase *ina sūqi*, both signifying an action which is performed publicly in the presence of witnesses (AASOR 16 p. 96, and cf. AHw 2 1061b sub *sūqu*). Note the use of the phrase *ina sūqi* in the lawsuit HSS 5 43:17 to describe a wound inflicted publicly. Another interpretation of the phrase *ištu sūqi* is that it signifies an action which is performed in an emergency under duress (CAD I 71b sub *ilimdu*; for the meaning of the term *ilimdumma epēšu* "to enter into a covenant, to make an oath," see F. Bush, A Grammer of the Hurrian Language [unpubl. Ph.D. diss., Brandeis University, 1964] pp. 184, 351). For the implication of the phrase *ina sūqi* in the Akkadian legal texts from Ras Shamra, see A. D. Kilmer, "Symbolic Gestures in Akkadian Contracts from Alalakh and Ugarit," JAOS 94 (1974) 181f.

49. The cuneiform reads (lines 8-10): *ša rāpisiya irappis ša ina anzariya inanṣaršu* "He shall attack those who attack me, he shall guard that which is in my storehouse(?)." Cf. Speiser, AASOR 10 p. 62, and Koschaker, ZA 41 (1933) 34.

50. Cf. JEN 434, in which a woman contracted her own marriage to a slave of Teḫip-tilla and received ten shekels of silver from Teḫip-tilla.

the future renumeration due him upon her marriage and presumably for the benefits of her labor and handiwork while in his household. This latter compensation may be reflected by the penalty fine of one slave girl for breach of contract.

In attempting to perceive the nature of the transaction recorded in this text, certain problems become apparent. The fact that her natural brother is to share in her future marriage price indicates that he has certain rights and obligations toward his sister. It may therefore be assumed that, prior to this sistership contract, the woman had not been freed from her brother's authority by a previous marriage or adoption as was deduced from text No. 3. If this be the case, the motivation for her desire to become the adopted sister of Akawa-til in view of the existence of her brother Elḫin-namar must be explored. One may conjecture that the motivation was based upon her desire to improve her social and economic station by being adopted by someone more affluent than her brother. Nuzi prosopographic data could perhaps support this conjecture since Akawa-til son of Elli appears as a creditor in two Nuzi contracts,[51] as the recipient of a girl in a *kallatūtu* transaction,[52] and as the purchaser of a female slave.[53] But even if the problem of motivation were solved, the question as to the woman's right to negotiate in the presence of her brother remains problematic. There are two possible solutions. One is to assume that in this deposition, unlike the preceding text, the woman is not contracting her own adoption but is rather stating her consent to the terms of adoption agreed to by Akawa-til and her brother. The second, in keeping with the active tenor of the woman's declaration, is to assume that the woman is negotiating her own sistership arrangement after having received her brother's permission to do so. It would be logical to assume that he would have granted such permisssion since on the basis of the first two texts the woman's consent seems to be a necessary prerequisite to any arrangement. In either case, economic constraints would seem to be the major reason compelling the brother to cede half of his sister's marriage price by giving her to another in sistership; and Akawa-til's attested interest in the acquisition of male and female labor would explain his motivation in adopting her.

5. HSS 19 70: Pukuli daughter of En-šaku declares her desire[54] to be adopted into sistership by Ḫaniu son of Arip-šelli. She also gave her daughter Malim-ninu to him in daughtership. Although the remaining portion of the text is badly damaged,[55] it seems to record that Ḫaniu, upon his giving Malim-ninu in marriage to an Arrapḫean,[56] shall receive her marriage price. Ḫaniu also seems to present Pukuli with a *qištu*-gift.[57] Pukuli further declares that she has released whatever of her daughter's monies which are to be bound in her hem to Ḫaniu.[58]

It should be noted that this text makes no reference to any natural brother. Since the woman has a daughter, it may be assumed that she had been previously married and hence is free to contract her own sistership transaction. By placing this transaction in juxtaposition with AASOR 16 No. 55, one can gain an added perspective since a contract similar to the one under discussion must have served as an antecedent to the arrangement recorded in AASOR 16 No. 55.

According to that text, Šukri-tešup gives Ḫaluya, his (adopted) sister,[59] in marriage to Zilip-kušuḫ for thirty shekels of silver. He also gives Ḫaluya's daughter in marriage to Zilip-kušuḫ's son for forty shekels, receiving only twenty shekels and releasing the remaining twenty shekels to the bride as custom dictated.[60] Šukri-

51. In HSS 5 28 Akawa-til lends four homers of barley and in HSS 5 40 he lends twelve minas of tin in a personal antichretic pledge transaction whereby he acquires the services of a harvester.

52. HSS 5 53.

53. HSS 5 8.

54. The expression is *laḫ alāku*, modified by the phrase *ina sūqi*.

55. The proposed restoration is as follows:

ù DUMU.SAL-*ti-ya* ^{f}*Ma-li-i*[*m-ni-nu*]
a-na ma-ar-tù-ti [*a-na* ^{m}*Ḫa-ni-ù*]
at-ta-din [*ù Ḫa-ni-ù*]
^{f}*Ma-li-im-*[*ni-nu a-na aš-šu-ti a-na* DUMU A]*r-ra-ap-ḫe*
i-na-an-din [*ù* KÙ.BABBAR.MEŠ-*šu*]
i-leq-qè [*ù* ^{m}*Ḫa-ni-ù*]
ki-ma [NÍG.BA-*šu* . . .]
1 IMER [ŠE(?) . . .]
a-na ^{f}[*Pu-ku-li i-na-an-din*]
šum-[*ma* . . .]
. . . . .
l.e. [*u*]*m-ma* ^{f}*Pu-ku-li-ma mi-nu-um-me-e* KÙ[.BABBAR.MEŠ]
[*š*]*a*! ^{f}*Ma-li-im-ni-nu a-na qa-an-ni-šu-ma* [*ra-ki-is*]
[*a-na*] ^{m}*Ḫa-ni-ù un-te-eš-ši-ir-šu-nu-*[*ti*].

56. Lines 9b-12. Cf. HSS 19 87:12b-13, which states *ù* ^{m}*Pa-ik-ku* ^{f}*Te-eš-ma-an-ni a-na aš-šu-ti a-na* DUMU *Ar-ra-ap-ḫe i-na-an-d*[*in*] [*a-na*] LÚ ÌR *la i-na-an-din*, "Paikku shall give Teš-menni in marriage to an Arrapḫean; he may not give her to a slave."

57. Lines 13-15. The damaged text does not permit the ascertaining of the value of the *qištu*-gift.

58. Lines 1′-3′ of the left edge. For the implication of this statement see below, the discussion of text no. 10.

59. Even if Šukri-tešup would have been Ḫaluya's natural brother, his fraternal rights to her would have had to have been re-established through a sistership adoption, since Ḫaluya had been previously married. Cf. text no. 3 above.

60. Lines 14-15: *ana qan*[*nišu*]*ma ra*[*k*]*is u ana* ^{f}PN *unteššir*, "He released to ^{f}PN (the money) bound in her hem." Although the

tešup's transaction ends with Ḫaluya's declaration of consent to the marriage arranged for her by her (adoptive) brother.[61] The text then records that Ḫaluya herself contracted with her prospective husband for the marriage and the adoption into daughtership for her remaining two daughters. Thus it seems that the original sistership agreement between Ḫaluya and Šukri-tešup had involved the giving of one of her three daughters to Šukri-tešup in daughtership at the time of her own adoption into sistership. Such an agreement is attested in HSS 19 70, the deposition under discussion, in which Ḫaniu adopts Pukuli in sistership and by the presentation of a *qištu*-gift, acquires sole right to the marriage price of her daughter Malim-ninu whom he adopts in daughtership. Šukri-tešup in AASOR 16 No. 55, acting in accord with stipulations parallel to those of the deposition under discussion, receives fifty shekels of silver for mother and daughter upon their marriages. Thus it seems that for the cost of the *qištu*-gift, Ḫaniu is able to anticipate a considerable gain. This profitable double adoption arrangement may have induced Ḫaniu to accept Pukuli's sistership proposal. In any event, it seems certain that Pukuli must have been in great economic or social need to relinquish her right to her daughter's marriage price for the received *qištu*-gift.

6. "Yale 12"[62]: Ḫinzuri daughter of Kakkassu declares her desire[63] to be adopted into sistership by Wanti-šenni son of Ḫašip-tilla. Wanti-šenni, upon giving her in marriage, shall receive one cow from her future husband. The remaining portion of the tablet is badly broken.[64]

Prosopographic data indicates that Wanti-šenni son of Ḫašip-tilla was a wealthy landowner with extensive real estate holdings and surpluses of grain and livestock.[65] Hence Ḫinzuri's motivation in becoming a member of his household is easily comprehended. It is not clear, however, whether Ḫinzuri is acting on her own initiative in this matter or whether her deposition represents only a statement of consent to an arrangement contracted for her by an unidentified natural brother. The fact that the deposition states that her adoptive brother will receive a fixed sum rather than the entire marriage price may indicate that her price is to be shared by an assumed natural brother.[66] Nevertheless, in AASOR 16 No. 54 (No. 3 above), in which the woman herself negotiated the arrangement, a fixed sum is also stipulated. In such cases, the difference between the fixed sum and the actual marriage price may have been given to the woman as a dowry. An alternative explanation would view the fixed sum as the minimum price for which the adoptive brother must agree to give her in marriage, thus protecting her from the avarice of her adoptive brother.

7. HSS 19 143: This deposition made by Šakuti[67] contains two statements which are difficult to interpret. The relevant passage of the cuneiform text reads: (3) ᵐ*Ki-ri-ip-še-ri a-na a-ḫa-*[*tu-t*]*i* (4) *i-te-pu-uš ù*! DAM *ṣú-ḫ*[*a-a*]*r*!*-ti* (5) *i-te-pu-uš a-na aš-šu-ti* (6) *a-na* LÚ DUMU.UŠ *a-na-an-*[*di*]*n-na-a*[*š-š*]*u* (7) *ù* KÙ.BABBAR-*ya i-ik-kál*. This passage seems to divide into two statements on the basis of its verbal structure. The first statement contains identical verbal forms in the perfect tense, while the second contains two verbal forms in the present tense.

The second statement is less problematic. In it Šakuti deposes that "I shall be given by him[68] (i.e., the

---

term for dowry in Nuzi is *mulūgu*, reference to a dowry is more frequently expressed as part of the bride price which is "bound in the bride's hem" (cf. BE 6/1 101:21 [=VAB 5 209:21] for similar Old Babylonian usage). That this money is to be identified with the *mulūgu* is apparent from HSS 5 80:12-14, which explicates this expression with the phrase *ana mulūgūti* "as dowry." Note, however, that the term *qannu* in Nuzi may refer to both a man's and a woman's personal belongings or "nest egg" (Paradise, Nuzi Inheritance Practices [unpubl. Ph.D. diss., University of Pennsylvania, 1972] p. 47). Cf. H. Petschow, "Gewand(saum) im Recht," RLA 3 321f.

61. Lines 17b-19a: *ra-ma-an-ni-ma a-na aš-šu-ti* [*a-na*] ᵐ*Zi-li-ik-ku-šu i-din*.MEŠ-*an*-[*ni-m*]*i*, "With my consent, he gave me into wifehood to Zilip-kušuḫ. Cf. Speiser, AASOR 16 pp. 105f. with n. 17.

62. This text (YBC 9112) is part of the Nuzi tablets in the Yale Babylonian Collection which are to be published by E. R. Lacheman. J. Breneman has presented a transliteration of this text (Nuzi Marriage Tablets p. 166), upon which I have relied here.

63. The transliteration *lalûšu attalkaššu*, modified by the phrase *ina sūqi*, reflects the underlying expression *lalû alāku*. Cf. above, n. 54.

64. Breneman's restoration (Nuzi Marriage Tablets p. 166) seems quite plausible: (11b) *ù šum-ma* (12) *a-na aš-šu-ti l*[*a i-na-an-din*] (13) *i-na* É-*šu* . . . (14) *aš-b*[*u* . . .], "But if he does n[ot give (me) into wifehood, in his house . . . I(!) shall remain . . ." There is no indication as to whether the second clause represents the apodosis or is to be understood as part of the protasis.

65. In the *tidennūtu* contracts RA 33 (1926) 142 no. 2; 143 no. 3; 149 no. 30; 154 nos. 47, 48; and TCL 9 16, he appears as a creditor in loans of barley and livestock which are secured by real estate. In TCL 9 9, he appears in a lawsuit concerning another real estate *tidennūtu* transaction. He is also a creditor in TCL 9 45, and the purchaser of a slave girl in TCL 9 46.

66. Cf. text no. 9 below.

67. In line 19 following the seal impression, she is identified as EN *awāti*, "the litigant."

68. Literally, "I shall give to him." This is an example of the confusion caused by the passival orientation of the Hurrian verb which would require the form "I shall be given by him." The Nuzi scribe mechanically translated this Hurrian form into Akkadian where the verbal construction is active. Other such instances are cited by Speiser, AASOR 16 pp. 136ff.; and by Wilhelm, Untersuchungen zum Hurro-akkadischen pp. 61ff.

adoptive brother) in wifehood to a man described by the term DUMU.UŠ, and he (i.e., the adoptive brother) shall use my (bride-)money." The term DUMU.UŠ occurs only once in Nuzi in the sense of *aplu*, "chief heir."[69] Its appearance in such a context as DUMU.UŠ.GAL[70] would seem to indicate that in Nuzi the term DUMU.UŠ could also alternate with DUMU, "son." However, the interpretation of this statement as the obligation of the adoptive brother to give the adopted sister to his own son or chief heir is negated by the subsequent reference to his utilization of her marriage price which normally would not be given under such circumstances. Thus it seems preferable to interpret the term DUMU.UŠ as descriptive of a social class, as one who inherits, or perhaps as an abbreviated reference to DUMU *Arrapḫe*. Accordingly, the adoptive brother must marry his adopted sister to a freeman.[71]

In the first statement, Šakuti deposes that "Kirip-šeriš has adopted (me) into sistership and has made me a you[ng gi]rl-wife." The meaning of the latter part of this statement is enigmatic. It cannot indicate that he has married her himself since the second statement clearly states that she is to be given to another in marriage. One possible explanation is to assume an haplography of the *zu*-sign, and read DAM-*sú* <*ṣú*>-*ḫ*[*a-a*]*r-ti i-te-pu-uš*, "his wife has made (me) a young (servant-)girl."[72] Thus, Kirib-šeriš adopted Šakuti in sistership, and while in his household she is to serve as his wife's personal servant.

After these two problematic statements, the deposition stipulates the penalty of one mina of silver and one mina of gold for breach of contract, and concludes with a *šūdūtu*-clause. Despite the textual difficulties which hamper a full understanding of the document, it is clear that it records the adoption of a woman into sistership by an adoptive brother who will benefit from her bride-price upon her future marriage. The woman in this text appears to have acted on her own in initiating the transaction.

C. *Uncertain deposition*

8. Gadd, RA 23 (1926) 149 No. 31: The preserved portion of this document records the granting of land as *mulūgu*-property[73] by Šalap-urḫe to his sister Ḫalaše, who presents him with a *qištu*-gift equivalent to fifteen shekels of silver. Since the opening lines of the text are destroyed, it is impossible to ascertain the exact nature of the sistership transaction which formed the prelude to the land transfer.[74] Since Šalap-urḫe is identified as the recipient of the *qištu*-gift, it is clear that he is the maker of the deposition concerning the land grant (lines 4b-20). Hence it would seem that Šalap-urḫe would also have made the following initial declaration (lines 1-4a), of which the opening section is destroyed: (1) [. . .] *ru* [. . . *š*]*a* ^{m}*Še-ka*$_4$*-a-a* (2) [*l*]*a-lu-ú-ya i-il-li-ik-šu-ma* (3) *ù a-na a-ḫa-tù-ti a-na ya-a-ši* (4) *i-te-pu-uš*, ". . . of Šekaya. My desire went to her and she was adopted by me into sistership."[75] Accordingly, Šalap-urḫe would be the adoptive brother of Ḫalaše. However, since the expression *lalû alāku* in the depositions HSS 19 70:5 and "Yale 12:4" is employed by the adopted sister, and the first line of the declaration may be read as [*a*]-*na*! *Še-ka*$_4$*-a-a*, the entire section may be interpreted as an

69. HSS 5 71:33. In Nuzi, the chief heir is usually indicated by the term DUMU.GAL = *māru rabû*. Cf. CAD A/1 174b.

70. RA 23 (1926) 143 no. 5:33.

71. Cf. text no. 5 above, with n. 56.

72. The interpretation of *ṣuḫārtu* as a servant girl seems preferable to that of a young girl, for some kinship term would have been expected if this transaction represented a real adoption by Kirip-šeriš's wife.

73. Cf. B. A. Levine, "*Mulūgu/Melûg*: The Origins of a Talmudic Legal Institution," JAOS 88 (1968) 271-85. The term *mulūgu* represents dowry property, consisting of either real estate, slaves, or mobilia, which was given to the bride by her family, and may have included the bride's marriage price. The purpose of this property was two-fold: to provide the woman with resources were she to leave her husband's household; and to insure the transfer of property from the bride's family to her progeny. Paradise (Nuzi Inheritance Practices pp. 335f.) has convincingly argued that a woman is forbidden to alienate her *mulūgu* property by selling it to an outsider. This is contrary to the opinions of Speiser (AASOR 10 p. 65) and Levine (JAOS 88 [1968] 277), whose conclusions were based upon a misinterpretation of HSS 5 11:10f. This text when correctly translated identifies the reputed outsider, to whom the *mulūgu* property is given, as a daughter-in-law (cf. Breneman, Nuzi Marriage Tablets p. 122, and Paradise, Nuzi Inheritance Practices p. 335). According to the provisions of this text, the daughter-in-law must retain the property for her children.

74. C. Gordon considered this *mulūgu* land transfer to represent a disguised sale (ZA 43 [1936] 158). He based his position upon Speiser, who maintained that texts recording the exchange of a *qištu*-gift for *mulūgu*-property represented fictitious *mulūgu* transactions in which the *qištu*-gift served as a disguised sale-price (AASOR 10 pp. 26f.). The provisions of the text under discussion, however, are similar to the *mulūgu*-property transfer in HSS 19 79 treated by B. Levine (JAOS 88 [1968] 275ff.), which is clearly not "fictitious" since the transferred land may not be alienated from the family. The original evidence adduced by Speiser for the fictitious nature of certain *mulūgu* transactions (HSS 5 11 with HSS 5 26) can no longer be maintained in view of his misinterpretation of the texts (see n. 73 above). Thus there exists no evidence to support the claim that certain *mulūgu* transactions in Nuzi functioned as disguised land sales comparable to the Nuzi sale-adoption transactions.

75. References listed in CAD L 49b sub *lalû* indicate that both male and female subjects may express their desire or willingness to do something in terms of the noun *lalû*.

inserted declaration of Ḫalaše: "My desire went to Šekaya and he adopted me into sistership." Thus Šalap-urḫe would be the natural brother of Ḫalaše, who is adopted by another in sistership.[76]

II. DOCUMENTS OF SISTERSHIP

9. HSS 19 67: Tarmiya son of Ḫuya[77] has adopted Azum-naya daughter of Ḫašeya into sistership. Upon giving her in marriage, he shall receive one ox from the groom.[78] The remainder of her marriage price is to be given to her brother, Ḫašip-tešup. The penalty for breach of contract is one mina of silver and one mina of gold. The document, written in Nuzi, concludes with a *šūdūtu*-clause.

This document does not name the contracting party who has given Azum-naya into sistership. Since Ḫašip-tešup, her brother, is to benefit from a portion of her marriage price, it may be assumed that either he had initiated the arrangement or that Azum-naya herself had negotiated the matter with her brother's prior approval.[79] It should also be noted that there is no mention of Azum-naya's consent to the sistership adoption in this contract.[80]

10. JEN 78: Zikipa son of Eḫel-tešup has given his sister Ḫinzuri in sistership to Ḫut-arrapḫe son of Tišam-mušni who shall give her in [marriage] to whomever he pleases and receive her marriage price. Ḫut-arrapḫe has given one ox, [x] sheep, one homer of barley, two minas of bronze, and nine minas of wool to Zikipa, equaling twenty shekels of silver. Zikipa then declares that he has released to Ḫut-arrapḫe twenty shekels of silver, the remaining portion of Ḫinzuri's money which has been bound in her hem. Zikipa also bears the responsibility to clear his sister from any prior claimants. In the presence of witnesses Ḫinzuri states that she has been given in sistership to Ḫut-arrapḫe with her consent. The penalty for breach of contract is one mina of silver and one mina of gold. The document, written in Nuzi, concludes with a *šūdūtu*-clause.

The first section of the contract is straightforward. Ḫut-arrapḫe adopted a woman in sistership, gaining sole right to her eventual marriage price by paying her brother twenty shekels of silver. This represents half the usual marriage payment in Nuzi. The import of the second section of the contract, however, is more difficult to ascertain. In this section, the brother declares (lines 12-16): 20 GÍN KÙ.BABBAR.MEŠ *reḫtu* [*š*]*a Ḫinzurim*[*a*! *a*]*ḫatiya ina qanni*[*š*]*uma ša Ḫinz*[*uri*] *irtaksunūti*(!)[81] *ana Ḫutarr*[*ap*]*ḫe untešširšunūti*, "I have released to Ḫut-arrapḫe twenty shekels of silver the remainder of my sister Ḫinzuri's money which I have (or he has) bound in her hem." The problem concerns both the origin and purpose of the twenty shekels under discussion. As to their origin, one may assume that they represent the twenty shekels of silver which Zikipa just received for giving his sister into adoption. Zikipa then declares that he is returning the received money to Ḫut-arrapḫe for the purpose of serving as a nest egg for his sister upon her future marriage.[82] This statement would thus be motivated by an altruistic brotherly concern for his sister's future welfare. Such an interpretation would gain support from JEN 636, discussed above,[83] which records Zikipa's redemption of his sister Ḫinzuri from a status of *kallatu* (daughter-in-law) or *amtu* (slave girl). Such an interpretation, however, involves two difficulties. One lies in the fact that the twenty shekels are described as *reḫtu*, "remaining portion," which in monetary contexts in Nuzi usually represents an unpaid balance of money.[84] The other difficulty is that this money is not released to the sister but to the adoptive brother, Ḫut-arrapḫe. These difficulties become more readily apparent when Zikipa's statement is juxtaposed with the provision recorded in AASOR 16 No. 55, in which Šukri-tešup has given Šeḫalitum in marriage to a son of Zilip-kušuḫ. Lines 10-16 of that text read: [*u Z*]*ilikkušu* 20 GÍN KÙ.[BABBAR.MEŠ *ḫašaḫu*]*šennu ana* ᵐ*Šuk*[*ri-tešup*] *inandin u* 20 GÍN [KÙ.BABBAR.MEŠ *r*]*eḫtu ša Šeḫalitum ana qan*[*nišu*]*ma ra*[*k*]*is u ana Šeḫ*[*ali*]*tum unteššir*, "Zilip-kušuḫ shall give twenty shekels of *ḫašaḫušennu*-silver to Šukri-tešup, and as for the remaining

76. Support for Skaist's interpretation of this document as one in which "provision is made for a *mulūgu* 'dowry' for the sister of the girl who gave herself in adoption" (JAOS 89 [1969] 17) seems lacking. For yet another interpretation of this document, see Koschaker, NRUA p. 91 and ZA 41 (1933) 28 n. 3.

77. There is a Tarmiya son of Ḫuya, who is known from JEN 370 as a canal inspector (*gukallu*). The text records a lawsuit concerning a canal in which Tarmiya is fined one ox. In the deathbed testament AASOR 16 no. 56, a Tarmiya son of Ḫuya received a slave girl as wife from his father. No definite connection can be established between all three texts which would clearly identify them as relating to the same person.

78. Line 7 reads *ašar* LÚ *ḫatāni*. The term *ḫatānu* is used to indicate a male relative by marriage (cf. CAD Ḫ 148).

79. For this latter alternative, cf. text no. 4 above. There is also the possibility that the brother may have been a minor. There is, however, no information with regard to a minor's fraternal rights to his sister.

80. See below n. 98.

81. The cuneiform reads *ir-ta-ak-su-nu-ti* for *irtakassunūti*.

82. Cf. the remarks of Speiser in AASOR 10 p. 22 n. 49, and in "Nuzi Marginalia," Or. NS 25 (1956) 12.

83. See pp. 48ff.

84. Cf. AASOR 16 no. 55:13; HSS 9 108:8; HSS 19 87:10 and 89:12.

twenty shekels due for Šeḫalitum, he shall release them to Šeḫalitum to be bound in her hem." Here the twenty shekels represent the remainder of the woman's marriage price and they are to be released directly to her.

Zikipa's statement in JEN 78, in line with the above provision of AASOR 16 No. 55, can be interpreted to mean that the twenty shekels of silver are the balance remaining from the full marriage price of forty shekels of silver which Ḫut-arrapḫe would eventually receive, after having deducted from it the payment which Ḫut-arrapḫe made to Zikipa upon adopting his sister. Upon the marriage of a free woman in Nuzi, these twenty shekels of silver would be bound in the bride's hem and released to her as her dowry by her father or guardian. However, Zikipa has declared that this money which *would have been bound* in his sister's hem has been released to Ḫut-arrapḫe, thus freeing Ḫut-arrapḫe from the obligation of providing Ḫinzuri with a dowry and enabling him to realize a profit of twenty shekels of silver from her marriage price.[85] According to this interpretation of the sistership adoption, Zikipa retains the received equivalent of twenty shekels of silver and Ḫut-arrapḫe acquires the services and handiwork of a woman for only twenty shekels of silver with an anticipated profit of twenty shekels of silver upon her future marriage. As for Ḫut-arrapḫe's interest in acquiring personal services, it is well attested in the Nuzi texts. JEN 2 179 records his purchase of a woman, who had been ransomed(?)[86] from the land of the Kassites, for forty shekels of silver, and JEN 3 290 records his securing the services of a carpenter for ten years by lending thirty shekels of silver and two homers of barley to the carpenter's master in a *tidennūtu* arrangement.

11. HSS 5 69: Akkul-enni son of Akiya has given his sister Bēlt-akkadi-ummi, in sistership to Ḫurazzi and has received forty shekels of silver from him. Akkul-enni bears the responsibility to clear his sister from any prior claim. The penalty for breach of contract is one mina of silver and one mina of gold. This document, written in Temtena, concludes with a *šūdūtu*-clause.

This contract of sistership is atypical in that it fails to make reference to the eventual marriage of the adopted sister and the right of her adoptive brother to her marriage price. It is also the only document in which the adoptive brother has paid the full sum of forty shekels of silver, equivalent to the average marriage payment for brides. This payment of the full sum for the acquisition of the woman in sistership may have clearly established the adoptive brother's right to her eventual marriage price and hence need not have been stressed by recording this right in the document.[87]

As mentioned in the beginning of this article, the nature of the transaction recorded in this text is further complicated by the fact that according to another document the same brother gave the same sister to the same adoptive brother in marriage. That document, HSS 5 80, records an agreement between Ḫurazzi and Akkul-enni in which Akkul-enni is to give[88] his sister Bēlt-akkadi-ummi in marriage to Ḫurazzi for twenty shekels of silver, with the remaining money to be bound in his sister's hem as her dowry. In addition, Akkul-enni also declares that he is giving another sister, Kapul-anza, to Ḫurazzi in daughtership. Akkul-enni will receive twenty shekels of silver from Ḫurazzi upon the consummation of Kapul-anza's marriage. Despite the fact that this marriage document contains a penalty clause for breach of contract, these stipulations do not seem to represent the final arrangements. According to a third document, HSS 5 25, Akkul-enni deposes that he has given[89] Bēlt-akkadi-ummi in marriage to Ḫurazzi, and that he has been paid forty shekels of silver. Bēlt-akkadi-ummi's consent to the marriage, arranged for her by her brother, is also recorded. Ḫurazzi then declares, however, that he shall not raise a claim against Akkul-enni concerning Kapl[u-anza].[90] This seems to indicate that Ḫurazzi had relinquished his contracted right to adopt Kapul-anza in daughtership, i.e., the deposition HSS 5 25 invalidated part of the marriage contract HSS 5 80. One could therefore argue that,

85. Cf. Breneman, Nuzi Marriage Tablets p. 166. Texts containing this provision similar to JEN 78 are: HSS 9 145; HSS 19 70, 86; and RA 23 (1926) 152 no. 42. Unlike the practice cited above n. 60, these texts state that the money bound in the girl's hem is released to her adoptive parent.

86. The term used is *ú-a-an-ta*, for which Speiser suggested the underlying meaning of "ransom" (Or. NS 25 [1956] 13 n. 5).

87. This interpretation is based on the assumption that the Nuzi legal document served as a summary of the orally concluded transaction, recording the names of the witnesses, rather than as a carefully formulated, all-inclusive written contract which created the reality of the transaction. Cf. Eichler, Indenture at Nuzi pp. 11f., and S. Greengus, "The Old Babylonian Marriage Contract," JAOS 89 (1969) 513.

88. Line 6 contains the verbal form SUM-*šu*. The verb is to be rendered in the present-future aspect, *inaddinšu*, rather than the perfect (Speiser, AASOR 10 p. 59), since the parallel verbal form in line 10 is *i-na-an-din*.

89. The verbal form in line 6 is in the perfect aspect (attadin). As for the chronological ordering of these three texts, see the discussion below with n. 92.

90. Based on context, it seems certain that this restored name is to be identified with ᶠKapul-anza of HSS 5 80. Cf. Gelb, Purves and MacRae, Nuzi Personal Names (Chicago, 1943) p. 80a.

similarly, Ḫurazzi had relinquished his contracted right to adopt Bēlt-akkadi-ummi in sistership prior to his marrying her, i.e., the marriage contract HSS 5 80 invalidated the sistership contract HSS 5 69.[91]

An alternative position is to assume the validity of both the marriage and the sistership arrangements. But even under this assumption, only the following alternative deductions can be made.[92] Positing the priority of the marriage contract, one may deduce that a husband could acquire from his wife's brother certain assumed fraternal rights and obligations which had not been abrogated by her marriage, by contracting a sistership adoption *in addition* to the original marriage agreement. According to the two extant contracts, the husband would have to make an additional payment for these fraternal rights over and above the marriage price. The nature of these fraternal rights and the advantages of such a costly arrangement accruing to the husband are unclear. Alternatively, by positing the priority of the sistership contract, one may deduce that an adoptive brother could marry his adopted sister by contracting a separate marriage agreement.[93] The existence of both documents indicates that the sistership contract alone did not grant marital rights to the adoptive brother. From the extant documents, it also appears that upon her marriage the adoptive brother had to make an additional payment to her natural brother over and above the adoption price. Unless motivated by an infatuating love, it is unclear why the adoptive brother would pay an additional twenty shekels of silver, totalling sixty shekels, to acquire his adopted sister as wife. It is also unclear why the additional marriage payment should be made to the adopted sister's natural brother, since in the other sistership transactions, the natural brother cedes to the adoptive brother the right of arranging for his sister's marriage and the receipt of her marriage price. It therefore seems necessary to assume the existence of another unpreserved contract in which the adoptive brother, desiring to marry his adopted sister, relinquished his acquired rights to his adopted sister with the concurrent return of the adoption price to her natural brother. This would form the intermediate stage between the sistership and marriage arrangements. Thus this alternative deduction in essence leads one to a conclusion which is tantamount to negating the validity of the original sistership contract which was proposed above. In any event, it is clear that the two related texts HSS 5 69 and 80 do not reasonably allow the equation of sistership with wifehood or the assertion that in all sistership transactions the adoptive brother had the concurrent status of husband.

Although there is no satisfactory resolution to the problems posed by the last cited sistership transaction, a summation of the constant data gleaned from the other sistership documents is in order. All of the other sistership adoptions clearly involve the transference of the privilege to negotiate the woman's marriage arrangements from the natural brother (or the woman herself) to the adoptive brother. With this transference the adoptive brother either gained the right to share in her future marriage price or obtained the sole right to the marriage price.[94] Presumably, while the adopted sister is yet unmarried and resides in his household, the adoptive brother would benefit from her services and handiwork.[95] The sistership adoption itself could be arranged either by the woman's brother or by the woman herself.[96] Circumstantial evidence suggests that the woman, in negotiating her own sistership adoption, may have had to obtain her brother's prior consent had she not been freed from his authority.[97] The documents however, clearly attest to the necessity of the woman's consent to the sistership adoption transacted by her brother.[98] The circumstances

91. Note, however, that unlike the former case, the verbal forms describing the transfer of the woman's status in the "invalidated" document are in the perfect aspect, and not in the present-future aspect. Therefore it is difficult to assume that the "invalidated" document merely stipulated a contractual right which was subsequently relinquished. It seems more probable to assume, with the alternative position discussed below, that an unpreserved document had cancelled the existing sistership contract. Cf. text TF 788=IM 73425 (A. Fadhil, Rechtsurkunden und Administrative Texte aus Kurruḫanni [Heidelberg, 1972] pp. 67f. no. 5), which cancels a marriage agreement with the return of the bride-price to the groom's family and the return of the bride to her family.

92. The fact that the sistership and marriage contracts were written in different cities, by different scribes, and with different sets of witnesses would seem to argue against the simultaneity or equation of the sistership and marriage transactions. But cf. Koschaker, ZA 41 (1933) 14 n. 2, who discusses the chronological ordering of the three texts. Gordon (ZA 43 [1936] 154 n. 1) and Lewy (Or. NS 10 [1941] 213) gave priority to the sistership contract, while Speiser (Oriental and Biblical Studies pp. 68f.) gave priority to the marriage contract.

93. Cf. Cassin, L'Adoption à Nuzi p. 304 and Van Seters, Abraham in History and Tradition p. 74.

94. Texts nos. 4 and 9 clearly indicate that the adoptive brother receives only a share of the marriage price, while in texts nos. 1, 2, 7 and 10 he receives the full marriage price. Texts nos 3 and 6 record that upon giving the adopted sister in marriage the adoptive brother is to receive a fixed sum.

95. See above, the discussions of texts nos. 4 and 7.

96. The adoption arrangements are made by the brother in texts nos. 1, 2, 10 and 11; and by the woman herself in texts nos. 3-7.

97. See above, the discussion of text no. 4.

98. Cf. Koschaker, NRUA p. 91 n. 1; and Skaist, JAOS 89 (1969) 11. Texts nos. 1, 2 and 10 record the sister's declaration of consent, while texts nos. 3-7 are depositions made by the woman herself and hence implicitly contain her consent to the arrangement. Only texts nos. 9 and 11 do not make mention of the sister's consent.

under which sistership adoptions were transacted are quite varied. However, in all cases, with the exception of the last, the woman or her brother must have been under severe socio-economic pressures, for it would have been more profitable for them to have negotiated the marriage themselves rather than transferring the right of negotiation to an adoptive brother.[99]

Since the sistership contracts represent the means by which an adoptive brother attains rights to his adopted sister's marriage price, they can afford little insight into the origin and extent of fraternal authority over one's natural sister.[100] The only available source material dealing with the issue is the Nuzi wills[101] recording the disposition of the testator regarding the fate of his property and of those persons under his authority. J. S. Paradise, in his study of Nuzi inheritance practices has discussed the evidence concerning the disposition of a male testator's daughter and her marriage price.[102] Assuming that the Nuzi documents provide evidence for the normal rather than exceptional practice, Paradise concludes that the testator's wife rather than his sons were invested with authority over his daughters.[103] His conclusion is based on the fact that three out of the four relevant texts record such a disposition.[104] In the fourth text,[105] although the testator had designated his wife guardian over his property, sons, and daughters, he nevertheless specifies that his sons shall give his daughters in marriage and receive their bride price.[106] From this text it is clear that fraternal authority to give one's sister in marriage and receive her bride price may derive directly from one's father. On the other hand, this authority may derive also from one's mother. In HSS 19 11 the female testator bequeaths her daughter to her son in sistership (*ana aḫātūti*).[107] Although it is impossible to ascertain whether the testator's wife or son would have prior claim to the testator's daughter,[108] inferential evidence indicates

Nevertheless, it should be noted that while the marriage contract HSS 5 80 does not record the woman's consent to the arrangement, the parallel deposition text HSS 5 25 does contain her declaration of consent. Hence it may be assumed that the sistership texts nos. 9 and 11 may have had accompanying deposition texts which did contain the sister's declaration of consent.

The woman's consent may have been prerequisite not only for the sistership transaction but for any arrangement made for her by her brother. For example, HSS 5 25:14-16 (*ana aššūti*) and AASOR 16 no. 23:2-4 (*ana mārtūti*). However, the other texts cited below, n. 111, do not contain the sister's declaration of consent.

99. This would argue against Speiser's position that the sistership arrangement represented an advantaged position bestowed upon women of high social status (Oriental and Biblical Studies pp. 71f., 75). Cf. the critical remarks of Mullo Weir, Transactions of the Glasgow University Oriental Society 22 (1967-68 [1970]) 19ff.

100. The only inference that can be made from the corpus is that according to texts nos. 3 and 5 it seems that a sister is freed from her brother's authority by a previous adoption or marriage. The corpus gives no indication as to whether an orphaned girl is freed upon reaching her majority or whether she is still under the authority of her brother even if he is a minor.

101. These texts take the form of depositions made by the testator or else they bear the superscription *ṭuppi šimti* "document of fate (or fixed decision)."

102. Nuzi Inheritance Practices pp. 297-300.

103. Nuzi Inheritance Practices p. 297. Paradise notes that this conclusion is contrary to the position taken by Skaist, JAOS 89 (1969) 16ff. Paradise also cautions, however, that the documentary evidence may attest to the exceptional rather than to normal practice. Cf. Greengus, JAOS 89 (1969) 512f.

104. HSS 19 10, 7, and 6. With regard to the last text, it must be noted that Paradise assumes that the female given to the testator's wife in daughtership is indeed the testator's daughter. To the corpus collected by Paradise, one should add the non-will texts JEN 482, in which a husband relinquishes two daughters to his wife, and HSS 19 91, in which a husband gives his daughter to his wife in daughtership. This daughter is subsequently given by her mother and brother to another person in daughtership (HSS 19 92).

105. HSS 19 19. Paradise, on the basis of circumstantial evidence, assumes that the text is dealing with the children of separate marriages (Nuzi Inheritance Practices pp. 78 and 299 n. 199).

106. Rather than assuming with Paradise that this text (HSS 19 19) is at variance with the three texts cited in n. 104, the following alternative explanation may be considered:

As indicated by this text, the wife's guardianship authority (*abbūtu*) over a daughter may never have entitled her to receive the daughter's marriage price. In fact, in the three texts cited above only HSS 19 6 mentions the receipt of the girl's marriage price by the testator's wife. Furthermore, it is the only text which does not mention that the wife has been appointed guardian but rather that the girl has been given to her in daughtership (as mentioned above in n. 104, Paradise only assumes that this girl is the testator's daughter). If text HSS 19 6 would be separated from the corpus, there would be no evidence of the wife's guardianship entitling her to receive the daughter's marriage price. If this be so, the nature of the wife's guardianship over the daughter would be similar to the wife's guardianship over the husband's property. Despite her appointment as guardian over the property, the wife is forbidden to alienate the property without the permission of her husband's sons (Paradise, Nuzi Inheritance Practices pp. 288ff.). Similarly, the wife's guardianship over the daughter would entitle her to the daughter's services and handiwork, while the sons would be responsible for arranging the daughter's marriage and would receive the bride price. The rationale for this differentiation would be due to the conception of the daughter's bride price as part of the paternal estate to be inherited by his sons.

107. This daughter is one of five daughters given to the woman together with other property by her husband in his will (HSS 19 10). The son who receives the daughter is named as PN the son of her husband, and hence may be the woman's natural son or stepson.

108. Cf. above n. 106, suggesting that the testator's wife, although receiving guardianship authority over a daughter, may have had to receive permission from her husband's son who would receive the girl's bride price in order to arrange for the girl's future. Evidence for this may be gleaned from JEN 120, in which a mother and brother arrange jointly for the girl's future marriage. Nevertheless, there are texts in which the mother alone arranges

that Nuzi society recognized the legitimacy of a brother's authority over his orphaned sister. The will HSS 19 7 stipulates that the testator's daughter, who is to be given to her mother, shall go free upon the death of her mother and none of her brothers may lay claim to her. Similarly, the daughtership contract TCL 9 7 contains a clause forbidding the girl's brothers from raising a future claim to their sister against her adoptive mother.[109]

In attempting to relate the Nuzi sistership transactions to the entire set of documents in which females are acquired for purposes of matrimony, only a superficial pattern emerges. In Nuzi, a father had three basic options in the disposition of his female children. He could arrange for their immediate marriage by giving them into wifehood (*ana aššūti*), or for their adoption into daughter or daughter-in-lawship (*ana mārtūti u kallatūti*) with the eventual purpose of marriage. He could also sell them into slavery (*ana amtūti*).[110] The Nuzi texts also attest to three options which a brother could exercise in the disposition of his presumably orphaned sister. Like the father, a brother could arrange either for her immediate marriage by giving her into wifehood (*ana aššūti*) or for her adoption into daughter and daughter-in-lawship (*ana mārtūti u kallatūti*).[111] The brother, however, also had the unique option of arranging for another type of adoption—that of sistership (*ana aḫātūti*) whereby he transfers his fraternal rights to an adoptive brother. The adoptive brother would than have the same options as had her natural brother—namely, giving her into wifehood or into adoption to a third party.[112] Unfortunately, the documentary evidence does not reveal the motivating factors operative in the choice of these various options.[113] This ignorance impairs a more profound understanding of the nature of the Nuzi sistership transaction which is attested at present only in the Nuzi legal texts.[114]

for her daughter's future (*ana mārtūti u kallatūti*: JEN 431; AASOR 16 nos. 30, 55; HSS 9 145; HSS 19 88). Perhaps in these cases the daughter had no brothers.

109. In lawsuit RA 34 (1926) 151 no. 35, a brother does raise such a claim to his sister whom the defendant contends had been given to him in daughtership by their father. His claim, however, may have arisen after the death of their mother.

110. E.g., *ana aššūti*: JEN 435; HSS 19 83, 85; TCL 9 41; *ana mārtūti u kallatūti*: JEN 26, 50, 433; HSS 9 119; HSS 13 15; HSS 19 89, 94, 145; AASOR 16 no. 52; TCL 9 7; *ana amtūti*: RA 23 (1926) 155 no. 52; HSS 19 117.

111. E.g., *ana aššūti*: JEN 441; HSS 5 25, 53, 80; HSS 9 24; HSS 19 84; TF_1 431=IM 70978 (Fadhil, Rechtsurkunden aus Kurruḫanni p. 63 no. 2); *ana mārtūti u kallatūti*: JEN 429, 437, 596; HSS 5 80; HSS 14 543; HSS 19 87, 100; AASOR 16 no. 23; TCL 9 6. There is no attested example of a brother giving his sister into slavery (*ana amtūti*).

112. E.g., *ana aššūti*: JEN 78; HSS 5 26; HSS 19 67-69, 143; AASOR 16 no. 54; *ana mārtūti u kallatūti*: HSS 5 79. In lines 27-28, the woman declares: *anāku aḫātūti ana Šar-tešup*, 'I am in sistership to Šar-tešup" (who has given her into a *kallatu* relationship in this contract).

113. A price analysis reveals that although forty shekels of silver is attested as payment for a female given *ana aššūti* (JEN 441), *ana mārtūti u kallatūti* (JEN 429) and *ana aḫātūti* (HSS 5 69), the average payment is higher in marriage contracts than in adoption contracts for purposes of matrimony. Within these adoption contracts, the payment tends to be somewhat higher in *mārtūtu u kallatūtu* transactions than in *aḫātūtu* transactions. In both transactions, the payment is sometimes postponed until the marriage of the female. At present it is impossible to ascertain why a brother would choose to give his sister *ana aḫātūti* or *ana mārtūti u kallatūti*, or what the essential difference is between them since both are adoptions for purposes of matrimony. Indeed, Skaist does not consider the terminology to represent different options but rather to reflect the vacillation of the scribes which may be due to the hypothesis that "patrilineal succession had only recently been discarded" (JAOS 89 [1969] 17). Gordon suggested that the use of terminology may be determined by the age of the adopter: a brother would give his sister to an older man *ana mārtūti u kallatūti* but to her contemporary *ana aḫātūti* (ZA 43 [1936] 155 n. 4). In addition, he speculated (ibid. p. 156) that a brother ceded all his rights to his sister given *ana mārtūti u kallatūti*, but shared his rights, when given *ana aḫātūti*. There is no documentary evidence to confirm any of these hypotheses.

114. The Old Babylonian, Neo-Babylonian, and Elephantine texts cited by Van Seters (Abraham in History and Tradition p. 74 n. 33) are only examples of brothers giving their sisters in marriage. They are not sistership adoptions involving the transference of the privilege to negotiate the woman's marriage arrangements from the natural brother to the adoptive brother. Similarly, the Old Babylonian *atḫūtu*-contract in which a woman adopts a "sister" as a second wife for her husband does not parallel the Nuzi sistership transaction since it establishes only a sororal relationship between two women. For the Babylonian parallels to the Nuzi *mārtūtu u kallatūtu* transaction, see Van Praag, Droit matrimonial p. 79; Cardascia, Revue historique de droit 37 (1959) 6 n. 22; Driver and Miles, The Babylonian Laws 1 (Oxford, 1956) 251f.; Landsberger, "Jungfräulichkeit," Symbolae Iuridicae et Historicae Martino David Dedicatae 2 (Leiden, 1968) 90 n. 3, 93f.; and CAD K 86a sub *kallūtu*.

LAND OF DEAD *rēdû*'s

Maria deJ. Ellis
The University Museum
University of Pennsylvania

Not long ago I completed a lengthy study concerned with general problems of land tenure in ancient Mesopotamia, including the evidence available for the administration of state fields during the Old Babylonian period.[1] That study developed in part from a dissertation produced under Jack Finkelstein's direction; shortly before his death, he asked me to speak about the subject as the topic for a session of the Assyriological Colloquium.[2] It therefore seems appropriate to offer here some additional material which I discovered after the larger work had gone to press. First, however, I will briefly trace the general outline of the Old Babylonian agricultural administrative system.

During the reign of Ḫammurapi, land under the ultimate control of the Old Babylonian state could be assigned as subsistence allotments to beneficiaries, who then cultivated the land. These beneficiaries were state personnel of various classes, above the level of ration-recipient. The land involved was variously referred to as *ilku*-land, *šukussu*-land, and *ṣibtu*-land. There were also certain people to whom subsistence allotments were assigned, but who could not—or did not—attend to the land's cultivation themselves. Land assigned to such people was retained by the state, and one of the officials in the state's agricultural hierarchy entered, as tenant, into a field lease contract with the beneficiary, who figured as the "field-owner." The land was then cultivated by state personnel, together with *biltu*-land—land that remained state land proper and whose total yield accrued to the state. Of the rental land, the one-third or one-half share of the harvest that was "rent" (*biltu*) was paid to the beneficiary, while the remaining two-thirds or one-half of the harvest went to the state after the deduction of production expenses. In cases of mismanagement on the part of the "tenant" (i.e., the state agricultural administrator), the "owner's" share of the harvest was referred to as *miksu* in letters of complaint by the owner. *Miksu* in this context carries its general meaning "share."[3]

The evidence upon which the description given above is based comes from southern Babylonia during Ḫammurapi's reign; the reconstruction is based primarily, but not exclusively, on the correspondence of Ḫammurapi's officials in Larsa, and on some documents from the Lagaš area. The latter texts show that the *iššakku*'s were in immediate charge of, and were accountable for, fields cultivated within the system.[4] A second body of evidence comes from northern Babylonia, from the reigns of Ḫammurapi's descendants Ammiditana and Ammiṣaduqa. These texts, which date about a century later, show that the same field categories still existed. However, the state's *biltu*-land, and the allotments not directly worked by their beneficiaries, were no longer cultivated by agricultural workers dependent on the state, as had been done in the time of Ḫammurapi. Instead, the official in charge of administering such lands (the *iššakku*) acted as middleman in the leasing of those allotment fields to third parties,[5] in the name of the nominal "owner" (beneficiary) of the field. To work the state's own *biltu*-fields, he hired labor crews, with capital provided by the state.[6]

It has been possible to reconstruct the system in general outlines, but how individual groups of workers were treated under it must still be determined. Here I will deal briefly with the fields alloted to *rēdû*'s, the "soldiers." Information comes from formal public documents such as the Code of Ḫammurapi and the Edict of Ammiṣaduqa, and from everyday records.

The Code of Ḫammurapi mentions land held by *rēdû*'s in return for their service to the state (*ilku*) in

1. Maria deJ. Ellis, Agriculture and the State in Ancient Mesopotamia: An Introduction to Problems of Land Tenure, Occasional Publications of the Babylonian Fund, 1 (Philadelphia, 1976).

2. Dissertation: Taxation and Land Revenues in the Old Babylonian Period (Yale University, 1969). Colloquium: "Land Tenure in Ancient Mesopotamia," 18 December 1974.

3. See in general Ellis, Agriculture. For another short overview of the problem, see Ellis, "Taxation in Ancient Mesopotamia: the History of the Term *miksu*," JCS 26 (1974) 214-15, in the context of a discussion of the term *miksu*, pp. 211-50.

4. The texts were published by M. Birot, in Tablettes as Nos. 1-11. For a discussion of the texts, see Ellis, Agriculture Chapter 2 Section A 2a (1) and Section A 4.

5. Often high officials, such as the *mu*ʾ*irru*, the *šāpiru*, and the *rabiānu* of Kish, acting in partnership. For texts, see e.g. YOS 13 48, 50, 56, 59, 79, 222, 223. For a discussion of the practice, see Ellis, Agriculture Chapter 2 Section A 2a (2a).

6. See Ellis, Agriculture Chapter 2 Section A 2a (2b) for a discussion of the contracts.

Ancient Near Eastern Studies in Memory of J. J. Finkelstein
Connecticut Academy of Arts and Sciences, Memoir 19

paragraphs 26ff. Those paragraphs describe in some detail the rights and obligations of the *rēdû*'s in *ilku*-land. The topics covered include how the landholding was affected in cases of a *rēdû*'s non-performance of service, by sending a substitute (§ 26); his being missing in the line of duty (§§ 27-29); and his relinquishment of his *ilku*-obligation and holding (§§ 30-31). There are also direct prohibitions against the sale of a *rēdû*'s *ilku*-land (§§ 36-37 and 41), and against its gift to a female family member (§ 38). The sale of *ilku*-land, incidentally, is specifically prohibited only for *rēdû*'s and *bāʾiru*'s ("fishermen"), but is allowed for other classes under *ilku*-obligation, with the proviso that the buyer assume the seller's *ilku*-duty.

Thus the Code of Ḫammurapi; the Edict of Ammiṣaduqa alludes to duties incumbent on *ilku*-lands, including those of *rēdû*'s, only in terms of their temporary remission. § 15 of the Edict reads:

[EN]KU(ZAG.ḪA) [š]*a* GÚ.U[N A.ŠÀ ŠE[7] Š]E.GIŠ.Ì *ù ṣe-eḫ-ḫe-er-tam*
[š]*a na-ši* GÚ.UN x [x] *ra-bi-i*
LÚ *mu-uš-ke-nim* AGA.UŠ ŠU.[ḪA]
ù il-ki-im a-ḫi-im ša K[Á].D[INGIR.R]A.KI
ù na-we-šu im-ma-ak-ku-su
aš-šum šar-rum mi-ša-ra-am a-na ma-tim iš-ku-nu
ú-u[*š*]*-šu-ur ú-ul im-ma-ak-ku-us*
še-e ši-mi-im ù ta-ak-ši-tim
ki-ma mi-ki-is la-bi-ir-tim im-ma-ak-ku-us

"The *mākisu* (tax collector), with whom the yield of the fields is divided, (namely) the barley and sesame and the minor crops of the *nāši bilti*, of the . . ., of the *muškēnu*, of the *rēdû*, of the *bāʾiru*, and of the holder of any other *ilku*-field in Babylon or its environs—because the king has instituted a *mīšaru* for the country—it shall not be so divided (with him). The barley for sale and for business purposes will be divided according to the usual division."

Some of the situations listed above are known from the private documents of the Old Babylonian period; the information gained from those documents does not always agree with the stipulations of the Code of Ḫammurapi. For example, §26 of the Code stipulates that a *rēdû* (or a *bāʾiru*) may not send a substitute to do his service; should he do so, he forfeits his holding. Yet the archive of the *rēdû* Ubarrum,[8] from the time of King Abiešuḫ, contains a number of texts which refer to arrangements made with a substitute. Those texts may reflect adjustments made to the regulations over the time span elapsed since Ḫammurapi's reign, but it is, of course, also possible that the rule in the Code of Ḫammurapi did not reflect usual practice even in its own time.

We have very little information about other aspects of the *rēdû*'s relation to *ilku*-land. The legal rules do not state in what manner land was assigned to members of this class, but we do have some indications about its assignment from letters. For example, OECT 3 11 and 16 both refer to assignments of land made to *rēdû*'s and their supervisors (PA.PA and NU.BANDA$_3$). The *rēdû*'s received two *iku*'s of land each, the NU.BANDA$_3$ four, and the PA.PA eight. Similarly OECT 3 40 refers to an ancient list of field assignments to *rēdû*'s. That list is called an old tablet of *ilku*'s (*tup-pí la-bi-ri-im ša* [*i*]*l-ka-tim* [line 17]); it listed the individual *ilku*-holders by name.

The question I would like to discuss briefly here concerns what happens when a *rēdû* dies without heirs who qualify in their turn to hold the land and perform the service (i.e., male heirs). The letter CT 6 27b (= AbB 1 76 No. 111) states that a field which had originally belonged to a *rēdû*, since deceased without heirs, had been given by "the city" to another *rēdû*. The latter had held it for thirty years. The complaint stated in the letter concerns the fact that the city had taken away half of that field while its current owner was on service (*ina ḫarrān bēlija*) in Sippar. The information contained in this letter, of course, nicely complements the rules from the Code: if there are no qualifying heirs, then the field is redistributed within the peer group, since it is held in return for service. It remains to be discovered what the mechanics of the redistribution are, and what happens to a field if there is no other qualifying holder immediately available.

Two tablets from the John Frederick Lewis Collection of the Free Library of Philadelphia give some information about the procedures involved. The tablets resemble each other in format, and are dated six days apart in Ḫammurapi's 33rd year. FLP 1738, dated to the 26th day of Ajaru, reads:

7. For the restoration see CAD Ṣ 174a and Ellis, Taxation p. 217 n. 35.

8. Last treated in detail by B. Landsberger, JCS 9 (1955) 121-31.

obv. 70 ŠE.GUR
GIŠ.BA.RÍ.GA ^{d}AMAR.UTU
ša AGA.UŠ.MEŠ *mi-tu-tim*
LÚ URU.KI GN *ša* I_7 GN
NÍG.ŠU PN
ša i-na GÚ I_7 GN
MAŠ.EN.KAK *i-ri-šu-ú-ma*
a-na NÍG.KUD ŠU.RI.A
iš-ša-ak-nu
ša a-na Ta-ri-bu-um
Á.GÁL
rev. *a-na šu-ud-du-nim*
na-ad-nu
É.GAL *i-ip-pa-al*

The only identifiable seal is that of Taribum.

FLP 1648, dated six days earlier than FLP 1738, is similar, but slightly more elaborate, since the barley accounted for was the responsibility of two individuals, named at the head of the text:

obv. 73 (GUR) 4 (BÁN) 7½ $SILA_3$ GUR.ŠE
NÍG.ŠU DUMU.UDAR
3 (GUR) 1 (BÁN) 6⅔ $SILA_3$ GUR NÍG.ŠU *Zi-kír*!*-ì-lí-šu*

---

76 (GUR) 1 (PI) 4 $SILA_3$ 10 GÍN ŠE.GUR
GIŠ.BA.RÍ.GA ^{d}AMAR.UTU
ša AGA.UŠ.MEŠ *mi-tu-tim*
LÚ URU GN
ù URU GN_2
ša i-na GÚ I_7 GN
MAŠ.EN.KAK *i-ri-šu-ma*
ana ŠU.RI.A *ša-ak-nu*
rev. *a-na* x x ⌜x⌝ IG? *ša* DUMU.UDAR
a-na šu-ud-du-nim na-ad-nu
É.GAL *i-ip-pa-lam*!

The tablet is sealed, but the impressions are not legible.

The texts both give the information that lands of deceased *rēdû*'s of several towns, all within the same area[9] (so far not further located) had been cultivated by a group of people generically described as *muškēnu*'s. The proceeds of the cultivation were subject to the one-half division, and both texts note that the palace had been paid. FLP 1738 contains the statement that the procedure had been handled by Taribum, the *muʾirru*.[10] In FLP 1648 the identity of the administrator must be hidden in the broken first line of the reverse.[11]

9. The lands mentioned in both texts are located on the same canal: I_7 *Ga-bu-ú*, FLP 1738:6, 1648:9.

10. Note the exceptional writing of the title, which in economic texts is usually written with variations of the formula GAL.UKKIN.NA ERÍN KA É.GAL; for the equation Á.GAL=(*mu-ʾi-ru*) see MSL 12 96 line 113. For examples of the *muʾirru*'s activities as they are attested in economic texts, cf. YOS 13 p. 81, index s.v., and, for example, the harvest labor contract YOS 13 59 and similarly formulated texts (discussed in Ellis, Agriculture Chapter 1 Section A 2a (2a), which list the *muʾirru* as the source of the harvest laborer's wages). The title *muʾirru* was treated by N. Yoffee, The Economic Role of the Crown in the Old Babylonian Period (Yale, unpubl. Ph.D. diss., 1973 [revised version to be published by Undena Publications, 1977]) Chapter 3. It must be noted that the FLP 1738 attestation is a very early reference to the title as used of an official, regardless of how it is written. The next occurrence known to me is found in some tablets dated to Samsuiluna's 23rd year; the texts are to be published as YOS 12 411-16; see now Ellis, Agriculture Chapter 2 Section A 2c.

11. I have no suggestions for the three signs following *a-na*, though one would expect either a personal name or a title. On the basis of the similar passage in FLP 1738, it might be suggested that ⌜x⌝ IG should be restored ⌜Á⌝.GAL, *muʾirru*, but I do not know of any *muʾirru* described as being *ša* PN.

One other text, YOS 13 41, dated to Samsu-ditana's second year, gives some information on how fields were administered in the interim period. The text records the lease of certain properties that had been assigned to now-deceased *rēdû*'s who had been under the command of a PA.PA. The lease ran for the term of one year; the lessees were partners, the *muʾirru* and the *šāpiru* of Kish. These two officials appear often as the tenants in lease contracts for fields handled by the state agricultural officials in the late Old Babylonian period. The official involved is usually the *iššakku*; *ana qabê* PN *iššakku*, "at the behest of PN, the *iššakku*" is the most common phrase found in such texts.[12] In YOS 13 41, however, the phrase *ana qabê* appears, but the two individuals mentioned are not given titles. We therefore do not know into which official hierarchy they fit.[13] YOS 13 41 is, of course, a late Old Babylonian text. We cannot infer from it how representative its stipulations are for the procedure that was usually followed in such cases.

The pattern shown by these texts—if one can speak of a pattern on the basis of three texts—is very interesting in that it overlaps with that observed for the administration of state lands in the time of Ḫammurapi and during the later part of the dynasty, respectively, as that administration was outlined above. The evidence from the reign of Ḫammurapi shows that in southern Babylonia at that time fields which were not directly cultivated by their holders were cultivated by members of the lower order of the state agricultural labor force, usually called *nāši bilti*'s in those texts. The two FLP texts show that in the case of vacancies caused by a death, the fields of *rēdû*'s were administered as if they were held by absentee owners (although in the case of the two FLP texts those who performed the actual work of cultivation were called *muškēnu*'s, not *nāši bilti*'s[14]). Records from Lagaš[15] show how such fields were accounted for within the internal archives of the state. At present I do not have any further suggestions for the provenience of FLP 1648 and 1738, but it is certainly interesting to note that the FLP collection contains several texts belonging to the same archive as the Lagaš texts published by Birot.[16]

YOS 13 41 indicates that near the end of the dynasty as well, fields fallen vacant because of the incumbent *rēdû*'s death without heirs were accounted for as if they were held by absentee holders. In that instance the text shows that the then usual practice of renting the land out to a third party was followed.

The vacated fields were obviously kept separate from general non-assigned state fields, i.e., they did not merely revert directly to the state land fund. That this was so for groups other than *rēdû*'s is attested by TCL 7 32. That letter contains a directive from Ḫammurapi to Šamaš-ḫazir and his colleagues to inform Ḫammurapi of the assignments recently made to *girsequ*'s. Ḫammurapi also wanted to know, however, which of the fields set aside for *girsequ*'s had not as yet been allotted and therefore were still available for assignment.

The *rēdû* texts discussed here do not indicate who received the "owner's income" from the vacant fields: the state at large, or the assignee's peer group. One problem is to determine what is meant by the statement that "the palace was paid." It is possible, but in my view not at all likely, that the statement refers to the destination of the "owner's share." More probably it is the palace's share of the harvest, or an impost exacted from the production, that is meant. After all, the Edict of Ammiṣaduqa, §15, cited above, refers to the payments incumbent upon, among others, *muškēnu*'s and *rēdû*'s.

12. See, e.g., YOS 13 330. I discussed the text category and its place in the Old Babylonian agricultural administration at length in Ellis, Agriculture Chapter 2 Section A 2a (2b).

13. I.e., that of the *rēdû*'s peer group, or that of the state agricultural administration. That *ana qabê* indicates action taken in the course of official functions was pointed out by B. Landsberger, JCS 9 (1955) 128.

14. Note TCL 17 76, the letter from Samsuiluna to Etel-pi-Marduk which refers to a *mīšaru* enacted by Samsuiluna; it mentions the *nāši bilti* in general, as well as specific categories of workers including the *iššakku*'s, and, specifically, the debts of *rēdû*'s, *bāʾiru*'s, and *muškēnu*'s.

15. Birot, Tablettes Nos. 1-11.

16. I recently found these texts in the process of conserving some tablets within the FLP collection; they will appear in JCS 29 (1977). I wish to thank Mr. H. Heaney, Rare Books Librarian of the Free Library of Philadelphia, for permission to publish these texts from that collection.

FLP 1738

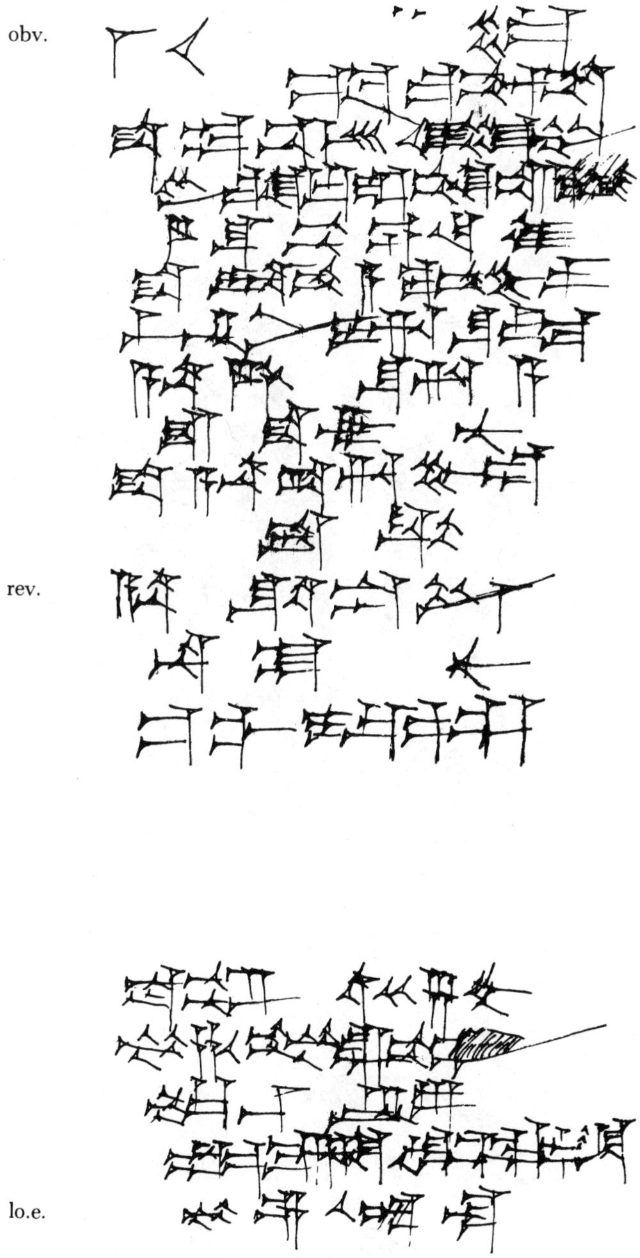

the tablet is rolled over its entire surface with the seal of

Ta]-*ri-bu-*[*um*
DUMU] x x [
ÌR] ^{d}[

FLP 1648

obv.

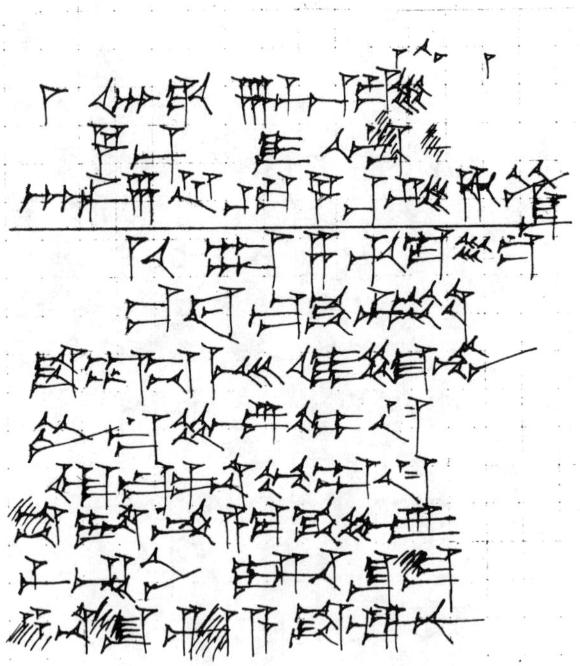

rev.

seals

seals are rolled over the entire surface of the tablet

"LION-MEN" IN ASSYRIA

Richard S. Ellis
Bryn Mawr College

The term "lion-man" is one that occurs frequently in the literature of Mesopotamian archaeology; unfortunately it refers to any of several different types of figures that combine human and leonine features in various ways. Examination of lion-human combinations in Neo-Assyrian art reveals the following types:

a) a man in a lion suit.

b) a being whose head is superficially leonine, but who has long, pointed, upright ears, and a feather ruff. His torso, arms, and legs are human; his feet are those of a bird of prey.

c) a being whose head and upper body are human, and whose lower body and legs are those of a lion.

d) a lion-centaur, with the body and all four legs of a lion, and a human thorax, arms, and head where the lion's head would normally be.

e) a human-headed lion.

In this paper I will try to distinguish types (a) and (b) as consistent iconographic types of lion-human combinations. I will also try to define the function of the man in the lion-suit, and to find out whether any references to him can be recognized in texts.

The man in the lion suit can be seen most clearly on reliefs of Assurnaṣirpal II and Tiglathpileser III. A slab on the east wall of Assurnaṣirpal's throne room, toward the southern end of the room—the end away from the throne—showed on its upper register, from left to right, a circular camp, a pavilion with horses in and in front of it and, at the door of the pavilion, a eunuch who faces to the right and is receiving a row of prisoners (fig. 1).[1] The prisoners and their conductors occupy only the lower part of the register: above them, next to the top of the pavilion, are three figures who appear to be dancing. The figure on the left is that of a bearded, bareheaded man wearing a short tunic, facing to the right. He is playing a banjo-like instrument with a long neck and a small sounding-box. His posture is that of running, though he is presumably dancing while providing music for the other two figures.

These two figures face each other, and are also in a kind of running posture, but the weight of each seems to be mostly on his rear foot, so that the posture looks more like kicking, and is presumably some sort of dance step. The two figures are close enough together that the forward, kicking legs overlap at the ankles. The man on the left is clapping his hands together. The one on the right holds in his right hand a whip with a rigid handle and a single thong; he holds his left hand to his mouth in a gesture of which the details are vague.[2] Both figures apparently wear fringed, knee-length tunics. Their heads are completely hidden by the lion masks that they wear, while long, open-fronted cloaks hang down their backs from the rear of the masks, and are visible between their legs. The cloaks are patterned in such a way as to suggest hairy pelts.[3] The lion masks have the mouths only slightly open. When they are compared with representations of real lions on Assurnaṣirpal's sculptures,[4] the muzzles of the masks seem a bit narrower. The stylization of the face seems basically the same, though a bit simpler, presumably because of the smaller scale of the masks. On both the masks and the real lions a curved line marks the transition from the face to the mane; in the case of the masks this is probably the point at which a flexible cloak is attached to the more rigid mask. On real lions a thicker ruff is shown just behind this line; this detail is not visible on the lion masks, nor do the masks appear to have any ears. The line of the head rises more above the face in the masks than in the real lions; this is probably an accurate feature of the representation, and is due to the presence of a man's head inside the mask. There is nothing to show whether the mask and cloak are made from a real lion skin, or are artificial.

The single lion-masked man shown on Tiglathpileser III's reliefs is on a slab whose specific context is, unfortunately, unknown,[5] but which may form part of a scene of tribute or triumph (fig. 2). The sculpture

1. E. A. W. Budge, Assyrian Sculptures in the British Museum: Reign of Ashur-nasir-pal, 885-860 B.C. (London, Trustees of the British Museum, 1914) pl. 16:1.

2. In the photo, Budge, Assyrian Sculptures pl. 16:1, the hand appears to be *behind* the jaw of the lion mask; in the drawing by T. Madhloom, The Chronology of Neo-Assyrian Art (London, Athlone Press, 1970) pl. 53:1, the position of the hand is not clear.

3. This detail is not visible on the photograph published in Budge, Assyrian Sculptures, but is shown by Madhloom, Chronology (see n. 2) in a drawing made from the original.

4. Budge, Assyrian Sculptures pls. 12:2 and especially 19:2, where the lion is dead, and his mouth is only partly open.

5. See R. D. Barnett and M. Falkner, The Sculptures of Aššur-naṣir-apli II (883-859 B.C.), Tiglath-pileser III (745-727 B.C.),

Ancient Near Eastern Studies in Memory of J. J. Finkelstein
Connecticut Academy of Arts and Sciences, Memoir 19

originally showed five figures walking toward the right; of these only the three left-most figures are now preserved.[6] The first four of the original figures were men in long fringed garments; the first and fourth were beardless, the second and third bearded. All are bare headed, and all are shown clapping their hands. The fifth figure is half a head or more shorter than the others, and wears a lion mask and cloak over a calf-length tunic. The lion mask is similar to those on Assurnaṣirpal's sculpture. The lips are open, but the teeth are clenched inside them. The face joins the cloak in a curved line. There is a curious rounded protuberance extending forward about three fingers' breadth from the lion's nose. It appears to be low and flat on the relief; its nature and purpose are unknown. As with Assurnaṣirpal's lion-cloaked men, no ears are shown, and the top of the cloak rises to accommodate the wearer's head, giving a contour that would be unnatural for a real lion. The cloak of the Tiglathpileser figure, however, is not patterned like a shaggy pelt, but is shown smooth, with two strings of connected triangles hanging down from the top of the head; one is shown in profile at the back of the cloak, and one is incised on the surface of the cloak facing the observer. The individual triangles hang with their bases down. They resemble the strings of tassels that are shown on other of Tiglathpileser's reliefs decorating horses' bridles and quiver covers.[7] This figure's hands are joined in front of his chest. He is not clapping; his fingers are extended but intertwined. He is probably snapping his fingers two-handed, as is still done by dancers in the Near East. Hanging downward from his hands, idle but ready to be used in another part of the ceremony, is a whip with a stiff handle and a thong that divides into two points.

In these palace reliefs both the appearance and the context of the lion-cloaked figure make it clear that we are dealing with a human being in fancy dress rather than with a composite creature. My impression is that the Assyrian artists were always explicit about this distinction; when they portrayed a man dressed up, as here, or in the case of the fish-cloaked man,[8] they leave no doubt of the artificiality of the combination. I believe that, in contrast, the eagle-headed man and the figure with "leonine" head and bird feet were always meant to represent supernatural beings, not men in masks.[9]

The man dressed as a lion appears also upon two smaller objects from first millennium Mesopotamia. One is a cylinder seal in the Southesk Collection, attributed to ninth-century Assyria (fig. 3).[10]

The scene depicts a goddess facing right seated on a throne, which in turn rests on a lion. She wears a cylindrical polos topped by a star. In her left hand she holds a ring of dots, and she raises her right hand in a gesture of greeting. Facing her a bearded human being, with long garments and bare head, makes the finger-pointing gesture of reverence with his right hand, while holding out his empty left hand with the palm upward. Above and between these two figures are the seven dots. Immediately behind the goddess are three large stars arranged vertically, then, at the top, a crescent, and then a man in a lion suit, facing the goddess and facing in the same direction as she. Between the backs of the lion-garbed man and the bearded worshipper are, above, a winged disk, and below, the symbols of Marduk and Nabu.

The lion-cloaked man here wears an ankle-length fringed garment instead of a shorter one, and his mask appears to have ears; otherwise he is much like the other representations we have mentioned. The mouth of the mask is wide open; a whip hangs downward from his right hand, and his left hand is raised to his mouth. It is not apparent whether he is accompanying the bearded figure in confronting the goddess, or whether he is an associate of the goddess. Since he appears on the palace reliefs as a real functionary, it is probable that here also he is a part of the personnel of the goddess' cult, rather than a supernatural companion. Frankfort identified the goddess as either Gula or Belit (Ninlil).[11] In view of the lion under her feet an identification with Ninlil and/or Ishtar of Nineveh seems likely.[12]

Esarhaddon (681-669 B.C.) from the Central and South-west Palaces at Nimrud (London, The Trustees of the British Museum, 1962) pls. 1-2 and 129, for its approximate position, based on information derived from Layard's "Original Drawings." It is shown as related to Tiglathpileser's first Babylonian campaign.

6. Barnett - Falkner, Sculptures pls. 1 and 2.

7. Barnett - Falkner, Sculptures pls. 65 and 55, respectively.

8. E.g., Walter Andrae, Das wiedererstandene Assur (Leipzig, J. C. Hinrichs, 1938) pl. 21.

9. See A. L. Oppenheim, "Akkadian *pul(u)ḫ(t)u* and *melammu*," JAOS 63 (1943) 32. While Oppenheim certainly showed that ritual masks were used, the passages he cites for *melammu* fit a meaning "radiance" better than one of "mask."

10. H. Frankfort, Cylinder Seals: A Documentary Essay on the Art and Religion of the Ancient Near East (London, Macmillan, 1939) pp. 193, 215; pl. 33g.

11. Frankfort, Cylinder Seals p. 215.

12. For the apparent identification of Ninlil with Ishtar of Nineveh as the consort of Aššur, see Knut Tallqvist, Der assyrische Gott, StOr 4/3 (1932) 21-22, and G. van Driel, The Cult of Aššur (Assen, van Gorkum, 1969) pp. 39-40 n. 36.

The only other relief representation of this figure known to me is on a bronze "incantation relief" in Istanbul (fig. 4).[13]

This relief is of a common type, with on one side a representation of a large animal-shaped demon who peers over the top of the plaque, and on the other registers showing, from the top down, 1) divine symbols, 2) a row of six animal-headed human figures in threatening poses, 3) a scene of Lamashtu kneeling in a boat, with the snakes and suckling animals that usually accompany her. Beside her to the right is a group of miscellaneous apotropaic objects. To the left is a figure that was identified by Frank as a seated dog, but which I think is undoubtedly a lion-cloaked man.[14] The human feet, in a striding position, can be seen as well as what is probably the hem of a knee-length garment. The lion head, its mouth open, is vague but easily recognizable; the cloak falls down the back of the figure in the characteristic form that is seen on the palace reliefs.

Here the man in the lion suit appears in an apotropaic context. As in the last instance, it seems here more likely that the lion-cloaked man represents someone taking part in the activity involved—the apotropaic conjuration—than a supernatural companion of Lamashtu.

So far it is pretty certain that these four figures are meant to represent the same type of person. The characteristic features are the presence of ordinary clothing beneath the lion costume, and the whip. There exist other representations in which these two features are not certainly present, but which I believe were meant to represent the man in the lion suit. These are clay figurines of lion-headed figures; I know of six to eight such figurines. Two are in the Iraq Museum; one is in the Louvre; one, from Khorsabad, has apparently been lost; two (or possibly only one) are from Assur, and are now in the Staatliches Museum in Berlin; one is from Nimrud and is now in the Institute of Archaeology of the University of London; and one was found at Uruk; its present location is unknown to me.

1 and 2 (figs. 5 and 6). These two figures in the Iraq Museum,[15] IM 9580 and IM 9583, are of unknown provenience. IM 9580 is 11.5 cm. high, IM 9583, 13 cm. Both stand on low round bases. The two are quite similar. Both are apparently of unbaked clay, and were covered completely with a thin black coating which is now rubbed off in places. The heads are identical in style, and are quite naturalistically depicted. The mouths are partly open, revealing the tongues and teeth. The noses are wrinkled. The heads are equipped with ears, small and folded back. The heads of both figures appear to look slightly upward.

Both figures wear robes that fall to the feet; human feet stick out from beneath the hem. The robe of IM 9580 is plain all over; that of IM 9583 is plain in front, but a vertical line is incised down each side, from the shoulders, behind the elbows, to the base. Behind these lines a crosshatched pattern is incised. This presumably represents a shaggy material, and serves to show that the lion suit is a separate costume worn over a normal garment.

Each figure has a pair of human hands, clasped in each other on the chest. Although the hands are modelled to show them folded in each other, the figurines originally each held some other object as well. A hole, circular in cross-section and 2-3 mm. in diameter, goes vertically through each pair of hands. Whatever was held is now gone, and since the bodies of the figures slope backward above and below the hands, there is no impression of the object on the bodies. Presumably the objects were made of wood or some similar material. In view of the representations on the palace reliefs we may suppose that they were whips.

3. The Louvre figurine, AO 19705, has been published and discussed by M. Rutten[16] and M.-T. Barrelet.[17] Like the Baghdad figures, it is of unknown provenience. It is 12.6 cm. high, of beige clay, painted black. It is similar to those in the Iraq Museum in most respects; the mouth is slightly open, the head has small round ears and looks upward slightly. The back is covered with "shaggy marks" to the bottom of the base. Human feet appear under the garment in front, and the hands are placed together in front of the chest. None of the descriptions mention anything held in the hands, but Rutten[18] mentions that the hands are broken, and a comparison of the published photographs[19] suggests that the figurine once held a small stick, possibly of

13. C. Frank, Die babylonische Beschwörungsreliefs, LSS 3/3 (1908) 84 pl. 3 Relief B.

14. This identification was also made by Unger in "Mummenschanz," RLV 8 (1927) 331 pl. 3c.

15. I would like to thank Dr. Faraj Basmaji, former Director of the Iraq Museum, for allowing me to examine these figurines in 1967.

16. "Deux terres cuites inédites du Musée du Louvre," RA 40 (1945-46) 99-103.

17. Figurines et reliefs en terre cuite de la Mésopotamie antique. I: Potiers, termes de métier, procédés de fabrication et production (Paris, Geuthner, 1968) no. 842, pp. 117, 420, pl. 84 no. 842.

18. RA 40 (1945-46) 99.

19. Rutten, RA 40 (1945-46) 100 fig. 1, and Barrelet, Figurines pl. 84 no. 842.

rectangular cross-section, and that the fronts of the hands are broken away through the hole left by this object. However, only careful examination of the object can decide this point.[20] There can be no doubt, at any rate, that this figure is of the same type as those in the Iraq Museum.

4. In Sargon's palace at Khorsabad P. E. Botta found a figurine that was apparently of the lion-man type (fig. 7). A drawing of it was published in Monument de Ninive.[21] Apparently the figure was lost before it reached Paris; no further information on it is available.[22] Flandin's illustration shows a human body in a long garment, with feet protruding at the bottom. The human arms show what seem to be sleeve hems above the elbows. The left arm is crossed over the chest, with the hand either lying flat against the right side of the chest, or with the fingers lightly clenched. The right arm hangs at the side; the hand holds an elongated object of some kind. The mouth of the lion face is wide open. The head seems to show few details; no ears are visible on the engraving. The ruff around the face falls to the shoulders, but it is not clear whether it continues as a cloak. No marks are visible on the back.

5 and 6. The clay apotropaic figurines from Assur were published by E. Klengel-Brandt.[23] More is known about the finding of these figures than in the case of the Baghdad and Paris examples, but it is still not enough to tell us much about their function.

5. Ass. 15503-VA Ass. 3602 is certainly a figure of the same type as those described above; it particularly resembles the figures in the Iraq Museum. It is 12.6 cm. high, of reddish-brown clay; no paint is visible on the photograph or mentioned by Klengel-Brandt. The mouth is slightly open; ears do not appear to be shown. Wrinkles on the muzzle and locks of the mane are represented by rather coarse incisions. Human feet are shown below the hem of the garment. The back is patterned with crosshatching of vertical and diagonal lines, the division between the smooth and the hatched portions passing behind the shoulders. The hands are joined on the chest. They are somewhat chipped, and it is impossible to see from the photograph whether they held any object; none is mentioned by Klengel-Brandt. This figure was found in an exploratory trench in hD10I, in the southern part of the inner town of Assur. The only indication of its architectural context given is that it was found at the level of a brick pavement.[24]

6. Ass. 14628-VA Ass. 3603[25] was found in KC9I, the "2. Arbeitsschicht" of an exploratory trench. This figure differs somewhat from the others described, and I cannot with the same confidence ascribe it to the same type and function. It shows a (presumably) human body with a lion's head. The mouth is slightly open. Small folded ears appear to be shown. Short vertical incisions on the back represent a shaggy surface. So far it is similar to the others. But no feet are shown in front, and the hands are not clasped on the chest. The right arm is broken close to the shoulder, but the upper arm appears to have been horizontal, as if the arms had been raised to brandish some object. If the left arm is preserved at all, it cannot be seen on the photographs. These differences could by stylistic rather than iconographical—the raised arm could have held the same object as the clasped hands of the others (a whip?), but we cannot tell. The fact that the lion head is rather shorter and the muzzle rounder, and that it does not gaze upward as do the others, could easily be stylistic variants with no iconographical significance.

7. The Nimrud figurine, ND 9342 (fig. 8)[26] was found in a corner of court S37 in Fort Shalmaneser. It was found in a brick box sunk into a layer of dirt above the pavement. According to Mallowan this secondary position indicates that the figure was deposited between the two destructions of the palace, in 614 and 612 B.C.[27] This figure has therefore the most precise date of its type, and its find-spot specifies its purpose. It was deposited in the same way as numerous figurines of other iconographic types, which had a clearly apotropaic purpose.[28] The figure was crudely made; the front looks as if it may have been pressed in a mold.

20. In 1967 I was able, by the kind permission of M. Pierre Amiet, to examine this figure. At the time I was not aware of Rutten's article and photograph, and my notes record the impression that there was no trace of an object held in the hands. I did not then see the break in the hands.

21. Vol. 2 pl. 152bis.

22. See Barrelet, Figurines I 114, 368. In E. Douglas Van Buren, Foundation Figurines and Offerings (Berlin, Hans Schoetz, 1931) p. 51 n. 4, the references given for this figure, except for that to Botta, belong in fact to the other "lion-headed figure" from Khorsabad, to be described below. It is worth noting that Botta himself makes no reference in his text to this figurine. We can only assume that his comments about the finding of the figurines in general apply to this one.

23. FuB 10 (1968) 19-37.

24. Klengel-Brandt, FuB 10 (1968) 26.

25. FuB 10 (1968) 27f. pl. 7:1.

26. I would like to thank Dr. Barbara Parker of the Institute of Archaeology of the University of London for providing me with a photograph of this object, and permitting me to publish it.

27. Mallowan, Nimrud and Its Remains 2 390.

28. For this type of figurine see O. R. Gurney, "Babylonian Prophylactic Figures and Their Rituals," AAA 22 (1935) 31-96 and my forthcoming book on apotropaic figurines, Domestic Spirits.

It represents, in full-face, a being whose body appears to be human, dressed in a long garment, below which his toes protrude. The right hand is held against the chest. Incised marks on the chest represent an object like a stick held in the hand. From the upper end of this object an incised line extends vertically downward, forking twice. The marks were apparently intended to represent a whip. The left arm apparently hangs at the side; it is impossible to see whether the hand holds anything. The front of the head is broken, but the degree to which the head extends forward, and what details are still visible show that the face was not human. Radiating lines visible on the sides of the face could be either the whiskers or the muzzle-folds of a lion. Behind the outline of the figure the rear portion extends outward like a narrow rim, and is rounded off in back. This back part is marked with rows of short vertical incisions, and looks like a shaggy cloak worn over the head and body. For all its crudity, this figure shows more details than the others: the whip, and the distinction between the ordinary human clothing and the shaggy cloak.

8. This figure (fig. 9) is still more enigmatic than No. 6, but may still belong to our group. It is also the only one of all these representations that is known to come from Babylonia rather than Assyria. It was found in one of the layers of debris comprising the western of the Freihat al-Nufeiji, a pair of burial tumuli, just north of the city wall of Uruk.[29] The dating of the tumulus is uncertain: no earlier than Seleucid, possibly as late as Sasanian.[30] Objects in the earth of which the mound was made must of course be earlier than its construction, but most of the sherds found in the mound were apparently no earlier than Seleucid.[31] The figurine[32] differs markedly in style from most of the others. It is sketchily done, and appears to have been made of relatively moist clay with a minimum of tool-work. A plain cylindrical body, showing no feet, is topped by a grotesque lion head. The muzzle is thrust forward; the eyes are apparently represented by impressed circles, the wrinkles on the muzzle by shallow incisions. The mouth is shown slightly open; a round pellet of clay is pressed into the front of the mouth. A heavy ruff stands up behind the face, and is set off from the face by a groove. No ears are shown. The back of the ruff, down to shoulder level, is decorated with several round pellets of clay pressed on. The right arm hangs downward, with the flat, unarticulated hand pressed against the front of the body. The left hand is pressed against the bottom of the jaw. The general impression is as if the person is about to be sick, but this is probably not what was intended. Although it differs stylistically from the other clay figures,[33] the similarity is great enough that both Falkenstein and Barrelet compared it to the Louvre figure (No. 3, above).[34] Curiously enough, two iconographic features may connect it more closely with the Assyrian palace reliefs than any of the other clay figures. It holds one hand to its mouth, like the lion-cloaked men on the relief of Assurnaṣirpal II, and on the Lamashtu plaque and the seal. The pellet of clay pressed into the mouth might have some connection with the curious protuberance on the muzzle of Tiglathpileser's lion-masked man, though, since we cannot interpret either one, this suggestion must be extremely tentative. The Babylonian piece certainly belongs to a different tradition of workmanship than the other figurines, but it may well reflect the same tradition of activity as the others.

To my mind there is no doubt that at least the first five of these clay figurines, and No. 7, represent the same type of functionary that is depicted on the palace reliefs cited. While in only one case are we certain that a clay figure carried a whip, the leonine head, the pattern shown on the back but not on the front of the figure, the human hands and feet—all show that the intention was to depict, not a composite creature, but a man in a lion mask and cloak.

The fact that figure No. 6 shows some anomalous features introduces the problem of the relationship of our figure to a "lion-headed" image that appears frequently in apotropaic contexts in Assyria and Babylonia, the one cited as type (b) at the beginning of this article.

Rutten, in discussing the Louvre figure,[35] compared it to a clay figurine that had been found buried under a pavement in the palace of Sargon II at Khorsabad. Her references are not to the Khorsabad figure listed as No. 4, above, but to another that is now preserved in the Louvre (fig. 10). This figure was not in perfect preservation when found, and has suffered since,[36] but several details can be seen. It resembles our "lion-

29. A. V. Müller, G. Peschken and A. Falkenstein, UVB 15 (1959) 27-35.

30. Falkenstein, UVB 15 (1959) 33-34. Cf. A. v. Haller, UVB 16 (1960) 29-30.

31. Falkenstein, UVB 15 (1959) 33.

32. W.18848, c. 10 cm. high; UVB 15 (1959) pl. 22c.

33. Falkenstein, UVB 15 (1959) 33, calls the Uruk example a "Tonfigur"; he does not say whether baked or not.

34. Falkenstein, UVB 15 (1959) 33 n. 60; Barrelet, Figurines p. 117.

35. RA 40 (1945-46) 101.

36. For progressive states see the engraving from Flandin's drawing published in Botta, Monument de Ninive 2 pl. 152; another engraving in Léon Heuzey, Les figurines antiques de terre cuite du Musée du Louvre (Paris, A. Morel, 1883) pl. 1:3; and the photograph in Barrelet, Figurines pl. 68 no. 723.

men" in having a human body and a lion-like head, but there are several differences. The ears are neither absent nor small and rounded; though now broken, they were originally tall, upright, and pointed.[37] The head has no bulky ruff falling to the shoulders; the neck, of human proportions, is visible between the head and shoulders. In place of a leonine mane, there is a curious rectangular protuberance on each side of the face. The dress of the figure is unclear. Heuzey and Van Buren state that the legs end in the claws of a bird of prey.[38]

The similarity between the man in the lion cloak and this creature consists only of the combination of a human torso and an (approximately) leonine head. The differences in the ears, mane, clothing, feet, and stance suggest that they were conceived by their makers as different types of beings. This contrast becomes clearer still when we look at the analogues of these creatures on relief sculpture. We have already discussed the lion-cloaked man on the sculptures of Assurnaṣirpal II and Tiglathpileser III. Several representations of a creature similar to our second type appear in Assyrian palace reliefs, as well as elsewhere. Fig. 11 shows an example from the palace of Sennacherib at Kuyunjik. The long pointed ears, the neck and shoulders bare and visible, the position of the hands, and the bird's feet, are elements of similarity to the long-eared "lion-man" from Khorsabad. The curious rectangular ruff does not of course project from the relief, but it is shown in elevation, so to speak; it is clear that it, together with the covering of the back of the head, is made of feathers.[39] This long-eared, bird-footed "lion-man" appears in the Old Babylonian period and persists through Neo-Assyrian times, with a brief afterlife at Pasargadae.[40] In Neo-Assyrian times both his iconography and his function are quite consistent. He is clearly a being of apotropaic power, since he appears on the door-jambs of palaces, on a bronze bell that was probably used for exorcism,[41] and on the same bronze Lamashtu-plaque on which one of our examples of the man in the lion cloak is depicted (fig. 4). His function overlaps partly with that of the lion-cloaked man, therefore, but is not identical. The long-eared bird-footed creature never appears in scenes of human activity, as the other does. The former is, in fact, a supernatural composite being; the latter is consistently and rather carefully shown as a man dressed up as a lion. There can be no question of the identity of the two types.

Let us see to which of these two types a few individual objects belong. As I have said, I believe Rutten's identification of the Louvre lion-cloaked man and the Khorsabad long-eared creature to be incorrect. The same identification of the two types has frequently been made.[42] Among other objects brought into the discussion are three clay figurines from Ur.[43] Woolley described these figures as having cat-like heads, except for one whose head is more like that of a bear.[44] They are all poorly preserved, and do not look as if they were ever very well made. They are shown with their right arms raised, brandishing what Woolley called clay clubs[45]; their left hands are pressed to their chests. The heads are clearly set off from the shoulders. U.6768B[46] is the best preserved of the three; its ears appear to be upright and pointed, though not very long. The feet of none of the three can be distinguished. Considering the pose and what can be seen of the shape of the head, it seems probable that all three of these figures are of one type, namely that of the long-eared, bird-footed "lion-man."

Two other clay figures that are clearly of this long-eared type were found in Fort Shalmaneser at Nimrud.[47]

37. Monument de Ninive 2 pl. 152.

38. Heuzey, Figurines antiques p. 1; Van Buren, Clay Figurines p. 227 no. 1110; Foundation Figurines p. 52. Botta did not mention this feature, which is not suggested on Flandin's drawing, Monument de Ninive 2 pl. 152; Barrelet, Figurines p. 372, states that the bird feet can no longer be seen. My own notes, made when I examined the figure in 1967 by the kind permission of M. Pierre Amiet, say "apparently bird feet."

39. It may be mentioned that the head and feet of this creature are virtually identical to those of two other beings: Lamashtu: Frank, Beschwörungsreliefs pls. 1, 3; and the figure identified by Landsberger WZKM 57 (1961) 18 as Anzu: H. Frankfort, Art and Architecture of the Ancient Orient (Baltimore, Penguin, 1954) fig. 38.

40. See Seidl, Bagh.Mitt. 4 (1968) 171-75 for a list of occurrences. For the creature at Pasargadae, see Carl Nylander, Ionians in Pasargadae (Uppsala, 1970) fig. 43. In this context the bird feet preserved are more likely to have belonged to the figure under discussion than to a monster like those at Persepolis, e.g. André Goddard, L'Art de Iran (Paris, 1962) pl. 72. Cf. Hartmut Schmökel, Ur, Assur und Babylon (Stuttgart, 1955) pl. 82 for the probable original appearance of the Pasargadae figures.

41. Schmökel, Ur, Assur und Babylon pl. 78. Here, however, the feet of the figures may be human.

42. E. Klengel-Brandt, FuB 10 (1968) 26 nn. 47-50; Madhloom, Chronology p. 80. The identity was denied by Weidner, Reliefs p. 8 n. 27.

43. C. L. Woolley, The Kassite Period and the Period of the Assyrian Kings, UE 8 (London, 1965) pl. 33, U.6768A,C, U.6769(!=U.6768B).

44. UE 8 94.

45. UE 8 94.

46. Woolley, UE 8 pl. 33, designated U.6769.

47. M. E. L. Mallowan, Nimrud and Its Remains 2 fig. 314 (ND 8190); ND 8181=IM 61854.

The apparently lion-headed figurines from Assur are hard to interpret. One of them, our no. 5 above, is clearly of the lion-cloaked variety. Another, unfortunately badly preserved, is probably of the long-eared type.[48] No. 6, above, is ambiguous; its head and garment resemble those of the lion-cloaked man, while the position of the arms is like that of the long-eared type. If it belongs to one of these two types, I would assign it to the lion-cloaked group. In the absence of more figures like it I would rather not create a third type for it to represent.

The identity of the long-eared creature has been discussed by others.[49] Less has been written about the lion-cloaked man; I would like to look briefly here at the evidence that we have for his identity and function.

The lion-cloaked man could be a real person, even if he was not always so. The lion-cloaked man does not appear in a clearly apotropaic role in the Assyrian palaces, unlike the long-eared "lion-man" and several other types, which were placed on door-jambs, clearly separated from the narrative scenes. The lion-cloaked men in the Northwest Palace at Nimrud appear to act in connection with the reception of prisoners after a military victory. The scene from Tiglathpileser III's reliefs seems to have some connection with a military campaign, but that is about all one can say. What the lion-cloaked man on the Southesk seal is doing is not clear, except that he apparently can play some part in the cult of Ishtar.

These circumstances are not enough by themselves to suggest an identity for the lion-cloaked man. We may, however, look in texts for references to those characteristics that are visible to us: the lion-cloak, the whip, and the dance. The last feature, of course, is certainly present only on the palace reliefs, while the whip can be seen there, on the seal, and on the Nimrud figurine (No. 7).

The "Epic of Era" contains several references to someone assuming *zīm labbi*, "the guise of a lion."[50] Three passages in the Epic use this expression. In one Anu instructs the third of the seven gods (ᵈ*Sibitti*) to "assume the guise of a lion, so that whoever sees you will dissolve (with fright)."[51] The second occurrence[52] is too fragmentary to be interpreted with certainty, but appears to refer to Era himself. In the third passage Ishum accuses Era of having put on the appearance of a lion and entered the palace of Babylon.[53] In these contexts the being who is disguised as a lion is hostile to mankind; the Sibitti are preparing to assist Era to bring plague upon mankind, and their equipment anticipates that of Era himself.[54] The function of the lion's guise in the context of the epic itself is not apotropaic. If it was regarded as typical of Era or the Sibitti, however, it could have been used in efforts to propitiate these gods, who controlled the effects of plague, or to bring about their forbearance by miming it. The use of the entire Epic of Era, or of excerpts of it as apotropaic, makes it plausible, though scarcely certain, that such expedients may have been resorted to.[55]

Another reference that may have something to do with our lion-cloaked man is found in an Assyrian ritual against ghosts.[56] After reciting three times an incantation addressed to an image of ᵈId, the river-god, the practitioner is to act as follows:

> IM KI.GAR K̆ÍD(*-iṣ*) NU [. . .]
> DIŠ(*-ú*) *la-an-šú* SAG.DU*-su ša* UR.MAḪ ŠU.II [. . .]
> IGI.MEŠ*-šu* IM.SA$_5$ ŠÉŠ *ina* IGI ZAG*-šú* [. . .][57]
>
> You pinch off clay from the clay-bed, (you make) a figure . . .
> Its body normal, its head that of a lion, its hands . . .
> You rub its eyes with dark clay, in its right eye . . .
> (or "in front of its right hand")

This sounds a good deal like our clay figurines; the "normal" body could refer to a human figure in a long

48. Klengel-Brandt, FuB 10 (1968) 27 pl. 7,2: Ass. 14660=VA Ass. 3730. The position of the arms and what appears to be the hem of a kilt support this identification, though details of the head and feet cannot be made out.

49. Particularly by Frank, Beschwörungsreliefs pp. 26-28. See Seidl, Bagh.Mitt. 4 (1968) 173-74 for a resume of opinions. My own, different, conclusions will be presented in my forthcoming book on apotropaic figurines, Domestic Spirits.

50. Another reference to *zi-i-mu la-ab-bi* is in ABL 1455 rev. 8. The letter is fragmentary and high-flown in style. It appears to be chiefly in praise of Assurbanipal; what the "lion's guise" means is obscure. It does not seem necessary to take it literally here, i.e., to associate it with anyone actually dressed as a lion.

51. I 34: P. F. Gössmann Das Era-Epos (Wurzburg, Augustinus, 1956) p. 9; the translation borrows from CAD Z 121b.

52. III 22.

53. IV 21: Gössmann, Era pp. 26-27, 52.

54. Cagni, Erra pp. 152-53.

55. For this use of the text of the epic, and for its rationale, see E. Reiner, "Plague Amulets and House Blessings," JNES 19 (1960) 148-55.

56. VAT 8910=KAR 227; E. Ebeling, Tod und Leben nach den Vorstellungen der Babylonier (Berlin, de Gruyter, 1931) pp. 122-33.

57. Ebeling, TuL pp. 125-26 lines 23-26.

coat. Unfortunately some details are broken, such as what its hands are like, and what it is doing with them. The being represented is not identified. Neither is it mentioned what was to be done with the figurine. Still, we do see here a figure involved in an exorcistic ritual that may have been like our lion-cloaked man.

Finally, the Seleucid text AO 7439, from Uruk, which describes the *akītu*-festival of Ishtar,[58] includes among the personnel that are to assemble for the procession "four lion-men from the temple of Birdu (dKAL.EDIN).[59] The word translated "lion-men" is written UR.MAḪ.LÚ.U_x.LU; the Akkadian reading *nēšu-amēlu* has been given for it.[60] There are other beings, however, whose names are constructed in the same way: GIR.TAB.LÚ.U_x.LU, the scorpion-man, and KU_6.LÚ.U_x.LU, the fish-man. Of these the latter was certainly read *kulīlu* or *kulullu*.[61] The readings *girtablīlu* for the scorpion-man[62] and *urmaḫlīlu* for the lion-man[63] have been suggested.

This passage again sounds promising, for the connection of these "lion-men" with a rite of Ishtar recalls the seal mentioned above, and their participation in a religious procession suggests that they might have been real men in costume. We cannot be certain of this, however; the other "personnel" assembled for the parade were apparently all deities—that is, presumably, statues. Therefore the "lion-men" might have been statues of composite creatures, rather than men in costume. Another circumstance that makes it difficult to posit a consistent identification of the UR.MAḪ.LÚ.U_x.LU with the lion-cloaked man is the possibility that he may be the lion-centaur, instead. For one thing, both the GIR.TAB.LÚ.U_x.LU and the KU_6.LÚ.U_x.LU are pretty certainly represented by beings with human heads and torsos, and animal hind-quarters.[64] It seems plausible that the UR.MAḪ.LÚ.U_x.LU would follow the same pattern. Of more importance, however, is the fact that the UR.MAḪ.LÚ.U_x.LU appears in KAR 298, the well-known text that describes apotropaic figures to be buried beneath buildings.[65] There is no description of the figure beyond its name, but it is to have an inscription upon it which Gurney reads *ta-par-ri-ik mukīl rêš lemutti*(=SAG.ḪUL.ḪA.ZA), "Bolt out the supporter of evil.[66] Recently E. Klengel-Brandt published a broken figurine of a quadruped from Assur, now in Berlin, with the suggestion that it might originally have been a lion-centaur.[67] The head is broken off and few details are clear, but it bears an inscription which Klengel-Brandt gives as:

dup-pir ri-qi SAG.ḪUL.ḪA.ZA "Go away, begone, Supporter of evil!"

The similarity of the two texts is striking; without collation it is impossible to say whether they are identical and, if so, which reading is correct. At any rate, the similarity is strong evidence for an identification of the UR.MAḪ.LÚ.U_x.LU with the lion-centaur. Two complete clay figurines of the type are IM 48299-48300, in the Iraq Museum.[68] The creature can be seen in more detail in the sculptures at the doors of the throneroom of the Northwest Palace at Nimrud,[69] and on a slab together with other apotropaic figures from Assurbanipal's palace at Nineveh.[70]

All this speaks against an *exclusive* identification between the UR.MAḪ.LÚ.U_x.LU and the lion-cloaked man. One might imagine that the latter was a mimic imitation of a supernatural being; but it seems to me that to imitate a being with a lion's body and human torso and head by a man with a lion's head would be too remote a copy to be effective.

These attempts to interpret the lion-cloaked man through his leonine aspect have yielded some rather vague support for the existence of lion-human images in contexts that could have been apotropaic, and have shown that some kind of lion-human creature was associated with the Ishtar cult at Uruk, though it was not necessarily a lion-cloaked man. We still have no real information about the name of this figure, and few of the

58. F. Thureau-Dangin, Racc. pp. 73, 114-18.
59. Obv. 10.
60. Racc. p. 114 line 10; Oppenheim, JAOS 63 (1943) 32.
61. CAD K 562b.
62. CAD Z 165b.
63. AHw. 2 783 sub *nēšu(m)*.
64. Schmökel, Ur, Assur und Babylon pl. 69 left. E. Strommenger, Fünf Jahrtausende Mesopotamien (Munich, Hirmer, 1962) pl. 229 at right.
65. Gurney, AAA 22 (1935) 72 rev. 15-16. The UR.MAḪ.LÚ.U_x.LU is also mentioned in the ritual for the substitute king published by W. G. Lambert in AfO 18 (1957-58) 111:30-34; 19 (1959-60) 119:30-34. Two figures were to be made of tamarisk-wood, with buckets in their hands. The text to be inscribed on them is not the same as that cited above.
66. AAA 22 (1935) 73 rev. 15. For this being, see Walter Farber, "Sagḫulḫaza *mukīl rēš lemutti*," ZA 64 (1975) 87-95.
67. FuB 10 (1968) 26 pl. 5:2. Cf. n. 56, above.
68. Yasin M. al-Khalesi, "Unpublished Clay Figurines in the Iraq Museum," (unpubl. MA thesis, Dept. of History and Archaeology, University of Baghdad, 1966) nos. 418-19, figs. 164-65. Klengel-Brandt compared IM 48299 to her figure Ass. 1836, considering them probably of the same type: FuB 10 (1968) 36 n. 104. These figures are apparently uninscribed; neither al-Khalesi nor Klengel-Brandt nor my own notes mention any inscription.
69. Madhloom, Chronology pl. 71:2-3
70. Madhloom, Chronology pl. 72:5.

connections discovered so far seem to have much to do with the activities shown on the palace reliefs. Let us then attack the problem from the other side, through the dance and the whip.

A whip is one of the utensils used by the exorcist in his trade. In the ritual text describing the use of figurines to protect a house, published by O. Gurney,[71] a whip (KUŠ.USUN, *qinnazu*) is listed among a large group of tools and materials used for purifying the house. In tablet "B" of the series UDUG.ḪUL, "Evil spirits," the practitioner claims to have made the demon smart with a whip, as though he were a stray donkey.[72] Marduk-šakin-šumi, an official of Esarhaddon, wrote to the king describing what was apparently the same ritual,[73] including the statement that the *mašmāšu* was to "strike with a whip."[74] These are not many occurrences, and none of them have any expressed connection with a lion disguise.[75] Still, the references establish that exorcists did use whips, and give us one possible function for the whips in the hands of the lion-cloaked men.

Another mention of a whip in a ritual context is found in a hymn to Nana from the time of Sargon II.[76] Among other celebrants are mentioned *kurgarru*'s, carrying whips (*tamšēru*'s), as well as spindles and other untranslatable objects. This connection, again, seems like a promising lead; the *kurgarru*, together with his colleague the *assinnu*, was associated with the cult of Ishtar and performed dances.[77] On some occasions he wore a mask or disguise, though the guise is specified as being that of the goddess Narudu, who we have no reason to think looked like a lion.[78]

It will be noticed that we have been dealing so far with a combination of Assyrian and Babylonian data, which should not be lumped together without consideration. All of the representations of lion-cloaked men whose proveniences are known are Assyrian, with the exception of the figurine from Uruk, no. 8, which may or may not belong to the group. This distribtution could mean that the functionary and custom represented were peculiarly Assyrian; but it could also be due to the greater prevalence of representational art in Assyria. Moreover, some of the clay figurines besides no. 8 could be from Babylonia, as far as anyone knows. Of the texts cited, most were at least known in Assyria.[79] This includes the texts cited in connection with apotropaic rites. References to the *kurgarru* and *assinnu*, on the other hand, are mostly from Babylonia,[80] and the references to the cult of Ishtar are not only from a late Babylonian text, but refer specifically to the cult of Ishtar of Uruk.[81] It is not clear to me how much similarity one may expect between the cults of Ishtar of Uruk and Ishtar of Nineveh. The figurine from Freihat al-Nufeiji may provide a link between the Babylonian texts and the Assyrian representations. Moreover, a personnel list of the reign of Sargon II from Nimrud[82] includes 56 *kugarru*'s among other functionaries. A connection between the lion-cloaked man and the *kurgarru* cannot be ruled out solely on the ground that they belonged to geographically separate traditions.

While we have no definite indication of who the man in the lion cloak was, the hints available point in two directions. The clay figurines and the figure on the Lamashtu plaque indicate an apotropaic function, while the palace reliefs suggest a cultic dance. The figure carries a whip in both of these circumstances. If we accept a connection with the activities of the *kurgarru* and *assinnu*, we would have also a link with the cult of Ishtar, which is suggested by the seal impression. All of these associations are tenuous enough that attempts to reconcile them could lead us astray. It may be pointed out, nonetheless, that the two functions—exorcism and cultic ceremonial—are not necessarily mutually exclusive. Could it be that the lion-cloaked dancers on Assurnaṣirpal's relief are performing a ritual to exorcise the ghosts of the enemy dead, as the scene

71. AAA 22 (1935) 58 rev. 57.

72. CT 16 29:77; R. C. Thompson, The Devils and Evil Spirits of Babylonia 1 (London, Luzac, 1903) 136-37.

73. ABL 24; Waterman, Royal Correspondence 1 20-21. The incipit of the incantation quoted by Marduk-šakin-šumi (ḪUL-GÁL.ḪÉ.ME.EN) is the same as that of UDUG.ḪUL tablet "B"; CT 16 27:1; Thompson, Devils 1 128.

74. [*ina qi-*]*na-zi i-maḫ*[*-ḫaṣ*], ABL 24 rev. 3.

75. Unless the *naḫlaptu santu ša puluḫti*, "the red cloak of terror," worn by the exorcist in UDUG.ḪUL (CT 16 29:69) was actually the lion cloak.

76. Macmillan, BA 5 626=Craig, ABRT 1 55 i 10, cited from CAD K 558; for the identification as a Nanâ hymn see Borger, HKL 1 327.

77. CAD K 557-59; A/2 341-42. It is possible that the long-necked instrument played by the man on the Assurnaṣirpal relief was also associated with Ishtar's cult—cf. its occurrence on the lead plaques with sexual scenes from Assur: W. Andrae, Die jüngeren Ischtar-Tempel in Assur, WVDOG 58 (Leipzig, J. C. Hinrichs, 1935) pl. 45c-d.

78. AO 7439 rev. 7: Racc. p. 115. Cf. CAD K 558a. This is the same text that mentions the UR.MAḪ.LÚ.U$_x$.LU, see n. 56, above. For what we do know about Narudu's appearance, see Gurney, AAA 22 (1935) 46-47 iii 1-4.

79. For instance, the Epic of Era is known mostly from Kuyunjik, Assur, and Sultantepe texts (Cagni, Erra pp. 13ff.), while the anti-ghost incantation cited, KAR 227, is of course from Assur.

80. See CAD A/2 341-42, K 557-59.

81. Racc. pp. 111-12.

82. Barbara Parker, "Administrative Tablets from the North-west Palace, Nimrud," Iraq 23 (1961) 35, ND 2491:1. The text itself is not dated, but all the dated tablets from the same room are from Sargon's reign.

immediately below shows the living captives being dealt with? The cult of Ishtar is not removed from exorcism, as is shown by the text KAR 42,[83] which has the form of a ritual dedicated to Ishtar and Dumuzi, but which is expressly stated to have an exorcistic purpose. In Maqlu, also,[84] the *kurgarru* is listed among a number of persons by whom the witches are cursed.

Most of these hints concerning the identity and function of the lion-cloaked man remain merely hints. I will be content with having—as I believe—demonstrated the consistency of the iconography of the figure in several media, and its distinctness from other types, and will leave the matter here. New data or other scholars may bring more explicit explanations.

83. Cf. Ebeling, MVAG 23/2 21ff.

84. Meier, Maqlu p. 31 IV 83, p. 50 VII 92, 96.

Fig. 1

Fig. 2

Fig. 3

Fig. 4

Fig. 5

Fig. 6

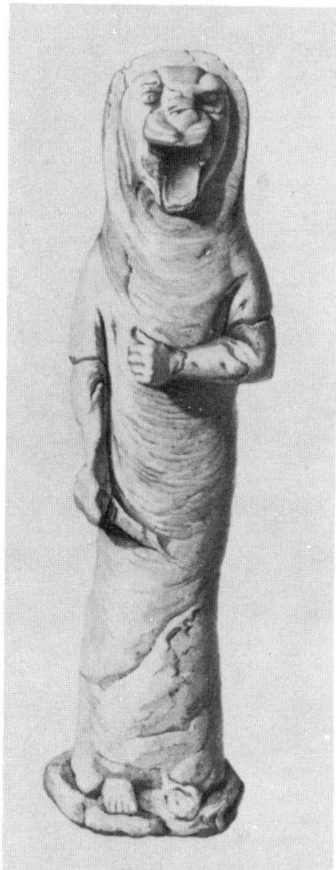

Fig. 7

Fig. 8

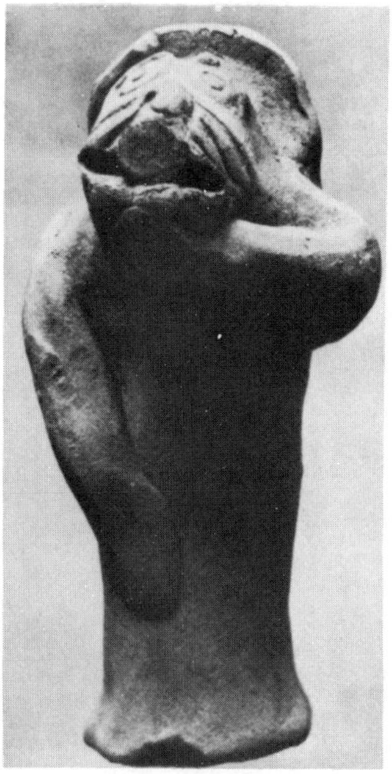

Fig. 9

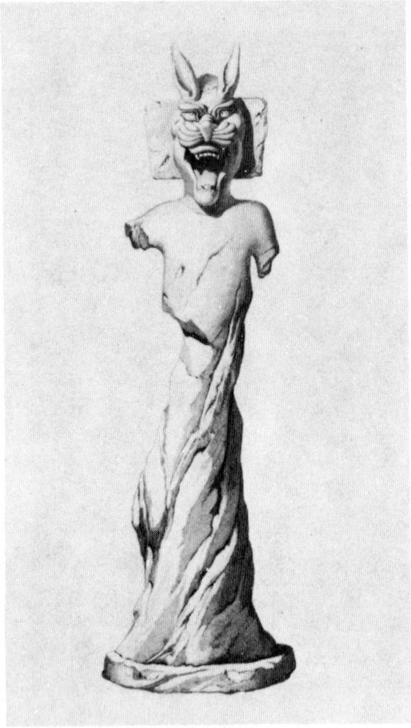

Fig. 10

Fig. 11

EA AND ṢALTU

Benjamin R. Foster
Yale University

This essay on the Agušaja Hymn is offered as a tribute to the late J. J. Finkelstein. Although he saw the primary focus of his academic concerns as "centered upon the legal phenomena in the ancient civilizations of Mesopotamia and surrounding regions,"[1] major and minor works of Akkadian literature were by no means peripheral to his interests. His approach to and understanding of them were unique and personal, and it is much to be regretted that he seldom chose to make his work on them public.[2] His view of this particular composition must remain unknown, for as the eminent jurist Sir Edward Coke wrote of his predecessor Sir Thomas Littleton, "Certain it is, that when a great learned Man (who is long in making) dieth, much Learning dieth with him."[3] Perhaps the most important lesson he left with his students in Akkadian literature is that understanding and interpretation are the results of a collective effort where some lead and others follow. Thus there can never be a definitive treatment of a problem or literary work, only successive stages in a continuing collective enterprise.

A particularly happy combination of erudition and technique allowed J. J. Finkelstein to demonstrate such remarkable research capacity as his essay on the goring ox,[4] and such superb skill in copying of cuneiform tablets as the plates of YOS 13.[5] This diversity of ability approached to some extent a Mesopotamian ideal of scholarship that was both knowledge of the way things are and mastery of how things should be done. Such was the ideal a Babylonian poet evoked in praise he bestowed on Nabu himself, the patron deity of letters: *mu-de-e al-ka-ka-ti la-mi-id ki-id-du-di.*[6]

Of all the figures in Mesopotamian tradition, Ea best exemplifies a unity of knowledge of the ways of things and how they can be manipulated. No better example of Ea's ingenuity can be found than his plan and procedure in the story of Agušaja. The purpose of this essay is to show the importance of Ea in the Agušaja story, what his plan was, and how he brought it to pass.

The mutilated condition of the text and the difficulty of the surviving portions stand in the way of a full appreciation of its sense and significance. The first part of the text was identified by Zimmern and treated by him in a model study entitled "Ištar und Ṣaltu, ein altakkadisches Lied."[7] A second tablet containing the rest of the composition was acquired by Scheil and published in photograph and transliteration in RA 15 (1918).[8]

The poetic dialect of the composition, to which Zimmern had already drawn attention,[9] was studied by von Soden in his treatment of the "hymnic-epic dialect" of Akkadian.[10] In 1971, Brigitte Groneberg took up this dialect in her Münster dissertation, Untersuchungen zum hymnisch-epischen Dialekt der altbabylonischen literarischen Texte; she was able to draw on von Soden's profound knowledge of this material, and to make a substantial contribution of her own towards understanding it and its poetic context.[11] Her book includes an up-to-date edition of the Agušaja hymn. This offers many original readings

1. Temple Law Quarterly 46 (1973) 169.

2. Some of his work on Atraḫasis, for example, was communicated privately to W. G. Lambert, who was then editing the texts. Cf. W. G. Lambert and A. R. Millard, Atra-ḫasīs: The Babylonian Story of the Flood (Oxford, 1969) p. v.

3. Sir Edward Coke, The First Part of the Institutions of the Laws of England: Or, a Commentary upon Littleton, Not in the Name of the Author only, but of the Law it self (London, 1737) p. vi, "Proemium," paraphrasing Seneca.

4. Temple Law Quarterly 46 (1973) 169-200.

5. Late Old Babylonian Documents and Letters, YOS 13 (New Haven, 1972).

6. KAR 104 25. A Babylonian origin for the poet is suggested by his dedicating the first fourteen lines of his hymn to Marduk (of Babylon), but only the next seven to Nabu (of Borsippa), even though both deities are invoked.

7. Berichte über die Verhandlungen der Königlichen Sächsischen Gesellschaft der Wissenschaften zu Leipzig, Phil.-hist. Klasse 68/1 (1916) 1-43 (with photo); hand copy in VAS 10 214.

8. "Le poème d'Agušaya," RA 15 (1918) 169-82 (with photo). The two tablets do not belong together. Note that in the Zimmern tablet Ṣaltu is not written with the determinative for deity, and Ea rarely, while the determinatives are used regularly in the Scheil tablet.

9. Ištar und Ṣaltu p. 1 n. 2.

10. W. von Soden, "Der hymnisch-epische Dialekt des Akkadischen," ZA 40 (1932) 163-227; ZA 41 (1933) 90-183.

11. Other discussions of this poetic usage include W. Ph. Römer, "Studien zu altbabylonischen hymnisch-epischen Texten," Heidelberger Studien zum alten Orient (Wiesbaden, 1967) 185-99; JAOS 86 (1966) 138-47; WO 4 (1967) 12-28; W. G. Lambert, "Studies in Nergal," BiOr 30 (1973) 358. With respect to Lambert's essay, it appears to me more probable that BM 120,003 refers to Naram-Sin of Eshnunna than to Naram-Sin of Agade.

Ancient Near Eastern Studies in Memory of J. J. Finkelstein
Connecticut Academy of Arts and Sciences, Memoir 19

and interpretations, and provides a sound basis for future work on the composition.[12] That I am unable to agree with her understanding of the story or her translation of key passages in no way lessens my debt to and admiration for her meticulous work.

The poem opens with a hymn of praise to Ishtar, inscrutable, warlike, and powerful, who runs down her enemies like an onrushing vehicle, to whom combat is a festival.[13] In the excess of her valor, she comes forth bellowing like a wild bull, seeking occasion to do battle. Her clamor exasperates Ea, and he resolves to bring it to an end.[14] He calls together the gods, explains that Ishtar's aggressiveness has become unbearable, and suggests that a suitable opponent be created for her (A v 6ff.):

[ši-i] lu ak-ṣa-at	She should be violent
[lu nu]-ku-la-at ša-ra-as-sà	She should be wonderfully hairy[15]
⌜*de?*⌝-*ši-it el ṣi-ip-pa-tim*	More luxuriant(?) than a garden.
bi-ni-tu-uš li-id-ni-in	Let her be massive of build.
li-id-bu-ub lu da-an-na-at	Let her complain—she should be strong
li-iḫ-zú la i-na-na-aḫ	Let her gasp for breath—she should not tire.

Ea is of course seeking general approval for a scheme he has already devised. Since no one but he is capable of bringing it to pass, the gods appeal to him to do as he has proposed (A v 18ff):

iš-ti-i-ka lu na-ṭú	You are suited to
an-nu-ú e-pé-šu-um	undertake this task.
a-na aš-ri-im ša la ka-at	Who will bring it to pass
i-ša-ka-an ma-an-nu-um	if not you?[16]

With the dirt of his nails Ea creates Ṣaltu, "powerful in her form, monstrous in her proportions" (*ab-ra-at ši-ik-na-as-sà šu-un-na-at mi-ni-a-tim*).[17]

The middle portion of the poem is a lengthy speech by Ea in which he prepares Ṣaltu for her confrontation with Ishtar. What remains of his speech can be divided into two main sections. In the first (A vi 17-49) Ea informs Ṣaltu of a certain goddess, whom he refers to not as Ishtar, but as Irnina, one of her by-names,[18] and tells Ṣaltu that her purpose is to humiliate this goddess. He describes their upcoming confrontation and how Ṣaltu should behave. She is to provoke the goddess by violating her privacy and rudely challenging her. In the second part of his speech (A vii 20-A viii 25) Ea goes on to tell Ṣaltu how she will recognize her opponent. He waxes eloquent in his description of Ishtar to make Ṣaltu angry and jealous, and devotes the last part of his speech to an invidious comparison of the two. In this comparison he subtly echoes his first speech, in which he envisaged their encounter, to mock Ṣaltu with her inferiority. He concludes by saying that Ṣaltu had better not proceed as the mere sight of her enemy will render her

12. Groneberg, Dialekt pp. 29-94, with collations of the Zimmern tablet. The Scheil tablet is now lost (Groneberg, Dialekt p. 31). Detailed discussion of the philological problems in the passages cited below will be found in her edition, and many of her readings have been adopted here without remark.

13. A iii 7ff. may be read:

i-si-in-ša ta-am-ḫa-ru
šu-ut-ra-aq-qú-⌜*du*⌝ *a-*<*na*>*-an-ti*
i-ša-tu ú-ul ta-am-ḫa-at a-li-li
i-ta-ar-ru da-aš-ni

Her festival is combat,
Battles make her dance with glee,
Nor in them does she hold back the battle cry,
Sweeping aside (her) assailants.

14. Similarly *rigmu*, "clamor," was the reason that Enlil sent a plague and the flood upon men, Atraḫasis I 358; for a discussion of this word see G. Pettinato, "Die Bestrafung des Menschengeschlechts durch die Sintflut," Or. NS 37 (1968) 165-200.

15. Thick hair of itself was considered a good physical characteristic; cf. Kraus, Texte 3b iii 4: *šumma šārat qaqqadi kuššu* UD.BI GÍD.DA *amēlūta illak* "if the hair of his head is thick, his life will be long; he will reach old age"; differently Kraus MVAG 40/2 (1935) 82. On the other hand, Enkidu's hairiness was characteristic of his outlandish appearance: *[šu]-ᵓu-ur šar-ta ka-lu zu-um-ri-šu*, Gilg. I ii 36. Ṣaltu's hair figures in a pretty chiasma, A v 43f.:

ši-ru-ša sà-ba-aᵓ-ú
ṣé-lu-ú ša-ra-as-sà

Her flesh is the melee,
The close fight her hair.

16. In a similar vein Nintu addresses the great gods when she is asked to create man, Atraḫasis I 200ff.:

it-ti-ia-ma la na-ṭú a-na e-pé-ši
it-ti ᵈ*En-ki-ma i-ba-aš-ši ši-ip-ru*

"By me alone he cannot be fashioned;
For Enki himself is a task at hand."

For the translation, see Moran, BASOR 200 (1970) 49. For the expression *ana ašrim šakānum*, cf. YOS 9 35:36ff.: *ša bi-bil li-ib-bi-ia a-na aš-ri-im ša-ka-nam mu-du-ú* "who knows how to realize my heart's desire" (Samsuiluna C).

17. A v 35f.

18. Ea may have chosen this name purposely to keep Ṣaltu in the dark as to whom he meant. For references to Irnina as an aspect of Ištar, see Tallqvist, Götterepitheta p. 329; see also below, n. 23.

helpless. Ea's purpose in his praise of Ishtar is obvious, and the poet is at pains to clarify Ea's real intentions, as will be shown below.

Ea's first speech reads as follows (A vi 17ff.):

qú-li uz-na-am šu-uk-ni	Keep quiet, listen
uṣ-ṣi-ri qí-bi-ti	Pay heed to what I say
ši-me-e si-iq-ri-ia	Hear my orders!
ša ú-a-wa-ru-ú-ki ep-ši-i	What I tell you, do!
iš-ti-a-at il-[tum] qar-da-at	There is a certain goddess
el ka-la [i]-la-tim	more valiant than all others,
šu-tu-qú na-ar-bu-ša	whose greatness is surpassing.
ša-ni ši-p[í-i]r-ša nu-uk-ku-úr	Strange and cunning are her deeds.
šu-u[m-š]a ^{d}Ir-ni-na	Her name is Irnina.
[ap?]-ra-at ap-lu-ḫa-tim	She is clad(?) in mail,
[be-le]-et be-le-e-tim	the supreme lady,
[te-l]i-tim bu-uk-ra-at ^{d}Nin-gal	lofty one, daughter of Ningal.
[ša]-⸢at⸣ a-ru-še-e-ša	I have created you
[ab]-ta-ni ka-a-ti	to humiliate her.
qú-úr-da-am du-un-na-am	Valor and might
i-na ne-me-qí ú-ṣí-ib	in my wisdom did I
la-ni-iš-ki	give your form in abundance.
i-na-an-na al-ki at-ti	Now be off,
at-ka-ši ta-i-iš-ša	Go off to her private chamber.[19]
pu-lu-uḫ-ta-am lu la-ab-ša-a-ti	You should be girded with aweful splendor.
ú-ta-e-ri-ši an-na	Accost her: "You there!"
ši-i uš-bi it-te-e-ki	She will bend down to you,
a-wa-ta i-qá-bi-i-ki	She will speak to you
i-ša-al-ki ar-da-at ma-aʾ-na	and ask, "See here, woman,
a-la-ak-ta-ak pu-uš-ri	explain your behavior!"
at-ti lu ša-ab-sa-at	But you, though she be furious,
la ta-ka-nu-ši-i-ši	Show no respect to her.
ša nu-pu-uš li-ib-bi	Whatever she utters,
la ta-ap-pa-li-i-ši a-wa-tim	answer her never a word.
ma-ti li-il-qé mi-im-ma-ki	What advantage shall she have of you?
bi-ni-it qá-ti-ia at-ti	You are the creature of my power.
ša-al-ṭi-iš ma-al pí-i-ki	Speak out proudly what is on your tongue,
ù ma-la-am ma-ḫa-ar-ša du-ub-bi	and as much (again) before her!

This concludes the first part of Ea's advice, in which he tells Ṣaltu what will happen and what he expects her to do.

The next portion of Ea's speech is set off from the first by a section of narrative which could be described as "formulaic." This need not be taken as evidence that this composition as it is now known can be analyzed as a fixed version of an oral poetic tradition.[20] Rather it appears to be the work of a creative artist who, though he may have used a traditional story and traditional poetic techniques, produced a work that appears to be individual and literary in character.[21]

As Ea begins the second part of his speech, the poet informs us that his purpose in saying what he does is to make Ṣaltu furious by praising her opponent, who is none other than Ishtar herself (A vii 2ff.):

19. In like manner Ištar's clamor had even reached Ea's dwelling (A iv 12f.):

i-šu-ub-ti ni-iš-ši-i-ki ^{d}É-a
pu-lu-uḫ-ta-am uṣ-re-e

In the dwelling of the *niššiku* Ea
Look out for her terror!

Thus Ea seems to have relished the idea that Ṣaltu would invade Ištar's household.

20. For "formulaic" usage in Mesopotamian literature, see B. Alster, Dumuzi's Dream: Aspects of Oral Poetry in a Sumerian Myth, Mesopotamia 1 (Copenhagen, 1972) 16ff.

21. For a study of this aspect of Mesopotamian creativity, see A. L. Oppenheim, "A New Prayer to the 'Gods of the Night'," AnBi 12 (1959) pp. 289ff. That the author was a court poet is suggested by B vii 23ff.: *ù šar-rum ša an-ni-a-am za-ma-ra-am . . . ta-ni-it-ta-ki iš-mu-ni* "and the king who hears (?) this song . . . your praise." For *iš-mu-ni*, see below, note 32.

šu!-pí-iš[22] *it-ta-zi-uz Ṣa-al-tum*
É-a qer-bu ap-su-ú
i-ši-wa-an-ši-im du-un-na-am
i-bu-uk-ma Ṣa-al-ta-am
šu-tu-ru bi-ni-an-nim
ú-ša-ar-ri-ir-ši am-ma-ag-ra-tim
qú-ul-lu-li-im ta-ar-ši-a-tim
É-a er-šu-ú ša šu-tu-ru ma-la-ak-šu
ú-ṣa-ab ú-re-ed-de a-wa-ta-am
a-na ka-ar-ši-ša
it-ti Ištar šar-ra-tim i-na-da-an-ši
Ištar-ma ga-aš-ra-at el ka-la
i-la-tim ši-i-ma
ú-e-di-ši na-ar-bi-ša
ša ba-aš-ti ú-ṭa-a-ab-ši
an-nu-um-ma aš-šu ša la i-pa-ṭa-ru ar-ka-nu-um
i-ta-at il-tum te-re-ta-ša ra-bi-a
be-le-et-mi la ip-ru-ku-[. . .]
pa-ni-iš-ša ma-am-ma-[*an*]

Proudly has Ṣaltu taken her stand
(while) Ea, in the midst of the *apsu*
gives her might.
So he dispatched Ṣaltu
extraordinary of form
making her tremble with insults,
contempt and calumny.
Ea the wise, whose reasoning is beyond all,
goes on to add yet a word
(that cuts) to her heart.
The sign of Ishtar the queen he gives her—
for it is Ishtar herself, greater than all the gods.[23]

He makes her know her grandeur.
He well describes to her that prideful self,
this lest she avoid (her) later.[24]
"The sign is a lady whose commands are mighty;
She is a lady whom no one
has obstructed . . ."

The continuation of Ea's speech, in which he gives Ṣaltu the signs of Ishtar, is broken, but it is clear his description of her leads up to a mocking comparison with Ṣaltu (A vii 36ff.):

pí-ki lu šu-tam-li te-r[*a-sà šu*]*-tu-ra-at*

⸢*at*⸣-⸢*ti*⸣ *lu ka-ad-ra-a-ti*
it-ti-it a-pa-ni-ša
uš-ta-ar-ra-aḫ el-ki-i
la ta-pa-aṭ-ṭa-ri bi-it ni-ši

"You may have much to say (but) [her com]mand is surpassing.[25]
You may be fierce
(but) she is unique in herself!
She is grander than you are.
Don't rush in where others fear to tread."[26]

In the next twenty lines, which are lost or fragmentary, Ea continues to taunt Ṣaltu, as in A viii 22ff.:

[*li*]*-ik-ta-aš-da-ak-ki*
[*li-ḫ*]*a-li-qú di-ib-bu-ki*
[*re-qé-et?*] *al-ka-ka-ti*
[*ša be*]*-le-et ni-ši te-li-ti*

"Let her but reach you,
your speech will fail;
[inscrutable?] are the ways
[of] the lady of the people, the lofty one."

The narrative resumes (A viii 26ff.):

[*Ṣa-a*]*l-tum uz-zi-iz iš-nu-ú*
[*pa*]*-nu-ša pa-al-ḫi-iš*
[*i?*]*-ta-a-ar ug-da-aš-ša-ar*
[*šu?*]*-qú-la-at ḫa-la-qí-iš*

Ṣaltu flew into a rage.
Her face altered horribly.
She turned, girded herself,
silent as a fugitive,[27] . . .

22. This reading is based on the corresponding description of Ištar in B ii 13f.: *šu-pí-iš du-un-ni-ša ša-ga-pu-ri-iš it-na-za-az*. Groneberg's reading *ṣubbiš*, "um zu prüfen," seems less likely (cf. Dialekt p. 83 n. 2).

23. The emphasis here seems to resume A xvi 25, as the poet seems to say that actually Ishtar was meant by what follows.

24. Groneberg's "Dieses (gilt) wegen dessen, das nicht gelöst werde später" (Dialekt p. 64) and CAD's "he (Anu) has made her (Ištar) distinguished by her size and enhanced whatever pertains to her dignity so that they (the described qualities) should not depart (from her) thereafter," (A/2 273b, B 143a) both seem to me wide of the mark. The poet emphasizes that Ea is saying these things to make sure Ṣaltu will be eager to challenge Ishtar and not lose her resolve. Note the admonition in Lambert, BWL p. 100:36: *ina pa-an ṣa-al-tim-ma pu-ṭur e tak-pu-ud* "When confronted with a dispute avoid (it); pay no attention."

25. Literally, "your mouth may be very full." This line ironically recalls A vi 48ff., where Ṣaltu is enjoined to speak whatever is on her mind: *ma-al pí-ki . . . du-ub-bi*.

26. Literally, "Don't break into a person's house." This line ironically recalls A vi 35, where Ṣaltu is urged to go right into Ishtar's private chamber: *at-ka-ši ta-i-iš-ša*. That it is a proverbial expression is shown by the Instructions of Šuruppak 33: — é na-an-ni-bùr-e-en mi-si-saḫar al nam-me "do not burst into a house, do not demand the sieve," B. Alster, The Instructions of Suruppak: A Sumerian Proverb Collection, Mesopotamia 2 (Copenhagen, 1974) 36. The sense seems to be that one should not look for trouble. "Demanding the sieve" may have been the Sumerian equivalent for "having a chip on one's shoulder" or "picking a fight."

27. That is, she is setting forth silent with grim resolve. One may compare the Biblical "like a thief in the night."

The remainder of the narrative is badly broken, but enough remains that the thread of the story can be reconstructed to some extent, and the point of the composition recovered. Ṣaltu goes forth in search of her enemy, and as the text resumes Ishtar has heard of her clamor for battle and sends out her messenger Ninšubur to find out about her (B i 5ff.):

i-da-at du-un-ni-ša	(. . .) the signs of her strength.
[a]r-ka-as-sà pu-ur-sà	Find out all about her,[28]
aš-ra-ta-ša a-li-ša-am-ma-a	her haunts, wherever they are(?).[29]
le-qé-a-am it-ta-ti-ša	Bring word of her signs;
šu-un-ni-a al-ka-as-sà	recount to me her ways.

Ninšubur goes out, catches sight of Ṣaltu, and is struck dumb with fear. She returns to Ishtar and stammers out a description of Ṣaltu (B i 20ff.):

ku-uk-ku-la-at e-pé-ša	She is b-bizarre in her actions
ú-ul im-la-al-lik ni-ši	she b-behaves unreasoningly(?).[30]
ši-ki-tu-uš ta-ak-la-ak	In her form she is m-mighty.
a-li-wi-tim ma-da-at	She makes many c-cries for battle.[31]
zu-ʾu-ú-na-at na-mu-la-ti	She is adorned in a-awesomeness.
at-bu-uš-ša šu-ul-lu-ma(?)	I came away from her(?) to save myself(?).[32]
[ga]-ṣa-at ša-li-a-at ù ra-aʾ-ba-at	She is murderous, bullying, vicious,
GURUŠ KI.SIKIL-*am i-šu*	has the young man and the maid . . .

The remarkable phonological distortions of this passage, *kukkulat* for *nukkulat, imlallik* for *imtallik, taklak* for *taklat, aliwītim* perhaps for *aliḫtim*, and *namulāti* for *namurrāti* are taken as corruptions or scribal errors by Groneberg (cf. p. 90) and others. Four "errors" of this kind could hardly occur one each in four successive lines. It seems preferable to interpret them as intentional distortion by the poet designed to convey Ninšubur's great agitation.

Ishtar was infuriated by this description (B ii 25f.):

ša-am-ri-iš i-sà-qá-ar	Angrily she exclaims,
ši-i i-da-at du-un-ni-ša	"those are the signs of her might?"

The climax of the narrative is lost. When the text resumes Ea is talking with Ishtar, now referred to by her war-like aspect as Agušaja (B vii 1ff.)[33]:

ta-aš-ta-ka-an na-ar-bi-[i-ša]	"You made her enormity,
ᵈ*Ṣa-al-tum ri-ig-[ma-am]*	Ṣaltu clamor
iš-ta-ka-an e-[li]-ia	has set against me.
li-tu-ur up-pí-iš-ša	Let her return to her hole."
ᵈ*É-a pa-a-šu i-pu-ša-ma*	Ea spoke and answered as follows;
a-na A-gu-ša-ia qá-ra-ad i-li i-sà-qar	to Agušaja, hero of the gods he says:
a-na sú-ur-ri ki-ma ta-aq-bi-i	"As soon as you say it,
e-pí-pu-uš-ma	then it's done and certain.
tu-ša-ar-ra-ri-in-ni-ma	You make me joyful
tu-ḫa-ad-[di]-i šu-ú-ṣú-uk-ki	and cause delight with your having done with it.[34]
ki-ma in-né-ep-šu-ú	The reason it was done

28. This passage would seem to contradict San Nicolò's assertion that *arkatam parāsu* meant "entscheiden" or "klarstellen," as against Landsberger, MSL 1 80ff. and 93, who understood it as "seine Sache (Angelegenheit) untersuchen," Babylonische Rechtsurkunden des ausgehenden 8. und 7. Jahrhunderts v. Chr., ABAW Phil.-hist. Kl. NF 34 (1951) 143 with note °°.

29. CAD A/1 350a emends to *aš-ra-ta-ša-a li-ta-am-ma-ad*!, which seems better than the original.

30. Literally, "she has not sought people's advice."

31. This takes *a-li-wi-tim* as a misformed plural of *a-li-li* "cry of triumph." An indeclinable form of this word occurs in the Old Babylonian epic of Sargon published by Nougayrol, RA 45 (1951) 169ff. line 36.

32. The enigmatic *at-bu-uš-ša* and *iš-mu-ni* (B vii 25) may both be solved by one explanation, if one accepts them as poetic variants of the expected *ê*-ending of the *e*-class verb: *atbê, išmê*. The photo supports Scheil's reading of the final word as *šu-ul-lu*-DI, rather than *šu-ul-ma*!-x. The final sign might also be *ša*. In any case the line remains obscure.

33. For the name Agušaja, see von Soden, MDOG 96 (1965) 45f., and Groneberg, Dialekt p. 42.

34. For the sense of this line see below.

ib-ba-nu-ú ^{d}*Ṣa-al-tum*	and Ṣaltu was created is
ki-mi-ni li-il-ma-da	that besides ourselves(?)
ni-šu ar-ki-a-tum	people of future days might know.
li-ib-ši ša-at-ti-ša	Let it be yearly
li-iš-ša-ki-in gu-uš-tu-ú	that a whirling dance be done[35]
i-pa-ar-zi-im ša-at-ti	in the . . . of the year.
bi-it-ri-i ni-ši-i gi-im-ra-as-sí-in	Look about at all the people!
li-me-el-lu i-sú-qí-im	Let them dance in the street.[36]
ši-me-e ri-gi-im-ši-in	Hear their clamor!
at-ti bi-it-ri-i em-qé-ta-ši-in	See for yourself the intelligent things they do.
⌈*ṭe*⌉*-em-ši-in ṭe?-em-ki-i*	Let their rationale(?) be yours."[37]

Ea's final speech reveals for the first time his purpose in creating Ṣaltu. Ishtar has just complained to him that he is responsible for producing this offensive monster, and she orders him to send it off. Ea answers that he is delighted to do so, for as soon as Ishtar has stopped acting as she has (*šuṣukki*) the offensive creature is gone. This brings home the purpose of his enterprise: he had in fact created a gross travesty of Ishtar herself, fierce and clamoring for a fight. The sight so revolted the goddess that she gave up her incessant clamor for battle, as such behavior was not a true sign of might. Ea's project succeeded admirably, so it remained only to soothe Ishtar's feelings. This he did by declaring that once a year people would dance madly about the streets, their uproar a reminder of the warlike aspect of the goddess: Agušaja. The rest of the year presumably Ea was left in peace.

The implications of this pacification of Ishtar remain a matter of speculation. It is not by chance that the poem begins with a lengthy encomium of Ishtar's valor but ends with Ea's conciliatory speech, the poet's etiological explanation of a peculiar holiday, and with the anger of the "lioness" being soothed. One may perhaps sense the artist's rightful pride at the conclusion of his work, if one allows that not only the occasion but the poem itself is referred to in the following lines:

^{d}*Ě-a ni-iš-ši-i-ki*	The *niššiku* Ea
i-da-at du-un-ni-ša	let all the people hear
kă-la ni-ši ú-še-eš-mi	the signs of her might.[38]

35. Groneberg and von Soden's emendation of *gu-uš-tu-ú* "whirling dance" to *gu-du*!*-tu-ú* "Räuchertisch" is unjustified. Scheil read *gu-uš-tu-ú*, but translated it as "offrande."

36. Dancing in the street was characteristic of the Sumerian Inanna, but this was seen by some poets as only girlish play: *i-na re-bé-tim im-me-li-il*, TuM NF 3 25, Akkadian gloss to line 15; cf. Wilcke, AfO 23 (1970) 85.

37. This reading is based on a suggestion of von Soden's, cf. Groneberg, Dialekt p. 93, although the first sign of the second word looks more like LI, as Scheil read it. Von Soden avoided this problem by reading it as $ṭe_4$, but this means the same word would be written two different ways in the same line. For the sense of *ṭēmu*, roughly "the reason someone does something," see for example Moran, BASOR 200 (1970) 52. Ea is chiding Ishtar for proclaiming her power by going about crying for a fight. Ṣaltu and the people demonstrate how foolish it looks.

38. In B vii 24 the poem is specifically called *i-da-at qú-ur-di-ki*, "a sign of your valor." With like pride, the Babylonian poet wrote *ú-šar-raḫ nak-liš* "I extol artfully" KAR 104:8.

NḤŠTK (Ezek. 16:36): ANOTHER HEBREW COGNATE OF AKKADIAN *naḫāšu*

Moshe Greenberg
The Hebrew University

In his study "Old Babylonian Herding Contract and Genesis 31:38ff.," J. J. Finkelstein argued forcefully that Hebrew *niḥeš* in Genesis 30:27 meant "grow rich." He admitted the difficulty that this interpretation assumes an otherwise unattested Hebrew cognate of Akkadian *naḫāšu* "be rich, abundant."[1] This note is offered, alas too late for him to receive it, as a mitigation of that difficulty. There is another candidate for derivation from a Hebrew *nḥš* "be abundant," whose case has been put forward before, but without notable success. In taking up the argument once more that *nḥšt* (in the form *nəḥuštek*) of Ezekiel 16:36 is best understood as a derivative from such a root,[2] I honor the memory of a dear friend.

The first part of chapter 16 of the book of Ezekiel is a lurid parable of Jerusalem as a foundling who grew up to be a nymphomaniacal harlot who left her husband to go whoring with any and all comers. The descriptions of the child as an infant and of the brazen harlot are couched in highly colored language; the naked goriness of the girl before she was married is emphasized, as is her wanton surrender of all her charms and her husband's gifts to her paramours. But more shocking language is to come.

In verse 36, the prophet begins to pronounce God-the-husband's sentence upon the wanton creature with an epitome of her outrageous behavior; here the crux of our study appears: *yaʿan hiššapek nəḥuštek wattiggale ʿerwatek*, "because your *nḥšt* poured out and your crotch was exposed." The reading *nḥštk* is firmly attested by Greek *ton chalkon sou*, Syriac *nḥšky*, and Latin *aes tuum*, all "your copper," which, though meaningless here, leave no doubt about the graph. While *hšpk* is rendered variously—Greek *execheas* "you poured out," Syriac *yhbty* "you gave," Latin *effusum est* "was poured out"—none of the renderings (nor all taken together) point decisively to a different Hebrew *vorlage*. Targum *ʾtgəliʾat bahatətik weʾitḥazi qəlanik* "your pudendum was exposed and your shame was seen" is a stock targumic rendition of several like expressions regardless of their exact sense and wording; cf. at 16:37 and 23:18. Hence one hesitates to base on it a change of *hiššapek* to *ḥospek* "your disclosing," all the more since it entails a second change of the next verb to *wattəgalli* "and you exposed."[3] Emendations must wait until the sense of the passage is clear, and that depends as much or more on the meaning assigned to *nḥšt*.

Of the ancient versions, only Targum tries to give a contextual rendering of the word, taking it simply as a synonym of Hebrew *ʿerwa*, "crotch," in the next clause. One possible road to this sense is given by Rashi and Kimḥi, who explain *nḥšt* as "bottom, nether-part," on the basis of a traditional interpretation of a technical term in the Mishnah, *nəḥušto šellətannur*, "the bottom of an oven."[4] But this late and obscure technical term hardly affords a secure foundation for interpreting the biblical word. In modern times, derivatives of Akkadian *naḫāšu* have been put forward as possible cognates. Older authorities adduced *nuḫšu*, "abundance, overflowing," in the pejorative sense of extravagance and prodigality (Cooke),[5] or as "abundance, luxury, liquid overflow," with a reference to "sexual fullness" (G. R. Driver).[6] Later on, *naḫšātu* was adduced, in the alleged sense of "menstruation" (Tournay[7]; Kohler-Baumgartner's Lexicon), only to be rejected as an irrelevant "gloss" (Fohrer[8]), or for being contextually improbable and otherwise

1. In JAOS 88 (1968) 30-36; for the argument for *niḥeš*="grow rich," see p. 34 n. 19.

2. The proposal to explain *nḥštk* in Ezek. 16:36 by reference to Akk. *nuḫšu* 'wealth, abundance" was made in 1884 by F. Delitzsch in his preface to S. Baer's Liber Ezechielis, pp. xiv-xv (Cooke's note, see below, n. 5). The entry in Brown-Driver-Briggs, Lexicon (1907) 639a ignores it, but it is noted by Gesenius-Buhl, Handwörterbuch (1915) 499b; for further history, see below.

3. See Geiger, Urschrift p. 391ff.

4. Mishnah, Kelim 8:3; 9:1. Geiger, Urschrift, p. 391ff. [Hebrew translation p. 252f.], derived this sense ultimately from Ezek. 24:11, interpreting *nəḥuštah* there as "bottom (of a copper pot)," whence the generalized usage in later Hebrew and the metaphor in Ezek. 16:36; Ben-Yehuda, Thesaurus s.v. follows suit. Citing the Targum, Geiger emended *hiššapek* to *ḥospek*, and the following verb to *wattəgalli* (cf. Syriac). For the Mishnaic term, see now Y. Brand, Klei Haḥeres Besifrut Hatalmud (Jerusalem, 1953) 554ff.

5. In The International Critical Commentary (1937) 174.

6. Biblica 19 (1938) 65; Driver himself abandoned the construction he there put on Ugaritic *mmlʾt dm* in his later Canaanite Myths and Legends, p. 31b (Keret I iii 10).

7. In a list of Akkadisms in Ezekiel, Biblica 60 (1953) 419.

8. In Handbuch zum Alten Testament (1955) p. 87 textual note to vs. 36: "Delete 'your menstruation (hap. leg.) was poured out' =variant gloss." This judgment runs counter to the essence of a gloss—"a brief explanation . . . of a difficult or obscure word or expression" (Webster). It is hard to believe that a hapax should be used for glossing; what difficult expression does it gloss?

Ancient Near Eastern Studies in Memory of J. J. Finkelstein
Connecticut Academy of Arts and Sciences, Memoir 19

unlikely, since Hebrew has its own perfectly adequate term for that, namely, *niddah* (Zimmerli[9]).

Recent translations have gone separate ways: Zimmerli emends to *ḥospek* and renders *nḥštk* "pudendum" according to context, giving up on an etymology. The New English Bible (1970) and the New American Bible (1970) render, respectively, "You have been prodigal in your excesses" (cf. Cooke), and "You poured out your lust."

Progress can be made by a closer look at Rashi and a more accurate definition of *naḫšātu*. After connecting *nḥštk* with the Mishnaic "bottom of an oven," Rashi glosses the entire phrase thus: "Out of great lust for fornication your 'fountain' flowed (*zab mᵊqorek*)."[10] What Rashi intended may be clarified by a talmudic anecdote in Sanhedrin 92b:

> Among the exiles carried off by Nebuchadnezzar were lads who put the sun to shame by their beauty. When the Chaldean women saw them, they began to discharge copiously (*šopᵊᶜot zabot*). They told it to their husbands, who told it to the king, who ordered that the lads be slain. Still the women kept discharging copiously [at the sight of the slain bodies], until the corpses were disfigured by trampling at the king's order.

The proper sense of *naḫšātu*, with all due respect to a scholarly tradition that is now embodied in von Soden's Akkadisches Handwörterbuch, cannot be menstruation, as the following citations from a text containing cures for women's ailments show:

> KAR 194 i 17 (=21): INIM.INIM MA *sinništu ša na-aḫ-šá-te marṣat*, "Incantation for a woman who suffers from *naḫšātu*."
>
> KAR 194 i 24: *na-aḫ-šá-tu ipparrasā*, "(then) the *naḫšātu* will stop."
>
> KAR 194 i 29: *ina šērim la patan išatti na-aḫ-šá-tu ipparrasā*, "[after going through the prescribed ritual] let her drink of it in the morning, not having eaten; the *naḫšātu* will then stop."[11]

From these citations it is certain that an abnormal discharge is meant. This is implied not only by the connection with *marāṣu* "be sick," but especially by the measures designed to put a stop to it: women do not resort to incantations and potions to put a stop to their normal monthly courses. Further evidence of the same is the appearance of the term in the apodosis of a liver omen (KAR 153 rev. 12: *bēltum muruṣ na-aḫ-šá-ti marṣat* "(this signifies that) the lady will be sick with the *naḫšātu* sickness."[12]

Rashi, the talmudic anecdote, and the Akkadian pathological term fall together. Hebrew *zwb* "flow," when used of a genital discharge, means always and only an abnormal one.[13] The anecdote's adverbial *šopᵊᶜot* "copiously" adds a detail that brings the *zabot* "discharging women" in question as close as possible to the basic sense of overflowing abundance underlying *naḫšātu*. Together, the data indicate that Hebrew *nḥšt* in Ezekiel 16 is a cognate of the Akkadian term,[14] and, like it, signifies an abnormal female genital outflow (conceived of as an excess or overflow, hence a derivative of *nḫš* = *naḫāšu* "be rich, abundant"). In the phrase *hiššapek nᵊḥuštek*, the sense is not pathological but erotic, a reference to an outpouring of the "distillation" of the lust-ridden harlot of the parable. The phrase may be rendered in more familiar terms "your 'juice' poured out."[15]

J. J. Finkelstein's lonely *niḫeš* of Genesis 30 thus acquires a racy etymological companion.

9. In Biblischer Kommentar (1958) p. 339.

10. Glossing *nḥštk* by "fountain" (i.e., the womb, the source of the discharge), Rashi obtains an acceptable construction with *hiššapek*. In Mishnaic Hebrew, a container can be *nišpak*, the reference being, of course, to its content: *ḥabit . . . šennišpᵊka* "a wine-cask that (=whose content) was poured out" (Terumot 11.7).

11. This tablet was republished in F. Köcher, Die babylonisch-assyrische Medizin 3 (Berlin, 1964) no. 237. Many years ago, Åke Sjöberg supplied these lines to me from the files of the CAD; before completing this article, I benefited from discussing them with Zvi Abusch. To both colleagues I give my thanks.

12. This reference was supplied to me by Åke Sjöberg. In his article "Frauenkrankheiten" in RLA 3 109, R. Labat defines *naḫšātu* as "excessively strong menstrual bleeding or leukorrhea"—two very different things! Labat connects "water issuing from the internal genitals of a woman," mentioned elsewhere on this tablet, with *naḫšātu*. The connection is not certain, but if it is correct, calling the issue water rather than blood works against defining it as menstrual. Blood is not mentioned in connection with any of the references to *naḫšātu* listed above.

13. In the case of a female, usually, but not necessarily, bloody; in Nidda 32b a white discharge (leukorrhea) is expressly distinguished from a bloody one, and declared non-polluting.

14. The vocalization *nᵊḥuštek* assimilates the word to the pattern of *nᵊḥošet* "copper." If it is indeed cognate with *naḫšātu*, it cannot be related to *nᵊḥošet*, for *nᵊḥuštek* has *ḫ* and *nᵊḥošet ḥ* underlying the present Hebrew homographs. The assimilation to "copper" may reflect a late speculative etymology similar to that of Geiger adduced in note 4 above. The formal Hebrew equivalent of the Akkadian *naḫšātu* (pl.) would be °*nᵊḫašot*; singular, with suffix (suiting the graph in Ezek. 16:36), °*naḫšatek*.

15. On distillation see Th. H. Van de Velde, Ideal Marriage (New York, 1970) pp. 137, 177. Copious distillation is a motif of hypersexuality in erotic literature (e.g., H. Miller, Tropic of Capricorn [New York, 1961] p. 182); is Ezek. 16:36 the earliest occurrence of this motif?

našû-nadānu AND ITS CONGENERS

Jonas C. Greenfield
The Hebrew University

J. J. Finkelstein is not usually thought of as a lexicographer, yet he was always interested in words, their meaning, impact and significance. Since he received early training in both Hebrew and Aramaic, he was always interested in the interrelationship between Akkadian and the West Semitic dialects; in almost all of his articles there is a contribution to lexicography, especially in the legal sphere.

1. The coordinate use of the verbs *našû-nadānu* to form a formula of conveyance and transfer of property is best known to Assyriologists from the Akkadian texts excavated at Ras Shamra. In these texts it is usually expressed as *išši/ittaši-iddin/ittadin* and is used for the royal grant. The formula caused some difficulty for J. Nougayrol who published and translated the texts containing this formula in PRU 3 (and subsequently in PRU 6)[1] and also to G. Boyer who provided the legal commentary to PRU 3.[2] It was E. A. Speiser, in his review of that volume, who clarified the usage of this formula with elegance and established its meaning with precision.[3] Only minor nuances have been added to his study by subsequent writers.[4] Boyer did a service to scholarship by calling attention to the *išši-iddin* formula in the Hittite landgrants which at that time were known primarily from the pioneering study of H. G. Güterbock.[5]

K. K. Riemschneider's "Die hethitischen Landschenkungsurkunden" made available all the texts then known and *inter alia* elucidated the use of the *išši-iddin* formula in these texts.[6] He compared the material from Ugarit, and pointed out that although the use of the formula was more limited in the Hittite texts, it was clear that there was a direct relationship between the use of the formula in the two groups of texts. Also, both used a royal seal to affirm the transaction. Many of the texts from Boğazköy are sealed with the Tabarna seal—that is, an archaic seal which does not mention a specific ruler—and the text itself does not identify the ruler who is bestowing the grant. Further texts were published in copy by H. Otten in an article on the seal of Taḫurwaili,[7] and a very interesting landgrant excavated at Inandik was published recently with detailed commentary by K. Balkan.[8] Güterbock, Riemschneider, T. Beran, and H. Otten were of the opinion that the landgrants with the Tabarna seal were executed during the second half of the sixteenth century B.C., considerably earlier than the material from Ugarit.[9] Balkan is of the opinion, based on paleographic and other considerations, that these landgrants are to be dated to Ḫattusilis I.[10] If this is correct then an even longer period is available for the development of the simple landgrant to the type known from the fourteenth-thirteenth centuries.

The basic pattern of these landgrants is: (a) introduction referring to the seal used; (b) item granted; (c) the *našû-nadānu* formula; (d) vindication clause; (e) sanctions; (f) place and name of witnesses and scribe. Clause (c) usually reads: LUGAL.GAL *išši-ma ana* PN *iddin*; clause (d): *urram šēram ana* PN *ana* DUMU.MEŠ-*šu mamman la iraggum*, "in the future no one will raise a claim against PN or his sons." Clause (e) contains the interesting remark that *awat Tabarna* LUGAL.GAL *ša* AN.BAR *ša la nadiam ša la šebērim ša ušpaḫḫu* SAG.DU-*šu inakkisu*, "the king's word is iron; it should not be thrown (into water); it should not be broken; he who changes it, his head will be cut off."[11] In some of the texts the item granted is simply stated, in others there is a detailed listing.

1. Cf. PRU 3 224.

2. See his "Etude Juridique" in PRU 3 283-308, particularly p. 286ff. (reprinted in his Mélanges d'histoire du droit oriental [Paris, 1965] pp. 111-51.

3. E. A. Speiser, "Akkadian Documents from Ras Shamra," JAOS 75 (1955) 154-65, particularly 157-61.

4. C. J. Labuschagne, "The *našû-nadānu* Formula and Its Biblical Equivalent," in Travels in the World of the Old Testament, Studies Presented to Prof. M. A. Beek at the Occasion of his 65th Birthday (Assen, 1974) pp. 176-80.

5. H. G. Güterbock, Siegel aus Bogazköy 1, AfO Beiheft 5 (194) 47-55.

6. K. K. Riemschneider, "Die hethitischen Landschenkungsurkunden," MIO 6 (1958) 321-81.

7. H. Otten, "Das Siegel des hethitischen Grosskönigs Taḫurwaili," MDOG 103 (1971) 59-68.

8. K. Balkan, Eine Schenkungsurkunde aus der althethitischen Zeit, Gefunden in Inandık, 1966, Anadolu Medeniyetlerini Araştırma vakfo yayınları 1 (Ankara, 1973).

9. Cf. Balkan, Schenkungsurkunde pp. 68-70 for a survey of opinions.

10. Balkan, Schenkungsurkunde pp. 70-77.

11. Cf. Balkan, Schenkungsurkunde p. 67 for variants. There is no reason to assume that the original was written on iron, as some scholars have done; the phrase refers simply to the immutability of the royal decree and its indestructible nature. Although *ša la nadiam* can be translated "sie sind nicht zu verwerfen," I prefer my translation since the two possible modes of destroying a clay tablet would be dissolving it in water or smashing it.

Ancient Near Eastern Studies in Memory of J. J. Finkelstein
Connecticut Academy of Arts and Sciences, Memoir 19

Balkan's landgrant text differs from the others published previously. It notes the occasion for the grant, an adoption-marriage, and the father-in-law's granting of a marriage gift (NÍG.BA). It also reports the granting, by the king, of the father-in-law's son to the household of a goddess.[12] The text contains the usual formulae clauses (c), (d), and (e). As Balkan pointed out, only one other known Hittite landgrant reports the circumstances of the grant (LS 19). That is also the only other text in which a person is granted by the king to the household of a temple. Its grant formula uses *leqû-nadānu* rather than the usual *našû-nadānu*. Balkan also discussed the variant formula *nadānu-šakānu* found in LS 3.[13] Riemschneider had proposed that that aberrant formula was due to the Hittite scribe's not knowing the correct translation for the underlying Hittite expression. But the recurrence of this formula (in all likelihood in LS 4 and LS 1312u) makes this unlikely.[14] It is also quite unlikely that Hittite formulae stood behind the text while the Akkadian formulae were operative in these texts.[15]

There are then three possible formulae in the grant section of these texts: (1) *našû-nadānu*; (2) *našû-šakānu* and (3) *leqû-nadānu*. Güterbock, in 1939, perceived that the first formula is used when property is granted to a person, and the second when property is granted to an institution.[16] To these should be added the third, used when a person is granted to an institution. One should also note that in LS 4:15-16 an enigmatic use of *leqû-nadānu* is found. The Hittite landgrant texts, as far as can be established, predate the Empire period, except for the grant dated to Arnuwandas I (LS 1).[17] There is a gap of almost two hundred years until we reach the texts in Hittite from the time of Ḫattusilis III-Tudḫaliyas IV, to be discussed below. For the history of landgrants and the *našû-nadānu* formula one must now turn to Ugarit.

2. The use of the royal seal and the *našû-nadānu* formula serve to bring together the texts from Ḫattusas and Ugarit under the rubric of royal grants, but there are differences between them. The Hittite texts are simpler in form and are simply grants. They are limited on the whole to real-estate; at times livestock and retainers associated with the household are also affected by the grant. None of the Hittite texts are commercial. Speiser, however, has shown that the situation in Ugarit is more complex, that the *našû-nadānu* formula was used for various types of transfer and conveyance, and that at times this included sale.[18] Since Speiser has analyzed these texts there is no need to go into detail here, but two texts should be mentioned since there will be occasion to refer to them below: (a) RS 16.244 (PRU 3 p. 93) in which the rights to the tithes of a city are granted; and (b) RS 16.356 (PRU 3 pp. 71-72) in which a document is granted.[19] Riemschneider has shown that there are similarities and differences in the formulation of the various clauses of the grants[20]; the usual non-royal grant at Ugarit is not witnessed while the royal grants are all witnessed. The texts from Ugarit are replete with information concerning the circumstances of the grant, concerning the social status of the participants and ensuing changes in their status, their duties and privileges. In these texts only real-estate is explicitly mentioned, although one may assume that produce, livestock and perhaps retainers (summed up in the heading *qadu gabbi mimmušu*) were also included in the transfer.

One may ask if the scribes of Ugarit were really at home with the *našû-nadānu* formula. It is true that they use it with more flexibility than the Hittite scribes who know only the preterite *iššî-iddin*; yet this may have become for the scribes of Ugarit a frozen formula which had only juridical meaning. Thus we find, as Speiser already noted, that along side of the *našû-nadānu* formula, there is a rarer *nadānu-nadānu* formula[21] which is reflected in the two royal grants in Ugaritic (PRU 2 8 and 9) where the king has *ytn* "taken" (lit. "given") the field of PN_1 and given it *ytn.nn* to PN_2. In the final clause of these grants, the clause prohibiting the alienation of the property from the grantee, the verb *našû* is not used, but in its stead we find *leqû*. The usual formula is: *urram šēram mannumma/mamman . . . ištu qati* PN *la ileqqi*, but at times the verb *leqû* is replaced by *ekēmu*, "to remove." This is phrased in Ugaritic as *šḥr ʿlmt bnš bnšm/mnk mnkm lyqḥnn/lyqḥ bd* PN . . . *ʿd ʿlm*, "in the future no one shall take it from the hand of PN . . . forever."

12. Is the son-in-law to replace the son as heir? Is the son given a prebend as a compensation?

13. Balkan, Schenkungsurkunde pp. 48-50.

14. Riemschneider, Landschenkungsurkunden p. 332 n. 41; the Hittite texts dealt with below show that the expression normally used was "to give," not "to place."

15. The practice of Hittitologists to transliterate the Akkadian texts in these landgrants as if they were composed of ideograms is misleading for these are essentially Akkadian texts based on Old Babylonian formulae.

16. Siegel 1 48 n. 178.

17. Güterbock, Siegel 1 32-38, argued cogently that this document belonged to Arnuwandas I. This has now been firmly established; cf. P. H. J. Houwink ten Cate, The Records of the Early Hittite Empire (c. 1450-1380 B.C.) (Istanbul, 1970) p. 81.

18. Speiser, JAOS 75 (1955) 159.

19. Speiser mistakenly refers to RS 16.353.

20. Riemschneider, Landschenkungsurkunden pp. 331-33.

21. E.g. RS 16.189, p. 92; RS 16.206, p. 106; RS 16.136, p. 142; RS 16.383, p. 164.

Thus it is quite possible that the scribes of Ugarit, if they were not bound by tradition, would have used *leqû-nadānu* rather than *našû-nadānu* as the natural way of expressing transfer or conveyance of property.

3. Similarly, when we examine a group of Hittite texts from Boğazköy in which the equivalent of *našû-nadānu* is found, we see that the Hittite scribes, freed from the bonds of tradition, used the simple formulation *arḫa da-/pai-* "to take/to give." This formula is found in a group of texts from the time of Ḫattusilis III and Tudḫaliyas IV which confirms the disposition of property and also grants certain privileges. These texts, studied thirty years ago by V. Korošec, are KUB 26 43 and KUB 26 58; they were characterised by Korošec as a sort of Freibrief.[22] The treaty of Ḫattusilis III (or Tudḫaliyas IV) with Ulmi-Tešup—KBo 4 10—contains similar phraseology. In KUB 26 43, the so-called Saḫurunuwa text, the division of property made by Saḫurunuwa, a wealthy Hittite of high rank, in favor of his children and grandchildren, is recorded and approved by royal authority, witnessed by important officials and sanctioned by divine curse. Various duties, privileges, and exemptions were granted as well as a change in status for some members of the family. In this text it is stated that even if punishment be meted out by the king to a member of the family (line 64) *pirmaššikan lē danzi nat damēdani lē piianzi*, "they shall not take away his estate (lit. house) and they shall not give it to anyone else." In the similar grant for GAL-ᵈIM-as (KUB 26 58) the phrase used is (18) . . . *pirmaššikan arḫa lē* (19) *danzi nat damēdani antuḫši* (20) *damēdani warwalani lē piianzi*, "they shall not take away his estate, they shall not give it to another man, to another family (lit. seed)." Similarly the treaty of Ḫattusilis with Ulmi-Tešup of Dattasa contains a clause which provides for the house and land of Ulmi-Tešup remaining in the family despite the crime that one of his descendants might commit: (10) *pirmaššikan utneia lē arḫa danzi nat damēl warwalanaš lē piianzi*, "the house and the land they shall not take away from him, they shall not give it to the family of another." Beside the use of a functional equivalent of the *našû-nadānu* formula the texts have much in common with the royal grants from Ugarit, for as noted above they grant privileges and exemptions and record changes in rank. They are quite different in matters of form, for they continue some aspects of the Hittite landgrants.[23] Among these are: (a) the document is declared to be *amat* AN.BAR *ša la šebērim u ša la nadiam*—note the use of Akkadian rather than Hittite!; and (b) a list is provided of those who witnessed the tablet. Yet there is a modern touch which unites, as Riemschneider has noted, both the earlier and the later uses in the Ulmi-Tešup treaty (KBo 4 10 rev. 22): *natkan ziladuwa* ŠA *Ulmi-Tešup warwalani arḫa lē kuiški dai ḫannariiaššikan lē kuiški*, "no one in the future (= *urram šēram*) shall take away (= *la ileqqi*) from the family of Ulmi-Tešup not shall any one lay claim (*la iraggum*)."

4. Speiser pointed to Mishnaic Hebrew *maśśāʾ umattān* (to which I shall return below), but was unaware of other possible parallels to the *našû-nadānu* formula in Hebrew. This writer in the course of teaching various Aramaic texts from Elephantine noted parallels in both Biblical Hebrew and Aramaic. The recent essay by C. J. Labuschagne, "The *našû-nadānu* formula and its Biblical equivalent," provides an excellent survey of the Biblical material which goes beyond my collection of examples.[24] Most of the parallels use—as could be expected—the formula *lqḥ-ntn*, but there are also examples of *nṣl-ntn*.[25] Among the texts that Labuschagne has noted as using the *lqḥ-ntn* formula, I would chose the following as being truly relevant:

(1) Gen. 20:14 Abimelech conveying movable property to Abraham; and

(2) Gen. 21:27 Abraham conveying movable property to Abimelech.

God's sovereign power is expressed by *lqḥ-ntn*:

(3) II Sam. 12:11 transferring the wives of X to Y;

(4) I Kings 11:35 transferring the kingdom to another.

God's absolute power over man's life:

(5) Job 1:21 *ʾadonāy nātan weʾadonāy lāqaḥ*.

22. V. Korošec, "Einige juristische Bemerkungen zur Saḫurunuva-Urkunde KUB 26 43 =Bo 2048)" in Münchener Beitr. zu Papyrusforsch. 35 (1945) 191-222. The Hittite texts quoted here are found in Korošec's article. He did not see the relationship between these texts and the landgrants. M. Weinfeld, "The Covenant of Grant in the Old Testament and in the Ancient Near East," JAOS 90 (1970) 184-203, esp. pp. 189-90, made use of these texts and discussed some of the terminology. The formulation *arha da - pai* is also found in KUB 16 32 vs. ii 2′-3′, where a house is given to a 'Totengeist,' and ii 24′-25′, where a city is given to a 'Totengeist.' Cf. Ahmet Ünal, Hattusilis III (Heidelberg, 1974) pp. 104-109.

23. But there is no sign of the use of a royal seal on either KUB 26 43 or 58; indeed the form is that of a direct grant of the ruler whose words are witnessed by his courtiers rather than being affirmed by his seal.

24. Cf. above, n. 4.

25. Labuschagne, Studies Beek p. 180, would also consider I Kings 9:16, where the combination *lkd - ntn* is found.

It is not surprising to find terms originally used of the "great king" applied to Yahweh.[26] A skillful inversion of *lqḥ-ntn* is found in Gen. 48:21: "and now I give you (*nōtēn ləkā*) one portion more than your brothers, which I took (*lāqaḥtī*) from the Amorites with my sword and with my bow."[27]

More complicated is the use of the *lqḥ-ntn* formula in I Sam. 8:10-18, the "rule of the king" pericope, where the people are warned by Samuel about the abuse of absolute power on the part of a future king. It has been shown by I. Mendelsohn and others that Samuel's words were based on Canaanite precedent.[28] Examination of the terminology used in this pericope shows that the writer was subtler than merely repeating *lqḥ* and *ntn*. In the following, the verses are set out schematically:

(1)	v. 11	*yiqqaḥ wəśām*	conscription of males to royal service
	v. 12	*wəlāśūm*	continuation of previous verse
	v. 13	*yiqqaḥ*	conscription of females to royal service
(2)	v. 14	*yiqqaḥ wənātan*	fields, vineyards, olive groves confiscted and granted to royal courtiers
(3)	v. 15	*yaᶜśor wənātan*	granting tithes to courtiers
(4)	v. 16	*yiqqaḥ wəᶜāśā limlaᶜkto*	confiscating staff, servants, and beasts for royal use.

The more familiar phrase *lqḥ-ntn* (no. 2) is limited in this pericope to the case of the king's transfer of land to his courtiers. It matches the use of *našû-nadānu* in the Hittite landgrants and in the Akkadian texts from Ugarit. The phrase *yaᶜśor wənātan* (no. 3) has no direct match in the texts from Ugarit, but at least one of the *našû-nadānu* texts (RS 16.244), referred to above, grants to the *rābiṣu* of a certain town various imposts as well as the *maᶜšaru* (= Heb. *maᶜaśer*) and this text may very will serve as a parallel to our no. (3).[29] The phrase *yiqqaḥ wəśam* which is found in v. 11 and in part in vv. 12-13, should be compared with *iššī-ma ana* X *iškun* found, as mentioned above, in LS 3. In that text property is granted to an institution rather than to a person. The use in I Sam. 8:11-13 is similar, for humans are not being granted to a particular person but are being conscripted to various services in the royal household; *śām*, the semantic equivalent of *šakānu*, is appropriate. The last phrase (4) which serves as the culmination of the king's power has no parallel in the landgrant texts.[30]

Labuschagne also pointed to the use of the *hiphil* of *nṣl*, usually "to deliver, save," as meaning "to take," i.e. equal to *našû* in Gen. 31:9. In this verse God has granted *hnṣl-ntn* Laban's wealth to Jacob; the use of this formula in Aramaic is discussed below.[31]

5. It is clear that *našû-nadānu* and its cognates are all from the West, but it is too early to speculate about the source of the phrase. Perhaps the discovery and publication of more texts in Akkadian from the Old Babylonian period or earlier from Syria will make it possible to pinpoint the source from which the Hittites derived the format and phraseology of their landgrants. It is, of course, not surprising that the phrase (*našû-nadānu*) is lacking in the texts recently studied and re-edited by Postgate in Neo-Assyrian Royal Grants and Decrees.[32] That these texts continue the tradition of royal grants known from the Hittite and Ugaritic texts may be seen from their general format and from the use of the royal seal. There is also evidence of Aramaic influence in the wording of the texts, yet the texts are Assyrian and not from the West. However, even in Assyrian texts, a reflex of the *našû-nadānu* may be discerned. In a series of legal texts the obligation of PN_1 to present PN_2—in all likelihood a slave—to PN_3 is recorded. In these texts, ARU 223, ARU 227 (and its duplicate ARU 228) and Tell Halaf no. 111, the formula preceding the penalty is *šumma*

26. Cf. Pss. 47 and 48, where the two West Semitic equivalents of LUGAL.GAL / *šarru rabû, melek rab* and *melek gādōl*, are found.

27. I owe this to my colleague Prof. M. Weinfeld of the Hebrew University.

28. Cf. I. Mendelsohn, BASOR 143 (1956) 17-22; Z. Ben-Barak, The Manner of the King and the Manner of the Kingdom (Hebrew University diss. [in Hebrew], 1972) pp. 117-19. Mrs. Ben-Barak's dissertation deals with these texts in detail.

29. For the tithe at Ugarit cf. Mrs. Ben-Barak's dissertation, and most recently, M. Heltzer, "On Tithe Paid in Grain in Ugarit," IEJ 25 (1975) 124-28.

30. For this phrase cf. P. A. H. de Boer, "I Samuel 8, verse 16b" in Studies Beek 27-29; J. C. Greenfield, "Iranian or Semitic," in Monumentum H. S. Nyberg 1 (Leiden, 1975) 311-16.

31. For a variety of reasons Num. 11:15, also suggested by Labuschagne, seems less likely. We shall see *nṣl - ntn* in an Aramaic text below. Is this an Aramaism in the speech of Laban's daughters?

32. (Rome, 1969). There is the distinct possibility that in these texts the phrase *ša ina ṣilliya iqnû*, "which he acquired under my protection" (Postgate, Royal Grants p. 28, 9:24) followed by *addin* (line 29) equals the *našû - nadānu* formula. As in the royal grants from Ugarit and in the Hittite texts, exemption from various taxes and services are part of the grant.

la naṣṣa la iddin, "if he has not handed over."[33] The exact circumstances are not clear in any of the texts. One of them—that from Tell Halaf—is clearly from an area in which there were many Arameans; it is quite possible that the same is true of the other texts. Be that as it may, the phrase has lost all of its legal significance. Riemschneider noted one occurrence in a Neo-Babylonian text. NRU 81 records the sale of a slave, previously held as a pledge. The contract also guarantees the delivery of the document recording that pledge to the purchaser of the slave: *uʾiltam . . . inaššī-ma ana* PN *inamdin*. The use of the *našû-nadānu* formula for the delivery of a document at Ugarit was mentioned above. In both cases the phrase simply means that the goods must be delivered.

6. In two documents of the Mibṭaḥia archive from Elephantine (CAP 8, 9) reflexes of the *našû-nadānu* formula are found, but two different formulae are used.[34] In CAP 8, a document recording the gift of a house by Maḥseia to his daughter Mibṭaḥia, the donor asserts that he no longer has the right to give the house to anyone else. This is phrased as follows (lines 18-19): *wʾp ʾnh mḥsyh mḥr ʾw ywm ʾḥrn lʾ ʾhnṣl mnky lmntn lʾḥrnn*, "Moreover, tomorrow or another day, I Maḥseia shall not give it to others." The verbs *hnṣl-ntn*, already met with above in Biblical Hebrew, are also used here. The other occurrence is CAP 9, where Mibṭaḥia's husband is granted certain privileges in the same house. Although the scribe is the same ʿAtarshuri bar Nabuzeribni, he chose a different phrase when limiting Mibṭaḥia's rights in the house (line 9): *lʾ šlyṭh hy lmlqḥh wlmntnh lʾḥrnn*, "she shall have no right to give it to others." The usual interpretation of *hnṣl* is "to remove by force," but it is clear that both phrases simply mean the transfer of property to another.

Outside of the legal document from Elephantine the phrase occurs in the Proverbs of Aḥiqar.[35] Without attempting to explicate the proverb in its entirety, I note that the phrase *lqḥ-ntn* is used in it. The text reads (lines 171-172): ***hn yʾḥdn ršyʿʾ bknpy lbšk šbq bydh ʾḥr ʾdny lšmš hw ylqḥ zylh wyntn lk***, "If the wicked man seizes the corner of your garment, leave it in his hand; then draw near to Shamash. He will grant you his." Although the last phrase could be simply translated "He will take his and give it to you," the sovereign power of Shamash, god of justice, emerges with greater clarity when the two verbs are seen as part of a formula with a legal past.[36]

7. Let us now return to the phrase *maśśāʾ umattān* with which Speiser compared the *našû-nadānu* formula. Speiser was aware of the fact that in Mishnaic Hebrew the phrase had lost any remnant of its significance as a term of transference or conveyance and had acquired the meaning "business, dealings, intercourse, affairs." But the antique flavor of the term may be felt by the use of *lāśēʾt wᵊlātēt*, the Biblical Hebrew infinitives, rather than the typically Mishnaic *liśśāʾ wᵊlittēn*.[37] In addition to *maśśāʾ umattān* there is also *miqqaḥ umimkār*, with the same meaning; it is obviously a later term. A reflex of the earlier use of these terms may be found in the *kyrieia* clause of Aramaic and Syriac sales documents in which the purchaser is fully empowered *lmqnh wlmzbn* /*lmqnʾ wlmzbnw*, which cannot mean "to acquire and to sell," but must mean "to dispose of freely." Further reflexes of *našû-nadānu* may be found in the formulae *nsb-yhb* and *šql-ṭry*, both frequently used in Jewish Palestinian and Jewish Babylonian Aramaic respectively, with the same meaning as ***maśśāʾ umattān***. The true equivalent of ***našû-nadānu*** in Mishnaic Hebrew is ***nṭl-ntn***, for ***nṭl*** has replaced ***lqḥ*** in Mishnaic Hebrew in most of the common usages of "to take." The phrase is found in apt usage in Genesis Rabba to Genesis 1:1 (ed. Theodor-Albeck p. 5), which declares that the world belongs to God "who when he wished he gave (*ntn*) it to you and when he wished he took (*nṭl*) it from you and gave (*ntn*) it to us." In this Midrash God functions as the "Great King," granting property to whomsoever he wishes. This usage of *ntn* - *nṭl* is found elsewhere in Mishnaic Hebrew.[38]

33. For the alleged verb *naṣṣ* as a form of *našû*, cf. S. Parpola, "The Alleged Middle/Neo-Assyrian Irregular Verb **naṣṣ* and the Assyrian Sound Change /š/ > /ṣ/," Assur 1/1 (1974).

34. Cf. B. Porten and J. C. Greenfield, Jews of Elephantine and Aramaeans of Syene (Jerusalem, 1974) pp. 8-15.

35. As E. Y. Kutscher and this writer have variously pointed out, the language of the proverbs differs from the language of the frame-work story. The proverbs are written in the dialect of North Syria - Assyria.

36. For the method, cf. J. C. Greenfield, "The Background and Parallel to a Proverb of Ahiqar," in Hommages à André Dupont-Sommer (Paris, 1971) pp. 49-59.

37. I owe this insight to Dr. M. Sokoloff.

38. Cf. Sifra Tsav, sec. 17:5 (ed. Weiss p. 44a).

INSCRIBED CYLINDERS AND CYLINDER FRAGMENTS IN THE ASHMOLEAN MUSEUM, OXFORD

O. R. Gurney
Oxford

This publication of all the inscribed cylinders and cylinder fragments in the Ashmolean Museum is dedicated to J. J. Finkelstein in memory of many happy months spent with him in Ankara in 1955, while working on the Sultantepe tablets, and again during his sabbatical leave in Oxford in 1974. They are listed roughly in chronological order.

1924-616. Part of an upright cylinder, inscribed (like a prism) in (probably six) columns, of which parts of the last three are preserved. Diam. 67 mm., ht. 55 mm. Sumerian. Provenance: Kish, Uhaimir, temple area, great wall E-F beneath brickwork. Exc. no. HMR 194. Plate I.

col. i′

[. . . . . .]-ra
[g]ù-dé-a
lugal dalla(?)
lugal íd.idigna
lugal NE-SAG(?)
x-NE-x
x me-te(?)-x

col. ii′

šul ka-tar-a x[
íd-dè nu-bal-a
lugal am-am kur um um
ká ki-bal-dím
giš.tukul-kiši-dím
dúb-dúb-a

col. iii′

x[
é(?) [
lú [
(end)

In the left column too little, unfortunately, is preserved to show whether gù-dé-a is the name of the famous Ensi of Lagash or an epithet, "eloquent," or the like, though it is perhaps unlikely that the name of the author(?) of the inscription would appear in the fourth column. The rest of the text seems to consist of (further?) epithets, the first two of these being "heroic king"[1] and "king of the River Tigris," both apparently unknown. The meaning of the middle column is not clear to me.

1924-263. Hollow barrel cylinder, complete. Length 137 mm., diam. 98 mm. Inscription of Sin-iddinam of Larsa, duplicate of "David hollow barrel cylinder" published by Langdon, OECT 2 7. Bought in Baghdad in 1923, provenance unknown. This cylinder is badly chipped and weathered and might repay further study by a Sumerologist. Variants: (i 16) ki(?)-bi-šè, (25) apparently gù-in-ne-ša$_6$-ša$_6$, (28) ba-al-la-da, (36) first line of col. ii, (ii 1) nothing after dingir-mu, (2) á-daḫ-mu-ta, nothing after this, (3) á-kal-maḫ-[d]nanna-dingir-kù-ta, (5) íd-ḫe-gál-la, (7) line omitted, (8) last sign mu, (16) in two lines, (19) sign after še appears to be the numeral 1, possibly followed by a damaged gur, (25-26) in one line, (32) in two lines. Not copied.

1924-621. Left end of barrel cylinder. Max. diam. c. 90 mm. Provenance: Kish, Uhaimir, house ruins, Exc. no. HMR 860. Samsuiluna, Inscr. 'C,' Akkadian, lines 4-14 and 57-65 (Sollberger, RA 63 [1969] 29ff.). Variants: (5) *in i-gi$_4$-gi$_4$*, (10) *šu-ba-as-su-nu.* Plate I.

1924-1545. Fragment from middle of barrel cylinder. Diam. 90 mm. Provenance: Kish, Uhaimir, surface. Exc. no. HMR 170. Samsuiluna, Inscr. 'C,' Sumerian, lines 22-35 and 80-89 (Sollberger, RA 63 [1969] 29ff.). The text restores the ends of lines corresponding to the Akkadian 22-31 and the beginnings of lines corresponding to Akkadian 84-89, which were previously missing. In line 81 lugal is absolutely clear, and 1929-137 (Sollberger's 'Sum. B') appears to have the same sign, as read by Langdon (collated). It is presumably a scribal error, since lú is undoubtedly required. Plate I.

1931-142. Fragment from left end of barrel cylinder. Max. diam. c. 80 mm. Provenance: Kish, Ingharra YW 0.50 m. Akkadian. The inscription resembles Samsuiluna Inscr. 'C,' lines 92-100. Plate I.

1′ [d]*en-líl er-ṣe-tim r*[*u- . . .*]
2′ GIŠ.TUKUL.GIŠ.TUKUL-*šu u*[*š?-te-še-ir* KASKAL-*am?*]
3′ *a-na ša-qá-áš za-i-ri ú-ša-a*[*r-di*]
4′ [d]*za-ba$_4$-ba$_4$ ù* [d]INANA EN.MEŠ [. . .]

1. Not listed by M.-J. Seux, Épithètes. Cf. AHw. s.v. *mamlu.*

Ancient Near Eastern Studies in Memory of J. J. Finkelstein
Connecticut Academy of Arts and Sciences, Memoir 19

[a-n]a šu-um-qú-ut a[-a-bi-šu]
[a-n]a ka-ša-ad! ir-ni-i[t-ti-šu]
[il]-li-ku re-ṣu-u[s-su]
[^{d}*na-bi-u]m-šu-mi-iš-ku-un* NUN [. . .]

ruler of the underworld [. . .]
He [prepared] his weapons, [an expedition(?)]
to crush his enemies he led.
Zababa and Ishtar, lords [. . .]
to overthrow [his] enemies [. . .]
to gain victory for him [. . .]
went to his aid. [. . .]
[Nabiu]m-šumi-iškun(?) the prince(?) [. . .]

If the restoration of line 8′ is correct, this would appear to give the name of the author of the inscription; yet names of this type are not attested till a much later period (Brinkman, Political History p. 224). The script of this cylinder is good Old Babylonian, and the provenance precludes a date later than this.[2]

1924-622. Part of a barrel cylinder with right end. Max. diam. 70 mm., min. diam. 40 mm., length 101 mm. Bought from Sheikh Attiyah who said it came from Khan Haswa, 25 miles NW of Kish. Old Babylonian funerary inscription, Akkadian. Previous publication: Langdon, Kish I 34 no. 2 (copy only). The inscription runs round the entire circumference without any indication of beginning and end. It has been assumed that Langdon assessed this correctly. The name ^{md}*Šamaš-illati(ti)* in the left column could well be that of the author of the inscription and owner of the grave. Plate II.

Right column:

(1) [*ša*] KI.MAḪ (2) [*an*]-*na-a* (3) *i!-pe-tu-ú*[3] (4) *a-na la-bi-ir-ti* (5) *ù-la i-ke-ši-ru* (6) ^{d}*a-nu-um* (7) ^{d}*en-líl* (8) *ù* ^{d}*é-a* (9) ŠE.NUMUN-*šu* (10) *li-il-qu-*tu_4 (11) ^{d}*a-nun-na* (12) *i-na ša-ap-la-ti* (13) *pe-ri-iḫ-šu* (14) [*li-ḫ*]*a-al-li-qu* (15-20) [. . .]

"Whoever opens this tomb and does not repair it for a long time,[4] may Anu, Enlil, and Ea destroy his progeny, may the Anunnaki in the netherworld annihilate his offspring."

1929-817. Fragment from the base of an upright cylinder, inscribed in columns. Diam. c. 110 mm., ht. 48 mm. Provenance: Kish, Ingharra, C-4, 2 m. Akkadian, perhaps Middle Babylonian (archaizing).[5] Plate II.

Right column:

(1′) ÌR *ša* [. . .] (2′) *ti-ri-iṣ* [*qa-at* . . .] (3′) *iṭ-ri-in-ni i-na* [. . .] (4′) *šu-zi-bi-ni i-na* PAP.[ḪAL . . .]

"servant of . . . , favourite of . . . , spare me from . . . , save me from trouble . . ."

1922-186. Fragment from middle of large hollow barrel cylinder. Diam. c. 200 mm., thickness c. 30 mm. Provenance unknown, Weld-Blundell collection. Nebuchadnezzar Cyl. III 3, according to the numeration of P. R. Berger, Die neubabylonischen Königsinschriften, AOAT 4/1 (= Langdon, no. 1), col. ii 14-24. Variant: (18) apparently *še-ip-šu* for *ki-bi-ir-šu* "its bank." Plate III.

1922-187. Fragment from middle of (apparently solid) barrel cylinder. Diam. 80 mm. Provenance unknown, Weld-Blundell collection. Nebuchadnezzar Cyl. III 1 (= Langdon, no. 12), col. i 4-11, ii 9-19. The script is contemporary (Neo-Babylonian), not archaizing. Variants: (5) *ki-it-tim,* (9) *ni-šì;* different division of lines in col. ii. Plate III.

1924-1245. Fragment of large hollow cylinder or truncated cone (two pieces joined). Diam. c. 210 mm., thickness 12 mm. Provenance: Kish, Uhaimir, house ruins, surface; exc. no. HMR 856 a, b. Nebuchadnezzar Cyl. III 8 (PBS 15 79, Langdon no. 20), col. i 1-7, 63-68, 68-74, col. ii 47-56, but col. ii begins in the middle of

2. For information on the provenance of the objects I am indebted to the researches of P. R. S. Moorey and McGuire Gibson. For Sounding Yw at Ingharra, see Moorey in Iraq 28 (1966) 32.

3. Read *ú-pe-tu-ú* by Langdon and CAD s.v. *kimāḫu*. The sign is badly worn.

4. So CAD s.v. *labirtu*, but "for the future" s.v. *kašāru*.

5. In the 'C' trenches "the tablets vary from archaic to Achaemenian texts" (Moorey, Iraq 28 [1966] 32). The material of this piece is coarse architectural clay (like a brick). Dr. Moorey suggests to me that it might be part of a clay nail. But the inscription in columns would be unusual.

line 68 of the Philadelphia cylinder and the line division is quite different. Variants: (i 1) *ru-ba-a*, (2) [*iš-š*]*a-ak-ku*, (4) *er-šu*, (6) [*ta-ši*]*m-tum*, (7) *aš-ri sa-an-qá*, (65) *ú-ra-at-tì*, (66) *pa-a-ti*, (68) *ù*, *ma-ri*, (72) *ek-du-tim*, *si-ip-pi-e*, (73) *e-ri-bi*, (ii 49) PA-RI-IM, (50) *ra-bí-tì*, (52) *ša-da-niš* (54) *e-pú-uš*. Plate III.

1924-1032. Right end of barrel cylinder, apparently solid. Diam. c. 160 mm. No excavation number or provenance recorded, but discovery mentioned by Langdon, JRAS 1929 379. Nebuchadnezzar Cyl. III 8, col. iii 66-81. Variants: (67) [*ú-ma-ì*]*r-an-*[*ni*], (73) [*ti-iz-qa*]*-ri*, (77-78) [^{d}*nabû-ap-lu-ú-ṣ*]*u-úr* LUGAL KÁ.DIN[GIR.RA], (80) [*é-dub-b*]*u*. Plate III.

1969-584. Small fragment of hollow barrel cylinder. 64×48 mm., thickness 10 mm. Provenance: Kish, no details. Nebuchadnezzar Cyl. III 8, col. i 27-35. Variant: (35) *zi-qu-rat*. Plate IV.

1939-432. Large cylinder, or truncated cone, complete. Max. diam. 130 mm., min. diam. 110 mm., length 195 mm. Presented by Mr. R. W. ffennell, provenance unknown. Duplicate of Nebuchadnezzar Cyl. III 2. Accession reported in Ashmolean Museum, Report of the Visitors 1939 11, with photograph. Not copied. Identical with Rm. 673 except for following variants (line numbers according to Langdon no. 1): (3) *iš-ša-ak-ka*, (11) *ra-bu-ù* over erasure, (ii 5) *še-lal-ti-šu*, (12) *ša ma-na-a-am šar ma-aḫ-ri-im*, (29) ^{d}LUGAL.A.TU.LIŠ, (38) *ši-bi-ir*$_{4}$*-ši-in*, (iii 3) *a-ba-ṭi-il-šu*.

1969-585. Small fragment from left end of small barrel cylinder. Max. diam. c. 40 mm., min. diam. c. 30 mm. Provenance: Kish, Mound W. Exc. no. 1657, registered in 1924. Duplicate of 1969-582. Inscription of Nabonidus, hitherto unknown.

1969-582. Fragment from left end of small barrel cylinder. Max. diam. c. 75 mm., min. diam. c. 40 mm. Provenance: Kish, no details. Duplicate of 1969-585.

[. . .] *x nu du ga ga*
[*ša a-na é-sag-í*]*l ù é-zi-*[*da*]
[*la ip-pa-r*]*a-ak-ku-ú ka-a-*[*a-na*][6]
[*a-n*]*a* DINGIR.GAL.GAL *su-ud-du-ru i-*[. . .]
ud-du-šu ma-ḫa-zi DINGIR.MEŠ *iš-te-ni-ʾ-*[*ú* . . .]
DUMU ^{md}*na-bi-um-ba-la-aṭ-su-*[*iq-bi*]
ru-bu-ú e-em-qá [*a-na-ku*]
i-nu-um ^{d}*marduk be-el ra-*[*bu-ú*]
a-na be-lu-ut ma-a-ti ib-bu-ú [*ni-bi-ti*]
i-na na-ap-ḫa-ar ṣa-al-ma-at qá-q[*á-di*]
⸢*ú-šar*⸣*-bu-ú zi-ik-ri*[7] [. . .]
ni-ši ki-ib-ra-a-ti ir-bi-i[*t-ti*]
[*a*]*-na re-é-ú-ti id-di-*[*nam*]
[. . .] *ba-ú-la-a-ti-šu*[. . .] *i-d*[*in*?]
. . . .
. . . .
[*ki-i*]*b-ra-at ir-bi*[*t-ti*]

. . . .
[who towards Esag]il and Ezida
constantly [does not] fail,
(who) to provide regularly [for] the gods (?) . . .
(and) to renew the shrines of the gods constantly seeks [. . .]
son of Nabu-balaṭsu-iqbi,
the wise prince [am I].
When Marduk, the great lord,
summoned [me] to rule the land (and)
among all the black-headed ones
glorified my name,
(and) gave [me] the people of the four quarters

6. Cf. VAB 4 262:19-20.

7. Variant: *zi-ik-r*[*a*].

to govern,
[. . .] the subject people [. . .] he gave(?)
15′. . . . .
. . . .
the four quarters [. . .]

1922-185. Small fragment from left end of hollow barrel cylinder. Diam. c. 50 mm. Weld-Blundell collection. Inscription completely illegible. Not copied.

Bodl. AB 239. Formerly W-B 4. Barrel cylinder, complete. Nabonidus Cyl. II 2 no. 5 (Berger) = Langdon, Nabonidus no. 5. Variants: (10-11) in one line, (14-16) in two lines, (19) *šu-a-ti*, (20) *il-li-ik*, (22-24) in two lines, (26-29) in three lines, (26) *u*, (27) *šu*, (ii 14) *rabītu(tú)*, (17-18) in one line, (24-25) in one line, (26-28) in two lines, (29-31) in one line.

The collection also contains the following previously published cylinders:

1929-137, 138, and 138bis. Fragments of barrel cylinders, exc. nos. V 232, KM 26, and V 203 respectively. Provenance: 137 and 138, Uhaimir, surface; 138 bis, Ingharra, C-2m. Samsuiluna, Inscr. 'C,' Sumerian (137) and Akkadian (138 and 138bis). Published by Sollberger, RA 63 (1969) 29ff.

1962-353. Part of barrel cylinder. Max. diam. c. 100 mm., min. diam. c. 80 mm. Provenance: Kish, no details recorded. Samsuiluna, Inscr. 'C,' Sumerian. Published by Sollberger, RA 63 (1969) 29ff.

1922-195. Inscription 'B' of Samsuiluna, published by Sollberger, RA 61 (1967) 39ff. (ms. 'F'). This object was described as a barrel cylinder by Langdon (OECT 1 60, reiterated RA 21 [1924] 125), and as the end of a flat-topped cone by Sidney Smith (RA 21 [1924] 75 note 1). It is, however, certainly the blunt end of a clay nail similar to that illustrated YOS 9 40, as seen by Sollberger (RA 61 [1967] 40). Diam. 72 mm.

1922-201. Formerly W-B 5.[8] Barrel cylinder, complete. Nabonidus Cyl. III 3. Published by Langdon, OECT 1 32 and pl. 23-28.

Bodl. D 1. Fragment of a cylinder. Nebuchadnezzar Cyl. Frag. II 2. Published by Langdon, PSBA 31 (1909) 325.

8. Not W-B 4, as given in Berger, Königsinschriften 376.

Plate I

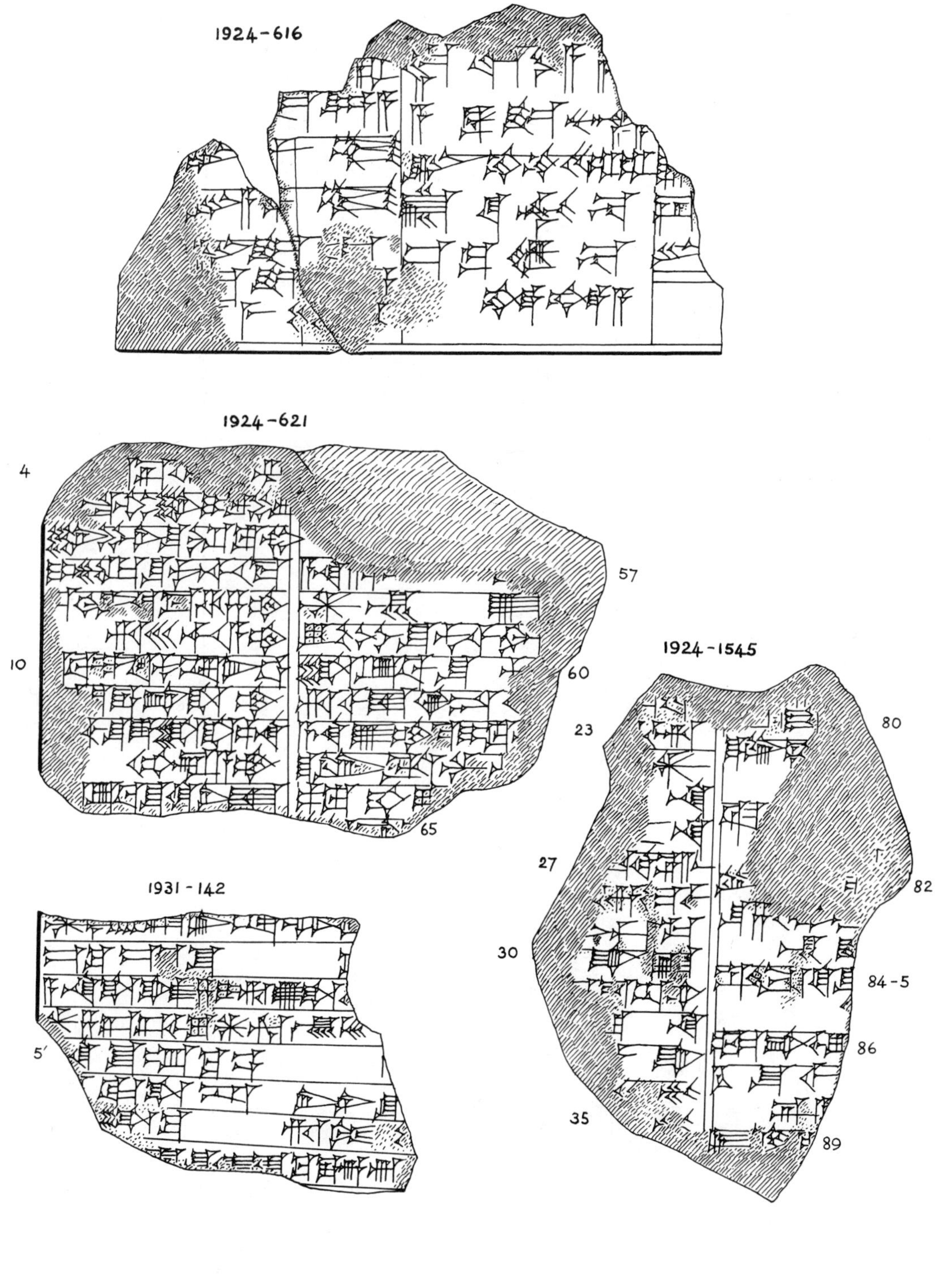
1924-616
1924-621
4
10
57
60
65
1924-1545
23
27
30
35
80
82
84-5
86
89
1931-142
5′

Plate II

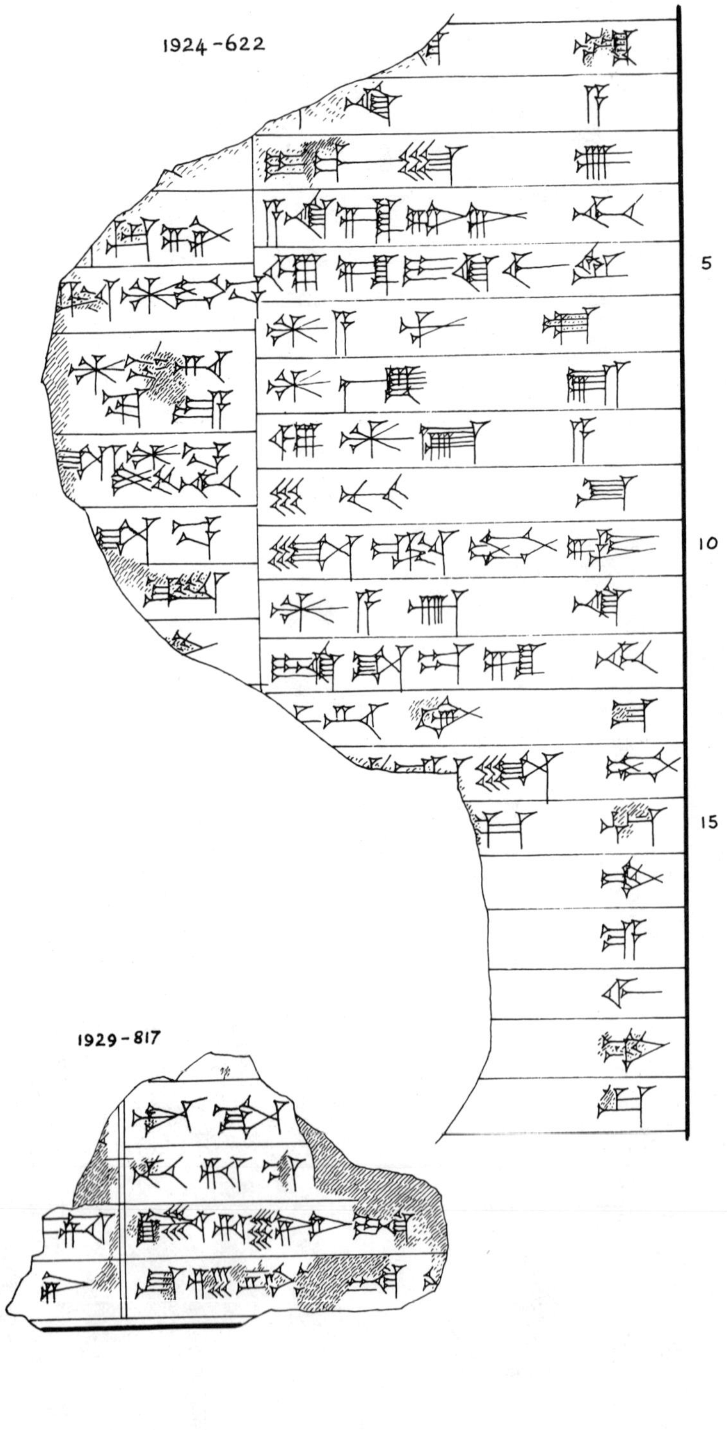

Plate III

1922-186

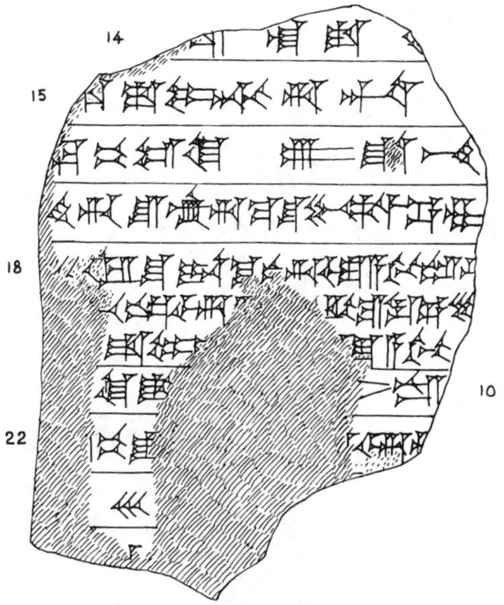

1922-187

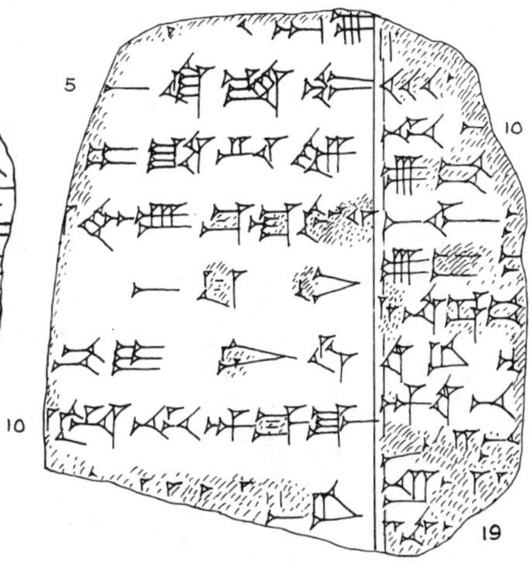

1924-1245

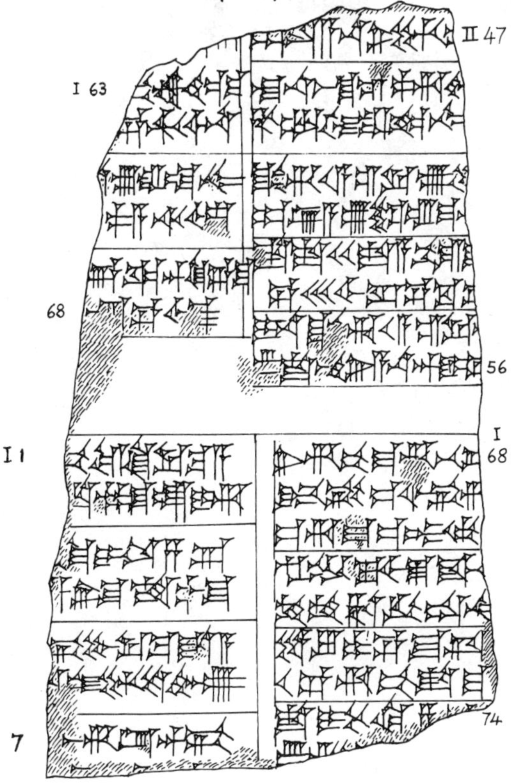

1924-1032

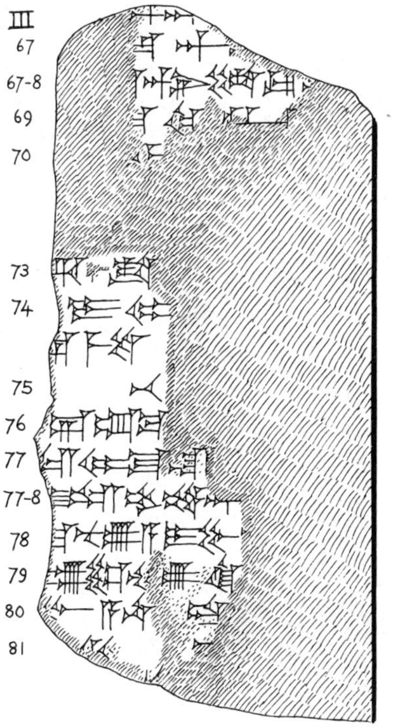

Plate IV

1969-584

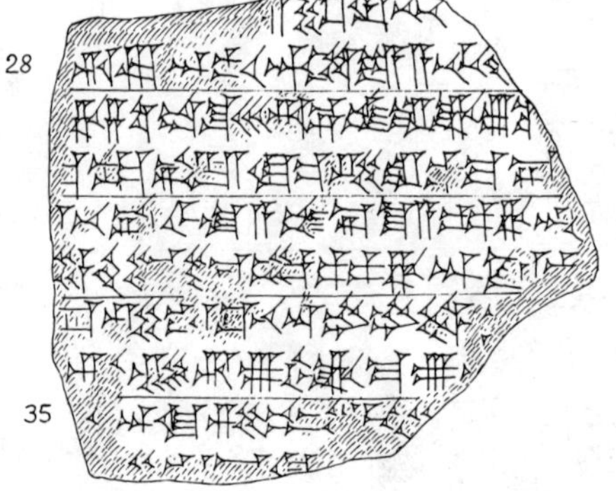

1969-585

1969-582

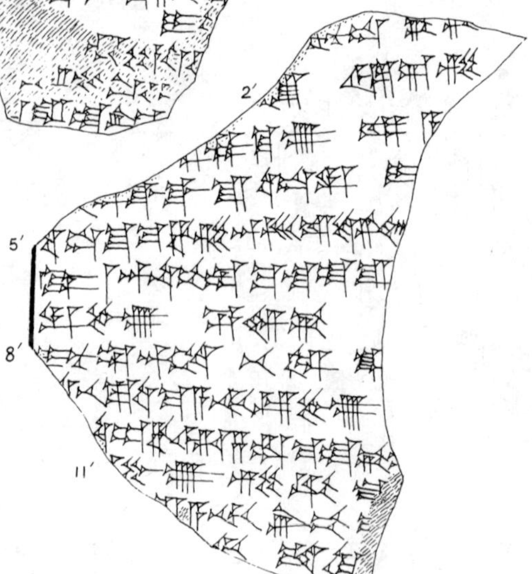

HAPLOGRAPHIC MARGINALIA

William W. Hallo
Yale University

Scribal mistakes call for scribal corrections. In the vast genre of archival texts, scribes often erred in their arithmetic and then corrected themselves by the time-honored device of an (intentional) compensating error to arrive at a proper total.[1] In literary texts, a common *lapsus calami* consisted of omitting an entire poetic line. In such a case, probably detected when the scribe counted his lines and entered their total in the colophon, a simple corrective was available: the left edge of the tablet. This was normally blank except where the scribe had used up the obverse, reverse, and bottom edge of the tablet and still needed more space for additional lines.[2] Otherwise he could use it to enter the missing line, normally (as far as can be seen from the published copies) in a downward direction relative to the point of insertion. When possible, a straight line before the entry indicated where on the obverse or reverse of the tablet it was to be inserted. The practice in question is already attested in Old Babylonian copies of Sumerian literary texts, where it was discovered by Kramer a quarter of a century ago. He wrote:[3]

> Line 59, as the copy shows, was written on the left edge, since it was accidentally omitted by the scribe who indicated by means of a short horizontal line the exact place where it belongs. This interesting scribal practice was relatively simple to figure out in the case of the Yale tablet as a result of a comparison of the passage beginning with line 54 with the parallel passages beginning with lines 30 and 45, not to mention the presence of the line in the duplicate, cf. line 327 of the restored text. There is at least one other example of this scribal device in the published Sumerian literary texts which has remained unrecognized hitherto because of lack of duplicating material. Thus in the all-important "deluge" tablet published in PBS V 1, the signs written on the left edge are preceded by a short line just as in the case of the Yale tablet; it is therefore not a colophon (cf. PBS IV 2, p. 63 and Heidel, The Gilgamesh Epic and Old Testament Parallels, p. 105) but a line that was accidentally omitted between lines 5(!) and 6(!) of col. vi., which might perhaps be restored to read: an-^{d}en-líl-li zi-u$_4$-sud$_x$-ra mí b[í-in-dug$_4$-ge-eš] "An and Enlil ch[erished] Ziusudra."

Commenting on the line from the Sumerian Flood Story, Civil stated in 1969: "Kramer's suggestion to insert here the line from the left edge of the tablet is in probability correct,"[4] but he assigned it the line number "255a" as an index of his hesitancy on this point.[5] The hesitation no longer seems necessary in view of the large number of additional examples of the identical practice now available. They are catalogued here in the context of the discussion of "scribal errors in cuneiform," the topic of the Assyriological Colloquium at Yale for December 16, 1975.[6]

Kramer himself noted a third instance in CT 42 (1959) 1: the fifth of the seven familiar "heroic epithets" of Enlil having been omitted inadvertently after line 6 of the obverse, the scribe inserted the missing line in the right edge.[7] The switch to the right edge in this case may be a function of the late date of the exemplar (on which see presently) or it may have been prompted by the enigmatic "musical" notations which pre-empted the left margin (edge?).[8]

The text in question is a-ab-ba ḫu-luḫ-ḫa, now edited by Kutscher.[9] The exemplar involved is said to be Neo-Babylonian in date.[10] Kutscher called attention to a second example of the practice in the same composition, for the Old Babylonian scribe of the Yale text YBC 4659 accidentally omitted line *155 and inserted it on the left edge, with a straight line "pointing to" line *156.[11]

The fifth example is provided by the Nippur text Ni. 4552, published by Kramer in 1963 and re-edited by

1. No example comes to mind at this writing.
2. See for example W. W. Hallo and J. J. A. van Dijk, The Exaltation of Inanna, YNER 3 (1968) pls. 5 and 9.
3. Samuel Noah Kramer, "'Inanna's Descent to the Nether World,' Continued and Revised," JCS 4 (1950) 206f. n. 45.
4. M. Civil, "The Sumerian Flood Story," apud Lambert-Millard, Atra-ḫasīs (1969) 172.
5. Civil, in Lambert-Millard, Atraḫasīs p. 145.
6. See Appendix to this article.
7. S. N. Kramer, "CT XLII: A Review Article," JCS 18 (1964) 36 n. 1.
8. On these notations see most recently W. G. Lambert, "The Converse Tablet: A Litany with Musical Instructions," apud H. Goedicke, ed., Near Eastern Studies in Honor of William Foxwell Albright (1971) 335-53.
9. Raphael Kutscher, Oh Angry Sea (a-ab-ba ḫu-luḫ-ḫa): The History of a Sumerian Congregational Lament, YNER 6 (1975) 68.
10. YNER 6 11 (quoting E. Sollberger).
11. YNER 6 107f.; cf. the hand-copy on plate 7 (!).

Ancient Near Eastern Studies in Memory of J. J. Finkelstein
Connecticut Academy of Arts and Sciences, Memoir 19

Jacobsen as "The Sister's Message."[12] The text can be reconstructed with the help of an unpublished Yale duplicate.[13] The omitted line is line 27 in Kramer's edition and line 11 of the restored text; it occurs at the indicated point of insertion in the Yale text as well as in the published duplicate (UM 29-16-8).

The sixth example occurs in another Nippur tablet, Ni. 4233, published on p. 74 of ISET (1969), as pointed out in my review of the volume.[14] The text is a hitherto unknown hymn to Nin-imma.

But the practice was not confined, even in Old Babylonian times, to texts from Nippur and whatever site was the provenience of the Yale texts. It was noted in a literary text from Ur by Kramer[15] and in one of unknown provenience by Limet.[16] These examples are particularly illuminating, the former because the omission occurred at the very end of the obverse and before the inscribed lower edge,[17] the latter because the insertion, coming as it does at line 26 of an obverse of 34 lines, had to continue along the bottom edge of the tablet.

A different solution was adopted by the scribe of MLC 1207, likewise of unknown provenience. Here the scribe squeezed the omitted line into two lines running down the left edge *before* the point of insertion which, as usual, was marked by a straight line. That line then *follows* the insert rather than preceding it.[18] A simpler, if less traditional, approach was employed at Kish, to judge by the only example from that scribal center in which the insert comes near the end of the obverse: here the scribe simply reversed the usual direction of the omitted line and wrote it *up* the left margin *above* the line of insertion.[19]

That the practice continued unabated into the first millennium, as demonstrated by the third example (above), was clearly recognized by C. Bezold long ago, as is amply demonstrated in the his Kouyunjik Catalogue (footnotes to pp. 543, 554 and passim thereafter). It has been less explicitly stated in more recent treatments. Thus Lambert noted that a Babylonian copy of a late Assyrian fire incantation "adds a whole line (III 27) in the left margin, while the duplicates have it in the text." But, he adds, "in this case it is not clear if the line was lacking from the basic copy used by the scribe . . ., or if the scribe of [the Babylonian copy] accidentally omitted it at first, but later discovered the fact when checking the work."[20] Even though the copy in question has other scribal notations in the form of textual variants, it seems clear that we have here another simple case of scribal correction comparable to the Sumerian precedents from the second millennium. Note only that, in distinction from those, the present tablet has two columns on each side and therefore the scribe availed himself of the space between the columns for his insertion. Moreover, his line runs *up*, rather than down this space. But it begins, as usual, at the point of insertion, and this point is clearly marked by a wedge, comparable to the straight line in the Old Babylonian convention.

Finally, the practice can be traced even beyond Mesopotamia as far west as Ugarit. The famous snake charm RS 24.244, first published by Virolleaud,[21] has three lines of text running down the left margin underneath a straight line which constitutes a simple extension of the line dividing the fifth and sixth stanzas of the text.[22] Virolleaud did not know what to make of these three lines of text,[23] but Astour, who first re-edited the composition, described them as "a summary of an omitted or additional incantation strophe; with it, the number of repetitions would amount to twelve."[24] More specifically, he compares the twelve pairs of deities in the related text RS 24.241 and says "the scribe of [RS 24.244] inserted a marginal note"[25] to be

12. S. N. Kramer in "Cuneiform Studies and the History of Literature: The Sumerian Sacred Marriage Texts," PAPS 107 (1963) 524; The Sacred Marriage Rite (1969) p. 103f.; T. Jacobsen, "The Sister's Message," The Gaster Festschrift, ANES 5 (1973) 199-212.

13. NBC 10923. This text shows that our bal-bal-e began at line 17 of the published editions with di-da-mu-dè di-da-mu-dè. Line 16 should, with the photograph and against the editions, probably be restored as [bal-bal-e-^{d}Inanna]-kam; to judge by the Yale text, it was probably preceded by Kramer's text no. 11.

14. W. W. Hallo, review of Çıg, Kızılyay and Kramer, Sumerian Literary Tablets and Fragments in the Archaeological Museums of Istanbul 1 (1969), in JCS 18 (1971) 39 n. 1.

15. See his remarks apud C. J. Gadd and S. N. Kramer, Literary and Religious Texts: First Part, UET 6 (1963) 35 (p. 5).

16. H. Limet, "Le poème épique 'Innina et Ebiḫ'," Or. NS 40 (1971) 14. For the (unknown) provenience of PUL 550, see p. 11, and Limet, RA 63 (1969) 5.

17. The copy does not show the exact placement of the insertion, except that it is located "on the left edge."

18. J. van Dijk, "Incantations accompagnant la naissance de l'homme," Or. NS 44 (1975) 65-69 and n. 35. The copy will appear in YOS 11.

19. Alster, Dumuzi's Dream p. 165 pl. 18. Alster's note, p. 55 line 23, seems unaware of the nature of the scribal practice involved.

20. W. G. Lambert, "Fire Incantations," AfO 23 (1970) 39.

21. Ch. Virolleaud, "Les nouveaux textes mythologiques et liturgiques . . .," Ugaritica 5 (1968) 567 no. 7.

22. This fact was called to my attention by David Wortman.

23. Ugaritica 5 574.

24. M. C. Astour, "Two Ugaritic Serpent Charms," JNES 27 (1968) 15.

25. JNES 27 (1968) 21.

translated "after (the strophe on) Rešeph, (insert that on) Astarte, (namely:) 'With Astarte in Mari / is the incantation for the bite of the serpent.'"[26]

A minor difficulty with this interpretation (from the point of view of the Mesopotamian scribal usage) is only that the insertion seems to be placed physically *before* the stanza on Resheph!

These examples should suffice to establish the chronological and geographical scope of a cuneiform scribal device intended to rectify the omission of lines from literary texts.

26. JNES 27 (1968) 22. Cf. now also T. H. Gaster, ANES 7 (1975) 33-51.

Appendix

The Assyriological Colloquium at Yale was conceived by J. J. Finkelstein in 1966. It continued to function under his leadership until his death, and in his spirit since then. The original conception of the Colloquium remains as stated in the invitation of September 15 1966: "a forum for informal and extended discussion of topics and problems in Assyriology which interest any of the participants . . . limited to Assyriologists within short rail or automobile travel distance to New Haven (and) Assyriologists from abroad or elsewhere in this country present in the area at the time of the meetings." Finkelstein sent invitations to A. Goetze, W. W. Hallo, T. Jacobsen, S. N. Kramer, W. L. Moran, O. Neugebauer, A. Sachs, Å. Sjöberg, and F. J. Stephens. All but one (Neugebauer) of these ten attended the first Colloquium, which since then has grown to include numbers of additional, and especially younger, participants without sacrificing its informal and intimate character. After a decade of meetings, it seems appropriate to list briefly the formal topics of each Colloquium in a volume dedicated to the memory of its founder.

1966 - no set topic
1967 - W. W. Hallo, Classification of the Lexical Texts
1968 - T. Jacobsen, Comments on Oppenheim's "Mesopotamian Religion"
1969 - A. J. Sachs, Astronomical Diaries
1970 - Å. W. Sjöberg, Examination Text A
1971 - W. L. Moran, Peripheral Akkadian
1972 - J. J. Finkelstein, The Goring Ox
1973 - S. J. Lieberman, Fragments of a Theory of Cuneiform Writing
1974 - M. deJ. Ellis, Land Tenure in the Old Babylonian Period
Minor communication: S. N. Kramer, The GIR_5 Profession
1975 - B. R. Foster, Sumerian Society under Sargonic Rule
Minor communication: J. Cooper, W. W. Hallo and A. J. Sachs, Scribal Errors in Cuneiform

HITTITE LEXICOGRAPHIC STUDIES, I

Harry A. Hoffner, Jr.
The University of Chicago

When I learned over a year ago that a volume was planned in memory of the late J. J. Finkelstein, I had hoped to contribute a study of an Akkadian literary text from Boğazköy which he and I had several times discussed and even planned to edit together. A heavy work load has not permitted me to finish that project in time for the memorial volume. Instead I offer several short studies of Hittite terms until now not correctly understood. Finkelstein took a lively interest in Hittite lexicography and for a time assisted the late A. Goetze in the preparation of materials for a Hittite Dictionary, which unfortunately never reached publication. I hope that these lines will prove adequate to express my own deep admiration for Jack Finkelstein and my acute sense of loss at his untimely death.

ekt- "(hunting) net"

S. Alp (apud H. G. Güterbock, Kumarbi p. 43) first proposed "Fuss(?)" for this word, and subsequently (Anatolia 2 27ff.) "Bein, Unterbein, Unterschenkel." Alp's translation was influenced by his, as it proves, incorrect assumption that *ekt-* and UZU.*ekdu-* represent the same word. These translations were listed by Friedrich in HWb 81 and HWb Suppl. 2 13, and have been accepted by Hittitologists up to the present. My re-examination of older occurrences led me to separate these two words and to translate *ekt-* "net." After this article was almost complete, H. Berman in looking through transliterations of unpublished /t and /u fragments in the possession of Prof. Güterbock came upon two further occurrences, (6) and (7), of which (6) provided a vivid confirmation of my new interpretation.

Documentation: **(1)** [. . . *-a*]*n*? *a-pít-ta pé-da-aḫ-ḫi* GIŠ.*kur-ta-al-li*.ḪI.A *ki-it-ta* [. . .]*x e-ek-za iš-pár-ra-an-za na-aš-ta* DUMU-*an* GIŠ.*kur-ta-li-aš* [. . .]*x pár-ku-nu-mi* (KBo 17 61 obv. 16-18). **(2)** *li-li-wa-an-za-ma-aš-ša-an ek-za-te-eš* KUR-*e kat-ta ḫu-u-up-pa-an ḫar-zi ek-ta-aš-ma-ad-du-uš-ša-an ir-ḫa-az Ú-UL na-aḫ-ša-ri-ia-wa-an-za ar-ḫa Ú-UL ú-iz-zi Ú-UL pít-tu-li-an-ta-an-ma an-da wa-ar-pí-iš-ki-ši*, "But your swift net holds the earth . . . -ed. Even he who is unafraid will not go forth (i.e., escape) from the circle of your net; you constantly enclose (therein) him who is unintimidated (by you)" (KBo 3 21 = BoTU 6 ii 15-19; cf. different translation by Alp, Anatolia 2 31); **(3)** 1 GA.KIN.AG 1 *EM-ṢÚ* 1 UDU.ÁŠ.SAL.GÀR 9 NINDA.ERÍN.MEŠ 2-*ŠÚ* 7 NINDA.SIG 1 UZU.ÚR.UDU È.A *e-ek-za dam*?*-me*?*-ku-ul te-pu* [. . .] *ku-un-ku-ma-a-an ḫa-aḫ-ḫa-al kar-aš* ḪAR.GÌR AN.B[AR . . .] (list of items in a ritual fragment; KUB 39 61 i 10′-12′). **(4)** [. . .]-*ŠU-NU da-a-i* [. . .]^{t}*an-zi nu e-ek-ta-an* [. . .   ]x?*-nu-zi nu-uš-ma-aš te-ez-zi* (KUB 48 76 i 1-3; communicated to me prior to publication by the courtesy of Prof. H. Klengel through the hands of Dr. H. Berman); **(5)** [*na*]*m-ma-wa ku-in :e-ek-ta-an ḫa-ma-x*[. . .] (KUB 31 68 27; reading *u-e-ek-ta-an* is also possible, although it yields no known word). **(6)** [. . . GIM-*an e-ek-ta-an* . . .]*-nu-wa-an-zi nu AR-NA-BU e-ek-te-et* [*ap-pa-an-zi* GIM-*an-ma* MU]Š?*-an kal-mu-ši-it iš-ḫi-eš-ni-it* [*ap-pa-an-zi nu* . . . *QA-TA*]*M-MA ap-pa-an-du na-at ḫar-ni-in-kán-du* (473/t obv.? left 13′-15′; passage noted by H. Berman and publication right granted by H. G. Güterbock; readings and restorations mine); **(7)** [. . . ME]Š?*-aš kat-ta-an* KUŠ?.BABBAR x[. . . KUR URU.*Ḫa-at-t*]*i*?*-ma-kán e-ek-za ḫu-u*[*p*?*-pa-an ḫar-zi* . . .] (1067/u 4′-5′; passage noted by H. Berman and publication right granted by Güterbock; readings and restorations mine).

Discussion of documentation: Of the six passages certainly the key ones are (6) and (2). The *ekza* is a kind of weapon of the storm god, by which (or in which) he encloses his opponent, and from which even the fearless enemy cannot escape. It forms a circle or enclosure (*irḫa-*) about the trapped person. It is called "swift" (*liliwant-*) because it is cast suddenly over the victim. Passage (2) is, of course, a Hittite translation of an Akkadian hymn to the storm god. It reflects ancient Mesopotamian concepts of divine combat. Perhaps the best single artistic representation of just such a scene is the "Stele of the Vultures" of Eannatum, which shows the god Ningirsu triumphant over the enemies of Lagash. His right hand holds a club, his left hand a net which encloses a large group of naked and defeated enemies. This interpretation of (2) also leads to suggestions for translating two somewhat difficult verbs: *katta ḫupp-* and *anda warpišk-*. Friedrich listed E. Sturtevant's translation "to assemble, heap up" in HWb 75, and A. Goetze's "toss, fling, throw" (JAOS 74 189) in HWb Erg. 1 7, but rejected both in favor of a unifying of this *ḫup(p)-* with *ḫuwap(p)-* and a translation

Ancient Near Eastern Studies in Memory of J. J. Finkelstein
Connecticut Academy of Arts and Sciences, Memoir 19

"mistreat, injure" for both (HWb Erg. 1 7). Friedrich made a generous use of question marks in proposing the unification and never gives specific textual evidence to show that the two writings denote the same verb. In fact, one can cite KUB 7 46 iv 9′-12′ (with restorations from B = IBoT 3 114 iv 1-3): *ku-iš-wa* [(*A-NA* LUGAL SAL)].LUGAL *a-ra-aḫ-zé-na-aš* UN-*aš* [(ḪUL-*lu ša-an-aḫ-zi n*)]*a-an ḫar-zi nu-wa-ra-a-an* DINGIR.MEŠ *QA-TAM-MA* [(IGI.ḪI.A-*wa kat*)]-*ta ḫu-u-wa-ap-pa-an-du*, "whatever foreigner seeks to harm the king (and) queen, he will hold him, and let the gods . . . him (on) the eyes!" The duplicate IBoT 3 114 iv 3 reads *ḫu-u-up-*[*pa-an-du*], which seems to confirm Friedrich's thesis that the two writings express the same verb. It is not evident, however, that a general translation "injure, damage" is to be expected here rather than something more specific. With respect to *katta ḫuppan* it is formally possible that the verb is *ḫuppa(i)-*, for the participles of *ḫupp-* and *ḫuppa(i)-* would be identical. A *ḫupai-* with one *p* is known from VBoT 58 iv 33 (cf. Laroche in RHA f.77, 86 with note 11). There it expresses an action performed upon various vessels (DUG's and GAL's). Its form, *ḫu-u-pa-i*[*z-zi*], marks it as a *mi*-verb. Possibly the same verb is found in *ki-nu-un-za ḫu-u-up-am-mi* (KUB 33 67 iv 18), which forms the third action in the sequence: "I will now eat and drink, I will now . . . ". This action, however, is not necessarily transitive. Similarly open to intransitive interpretation is the form in *nam-ma* LÚ.MEŠ BALAG.DI *ḫu-u-pí-is-kán-zi* (KBo 15 69 i 11). With a double writing of the *p* but showing the *-a(i)-* stem ending is the verb in the phrase: *nu* EN.SISKUR 7-*ŠU ḫu-u-up-pa-a-iz-zi nu* [. . .] *ša-ra-pí nu pa-a-ši* (KUB 27 29++ iii 8-9). Despite the single and double writings of the *p*, I am inclined to agree with Laroche (RHA f. 77 86 note 11) that the three forms belong to the same verb. The form *katta ḫuppan*, however, in my opinion should be kept apart from this *ḫup(p)a(i)-*, and should be considered as belonging to the stem *ḫupp-/ḫuwapp-*. This does not mean, however, that all *ḫuwapp-* and *ḫupp-* forms must belong to one verb with a unified meaning. Many can be subsumed under a general translation "to injure, harm, damage," as already assumed in the dictionaries and translations (HWb 79). Other passages do not lend themselves to such a translation. Without undertaking here an exhaustive study of all *ḫuwapp-* forms, I should like to merely sketch the outlines of the case for keeping some *ḫuwapp-* forms distinct.

All forms of *ḫuwapp-* without preverb can be explained and translated as "to be hostile or ill-willed toward, do evil against." These forms always take the logical object in the dative-locative rather that accusative case: *-šmaš* rather than *-uš* or *-aš* (KUB 26 43 obv. 62), *-ši* rather than *-an* (KUB 26 1++ iii 43; von Schuler, Dienstanw. 13-14), *A-NA* ᵐ*Am-mi-*ŠEŠ-*ma*[*-ká*]*n* (KUB 13 34++ i 13f.; Werner, StBoT 4 38f.), [KU]R-*e ḫu-u-wa-ap-pí-iš* (KUB 43 75 obv. 19′; *utne* as dative-locative rather than nominative-accusative), *-mu* can be either accusative or dative-locative in Hatt. i 34, KUB 21 17 i 9. The absence of clear accusative forms and the presence of clear dative-locative ones leads us to the conclusion that *ḫuwapp-* "to be/do evil towards" always governs the dative-locative case. *kuitki* in KUB 26 1++ iii 43 is adverbial, as recognized by von Schuler. Several passages (KUB 13 34++ i 13f., KUB 26 1++ iii 37-44) suggest a translation "to seek to incriminate, cast aspersions on," fitting also for Hatt. i 34 and KUB 21 17 i 9.

On the other hand, the forms of *ḫupp-* and *ḫuwapp-* with preverbs govern objects in the accusative case: KUB 7 46 iv 9′-12′ (see transliteration, translation, and discussion above), *nu ku-wa-bi an-da ḫu-u-up-pa-an-du-uš* NA_4.ḪI.A *ú-e-mi-ia-an-zi* (VBoT 24 ii 20, passive participle modifying NA_4.ḪI.A). These latter verb forms resemble syntactically the forms of *ḫupp-* without preverb which likewise take an object in the accusative: *še pa-a-ir* ḪUR.SAG-*i* [. . .] *pa-aḫ-ḫu-ur pa-ri-ir še* LÚ.NINDA.DÙ.DÙ *ḫu-u-up-pí-ir ku-i-da*[- . . *pa-aš-ši*]*-la-an šal-li-in ša-an ḫa-at-ta-an-ni-ir ša-an ša-mi*[*-nu-ir*] (KBo 3 34:2ff. = BoTU 12A §1), where I construe *ḫuppir* with [*pašši*]*lan šallin*. Since there seems to be a noun *ḫuppa-* (stem vowel uncertain) which designates an object into (or onto) which items can be poured or heaped up (*ḫu-u-up-pí-iš-ši šu-uḫ-ḫa-an-z*[*i*] (KUB 43 30 iii 15′ and 17′, cf. also KUB 27 29++ iii 7-8), which could be something like a "pile(?)," or "heap(?)," both *ḫupp-* and *ḫuppai-* (for the latter KUB 27 29++ iii 8 immediately after *ḫuppešš*[*i šuḫḫai*]) could denote piling, heaping up, stacking, or gathering into a pile. *anda ḫuppanzi* also occurs in KBo 10 27 iv 32′, but the context is not decisive for determining meaning. *katta ḫuwapp-* occurs in three passages in which there is insufficient context to determine meaning (KUB 10 63 ii 8′, KUB 35 148 iii 42, and KUB 7 57 i 7). In a fourth (KUB 7 46 iv 9-12 transliterated and discussed above) the gods are to perform this action on a person's eyes. *katta ḫupp-* occurs finally in the passage from which our discussion departed, KBo 3 21 ii 14-16, in which a translation "your swift net holds the (inhabitants of the) land heaped up" is certainly possible. The scene from the Stele of the Vultures shows the god's net enclosing a heap of enemy soldiers. If the verb *ḫupp-* does mean "to gather together into a pile," one might connect it with the glossed word *ḫupala-*, "fishing net" (KBo 6 29+ ii 34; Güterbock, Oriens 10 353, 362).

KBo 3 21 ii 15-19 also contains the verb *anda warpiškiši*, which I translated "you constantly enclose." For this translation I must make some justification, since the HWb gives for *anda warp-* "drinnen baden" (p. 246 s.v. *warp-*). There simply is no evidence (contra HWb 246) for preverbs with the verb *warp-* "to wash." *appanda warp-* is based upon passages such as KUB 13 2++ iii 14 (for which see H. Hoffner, AOAT 22 85 n. 23), where EGIR-*anda* is adverbial ("furthermore afterwards let the city bathe itself!"). *piran para* in KUB 29 4 i 53-54 is also clearly adverbial and not preverbial. *katta warappiškizi* in KUB 45 5 ii 19′ could be a preverb construction, but the broken context does not make it possible to reconstruct the action being described. Is it really "washing" here? As for *anda warp-*, I am inclined to connect the verbal element with the root underlying the expression *warpa dai-/tiya-* "to surround, enclose" (Goetze AM 237f., HWb 246). *anda warp-* occurs in two other passages: (1) *tu-zi-ma-aš-kán iš-pa-ta-za an-da* [. . . -*k*]*a*?-*li* GIM-*an* GÌR-*it an-da wa-ar-pa-nu-un* (KBo 3 13 = BoTU 3 rev. 3′f.; ZA 44 70f.), which may describe a military maneuver in which a foe is surrounded, and (2) ("various colored wools she takes and") *na-at* EGIR-*pa pár-za ma-la-ak-zi nam-ma-at pa-ra-a ḫa-an-da-a-an an-da tar-na-i na-x-x an-da* ŠA GI *ḫa-pu-ú-še-eš-šar* Ù [(ŠA GIŠ.TÚG *pa-an-za-ki-i)*]*t-ti-in wa-ra-ap-zi na-an an-da* [*(na-a-i na-)*]*at ša-an A-NA* NINDA.KUR$_4$.RA *da-a-i* (KUB 7 1+ ii 14f. restored from duplicate KBo 22 145 ii), a very difficult passage to be treated in detail below. It is my opinion that this verb is based on the same proto-Indo-European root as Lithuanian *verpti*, Greek *raptō*, and Anglo-Saxon *wearp*, a verb used to describe actions of spinning, weaving, etc. In Hittite it describes winding cord about something or enclosing as in a net or snare.

Returning to the discussion of the *ekt-* documentation, the trace before the *nu* in the verb of (4) is the same as in the first verb of (6). I assume it is the same verb. Because of *išparranza* in (1), I had once thought of restoring the verb *išparnu-* in both passages. But *išparnu-* takes *watar* as its most usual object and should be translated "sprinkle," and once persons are "besprinkled" (KUB 7 57 i 8). It does not mean "veranlassen hinzubreiten; (Brücke) anlegen lassen" (HWb 90)—the object of the verb in KUB 19 9 iv 10-12 is not the bridge! Therefore *išparnu-* does not mean "to spread out" and is inappropriate as the verb taking "net" as its object. The trace in both (4) and (6) shows the extreme righthand margin of the sign had a single horizontal wedge: *ši*, *wa*, *aš*, *nu*, and even *ni* are possible.

The unpublished fragment (6) offers welcome evidence that the *ekt-* was used in hunting, for here someone catches a hare with it. Here the net would not be thrown but rather concealed under leaves, soil, or other cover and used as a snare or trap. One cannot translate "[they catch] a hare by (its) leg," for the following lines show the instrumentals are really the inplements used to catch the prey (*kalmušit*, *išḫešnit*). Passage (7) is less helpful because of its fragmentary state. It is barely possible that the word following *e-ek-za* is the verb *ḫup-* discussed above and describing the action of the *ekt-* in (2).

In (5) the verb may be some form of *ḫamenk-/ḫamank-* "to bind," perfectly appropriate for a net. In fact Alp (Anatolia 2 29) restored *hamank-* here. The presence of the single Glossenkeil might indicate that the word *ektan* is Luwian. But, as Berman has reminded me, the *e* vocalization is not expected in Luwian, since Nesite *e* regularly has *a* as its Luwian counterpart (cf. Laroche, DLL 134, §16). Berman and I jointly recalled the glossed *aggati-* from the Hittite translation of the Gilgamesh Epic (cf. Hoffner, Al. Heth. 125 with note 191, and now Kammenhuber, HW² 53; not in Laroche, DLL). *aggati-* translates Akkadian *nuballu*, which von Soden (AHw 2 799b s.v. "als Fangnetze") indicates can denote a net for trapping. The Luwian word is based upon the same Indo-European root (perhaps the verb **yē-* with *-k-* enlargement; cf. Latin *iaciō*, *iēcī*, and A. Walde and J. Pokorny, Vergleichendes Wörterbuch der Indogermanischen Sprachen 1 199), and has nominalized with the same dental suffix, but with a vocalic insert *a*. The Luwian noun is thematic (i-stem), while the Nesite noun is consonantal stem. All of these features are regular for the two languages respectively. Since not all glossed words in Nesite texts are necessarily non-Nesite (*šakuwa* "eyes" and *šanḫeškimi* "I keep seeking" cited in HWb 332-3), we would prefer to consider *ekt-* as a genuinely Nesite word, and *aggati-* its Luwian counterpart. Proto-Indo-European **ye-* seems always to appear as *-e* in Nesite; cf. *ega-* "ice" from Proto-Indo-European **yeg-* (Walde-Pokorny 1 206).

Since S. Alp's 1957 study in Anatolia 2 27-31, it has been customary to regard *ekt-* and UZU.*ekdu-* as virtually synonymous. I do not agree. *ekt-* never bears the UZU determinative. Furthermore, the addition of the u-stem vowel has never been explained. At present, I have no objections to Alp's rendering of UZU.*ekdu-* as "Bein, Unterbein, Unterschenkel" (p. 28); for now I only maintain that *ekt-* be recognized as a different word, whose meaning seems quite remote from that of UZU.*ekdu-*.

(GIŠ).*ḫueša*- "distaff"

Based upon its occurrence in passages describing typical women's utensils, Heinrich Zimmern (ZA 35 [1924] 183 n. 1) suggested that the *ḫueša*- was a mirror. Hans Ehelolf (foreword to KUB 29, p. iii note 2) accepted the translation and added a semantic parallel from ancient Egyptian hieroglyphics, where the same triconsonantal root denoted both "to live" and "mirror." My discovery of a duplicate to text (6) discussed below allowed me to make the equation GIŠ.*ḫueša*- = GIŠ.TÚG, "distaff," and led to a thorough reassessment of the existing documentary evidence for the word.

Documentation: **(1)** *nu* TÚG.NÍG.MÍ GIŠ.*ḫu-la-a-li* GIŠ.*ḫu-e-ša-an-na ú-da-an-zi* "they bring women's attire, spindle and distaff (and they break the arrow and you speak thus to them: 'What is this? Is it not women's attire?')" (KBo 6 34 ii 42ff.; Soldier's Oath); **(2)** *a-pé-da-aš-ma-kán* ŠU-*i* ŠA MÍ-*TI* GIŠ.*ḫu-u-la-li* GIŠ.*ḫu-i-ša-an-na da-a-i nu-uš* MÍ-*ni-li ú-e-eš-ši-ia* "put into their hands a woman's spindle and distaff and dress them like women!" (KBo 2 9 i 27ff.; ritual and prayer to Ishtar of Nineveh); **(3)** EN.SISKUR.SISKUR GIŠ.*ḫu-u-i-ša-an* GIŠ.*ḫu-u-la-li-ia* [ŠU-*i*] *an-da te-eḫ-ḫi . . . nu-uš-ši-iš-ša-an* GIŠ.*ḫu-u-e-ša*[*-an* GIŠ.]*ḫu-u-la-li-ia ar-ḫa pé-eḫ-ḫi* (mistake for *da-aḫ-ḫi*?) "I put into the hand of the patient distaff and spindle . . . I take the distaff and spindle away from him" (KUB 9 27+ i 20-24; ritual of Paškuwatti); **(4)** [. . .] *PA-NI* DINGIR-*LIM-ia ku-it* TÚG.*ku-re-eš*[*-šar* . . . GIŠ.*ḫu-u-la-l*]*i* GIŠ.*ḫu-u-i-ša-an Ú-NU-UT* AD.KID [. . .] (ABoT 26 8′ff.); **(5)** EGIR-*pa!-ma te-ez-zi nu ku-it iš-ša-an-zi a-pa-ša-aš-ši* EGIR-*pa te-ez-zi* GIŠ.*ḫu-u-la-li ḫar-zi* GIŠ.*ḫu-u-šu-uš šu-u-wa-du-uš ḫar-kán-zi nu* LUGAL-*wa-aš* MU.KAM.ḪI.A-*uš ma-al-ki-ia-an-zi* "he replies: 'What are they doing?' He to him replies: 'One holds the spindle; (others) hold full distaffs. They are spinning the years of the king." (KUB 29 1 ii 5-8); **(6)** *ki-i-ma ḫu-u-ga-an-da*[1]*-aš da-a-i* SÍG.GE$_6$ SÍG.SIG$_7$ SÍG.SA$_5$ SÍG.ZA.GÌN *da-a-i na-at* EGIR-*pa*[2] *pár-za ma-la-ak-zi nam-ma-at pa-ra-a ḫa-an-da-a-an an-da tar-na-i na-x-x an-da* ŠA GI *ḫa-pu-ú-še-eš-šar Ù* [(ŠA GIŠ.TÚG *pa-an-za-ki-i*)]*t-ti-in wa-ra-ap-zi na-an an-da* [(*na-a-i na-*)]*at-ša-an A-NA* NINDA.KUR$_4$.RA *da-a-i* "He takes these (items) of the enchanted person. He takes black, green, red, and blue wool and unravels(?) them and lays them together stretched out straight. The *ḫ*. of reed and the roping of the distaff he intertwines(?). He turns them together and puts them upon the thick bread." (KUB 7 1+ ii 13-18 restored from duplicate KBo 22 145 ii); **(7)** *ḫu-i-ša-aš-wa pa-an-za-ki-it-ti-iš* GIM-*an ú-e-ḫa-at-ta* DUMU-*li-ia i-da-a-la-u-eš ka-ra-a-te-eš kat-ta-an ar-ḫa a-pé-ni-eš-ša-an wa-ḫa-an-du* "As the skein(?) of the distaff turns, so in the same way let the evil *karateš* turn down away from the child!" (KUB 7 1+ ii 32ff.); **(8)** [GIŠ.*ḫu-u-la-*]*li* GIŠ.*ḫu-e-ša-aš* GIŠ.GA.ZUM (164/d rev. 10 as cited by Ehelolf in KUB 29 p. iii).

Discussion of documentation: As is already well known, the *ḫueša*- is paired with the *ḫulali*- and other characteristic female attire (passages (1), (2), (3), (4), especially). At least once (164/d rev. 10 as cited by Ehelolf in KUB 29 p. iii) it is also grouped with the comb (GIŠ.GA.ZUM). In (5), several deities are engaged in spinning the king's years. One of them holds the *ḫulali*, which all agree is the spindle. Others (note the plural verb) hold GIŠ.*ḫušuš šuwaduš*. Goetze (ANET 357) translated "mirrors (and) combs." But mirrors and combs are not used in spinning, and the following *malkiyanzi* indicates that all persons being described are cooperating in spinning the king's years. Güterbock (in RHA 14 [fasc. 58; 1956] 25 note 6, and in S. N. Kramer, Mythologies of the Ancient World, p. 149) hit upon the correct understanding of *šuwaduš*, when he translated "filled." *šuwaduš* is simply the denasalized form of *šuwanduš*. The scene can best be understood in the light of pictorial representations of spinning from ancient Egypt. These show strands of roping drawn from several distaffs being spun onto a single spindle (A. Linder, Spinnen und Weben Einst und Jetzt [Verlag C. J. Bucher, Luzern und Frankfort/M., 1967] p. 7). Several wool sources (i.e., distaffs) are supplying the raw material for the strong yarn of the king's life. Because as the text proceeds to say there is no end of the yarn, it is also necessary to observe that the distaffs are full. Supporting this interpretation is the observation that in Latin the distaff is occasionally characterized as "full" (*colus plena*). Because of the pairing of the *ḫapušeššar* of reed and the *panzakitti*- of GIŠ.TÚG in (6) and the juxtaposition of paragraphs discussing the *ḫuišaš panzakitti*- (7) and the *ḫapušaššanza* of reed later in the same column of the same text, it is safe to make the equation ŠA GIŠ.TÚG = *ḫuišaš*. Thus we may dispense with E. Neu's objection (StBoT 5 196, 198-9) that the form lacks the GIŠ determinative. Neu's own translation "Wie des rohen (Fleisches)(?) *panzakittiš* . . . " would require *ḫuišawaš*, since the adjective is a u-stem. I have not yet seen N. Oettinger's discussion of *ḫueša*- in StBoT 22, on which E. Neu's rendering

1. Dupl. KBo 22 145 II 5′: *-ta-*.

2. Dupl. *a-a*[*p-pa*].

"Wirtel" (StBoT 18 94) is based. But from the evidence which I have adduced I cannot accept the explanation of (GIŠ).*ḫueša-* as a "spindle whorl." As for *panzakitti-*, it is known to me only from the two passages cited here, (6) and (7). Neu cited "Bruchstückhaftes *pa-an-za-ki-id-d[u(-)]* 259/i, 3" in StBoT 5 199, but this unpublished fragment has not been available to me. The Sumerogram GIŠ.TÚG normally denotes the "boxwood tree" or its wood (Akkadian *taskarinnu*), on which see MSL 5 92 (Hh III 1) and R. C. Thompson (1949) 348 (reading *taskarinnu* instead of older *urkarinnu* established by B. Landsberger in WO 5 368ff.). On the basis of this equation one ought to regard GIŠ.*ḫueša-* in the first instance as the name of a tree and its wood, most likely the box (*buxus longifolia*), and secondly as the name for the distaff as an item customarily made from that wood. In Latin *buxum* denotes first the wood of the box tree, and second "flute," "pipe," or "comb," as made from boxwood. Any connection between GIŠ.*ḫueša-* and the verb *ḫuiš-* "to live" would probably concern the box tree's status as an evergreen, and therefore as a perennial symbol of life.

ḫupp- and *ḫuwapp-*

See above in discussion of *ekt-* "(hunting) net."

SÍG.*maišta-* "strand of yarn"

Documentation: **(1)** [*ma*]-*a-an* SÍG.*ma-iš-ta-an-na ma-ši-wa-an-ta-an wa-aš-ta-an-zi* "If they offend in respect to so much as a strand of yarn, (I, His Majesty, will make war from this side and you [the treaty partner] make war from the other side!" (KBo 16 47:8′ff.; Otten, Ist.Mitt. 17 [1967] 56-57 and note 8); **(2)** [SÍG.*ma-iš-ta-*]*an ma-ši-wa-an-ta-an le-e ap-te-ni* "Ye shall not seize so much as a [strand of yar]n!" (1684/u + KUB 23 72 obv. 42; join and restoration after Hoffner JCS 28 [1976] 60f.); **(3)** *a-ap-pa* SÍG.*ma-iš-t*[*a-a*]*n ma-ši-wá-an-ta-an Ú-UL ap*[*-pa-an-zi*] "and they do not seize so much as a strand of ya[r]n." (KUB 23 72 rev. 8); **(4)** *a-ap-pa* SÍG.[*ma-iš-ta-an Ú-UL ap-pa-an-zi*] (KUB 23 72 rev. 15).

The identification of the SÍG sign is clear from texts (3) and (4). On the basis of the expression SÍG.*maištan mašiwantan* it is unlikely that the determinative should be read otherwise in (1), as Otten proposed in Ist.Mitt. 17. The use of *mašiwant-* suggests that the item is one of nugatory value, much as in the expression ŠA KISLAḪ *ezzan taru*. To be compared is the biblical passage in Gen. 14:23 (Hebrew *ḥūṭ*); see also M. Tsevat, JBL 87 (1968) 460, and Hoffner, Al. Heth. 33ff. The Luwian passive participle *maštaimi-* may be related, as suggested by E. Laroche (DLL p. 70 s.v.).

panzakitti- "roping(?)"

See above in discussion of GIŠ.*ḫueša-* "distaff."

šemeḫuna- (a foodstuff)

Documentation: **(1)** *še-me-e-na-aš ḫu-u-up-pa-ra-aš šu-u-uš* [. . .] . . . *še-me-ḫu-ni-it šu-u-uš* (KBo 20 8 rev.? 4′-6′; typical old ductus); **(2)** A-*NA* LÚ.MEŠ *a-šu-ša-a-la-aš ša-me-ḫu-na-a*[*n* . . .] *še-e-ek-ti-i-iš-mi iš-ḫi-iš-kán*[*-zi*] . . . *nu-uk-kán ša-me-ḫu-na-an še-e-*[*ek-ta-az-mi-it*] *la-a-an-zi* (KBo 17 37 rev. right 4′-8′); **(3)** [*še-me-ḫu*]*-u-na-an* BAR NINDA *ḫar-ši-in kat-ta-an ar-ḫa* [. . .] . . . *me-ma-al še-me-ḫu-na-an* UZU.NÍG.GI[G . . . A-*NA* L]Ú.MEŠ Ú.ḪÚB *ḫu-u-up-pí-iš-ši šu-uḫ-ḫa-an-z*[*i*] (KUB 43 30 iii 14′-17′); **(4)** 10 PA ZÌ.DA *še-ep-pí-it ḫa-a-ta-an-ta-aš ša-me-e-ḫu-ni* 3 PA ZÌ.DA ZÍZ *ḫa-a-ta-an-ta-aš* (KUB 42 107 iii 8-9); **(5)** 1 DUG.LIŠ.GAL TU_7 *še-me-ḫu-na-aš ḫa-az-zi-la-aš* (KBo 16 49 iv 6′); **(6)** KUŠ UR.MAḪ *ša-me-ḫu-u-wa-an* [. . .] (KUB 17 34 iv 5; only remotely possible!); **(7)** [. . . P]A *še-me-e-ḫu-na-aš ḫa-az-zi-l*[*a-aš*] (KBo 16 78 iv 20).

That this is a foodstuff is clear from (5), where a soup or stew (TU_7) is made from it, and from (3) and (4), where it is grouped with meal and grains. The writings taken all together eliminate the possibilities that one read ŠE *me-ḫu-na-aš* (5) as "grain of the season" (so Kammenhuber in Or NS 39 [1970] 558), or ŠA *me-e-ḫu-na-an* as some form of the genitive. Rather the various writings suggest a vowel of indistinct quality in the initial syllable. Perhaps the word even began with a cluster *šm*, although for this one might expect a prothetic vowel, *išmeḫuna-*.

anda šekuwa-

Cornelia Burde in her monograph on the Hittite "medical" rituals (StBoT 19 [1974] 20 and 72) notes a verb *anda šikuwa-* in a broken context, for which she knew only one further, unpublished occurrence (Bo 69/556; StBoT 19 72 note t). She left the verb untranslated, but several further occurrences in published texts allow us to propose a translation for it.

Documentation: (1) [. . .] . . . *nu tar-na-aš-še-et* TÚG-*an ma-a-an* [. . .] *an-da- še-e-ku-e-er tar-na-aš-ša!*(KUB: *ta*)-*an* ᵈ*Ku-mar-bi-in* [. . . *pé*]-*e-da-az* UR.SAG-*iš* ᵈIM-*aš pa-ra-a ú-it* "His skull like a garment [. . .] they sewed up (i.e., closed up the hole made in ii 36ff.). He left him, Kumarbi, [and from the 'good pl]ace' the valiant storm god came forth." (KUB 33 120 ii 73-75; cf. Goetze in ANET 121a, "they made Kumarbi's [*tarnassas*] secure"; P. Meriggi, Athenaeum NS 31 120ff. with note 47: "dilatare"); (2) *nu-uš-ši-kán ŠU-UR-ŠA-ŠU ar-ḫa da-a*[*-i* . . .] *an-da ši-ku-wa-iz-zi A-NA* KUŠ.*MA-AD*?-[. . .] PIRIG.TUR *ku-it ku-na-an ḫar-zi* "He takes from it (a plant?) its roots [. . . and the cavity (from which the plant was removed?)] he *repairs* (i.e., fills in again?). To the [. . .] because he has killed a panther . . ." (KUB 44 61 rev. 12′ff.; StBoT 19 20); (3) 1 GIŠ.*pa-aḫ-ḫi-ša* 3 GIŠ.x[. . .] *še-e-ku-wa-an-za na-aš x*[. . .] (KBo 22 135 i 3′-4′).

Discussion: None of the three passages in which this verb appears is without difficulties. In some ways (1) is the clearest. As Meriggi noted (Athenaeum NS 31 121 note 47), the "birth" of the previous god ᵈKA.ZAL, in col. ii 36ff., gives light on ii 73ff. In the former place someone split open (*paršanu-*) Kumarbi's skull (*tarna-*) like a stone, and the god KA.ZAL came forth. Since in ii 73ff., it is desired to prevent the storm god from exiting from the same orifice, certain persons *anda šekuer* the skull, i.e., "mend" or "seal it up." Thus Goetze's "they made . . . secure" was quite appropriate, and Meriggi's "dilatere" was wide of the mark. (2) is difficult, and my interpretation open to many questions. But I would suggest that the hole left by the removal of the "root(s)" was closed or filled in, and that such a closing of the orifice is what is connoted by the *anda šekuwa-*. (3) is simply too broken; it seems that we have a passive participle there. I am reluctant to follow Meriggi's proposal that the verb is a variant of the verb *šakuwai-*, since the spellings with both *e* and *i* should not go with verb forms showing *a*. I do not think we have an ablauting verb here. Until one can show a closeness of meaning between the *šekuwa-/šikuwa-* verb and the *šakuwa(i)-* verb, they must remain separate.

tarna- "skull"; *tarašna-* "throat"

The problem of *tarna-* and *tar(a)šna-* is quite complicated and has most recently been discussed by E. Laroche (RHA f. 79 162). The nominative singular form *tar-na-aš* in KUB 9 34 ii 38 is to my knowledge the only form of the body-part noun *tarna-* (as opposed to the unit of measure *tarna-*) which is clearly common gender. On the basis of this *tarnaš*, common gender nominative singular, Laroche restored the vocabulary passage as [*mu-u*]*ḫ-ḫu* = *tar-na-a-*[*aš*] (KUB 3 103 rev. 9). Laroche himself acknowledged, however, (RHA f. 79 162) that since the parallel passage in KUB 9 4 i 23 has *tar-aš-na-aš*, the scribe of KUB 9 34 may have made a mistake, writing *tar-na-aš tar-na-aš-ša* GIG-*an* instead of the correct *tar-aš-na-aš tar-aš-na-aš-ša* GIG-*an*. If Meriggi's suggested reading (Athenaeum 31 [1953] 104 and note 11) [*tar*]-*na-aš-ša-an a-aḫ-ra-ma-an* in KUB 9 34 i 22 is correct, the KUB 9 34 scribe consistently wrote *tarna-* for KUB 9 4 scribe's *tarašna-*. There is no reason to assume that the two writings are the same word. Aside from the obvious correspondences between the parallel passages in KUB 9 4 and 9 34 just noted, all occurrences of *tarašna-* point to the throat or esophagus or larynx: *tar-aš-na-aš ta-aš-ku-pí-ma-an* (KUB 9 4 iii 36) and *tar-aš-ša-na-aš!*(KBo: *-ni*) *ta-a-aš-ku-pí-ma-an* (KBo 17 54 i 9′-10′ = 165/d cited in RHA f. 79), "the wailing of the throat/larynx(?)." Those of tarna-, on the contrary, point to the skull or cranium. Laroche (RHA f. 79 162) admits this, but he overlooks a strong argument in favor of keeping the two words apart: the word *tarnaššet* in KUB 33 120 ii 73f. (unlike the *tar-na-aš-ši-ta* in ii 38) has to be accusative singular and thus a neuter! The verb *anda šekuer* governs it directly. I would translate the context: "They closed up his skull (which had been opened—*paršanut* (ii 36-37)—to allow the god KA.ZAL to come out) like a (torn) garment (reading: TÚG-*an ma-a-an*). He left him (namely left) Kumarbi, [and] from [the good] place valiant storm god came forth" (KUB 33 120 ii 73-75). Güterbock suggested analyzing *tarnaššan* ᵈ*Kumarbin* as "he left him [*tarnaš-an*] (namely) Kumarbi," a very satisfying solution, which works also in ii 37, and which eliminates a senseless vacillation in the gender of *tarna-* within the same column of the same tablet. He also suggests that *tar-na-aš-ši-ta ú-it* (ii 38) is an assimilated *tarna(z)-šit-a* "and from his *t*." If the few *tarna-* forms of KUB 9 34 are mistakes for the *tarašna-* of KUB 9 4, and the two words are distinct, then all *tarna-* forms are neuter and all *tarašna-* forms common gender. This would mean restoring the KUB 3 103 rev. 9 vocabulary passage as [*mu-u*]*ḫ-ḫu* = *tar-na-a-*[*an*].

A further argument for keeping *tarašna-* separate as "throat" is the adjectival form *tar-aš-ga-ni-ia-u-wa-an-za*, which occurs twice (KBo 10 37 ii 24, iii 49) in conjunction with *šeḫuganiyawanza* "defiled with urine" and *šakki*[*ganiyawanza*] "defiled with feces" (see Goetze, JCS 16 30 and 22 20). Since both *šakkar* and *šeḫur* are r/n-stems, an *n* has been lost in composition in these adjectives. The bodily issue *tar-aš*, which here, like urine and feces contaminates, seems to have given the name to the *tarašna-* "throat, gullet." Since it is the anus region (*arrišmet*) which is defiled with urine and feces, while it is the mouth (*aišmit*) which is *tarašganiyawanza*, it would seem that the contaminating bodily issue is phlegm/mucus from the throat. Certainly it can be nothing from the skull/cranium (*tarna-*), and "spittle" is *iššalli* in Hittite. The *tarašа-* (common gender) of KBo 17 61 obv. 5 and 18 may be an animal of some kind and surely need not be related to *tar-aš* "mucus." The *taraššawala* of the Targašnalli treaty is also unrelated. The *tar(r)aškanza* MÍ-*za* in KUB 33 86++ iii 13 (StBoT 14 56ff.), KUB 33 120 ii 34f., and possibly in Song of Ullik., 1st Tabl. A iii 34, is (in KUB 33 120 ii 34f.) a source of defilement (*aḫ-ḫu-iš-ki-iz-zi*), and *might* be the woman who by menstruation sheds the mucus lining of her uterus. But this last is *quite uncertain.*

Inuma Ilu awīlum

Thorkild Jacobsen
Harvard University

The Problem

The introductory line of the Atraḫasīs story is a difficult one, so much so that its correct interpretation became a major point at issue in a spirited Assyriological debate between W. G. Lambert and Wolfram von Soden some years ago.[1]

Lambert, translating the line in his and A. R. Millard's edition of the story,[2] took the last word, *awīlum*, to be an adverb ending in the adverbial ending *-um* and assigned to that ending not only its well attested locative meaning, but similative force as well.[3] He accordingly rendered the beginning lines of the story:

i-nu-ma i-lu a-wi-lum	as:	"When the gods like men
ub-lu du-ul-la iz-bi-lu šu-up-ši-[i]k-ka		Bore the work and suffered the toil . . . "[4]

Von Soden, in an article published in Orientalia shortly after Lambert's translation had appeared,[5] vigorously opposed this interpretation and the proposed similative force of *-um*. Instead, he suggested that *awīlum* should be considered the predicate of a nominal sentence the subject of which was *ilū*. He therefore translated:

"Als die Götter Mensch waren
trugen sie die Mühsal, schleppten den Ziegelbrett . . . "

He interpreted this to mean that originally the gods had human as well as divine characteristics, becoming fully differentiated as divine beings only later. The grammatical difficulty presented by a sentence with plural subject and singular predicate he recognized, but he saw it as an instance of provocative language deliberately used by the poet to gain the attention of his audience. Von Soden further argued that the singular was used as a collective and that the use of a collective rather that a plural would predicate only partial, not complete, identity of subject and predicate.[6]

In a reply to von Soden Lambert defended his interpretation and called attention to a Neo-Assyrian fragment of the story from the library of Ashurbanipal which actually does give the incipit of the story in its colophon as:

e-⌜*nu*⌝*-[ma] ilū*(DINGIR.MEŠ) *ki-i a-mi-li*	"When the gods like men . . . etc."

explicitly agreeing with his rendering.[7]

In a subsequent rejoinder, however, von Soden pointed out that the emendations of later copyists trying to make sense of archaic language unfamiliar to them are not implicitly to be trusted, and also that the text of the version underlying this particular copy may have differed from that of the Old Babylonian version we have.[8]

Other scholars have in the main sided with one or the other of these two basic views. Pettinato, van Dijk, and Matouš take with Lambert *awīlum* to be a similative adverbial form,[9] while Moran leans toward von Soden's view, translating:

"When (some) gods were mankind"[10]

It is not the purpose here to go over once more the pros and cons of the arguments advanced by the two sides. Both solutions still seem to us to wrestle with serious difficulties: Lambert's with the need to document conclusively a similative use of the locative *-um*; von Soden's with the uncomfortable assumption of a

1. The literature on the debate and other comments on the line is conveniently listed by Borger in HKL 2 (1975) 157.

2. Lambert-Millard, Atra-ḫasīs. Unless otherwise indicated all quotations from the story are from this publication. We have, however, felt free to adapt transliterations to our own style.

3. Lambert-Millard, Atra-ḫasīs p. 146.

4. Lambert-Millard, Atra-ḫasīs p. 43.

5. W. von Soden, "'Als die Götter (auch noch) Mensch waren': Einige Grundgedanken des altbabylonischen Atramḫasīs-Mythus," Or. NS 38 (1969) 415-32.

6. Or. NS 38 (1969) 416-18.

7. W. G. Lambert, "New Evidence for the First Line of *Atra-ḫasīs*," Or. NS 38 (1969) 533-38.

8. W. von Soden, "Grundsätzliches zur Interpretation des babylonischen Atramḫasīs-Mythus," Or. NS 39 (1970) 311-14; see specifically pages 311-12. Lambert answered in "Critical Notes on Recent Publications," Or. NS 40 (1971) 90-98, on pages 95-98.

9. See von Soden, Or. NS 38 (1969) 416.

10. William L. Moran, "Atraḫasīs: The Babylonian Story of the Flood," Biblica 52 (1971) 51-61. See especially p. 59 n. 2.

Ancient Near Eastern Studies in Memory of J. J. Finkelstein
Connecticut Academy of Arts and Sciences, Memoir 19

nominal sentence with plural subject and singular predicate. It might therefore, perhaps, not be amiss to try to look beyond them to see whether there could be other possible approaches to understanding the line, and if so to explore them further. If nothing else, such an attempt might at least serve to diversify and broaden the compass of the discussion.

The Term *i-lu*

As point of departure we may take von Soden's suggestion that the disputed line constitutes a nominal sentence with *i-lu* as subject and a singular, *a-wi-lum*, as predicate and go on from there to ask whether elsewhere in the text there are other sentences in which likewise *i-lu* as subject is governed by a singular predicate.

As far as we can see there are at least two such cases.[11] In the passage I 70-73 we have:

mi-ši-il ma-aṣ-ṣa-ar-ti mu-šum i-ba-aš-ši	"It was the middle of the watch in the night,
bîtum(É) *la-wi i-lu ú-ul i-di*	the house was surrounded, (but) *i-lu* did not know.
mi-ši-il ma-aṣ-ṣa-ar-ti mu-šum i-ba-aš-ši	It was the middle of the watch in the night,
É-kur la-wi ᵈEN.LÍL *ú-ul i-di*	Ekur was surrounded, (but) ᵈEN.LÍL did not know."

Here, in *i-lu ú-ul i-di, i-lu* is clearly construed with a predicate in the singular, the verb *i-di*, and as the following parallel lines plainly show it constitutes another designation of Enlil.

The second passage, II 4-5, is similar:

[*i-n*]*a ḫu-bu-ri-ši-na i-lu it-ta-aʾ-da-ar*	"At their noise *i-lu* became distressed,
ᵈEN.LÍL *iš-te-me ri-gi-im-ši-in*	ᵈEN.LÍL heard their clamor."

Here too *i-lu* is construed with a predicate in the singular, *ittaʾdar*, and likewise plainly refers to Enlil.

The fact that *i-lu* in these passages must refer to Enlil does not, of course, by itself fully clarify the term. Is it to be considered a mere general term applicable to him, or is it more specific in character, an epithet or even a proper name for him; and how is the absence of mimation to be rated?

In Lambert's translation of the two passages *i-lu* is rendered "the god," suggesting that Lambert considers it an instance of the general term *i-lu* "god" written as the word was spoken after mimation had been lost. This is, of course, a perfectly possible interpretation, for though the scribe in many cases retains mimation he is anything but consistent and very often omits it. It seems odd, though, on this interpretation, that in a setting dealing exclusively with gods Enlil would need to be described as one. Something more specific is surely called for. It seems worth noting, therefore, that Old Babylonian knew a form for divine proper names which had case-endings but not mimation, a form that could be used as an alternative to the more common completely endingless form. Thus the Meissner fragment of the Gilgamesh Epic[12] writes the name of the sungod, Šamaš, with case vowel but without mimation as *Šamšu*(ᵈUTU-*šu*) in i 5, and in the genitive as *Šamši* (ᵈUTU-*ši*) in i 15 and iv 11, but the word for "sun" with mimation as *ša-am-ša-am* in i 13. Note also *bît*(É) *Ani*(AN-*ni*) in iv 9. This variant form for divine proper names seems to be old in Akkadian for, as von Soden has pointed out,[13] Old Akkadian personal names use mimationless forms of words like *abum* "father" and *aḫum* "brother" when they serve as appellations of the family god. Here belongs also the form *Ilu* which occurs with its predicate in the singular in names such as *I-lu-da-lil* and *I-lu-il*(DINGIR) and which has recently been discussed by J. J. M. Roberts.[14] Roberts sees it, undoubtedly correctly, as a variant of the divine name Il, the Akkadian equivalent of West-Semitic El. All of this makes it attractive to interpret also *i-lu* in the Atraḫasīs story in this way, as a variant of Il/El; its use as a by-name for Enlil indicating that he was identified with Il. One may perhaps even go a step farther and assume that by popular etymology Sumerian *Illil* would have been interpreted among speakers of Akkadian on the analogy of names like *Il-Aba (Il-A-ba)*, "God

11. A third such sentence is almost certainly II vi (D) 15 of the passage in lines 15-18: [*i-lu*]-*ma i-ta-šu-uš a-ša-ba-am* / [*i-n*]*a pu-úḫ-ri ša i-li ṣe-eḫ-tum i-ku-ul-šu* / [ᵈEN-LÍL-*ma*] *i-ta-šu-uš a-ša-ba-am* / *i-na pu-úḫ-ri ša i-li ṣe-eḫ-tum i-ku-ul-šu*, "Ilu alone fretted about sitting idle / the laughter in the assembly of the gods stung him / Enlil alone fretted about sitting idle / the laughter in the assembly of the gods stung him." We have restored [ᵈEN-LÍL-*ma*] rather than [ᵈ*En-ki*] at the beginning of line 17 assuming that the line refers to the ill-concealed amusement of the gods at Enlil's discomfiture when Enki caused his plan to wipe out mankind to fail. The ridicule spurs Enlil to his supreme effort, the Flood.

12. Bruno Meissner, "Ein altbabylonisches Fragment des Gilgamos-Epos," MVAG 7/1 (Berlin, 1902).

13. Grundriss der akkadischen Grammatik (Rome, 1952) §63d.

14. J. J. M. Roberts, The Earliest Semitic Pantheon (Baltimore, 1972) p. 134. Roberts carefully distinguishes these names from names in which *i-lu* stands for a plural nominative and construes with plural predicate; he considers the possibility that a pluralis majestatis may be involved.

Aba," *Il-Abrat* "God Abrat," etc. as *Il-Il* "God Il" with variant *Il-Ilu* "God Ilu," for such a form would seem to underlie the puzzling AN-AN which occurs as a theophoric element in Old Akkadian personal names with predicate in the singular.[15] It may be read *Il-Il* or *Il-Ilu*. In favor of assuming a form *Il-Ilu* is the parallelism in the Atraḫasīs story of *i-lu* and ^{d}EN.LÍL, for it is tempting to read a stanza like I 70-73 as:

> "It was the middle of the watch in the night
> the house was surrounded, (but) Ilu did not know,
> It was the middle of the watch in the night,
> Ekur was surrounded, (but) Il-Ilu [Illil(u)] did not know."

with Ilu of line 71 elaborated to Il-Ilu "God Ilu" in line 73.

However, be that as it may—the basic fact that *i-lu* in the Atraḫasīs story can serve as an appellation, most likely a by-name, of Enlil is not to be doubted.

The Term *a-wi-lum*

Returning, then, with this possible alternative meaning of *i-lu* in mind to consideration of the first line of the story to see whether *i-lu* here, as in the other passages where it construes with singular predicate, may perhaps refer to Enlil, we must obviously examine more closely the possible meanings of its predicate *awīlum*.[16]

15. See *Iš-ṭup*-AN-AN and *I-dí*-AN-AN in Roberts, Pantheon p. 134.

16. We hope at some later time to be able to discuss the system of meanings of *awīlum* in some detail and give here merely a bare outline. Guiding us is de Saussure's dictum that concepts "sont purement différentiels, definis non pas positivement par leur contenu, mais negativement par leur rapports avec les autre termes du systême. Leur plus exacte characteristique est d'etre ce que les autres ne sont pas." (Cours de linguistique générale [ed. Bally and Sechehay, 2nd. ed., 1922] p. 162). In the case of a term like *awīlum* the various meanings which it can have are each members of subsystems of their own and derive their precise denotation from contrast with other possible terms of their subsystems. The various subsystems of "horizons" of reference of speaker and hearer form a hierarchy of progressively narrower compass, so that what *awīlum* specifies within one horizon will itself become a horizon when a new narrower meaning is specified. Primary is a division into classifying (I) and individualizing (II) use of the term. That is, it may be used interconceptually to set off the class—or an individual of the class—*awīlum* against other classes or individuals belonging to them, or it may be used intra-conceptually to set off one individual of the class *awīlum* against other individuals of that class, which gives it almost pronominal character: "man" = a single individual, or even "one" (cf. German "man"<Mann). Horizon for *awīlum* in classifying use is at its widest (A) "Living Beings" (*šiknāt napištim*) within which it specifies "Human Being" in contrast, e.g., to "God" or "Animal." The sense "Human Being" can then itself serve as horizon, within which *awīlum* will specify (a) "Authority Figure," head of a private or a commercial house or of a public administrative unit. The sense "Authority Figure" in its turn can serve as a new horizon (a′) within which *awīlum* will specify "Good Authority Wielder," "Respected Authority Wielder." The system may be set out as follows:

I. *Classifying, i.e., interconceptually distinctive meanings*
  A. Horizon: "*Living Beings*"
    Meaning: "Human Being," Man." Member, mostly male, of the *genus homo* (MB and later). Contrasts are *ilum* "God" and terms for animals. As a collective "Man," "Mankind." Compare *awīlûtum* which can have similar meaning.
  a. Horizon: "*Human Being*"
    Meanings: "Authority Figure." Specifically (1) "Householder," "Citizen," "Townsman," "Notable" (OA, OB, Mari). Typically the free householder *sui juris* with *patria potestas* and *dominium* over his household. Contrasts are socially: *muškēnum* "Client," and *wardum* "Slave"; domestically: *aššat awīlim* "Wife of an a.," *mār awīlim* "Son of an a.," *warad awīlim* "Slave of an a.," *amat awīlim* "Slave Woman of an a.," and the collective *nišē* "(Women) Folks," Dependents," and the plural *iššū* "The Women (Folk)." As a collective, *awīlum* denotes within this horizon "The Citizenry," "The Townsmen." (2) "The Principal" (OA, OB). Head of a commercial house or other private economic establishment. Contrasts are: *ṣuḫārum* "Apprentice," "Junior," and *mārum* "Son," also used for the apprentice. (3) "Magistrate" (OB, Mari). Man having control and authority over a public administrative unit such as, e.g., a district or a city, in which latter case *awīlum* can denote the "Ruler." Contrast is, e.g., *awīlû* "Notables."
  a′. Horizon: "*Authority Figure*"
    Meanings: (1) As title of respect. Private sphere: "The Master," "(My) Lord and Master" (OB). Title used for the head of a private household by its members. Public sphere: "His Honor," "The Magistrate" (OB). Title of respect used for high officials wielding judiciary and disciplinary powers. (2) As a standard of gentility (OA). Private sphere: "Gentleman," "Pukka Sahib." A person, often a patron, of probity; dependable, trustworthy. Contrast *la awīlum* "Untrustworthy, Ignoble Person." As a standard of virility: (Mari, Amarna, perhaps a West Semitic calque) "Man," a man of manly, warlike virtues. As standard of appearance: "Fine Gentleman" (OB). A man of well groomed appearance.

II. *Individualizing, i.e., intra-conceptually distinctive meanings*
  a. Horizon: "*Human Being*"
    Meanings: (1) "Man" as an individual man distinguished from other individual men as one unit from others (OAkk and onwards), "Person," "Worker," "Member of a Group" (with following genitive or possessive pronoun often "Liege-man"). In this meaning *awīlum* often serves as singular to *ṣabum*. In MB and later: "Slave." (2) "One." As a mere syntactic prop-word for adjective or genitive

Previous translations of the line have uniformly understood that term as being in contrast with the preceding *i-lu* read as *ilū* "the gods," and have accordingly rendered it in its connotation of "human," "mortal," and—as suggested by the following lines—"toiler." If, however, *i-lu* need not mean "the gods" but can refer to Enlil, that contrast no longer imposes itself and other meanings of *awīlum* in Old Babylonian come into consideration, especially, of course, such as seem applicable to Enlil in his rôle in the context.

Relevant here is particularly one meaning which may be rendered approximately as "magistrate." In this use *awīlum* designates a person having control and authority over a public administrative unit such as a district or a city, in which latter case it serves as a colloquial term for "ruler."[17] Since in the beginning of the Atraḫasīs story Enlil is the person in authority on earth and in charge of public works, corvée, such as canal digging, the term fits him and his rôle perfectly. Seeking a suitable translation one may consider terms such as "master," "task-master," or "boss," for since the plot of the story has its focus on Enlil's rôle as imposer of heavy labor it seems best to remain within the purview of labor relation terms. In view of the colloquial overtones of *awīlum* in this use, further, "boss" is perhaps to be preferred.[18]

As an alternative rendering of the beginning of the Atraḫasīs story we would thus seriously consider:

i-nu-ma i-lu a-wi-lum	When Ilu was the boss
ub-lu du-ul-la iz-bi-lu šu-up-ši-[i]k-ka	they were burdened with corvée, toted the work-basket;
šu-up-ši-ik i-li ra-bi-[m]a	the gods' work-basket was large, so that
du-ul-lu-um ka-bi-it ma-a-ad ša-ap-ša-qum	the misery was heavy, the distress much,
ra-bu-tum ^{d}*a-nun-na-ku si-bi-it-tam*	the senior *annunakū* were burdening
du-ul-lam ú-ša-az-ba-lu ^{d}*i-⸢gi-gi⸣*	the seven *igigû* with corvée.

The Context

A few comments on the context in which the intial line occurs, and on some of the terms used may be added.

The parallelism with *šupšikkum* suggests that *dullum* in line 2 has its specialized sense of corvée, a sense otherwise attested in Old Babylonian only in Elam.[19] The word *šupšikkum* denotes basically a carrying pad and looks like a loan from a Sumerian *dub-síg "wool pad," not yet, as far as we know, attested. Its normal Sumerian correspondent is dusu, for which we can suggest no etymology. The older forms of the sign for it, ÎL, show a basket standing on a pad-like structure with a hollow for the top of the head to fit into, and it in turn rests on a human head. Von Soden calls attention to a statuette in the Metropolitan Museum in New York, published by Crawford, which seems to have it in the form of a box, presumably filled with wool or other padding, which would agree well with the form depicted in the sign.[20] Other representations, e.g., on the foundation figures of Ur-Nammu from Nippur, show it as a ring of some, presumably soft, material.[21] The sign, and the fact that the word is often written with the determinative for reed, GI, suggest that the term could be used not only for the pad, but for the whole carrying rig including the basket. Work-basket seems therefore a permissible and immediately understandable translation. Since the corvée of the gods consisted in the digging of canals—more precisely, in digging out the beds of the Euphrates and the Tigris—the *šupšikkum* would be used for transporting excavated earth and not, as on other occasions, to carry bricks up to the bricklayers. A translation "hod" in English, "Ziegelbrett" in German, seems therefore less apt in this passage.

The conceptual structure of the stanza is very fine. The fact of corvée work bossed by Ilu is objectively stated of an unidentified "they" in lines 1-2; the general term *dullum* is made more vivid by the pregnant

carrying the actual meaning (OAkk. and onwards). Frequent as formant in terms for occupations. With negation "No-one," "No-man" (OAkk. and onwards). (3) "One (the Other)" with force of reciprocal pronoun (OB and onwards). (4) With *ištēn* "one" *awīlum* can serve as term for the distributive "Each One" (OAkk. and onwards), or to stress singularity: "Single One."

17. See for instance ARM 5 24:5-24, in which the office of the deceased *awīl Ti-iz-ra-aḫ*.KI is referred to as *ša-pi-ru-ti-ni* "governorship over us" (line 11) and as *su-qá-[q]ù-tim* "headmanship" (line 20), or Fish, Letters 1:5-14, in which the *šāpir mātim*, "the governor," to whom the letter is addressed, is referred to in the body of it as *awīlum*. Judiciary and police powers of the *awīlum* are referred to in PBS 7 101:1-2 and 24-28, YOS 2 40:24-28, CT 4 i 24. Many other passages could be cited.

18. For the colloquial character of this usage see von Soden, AHw. 1 90 s.v. *awīlum* B.2b.

19. See CAD D 177 s.v. *dullu*.

20. Or. NS 38 (1969) 420 n. 1.

21. See the photograph in S. N. Kramer, The Sumerians (Chicago, 1963) on top of fourth page after page 64.

image of the work-basket which parallels it. Line 3 then identifies the general "they" as "the gods"[22] and the work-basket as "large"—and so excessively hard to carry—in the manner of a "particularizing stanza."[23] It then uses the final *-ma* "so that" to lead from purely objective description, as seen from outside, to the subjective emotional plane, telling of the effect the conditions had on the gods. In so doing the poet skillfully develops, as it were, aspects inherent in the objectively descriptive terms he has just used: *dullum* is now given its meaning "misery," *šapšaqum* serves as meaningful pun on *šupšikkum*.[24] The external closeness of this language to that of line 2 has the effect of suggesting at first blush mere repetition; then of giving unexpected pleasure as it dawns on the hearer that a new content is being unfolded. Lines 5-6 continue the gradual exposition by particularizing still further the gods of line 3 as the *igigû* and setting forth the administrative power-structure behind Ilu/Enlil and the corvée work, the senior gods, whom the poet then goes on to list by names and offices.

Grammatically the seeming difficulties created by the accusative *sibittam* were solved by von Soden,[25] who suggested that the poet here uses enjambment so that *sibittam* belongs with ^{d}*i-gi-gi* of line 6 and not with the immediately preceding ^{d}*a-nun-na-ku*. His suggestion is unaffected by the texts quoted by Borger (BRM 4 2 i 10 *si-bi-te*!, cf. GAG §69a[8]; RA 46 90 "(as) seven in war," cf. GAG §147).[26] The number seven does, indeed, characterize the *igigû* well, for it seems to have been constitutive for the very notion of that term, which appears to consist of the Sumerian word for five: i written with five horizontal wedges plus gi-gi "and one and one" i.e. 5+1+1=7. Note gi-e . . . = *iš-ten* Ea II 54, gi = *iš*[*-te-en*] Antagal C 52, gi-e . . . = *iš-ten* Ea II 202 and the formation of the numerals peš = *ša-la-aš-ti* (=3) peš-bal = *ir-bi-it* ("3 and over" = 4), peš-bal-gi_4 = *ḫa-an-še-et* (=3 and over and one"=5), peš-bal-gi_4-gi_4=*ši-iš-še-et* (+1+1=6), peš-peš-gi_4 = *si-bi-it* ("3 and 3 and 1" = 7), peš-bi = *ša-al-šu* "the third," peš-gi_4-bi = *ri-bu-u* "the fourth" MSL 4 164f. 41-47. That the basic meaning of *igigû* is "the seven" is also indicated by the well known variant writing DINGIR-Ì-MIN to be read ^{d}*í-gì-gì* "the seven."

As for the implications of this designation, it would seem first of all that since the term is Sumerian it most likely refers to Sumerian deities and—in view of the variant designation ^{d}nun-gal "the great divine princes"—deities of at least as high rank as the *anunnakū*, who are only "the sons of princes." Most likely, since the notion "seven" could convey the idea of totality in Sumerian (imin = *kiššatu*, see CAD K 457), dingir igigi may have stood for "the totality of the gods," and the term would appear to be originally a simple synonym of *anunnakū* as a term for the gods as a whole.[27] This has a degree of support from the fact that in later times it was felt necessary to reinterpret the writing ^{d}Ì-MIN as the higher number 5×60×2=600.

The existence side by side of two synonymous terms for the gods as a whole also led later on, as the astral tendency in Babylonian-Assyrian religion became more pronounced, to a secondary differentiation of meaning: the term *anunnakū* tended to be used of the chtonic, *igigû* of the celestial, deities in the pantheon.[28]

In the Atraḫasīs passage, apparently, this differentiation has not yet taken place; *anunnakū* and *igigû* are here synonymous terms, used by the poet for the sake of variety of expression. The distinction of lines 5-6 is thus to be sought for in *rabûtum* "the senior," i.e. the authoritative, governing, gods, to wit those listed in lines 7-15, as over against the general run of gods.

22. One could of course consider reading *i-li* here not as *ilū* "the gods" but as genitive of *i-lu* in line 1, and translate "Ilu's work basket was large." William Moran calls my attention to I 196-97, *ap-ša-nam li-bi-il ši-pí-ir* ^{d}EN-LÍL / *šu-up-ši-ik ilim*(DINGIR) *a-wi-lum li-iš-ši*, "let him bear the yoke, the task imposed by Enlil, / let man take up the god's work basket," where both orthography, DINGIR, and the contrast with the following *a-wi-lum*, "man," indicate that *ilū* is intended. We therefore provisionally take *šu-up-ši-ik i-li* in line 3 as meaning "the work-basket of the gods" also.

23. See JNES 12 (1953) 162 n. 5=Image of Tammuz, p. 334 n. 5.

24. That a "pun" is involved here was seen independently also by William Moran.

25. Or. NS 38 (1969) 420.

26. Borger, HKL 2 157.

27. This was seen already by Kienast, Studies Landsberger 16 (1965) 157f.

28. See Kienast, Studies Landsberger 16 (1965) 157f.

AN ASSYRO-ARAMAIC *egirtu ša šulmu*

Stephen A. Kaufman
The University of Chicago - Haifa University

Cuneiform law, seen as a reflection and expression of the fundamental principles of Mesopotamian society, served as one of Prof. J. J. Finkelstein's major focal points in the scholarly pursuits. His masterful, indeed incomparable "The Goring Ox" (part of a larger, still unpublished study) in which with broad strokes and pointed purpose he scanned the entire history of the concepts of forfeiture and sovereignty in western jurisprudence, is unquestionably the most ambitious and noteworthy example of that trend of scholarship in the field of Ancient Near Eastern law that attempts to delineate the complicated history of the development and spread of legal institutions, formulary and conceptual frameworks. It is thus especially gratifying for me to be able to offer a small contribution to the study of Mesopotamian law to the memory of this dearly missed mentor and friend.

The inter-relationships among the various systems, procedures and formularies of cuneiform law, and their connections with and influence upon those of its postulated successor, Aramaic common law, have been the object of increasingly perceptive scholarly inquiry in recent years.[1] Proximate cuneiform models for various formulae known from the Aramaic legal documents from Elephantine have been sought in an effort to clarify the still hazy picture of Ancient Near Eastern legal history. Such models have been found in nearly every cuneiform archive, from both core and peripheral areas; yet up until recently the evidence for Neo-Assyrian parallels was surprisingly meagre, although historical considerations suggest that the legal system of the Neo-Assyrian empire should have played a key role in the development of the subsequent Aramaic patterns.

In his attempt to correct the former picture of this relationship, Y. Muffs has argued that 'in all probability, it was from Neo-Assyrian models that the Aramaic formulary was derived."[2] Such conclusions as those reached by Muffs, however, have necessarily been based, from the Aramaic side, almost exclusively on texts from a later period. Aside from a small but steadily growing number of brief Aramaic dockets on Akkadian economic texts and a few brief Aramaic loan records from Assur, Nineveh, and Tell Halaf,[3] only Akkadian texts have heretofore been known from that period which both historical and linguistic evidence indicates was the time of Aramaic-Assyrian symbiosis[4]; thus the extent to which Neo-Assyrian cuneiform texts reflect unknown Aramaic elements rather than ancient Mesopotamian traditions remains in many cases a moot point. Indeed, the fact that Neo-Assyrian law has much in common with that of earlier peripheral regions rather than with the core region[5] suggests that Aramaic may frequently have served as the vehicle responsible for the reappearance of archaic features in isolated Neo-Assyrian documents and archives.

This situation has been modified by the recent publication of the tablet studied here (Louvre AO 25.341), which represents the first known significant Aramaic legal document from the pre-Achaemenid period. The Aramaic text is carefully inscribed on a beautifully made, highly polished dark clay tablet of unreported provenience (though internal evidence suggests the region of Harran; v. infra). Although from the photographs it would appear to be somewhat more carefully made than the normal cuneiform-inscribed tablet of the same type and period (mid-seventh century B.C.), its shape and size are standard, and its physical format, a thrice-repeated stamp seal impression on the obverse below the introductory three or four lines of text, is well-known from late Neo-Assyrian private documents of similar content and provenience.[6] The ductus of the inscribed text is similar to, though not identical with, other known "argillary" Aramaic

1. Notably in Yochanan Muffs' outstanding monograph, Studies in the Aramaic Legal Papyri from Elephantine (Leiden, 1969). For previous scholarly opinions, see his discussion pp. 3ff.

2. Muffs, Elephantine p. 186.

3. See F. Vattioni, "Epigrafia aramaica," Augustinianum 10 (1970) 493-532, and the new material published by A. R. Millard, "Some Aramaic Epigraphs," Iraq 34 (1972) 131-37. A substantial new collection of similar Aramaic tablets in the possession of the Koninklijke Musea voor Kunst en Geschiedenis in Brussels is to be published by Edward Lipiński.

4. For the linguistic evidence see Stephen A. Kaufman, The Akkadian Influences on Aramaic, AS 19 (Chicago, 1974).

5. Cf. Muffs, Elephantine pp. 15f., 90f., 186, and especially p. 195 to p. 15 n. 3.

6. Cf., e.g., Tell Halaf tablets nos. 102ff.; Millard, Iraq 34 (1972) 131-37 no. 7; Barbara Parker, "Excavations at Nimrud, 1949-53 — Seals and Seals Impressions," Iraq 17 (1955) xxiv no. 1 (see p. 115) and 119f., figs. 14-15. For the type of seal itself ("mixed object type"), see the discussion by Parker, p. 115.

Ancient Near Eastern Studies in Memory of J. J. Finkelstein
Connecticut Academy of Arts and Sciences, Memoir 19

scripts of the same period.[7] The reading and interpretation offered below differ in several significant respects from that of the *editio princeps*.[8]

TEXT

obv. ⌜*k*⌝*lbyd*ʾ*l w*ʿ*zrn*ʾ*l*
ʾ*mhm śmw*
qdm nsḥnghy
seals
*bl*ʾ*m srgrnr*
*l*ʾ*m hṭ*ʿ*m lḥm*
*wšqlw klbyd*ʾ*l*
*w*ʿ*zrn*ʾ*l*

rev. *ksp šql*⌜*n*⌝ [ ]
wzwz lnsḥnghy
wśmw šlm bynyhm
mn ʿ*l mn.yšb*
⌜*ḥyy*⌝ *śhr wḥyy*
[*ml*]*k*ʾ *śhdn*
⌜*nsxx*⌝*yb w*ʿ*wyd*
*w*ʾ*drmny*
w⌜xx⌝*dšyb*
*w*ʾ*l*⌜xx⌝*n*

TRANSLATION

KLBYDʾL and ʿZRNʾL (2) made their declaration (3) before NSḤNGHY (4) in the eponym-year of Aššur-gārûa-nēri (5) as follows: "Here, eat bread." (6-7) And KLBYDʾL and ʿZRNʾL paid out (8) [x] shekels of silver (9) and a half-shekel to NSḤNGHY (10) and made a settlement.

(11) Whoever returns (in suit) against the other, (12) (may he be cursed) by the life of Śehr and the life of (13) the king. Witnesses: (14) NSxxYB and ʿWYD (15) and Addu-rēmanni (16) and xxDŠYB (17) and ʾLxxN.

TEXTUAL NOTES

Line 1. KLBYDʾL: "All is in the hand of God"—Previously known from the transliteration *kul-ba-ia-di-*[AN?],[9] this personal name is closely related to the well-known West-Semitic names *byd*ʾ*l, bd*ʾ*l, bd*-DN.[10] Precisely the same sentiment is found expressed in the contemporary Akkadian name *Gabbu/i-ina-qātē-il*/DN and its several variants attested in both Assyria and Babylonia.[11] It is doubtful whether the fatalistic sense of the English rendering was present in the original; Semitic *byd/ina qātē* expressed rather the sense "in the care of."[12]

Line 2. ʾ*mhm*: "their statement"—See below s.v. *l*ʾ*m*, line 5.

śmw: Note the position of the verb after both subject and object as opposed to the other two main verbs in the text (lines 6, 10) both of which begin their sentences. This text is thus good evidence for the generally free word order of Mesopotamian Aramaic of this period, a feature that should be ascribed to the influence

7. The forms of *ṭet*, *mem*, and *ḥet* are worthy of particular note. Two studies have been devoted to the analysis of the Aramaic scripts of the period: Stephen J. Lieberman, "The Aramaic Argillary Script in the Seventh Century," BASOR 192 (1965) 25-31, and Y. Naveh, The Development of the Aramaic Script (Jerusalem, 1970). Detailed comparison of letter forms still entails reference to the original publications, however, for there is a significant lack of agreement between the two studies, and details are often overlooked. Comparing their treatments of the Assur tablets, for example (Lieberman fig. 1:7, Naveh fig. 2:5-6), one notes: Lieberman's rendering of the *samekh* from tablet 4 is extremely inaccurate; Naveh misses the shallow *shin* of tablet 5. The unusual *ḥet* of 4:2 is drawn by neither (for the reading, see Lipiński, Studies in Aramaic Inscriptions and Onomastics 1, Orientalia Lovaniensia Analecta 1 [Leuven, 1975] 97 and the further proof in Kaufman, Influences p. 104 n. 364); and the special character of the *mem* (frequently drawn with ʿ*ayin*-shaped upper strokes totally separate from the main vertical as in our tablet) is not made evident in either's rendition.

8. Pierre Bordreuil, "Une tablette araméenne inédite de 635 av. J.C.," Semitica 23 (1973) 96-102. The plates of photographs accompanying the article are of superb quality, totally obviating a hand-drawn copy. This collection of full and detailed views of both the original and a cast might well serve as a model for future publications of similar texts.

9. Tallqvist, APN p. 117; cf. *Ba-a-a-di-il*, p. 49.

10. See Bordreuil, Semitica 23 (1973) 97 nn. 7-10. An additional Ammonite example of *byd*ʾ*l* is now found on a seal published by F. M. Cross, "Leaves from an Epigraphist's Notebook," CBQ 36 (1974) 490. See, too, the Palmyran hypocoristicon *byd*ʾ (J. K. Stark, Personal Names in Palmyrene Inscriptions [Oxford, 1971] p. 76).

11. Tallqvist, APN p. 78; cf. in APN *Gabbu-qātē-il, Ina-qātē-ilāni, Qa-ti-il*; Tallqvist, NBN p. 62, Gabbi-in-qāti, Gabbi-ina-qāti-Šamaš.

12. The translation suggested by Frank L. Benz in Personal Names in the Phoenician and Punic Inscriptions, Studia Pohl 8 (Rome, 1972) 285: "from/by the hand(s) of" misses the sense entirely, as is proven by the related names *Gabbu-ana-Aššur*, "all belongs to Aššur" and *Gabbu-ana-Ištar*, "all belongs to Ištar" APN p. 78.

of Akkadian[13]; it by no means implies a word-for-word translation from Akkadian, however.

Line 3. NSḤNGHY: "Nasuḥ is my splendor"[14]—NSḤ is the alphabetic form of the divine name found in numerous cuneiform spellings as *Na-aš-ḫu* or *Na-šuḫ* used in both Aramaic and Akkadian names and generally explained as an Aramaic by-form of Akkadian *Nusku*[15]; but the fact that *Nusku* (i.e. *nšk*) also appears in Aramaic contexts and the nature of the phonetic differences suggest a long period of independent development of the two forms.[16] NGHY, from the root *ngh* "to be bright," relatively rare in attested personal names, appears in cuneiform transcription as *na-gi* (e.g. *Adad-na-gi*) and *na-ga-ḫi-i.*[17]

Line 4. *blʾm*: The alphabetic spelling with internal *aleph* for Assyrian *limmu/līmu* was known previously.[18]

SRGRNR is the Akkadian name *Aššur-gārûa-nēri*, "O Aššur, kill my enemies," an eponym of the post-canonical period assigned by M. Falkner to the year 635 B.C.[19] The alphabetic spelling is noteworthy for the lack of initial *aleph* and its failure to indicate the glide in *gārûa*. The former may be explained by elision owing to the presumably junctureless connection between the name and the word "eponym," for internal *aleph* is frequently omitted in alphabetic transcriptions of Akkadian names.[20] The latter may be similarly accounted for; elision would not be unusual in a frequent and thoughtlessly used expression such as a date.[21]

Line 5. *lʾm*: "to say"—This word is to be understood as the intermediate stage between the old *lʾmr* (attested in the ostracon from Assur[22] as well as in Imperial Aramaic) and the particle *lm* found in Imperial Aramaic and Syriac (*lam*) as a marker of direct and indirect speech.[23] That *lʾmr* and *lm* can be identical in their usage is proven by the parallel clauses:

lʾ ʾkhl ʾmr lmḥsh lʾmr . . . (AP 5:11-12)

lʾ ʾkl ʾmr lk lm . . . (AP 10:11)[24]

The form in our text confirms that the latter is actually a phonetic development of the former. In fact another example of this intermediate form is found in Imperial Aramaic; for the heretofore obscure *lʾm* of AP 46:7 can now be identified with our word.[25]

If *lʾm* is a development of *lʾmr*, it would seem not totally unreasonable to suggest that *ʾm* in line 2 can

13. See Kaufman, Influences p. 132.

14. This personal name was not recognized as such by Bordreuil. The correct interpretation was independently noted by F. M. Fales in "West Semitic Names from the Governor's Palace," Annali di Ca' Foscari 13/3 (Serie Orientale 5, 1974) 188 n. 7.

15. For the correspondence between the transliteration *š* of the Assyrian cuneiform and alphabetic *s* (and the reverse), see Kaufman, Influences pp. 140ff.

16. In the Nerab inscriptions (KAI 225:9, 226:9) and in the personal name *nškly*, DEA 26.

17. Cf. Tallqvist, APN p. 296 and the additional bibliography cited CCNA 185,27. The forms *na-ga-a-a* and *na-ga-ha* are to be understood as perfect verbs. The final *a-a* of the former indicates *-ah* as in the frequent spelling of the Aramaic name-element *-ʾlh* as DINGIR-*a-a*.

18. See Bordreuil, Semitica 23 (1973) 100 n. 1. For a parallel and possible explanation, see Kaufman, Influences p. 67 n. 180.

19. "Die Eponymen des spätassyrischen Zeit," AfO 17 (1954) 118.

20. E.g., *ʾsrslmḥ* for *Aššur-šallim-aḫḫe* in M. Lidzbarski, Altaramäische Urkunden aus Assur (Leipzig, 1921) pp. 15ff., nos. 1, 2, 3; cf. S. Kaufman, JAOS 90 (1970) 270f. This very name is given by Bordreuil (Semitica 23 [1973] 100) and Lipiński (Studies pp. 89f.) as another example of the omission of initial *aleph*, for in tablet no. 2:2 the same name is apparently spelled *srslmḥ*. The first letter is rather severely abraded, however, and shows traces of a diagonal that could only belong to an *aleph*. One suspects an error, or even one letter inscribed upon another. Lipiński's argument (Studies pp. 89f.) that *ddbn* in tablet no. 1 represents *Adad-ibni* is equally untenable in light of the Assyrian name-element ᵈDaddi (Tallqvist, APN p. 67) and the probable pronunciation of *Adad* as *Addu/a*" (see below to line 15).

21. Of course there are other possibilities. The scribe may simply have been unable to indicate a glide sound which was neither *waw* nor *aleph*; or the final *a* may no longer have been pronounced. (Cf. the rare spellings *aš-šur-gārû-ni-ri* and *aš-šur-ga-ri-ni-ri* listed by Falkner, AfO 17 [1954] 101.

22. Cf. A. Dupont-Sommer, "L'ostracon araméen d'Assour," Syria 24 (1944-45) 38f.

23. See, too, Syriac (and Rabbinic Hebrew) *lamlem*, "to speak," and related nouns.

24. A Cowley, Aramaic Papyri of the Fifth Century B.C. (Oxford, 1923). Note that the initial quote of the lender in AP 10:3 is introduced by *lʾmr*! The following syntactic development of *lm* within Imperial Aramaic can be suggested: first, like *lʾmr*, as a particle preceding direct speech (AP 10:11, 13; 26:21; 30:6; Behistun 39 [=Akkadian *umma*]; Ahiqar 60, 165); then as an enclitic marker of direct speech (AP 32:2; AD 12:1, 5; 10:1; Ahiqar 20, 54); and finally as a general enclitic adverbial particle "then" (Ahiqar 39, 45). The meaning "indeed" suggested by Cowley, DISO and Driver (Aramaic Documents of the Fifth Century B.C. p. 58) is without foundation.

25. I owe this interpretation to a suggestion of Dr. Y. Naveh. I had originally proposed to read simply *lʾmr* instead of the current *lʾm h-*. Naveh argues convincingly that since our scribe is otherwise careful in his separation of words and that since, according to one of the photographs of the cast, the letter in question has a closed top and open bottom, the fourth letter of line 5 must be a *heh* and must connect with what follows. In sum, however, the letter is quite clearly malformed.

Those who would understand *lʾm* of line 5 as a repetition of the word *lʾm* of the previous line must assume scribal error. The *limmu* himself (*rab šāqê* of Aššurbanipal) could hardly be the subject of the following verb.

represent *ʾmr*, i.e. later Aramaic *mʾmr*. Thus *ʾmhm* would be "their word" or "their statement." Other than to note the parallel disappearance of the final *reš* of the root *ʾmr* in much later Babylonian Aramaic and the possible parallel of Biblical Aramaic *kᵊnēmā*, "thus" (Imperial Aramaic *knm*),[26] I can offer no satisfactory explanation for the loss of final *reš* in either of these forms.

For those who accept my general interpretation of the text but would hesitate to force the analogy *lʾm* : *lʾmr* :: *ʾm* : *ʾmr*, the enigmatic *ʾm* may be translated simply "conciliatory offer" and left without etymology. Previously attempted explanations fall far short of the mark: Bordreuil, with due caution, compares Akkadian *amātu*, "word," translating "affaire." It is not clear whether he thinks it to be a loanword or a cognate, but neither is phonetically possible. *Waw* is the original second consonant of this root, and subsequent Akkadian orthographies (Babylonian *m*, Assyrian *b*) continue to indicate a pronounced *waw*.[27] His understanding of the sense, however, is basically correct.

E. Lipińsky (see below, n. 32) takes *ʾmhm śmw* to mean "fixed their cubits." True, *ʾammā*, "cubit," frequently takes the masculine plural ending, but the expected form is *ʾmyhm*, and the omission of the plural marker *yod* before the suffix is unparalleled. Furthermore, the meaning "fixed" for *śmw* is tortured. Most importantly, the whole concept rests on an unacceptable reading and interpretation of line 5.[28]

Yet other suggestions may be offered. A comparison between *ʾm* and Akkadian *umma*, "thus," comes immediately to mind and would involve no change in our interpretation. But *umma* is never nominalized in Akkadian, and it is not frequent in texts from this period. Most reasonable of the doubtful suggestions is the obvious translation of *ʾm* as "mother." Our tablet would then be understood to deal with arrangements for support of an elderly parent (with *hṭʿm* of line 5 to be taken as "he fed"). The major difficulties with this interpretation are the non-determined form of *ʾm* in line 5, the unusual use of the preposition *qdm* in line 3 and the fact that the formulae of the tablet give clear evidence as to the nature of the transaction, and a "care for the aged" contract is just not indicated.

hṭʿm lḥm: Bordreuil reads the final word as *tḥm*, "boundary." That mark which he interprets as the vertical of the *taw*, however, is certainly nothing more than the continuation of a long scratch beginning far above the line, and the tick which appears at the bottom of this "vertical" is only one of a whole series of such indentations extending across the width of the tablet at this level. Furthermore, one would expect the tail of a *taw* to extend considerably below the base line of the neighboring *ḥet*. Eliminating these extraneous features, an absolutely clear *lamed* comes into view. Thus orthographic considerations, coupled with the proximity of the verb *ṭʿm*, "to taste, eat," permit little doubt as to the aptness of the reading *lḥm*, "bread."

The word *hṭʿm* at first glance appears to be a *hafel* of the common Aramaic root *ṭʿm*, "to taste" or simply "to eat." Since this yields little sense, [29] I have taken it to be the imperative of the simple stem preceded by the Old Aramaic spelling of later *hʾ*, "behold," a particle which frequently introduces messages or new subjects. The spelling without *aleph* is paralleled by the spelling of negative *lʾ* as *l-*, in the Sefire and Nerab inscriptions and in the ostracon from Assur.[30] The interpretation of *hṭʿm (tḥm)* advanced by Bordreuil and, following him, E. Lipiński, "he made (them) agree on a boundary" is without philological foundation,[31] and, moreover, lacks a subject for the verb.[32]

26. Cf. L. Koehler and W. Baumgartner, Lexicon in Veteris Testamenti Libros (Leiden, 1958) p. 1086.

27. See Kaufman, Influences p. 143.

28. Should further paleographic investigation be after all able to corroborate Bordreuil's reading *tḥm* in line 5, it would be best to relate *ʾm* to the Babylonian use of *ummu*, "mother," as something like an original deed of purchase in real-estate transactions. See especially Neo-Babylonian *ummi eqli* (NRVU pp. 145f., 612). Our tablet would thus refer to the use of such an *ummi eqli* to settle a boundary dispute between KLBYDʾL and ʿZRNʾL (brothers?) and NSḤNGHY (the original owner of the property); cf. Schorr, VAB 5 275ff., and note the rather small sums involved in the Old Babylonian examples, just as in our tablet. If one then assumes the meaning for *hṭʿm* rejected in n. 31, line 5 could be translated "He made boundary conform to original tablet."

29. Unless one accepts the translation "mother" for *ʾm*; see above.

30. This idea, too, was first suggested by Y. Naveh. For the specific nuance "here, take it" for *hʾ*, cf. the use of *hā* in the modern Arabic dialects as noted by Wolfdietrich Fischer, Die demonstrativen Bildungen der neuarabischen Dialekte (The Hague, 1959) pp. 158f.

31. It is ostensibly based on Dupont-Sommer's similar interpretation of the verb *ytʿm* in the Assur ostracon (line 8), apparently based on the usage of the noun *ṭʿm* in the meaning "sense." But there are no further Aramaic parallels to such a meaning, and in the ostracon itself, broken as it is, only a great imagination would divorce a verb preceded by "grinding" (*lṭḥnw*) and followed by "olives" (*bzyt*) from a connection with food.

32. Prof. Lipiński presented his interpretation in a paper read at Budapest in 1974, the essence of which he was kind enough to transmit to me in a letter (20.6.75). Both Bordreuil and Lipiński understand NSḤNGHY to be the subject of the verb, that is to say the judge in a boundary dispute. (Bordreuil's erroneous interpretation of this name as "le gouverneur du district" no doubt

Line 9. *wzwz*: In Akkadian the word *zūzu*, "half-shekel," is attested outside of lexical texts only in Middle Babylonian and Nuzi documents (CAD Z p. 170b). Rather than posit a very early (i.e. Middle Babylonian) loan into Aramaic, I prefer to take the evidence of our text to indicate that the word was current in Neo-Assyrian but merely unattested in syllabic writing.[33]

Line 11. *mn ʿl mn yšb*: Bordreuil reads *mn ʿlmn*, "depuis toujours," but the correct reading is clear from the Akkadian parallels discussed below.[34]

Line 12. *śhr*: *Śehr* is the Aramaic moon god, attested in cuneiform sources as *Šēr*, worshipped throughout the Aramaean region from the moon-cult city of Harran to Nerab (i.e., Aleppo) and Damascus.[35] Its use here as the only god invoked in the curse formula is strongly suggestive of the region of Harran as the origin of the tablet.

Line 14. *ʿwyd*: A hypocoristicon well-known from Palmyran.[36]

Line 15. *ʾdrmny*: The longer tail of the *reš* is no longer visible because of severe damage to the tablet at this point, as is clear from the photograph of the cast. Bordreuil's reading *ʾddmny* is problematic on two counts: The expected form of the Aramaic preterite element is *mnny*[37]; *mny* makes no sense. In the divine name one would expect the usual Aramaic spelling of the Aramaic god as *hdd*. The name is rather the Akkadian *Adad-rēmanni*. Instead of Aramaization of the Akkadian divine name (i.e. *hdd*), the scribe has rendered phonetically *ʾd*, representing the actual Akkadian pronunciation *Addu*.

Addu (or simply *Ad*) is apparently a development of the Amorite pronunciation of the name of the storm god as *Haddu* as at Mari and Ugarit.[38] Its preservation in the Akkadian of the middle Euphrates region (and Assyria?) is further demonstrated by the personal name ᵐU-*ḫa-ri* in the late Neo-Assyrian documents from Tell Halaf (101,103-6), appearing as *ʾdʿr* in an Aramaic document from the same archive. (The reading is clear, although not previously recognized.) See, too, the divine name Apil-Adad, attested in alphabetic transcription as *ʾpld* and in later Hellenistic times as Aphlad and variants thereof.[39] Note the numerous additional Aramaic names with *ʾd* as the initial element collected by Lipiński, though, as demonstrated by the Tell Halaf name cited above, his attempt to disassociate this element from the name *Addu* cannot be accepted.[40]

COMMENTARY

Our tablet is the record of the legal settlement of a dispute between KLBYDʾL and ʿZRNʾL on the one hand and NSḤNGHY on the other. Such settlements, which constitute a substantial percentage of the still rather limited corpus of Neo-Assyrian *Prozessurkunden*,[41] are characterized by the phrase *šulmu (ina) birtešunu*, "there is agreement ("peace") between them" corresponding to *wśmw šlm bynyhm* in line 10 of the Aramaic

---

contributed to this misunderstanding, as did the admittedly suggestive use of the preposition *qdm* in line 3.) The major difficulty with their interpretation is the fact that NSḤNGHY receives money from the other principals. Based on the immediate Neo-Assyrian parallels discussed below and, indeed, upon known cuneiform legal practice, this can only mean that N is a party to the settled dispute. Disputants may well have had to pay for "legal services," but if so we know nothing about it. It was totally irrelevant to the recording process.

33. Cf. Kaufman, Influences p. 114.

34. The correct reading of lines 11-13 was also noted by E. Lipiński; see n. 32.

35. See J. Lewy, "The Late Assyro-Babylonian Cult of the Moon and Its Culmination at the Time of Nabonidus," HUCA 19 (1945-46) 430 n. 136 and F. M. Fales, CCNA p. 18.

In Neo-Babylonian orthography the name of this god is regularly spelled *il-te-ri*. As I have shown elsewhere (Influences pp. 141f.), written Babylonian *lt* corresponds to phonetic *št*. I thus would understand the Babylonian form merely as a somewhat playful writing attempting to indicate the *śin* of *Śehr*. (Similarly, the Neo-Babylonian renderings of the Aramaic sun god as ᵈ*il-ta-meš*, etc., show that in Aramaic the original sibilant is *śin* as in Arabic *šams*.) *Il-te-ri* must be distinguished from *te-eḫ-ri*, *te-er-ḫi* (never *il-te-eḫ-ri*!), a divinity I would associate with the Old Testament name Teraḥ. On the other hand, the idiosyncratic writing *Te-er* by some Neo-Assyrian scribes probably is an attempt, like Babylonian *ilt-*, to indicate the foreign *śin* of *Śehr*.

36. See Stark, Names pp. 104f.

37. Cf. *ʾlmnny*: *Ilu-ma-na-ni* in Tell Halaf nos. 101ff. and CCNA 40.

38. See Herbert B. Huffmon, Amorite Personal Names in the Mari Texts (Baltimore, 1965) p. 156, and Frauke Gröndahl, Die Personennamen der Texte aus Ugarit (Rome, 1967) pp. 131ff. Cf. Amarna *Ad-da-da-ni*=ᵈIM-DI.KUD (Tallqvist, APN p. 12); *Ri-ib-ad-da/i*=*Ri-ib-*ᵈIM (Tallqvist, APN p. 186); etc.

39. See Lipiński, Studies p. 105. Cf. CCNA 69.

40. Lipiński, Studies p. 101 n. 6. Cf. CCNA 76 on *Man-nu-ki-ia-da*.

41. The published archives of Neo-Assyrian legal texts and private documents are those of Nineveh (ADD; AJSL 42 [1942] 170ff.; RA 24 [1927] 111ff. and Iraq 32 [1970] 292ff.), Nimrud (ND), Tell Halaf, and a few tablets from Sultantepe (J. J. Finkelstein, "Assyrian Contracts from Sultantepe," AnSt 7 [1957] 137ff.). The material stands to be substantially increased by the archive from Assur being studied by K. Deller; see 'Zur Terminologie neuassyrischer Urkunden," WZKM 57 (1961) 29ff.

text.[42] That "peace" is indeed the operative factor in these documents is demonstrated by the contemporary term for such texts which has been preserved for us in both its Akkadian and Aramaic forms: *egirtu ša šulmu*,[43] *spr šlm*.[44]

Such an *egirtu ša šulmu*[45] usually records the conclusion of a dispute as determined by court action (*dēnu*),[46] but may also serve as the official record of an "out-of-court" settlement.[47] In the latter case it may be distinguished from a simple quittance in that a settlement presupposes some complicating factor, be it a debt that has become overdue and the resultant penalty agreed upon,[48] an agreement for payment by or transfer of the obligation to a third party, or simply a prior disagreement over the terms. As a group, settlements differ from ordinary litigation records which detail the judgement and dictate the penalty for failure to comply but do not record actual compliance[49] and from records of debts settled by the incurrence of new obligations.[50]

The phrasing of the second half of the Aramaic text corresponds closely with the parallel terminology on late Assyrian (seventh century) cuneiform settlement documents:

Line 10. *wśmw šlm bynyhm*: As noted above, the Akkadian texts have *šulmu (ina) birti/e/ušunu*. Only one example, Tell Halaf 106, has phraseology paralleling the Aramaic use of the verb: *šulmu ina birtešunu issakanū*.

Line 11. *mn ʿl mn yšb*: This is the protasis of the guarantee clause, usually expressed in Akkadian by *mannu ša i-parrik*(GIB)*-u-ni*, "whoever interferes," or by *mannu ša ibbalakkatuni*. Only infrequently do we encounter the much closer parallel *mannu ša ina eli mannu ibbalakkatuni*.[51] The use of the verb *nabalkutu* in

42. ND 2337 is the only Neo-Assyrian settlement text known to me that does not have this phrase.

43. Tell Halaf 106:5. Cf. the similar expressions *egirtu ša dēnē ina birtušunu issaṭrū* (RA 22 [1925] 147; 648 B.C.), *ʾgrt kspʾ* in the Aramaic docket on ARU 268 (DEA 19) and S.U. 51/44 5ff.: *egirtu ša eqlēte* KIMIN (see K. Deller, Or. NS 34 [1965] 469) *ša* É, 2 *egir<āte> ša kaspi*. *Egirtu* seems to be distinguished from the more usual Neo-Assyrian legal term *dannatu*, "valid document." One may suggest that *dannatu* is a specific term, a record of either a sale or loan prepared at the time of the transaction itself (cf. Millard, Iraq 34 [1972] 137; Kaufman, Influences p. 46). As a more general term, *egirtu* may be equivalent to *dannatu* (as in S.U. 51/44) or may be used where the latter is inappropriate, as in the other cases where it is a record of the settlement of previously incurred obligations. See n. 44.

44. Found as part of the docket of the cuneiform tablet republished by Millard in Iraq 34 (1972) 131-37 no. 7 (ca. 617 B.C.): *spr šlm zy ḥzʾl*.

The correspondence *egirtu*: *spr* should serve to finally settle the dispute over the etymology of *egirtu*, Aramaic *ʾgrt/h* (see Kaufman, Influences p. 48). Were *egirtu* originally an Aramaic word there would be no reason to use the Aramaic *spr* instead of *ʾgrt* to translate it. Thus we are forced to posit an Akkadian etymology for *egirtu*. Morphologically, there is no problem in seeing it as the feminine verbal adjective of the verb *egēru*, "to be crossed (see AHw. s.v.), twisted"; indeed, it is the only possibility. The semantic difficulties are of a more serious nature. One wonders if it may not first have been used to refer to a specific type of tablet written or shaped in an unusual fashion. Bearing in mind the reference to an *egirtu armītu*, "Aramaic *egirtu*," in ABL 872:10, one might even suggest that *egirtu* originally referred to a document written in alphabetic script, from right to left, and thus "twisted" from the cuneiform point of view or even more literally "crosswise" to the original direction of cuneiform writing from top to bottom. (For the latter, see Falkenstein, ATU p. 10.) The chronological difficulties attendant on the positing of an alphabetic contemporary with top-to-bottom writing are admittedly substantial, but they are lessened somewhat by the observation that even in later periods tablets were probably held somewhat at an angle to the horizontal (cf. B. Meissner and K. Oberhuber, Die Keilschrift [1967] p. 22).

45. Since Neo-Assyrian regularly distinguishes between nominative/accusative and genitive, one expects rather *šulmi*. Apparently the standard writing SILIM-*mu* attained the status of a pseudo-logogram.

46. ARU 650, 651; VAT 14438; Tell Halaf 106, 107, 110; RA 24 (1927) 111ff. nos. 1, 2. Note that a settlement need not deal with strictly financial matters: RA 24 no. 1 is a judgment concerning betrothal rights.

47. ADD 780; Millard, Iraq 34 (1972) 131-37 No. 7; S.U. 51/44; RA 24 no. 8, and, probably, ND 2301. Compare the distinction drawn by Paul Koschaker between Old Babylonian ("*mitguru* bezeichnet vor allem die Tätigkeit der Parteien beim prozessbeendenden Vergleich") and Nuzi ("*tamgurtu* ist ein Vertrag, der ein konkretes unter den Parteien bereits vorhandenes Rechtsverhältnis regelt"), "Drei Rechtsurkunden aus Arrapḫa," ZA 48 (1944) 220. Cf. Muffs, Elephantine pp. 81ff.

48. Such a penalty is termed *sartu*; cf. K. Deller, "LÚ.LUL=LÚ.*parriṣu* und LÚ.*sarru*," Or. NS 30 (1961) 205ff.

49. E.g., ARU 643-49, 655; ND 2091, 2095. The litigation itself may entail an agreement between the parties as to future payment or work in lieu of payment, e.g. ARU 655; but such an agreement is not referred to by *šulmu*, which apparently carries the very specific legal connotation "settlement." Indeed, the presence of the *šulmu* clause in several texts seems to imply payment even when the operative clause PN_1 *ana* PN_2 *ussallim ittidin*, "PN_1 has paid PN_2 in full," is absent (e.g., Tell Halaf 107, 110; VAT 14438; in Tell Halaf 106:13 read ⌈*ú/us*⌉-[*sal*]-*lim*!). On the other hand, in the litigation report ARU 182 payment for a disabled slave is made, but the *šulmu* phrase is absent as is the formula of mutual "satisfaction," *uṭṭurū issi pān aḫîš*. Inasmuch as the recorded payment is one mina out of a total ordered payment of one and one-half, this text is a record of partial payment only; hence the absence of concluding clauses.

50. Cf. ARU 656 and RA 22 (1925) 147.

51. ADD 780, ARU 650, and also ARU 659:11. The use of the preposition *ʿl* in the Aramaic equivalent indicates that the cuneiform AŠ UGU is to be read *ina eli* with Ungnad, rather than *ana muḫḫi* with AHw. 1 695.

this context is well established in the cuneiform legal tradition,[52] and the accepted translation "vertragbrüchig werden" may be applied to Aramaic *św̌b* in this instance. The choice of this specific Aramaic verb, however, indicates that the basic meaning of the Akkadian in this period was understood to be "to turn around" (AHw 2 695b sub 9).[53]

The syntax of the Aramaic formulation is worthy of note. On the one hand, the verb concludes the phrase as in Akkadian[54]; on the other, the use of *mn*, as in Old Aramaic in general, obviates the need for the separate relative pronoun of the Akkadian.[55]

Lines 12-13. *ḥyy śhr wḥyy mlkʾ*: The standard formula in this position in the late Assyrian settlements is *Aššur Šamaš lū bēl dēnišu*, "may Aššur and Šamaš be his adversary" (with the possible addition or substitution of other divine names and the inclusion of an exorbitant monetary fine as well). In its place an expression similar to the Aramaic occurs only in Tell Halaf 107: TI *ša šarri ša mār šarri ina qātē<šu> ubaʾʾûni*. (Since TI is the logogram for *balāṭu*, "life," the first three words of this formula are totally equivalent to the Aramaic *ḥyy mlkʾ*.[56]) The clue to the proper interpretation of this clause was noted by Deller, who showed that it is merely a variant of the more familiar (though not found in settlements!) *adê ša šarri ina qātēšu lu/ubaʾʾû(ni)*, "may they/they will (i.e. the gods, see n. 56) hold him accountable for the oath of the king."[57] The link between *adê* and TI/*ḥyy* is to be sought in the term *nīšu*, "oath," used commonly in the Old and Middle dialects of Akkadian but largely replaced by *adê* in first millennium texts other than those in Standard Babylonian. The original meaning of *nīšu* is "life"; thus, as elsewhere in the Semitic world, an oath was frequently sworn by the life of the ruler or the god.[58] It is almost certainly wrong to assume that *adê* preserves this nuance, however. In fact the expression *ḥyy śhr wḥyy mlkʾ* of the Aramaic text lacks an exact parallel in the attested Neo-Assyrian formulary, but is clearly related to (if not ultimately derived from) the usual phrasing of the oath binding the litigants in Old Babylonian texts which may be generalized as *nīš* DN (DN *u* DN) *u* RN *(šarrim) itmû*. It would seem then that the Aramaic preserves an ancient usage and meaning and may have served as an intermediary introducing the equivalence "oath" = "life" into Neo-Assyrian cuneiform.

In what context, then, is *ḥyy śhr wḥyy mlkʾ* to be understood? A simple, unexpressed "they swore" is insufficient, for the Neo-Assyrian parallels suggest rather something corresponding to *ina qātēšu ubaʾʾûni*. Even in the latter case the meaning would at first seem to be that the parties have sworn not to reinstigate suit, and the omission of a concluding operative clause could be ascribed to the necessity for conciseness in writing on a less than ideal medium.[59] The more usual expression in this position, however, DN *lū bēl dēnišu*, makes no mention of an oath; it is merely a curse formula. That the parallel clauses, both Akkadian and Aramaic, must be similarly understood is demonstrated by the parallel terminology in Neo-Assyrian royal grants reminiscent of our Akkadian text in its apparent incompleteness: *u lū šarru u lū rubû ša pī dannite šuātu ušannû nīš Aššur Adad Ber Enlil aššurû Ištar aššurītu*: "Whether it be king or prince who changes the wording of that document, the oath by Aššur, Adad, Ber, the Assyrian Enlil and the Assyrian Ištar."[60] Since future kings and princes cannot have already sworn, it follows that in our case, and one may generalize for Neo-Assyrian law, the litigants do not necessarily take a common binding oath, but, as in the case of the royal grant, the tablet itself serves as an imprecation; thus the translation "(may he be cursed by)" offered above.[61]

52. See AHw. 1 695:8.

53. Note the Neo-Assyrian distinction between *nabalkutu*, used only of the reinstigation of a previously settled suit, and *tuāru* in the phrase *tuāru dabābu laššu*, "there shall be no return in suit," which occurs ubiquitously in sales contracts where no previous court action exists.

54. See above to line 2.

55. See R. Degen, Altaramäische Grammatik, AbKM 38/3 130.

56. As noted by Deller, WZKM 57 (1961) 32, TI is also to be read in ARU 47:22f.: *Aššur Sîn Šamaš Bēl Nabû* TI.MEŠ *ša šarri ina qātēšu lubaʾʾû*.

57. WZKM 57 (1961) 32. For *buʾʾû* in imprecations, cf. the use of *bʿh* in two Aramaic funerary inscriptions from Asia Minor: Keseçek Köyü lines 3-5: *wmn byš yʿbd ʿm ptkr znh wybʿh lh śhr wšmš*, "whoever does ill to this statue, Śehr and Šamaš will hold him responsible," and Gözne lines 2-4: *wybʿwn lh bʿlšmyn rbʾ śhr wšmš wlzrʿʾ zy lh*, "the great Baʿalšamayin, Śehr and Šamaš will hold him responsible as well as his progeny." Cf. Richard S. Hanson, "Aramaic Funerary and Boundary Inscriptions from Asia Minor," BASOR 192 (1968) 9ff.; contra Lipiński, Studies p. 150.

58. Cf. M. Greenberg, "The Hebrew Oath Particle *ḥay/ḥē*," JBL 76 (1957) 34ff.

59. Abbreviated formulae are encountered in cuneiform texts as well; the unusually brief ND 2301 concludes simply *mannu ša iparrikuni*. But the nature of alphabetic writing is certainly a factor. The Aramaic loan records on clay "olives" from Nineveh and Assur are paralleled by similar brief Akkadian texts (ARU nos. 304ff.), but the Aramaic versions are usually considerably more concise than the Akkadian.

60. E.g. Postgate, Royal Grants no. 9:65f.; cf. also no. 1:5ff.

61. Postgate, Royal Grants p. 37.

It has been demonstrated that each of the three clauses of lines 10-13 has a close parallel in the late Neo-Assyrian cuneiform sources. In each case, however, the closest parallel is to be found in a different source; in one case (*mn ʿl mn*) in some of the Nineveh texts and in the others in texts from provincial Gozan. In no case, though, can the Aramaic be described merely as a word for word translation of the Akkadian formula. In both *śmy šlm bynyhm* (position of the verb) and *mn ʿl mn yšb* (*mn* for *mannu ša*) the Aramaic demonstrates a certain linguistic authenticity which may be taken as indicative of some degree of independence in its legal terminology. For *ḥyy śhr wḥyy mlkʾ* it has been suggested that the Aramaic formula preserved a more archaic cuneiform model. Taken as a whole, the differences between the functional unit formed by lines 10-13 and cuneiform settlements are even more evident. The equivalent section of Neo-Assyrian settlements may be generalized as: (1) *uṭṭurū issi pān aḫîš*, (2) *šulmu ina birtešunu*, (3) *mamma issi mamma lā idabbubū*, (4) *mannu ša ibbalakkatuni/iparrikuni*, (5) *Aššur* (DN *u* DN) *lū bēl dēnišu*; with certain alterations possible in the order of the first three clauses. Thus the statement of mutual satisfaction (1) and the prohibition of further suit (3) are notably absent from the Aramaic version. Again the necessity for brevity may be responsible, although it must be noted that both clauses are also missing in ND 2301, Halaf 107, and S.U. 51/44.[62]

The other sections of the Aramaic text show little, if any, dependence upon Assyrian models. The list of witnesses appears, to be sure, at the end of the document; but, in contrast to the normative cuneiform tradition in which each name is preceded by the preposition *maḫar*, "before," the entire list is simply introduced by the word *śhdn*, "witnesses." This is nearly uniform practice in the published Mesopotamian Aramaic documents.[63] Its cuneiform parallel is to be found only in Neo- and Late Babylonian documents where, in the usual pattern, the list of witnesses is introduced by the word *mukinnū/ē* corresponding to Aramaic *śhdn*.[64] In light of the novelty of the Neo- and Late Babylonian structure within the cuneiform tradition, the assumption that its origin is to be sought in the native Aramaic tradition is warranted.

The Aramaic tablet is dated according to the eponym system we would expect to find in use anywhere under direct Assyrian political control, but only the year is mentioned, not the exact date usually found in the cuneiform documents. Again the need for brevity would seem to be decisive here. The position of the date in the body of the text itself is unusual. In Neo-Assyrian documents the date regularly appears either immediately before or after the list of witnesses. In the case of the Aramaic document, the nature of the document itself, as a record of a direct quotation, could be responsible for the position of the date within the framework clause introducing the quotation itself. Indeed, from the format of our text it is only a short step to the well-known pattern of the Aramaic "dialogue documents" from Elephantine: "On such and such a date, PN said to PN."

What is the meaning and function of the quotation "Here, eat bread" in our document? In light of the function of the tablet as a settlement record as determined from other internal criteria, the quotation must be interpreted as a subjective record of the agreement of the debtors to pay their previously contested obligation, thus ending their dispute. I take the statement to be a reference to a symbolic action finalizing the agreement, such as those known from elsewhere in Near Eastern law. The sharing of food and drink, especially "bread" (*lḥm/aklu*), was a widespread sign of friendship and alliance in the Ancient Near East. In Aramaic sources, note the use of the expression *nsk lḥm*, "to provide food," as a sign of alliance, in the Sefire inscriptions (III 5, 7; I B 37)[65] and Ahiqar 33: [*ḥ*]*d mn rby ʾby zy lḥm ʾby* [*ʾkl/ṭʿm*], "one of my father's nobles who ate my father's bread."[66] Of the many cuneiform examples it suffices to note Knudson Gebete 108:4: *lu*

62. The prohibition clause alone is missing in Tell Halaf 110. I have no explanation for the fact that except for the *šulmu* clause (and *issi pān aḫî*[*š uṭṭurū*?] in no. 1:10) none of these characteristic clauses appear in the tablets published in RA 24 (1927) 111ff.

63. The normative cuneiform pattern does appear in three early Aramaic texts, however. In Tell Halaf 2, Assur 6 and the tablet from the 34th year of Nebuchadnezzar II published by J. Starcky (Syria 37 [1960] 99-115) the name of each witness is preceded by the word *śhd*. That this is a conscious imitation of a non-Aramaic model is suggested by E. Lipiński's observation (Studies p. 110) that in Assur 6:5 "the scribe has automatically written *śhdn*, "witnesses," but he has immediately corrected the *n* into a *h*, since he intended to write *śhd* in front of the name of each witness." Two documents from Elephantine (AP 6, 20) still preserve this pattern, but the bulk of the Egyptian Aramaic texts show a three-stage development of the introductory *śhdn* type: *śhdyʾ* alone (note the emphatic form, and cf. *ʾlh śhdyʾ* in the Bauer-Meissner papyrus line 15 [SPAW, phil.-hist. Kl. 72 (1936) 414]); *śhdyʾ bgw* (cf. Reuven Yaron, Introduction to the Law of the Aramaic Papyri [Oxford, 1961] pp. 16ff.) and a combined form, in which *śhdyʾ bgw* precedes the entire list, but the name of each of the witnesses (with the possible exception of the first) may, in addition, be preceded by the word *śhd*. It would seem that the pattern familiar from subsequent Middle Aramaic documents from Judea and Palmyra, in which *śhd* follows each name, is derived from a different source.

64. For the various spellings see AHw 1 670.

65. See J. A. Fitzmyer, The Aramaic Inscriptions of Sefire, Biblica et Orientalia 19 (Rome, 1967).

66. AP p. 213.

EN MUN.MEŠ-*šú-un lu* EN NINDA.MEŠ-*šú-un*, where the meaning is clearly "their allies,"[67] and, from the Vassal Treaties of Esarhaddon (II 153-4), *šumma . . . adê ina pān ilāni (tašakkanu)-ni ina rikis paššūri šatê kāsi*, "You will not make a treaty by setting the table, by drinking the cup."[68] Banquets celebrating and symbolizing the making of a covenant between individuals are particularly well attested in biblical sources: e.g., Gen. 26:30; 31:54; Josh. 9:14. A symbolic banquet at the conclusion of a contract is actually attested in Mesopotamia, notably in a legal text from Mari, almost certainly indicative of a West Semitic tradition. The text, a sale of developed land (5 sar é.dù.a), concludes: *karram īkulū kāsam ištû u šamnam iptaššū*, "they ate the meat(?), drank the cup and rubbed themselves with oil."[69]

The subjective format of our tablet is without a precise parallel in either cuneiform or Aramaic sources. Such first-person formulations are generally not found at all in Neo-Assyrian legal documents (excluding royal grants and decrees). Quotations are known, to be sure, from some settlement records and litigations, but there they represent the testimony of the litigants. In one case, however, in the unfortunately damaged Tell Halaf 110, the concluding phrase of the debtor's testimony (*ina qātē* LÚ.LAL.MEŠ-*ú-a alik ba*ʾʾ*e*, "Go, demand it from my debtors")[70] is possibly to be understood as an agreement to pay, since it is followed immediately by the settlement clauses. The quotations embodied in the "dialogue documents" of Neo- and Late Babylonian times and in Elephantine Aramaic, in which the details of the entire transaction are contained in a statement by one of the principals, are of a much greater scope than the simple quotation on the Aramaic tablet.[71] Since the transactions involved are of a totally different type as well, no direct connection between the two can be demonstrated (aside from the position of the date in the tablet and at Elephantine, as mentioned above), and the origin of the "dialogue document" remains obscure.[72]

In sum, this Aramaic *spr šlm*, with its mixture of Neo-Assyrian features and elements which must be ascribed to native Aramaic legal practice, is further evidence of the mutually contributive nature of the Aramaic-Assyrian symbiosis and is an important piece of evidence in the reconstruction of the complex history of Aramaic common law.

67. MUN/*ṭābtu* in this context normally means "good" (cf. Postgate, Royal Grants no. 10:13, where *bēl ṭābti* is parallel to *bēl dêqti*), but the use of "bread" suggests that a play on the double meaning "salt, good" is intended. Cf. *bᵊrīt melaḥ* (Nu. 18:19; II Chron. 13:5), *melaḥ bᵊrīt* (Lev. 2:13).

68. D. J. Wiseman, Iraq 20 (1958) 39.

69. ARM 8 13:11ff. (this text was brought to my attention by Prof. Jonas C. Greenfield). The reading and meaning of the first word are uncertain. AHw. 1 468a considers it to be the equivalent of OAkk. *kerrum*, a kind of sheep or "ram." CAD K 239b reads *kāram*, translating "a platter or bowl"; their translation of the sentence almost certainly implies more than the text itself does in their assumption that the eating and drinking are done out of shared utensils. In CAD K 222a top, however, *ṭābiḫ kārī* is rendered "slaughterer and seller of prepared meat dishes," yet no such *kāru* is listed in the volume. Perhaps a simple emendation <*ka*>-*ka-ra-am* is required, as apparently assumed by Boyer's translation "pain."

70. For the translation see Deller, Or. NS 30 (1961) 205ff.

71. See H. Petschow, "Die neubabylonische Zwiegesprächsurkunde und Genesis 23," JCS 19 (1965) 103ff.; Muffs, Elephantine pp. 175ff.; Weisberg, YNER 1 129ff. Note especially the distinction drawn by Petschow (p. 108) between the common petitionary format of leases and betrothals and the less frequent pattern of sales where the quotation is that of the seller rather than the purchaser. If at all comparable, our tablet is similar only to the former, whereas the latter is paralleled in the Elephantine pattern.

72. Petschow's attempt to adduce Middle Babylonian antecedents for the dialogue document is unsuccessful (Mittelbabylonische Rechts- und Wirtschaftsurkunden der Hilprecht-Sammlung Jena [Berlin, 1974] pp. 38f.). The two groups of documents bear little resemblance to each other. The Middle Babylonian material belongs rather to that group of texts which record the statements of parties to disputes over existing obligations, not the making of new contracts.

NOTES ON AKKADIAN *uppu*

Anne D. Kilmer
University of California, Berkeley

Jack Finkelstein was deeply interested in the Atraḫasis Epic.[1] One lengthy conversation with him about it, shortly after CT 46 appeared, is vividly remembered. He was especially intrigued by the circumstances surrounding the slaying of divinity that was necessary to the creation of man from clay, and by the possibility that the god who was slain was one who possessed "intelligence"—or at least that a unique quality was passed from the gods to man and to no other creature of the earth.[2] It was partially in response to his stimulating speculations that the present writer attempted an exegesis of the Atraḫasis passage I 214-239 and pursued the question of the meaning of the terms *uppu* and *ṭēmu* in the primary creation scene. Because of Jack Finkelstein's abiding interest in these matters, it was decided to present a discussion of one of the terms, *uppu*, in this volume.

Whatever be the correct literal translation of the thought-provoking lines of Atraḫasis I, it seems clear that they deal with life and death: the drum of dirges, ghost and spirit, the sign of life, and the concept of remembrance.

Old Babylonian Atraḫasis Epic tablet I:

	aḫ-ri-a-ti-iš u_4*-mi up-pa i ni-iš-me*	Forever after, let us hear the *uppu*.
215.	*i-na ši-i-ir i-li e-ṭe-em-mu li-ib-ši*	From the flesh of the god, let there be Spirit;
	ba-al-ṭa it-ta-šu li-še-di-⌜šu⌝-ma	Let *it* make known the Living (being) (of which it is) its sign;
	aš-šu la mu-uš-ši-i e-ṭé-em-mu li-ib-ši	For the sake of never forgetting, let there be Spirit.
	. . . . .	. . . . . .
	^{d}*We-e(-)i-la ša i-šu-⌜ú⌝ ṭe*$_4$*-e-ma*	Wê (the) god who had *ṭēmu*
	i-na pu-úḫ-ri-šu-nu iṭ-ṭa-ab-ḫu	They slaughtered in their assembly.
225.	*i-na ši-ri-šu ù da-mi-šu*	With his flesh and his blood
	^{d}*Nin-tu ú-⌜ba⌝-li-il ṭi-iṭ-ṭa*	Nintu mixed the clay.
	aḫ-ri-a-t[i-iš u_4*-mi up-pa iš-mu]-⌜ú⌝*	Forever after, they heard the *uppu*.
	i-na ši-i-ir i-li e-ṭe-[em-mu ib-ši]	From the flesh of the god there was Spirit;
	ba-al-ṭa it-ta-šu ú-še-di-š[u-ma]	It made known the Living (being) (of which it is) its sign;
230.	*aš-šu la mu-uš-ši-i e-ṭe-em-mu [ib-ši]*	For the sake of never forgetting, there was Spirit.
	. . . . . .	. . . . . .
239.	*i-lam ta-aṭ-bu-ḫa qá-du ṭe*$_4$*-mi-šu*	"You slaughtered a god together with his *ṭēmu*."

THE MEANING OF *uppu*:

The brief discussion in Or N.S. 41 (1972) 163 of the meaning of *uppu* in our passage defended the suggestion that the sound should refer to the heartbeat.

Line 214, apparently, does refer to a sound connected with the creation of a new being.[3] It would appear

1. Much of this material was collected in connection with the writer's article "The Mesopotamian Concept of Overpopulation and Its Solution as Reflected in the Mythologies," Or. NS 41 (1972) 160-77 (see p. 163 with n. 13 and p. 165 with n. 25), and formed part of the original manuscript as submitted to press. Because of its length, however, and because it was still in an (even more) undigested state, the material referring to *uppu* (and to *ṭēmu*) was deleted. The material has been studied since then, and revised, and has benefited not only from the use of CAD files, but also from the remarks of Professor William Moran to whom the writer had sent the original manuscript. Moreover, in view of the articles by W. Moran, BASOR 200 (1970) 47-56; Biblica 52 (1971) 51-61; W. von Soden (1973); and W. F. Albright (1973), the present contribution excludes comment on the meaning of *ṭēmu*, which still needs further study.

References follow Lambert-Millard, Atra-ḫasīs.

2. See J. J. Finkelstein, "Ancient Mesopotamian Religion," Dartmouth College, Comparative Studies Center, Report of the 1965-66 Seminar on Religion in Antiquity, ed. J. Neusner (in private circulation, 1966) pp. 93-95.

3. Note that the sound is mentioned as soon as the "dough" is fully mixed—the clay-cum-god matrix from which, later, individual pieces are separated, and from which, in turn, individual humans are made. It is also interesting that the mother goddess takes credit (lines 240-47) for having solved the gods' labor problem at the same point—already when the dough is mixed, and before any individuals have been formed (after line 256).

Ancient Near Eastern Studies in Memory of J. J. Finkelstein
Connecticut Academy of Arts and Sciences, Memoir 19

that this is a newly commenced sound that functions as a sign of aliveness.[4] If that is so, it is more logical to assume that this new sound is a physiological characteristic of the new creation rather than a sound emitted from a dirge drum, although that translation may still be the correct one even though reference to heartbeat is to be understood.

In an effort to look for a parallel use of *uppu* in other contexts, a thorough investigation of the word became necessary. Though the following collection of references is not complete, it is hoped that, at the worst, the discussion of this very difficult and very interesting word *uppu*[5] will be useful, and that, at best, the meaning will be clarified to some extent. This collection of material proposes to demonstrate that: (A) The basic meaning of MUD=*uppu* is "socket," "concavity"; further, *uppu* "hole/pit" may be related to this basic meaning; (B) ÙB=*uppu* "percussion instrument" may be an onomatopoeic word based on phonetic Sumerian ab; if not, the Akkadian word may be related to the basic meaning "concavity." In addition, questions will be raised as to the meaning of other *uppu*'s, and general references to the heartbeat will be discussed.

Sources

A. *uppu* basic meaning "socket, concavity"

1. MUD=*uppu* "socket"[6]

1.1. latch-socket, join-socket [instead of older translations "handle," "key," "strap"]

1.1.1. referring to the door latch (i.e. the part of a lock mechanism which receives a bolt).[7] See fig. 1.[8]

CT 18 4 rev. ii 13-15 (Explicit Malku III): *né-ep-tu-ú=mu-še-lu-ú, up-pu*=MIN, *nam-za-qu*=MIN, *ga-mi-ru=gi-iš-ru* "opening-place/catch=lifter (i.e. that which makes go up/off)," "latch-socket=ditto," "latch-bolt=ditto," "lock-bolt=lock-pin." [CAD G *gišru* A and B should probably be combined, since "lock-pin/beam/barricades is conceptually the same as "bridge."] The comparable section in Malku is mš III 205f.: *ka-nu-ku*=[. . .], *up-pu*=[. . .].

Cf. LÚ.MUD=*ša up-pi* in the sequence of gatekeepers in LÚ=*ša* II 5-10 (MSL 12 116f.).

KAR 323:5: *na-an-za-aq up-pi ù*! *sikkatu* [*anāku*] "the bolt of the latch-socket and the peg [am I]."

VAB 2 357:52f. (Nergal and Ereškigal): *a-*[*t*]*u-ú* [*pi-ta*]*-a ba-ab-ka up-pí ru-um-mi-ma a-na-ku lu-ru-ú-ub* "Gatekeeper, open your gate! Disengage the latch-socket that I may enter!"

In omen protases from CT 40 12-13 (Šumma ālu XI) passim in lines 3-48, *uppi aškutti* (GIŠ.MUD.Á.SUKÚ) could mean "socket of the wedge(?)."[9] See CAD A/2 under *aškuttu* "(a device to bar a door)," and cf. von Soden, Or NS 27 (1958) 253.

See Ḫḫ V 276-299a (MSL 6 28ff.) for locks and lock parts; in Ḫḫ V 278ff., the *aškuttu* is provided with a *sikkatu* "nail/peg," an *eblu* "cord/rope," and an *uppu* "socket."

In the hymn BWL p. 136:183, the sequence is [. . . *u*]*p-pi*(GIŠ.MUD) *sik-ka-ta*(GIŠ.KAK) *nam-za-qí*(GIŠ.E_{11}) *áš-kut-ta*(GIŠ.Á.ŠUKÚ) ". . . latch-socket, nail/peg, latch-bolt, wedge(?)." Contrast the translations of CAD ". . . handle, lock-pin(?), latch(?), bar" and BWL ". . . thong, lock-pin, latch and door handle."

PBS 15 79 i 48f. (Nbk.): *e-la-an e-ra-a iškura*(DUḪ.LÀL) *ki-ma up-pi ú-ki-in ṣer-ru-uš-šu-un* "on top of the copper I put wax on them, like (on) a latch-socket"; see CAD I/J under *iškuru* (and contrast the CAD translation: "over them (the beams) I put wax as a protective coat(?) over the copper." The passage could mean that even the copper covering (of what?—surely not something exposed to the sun) was waxed (to keep from tarnishing?) as was done, perhaps with (fancy) metal latch-sockets. Note MUD.MEŠ.GUŠKIN in a temple treasury, VAT 13718 ii 8 (Or NS 17/2 [1948] pl. 37).

4. I. M. Kikawada points out that the *uppu* line, Atraḫasis I 214 (and 227) belongs to a quatrain of the ABAB pattern (see W. Moran, BASOR 200 [1970] 48-56); he observes that meaning must be derived from the literary unit; cf. his "The Shape of Genesis 11:1-9" in Rhetorical Criticism (ed. Jackson and Kessler, Pittsburgh, 1974) pp. 18-32; also "Some Proposals for a Definition of Rhetorical Criticism," Semitics 5 (1976, forthcoming).

5. See the Selected Bibliography at the end of this article for earlier studies.

6. Cf., for example, English door-socket, ball-and-socket joint, eye-socket, arm-socket; socket of a tooth, dry socket; axe-socket. The socket is the receiving part in which other parts fit, pivot or revolve in an articulation, mechanism or tool.

7. A meaning "bolt-chamber" for *kim/nṣu* does not seem defensible. See Salonen, Türen p. 77, and cf. CAD s.v. *kimṣu*.

8. The drawings in figs. 1-8 are intended only as visual aids to the discussion. Figs. 1, 2, 3, 6, and 8 do not represent known archaeological finds, while fig. 4 represents a type of axe-socket known from ancient Near Eastern sites. Drawings by Joyce Stark.

9. Note that Á.SUKÚ is also equated with *kiṣir ammati* "elbow joint(?)," which may, since the bent elbow forms a wedge, support the translation "wedge" for *aškuttu*.

1.1.2. referring to the oar-lock (part of an oarlock). See fig. 2.

Ḫḫ IV 412, 414f. lists the parts of an oar (see CAD G under *gišallu*): GIŠ.GISAL.MUD=MIN (=*gišallu*) *up-pi* "(oar-)socket," GIŠ.GISAL.LÍM.MA=*giš-ru up-pi* "oar-socket lock-pin/draw-pin" (Sum. obscure), GIŠ.KUL.GISAL=*šu-mu-u šá gi-šal-li* "oar-lock."

1.1.3. referring to part(s) of the chariot

Ḫḫ V 45, 45a, 46: GIŠ.MUD.GIGIR=*up-pu* "(chariot-)socket," GIŠ.KAK.MUD.GIGIR=(blank) "nail/peg of the chariot socket," GIŠ.MU.GÍD.GIGIR=*ma-šad-du* "(chariot-)shaft" (following the edition of Salonen, Landfahrzeuge p. 173; see p. 97 for his suggestion "handle" or "brake-handle" for this *uppu*). The exact part of the *narkabtu* is not discernible, but three possibilities come to mind for *uppu*: axle-socket; socket for the pole (possibly with rotary movement in one axis) at the juncture of the wagon body or the axle and the pole, see fig. 3; or the juncture of the yoke with the pole (i.e. pin into socket).

1.1.4. referring to a tool

Ḫḫ VIIA 245-251: GIŠ.NÍG.GUL=*ak-kul-lum* "pickaxe," GIŠ.NÍG.GUL.ŠU=MIN *qa-at* "ditto of the hand," GIŠ.NÍG.GUL.MUD=MIN *up-pu* "ditto of the axe-socket(?)," GIŠ.NÍG.GUL.A.ŠÀ.GA=MIN *eq-lu* "ditto of the field," GIŠ.NÍG.GUL.GIŠ.SAR=MIN *ki-ri-i* "ditto of the garden," GIŠ.SAG.NÍG.GUL=*qaq-qa-du ak-kul-lum* "head of the pickaxe," GIŠ.MUD.NÍG.GUL=*up!-pi!* MIN "socket of the pickaxe" (i.e. where the wooden handle inserts into the head). See fig. 4. (Note already Wilcke RLA 4 35b sub "Hacke": *uppu* "die Tülle?")

1.2. socket-joint of the body, i.e. articulation that is a ball-and-socket joint [instead of older translations "shoulder," "clavicle," etc.]; possibly also said of pivot-joints. See fig. 5.

1.2.1. MUD.Á=*uppi aḫi* "shoulder-joint, arm-socket, armpit"

In most passages of medical texts, a distinction between the older translations and "shoulder-joint" or "arm-socket" does not help us much. Note, however, in Labat TDP Tablet XXVI 5f., that "joint" may make more sense than, e.g., "clavicle" or "shoulder": (5) *šumma mi-šit-ti im-šid-su-ma lu imitta lu šumēla maḫiṣ(iṣ) uppi aḫi-šú la pa-ṭir* "If he suffered a stroke and either right or left is affected; his shoulder-joint is immobilized/doesn't move (freely)/is not loose.

1.2.2. MUD.KUŠ=*uppi aḫi* "elbow-joint(?)"

Antagal G 219 (see CAD A/1 under *aḫu* B, lex.): mud$^{ku.uš}$KUŠ=*up-pi a-ḫu*.

1.2.3. [*knee-joint. In the commentary on Šumma ālu for the word *uppu* "pit, hole in the ground," MUD.DÙG seems to have nothing to do with knees. See below, section 2.]

1.3. socket-like container/cylinder/applicator (with plunger or stick?) [instead of older "tube"] for medicaments.[10] See figure 6. In medical texts:

KAR 155:24-26: Ú *pu-qut-tu tasâk ina šamni ḫalṣi tapâš ina uppi*(MUD) *siparri*(ZABAR) *ana libbi išarišu tašappak* "You shall crush *puquttu*-thorn, you shall pound/mix (it) with purified oil, you shall expel (lit. 'pour' it) from a bronze applicator into/onto his penis."

Thompson AMT 59 1 i 23: Ú UD *tasâk ina šamni tuballal ina uppi*(MUD) *siparri*(ZABAR) *ana muštinnišu tanappaḫ* "You shall crush styrax(?), you shall mix (it) with oil, you shall expel (lit. 'blow' it) from a bronze applicator into his ureter."

AMT 9 1 40: *ina uppi*(MUD) *siparri*(ZABAR) *ana libbi inīšu tanappaḫ* "From a bronze applicator you shall 'blow' (it) into his eyes."

AMT 77 i 12: *ba-aḫ-ru-su ina maški teṭerri*(SUR-*ri*) *ištu*(TA) *uppi*(MUD) "You shall smear (it) hot on the skin(-plaster) from an applicator."

KAR 195:8: . . . *išteniš tuštabbal ina uppi*(MUD) *abari*(A.BÁR) *ana pagriša inappaḫma* . . . ". . . you shall mix together, from the lead applicator you shall 'blow' it on her body . . ."

1.3.1. socket-sheath for a pointed stick(?)[10]

BWL 242 19-20 (proverb): igi-gu$_4$-da du-a mud-šè bí-íb-ra-ra=*pa-an al-pi a-li-ki ina up-pi ta-rap-pi-is* "Do

10. Prof. G. Azarpay has called to my attention the bronze cylindrical tubes from Luristan that appear to have been the holders of applicator-sticks; see P. R. R. Moorey, Catalogue of Ancient Persian Bronzes in the Ashmolean Museum, plates 34 and 38-39 (similar small applicators were apparently used for eye make-up); but such sticks must dip out the substance rather than expel it. Cf. also the conical gold cosmetic kit from Ur (Royal Treasury, in the British Museum) as holder for tweezers and applicator-stick/pin.

you divert/push away the face of an on-coming bull with a socket?" (i.e., don't use the sheath instead of the stick). Cf. *uppu* coupled with *pulukku* in BULUG.ŠÀ.GUD.RA.ZABAR, a pointed metal stick/goad used by oxherds to drive cattle (gud~ra) Wiseman, BSOAS 30 501 (reference courtesy R. Caplice); cf. Ḫḫ XII 75 (MSL 9 205): BULUG.BÚR.RA.ZABAR=*up-pu*. Contrast the translation of BWL: "Do you strike the face of a moving ox with a *strap*?"

1.4. "socket/apex/cavity containing apical meristem"[11] of the date palm [instead of "pith," "stalk," "core," or "frond base"]. See fig. 7.

Ḫḫ III 398-400: GIŠ.MUD.GIŠIMMAR=*up-[pu]*, GIŠ.MUD.AL.GAZ.GIŠIMMAR=MIN *di-i-ku*, GIŠ.TÙN.DUL.GIŠIMMAR=MIN MIN "socket (of the date palm)," "killed socket," "ditto." Hg A 29 to Ḫḫ III: GIŠ.BAR.DA.GIŠIMMAR=*ta-[ri]-tum=mar-ti up-pi* "pruned-away (thing)=daughter of the socket" (referring to a shoot that may appear in a "killed" apex; cf. Landsberger Date Palm p. 35). CT 41 29 rev. 8 (Šumma ālu comm.): *ta-ri-tum*=DUMU.SAL *up-pi*.

2. *uppu/ḫuppu* "pit," "hole (in the ground)," "concavity." See CAD *ḫuppu* B "hole, depression,"[12] and AHw *ḫuppu(m)* II, *uppu(m)* II (Sum. Lw.) "Vertiefung."

MSL 2 128:14-16 (Proto-Ea): ub PÚ=*up-pu-um* "pit/hole," pu-un PÚ=*bu-ur-tum* "well," tu-ul PÚ=*is-sú-ú* "(clay) pit." MSL 3 217:3-5 (dupl. to above): ub PÚ=*bu-[ur-tum]*, ub PÚ=*up-pu-[um]*, tu-ul PÚ=*is-sú-[ú]*.

Ea I 51-53: pu-ú PÚ=*bu-ur-tu*, tu-ul PÚ=*is-su-u*, ub PÚ=*up-pu*.

A I/2 169-177: ub PÚ=*bur-tum, mi-iḫ-ṣu, laḫ-tum, up-pu, ḫu-up-pu, ḫu!-bal-lum, šu-up-lu, šu-ut-ta-tum, ḫa-ab-bu*.

CT 39 32:25 (Šumma ālu): *šumma up-pu ina qabal āli puttû* "If a hole-in-the-ground opened up in the city." CT 41 26f.:10-11 (Šumma ālu comm.): MUD.DÙG/ḪI=*piṭ-ru* [. . .], *up-pu=pi-iṭ-[ru]* "pit, fissure." See von Soden Or NS 26 (1957) 137.

Wiseman Treaties 641f.: *kî ša libbu ša ḫu-up-pu rāquni libbikunu liriqu* "Just as the inside of a hole is empty, so should your inside be empty."

For the passage OB Atraḫasis II vii 37, von Soden, Or NS 28 (1969) 430, suggests restoring *ši-[i] li-tu-ur a-na up-[pí-ša?-ma?]* "Let (mankind) return to its hole" (followed by Moran BASOR 200 [1970] 54 n. 23); he cites Iraq 15 123:6 (NB): *[sa]-mit-su iḫ-ḫar-mi-mu-ma i-tu-ru up-pú-uš-šú* "the 'Mauersockel' fell into decay and returned to its hole"; further AfO 17 (1954-6) 313 Text C:10 and p. 317: *ana-ku* DN *šá ina pu-luḫ-ti-šú mim-ma lim-nu i-tur-ru up-pu-uš-šú* "I am DN by whose awesomeness 'Every Evil' returns to its hole." In the Atraḫasis passage, the *šî* must refer directly to the *urtu*, the god's original decision (when they all said 'aye' in the assembly) to create mankind, and only indirectly to mankind itself. The force of the line is (like the AfO 17 passage said of evil things) "May that (ill-fated/evil?) decision return to its hole."

B. *uppu* "drum"

1. ÁB×ŠÀ=ùb=*uppu* name of a small percussion instrument[13]; hand frame-drum/tambour.

Lexical passages: S bII 253-258 (MSL 3 145): li-biš ÁB×ŠÀ=*lib-bu* "heart/inner," ub ÁB×ŠÀ=*up-pu* "hand frame-drum," ki-ir ÁB×ŠÁ=*ki-i-ru* "*k*.-vessel" (or a name for a "kettle-drum" here?), še-em ÁB×ŠÀ=*ḫal-ḫal-la-tu* "*ḫ*.-drum," me-zé ÁB×ME.EN=*man-zu-u* "*m*.-drum," li-li-is ÁB×BALAG=*li-li-su* "*l*.-drum."

11. Specifically, the cavity enclosed by the older fronds which contain the young fronds and the apical meristem. I thank Prof. R. B. Park and Dr. Bruce Bartholomew for enlightening me concerning the date palm.

12. BRM 4 32:4 (sub CAD *ḫuppu* B): *ḫu-up* IGI = *šu-up-lu* IGI, "eye-socket," is a good reference for *uppu*, "socket," but should probably be read *ḫu-up-pat* and placed under *ḫuptu* B, "hole/cavity." But how are *ḫuptu* and *(h)uppu* related? Moreover, what is the relationship between *uppu*, "pit/hole," *ḫabbu*, "pit," and *apu/abu*, "hole"? See H. Hoffner, JBL 86 385-401 on Heb. *ʾōv*, Hurro-Hitt. *a-a-bi*, Ug. *ib*, and Sumerian ab, all ritual or "sacrificial" or conjuring pits. Note especially honey and fat poured into a *ḫuptu* (see CAD sub *ḫuptu* B).

13. Sumerian hymnic/literary references for (kuš.)ùb(ÁB×ŠÀKÁR/TAG$_4$) "percussion instrument" are many; see Römer Königshymnen p. 157 and Sjöberg Temple Hymns p. 75, to which may be added "Inanna and Enki" II vi 24 (ed. G. Farber-Flügge, Inanna und Enki, Studia Pohl 10) and TCL 6 56:17. For the problem of ùb vs. šèm, see especially Römer, Königshymnen p. 167. Note also the following passages in which an ùb is apparently struck with a stick: "Ninmulangim" 49 (Hallo, 17 RAI 125): ùb-ba [. . .] KU [. . .] PA sìg-[gal]-a-né 'The ùb-drum . . . when he strikes it with the stick(?)"; TuM NF 3 25:16 (Kramer, PAPS 107 499, and Wilcke, AfO 23 84-87): ùb GIŠ PA e-ne-di-da ḫúb mu-di-ni-in-gub, with Akkadian gloss *i-na up?-pi lu?-pu?-tim i-na me-lu-ul-tim i-ra-[(aq)-q]u-ud* (contra Wilcke and AHw 2 954a: *i-ra-[ap]-pu!-ud*) "Striking an *uppu*, playfully, she dances."

For occurrences of ùb made of metals that are probably not to be taken as drums, see sub section C 9 below.

I wish to thank Dr. D. A. Foxvog for his able and patient assistance with the preparation of this article, and especially for bringing many of the Sumerian passages to my attention.

Because so many of the drum names have ÁB as the logographic base, it seems possible that ÁB was used as a phonetic sign (sound ᵊb-ᵊb-ᵊb). (It is difficult to see a drum in the early pictograph.) If so, (ÙB)/*uppu* could be the Akkadian onomatopoeic name of one of the instruments. In the Old Babylonian period, both ÙB and ŠÈM are written ÁB×GANÁ-*tenû,* see Krecher, Kultlyrik p. 220 n. 636. Note that *ḫalḫallatu* may also be written šem$_4$(ÁB×ME.EN), as in TCL 6 56 rev. 3: ér-šem$_4$-ma.

Hg 190 to Ḫḫ XI (MSL 7 153): KUŠ.ÙB=*up-pu*=*li-li-is-su.* OB forerunner to Ḫḫ XI, 123f. (MSL 7 221): kuš.ÁB×ŠE!?, kuš.ub. Cf. A VIII/3 2 (CAD Ḫ sub *ḫuppu* E): ub ÁB×ME.EN=*ḫu-up-pu*//*maš-ku šá li-l*[*i-si*] "*ḫuppu*//skin of the *l.*-drum" (i.e., the drumhead).

In a list of laments, Proto-Kagal 361-365 (MSL 13 77): ér-balag-gá, ér-ùb-a, ér-šèm-ma, ér-gi-di, ér-ḫul.

SBH 23 rev. 14f.: kuš.ùb-kù li-li-ìs-kù mu [. . .]=*ina up-pi el-lu li-li-is el-lu* [. . .] "with the pure *uppu* (and) the pure *lilissu* . . ."

KAR 16 rev. 15f. (= 15 rev. 1f.): kuš.ub-kù balag-kù-ge šu mu-un-tag-g[e]=*i-na up-pi eb-bi ba-lam-gi el-li ú-la-pa-tu-ši* "They play for her on the holy *uppu*-drum, on the pure *balaggu*-harp."

The instrument ÁB×ŠÀ.ZABAR occurs in the Kalû-Ritual (see RAcc. 10ff.); Thureau-Dangin reads *uppu* (see his note 6), but the instrument could be a *ḫalḫallatu.*

Our translation "hand frame-drum" derives from a guess that *uppu* was a small instrument. Several literary passages support such a guess. CT 42 18:14: gaba-ni kuš.ùb-kù-ga ì-sìg-ge ér-gig ì-še$_8$-še$_8$ "She beats her breast (like) a holy *uppu,* she cries bitterly." CT 42 30b rev. 7f.: gaba-a-ni kuš.ù[b . . .]=*i-rat-su ki-ma up-*[*pi* . . .] "Her breast beat like an *uppu* [she beats(?)]." Likewise, 1 LU 300 (ed. S. Kramer, AS 12): gaba-ni ùb!-kù-ga-àm ì-sìg-ge. One imagines a *mea culpa* gesture. (See below).

2. [derived use, referring to an involuntary body-sound; heartbeat(?)]

Ḫḫ XV 114-116 (MSL 9 10): UZU.ŠÀ.LUGAL.NU.TUKU=*pi-i šu-uḫ-ḫu,* MIN *up-p*[*i*], MIN *kar-ši* "internal organ having no master"="voice of the anus," "voice of the heartbeat(?)," "voice of the stomach." Or: "mouth of the anus," "mouth of the *uppu*-organ" see below under section C), "mouth of the stomach (duodenum or the like?)," i.e., translate *pû* as "mouth, opening" with AHw [but AHw's *uppu* as "Achselhöhle(?)," when the armpit has neither opening nor voice, is unlikely to be grouped with internal organs]. Cf. *pî ḫašû*: if not "sound of breathing," then is the esophageal opening meant? The Sumerian may make more sense with "sound" than with "opening." Cf. TCL 9 141:42 (LB, cited AHw 2 874, "unklar"): *a-na pi-i lìb-bi-ka* "according to your wish(?)."

OB Atraḫasis I 214: *up-pu i ni-iš-me* (also 227: [*up-pa iš-mu*]-*ú*) "Let us hear the *uppu,*" meaning either the heartbeat or the sound of the *uppu*-drum as referring to heartbeat. Cf. KAR 307:11: LILIS$^{li-li-su}$ ŠÀ-*šú* "his (the god's) heart is a *lilissu*-drum," see Ebeling, TuL pp. 28-32.]

C. *uppu* of uncertain meaning or unclear relation to A or B above

1. *uppu* as an abdominal organ, or part or characteristic of the intestines

Hg D 58-62 to Ḫḫ XV (MSL 9 37): [UZU],ŠÀ.MAḪ=ŠU-*ḫu*=*ir-ru kab-ru,* "*šamaḫḫû*=thick intestines," [UZU.Š[À.LU.ÚB=ŠU-*u*=*up-pu,* "*šalubbû*=*uppu,*" [UZU.ŠÀ.AL].ÚS.SA=ŠU-*u*=MIN "*šalussû*=*uppu,*" [UZU].ŠÀ.ŠU.NIGIN=*ir-ru sa-ḫi-ru-tú*=*ti-ra-nu* "convoluted intestines=*tīrānu,*" [UZ]U.ŠÀ.SÈ.SÈ.KE= *pir-su*=MIN *šin-ni* "*pirsu*=ditto, of urine [=bladder?]."

On the basis of this passage, Langdon, RA 34 (1937) 73 n. 7 (following Barton), suggested "womb" (a synonym of *biṣṣuru*) for *uppu.* "Womb" was rejected by S. Smith already in RA 21 (1924) 81, and presumably by every one else in the meantime. Cf. AHW *šalubbû* and *šalussû* "ein Teil der Gedärme?" Based on the Sumerian, ŠÀ.LU.ÚB "intestinal sack," ŠÀ.AL.ÚS.SA "that which lies next to the intestines," one might venture a translation "peritoneum."

For UZU.ŠÀ.LUGAL.NU.TUKU=*pî šuḫḫu, pî uppi, pî karši* of Ḫḫ XV 114-116, see above, section B 2.

2. *uppu*/*ḫuppu* as a gesture connected with mourning or anger

A I/1 141: i[r] A×IGI = *ḫu-up-pu.* Note passages collected CAD A/1 under *ḫuppu* C and *ḫuppû.* (AHw 1 places this sub *ḫuppu* II, *uppu* II "Vertiefung," translates "eine Beinhaltung," and separates from *ḫuppû* II, *ḫuppu* IV "ein Kulttänzer.") If this is to be connected with any of the *uppu*'s, perhaps with a breast-beating action and the *uppu* hand-drum. Cf. the passage CT 42 18:14 cited above in section B 1. Otherwise, if leg/foot movement, connect with "*ḫuppû*" and *ḫuppu*=stamping of feet or running about (excitedly); cf. the playing of an ùb together with húb ~ gub movement in the Dumuzi-Inanna tigi-composition, TuM NF 3 25:16 (see Wilcke, AfO 23 88 with n. 4).

3. Ḫḫ XI 257 (MSL 9 201): KUŠ.ÙB=*up-pu* "(a worked piece of leather)." Probably the drum-skin (see sub B above).

4. *uppu* as a gift article

TCL 18 87:48: . . . *lu*! *ba-al-ṭà-ta up-pa-am* PN *uš-ta-bi-la-kum* TÚG [*ki*]*p*?-*pu uš-ta-bi-*[*l*]*a-kum* "Be well! I sent you an *uppu* (via) PN (and) I sent you a . . ."

5. Uncertain: [. . .] *lu up-pi* KUR-*i akšud* ". . . indeed I reached the (very) *uppu* of the country," Iraq 18 (1956) 124:10′ (Tigl. III); "latch-socket" is possible, but seems unlikely, even if the reading is correct.

6. ÙB=*uppu* not a percussion instrument?

The following references have generally been taken to refer to the percussion instrument ("drum"), but the contexts as well as the materials (metals) support the possibility that sockets (or other utilitarian *uppu*'s) are meant instead. If so, then the logogram ÙB for the "socket" would have been in use earlier than MUD. (Passages included in Limet, Métal, e.g. pp. 206, 231f.)

6.1 ÙB=*uppu* references where latch-part is highly probable (cf. section A 1.1.1 above):

zabar sag.kul . . . ù zabar ùb "bronze (for a) lock . . . and bronze (for an) *uppu*" UET 3 602:3f. (cf. nos. 682:2f., 730 ii 3). 1 urudu.gu_4.ùb.ba, 1 urudu.ùb, 1 urudu.kak.ùb.ba "1 copper bull of the *uppu*, 1 copper *uppu*, 1 copper nail of the *uppu*" UET 3 752 rev. ii 9-11 (note that ùb is written here ÁB×TAG_4).

8 giš.ùr.te? [. . .], 40 giš.é.da, 7 giš.ká.na, 25 sa gi.NE, 30 sa A.$\frac{\text{ZI}}{\text{ZI}}$.A, nì.ùb!.ba.šè ba.ak "8 wooden roof-beams, 40 wooden side-planks, 7 wooden sills, 25 bundles of . . .-reed, 30 bundles of . . .-grass make into (an) *uppu*-thing(s)" UET 3 781.

Cf. *ub-bu* in Gelb, OAIC No. 43, 15 (OAkk.).

6.2. ÙB=*uppu* passage where "axe-socket" or other device is probable:

ùb.zabar, ùb.ama_5(É×SAL).zabar "bronze ùb, bronze ùb of the *cavity*/chamber" OB forerunner to Ḫḫ XII (MSL 7 232:12f.), in sequence followed by "axe."

6.3. Uncertain: urudu.ub-nun "copper princely ub" (described as nì.nam.EN.Eridu.ki.kam), UET 3 296.

6.4. Standard form for transporting tin in LB Tribute List: 5 *lim up*?-*pu* AN.NA, Wiseman BSOAS 30 497 BM 82684 ii 13′, with discussion p. 501.

√**apāpu*

A verb *apāpu* may not exist at all in Akkadian; if it does, it is attested only in Mari, once in N-stem, and possibly once in G; see AHw 1 57 and CAD A/2 166. See already S. Smith, RA 21 (1924) 81. While the semitic root meaning "to revolve, turn around" is rather tempting in relation to *uppu* "socket," "place in which something turns/fits closely," there is no ready relation to "concavity" or "percussion instrument." Likewise, if *uppu* "percussion instrument" were of onomatopoeic derivation, there would be no ready relation to *uppu* "socket/concavity."

Synthesis

Several questions arise in connection with *uppu*, the small percussion instrument, on the one hand, and *uppu* "socket" on the other:

1. Is there any relationship that could be based on the notion of "concavity"?
2. If so, are there any known ancient Near Eastern percussion instruments that exhibit such a characteristic?

Tentative answers, and further problems, are offered:

Only one type of percussion instrument that could probe the question is known to the present writer, viz. the concave object said to be a timbrel or small tambour that is held and played by a female figure, close to the chest, in the left hand, and struck with the right. See figures 9 and 10. B. Bayer (Encyclopedia Mikraʾit 5 775f.) has suggested (although not in dealing with the question of concavity) that small hand drums may be identified with Biblical *tof* (an onomatopoeic term). Note the ubiquitous *duff* of the modern Middle East. Supporting an identification of *uppu* with these small tambours (i.e., whether or not they appear concave) are such passages as CT 42 18:14, CT 42 30b rev. 7f., and 1 LU 300 (see above, section B 1). See already Spycket, Journal des Savants (1972) 178-81. Cf. the discussion of Rashid, ZA 61 (1971) 92-94. For the small tambour struck with a stick, see Spycket, Journal des Savants (1972) 169 and cf. passages in which ùb occurs with (GIŠ.)PA, cited in n. 11.

Note also HAV 13 rev. 14f.: balag-a-ni gi_4-ér-ra-an-um-ma ga-ša-an-gá kuš.ùb-an-ni <<balag>> li-li-ìs-àm "Her (Sumerian) *balag*-lament is an (Akkadian) *gerrānu*-lament, my lady's *ùb* is a *lilissu*." Is the emphasis on Sumerian vs. Akkadian, or small vs. big? It is always suggested that the *lilissu* is one of the large percussion instruments (see, e.g., CAD, Spycket, Rashid, and others), based on the illustration accompanying the late ritual text TCL 6 47 (Thureau-Dangin, RA 16 [1919] 145; see Spycket, Journal des Savants [1972] fig. 42). Note that a *lilissu* weighs ca. 2 lbs. in an OAkk. text (TCL 5 6055 ii 9, see CAD sub *lilissu*).

Since it is generally believed that *uppu* and *lilissu* are dirge-instruments, it is contrary to associate these female (sometimes male) figurines, usually thought to be entertaining themselves or others, with anything mournful. Note, however, 1 LU 356: kuš.ùb(ÁB×KÁR) á-lá-e nì-šà-ḫul-le-da "with the *ùb* and *á-lá* which rejoice the heart" (or is it the *šèm* and the *á-lá*?).

If the *uppu*-instrument could safely be identified with the small tambour or timbrel, and if the passage "She beats her breast like the holy *uppu*" (CT 42 18:14, cited above) were germane, we would be encouraged in the assumption that *uppu* in Atraḫasis I has reference to the heartbeat; further, if *uppu* had reference to a concave timbrel, then we would be inclined to believe that a basic notion of "concavity" underlies all the *uppu*'s.

3. If the ancient representations of a concave timbrel are even approximately accurate, how could such a shallow bowl-like percussion instrument be made?

If metal or clay, one can understand such a bowl being tapped, even though the holding of it in one hand would dampen the vibrations/resonance. If made of skin, it could have been a skin stretched over and tied to a bowl-like frame, e.g. a basket-like structure.[14] But it is unlikely that such an instrument was made.

Perhaps a simple solution is to be found by assuming that, as Hg instructs us, the *uppu* is a drum-*head* and not a drum; that is, a tambour/frame-drum could have been referred to as a drum-skin, the part that is struck. Further, it is conceivable that "concavity" derives from the open frame with skin stretched on one side only; see fig. 8 and the modern *duff* in fig. 11. The clay figurines that seem to display concavity would then be imprecisely rendered. Moreover, the figurines would imply that the hand or fingers tapped the skin either from the "front" or from the "back" side. But it may be wishful thinking to solve so many problems so simply. Further, if all the meanings of *uppu* are indeed related to the basic notion of concavity, then we conclude that *uppu* is a loanword from Sumerian.

Returning to the starting point of this investigation, the notion of "heartbeat," it may be useful to observe those passages that are relevant. In many languages, there exist verbs to express the beating of the heart, but not a specialized noun, e.g. English "heart" + "beat." In Akkadian we have the relatively common verbs "to beat," said of the heart, as *nakādu* and *tarāku* (see AHw 1 549 sub 2b; AHw 1 717). Both verbs, however, relate primarily to the heart's beating fast or hard, thus indicating excitement resulting from fear, anger, etc. Nevertheless, the meaning of *nakādu* is completely clear in the case of the dead Enkidu: *ilput libbašuma ul inakkad* "He (Gilgameš) felt his (Enkidu's) heart, and it did not beat" (Gilg. VIII ii 16). [The verb *labābu* "to be angry" is interesting in this connection (i.e. the fast heartbeat or pounding heart), especially in view of the notion of its being a "privative denominative" from *libbu*, as may be the case with *labbu* "dead, withered" (discussed by Landsberger, Date Palm p. 15 with fn. 42; cf. p. 35).][15]

Note the following uses of lipiš(ÁB×ŠÀ) "heart" in connection with notions of anger or fear:

SP 1.141 (Gordon, Sumerian Proverbs p. 110): [. . .]-te šeš-e lipiš-ta é?-ad-da-ne-ne in-gul-lu-uš ". . . the brothers, in anger(?), have destroyed the estate of their father."

14. Though it could be profitable to investigate properly *ḫuppu* "basket," *ḫuptu* "hole, socket," and even *ḫupḫuppu* "a container or tube," time, space, and the reader's patience do not permit.

15. It may be useful to observe the occurrences in Hebrew. Verb(s): "to beat," said of the heart, e.g., common *libbō dāfaq* "his heart beat," or *halmūt lēb* "pounding of the heart." [Note, too, *libbēb* "to hurt the heart(?)" (included in Landsberger's discussion of privative denominative forms from *libbu*, Landsberger, Date Palm 15 n. 42).] Hebrew also lacks a specialized noun for heartbeat. Note Bibl. *paʿam* "time, step, beat," etc.; *paʿamōn* "percussive instrument, bell (used in the cult)" of Ex. 28:33f., 39:25f. Can a peripheral notion of "heartbeat" be seen in *paʿam*, in view of the use of the verb *pʿm* when it means "to be agitated, troubled; to have an anxious spirit," i.e., does "to have one's heart pound/beat fast" lie behind the meaning? Gen. 41:8 *wattipāʿem ruḥō* "his spirit/emotion was agitated" (cf. Dan. 2:1, 3); Ps. 77:5 *nifʿamti wəlōʾ ʾadabbēr* "I am agitated and cannot speak." [Cf. Mod. Heb. *pəʿimōt lēb* "heartbeat."] I thank Prof. Jonas C. Greenfield for mentioning these passages.

lipiš-bal=*uzzatum* "anger" (Erimḫuš V 177, cited CAD A/1 sub *agāgu*, lex.); ŠL 424, 10: lipiš-bal-a-ni=*uzzat libbišu*.

"Dumuzi's Dream" 79 (Alster, Mesopotamia 1 62): àm?-ma?-an-gig lipiš-b[al]-nam-lú-u[lu$_x$-ke$_x$-ne] "The evil *ones*, hated by men."

TuM NF 3 2 iv 6′ (Inanna's Descent): [a-a ^{d}]en-lìl lipiš-bal-a-ni ^{d}nin-[šubur-ra] mu-[na-ni-ib-gi$_4$-gi$_4$] "Father Enlil answered Ninšubur angrily."

lipiš-gig=*kīs libbi* "heart spasm" (see CAD K sub *kīsu* and Landsberger, Date Palm 15 n. 38).

lipiš-tuku$_4$-tuku$_4$=*râdu* "to quake" (Erimḫuš, cited AHw 2 sub *râdu*); lipiš-tuku-tuku=*nazarbubu* (Erimḫuš, cited AHw 2 sub *nazarbubu* "etwa 'vor Ungestüm beben'").

In Sumerian, one may note the expressions denoting anger, disquiet, that also derive from heart-pounding, fast heartbeat, etc.

šà~sìg ("heart—to beat, strike") as in, e.g., "Curse over Akkad" 256: é-gal šà-ḫúl-la dù-a nì-šà-sìg ḫé-en-šub "Auf (deinen) Palast, der zur Herzensfreude gebaut worden ist, möge Herzensangst gelegt werden" (A. Falkenstein, ZA NF 23 [1965] 63; see p. 120 for further references for šà~sìg).

šà.sìg.ga=*šutaktutu* "sich beunruhigen" (Erimḫuš, cited AHw 1 sub *katātu*). [Cf. šà.sìg.(ga)=*ṣurup libbi* "heartache," CAD Ṣ sub *ṣurpu*; sìg=*ṣarāpu ša libbi*, CAD Ṣ sub *ṣarāpu*; but the basic meaning of *ṣarāpu* is "to burn."]

Note also "Lugalbanda Epic" 338f.: šà-gù-di-šeš-a-ne-ne-ta šà-sìg-ku-li-ne-ne-ta "Während die Herzen seiner Brüder laut pochten, während die Herzen seiner Freunde unruhig schlugen" (C. Wilcke, Lugalbandaepos [Wiesbaden, 1969] 120).

Referring to heart-pounding from fear, cf. "Schooldays" 23: ní ba-te šà-mu ba-dar "Fear overcame me, my heart 'split(?)'" (see S. Kramer, Schooldays [Philadelphia, 1949] p. 5, who translates "my heart beat fast"). Cf. JCS 25 (1973) 193 note to line 41: balag-kù li-li-ìs-kù šu mu-na-dar-e.

For another expression denoting excitement, possibly heart-pounding, cf. "Enlil and Ninlil II" 27: en gal-an-zu šà-ní-te-na-ka dum-dam mu-un-da-ab-za=[*be-lu*]*m mu-du-ú ina lìb-bi ra-ma-ni-š*[*u* (x) x]-*im-ma iḫ-taš-ša-ši* (M. Civil, JNES 26 [1967] 203, translates: "The all-wise lord rejoiced abundantly in his heart." Cf. Wilcke's translation, Lugalbandaepos p. 133: "der (sonst) weise Herr bekam um ihretwegen Herzklopfen (Akk. 'freute sich über sie')"). For uses of dum-dam~za "to clamor, rumble" in connection with anger, see Civil, JCS 20 (1966) 119f.

By way of conclusion, we may assert that the heartbeat, obviously, was known; it must have been distinguished from the observation of the flow of blood in the veins and arteries.[16]

Although not a single clear occurence is at hand either for *uppu*="heartbeat" or for any common Akkadian or Sumerian noun designating the heartbeat, the passage in Atraḫasis I, in connection with which the above investigation has been carried out, makes good sense only if one understands *uppu i nišme*—whether one translates *uppu* as "dirge-drum" or as "*uppu*-sound"—as referring to the heartbeat, the sound that was heard in the new creature that was to be a reminder forever of the death inherent in it.

16. See A. L. Oppenheim, "On the Observation of the Pulse in Mesopotamian Medicine," Or. NS 31 (1962) 27-33.

SELECTED BIBLIOGRAPHY

I. Additions to Or. NS 41 (1972) 176f. Bibliography pertaining to the Atraḫasis Epic:

1. L. Matouš, 1970 Review of Lambert and Millard, Atra-ḫasīs. ArOr 38 74-76.
2. J. Siegelová, 1970 "Ein hethitisches Fragment des Atra-Ḫasīs Epos," ArOr 38 135-39.
3. W. F. Albright, 1973 "From the Patriarchs to Moses: I. From Abraham to Joseph," BiAr 38/1 22-26.
4. J. van Dijk, 1973 "Une incantation accompagnant la naissance de l'homme," Or. NS 42 505-507.
5. W. von Soden, 1973 "Der Mensch bescheidet sich nicht—Überlegungen zu Schöpfungserzählungen in Babylonien und Israel," Symbolae de Liagre Böhl pp. 349-358.
6. S. A. Picchioni, 1974 "Principi di Etica Sociale nel Poema di Atraḫasīs," OrAnt. 13 81-111.
7. I. M. Kikawada, 1975 "Literary Convention of the Primaeval History," Annual of the Japanese Biblical Institute 1 3-21.
8. H. Hoffner, 1976 "Enki's Command to Atraḫasīs," AOAT 25 241-45.
9. A. D. Kilmer, 1976 "Speculations on Umul, the First Baby," AOAT 25 265-70.

II. Discussions of *uppu*:

1. S. Smith, 1924 "Miscellanea," RA 21 79-81 and 155.
2. A. Salonen, 1939 Die Wasserfahrzeuge in Babylonien. StOr 8/4 130.
3. A. Salonen, 1951 Die Landfahrzeuge des alten Mesopotamien. AASF B 72/3 97.
4. W. von Soden, 1957 "Zum akkadischen Wörterbuch," Or. NS 26 137.
5. W. von Soden, 1957 "Zu einigen altbabylonischen Dichtungen," Or. NS 26 308f., 313.

6. W. Lambert, 1960 Babylonian Wisdom Literature p. 248f.
7. A. Salonen, 1961 Die Türen des alten Mesopotamien. AASF B 124 159 and passim.
8. B. Landsberger, 1967 The Date Palm and Its By-Products, AfO Beiheft 17 35 with n. 115.
9. D. J. Wiseman, 1967 "A Late Babylonian Tribute List?," BSOAS 30 501.
10. W. von Soden, 1969 "Als die Götter (auch noch) Mensch waren . . . ," Or. NS 38 430.

III. Discussions of drums:

1. H. Hartmann, 1960 Die Musik der sumerischen Kultur pp. 37-43 and 79f.
2. B. Bayer, 1968 "Playing Music and Singing," Encyclopedia Mikraʾit 5 765-76.
3. W. Stauder, 1970 "Die Musik der Sumerer, Babylonier und Assyrer," Handbuch der Orientalistik, Abt. 1 Supp. 4 182-85, 197-200, 207f., 218f.
4. S. A. Rashid, 1971 "Zur Datierung der mesopotamischen Trommeln und Becken," ZA 61 89-105.
5. A. Spycket, 1972 "La Musique instrumentale mésopotamienne," Journal des Savants 153-209.

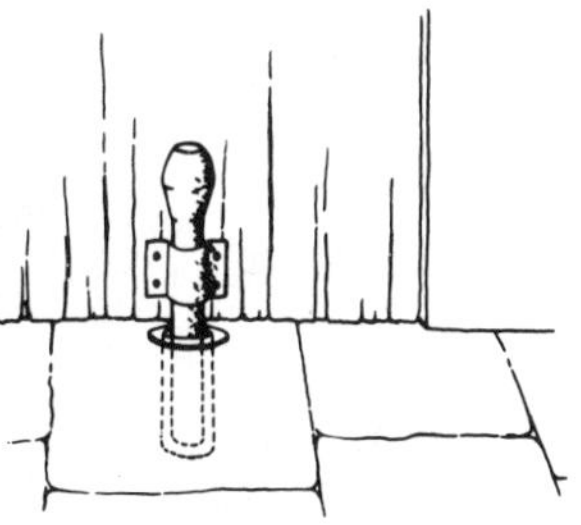
Fig. 1

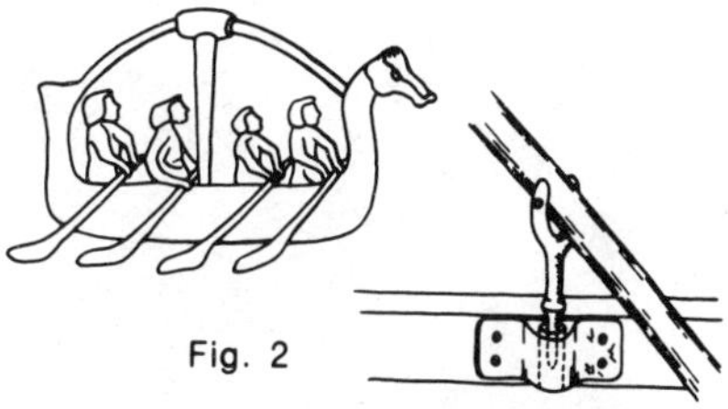
Fig. 2

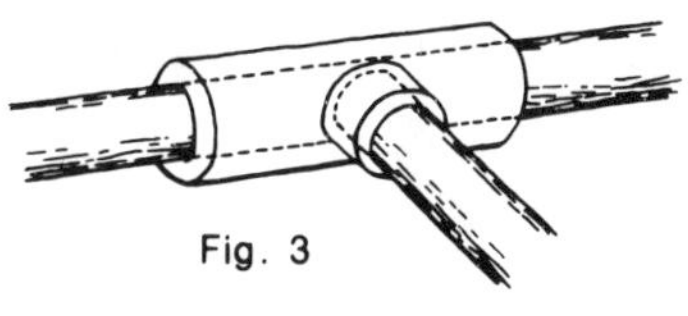
Fig. 3

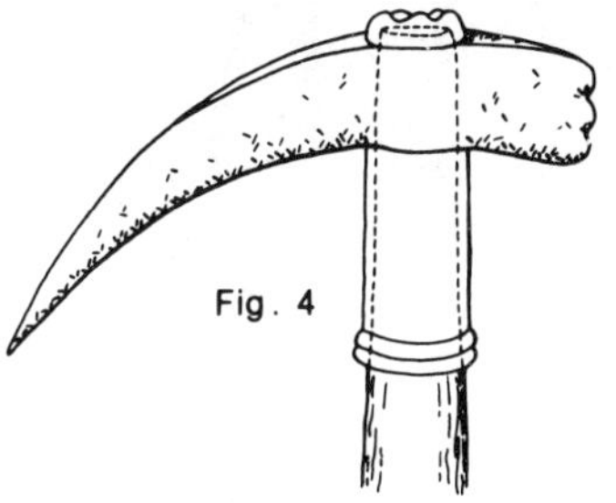
Fig. 4

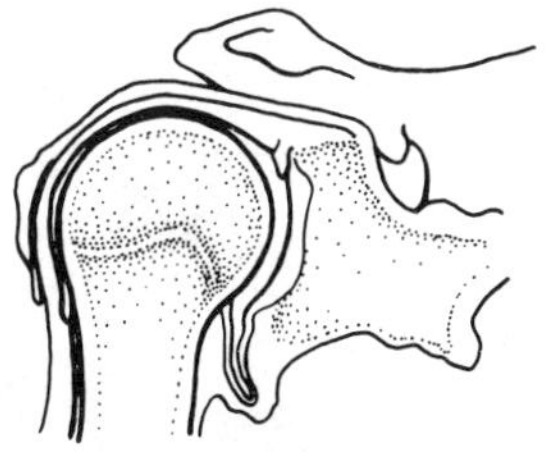
Fig. 5

Fig. 6

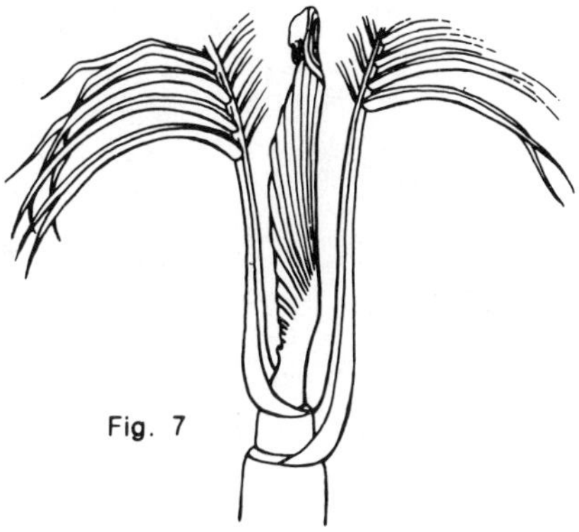
Fig. 7

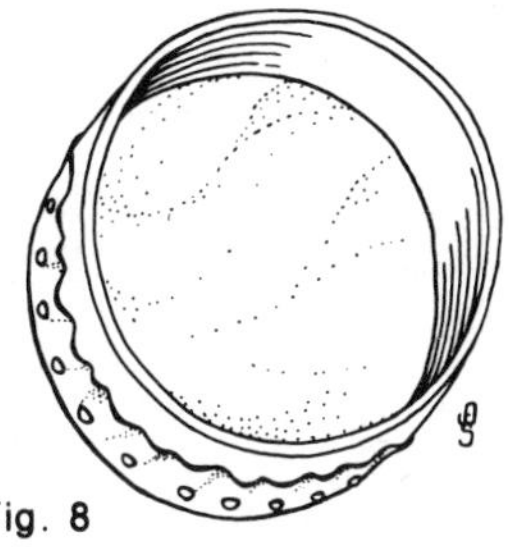
Fig. 8

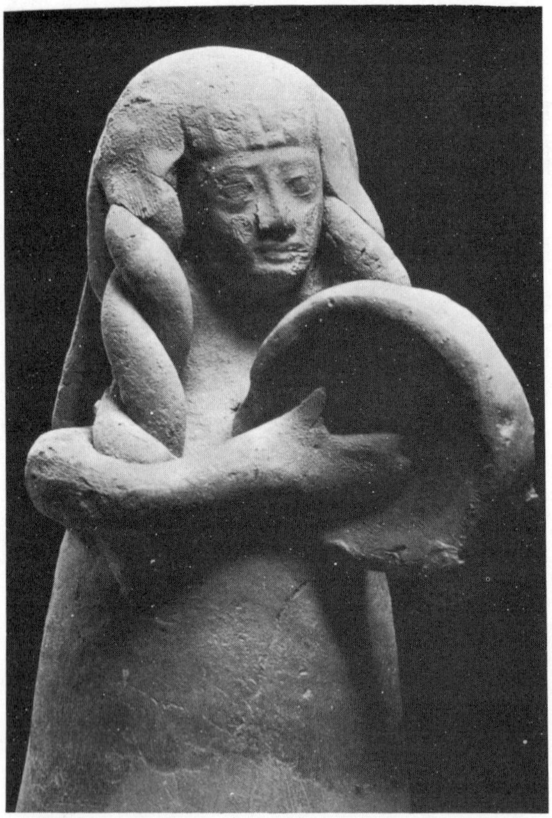

Fig. 9: Pottery figurine from Shikmona (HMAA,H24). Photo from Catalogue of the Haifa Music Museum, Music in Ancient Israel (1972/73)

Fig. 10: Terracotta relief (AO 12205). Photo from ZA 61 (1971) 90.

Fig. 11: A *duff* as used today in Pakistan. Photo taken from Jean Jenkins and P. R. Olsen, Music and Musical Instruments in the World of Islam (catalogue of Horniman Museum, London, exhibit for World of Islam Festival, 1976) p. 83.

THE GIR_5 AND THE ki-sikil: A NEW SUMERIAN ELEGY

Samuel Noah Kramer
The University of Pennsylvania

BM 24975 is a well-nigh perfectly preserved tablet 13×7 cm. in size, inscribed with a poetic composition that seems to be a funeral chant for a GIR_5 who was an intimate of a ki-sikil and beloved by her.[1] Most of the text of the composition can be transliterated with reasonable certainty, and much of it can be translated with a fair degree of assuredness. Nevertheless, its intent and purpose are difficult to fathom, and its real meaning remains doubtful. Primarily this is due to the ambiguity of the key-word, GIR_5,[2] a substantive that designates an individual whose status, function, and precise relationship to the ki-sikil[3] remain enigmatic throughout the composition, despite the fact that he is depicted in considerable detail, both realistically and metaphorically. In addition, there are a number of crucial textual and contextual problems which, as will become evident in the course of this paper, cannot be resolved satisfactorily at present.

The composition may be described as a playlet featuring two protagonists: the ki-sikil and an unnamed friend or adviser.[4] It begins with an address by the latter, consisting of 19 lines, in which he (or she) first exhorts the ki-sikil to prepare herself for the GIR_5's imminent arrival (lines 1-3), and then proceeds to depict him as one who has travelled far afield to distant places (lines 4-6); as an ill-fated, tearful, suffering individual whose stricken body is floating helplessly on the voracious flood-waters (lines 14-19). Though some of the renderings throughout this passage are rather uncertain, it is reasonably clear that the friend is apprizing the ki-sikil in oblique, poetic language, of the violent death of her beloved GIR_5 in some distant land. The death of the GIR_5 and the return of his corpse via mountain and river to the home of the ki-sikil whence he had presumably begun his disastrous journey, are also described in rather enigmatic, metaphorical language in lines 7-13, where he is depicted as a swallow who has disappeared; as a dragonfly adrift on the river; as mist(?) drifting over the mountain ranges; as grass floating on the river; as an ibex traversing mountains.[5]

The response of the ki-sikil constitutes the entire remainder of the composition (lines 20-49). If I understand it correctly, it consists of two sections. In the first (lines 20-37), she itemizes all the great things she will do for her GIR_5, presumably as cult offerings to his ghost[6]: cakes, fruits of the field, roasted barley, dates, beer, grapes on the vine, apples and figs, honey and wine, hot and cold water, a rein and whip, a clean garment, fine oil, a chair, footstool and bed, cream and milk. The second section begins with the ki-sikil's melancholy portrayal of the dead GIR_5 upon his arrival: he cannot walk, see, or speak (lines 38-40). She then continues with a description of the funerary ritual she performed immediately upon the dead GIR_5's arrival (lines 41-47), and concludes with the bitter realization that her smitten GIR_5 lay dead, and that his spirit had only just arrived with his body, had—now that he had been liberated from the corpse by the funerary rite—departed from her house (lines 48-49).

1. The first draft of this paper was prepared at the invitation of Jack Finkelstein several weeks before his death, and was read at the Yale Assyriological colloquium that met to do him homage after his death.

2. The best known meaning of GIR_5 when it refers to a person is "stranger," "alien" (cf. last Krecher, Kultlyrik pp. 218-19), but at least on the surface this hardly fits such expressions as GIR_5-zu (lines 1-2), GIR_5-kal-la-zu (line 3), GIR_5-mu (lines 20, 31, 38, 41, 49), unless it is assumed that the designation "stranger" is here used rather reproachfully and poignantly, because he had been away too long from the home of the ki-sikil. Thorkild Jacobsen, who studied the composition at my request, and to whom I am indebted for some of the more successful translations and interpretations in this paper, suggests a rather neutral rendering such as "traveller" for GIR_5, or perhaps even more specifically, "courier." Because of the numerous uncertainties involved, it seemed wiser to leave this crucial word untranslated for the present.

3. The ki-sikil, too, is not further identified in the composition; it is not impossible that the complex is here used as an epithet referring to Inanna, and if so, the GIR_5 may be Dumuzi, or some deity whose fate was identified with that of Dumuzi, or perhaps even the ruler as an avatar of Dumuzi, who may have been killed in the course of an expedition to a foreign land.

4. Both the ki-sikil and the friend speak in the Emesal dialect, with some rare lapses into Emegir.

5. There are two additional, but quite obscure, metaphorical descriptions of the GIR_5 (lines 12-13), where the initial IM-sag may perhaps be rendered as "early rain."

6. If the surmise that this passage indicates the introduction of a cult for the dead GIR_5 should turn out to be correct, it would corroborate the suggestion made in note 3 above, that the GIR_5 is a deity such as Dumuzi, or a king as Dumuzi incarnate. Jacobsen, on the other hand, interprets the contents of lines 20-37 as an emotional outburst of love on the part of the ki-sikil ("she would give him everything," "she would give him the world if she could") which is then choked off by the full realization that he is dead—he cannot walk, cannot see, cannot talk any more (lines 38-40).

Ancient Near Eastern Studies in Memory of J. J. Finkelstein
Connecticut Academy of Arts and Sciences, Memoir 19

BM 24975

obv.

rev.

TRANSLITERATION

obverse

1. GIR$_5$-mu im-ma-te ní-zu sa-gi$_4$-bi
2. ki-sikil GIR$_5$-zu im-ma-te ní-zu sa-gi$_4$-bi
3. GIR$_5$-kal-la-zu im-ma-te ní-zu sa-gi$_4$-bi
4. a-GIR$_5$ a-GIR$_5$
5. GIR$_5$-mu-lu-ki-bad-DU-zu
6. GIR$_5$-a-šà-sù-DU-kaskal-bar-ra-zu
7. sim.mušen-u$_4$-sù-da-nu-è-da-zu
8. ku-li-li-a-zi-ga-íd-dè-dirig-ga-zu
9. aḫḫur-ḫur-sag-e-dirig-dirig-ga-zu
10. ú-íd-šú-kur-ra-íd-dè-šú-a-zu
11. dara-kur-ra-dirig-ga-zu
12. IM-sag-sag-DU.DU.DU.DU-a-zu
13. IM-sag-e-líl-e-šú-a-zu
14. GIR$_5$-mu-lu-giskim-ḫul-a-zu
15. GIR$_5$-i-bí-ír-ra-ma-al-la-zu
16. GIR$_5$-mu-lu-šà-ḫul-ma-al-la-zu
17. GIR$_5$-a-me-EN-gír-kú-a-zu
18. GIR$_5$-šú-a-me-EN-sag-LÁ-LÁ-zu
19. GIR$_5$-gaba-da-ma-al-la-sìg-ga-zu
20. GIR$_5$-mu im-gen-na-ta ág ga-mu-na-ab-gu-ul-gu-ul
21. ninda-gúg-gúg ú-tir-ki ga-mu-un-na-ab-tag[7]
22. ág-sa-sa-ḫa-a-sà-ga ga-mu-un-na-me-ir
23. še-sa-a su$_{11}$-lum-ma ga-mu-un-na-me-ir
24. didaimgágá ga-mu-un-na-me-ir[8]
25. mu-tin pa-pa-al-la ga-mu-un-na-me-ir
26. giš.ḫašḫur ki-dagal-la ga-mu-un-na-me-ir
27. mu.ma ki-dagal-la ga-mu-un-na-me-ir

reverse

28. še-ir-gu-mu.ma-a ga-mu-un-na-me-ir
29. su$_{11}$-lum á-an-sur-ba ga-mu-un-na-me-ir
30. pú-kiri$_6$ làl-geštin ga-mu-un-na-me-ir
31. GIR$_5$-mu ì-gen-na-ta ág ga-mu-na-ab-gu-ul-gu-ul
32. a-kúm a-šed$_7$ ga-mu-un-na-me-ir
33. ad-tab ešé-íb-lá ga-mu-un-na-me-ir
34. túg-tán(!?)-na u$_5$-zé-ba ga-mu-un-na-me-ir
35. giš.gu-za mu.me-ri-gub ga-mu-un-na-me-ir
36. mu.ná-gi-rin-na ga-mu-un-na-me-ir
37. u$_5$-ga-tùr-amaš-a ga-mu-un-na-me-ir
38. GIR$_5$-mu gen-na-ni nu-um-gen gen-na-ni nu-um-gen
39. igi in-tuku igi nu-mu-ni-du$_8$-a
40. ka in-tuku ka nu-mu-da-ba-e
41. GIR$_5$-mu i-im-gen te-e-a in-ga-ba-gen te-e-a
42. ninda ì-sì šu bí-ib-gur
43. utúl-ma-al-tum-ma al nu-ub-du$_8$-a
44. GI.ESIR šu-um-du-um-bi nu-pil-la
45. a íb-ta-dé ki-in-dé ba-ab-nag
46. u$_5$-zé-ba-mu é-gar$_8$ mu-un-na-šéš
47. túg-gibil-mà giš.gu-za ba-an-mu$_4$-mu$_4$
48. im i-ku$_4$-ku$_4$ im ba-ra-è
49. GIR$_5$-mu kur-ra kur-šà-ba šu ba-an-tún ba-ná

TRANSLATION

obverse

1. "Your GIR$_5$ is approaching, prepare yourself,[9]
2. Oh ki-sikil, your GIR$_5$ is approaching, prepare yourself,
3. Your dear GIR$_5$ is approaching, prepare yourself.
4. Oh the GIR$_5$! Oh the GIR$_5$!
5. Your GIR$_5$, he of the far-away place,[10]
6. Your GIR$_5$, (he) of the distant fields, of alien roads,
7. Your swallow that will not come out unto distant days,[11]
8. Your dragonfly of the rising waters, adrift on the river,
9. Your mist(?) drifting over the mountain ranges,[12]
10. Your river-crossing grass floating on the river,[13]
11. Your ibex traversing the mountains,
12. Your . . . .,
13. Your . . . .,
14. Your GIR$_5$, he of evil omen,
15. Your GIR$_5$, (he) of weeping eyes,
16. Your GIR$_5$, he of grievous heart,
17. Your GIR$_5$, (he) whose bones were devoured by the high flood,[14]
18. Your floating GIR$_5$, (he) whose head was tossed about(?) by the high flood,[15]
19. Your GIR$_5$, (he) who has been struck in (his) broad chest."
20. "After my GIR$_5$ has come, I will do great things for him:
21. I will offer(?) him cakes (and) ú-tir,[16]
22. I will provide for him the fruits of the field,[17]

7. Between the signs U and TIR is an erased SA.

8. Under the U.SA of KAS.U.SA there is the gloss ga-ga.

9. The verbal form sa-gi$_4$-bi is assumed to be an imperative, the Emesal -bi corresponding to the Emegir bí (but cf. line 42, where the verb is introduced by bí, not bi).

10. Cf. the introductory lines in "Two Elegies on a Pushkin Museum Tablet," and in "The Message of Ludingirra to his Mother." Note, too, that Damu is depicted as "one of a far-away place" (cf. CT 15 26:1-4=TCL 15 9:64ff.).

11. Literally perhaps "Your swallow that will not come forth unto(?) distant days." Perhaps u$_4$-sù-DU modifies sim.mušen and the rendering should be "Your swallow of distant days (that is: of days gone by) will no longer appear."

12. The rendering "mist" for aḫḫur is a guess based on the context.

13. The rendering treats šú as *katāmu* and šú-a as *neqelpû*.

14. For gír cf. CAD E sub *eṣemtu*. Note that the rendering "by the high flood" in this and the following line assumes that the agentive -e is to be understood after a-me-EN (for a-mi-EN cf. now Sjöberg, Temple Hymns pp. 63-64).

15. Transliterations and translation of the line are quite uncertain.

16. For ú-tir cf. ŠL 375:11. The rendering "offer" for ki~tag is a guess based on the context (cf. BE 31 4 rev. 2, 6, and 10, where it may have the same meaning). Note that at least on the surface there seems to be no special reason for the use in this line of the verbal form ki ga-mu-un-na-ab-tag instead of the ga-mu-un-na-me-ir of the following lines; also that the ga- introducing the verb is Emegir, not Emesal.

17. For ág-sa-sa-ḫa, cf. AHw 2 sub *mutḫummu*. The rendering "provide" for the root me-ir is a guess based on the context.

23. I will provide for him roasted barley (and) dates,
24. I will provide for him bitter-sweet beer,[18]
25. I will provide for him grapes on the vine,[19]
26. I will provide for him apples of the wide earth,[20]
27. I will provide for him figs of the wide earth,
28. I will provide for him the še-ir-gu of the fig tree,[21]
29. I will provide for him dates on their cluster,[22]
30. I will provide for him the orchard's honey (and) wine.[23]
31. After my GIR_5 has come, I will do great things for him[24]:
32. I will provide for him hot water (and) cold water,
33. I will provide for him rein (and) whip,[25]
34. I will provide for him a clean(?) garment (and) fine oil,[26]
35. I will provide for him a chair (and) a footstool,[27]
36. I will provide for him a gi-rin bed,[28]
37. I will provide for him cream (and) milk of stall and fold.
38. My GIR_5—he has come (but) he walks not, he has come (but) he walks not,[29]
39. He has eyes but he cannot see me,[30]
40. He has a mouth but he cannot converse with me.[31]
41. My GIR_5 has come—approach! He has indeed come—approach![32]
42. I have cast down bread, wiped him clean with it.[33]
43. From a drinking cup that has not been contaminated(?),[34]
44. From a bowl that has not been defiled,[35]
45. I poured water—the place where the water was poured(?) 'drank it up'.[36]
46. With my fine oil I anointed the wall for him,[37]
47. In my new garment I clothed (his) chair.[38]
48. The spirit has entered, the spirit has departed.[39]
49. My GIR_5 was struck down in the mountain, in the heart of the mountain, (and now) he lies (dead)."[40]

18. For didaimgágá (note, however, the gloss ga-ga in our text), cf. CAD A/1 sub *alappānu*.

19. For pa-pa-al see AHw 2 sub *papallu*.

20. In this line note the use of the Emegir giš (also in lines 30 and 47) for the Emesal mu (lines 25, 27, 28, 36); line 35 has both giš and mu. The phrase "wide earth" in this and the following line is found repeatedly in the literary texts, and is probably used here without any special contextual significance.

21. For še-ir-gu in connection with the fig tree, cf. ŠL 367:143 and MSL 5 96 n. 30e.

22. For á-an-sur, cf. Landsberger, Date Palm p. 37. Jacobsen suggests that á-an-sur may be an orthographic variant for an-sur (cf. AHw 2 sub *sissinnu*).

23. The rendering treats làl-geštin as if it were followed by the possessive -bi.

24. This line, which is virtually a repetition of line 20, seems to serve to separate the food provisions from a varied assortment of personal furnishings. Note, however, that line 37 seems to relate once again to food provisions).

25. For ad-tab, cf. Salonen, Hippologica pp. 119-20; for íb-lá (without preceding ešé), cf. ibid. p. 152.

26. The sign TÁN(!?) seems to be written over an erasure.

27. Note that the determinative is written both as giš and mu in this line (cf. n. 20, above).

28. For references to the equivocal girin, cf. last Hallo and van Dijk, The Exaltation of Inanna p. 76.

29. "He has come" renders gen-na-ni (literally "at his coming"; nu-um-gen is assumed to be grammatically nu-(i)m(i)-gen.

30. Note the Emegir igi for i-bi, and the unexpected final -a (for -e) of the verbal form.

31. With this line compare especially "La Passion de dieu Lillu" (RA 19 [1922] 184ff.) rev. 12ff.

32. If the rendering "approach" for te-e-a is correct, it may be an exclamatory word addressed by the ki-sikil to the dead GIR_5 in a moment of deep emotional stress. Jacobsen suggests that it may have been addressed to those who brought the corpse to the home of the ki-sikil, and should therefore be rendered "bring it close." Note that preceding the second te-e-a is the verbal form in-ga-ba-gen where the -ba-gen is probably semantically identical with the i-im-gen that preceded the first te-e-a.

33. For the ritual involved cf. CAD K sub *kapāru*.

34. The rendering "contaminate" for al~du_8 is a guess based on the context.

35. GI.ESIR is assumed to be a variant of GI.EŠIR=*kuninnu*.

36. The rendering of ki-in-dé as if it read ki-in-dé-a may be quite unjustified.

37. If "wall" renders é-gar_8 correctly (note that it may also be equated with *lanu* "body"), it presumably refers to the wall of the place where the water-libation rite was performed.

38. The "chair" may be the chair for ghosts (cf. CAD E sub *eṭemmu*), but the nature of the ritual act performed is not too clear.

39. The rendering of this line assumes that im i-ku_4-ku_4 (the reduplication of the root seems inexplicable) refers to the spirit in the corpse when it arrived at the home of the ki-sikil, and that im ba-ra-è refers to the spirit after it had been released from the body following the performance of the funerary rites.

40. While the rendering of the individual complexes in this line seems reasonably assured, its contextual implications are quite uncertain.

LITERARY NOTES

Erle Leichty
University of Pennsylvania

SMOKE OMENS

Smoke omens are very rare in Akkadian. So far they exist on only three tablets, all from the Old Babylonian period. It is probable that the paucity of such omens is a result of the low esteem in which they were held in antiquity. Like the oil omens, they deal almost exclusively with personal fortunes and they seem to have been thought of as "fortune-telling" and "unscientific." These omens were not incorporated into the later "canonical" collections of omens.

It is most likely that diviners who worked with oil and smoke were similar to modern palmists. They probably set up shop in the market or other public areas where they read individual fortunes by means of patterns formed by smoke rising from a censer or oil dropped on water.

Despite the rarity of smoke omens, they have received a substantial amount of attention. The two largest tablets were first published by Lutz, one in PBS 1/2 99 (= CBS 14089) where it was misidentified as "Fragment of a Semitic Code of Laws" and the other in UCP 95 367ff. (= UCLM 9-2433) where Lutz correctly identified the text as "Divination," but did not understand that it dealt with smoke. In 1935, Ebeling correctly identified these two texts and published an edition of them in his article, Weissagung aus Weihrauch im alten Babylonien, Sitzungsberichte der Preussischen Akademie der Wissenschaften, Philosophische-historische Klasse (SPAW) 29 869-880. More recently, Pettinato republished the texts in his article Libanomanzia presso i Babilonesi, Rivista Degli Studi Orientali 41 (1966) 303-327. Unfortunately, Pettinato did not collate the texts, and even though his edition was an improvement on that of Ebeling, there was still room for advancements. Recognizing this, Biggs collated the texts and published his improved readings in RA 63 (1969) 73-74.

The third text was identified by the author a few years ago and is published below with the kind permission of Åke W. Sjöberg, Curator of Tablet Collections in the University Museum. It is not my intention to burden the Assyriological.world with yet another edition of the smoke omens. Instead, I offer my colleagues further collations of the published texts and a transliteration and translation of the new text.

CBS 14089 (=PBS 12 99)

Since Biggs collated this text, I have had the opportunity to have the text baked and cleaned. As a result, a number of new readings have emerged. The line numbering follows Biggs.

i 6: This is one of the most difficult spots on the tablet. The signs, as preserved, do not support Biggs' reading. The first sign could be *ma-*, but only if written over another sign. The second sign appears to be a clear PAB. Sign three is *ri*. The fourth sign appears to be BA or KU, but not *šu*. The reading of Biggs makes sense, but is badly forced. I would not, however, rule it out because the tablet is very badly written.

i 9: Biggs accepts the emendation of CAD which suggests the metathesis of the *i* and *ni* signs. However, there is a clear space between *za-ra-a* and *i-ni-šu*. As a consequence, I would be inclined to assume a metathesis between the words rather than the two signs. This despite the possible parallel given in CAD. I would render the passage as "its interstices are scattered" or something similar.

i 10: The end of the line reads *i-na aq bi im*. I am very hesitant to render this line. Could it possibly be "Inanna is resident in the <*na*>*qbû*?

ii 8: At the end of the line I read *i-na-an-*[*di*].

ii 16: I read *ši-ir a-wi-li da-*[*mi-iq*].

ii 17: I read ⌜*šum-ma qú-ut*⌝-[*ri*]-⌜*nu*⌝-[*um*].

iii 1: The sign remaining does not appear to be *as*, but rather the combination of the end of one sign and the beginning of another.

iii 2: I read [*a-na ḫa*]-⌜*ra*⌝-*ni-im*.

iii 3: I read ⌜*šum*⌝-*ma a-la-ak-šu*.

iii 5: I read *mu-ur-ṣú i-ba-aš-ši*. The *mu* is written over an erasure and the *ṣú* is less than clear.

iii 7: Clearly *ka-pí-ip-ma*.

Ancient Near Eastern Studies in Memory of J. J. Finkelstein
Connecticut Academy of Arts and Sciences, Memoir 19

iii 9: As noted by Biggs, the text has a clear *i* rather than *šu*.
iv 3: I read *a-la-ak-*⸢*šu*⸣ [*a-na*].
iv 4: I read *ma-aḫ-ri-*[*šu*].
iv 5: The text has clearly *da-ḫi-im*, but the root *da'āmu* must still be correct.

UCLM 9-2433 (= UCP 9/5 373-377)

I have worked with a photograph of this text and Anne D. Kilmer has been kind enough to collate occasional passages for me. Line numbers are according to Pettinato. I note only those lines where I differ with Pettinato or Biggs. I accept the readings of Biggs unless otherwise noted.

2: I read *um-ma-<na>-at-ka na-a*[*k-ru-ka i-da*]*-a-ak*.
5: I read *mi-qí-it-ti*.
9: I read *i-bi-sú-um ù ṣi-it* GUD.
12: I read *qá-ta-an*.
23: I read *ki-na-tim*.
24: I read *i-bi-sú-ú-um*.
27: I read *um-ma-ni-*[*ia*].
32: *ṣi-it* is on the tablet and needs no emendation.

CBS 156

Like the other two texts, CBS 156 is very poorly written and needs frequent emendation. All six omens on this tablet are duplicated on UCLM 9-2433.

qú-<ut>-ri-nam i-<na> sa-ra-⸢*qí*⸣-[*ka i-mi-ta-šu*]
i-la-ak-ma šu-mi-<el>-šu la i-[*la-ak*]
UGU *be-el li-mu-ti-ka ta-za-*⸢*az*⸣
šu-mi-<el>-šu i-la-ak-ma i-mi-ta-šu [*la i-la-ak*]
UGU *be-el li-mu-ti-ka ta-za-az*
a-na È ⸢^{d}UTU⸣ *i-la-ak-ma a-<na> ḫal-li ba-ri-im <la> i-la-ak*
UGU *be-el li-mu-ti-ka ta-za-az*

---

r. [*a-na ḫal-li ba-ri-im i-la*]*-ak-ma*
⸢*a-na* È ^{d}UTU *la*⸣ *i-la-ak* UGU *be-el <li>-mu-ti-ka*
ta-⸢*za*⸣*-az*
mu-úḫ-ḫa-šu iḫ-pí ⸢*i*⸣-[*bi*]-⸢*su*⸣ *ù ṣí-<it>* GUD <<*ma*>>
i-na È *a-*⸢*wi*⸣-[*lim ib-ba-aš*]*-ši*
mu-úḫ-ḫa-šu iḫ-pí ⸢*uš*⸣ [. . .] ⸢x⸣
ul i-[x x] ⸢*du*⸣ [. . .]

---

1) (If) the smoke, when you pour (on incense), goes to his right but not to his left—you will prevail over your adversary.
2) (If the smoke, when you pour on incense), goes to his left but not to his right—you will prevail over your adversary.
3) (If the smoke, when you pour on incense), goes to the east but not toward the crotch of the diviner—you will prevail over your adversary.
r. 1) (If the smoke, when you pour on incense), goes toward the crotch of the diviner but not toward the east—you will prevail over your adversary.
2) (If) the top (of the smoke) splits—there will be losses and loss of cattle in the house of the man.
3) (If) the top (of the smoke) splits . . .

LUDLUL BĒL NĒMEQI

In the course of cataloguing Neo-Babylonian economic texts from Sippar in the British Museum, I ran across a small fragment of a tablet containing literary extracts. The fragment, of which only one side is preserved, is divided into five line sections each of which is extracted from a literary composition.

I am unable to identify the source of the first section. The second section is extracted from Enūma Eliš and is a duplicate of tablet V 8-12. It contains variants but adds nothing new.

The third section comes from Ludlul Bēl Nēmeqi I 88-92, and supplies the correct reading for lines 88 and 90. Interestingly enough, Deller had already correctly guessed the reading of line 90 in his review of BWL in AfO 20 167. Line 88 furnishes a new attestation of ***kurruṣu*** in the sense of 'to slander."

I have been unable to identify the fourth section despite the fact that it is rather well preserved.

The text, BM 61433, is published below with the kind permission of E. Sollberger, Keeper of Western Asiatic Antiquities and the Trustees of the British Museum.

[. . .] ⌜x x x x⌝ [. . .]
[. . .] ⌜x⌝ *ga* ᵈLAMMA ⌜SIG$_5$⌝ [. . .]

[*man*]-⌜*za*⌝-*za* ᵈEN.LÍL *ù* ᵈ[*É-a ú-kin it-ti-šú*]
[*ip-te*]-*e-ma* KÁ.GAL.MEŠ *i-na* ⌜*ṣi*⌝-[*li ki-lal-la-an*]
[*ši*]-*ga-ri ú-dan-ni-ma šu-me-lu* [*u im-na*]
[*i*]-*na ka-bat-ti-šu-ma iš-ta-ka*-[*an e-la-a-ti*]
ᵈŠEŠ.KI-*ru uš-te-pa-a mu-ša iq*-[*ti-pa*]

---

ru-ú-a ṭa-a-bi ú-kar-ra-ṣa na-[*piš-ti*]
šu-piš ina UKKIN *i-ru-ra-an-ni ár*-[*di*]
GEMÉ-*ia*$_5$ *ina* IGI *um-ma-nu ṭa-pil-tum iq*-[*bi*]
i-mu-ra-an-ni-ma mu-du-ú šá-ḫa-tum ⌜*i*⌝-[*mid*]
a-na la UZU.MEŠ-*šú iš-ku-na-an-ni kim*-[*ti*]

---

[x] *li ki pa-an ina* ⌜x⌝ [x]
⌜x⌝ *ú-sa-ta*- DINGIR DINGIR-*šú ri*-⌜*ṣu*⌝-[x x]
⌜x⌝ *e kal uš-šú i-ta*-⌜x⌝ [. . .]
⌜x⌝ *i-ra-am* [. . .]
[. . .] ⌜x x x⌝ [. . .]

POOR MAN OF NIPPUR

At the end of the Poor Man of Nippur, the poor man, Gimil-Ninurta, has beaten the Mayor twice and we find him in a quandary as to how to complete his revenge. In line 140 Gimil-Ninurta is disturbed and "like a dog . . ." I cannot read the traces at the end of the line, but we certainly do not expect a negative phrase. I am tempted to read *ul-li* GEŠTU.II-*šú* and translate "like a dog he raised his ears," i.e. "he paid attention." However, to the best of my knowledge, that idiom is not attested in Akkadian. The text then goes on and says that Gimil-Ninurta watched all of the people.

At the beginning of line 142 I cannot make out a verb, but the context demands a verb meaning "to select," and the first two signs, *i-bar*, point to ***bêru*** or ***baʾāru***. The rest of the line is equally difficult. From the copy, we cannot escape the mayor of Nippur at the end of the line. That leaves the traces between *eṭlu* and *ḫazannu*. I would expect something like "unknown to" or "foreign to."

The next line, 143, I read as *i-qis-su-ma ana qiš-ti* [*en*]-⌜*za*⌝-*a* or ⌜*en*!⌝-*za*! "He gave him a goat as a gift." The former suggestion fits the traces well, but the long *a* vowel is difficult to explain. After this, Gimil-Ninurta tells the young man to go to the gate of the house of the mayor and set up a commotion so that all the people gather. The young man goes out and shouts "I am the one with the goat" (*anāku ša enzi*).

This interpretation of these few lines is based on the story plot. If the young man knew that he was going to be chased and probably beaten by an angry mob from the mayor's house, he would hardly have been foolish enough to take part in this adventure. Therefore, Gimil-Ninurta tricked him. He gave him a goat as a present and all the young man had to do was to take the goat to the gate of the mayor's house and shout "I am the one with the goat." He must have been rather surprised when the angry mob descended on him.

I believe that this reading of line 143 clarifies, at least in part, the ending of our tale.

THE NAMES OF THE CUNEIFORM GRAPHEMES IN OLD BABYLONIAN AKKADIAN

Stephen J. Lieberman
The University Museum
University of Pennsylvania

The names of the letters of the Greek alphabet are part of the evidence which has been adduced to bolster the contention that the "alphabet" was invented by speakers of North-West Semitic and spread from them to the Greeks.[1] As is well known, many of the Greek letter-names were borrowed from North-West Semitic; this, along with other indications, makes it clear that the Greeks were correct in asserting that they received their letters from the East.

The names by which the speakers of Akkadian designated the cuneiform graphemes were treated by V. Christian in 1913 in Die Namen der assyrisch-babylonischen Keilschriftzeichen.[2] Despite the fact that this study is now clearly dated, it remains the most recent systematic treatment of the grapheme names.[3] Since Christian's publication, the grapheme names have largely been ignored, save for A. Deimel's listing of them in the first volume of his Šumerisches Lexikon.[4] The present study treats the use of grapheme names in Old Babylonian times.[5] At the time of Christian's study, none of the Old Babylonian occurrences of grapheme names treated here had been published.

Despite the fact that there has been no systematic treatment of grapheme names, three words in Old Babylonian have previously been identified as such names. The first of these grapheme names (l), is *i-ti-ma-am*, from Sumerian IDIM.[6] It occurs in a school text which was found at Susa, and first published by V. Scheil.[7] Another word was interpreted as a grapheme name by B. Landsberger and M. Civil, in their publication of the tablet which they dubbed "Proto-Aa"[8] because they saw in it a precursor of the lexical series á=A=*nâqu*. This grapheme (b), which commonly has the reading lá, meaning "to raise" is here defined as ⌜*su/sú*⌝*-ru-ú* (MSL 9 126-37 i "56"), a word which was borrowed from Sumerian $ZURU_5$.[9]

The third previously identified occurrence of a grapheme name in an Old Babylonian text is found in the liver omen YOS 10 61 omen no. 7, where we read: *šum-ma i-na ma-aš-ka-an* <<DELE>> *šu-ul-mi-im* [*ḫ*]*a-lu-um pa-li A-k*⌜*a*⌝*-di-*⌜*i*⌝*m ga-mi-ir*, "when in (the) place of the *šulmum*[10] (there is a) (grapheme f) ḪAL, (then) the dynasty of Akkad is ended." J. Nougayrol's interpretation of the word *ḫallum* as the name of the grapheme (f) ḪAL[11] is confirmed by the occurrence of the grapheme in the omen which precedes this one (YOS 10 61 omen no. 6): *šum-ma i-na ma-aš-ka-an šu-ul-mi-im* ḪAL LUGAL (*šar*) *ki-ša-ti*. . ., "when in (the) place of the *šulmum* (there is a) ḪAL, (then) the king of (the) world . . ." This interpretation has been accepted by the dictionaries.[12]

A closer look at the Old Babylonian omens reveals some other terms that are actually best understood as grapheme names, but have previously been overlooked, or interpreted differently.

In the Standard Babylonian hepatoscopy text K.85,[13] we have a systematic listing of graphemes which are

1. The substance of this paper was read at a session of the American Oriental Society in April 1970, which was chaired by J. J. Finkelstein. The lettered references to graphemes refer to the sketches on page 150.

2. MVAG 18/1 (1913).

3. We hope in due course to devote a monograph to the study of the post-Old Babylonian grapheme-names.

4. The second edition, published by the Pontifical Biblical Institute in Rome in 1930, included references to the sources from which the grapheme names were cited. Unfortunately, all references were deleted in the third edition, which was published by the same institute in 1947, with the assistance of P. Gössmann.

5. We shall here limit ourselves to the identification of the grapheme names and some other matters. For further evidence concerning these words see Lieberman, The Sumerian Loanwords in Old-Babylonian Akkadian (hereafter referred to as SLOB). References below in boldface refer to the evidence cited in chapter 3 of the first volume of that work (HSS 22, 1977) and to the developmental charts in the second volume (HSS, forthcoming); for linguistic aspects of the words, see particularly the treatment in the second volume.

6. SLOB **342.idim**$_x$.

7. "Quelques particularités du sumérien en Elam," RA 22 (1925) 45-53, where it was number 8 on p. 51. The text was republished by G. Dossin as MDP 18 59.

8. MAH 15.850+16.061+16.078, published in MSL 9 p. 126-37.

9. Cf. SLOB **(L)741.zuru**$_5$, and below.

10. The *processus papillaris*, according to A. Goetze, YOS 10 pp. 6-7; the portal vein, according to M. Hussey, "Anatomical Nomenclature in an Akkadian Omen Text," JCS 2 (1948) 21-32, at 28.

11. In his review of YOS 10, published in JAOS 70 (1950) 110-13, n. 9 on p. 113.

12. Cf. SLOB **308.ḫal**.

13. Published in CT 30 1a.

Ancient Near Eastern Studies in Memory of J. J. Finkelstein
Connecticut Academy of Arts and Sciences, Memoir 19

said to be found on the liver. The first four of these graphemes are given below as (e) through (h). The first three of these graphemes consist of single "wedges" crossing.[14] In grapheme (e), four wedges cross, three in (f), and two in (g). It seems likely that what was actually seen on the livers was the lesions or cysts left after the sheep had been infested by worms[15] or perhaps other parasites, which ate their way through the livers and left straight paths. If two of these intersected at an angle, grapheme (g) would be formed, if three (f), and so on. In the lexical texts we find grapheme (e) followed by (f),[16] and elsewhere we have (g) followed by (h),[17] but as far as we can see four graphemes are not found together in the sequence of K.85 in the lexicons which are "arranged by graphemes."[18]

Grapheme (e) may well be designated by the word *kakkabum* "star" which is found in the Old Babylonian omens. We have already mentioned grapheme (f) and its name, *ḫallum*.

Grapheme (g) is PAB (PAP), and we read in a liver omen (YOS 10 17:47): "when (the) lobe (*naplastum*) is like a *pappum* (*ki-ma pa-ap-pi-im*), (then) the god wants an *ugbabtum*-priestess."[19] The word *pappum* is to be interpreted as the name of the grapheme PAB[20] here,[21] for the name of the grapheme (g) is known to be *pa-ap-pu* from later texts (S a 245, etc.).

The next omen in the text (YOS 10 17:48) reads DIŠ (*šumma*) IGI-BAR (*naplastum*) *ki-ma ka-aš-ka-aš* dIŠKUR (*Adad*) *i-ra-ḫi-iṣ*,[22] "when (the) lobe is like a *kaškaš*,[23] (then) Adad (the storm god) will inundate (with rain)."[24] It seems likely that this is the Old Babylonian form of the name of grapheme (h), for we have seen that this same sequence of grapheme (g) followed by grapheme (h) is attested in K.85 and elsewhere.[25] The suggestion[26] that this is the name of grapheme (h) is bolstered, as well, by another Old Babylonian omen (YOS 10:8-9) where we read: "when (the) lobe is like GRAPHEME (h) [here we have the grapheme, not its name], then the king will kill his favorites in order to allocate their goods to the temples of the gods."[27] The relationship between the protasis and apodosis of this omen would seem, again, to be based on paranomasia, namely on a comparison between the grapheme name *kaškaš(um)* and the verb *kašāšum* "to exact services for a debt or fine, to hold sway, to master."[28] The grapheme in question is known to have the reading kas,[29]

14. As Nougayrol has observed in his "Textes hépatoscopiques d'époque ancienne conservés au musée du Louvre (II)," RA 40 (1945-46) 56-97, esp. 79 n. 1, the graphemes whose forms the scribes refer to are the old forms, not the Neo-Assyrian (or other late) forms. It is therefore significant that K.85 uses these archaic forms for the graphemes in question, even though it is otherwise inscribed in a Neo-Assyrian ductus. The other texts which Nougayrol has noted as having grapheme forms (RA 40 [1945-46] 79) do not use archaic forms. For the archaic grapheme forms in K.2787 (republished as Kraus, Texte 27a), cf. F. R. Kraus, MVAG 40/2 (1935) 49-50. Note that this text sometimes uses grapheme names in descriptions, as well. For comparison in omens, cf. J. Nougayrol, "Les 'silhouettes de référence' de l'haruspicine," AOAT 25 (1976) 343-50, esp. 348 I.

The study of ancient grapheme forms was part of the curriculum of the schools known from texts found at Ugarit, as well as from later times.

15. Cf. M. Hussey, JCS 2 (1948) 26.

16. Proto-Ea 134-41a followed by 142 and Sa 87-90 followed by 91-92. Note that in Zimolong, Vokabular iv 18-31 (Ea II 266-81) and CT 12 4-5 i and ii (A II/6 i and ii), this sequence is reversed (DIĞIR followed by ḪAL), but in the Zimolong manuscript DIĞIR and ḪAL form a single section, marked off by lines.

17. We have this sequence in YOS 1 253 "220"-"240" // CT 35 1-8 (r) iii 54-70 (Ea I 260-84), CT 12 16a-17a i (A I/6), and elsewhere. Note that in the CT 35 text the section is marked off by lines, and that in all of these texts, SILA$_3$ intrudes in the PAB sequence, between simple PAB and graphemes composed of PAB and another grapheme.

18. Cf. H. S. Schuster, "Die nach Zeichen geordneten sumerisch-akkadischen Vokabulare," ZA 44 (1938) 217-70, esp. 224-27, 236-38, 250-52.

19. Doubtless the relationship between the protasis and apodosis is based in the paranomasia between the grapheme name and the second syllable of *ugbabtum*.

20. SLOB **542.pab**.

21. AHw 2 824b seems to take this as an occurrence of the word "locks," even though it says that that word is "Pl." (plural) and our word has mimation.

22. Another explanation, partially destroyed, follows.

23. AHw 1 462b s.v. **kaškaššu(m)** 2 takes this as "ein Werkzeug v[on] Göttern (Flutsturm??)" and apparently understands *kaškaš* as being in construct with the following divine name, but this is not admissible, because that would leave no subject for the verb *iraḫḫiṣ*.

It is to be noted that the word is not declined and in the genitive case, as one would expect following a preposition, but rather is an endingless form, formally identical with the *status absolutus*. For such forms, cf. SLOB vol. 2.

24. The relationship between the protasis and apodosis would again seem to be paranomastic, comparing the grapheme name *kaškaš* with *kaškaššu*, which is an epithet used of the storm-god Adad, cf. CAD K 290a.

25. Unfortunately, this is, as far as we can see, known only from post-Old Babylonian texts. Proto-Ea does not list grapheme (h).

26. SLOB **382.kaskas**. This interpretation has now been adopted by CAD K (1971, issued in 1972), p. 290.

27. When there was no ambiguity, this grapheme (h) could, however, be used in the omen texts for other words: *ḫarrānum* (e.g., YOS 10 18:56) and *padānum* (e.g., JCS 21 [1967, issued 1969] 228:11; cf. Nougayrol, ibid. p. 227 n. 61).

28. CAD K 286a.

29. SLOB **°381.kas**. This grapheme is used to write the word for "beer" (usually spelled kaš), for instance in Sollberger, Corpus Ukg. 4-5 C vi 8, as already noted by F. Thureau-Dangin, SAKI 48 n. m); cf. A. Deimel, Or. 32 (1928) 48. The spelling ^{ga}kas—bar has been shown to be equivalent to ka-aš—bar "decide" by J. Klein, "Sum. ga-raš=Akk. *purussû*," JCS 23 (1971) 118-22.

and the etymon of the Old Babylonian grapheme name would seem to be a reduplication of this (/kaskas/),[30] but it should be noted that the name of the grapheme in later texts is *kaskallu*, and we know of no evidence in the lexical texts for a reading *kaskas.[31]

In the omen immediately preceding the last, that in which we find grapheme (h), we find the lobe compared to the grapheme (a), BAD (= BAŘ$_4$) (YOS 10 14:6; cf. also 5, 14, and probably 15), the later name of which is *ba-aṭ-ṭu* (S a329). It is worth noting that in one Standard Babylonian liver omen text (CT 20 43-48 i 1-3) we have this grapheme following ḪAL (f), giving us the sequence (e)-(f)-(a), and replacing the PAB grapheme (g) of the sequence of K.85 with grapheme (a). Using the Old Babylonian sequence as a link, we may presume an order *(e)-(f)-(a)-(h) which was a variant to the tradition of (e)-(f)-(g)-(h). We should note that evidence for both of these already dates to Old Babylonian times. The connection between protasis and apodosis of the aforementioned omens which use the grapheme (a) in description may well result from a paranomastic relationship between the verb *bâtum* "to stay overnight, spend the night, to delay" (CAD B 169) and the grapheme name, for which we expect an Old Babylonian form **battum*. (Contrast grapheme (l), for the name of which see above.)

We also find other graphemes used for descriptions in the omens, such as grapheme (c) in YOS 10 61:1, the text where Nougayrol first identified the word *ḫallum* as a grapheme name.

The most frequently attested grapheme name in Old Babylonian is *kakkum*, which according to the texts often appears on various parts of the liver, and is from Sumerian GAG.[32] This is the name of the GAG grapheme (i), which we know from the later texts as *ga-ag-gu*[33] and GAG-*qu*.[34] The word *kakkum* is best translated as "the grapheme GAG," rather than "mace" or "weapon" because one expects an exact designation of a phenomenon in the terminology of the precise science of hepatoscopy, rather than some hallucinated "weapon."[35] This interpretation of the word is confirmed by the models of livers from Boğazköy showing the form of *kakku* to which A. Goetze has called attention,[36] and by K.2086 + 82-3-23,26 + 83-1-18,421 + 83-1-18,422[37] which not only shows a sketch of a single *kakku*, written GIŠ-TUKUL (r.! i! 4), but also has a sketch of how it looks if there are two (r.! ii! 2-3)[38] or three (r.! ii! 13-14) of them. There are other first millennium texts, as well, where sketches on the tablet make the identification of the form clear.[39] A. Boissier had already reached the correct conclusion in 1905 that what was involved was the presence on the liver of something which, at least in origin, was viewed as a cuneiform grapheme. He did not, however, identify the grapheme correctly, for he read GIŠ-TUKUL as IS-KU and he took it as a spelling for **zibu*,[40] even though he translated the word as "pointe."[41] This grapheme probably gained the importance which it had in the omens because of the fact that the word *kakkum* means "mace,"[42] in specific, and "weapon," in general, as well as "GAG-grapheme," and the omens often deal with matters military.

It is noteworthy that the graphemes and grapheme names, other than *kakku*, almost always occur in the

30. The grapheme represents an intersection of two roads.

31. For instance, *ka-as-kal*, CT 12 6-7 iv 20′ (A III/3 207) in a compound name.

One might have considered this a back-formation from our grapheme name plus a feminine ending (**kaškaš*+*tu* >**kaškaštu* >**kaškaltu* > **kaškal(l)u*), but for the sibilant, and the fact that a Sumerian word for "road" can be shown to have ended in /l/ already in Old Babylonian times, e.g., SRT 1 iv 26, where grapheme (h) is followed by the syllable grapheme -la.

32. SLOB **201.gag**.

33. CT 11 13b i′ 17′, etc. (Sa 194).

34. CT 11 6a-7b r i 9, etc. (Sa 194). Grapheme names compounded from this name and another component include such forms as . . . GAG-*qa-ku*, CT 11 45-48 iv, the fourth line before the catchline (Diri IV 313).

35. Note the use of GIŠ-TUKUL (*kakku*) in a description of a *kukku*, which was a baked product with a specific shape, Rm. 2 102 (Boissier, DA 11-19) col. "A" 16 and presumably K.6988 iii 1′f., cited as another manuscript with this omen by CAD Z 56a.

36. JCS 11 (1957) 96 n. 49; the texts are KUB 37 216 and 228.

37. First published by A. Boissier, Choix 137-44, with photographs on pls. 3 and 4. A new copy was given by P. Handcock in CT 31 9-12.

38. Also in the other manuscript (79-7-8,110) which covers this part of the text, published in CT 30 34b.

39. Cf. Sm. 1335 in Boissier, Choix p. 153; K.99 in Lenormant, Choix 94, republished by A. Sayce, TSBA 4 (1876) 304-305; and the texts published (or republished) in CT 31 14-15. The other side of K.2092 (CT 31 15) is now visible, and has been published by J. Nougayrol, "Deux figures oubliées (K.2092)," RA 68 (1974) 61-68. Some of the unpublished diagrams may be relevant.

40. Boissier, Choix pp. 151-52. It is of some curiosity to note that his translation (pp. 74-75) was not based on the sketches, but on philological grounds which were in error, as A. Ungnad showed, Babyloniaca 2 (1908) 265-67.

41. In the sketches of the forms of *kakku* to which we have referred, a single *kakku* is shown as a triangle, but when there are more than one, only the two longer sides of the triangle are inscribed.

42. It was so named after the macehead whose representation lay behind the grapheme GAG. As has long been known, the grapheme GAG+ČEŠ (REC 318), which is used to write the word "mace" in Sumerian, consists of the business end of a mace (the triangle GAG) and its wooden handle. The head of an arrow was likewise triangular (pointed in the opposite direction), and written with the grapheme GAG.

omens not in isolation, but rather in short sections dealing with more than one grapheme. (There are many such sections dealing with *kakku*, of course.) This could possibly reflect the types of sources used by the scribes who compiled the omen handbooks, but only a detailed investigation of the history of the organization of the collections of omens could verify any such suggestion.

If we recall that the god Šamaš (and sometimes Adad as well) is said to *write* the messages in the sheep used for omen-taking,[43] we will not be surprised to find that the diviners saw cuneiform graphemes written there.[44] One of the concomitants of a writing system is the vocabulary which is used in teaching it, and the grapheme names were used in describing what was seen on the livers. As we have seen, even the order of the graphemes which we find in the omens may be the same as that of the school traditions which we know from the lexical texts.

SKETCHES OF GRAPHEMES

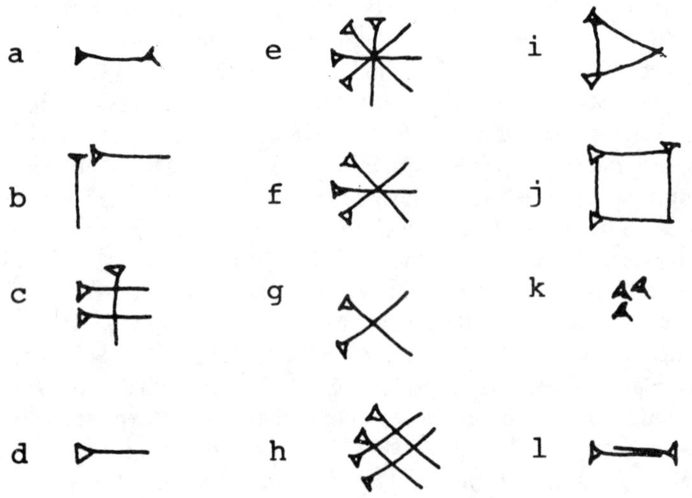

It is in the post-Old Babylonian lexical texts that we find most of the known occurrences of grapheme names. The scheme of those lexical texts which regularly provide grapheme names is shown here as our chart, along with the forms they have in Old Babylonian times.[45]

43. For instance, in the following line addressed to Šamaš: *ina* ŠA_3(*libbi*){var. *-bi*} UDU-NITA_2(*immeri*) {var. -MEŠ(*immerī*)} *ta-šaṭ*{var. *ša*}*-ṭar* UZU(*šēra*){var. -MEŠ(*šērī*)} PBS 1/1 12:14 (Šamaš-šum-ukin) // STT 1 60:15 // STT 1 61:15 // BMS 6 110 //OECT 6 30c:12′ (cf. Ebeling, Handerhebung 48 line 110) "in the belly of (the) sheep you write (the) portent{s}." Comparable uses of the verb *šaṭāru* "to write" in describing the process by which an oracular message was vouchsafed to the *amūtu* "liver, omen" can be found in TCL 3 319 (Sargon II), KAH 1 51 iii′ 3′ and other manuscripts (Borger, Esarh. p. 3 iv 6), 1 R 49 iii 24 and other manuscripts (Borger, Esarh. p. 19 Ep. 17 Fassung a 16) and BA 3 (1898) 312-13 r. 10′ (Borger, Esarh. p. 19 Ep. 17 Fassung b 10) (all Esarhaddon), and YOS 1 45 i 16 (Nabonidus). For a discussion of the relationship between writing and the omens, cf. J. Bottéro, "Symptômes, signes, écritures en Mésopotamie ancienne" in J. P. Vernant et al., Divination et Rationalité (Paris, du Seuil, 1974), esp. pp. 154-68.

44. It seems probable that the use of graphemes and grapheme names to describe the phenomena in the omens resulted in calling what the god or gods did to the liver in order to convey a message "writing," rather than vice versa. The use of graphemes and grapheme names is attested already in the Old Babylonian period, but the use of the verb *šaṭāru* as a metaphor for the imparting of the message is known, so far as we can see, only from the first millennium (for references cf. n. 43).

45. There are sporadic uses of grapheme names in other lexical texts, such as UET 7 126 ii 7′ (Nabnitu XXXII), MAOG 1/2 (1924) 53-56 ii 27′-29′ (Nabnitu A 178-80), 5R 19 3:16′-19′ (Hh XXIV 257-58), and CT 25 1-6 ii 39 etc. // LKU 7:5 etc 'An-Anum; also sporadically in other passages and manuscripts).

THE SCHEME OF LEXICAL TEXTS WITH GRAPHEME NAMES

	Text	I Sumerian Pronunciation	II Sumerian Spelling	III Grapheme Name	IV Akkadian Definition
Old Babylonian	Proto-Aa	(+)	+	-	+
	Monolingual Proto-Ea[46]	(+)[47]	+	-	-
	Bilingual Proto-Ea	+[47]	+	-	+
	Proto-Diri	(+)	+	-	+
	Boghazköy Diri	all written in a single column			+
Standard Babylonian	Aa	+	+	(+)[48]	+
	Ea	+	+	(+)	+
	Diri	+	+	(+)	+
	Idu	+	+	(+)	+
	Sa[49]	+	+	+	-
	Sb (except some school texts)[49]	+	+	-	+
	Sb (certain school texts)	+	+	+	+

( ) = column not present in some exemplars

As the chart shows, in the Old Babylonian lexicons we have no column with grapheme names (III). Many of the post-Old Babylonian tablets with copies of the Ea, Aa, Diri, and Idu, provide, in addition to a Sumerian pronunciation as column I, the grapheme or grapheme-complex being defined as column II and Akkadian translations as column IV, a description or name of the grapheme being defined as column III. In the primer commonly called Sa, the whole of the explanation of the grapheme consists of the grapheme name column, and no separate Akkadian translations are given,[50] while in some schoolboys' copies of Sb we have

46. Some manuscripts have graphemes only (II).

It is interesting to note that in Ni 5365 the writer inscribed four columns of graphemes, but did not finish putting in all of the syllabic spellings: he wrote two and a half of the columns of the pronunciation column, but did not complete the rest. Did the student who wrote this exercise tablet come to the end of the time allowed for an exam? Or did he drop his exercise as soon as the teacher announced that it was time to go home at the end of the day? It *is* important to note that the graphemes were repeated the number of times necessary to allow for the insertion of the various pronunciations which we find in the other manuscripts which cover this part of Proto-Ea, even though the text does not always have all of the grapheme-sections found in the other manuscripts (the passage without pronunciation is Proto-Ea 694-98 and 716-30, that which comes between these passages is broken off from the tablet).

47. This column is blank for some entries, cf. below.

48. Some manuscripts have II and III written in a single column.

49. There are also manuscripts which have only graphemes.

50. The equivalents in Sa are usually all interpreted as grapheme names, and clearly the vast majority of them are grapheme names. However, the identification of the equivalents which are not Sumerian in origin, but come, rather, from Semitic, constitutes a problem. V. Christian, and others, have understood these as Semitic grapheme names, but this is far from certain. First, it should be noted that most of these words follow occurrences of the usual Sumerian-based grapheme names (thus in lines 53, 68, 168 [note CT 11 13b ii′ 3′], 313, 345, 352, 379, and 385 of R. T. Hallock's reconstruction in MSL 3). It might, therefore, be best to take them not as grapheme names, but as translations. Two of the others (334 *kaspu* and 341 *aplu*) are given as equivalents of compound graphemes, and one (128 *ṣābu*) is also called by its Sumerian-based name in a compound grapheme

grapheme names as well as the usual Akkadian translations. These grapheme name columns are the principal source of our knowledge of the names of cuneiform graphemes in post-Old Babylonian times.[51]

The grapheme name column of these texts was added in post-Old Babylonian times, but the presence of grapheme names in the copies of the lexical text Diri found at Boğazköy seems to indicate that the grapheme names were part of the Old Babylonian school tradition. While the Sumerian grapheme complexes, readings, and names in Boğazköy Diri texts are not arranged in the separate columns which we find in the later lexicons, the presence in the Hittite schools of the knowledge of the names of the cuneiform graphemes makes it likely that they were part of an oral tradition learned from the Mesopotamian scribes. In fact, the linguistic forms of the names recorded by the Hittite scribes reflect developments in Sumerian which are not found in later Mesopotamian usage, but were normal phonological changes in Sumerian.[52] We have already seen from the omen texts that the grapheme names were used in Old Babylonian times, and that that tradition was connected, at least by the order of the graphemes, with the lexicons.

If, then, the Old Babylonian lexicographers did in fact use grapheme names, as did their colleagues in hepatoscopy, where did they hide them? Or were they left to the oral tradition alone?

We suspect that a number of the words in the Akkadian column of bilingual Ea and Aa texts from the Old Babylonian period ("Proto-Ea" and "Proto-Aa") may be interpreted as grapheme names, and that these words were later gathered into a distinct separate column for grapheme names. The problem in identifying the meanings of words in lexical texts is that one has nothing other than the Sumerian grapheme and its reading as a guide.[53]

We have already mentioned that Landsberger and Civil interpreted the word *surû* in Proto-Aa as a grapheme name. Another possible instance of a grapheme name is to be found in *ku-ru-um*, in a bilingual version of Proto-Ea.[54] In his treatment of this text, Landsberger refrained from translation. The word has since been interpreted as an occurrence of the word *kūru*, "ein Stück von Stamm (Holz od[er] Rohr)?" (AHw 1 512b), but a glance at the dictionary will reveal that that word was borrowed from Sumerian kur_4 (j). Another interpretation has been offered by the Chicago Assyrian Dictionary (K 570b), where it is taken as an occurrence of the word *kūru*, "daze." Again, however, there is no known evidence for Sumerian kur,[55] "mountain," or some homonym of it, being semantically related to the verb *kâru* from which that word is derived, and it is the grapheme (k) KUR which is being defined.[56] The grapheme name *ku-ú-ru* (Sa 318) is, however, well known from later texts to be the name of this grapheme. In the light of this, we might well interpret the word as the grapheme name, since words in lexical texts (as elsewhere) should be interpreted in the light of our knowledge of the rest of the Akkadian vocabulary combined with context, but it is possible that the word is simply to be taken as an (otherwise unattested) word for "mountain."[57]

The fact that this word, *ku-ru-um*, is to be interpreted as a grapheme name would seem to be confirmed by the fact that the left-most column of the equation is left blank, rather than providing a Sumerian pronunciation. B. Landsberger has suggested that a blank pronunciation column in Proto-Ea texts may be used for values which stand behind grapheme names.[58] Although it is hard to be certain, considering the

---

(351: *i-gi-e-ri-in-nu*). For all but two of the others (71 *ālu*, 397 *qištu*, 399 *ezibu*) we know of grapheme names from elsewhere which are Sumerian in origin (so also the variants to 314 in OECT 4 32 "313" and a Ni fragment: *ummu*). The grapheme names of the remaining two (262 ú and 283 é) remain a problem; for them, cf. SLOB vol. 1 notes 208 and 226. It should be observed that there is no consonant to reflect in any Akkadian borrowing of these last two Sumerian words. This would pose a problem if nominative *-u* were simply added, since we might well expect both to show up simply as *û*, but that difficulty does not seem to have prevented the creation of the name for the grapheme A from Sumerian /a/ (cf. Sa 1).

51. In addition to omens (cf. n. 14), grapheme names are attested in commentary texts (K.49, published in CT 18 49-50 passim, and JNES 33 [1974] 331-33, with M. Civil's remarks p. 329) and "esoteric texts" (CT 25 50 [with collation CT 46 54] 2, where we read ka-ra *ga-na-te-nu-ú*). For a possible occurrence of what may be a grapheme name in what seems to be an Old Babylonian commentary text, cf. n. 75.

52. We refer to the development of Sumerian /araguba/ to /raguba/, which we find reflected in the grapheme name *ra-an-ku-ub-bu* in KBo 1 48:8. For the form of this grapheme name in the post-Old Babylonian texts (and perhaps, in Old Babylonian as well), cf. n. 80.

53. Excluding, of course, those lexicons which are organized by semantic categories.

54. RA 9 (1912) 77-78 i 2; cf. MSL 2 p. 142. The line reads: (blank)=KUR=*ku-ru-um*.

55. For which see SLOB (L)**418.kur**.

56. The interpretation of (blank)=KUR=*ka-a-rum* remains a problem, but this line would seem to have been attracted to the passage by *ku-ru-um*, not vice versa.

57. It is possible that UET 6/2 375:10′ (Proto-Izi 226a) contains another occurrence of this word, if we are to restore KUR=*ku-*[*ru*(*-u*)*m*]. (N.B. the order of this manuscript of Proto-Izi is actually . . . 219-226-226a-224-225-227.)

58. In MSL 2 31 3). Landsberger suggests there, under 2), that in AO 5400 (published in RA 9 [1912] 77-78) the pronunciation

manner in which Proto-Ea was published,[59] the practice does not seem to be consistent. For there are instances of a blank pronunciation column where other manuscripts do not have the Sumerian etymon of the later grapheme name, but another value, such as Proto-Ea 271, and Proto-Ea 562 (MSL 3 p. 209).

It does seem reasonable, however, to interpret a word such as *di-e-lu-um* PBS 5 102 v 3[60] which is known from later texts as the name of the grapheme (d) DELE as a grapheme name in the light of such a blank pronunciation column.[61] Nonetheless, it could well have had another meaning, since the Sumerian etymon obviously did. The danger in contending that such words are grapheme names is that the Sumerian etymon always had a concrete meaning which was reflected in the grapheme which depicted it. We frequently encounter these common nouns as grapheme names in the later texts. Unfortunately, their identification as grapheme names must remain problematic, particularly since some of them are known as common nouns in Old Babylonian, elsewhere. Such words include *e-pe-nu-um*[62] known to be the later name of the grapheme APEN,[63] *i-si-nu* from IZEN,[64] *ka-ap-p[u-um]*[65] from KAB,[66] *k[a]-ar-rum*[67] from GAR_3,[68] *ki-sa-lum from* KIŽAL (= KISAL),[69] *la-gáb-bu*[70] from LAGAB (j),[71] *la-gal-l[um]* from $LAGAL_x$ (=$NAGAL_x$=LAGAR),[72] [*ma*]-*šum* from MAŠ,[73] [*me*]-*e-su-um* from MEŽ (= $MEŠ_3$),[74] *nu-un-nu-um* from NUN,[75], *sú-ma-šum* from $ZUMAŠ_x$ (= LAK 226),[76] *ša-ḫu-ru-um* from $ŠAḪUR_x$ (= LAK 227),[77] and *ú-mu-um*[78] from UM.[79]

There is some evidence for these words being grapheme names, and there may be others hidden elsewhere in Proto-Ea, Proto-Aa, and possibly in other lexical texts from the Old Babylonian period,[80] but

---

column is left blank because the pronunciation could only be given by repeating the grapheme being defined. He explains most of the blank pronuncation columns in this same fashion (MSL 2 pp. 30-31). This is, however, hardly convincing: the scribe could certainly have given the pronunciation of kur as ku-ur, as indeed a glance at unilingual Proto-Ea 447 will show some scribes did. The same can be said of the rest of the lines he cites (V-VC for VC, CV-V for CV, CV-VC for CVC, etc.). In fact, as a check of a number of lines of Proto-Ea will show, the scribes did not refrain from using the same grapheme in the pronunciation column as that being defined (note particularly Ni 5188 i 3′ where the equation a=A of Proto-Ea 5 is found, and the grapheme in the left column is written smaller than that of the right column).

The addendum to p. 31 of MSL 2, which was apparently supposed to appear in MSL 3 and deal with grapheme names (cf. MSL 3 p. 167 ad S. 34 g 3), p. 189 ad 174, and p. 206 ad 492a), did not appear there or in MSL 9.

59. We have collated the Istanbul manuscripts and checked all published copies and photographs.

Obviously, it is dangerous to base far-reaching conclusions on the omission of materials in texts which were students' copies revealing varying states of acumen and accuracy and were frequently folded, rubbed, cut, or otherwise mutilated between their use as exercises and their present enshrinement in museums.

60. MSL 3 p. 218.

61. Cf. SLOB **(L)135.dele**, the grapheme name *de-lu-ú* Sa 125, and Proto-Ea 100 (N 6113, cited as blank in MSL 2 p. 42). A translation such as "single," which Landsberger suggests in MSL 2, seems possible.

62. RA 21 (1924) 178 ii 3; cf. MSL 2 p. 147.

63. Cf. SLOB **58.apen**, the grapheme name *e-pe-en₆-nu* CT 12 31b ii′ 5 (Sb B 288) and Proto-Ea 523 (3 N-T 563, cited as blank in MSL 3 p. 208). The word could mean "seeder plow."

64. MSL 9 pp. 126-37 x "683." Cf. SLOB **366.izen**, and the grapheme names *e-ze-en-nu* Sa 382 (JCS 8 [1954] 144-45 no. 24 i 5) and *i-zu-un-nu* Sa 381. The occurrence could mean "(offering for) festival."

65. PBS 5 103 "r" ii′ 9; cf. MSL 2 p. 139.

66. Cf. SLOB **(L)370.kab** and the grapheme names *ka-ap-pu* Sb B 272 and KAB-*pu* Sa 395. The occurrence could also mean "wing" or "(part of a horse bit)."

67. RA 9 (1912) 77-78 i 20; cf. MSL 2 p. 143. The line actually reads (blank)=⸢GAR_3⸣=*k*[*a*]-*ar-rum*.

68. Cf. SLOB **213.gàr**, the grapheme name *qa-a-ri* Sa 235 and the blank space in the left column of the text which parallels Proto-Ea 472, and is cited in full in n. 67. The occurrence could mean "knob."

69. MSL 3 pp. 218-21 G_6 r ii 1′. Cf. SLOB **404.kižal**, and the grapheme name *ki-sal-lu* Sa 284. The occurrence could also mean "courtyard."

70. PBS 5 102 ii 11; cf. MSL 2 p. 126.

71. Cf. SLOB **(L)427.lagab**, the grapheme names *la-ga-bu* Sa 172, *la-gáb-*. . . KBo 7 12:4′ (in a phrase name) and some other instances cited in CAD L 37a, and Proto-Ea 33 (3 N-T 563, cited as blank in MSL 3 p. 183). The occurrence could also mean "clump" which it does in Nigga 289.

72. MSL 2 pp. 126-34 viii "50." Cf. SLOB **493.nagal$_x$**, and *la-ga-rak-ku* in a compound grapheme name in CT 11 45-48 (r) iii 39-40 (Diri IV 244). The occurrence could also mean "(a priest)."

73. MSL 9 pp. 126-37 iv "239." Cf. SLOB **467.maš**, the grapheme name *ma-a-šú* Sa 254, and Proto-Ea 118 (3 N-T 563, cited as blank in MSL 3 p. 186; perhaps likewise PBS 12/1 55 [MSL 2 pl. VII°-VIII°] ii 12′). The occurrence could mean "twin."

74. MSL 2 p. 135-36 o. Cf. SLOB **(L)475.mež** and the grapheme name *me-e-su* Sa 142. The occurrence could also mean "Celtis (tree)."

75. UET 6/2 379:5. Also, perhaps, *nu-un-*[. . .] OBGT XVII 17, which may well be a commentary text, cf. SLOB vol. 1 n. 70, with references. Cf. SLOB **(L)518.nin$_x$**, and the grapheme name *nu-ú-nu* Sa 150. The occurrence could possibly mean "(copper object)."

76. MSL 3 p. 223 G_9 9′. Cf. SLOB **(L)737.zumaš$_x$**, although the grapheme name in JAOS 65 (1945) foll. 224 12 (Diri VI), which Landsberger (MSL 3 p. 216, top) reads as [*su-m*]*a-as*!-*ku-ú-a-ku*, is shown by collation to have [x]-⸢x⸣-*e-ku-ú-a-ku*. The word could mean "(a fish)."

77. MSL 3 223 G_9 8′. Cf. SLOB **(L)619.šaḫur$_x$**, and *su-ḫu-ru* in a complex grapheme name, YOS 1 53 "186" (Ea I 219). The occurrence could also mean "(a fish)."

78. MSL 2 pp. 135-36 i (G_2 1). Not preserved in PBS 5 102+Ni 1141+Ni 2203.

79. Cf. SLOB **(L)686.um**, the grapheme name *um-mu* Sa 140, and Proto-Ea 184 (3 N-T 719, cited as blank in MSL 3 p. 190). The occurrence could mean "(reed implement)."

80. Such as *a-ra-gu-b*[*u*!-*u₄*] (PBS 5 148:22 [Proto-Kagal Bil.

their identification as grapheme names remains speculative. This is particularly true of words such as *surû* for which the meaning "name of the grapheme (b) LA_2" has been suggested,[81] since we know that the later name of that grapheme was *la-al-lu*.[82]

In the Old Babylonian texts presently available there are only simple grapheme names, but the presence of complex names in the Boğazköy materials makes it likely that they, as well, stem from Old Babylonian times. In later times, we have grapheme names formed from reduplication of Consonant-Vowel graphemes,[83] names formed by the addition of various adjectival phrases,[84] stringing together of basic names, with or without the addition of *-akku*, and phrase names.

We would like to refer to two facets of the study of the grapheme names which show their importance. These aspects cannot be discussed more fully here because of the exigencies of space. They must be dealt with in a treatment of all of the grapheme names,[85] rather than in the present investigation of the Old Babylonian names.

The grapheme names are sometimes useful in determing the phonology of particular Sumerian words, since they reflect ancient traditions. Thus, they often present us with evidence for the final consonant of a Sumerian vocable, which can be added to the other varieties of evidence available for the reconstruction of the pronunciation of Sumerian words.[86] For instance, the name of the grapheme KA, *ka-a-gu* (S a105), shows that the Sumerian word for "mouth" ended in a /g/, and this surmise can be supported by other evidence.[87]

Finally, it is noteworthy that the grapheme names are (nearly) all based on Sumerian words. The objects of which the cuneiform graphemes were originally depictions had Sumerian names, and those Sumerian names were passed on along with the graphemes. This, granted the validity of the analogy of the names of the letters of the "alphabet" to which we have alluded, is evidence for the question of who originated cuneiform script.

Section B 22; for the restoration, cf. SLOB vol. 1 n. 386]), for which cf. SLOB **(L)61.a-řá-guba$_x$** and the grapheme name *a-ra-gub-bu-ú* in Sa 113, etc.; *p*[*a*]*-ar-r*[*u*] (Proto-Izi II 325), for which cf. SLOB **(L)88.bar** and the grapheme name *ba-a-ru* Sa 248. Cf. also notes 57 and 75 above.

81. Cf. above, with n. 8. AHw 2 1063 has interpreted this line as perhaps ("dazu?") an occurrence of *surû(m), sūru II "ein Fremdling."* We know of no evidence in support of a connection of the Sumerian etymon $zuru_5$ and the Akkadian word with which this word is thus identified, and indeed AHw marks the word as "u[nbekannter] H[erkunft]." We do certainly have a Sumerian loanword here, as is evident from the equation of which it is a part: ⌜$zuru_5$⌝=⌜*su/sú*⌝*-ru-ú* (MSL 9 pp. 126-37 i "56"), and it is doubtless the object of which the grapheme (b) is a depiction, which seems to be a device that was bound on in order to aid in carrying.

82. YOS 1 53 "207" (Ea I 246). Note the contrast with *la-lu-ú* Sa 42 as the name of the grapheme LA, which results from reduplication.

83. Such as the name of the grapheme LA, cited in n. 82.

84. For most of these, and the modern conventions used to represent them, cf. SLOB vol. 1 2.064-2.067.

85. Cf. n. 3 above.

86. For a survey of these, cf. SLOB vol. 1 1.046-1.087.

87. Cf. SLOB°**387.kag$_x$**.

AMAR-SU'ENA AND THE HISTORICAL TRADITION

Piotr Michalowski
University of California, Los Angeles

Following the death of king Šulgi the throne of Ur passed to two of his sons, first Amar-Su'ena, then Šu-Sin. The long-lived king had sired quite a brood of children during his forty-eight year reign,[1] and it remains to be discovered why these two particular individuals out of all the others were entitled to the succession. Unfortunately our knowledge stems from economic documents which simply mention the fact that a given individual was a royal son or daughter (dumu/dumu munus lugal), without any qualification as to official status or name of the mother. No documents have survived which could explain the nature of royal succession during the Ur III period.

Amar-Su'ena, Šulgi's first successor, remains a mysterious figure to the modern investigator. Not once does his name appear in economic documents dated to the time of Šulgi. We do know, however, that his brother Šu-Sin held the office of military governor of Uruk during his father's reign.[2] With the exception of a number of building inscriptions,[3] little historical documentation has survived from Amar-Su'ena's nine-year tenure as king of Ur.

More important than the contemporary documentation for this ruler is the peculiar tradition relating to him which may be reconstructed from texts preserved in the Old Babylonian academy. We possess Old Babylonian copies of royal hymns in honor of all the other rulers of the Ur III dynasty, but not a single one in the name of Amar-Su'ena. Likewise, the royal correspondence of Šulgi, Šu-Sin and Ibbi-Sin was copied in the academy, but the only letters of Amar-Su'ena known at the present time date from the time of Šulgi and should properly be listed among that ruler's epistolary works.[4] In contrast to the majority of the other preserved letters of the Ur III kings, which deal primarily with military matters, these two letters appear to refer to the maintaining of waterworks in the region of Karkar[5] and the manumission of slaves.[6] Unfortunately the state of preservation of these texts does not allow a fuller analysis, and it is thus impossible to establish the position which Amar-Su'ena held during the reign of his father.

While the scribes of the Old Babylonian period did not, apparently, preserve any royal hymns of Amar-Su'ena, they did leave behind two texts of a most unusual nature that refer to him. Both of these texts,[7] which may actually turn out to be part of the same composition, describe this ruler's inability to rebuild a temple of the god Enki. To illustrate the nature of the narrative, we present here an edition of the more intelligible part of one of these texts, UET 8 33[8]:

> ⌜é-e mu⌝ 1-kam-ma ba-an-šub ki-bi nu-m[u-un-gi₄]
> ᵈamar-ᵈen.zu-na me nam-lugal-la na-x[. . .]
> 10′. mu 2-kam-ma b[a-an-šu]b ki-bi-šè nu-mu-u[n-gi₄]
> ᵈamar-ᵈen.zu-⌜na⌝ lu-bu-uš-tum nam-l[ugal-la-ka]-ni túg-mu-sír-ra b[a]-an-[ku₄]⁹
> mu 3-kam-ma ba-a[n]-šub ki-bi-šè nu-mu-u[n-gi₄]
> ᵈamar-ᵈ⌜en.zu-na⌝ giš-hur-hur na-[x.x.x.-p]àd
> mu 4-kam-⌜ma ba-an-šub⌝ ki-bi-šè nu-mu-un-gi₄
> 15′. abgal-e zú ⌜giš-al⌝-[la]-na-ka¹⁰ giš-hur é-e pa-è nu-mu-un-ak-e
> mu 5-kam-ma ba-an-šub ki-bi-šè nu-mu-un-gi₄
> èš-e abzu-a ᵈlama-bi-šè šu mu-ra-ra-e-ne

1. For a list of Šulgi's children see E. Sollberger, AfO 17 (1954-56) 21.

2. See A. Goetze, JCS 17 (1963) 15.

3. For a list of these texts see W. W. Hallo, HUCA 33 (1962) 35ff.

4. Ni 3083 (Or. NS 22 [1953] pl. 39) iii 2′-8′ with the unpublished duplicate N 2901 (identified by M. Civil), to Šulgi. The answer is preserved in the following lines of Ni 3083.

5. Letter to Šulgi, line 4.

6. Letter to Amar-Su'ena, line 3.

7. UET 8 32 and 33. For the former see A. Falkenstein, "Wahrsagung in der sumerischen Überlieferung," 14 CRRAI (1966) 50. The second text has been summarized by E. Sollberger in UET 8 p. 7. Both tablets have now been edited by Margaret Green, Eridu in Sumerian Literature (unpubl. Ph.D. diss., University of Chicago, 1975) pp. 58ff.

8. I wish to express my gratitude to Th. Jacobsen for a number of helpful suggestions concerning this difficult text as well as to M. Green who provided me with a copy of her unpublished dissertation.

9. Restoration according to M. Green, Eridu p. 58.

10. The reading of this complex was proposed by Th. Jacobsen.

Ancient Near Eastern Studies in Memory of J. J. Finkelstein
Connecticut Academy of Arts and Sciences, Memoir 19
© Connecticut Academy of Arts and Sciences, 1977

mu 6-kam-ma ba-an-šub ki-bi-šè nu-mu-un-gi$_4$
giš-hur é-e mu-un-kin-kin-e nu-mu-ni-in-pàd-dè
mu 7-kam-ma ba-an-šub ki-bi-šè nu-mu-un-gi$_4$
^{d}en-ki-ke$_4$ é-bi-šè é nu-me-a ba-an-na-dug$_4$
mu 8-kam-ma-ta é-ni dù-ù-dè šu-ni mu-un-gar
mu 9-kam-ma-ta ^{d}⸢amar-^{d}en.zu-na⸣ lugal-e
é udun-na ⸢šà?-gal?⸣ AN.ZU àr?-ra-gin$_x$ ba-dù

"That temple, during the first year, was in ruins, he did not restore it.
Amar-Suʾena did not . . . the me's of kingship.
In the second year it remained in ruins, he did not restore it.
Amar-Suʾena [exchanged?] his robe of kingship for a mourning garment.
In the third year it remained in ruins, he did not restore it.
Amar-Suʾena was [not able to] find its ground plans.
In the fourth year it remained in ruins, he did not restore it.
The master craftsman was not (able to) bring into view the ground plan of that temple with the end of his pick.
In the fifth year it remained in ruins, he did not restore it.
In the Deep they (i.e., the gods) refused the provision of protective deities for that shrine.[11]
In the sixth year it remained in ruins, he did not restore it.
He went on searching (ever still) for the ground plan of that temple (but) he (could) not find it.
In the seventh year it remained in ruins, he did not restore it.
(Finally) Enki, (although) without a temple, spoke to him about this temple.
As from? the eighth year he set his hand to the building of his temple.
With? the ninth year the king Amar-Suʾena built the 'oven-temple,'[12] like a . . . ."

The second of these two texts, UET 8 32, demonstrates that in deciding to rebuild a temple for Enki, perhaps the very same one mentioned in the text edited above, Amar-Suʾena in vain attempted to consult the will of the gods through divination.[13]

The true significance of these two documents escapes us at the present time. It is of importance, however, to note that in another text well known to the Old Babylonian scribes, the so-called "Curse of Agade," Naram-Sin's troubles begin with the refusal of the gods to grant permission for the rebuilding of the Ekur. As in the case of Amar-Suʾena, Naram-Sin's request for permission to rebuild a temple was worded in the form of an oracle inquiry.[14] It is also noteworthy that Amar-Suʾena attempted to pacify the gods by dressing in a mourning garment, in precisely the same manner as did Naram-Sin.[15] In the Neo-Assyrian version of the text known as "The Cuthean Legend of Naram-Sin," the ruler of Akkad also encounters unfavorable omens, and, just as in the "Curse of Agade," he acts against the will of the gods, bringing calamity upon his land.[16] Finally, we may note the fact that the Old Babylonian scribes also knew of the omen tradition which described the inglorious death of Amar-Suʾena as a result of a foot infection.[17]

Clearly we are dealing here with the beginnings of the historiographical tradition of the "Unheilsherrscher," the calamitous ruler who by his impiety brings destruction upon the land.[18] This tradition may be traced back to the "Curse of Agade," composed during the Ur III period,[19] and finds its full expression in the texts concerning Naram-Sin written in Akkadian, as well as in the composition known as the "Weidner Chronicle."[20] This tradition was, as J. J. Finkelstein stressed in his study of Mesopotamian

11. For the difficult šu . . . ra-ra, cf. perhaps Akkadian *qātam maḫāṣum*, AHw 1 580b (courtesy Th. Jacobsen).

12. It is not clear whether this is the proper name of the building. Note that the temple of Enki at Eridu is described in the cycle of Temple Hymns as the place "where the oven brings bread, (good) to eat" (gir$_4$ ninda íli ú-sù-sù-za, Sjöberg, Temple Hymns p. 17 line 17) and that Adapa bakes bread in Eridu for Enki in the "Myth of Adapa" (ANET^3 p. 101, text A lines 10ff.).

13. In UET 8 32 both a temple of Enki and one of Enlil are mentioned.

14. "Curse of Agade" lines 97-99, discussed by A. Falkenstein, 14 CRRAI (1966) 49.

15. Line 90: nam é-kur-ra-šè túg-mu-sír-ra ba-an-mu$_4$, "On account of the Ekur he donned a mourning garment"; see A. Falkenstein, ZA 57 (1965) 54. Cf. line 11′ of UET 8 33, edited above.

16. O. R. Gurney, AnSt. 5 (1955) 102 lines 75ff.

17. For this omen see A. Goetze, JCS 1 (1947) 261.

18. See H. G. Güterbock, ZA 42 (1934) 75.

19. According to Sjöberg, Temple Hymns p. 7, there exists an unpublished Ur III duplicate of this composition.

20. Now re-edited by A. K. Grayson, Assyrian and Babylonian Chronicles, TCS 5 (Locust Valley, 1975) 145ff.

historiography, but one aspect of a specific paradigm which contrasted good and bad rulers of the ancient past which centered mainly on the kings of the Akkad dynasty.[21]

The tradition of the "Unheilsherrscher" is known to us mainly from texts dating to Kassite and later times. The Old Babylonian texts which could be interpreted to fall into the category describe calamitous events which befell Ur-Nammu[22] and Ibbi-Sin[23] as well as Naram-Sin and Amar-Suᵓena. The later tradition includes only the Akkad rulers and Šulgi in this role.[24] This fact is in itself not surprising as after the Old Babylonian period the scholars of Mesopotamia appear to have singled out only certain historical moments and personages for inclusion in the tradition, telescoping history to fit their own needs. In this telescoping of the tradition, however, there was no longer any room for the person of Amar-Suᵓena. In fact, the whole Ur III period was designated in one text as the "reign of Šulgi," clearly indicating that other rulers of this dynasty were of little importance from the point of view of the later scribes.[25] Indeed, in the Neo-Assyrian period the paradigm of the tradition referring to the Sargonic period was extended to cover the Ur III period, in the person of king Šulgi. By that time historiography had been channeled into textual types which we at present designate as chronicles, pseudo-autobiographies, and prophecies,[26] and thus a fictitious autobiography[27] as well as a chronicle[28] were composed for Šulgi, matching the texts which described the deeds of the Akkad rulers. It is noteworthy that the only connection which survives between the Sumerian texts of Old Babylonian times which describe calamitous rulers and those of the later period is to be found in the motif of the unheeded omen, which we have described above.

It remains to be discovered why Amar-Suᵓena was chosen for the role of luckless ruler by the Old Babylonian scribes. From what little information is currently available on the texts found at Ebla, it appears that the troubles described in later compositions referring to the Sargonic rulers may have actually been based on historical fact. It would therefore be reasonable to assume that the tradition about Amar-Suᵓena should also go back to actual events of his reign. What these may have been cannot, however, be said at the present time.

21. "Mesopotamian Historiography," PAPS 107 (1963) 469ff.

22. See S. N. Kramer, "The Death of Ur-Nammu and his Descent to the Netherworld," JCS 21 (1967) 104-122.

23. "The Lamentation over the Destruction of Sumer and Ur." Translated by S. N. Kramer, ANET[3] pp. 611-19. The published Sumerian sources are listed by D. O. Edzard, AfO 23 (1970) 92.

24. Ibbi-Sin is remembered only in the omen literature. Other early kings which are mentioned in the later tradition do not concern us here as no historiographic paradigm was built around them.

25. BAL-*e* ᵈšul-gi, tablet II line 18 of the series MUL.APIN, cited by J. J. Finkelstein, JCS 20 (1966) 104.

26. On these texts see now A. K. Grayson, Babylonian Historical-Literary Texts (Toronto, 1975) pp. 13ff. with previous literature.

27. Edited by R. Borger, "Gott Marduk and Gott-König Šulgi als Propheten: Zwei prophetische Texte," BiOr 28 (1971) 14ff.

28. The Šulgi chronicle was found at Uruk during the 1969 campaign, and will be published by H. Hunger. See J. Schmidt, AfO 23 (1970) 130. This composition includes references to some misdeeds of the Ur III king. I am grateful to H. Hunger for allowing me to cite this text before publication.

"DEATH FOR DEFAULT"

David I. Owen
Cornell University

The recent study by H. Limet, "La clause du double en droit néo-sumérien,"[1] has provided an excellent and up-to-date survey and analysis of the most severe penalty for default in use during the Ur III period and known primarily from the documentation from Nippur.[2] Since the appearance of Limet's article I have identified a significant number of new examples of loans and contracts which incorporate the "double penalty clause" among the unpublished Nippur texts in the collections of the University Museum[3] and the Free Library of Philadelphia.[4] These texts support and augment the observations and conclusions set out by Limet and further demonstrate the special nature of the documentation from Nippur. In addition I have discovered a loan document which contains an unusual and so far unique death penalty for default. This text is presented below in transliteration, translation, copy, photo and commentary.[5]

In presenting this text in a volume dedicated to the memory of our colleague and friend, J. J. Finkelstein, we take note of his deep interest in and profound contribution to the field of Sumerian and Babylonian law. I take some satisfaction in having been able to discuss this text at some length with Jack, and know how interested and excited he was over its contents.[6]

CBS 13715

[40?].0.0. še gur
ki ba-la-a-ta
a-bí-a-ti
šu ba-ti
iti du$_6$-kù-ga
u$_4$ 30 ba-zal-la
ge$_4$-ge$_4$-dam
tukumbi!(=ŠU.LÁ.TUR) nu-na-ág
gaza-da
mu-lugal-bi in-pà
igi lú-4 lú-kin-ge$_4$-a lugal-šè
igi lú-^{d}gi-gi-lu-šè
igi u$_4$-da-ga-šè
igi lugal-pa-è-šè
igi ur-^{d}nin-tur-ra-šè
šà nibru.ki ág-e-dam
[mu] en-^{d}inanna unug.ki-ga máš-e ì-pà

obv.

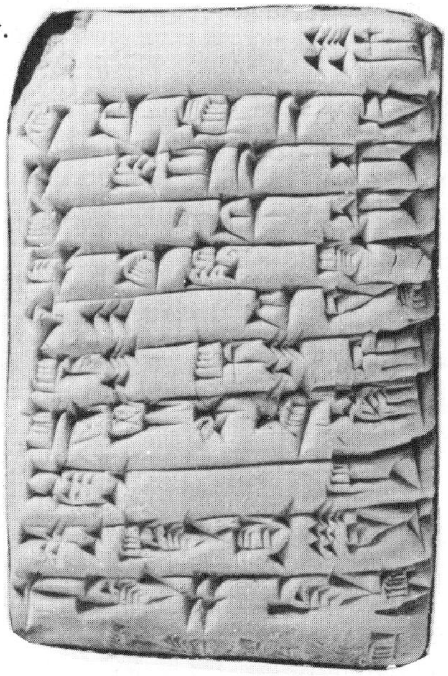

40? gur of barley Abi-ati received from Bala'a. At the end of the 30th day of the month of Dukuga he shall return (the 40 gur of barley). If he does not return it, he will be killed. In the name of the king he swore. Witnessed by four men, messengers of the king (who are): witnessed by Lu-Gi(r)gilu,

1. Or. NS 38 (1969) 520-32.
2. Or. NS 38 (1969) 532.
3. All of the texts in the collection of the University Museum have been copied and will soon appear in my Neo-Sumerian Archival Texts Primarily from Nippur in the University Museum, Part I: Catalogue and Texts (Paris, Geuthner, in press). The following texts contain penalty clauses: 94, 98 (double clause), 256, 260 (double clause), 268 (double clause), 281 (interest penalty), 293 (double clause?), 345 (double clause), 421 (interest penalty), 552 (double clause).
4. Two texts from the Free Library of Philadelphia have now been published in Owen, The John Frederick Lewis Collection, Materiali per il Vocabolario Neosumerico 3 (Rome, Multigrafica Editrice, 1975) as nos. 263 (double clause) and 317 (double clause).
5. The text is published with the permission of Åke W. Sjöberg, Curator of Tablet Collections, University Museum.
6. It should perhaps be pointed out that J. J. Finkelstein was of the opinion that the death penalty here was not to be taken literally. He did not believe that such a punishment would have been carried out for the default of a loan. However, in view of the contractual nature of the text and the special character of the witnesses, I have no reason to doubt that the punishment, as specified, would have been carried out.

Ancient Near Eastern Studies in Memory of J. J. Finkelstein
Connecticut Academy of Arts and Sciences, Memoir 19

witnessed by Udaga, witnessed by Lugal-pae, witnessed by Ur-Nintura. In Nippur he shall pay back (the barley). IS 2.

COMMENTARY

Line 1. The restoration is not certain. Traces of two Winkelhacken can be seen. The damaged area would have contained a number no less than 40, but perhaps considerably larger. See photo.

Line 2. Ba-la-a appears to be new to the Nippur onomastica. A man of this name does occur at Puzriš-Dagan in the reign of Šulgi as does his wife (BIN 5 11 [Š 32]); perhaps he is the singer/musician of the same name at Puzriš-Dagan alter in the reign of Šulgi (Eames Coll. E 2 (Š 43]). For additional references to this name see Limet, Anthroponomie p. 384.

Line 3. For this name see MAD 3 10 sub *abum* and 82 sub $^{\prime}{}_{x}T^{\prime}{}_{x}$. He does not occur elsewhere among the Nippur onomastica and may have been from another town, hence the stipulation that he had to repay the loan in Nippur. He may, in fact, be the Abi-ati known from Šuruppak(?) (TCS 1 text no. 13).

Line 8. For defective writings of tukumbi see H. Sauren, ZA 59 (1969) 56. Numerous additional examples occur among the unpublished Nippur texts.

Line 9. The introduction of this penalty clause, gaza-da, is unique among the loans and contracts so far available from the Ur III period. Generally the worst punishment for default, particularly from Nippur, is the requirement that the borrower return double the amount. H. Limet (Or. NS 38 [1969] 520-32) has provided an excellent survey of the use of the "double clause" in neo-Sumerian law, and noted that the use of the "double clause" is nearly confined to Nippur (ibid. p. 532). However, a punishment for default as severe as the death penalty, whether it was really to be executed or merely a threat, is unknown from contemporary texts as well as from the law codes. For the meaning of GAZA=*dâku*, "to be killed, to be executed," see CAD D 35ff. sub *dâku*, lexical section and 42a. The form appears to be a passive *marû*-form which may be analyzed as gaza+ed+a (D. O. Edzard, ZA 62 [1972] 29).

Line 10. For the traditional oath formula solemnizing the contract see Limet, Or. NS 38 (1969) 531.

Line 11. The special nature of this contract/loan is indicated by the unusual statement that the four witnesses were representatives of the king. In the hundreds of loan contracts from Nippur and elsewhere that I have examined, I have not come across a similar statement. Why this particular agreement needed special witnesses is not clear and no other texts that I am aware of relate to this agreement. Clearly, the severity of the penalty must, in some way, be related to the presence of the royal messengers. In view of the isolated instance of the threatened death penalty it would seem that the punishment would, in fact, have been meted out had Abi-ati defaulted on the loan.

Line 12. Lú-^{d}gi-gi-lu, if he is to be identified with the better-known Lú-gir-gi$_{4}$-lu(.ki) from Nippur (see the references in Limet, Anthroponomie pp. 477-78 and D. O. Edzard and G. Farber, Rép.Géog. 2 sub Girgilum; he is also known from additional unpublished Nippur texts) was very active at Nippur, and a number of loans may be attributed to him. However, in none of them is he ever distinguished as a royal messenger/representative. The name is curiously written here in a syllabic form and the city name is deified. I am not aware of a deity of this name.

Line 13. U$_{4}$-da-ga is also well-known in the Nippur archives. The form of the name occurs in Çığ-Kızılyay, NRVN 1 208, where the seal inscription confirms it as but a syllabic writing for the more common un-da-ga heretofore read as kalam-da-ga (see Limet, Anthroponomie p. 442). In both the published and unpublished texts in which he occurs he is never identified as a royal messenger/representative. In one text, CBS 3841 (IS 2), he is listed as an ašgab, but we may not be dealing with the same individual.

Line 14. There are a number of individuals by the name of Lugal-pa-è who are active in Nippur. Once again none is designated as a royal representative/messenger (Limet, Anthroponomie p. 471).

Line 15. The full syllabic spelling of the name Ur-^{d}nin-tur-ra confirms the view of T. Jacobsen (Or. NS 42 [1973] 277-81) that the divine name should be read as ^{d}nin-tur$_{5}$. The name Ur-^{d}nin-tur$_{5}$ does occasionally appear in the Nippur texts, mostly in unpublished documents. But, as with the others mentioned above, he is never qualified as a lú-kin-ge$_{4}$-a lugal.

Line 16. The stipulation that loans had to be repaid in a specific locale occurs infrequently, but coupled with the other unusual features of our text it lends additional force to the threatened punishment, should default take place. For the *marû*-form ág-e-da, see Edzard, ZA 62 (1972) 25.

CBS 13715

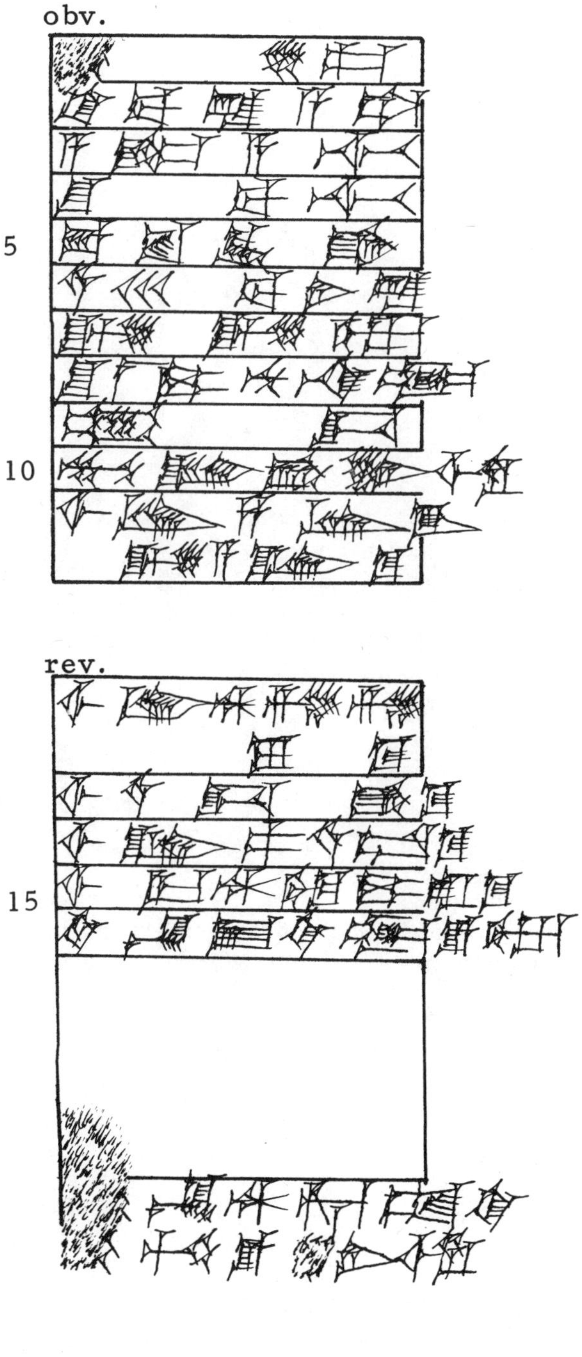

NOTES ON THE REPHAIM TEXTS FROM UGARIT

Marvin H. Pope
Yale University

Jacob Joel Finkelstein's article "The Genealogy of the Hammurapi Dynasty"[1] serves as the startingpoint for this offering in his memory. The Akkadian document treated by Finkelstein begins with a list of twenty-six ancestors of King Ammiṣaduqa of the First Dynasty of Babylon and goes on to invoke related dynasts and eponyms, named and unnamed, as well as the soldier who perished on perilous campaign, princes and princesses, persons in general from East to West, any and everyone deprived of an attendant or caretaker (to look after their postmortem needs). All the aforementioned are invited to a feast:

"Come ye, eat this, drink this (and) bless Ammiṣaduqa, the son of Ammiditana, King of Babylon."[2]

Although the term is not used, there can be no doubt that Finkelstein was right in regarding the banquet in question as a ***kispum***, a feast for the dead.[3] The meal in question, however, was apparently not one of the regular fortnightly feasts, but a general celebration for all the dead. Thus we have an Old Babylonian All Souls Feast intended to provide particularly for those of the dead who might be neglected. The care and feeding of the dead was an important concern since the welfare of the living and of the dead were believed to be inextricably linked.

The guests invited to the great feast provided by the Babylonian ruler are not designated by any single collective term, but it is clear that they are the spirits of the dead, the denizens of the netherworld, the heroes of generations past, those who are called in the Bible Rephaim (RĕPāAîYM) and in Ugaritic RPUM/RPIM. It is not intended here to deal in detail with all the Ugaritic texts and passages relating to the Rephaim, nor to review or summarize previous studies. It must suffice for the present to translate and comment on the two best preserved texts (22.2[124] and RS 34.126) and to intersperse notes on other relevant Ugaritic and biblical passages.

The Ugaritic Rephaim Texts[4] were from the first recognized as integrally related to the Aqht Epic, the story of the hero Danel and his ill-fated son Aqht. Danel has no son and seeks divine help in an incubation rite. Baal answers the suppliant and intercedes with El on Danel's behalf. El revives Danel's ardor (NPŠ) so that he is able to sire the desired heir. The duties of the son are four times specified, with minor variations,[5] and it will suffice to render a conflation of the lists, in Danel's grateful response to the blessed birth:

AṮBN ANK WANẖN	I will return and rest,
WTNẖ BIRTY NPŠ	And my soul repose in my breast,
KYLD BN LY KM AẖY	For a son is born me like my brothers,
WŠRŠ KM ARYY	A root like my kindred,
NṢB SKN ILIBY	Who sets up my ancestral stela,
BQDŠ ZTR OMY	In the sanctuary drops thyme toward me,
LARṢ MŠṢU QṬRY	To Earth sends forth my spice,
LOPR ḎMR AṮRY	To the Dust sings toward me,
ṬBQ LḤT NIṢY	Counters the insults of my enemies,
GRŠ DOŠY LN	Repulses him who acts against me,
AẖD YDY BŠKRN	Holds my hand when I'm drunk,
MOMSY KŠBOT YN	Lifts me when I'm sated with wine,
SPU KSMY BT BOL	Eats my piece in the house of Baal,
MNTY BT IL	My portion in the House of El,
ṮẖGGY BYM ṮIṮ	Smears my roof on a mud day,
RḤṢ NPṢY BYM RṮṮ	Washes my clothes on a filth day.

1. JCS 20 (1966) 95-118. This document, along with other genealogical materials from the ancient Near East, is treated in detail in a monograph by R. R. Wilson, Genealogy and History in the Biblical World (New Haven, Yale University Press, 1977) 107-114.
2. Wilson, Genealogy and History p. 97.
3. Wilson, Genealogy and History pp. 113-18.
4. CTA 20-22, UT 121-124, cited hereafter according to the reference system of R. E. Whitaker, A Concordance of the Ugaritic Literature (Cambridge, Mass., Harvard University Press, 1972).
5. 17[2 AQHT].1.27-34,45-48, 2.1-8,13-23.

Ancient Near Eastern Studies in Memory of J. J. Finkelstein
Connecticut Academy of Arts and Sciences, Memoir 19

Line 6. The meaning of ZTR has remained conjectural. M. Tsevat[6] suggested that it is a loanword from Hittite *sittar(i)*, "votive (sun)disk." Tsevat accordingly translated

NṢB SKN ILIBH	Who sets up the stela of his paternal god,
BQDŠ ZTR OMH	In the sanctuary the sun emblem of his kindred (deity).

While it is quite true, as Tsevat affirms, that OM is a well-known divive epithet attested at Ugarit, Mari, and elsewhere as a component of personal names, it is also true that, apart from the present alleged instance, there is not another use of OM with this meaning in the Ugaritic texts. In more than 150 occurrences of OM it is the preposition meaning "with," or, when used with a verb of motion, "toward," and there is no sure attestation of any other meaning. Aistleitner[7] took OM here as a synonym of QṬR, "incense," connecting it with Arabic *ġaym* "cloud." ZTR Aistleitner[8] construed as an active participle meaning "ausgehen lassen," and so translated ZTR OMH LARṢ "der ausströmen lässt meinen Weihrauch vom Boden." No cognate of ZTR in the sense "let go forth" was suggested by Aistleitner for the simple reason that none can be found. Even though two of the three words of the line were wrongly construed by Aistleitner, the approximate sense was nevertheless divined on the basis of the next line LARṢ MŠṢU QṬRY, "to/from Earth sends forth my incense." The connection of OM with Arabic *ġaym*, "cloud," is, however, highly dubious because Ugaritic would have Ó instead of O. On the assumption that the sense of BQDŠ ZTR OMY is similar to that of LARṢ MŠṢU QṬRY, and that both refer to incense offerings for the dead, we find a plausible cognate for ZTR in Akkadian *zateru*,[9] "thyme," Arabic *zaʿtar*. We have to assume also that ZTR here has the sense of Arabic QṬR, "drop (*quṭur*, i.e., aloes or other spices)," both verbs being denominative from the terms for the balsam or spices trickled down into the grave. Thus OMY "toward me" has its regular sense, just as in PONK TLSMN OMY, "let your feet run toward me," 3[ONT].3.16. The balsam and spices are directed toward the dead and not sent up from the tomb.

Line 8. *sings*: ḎMR here has been connected with Arabic *ḏmr*, "be brave, guard, protect," and the like. From UG 5.2.1.3, however, we see that ḎMR can also mean "sing," "chant": IL . . . DYŠR WYḎMR, "the god . . . who sings and chants." B. Bandstra, in an unpublished paper, has applied the meaning "sing" to the present context on the basis of a striking reference to song in the Akkadian funerary ritual KAR 146: *šarru* . . . ᵈ*Lisikūtu ušākal nāru . . . izammur zu-ma-ra ikaššada ina libbi api ikarrar*, "(with an iron knife) the king makes food portions for the *Lisikūtu*-spirits (possibly ancestral spirits) (while) the singer sings (the song indicated), when he (the singer) has reached the refrain, he (the king) throws (the pieces of meat) into the opening (of a conduit through which previously . . . blood, honey, oil, beer and wine were poured)."[10] We assume that the song is directed toward the honored dead, whether the singer is above or beside the bier.

Lines 11ff. Drinking to satiety (OD ŠBO) and to drunkenness (OD ŠKR) was customary and apparently *de rigueur* in the MRZḤ feast.[11] Sometimes the drinking went beyond simple inebriation to alcoholic delirium and unconsciousness, as with El (UG 5.1[RS 24.258]1.15-22):

IL YṮB BMRZḤH	El sat in his MRZḤ.
YŠT IL YN OD ŠBO	El drank wine to satiety,
TRṮ OD ŠKR	Must to drunkenness.
IL HLK LBTH	El would go to his house,
YŠTQL LHṬRH	Descend to his court.
YOMSN.NN ṮKMN WŠNM	ṮKMN-and ŠNM bore him up.
WNGŠNN ḤBY	There accosted him a "creeper"
BOL QRNM WḎNB	With two horns and a tail.
YLŠN BḪRIH WṮNTH	He floundered in his excrement and urine.
QL IL IL KYRDM ARṢ	El collapsed, El like those who descend to Earth.

The root RZḤ in Arabic means "to collapse from exhaustion," a *marzaḥ* being a place where a camel falls from fatigue. Collapse could also be brought on by causes other than fatigue, one of the commonest means of

6. M. Tsevat, "Traces of Hittite at the Beginning of the Ugaritic Epic of Aqht," UF 3 (1971) 351-52.

7. J. Aistleitner, Wörterbuch der ugaritischen Sprache (1963) p. 234, 2043. *ʿm* II.

8. Aistleitner, Wörterbuch p. 98, 890 *ztr*.

9. CAD Z 74a s.v. *zateru*.

10. CAD Z 154b s.v. *zumāru*.

11. Cf. M. Pope, "A Divine Banquet at Ugarit," in The Use of the Old Testament in the New and Other Essays: Studies in Honor of Wm. F. Stinespring, ed. J. M. Efird (Durham, N.C., Duke University Press, 1972) 170-203.

achieving such a state being alcoholic excess, a vice and device common among gods and men but rarely used by camels or other animals except when aided and abetted, induced and seduced, by man for morbid amusement. The duty of the faithful son to hold the hand of a besotted father and bear him up when he collapses is performed in El's MRZḤ by the divine pair(?) ṮKMN-W-ŠNM.[12] From a biblical allusion we gather that mother as well as father was entitled to similar consideration and assistance. In Isa. 51:17f. Jerusalem is depicted as a drunken woman with none to guide her or hold her hand of all the sons she had borne and reared. Ham's sin (Gen. 9:20ff.) was failure to care for father Noah when he lay in drunken stupor in order to protect him from indecency or perhaps worse.[13] At a funeral feast it was apparently obligatory to drink to inebriation or beyond. Augustine was ashamed of Christians who got drunk at the martyrs' graves. These were carnal and ignorant folk who supposed that their drunken carousals in the cemeteries[14] honored the martyrs and refreshed the departed, but still Augustine thought it better that one go home with a headache, than that he, like some others, should offer sacrifices to the dead. This self-indulgence at the tombs was simply the old-time religion in which people buried themselves on the graves in gluttony and drunkenness and called it religion.[15] It is interesting in this connection that in Judaism the single occasion on which it is permissible, even obligatory, to get drunk is at the festival of Purim which has been thought to derive from the old Persian funeral feast.[16] On Purim one should drink until he can no longer distinguish between blessed Mordechai and accursed Haman.[17] Augustine's condemnation of the fleshly foulness and sickness [*carnales foeditates et agritudines*][18] which disgraced the feasts of Christians in North Africa suggests that offenses grosser than mere gluttony and drunkenness were perpetrated on the graves. The allegation that incest and other improper sexual activities, child sacrifice and cannibalism characterize funeral feasts has persisted from the time of Israel's encounter with Moabite worship of Baal Peor (Num. 25; Ps. 106:28), to the efforts of Tertullian and Minucius Felix to counter such accusations against Christians.[19] The language of the Epistle of Jude with respect to the impurities of those who were blemishes or shoals (*spilades*) in the love feasts suggests offenses such as sin of the angels (Gen. 6:14), or the unnatural lusts of Sodom and Gomorrah.

Lines 15ff. The roof plastering and clothes washing mentioned among the filial duties seem at first blush to be merely menial housekeeping chores. It may be, however, that these too were sacral obligations connected with funeral feasts. The roof to be plastered might belong to the tomb and the laundry could also be a need occasioned by the orgiastic character of the feast. Old Sumerian texts from Lagash dealing with the cult of the dead mention a certain "Saggalube the washer" and J. Bauer[20] suggests that one of the references indicates that clothes were received for cleaning. It is not immediately apparent why the dead would need laundry service, but the survivors' participation in the feast might well necessitate post-prandial cleansing. In the feast provided by El for his fellow gods all tope to satiety and drunkenness, but the symposiarch El sits in his MRZḤ and drinks to delirium and beyond that to helpless floundering in his own excrement and urine and finally collapses as if dead. The situation recalls that depicted in Isa. 28:7-8 in which the celebrants, rulers, priests, prophets and people reel in vomit and filth. The clean-up after such a debauch would require some laundry work.

Before turning to consideration of text 22.2[124], it may be worthwhile to comment on some items of 20[121], 21]122], and 22.1[123]. These texts are too fragmentary to provide complete parallel lines, without which it is virtually impossible to confirm the sense. Nevertheless many key words and phrases are preserved.

It is clear in the first column of text 20[121] that the topic is a feast of the Rephaim. The phrase "on a summer day" (line 5) may supply the temporal setting. In line 8 there is the enigmatic expression IL

12. On this deity or pair of deities, cf. M. Pope, Studies Stinespring p. 194 nn. 49, 50.

13. Cf. H. H. Cohen, The Drunkenness of Noah (1974) chapters 1-3 on Noah's drunkenness, nakedness, and possible sexual connotation of some of the terminology.

14. Cf. F. van der Meer, Augustine the Bishop, tr. B. Battershaw and G. R. Lamb (1961) p. 517f.

15. Van der Meer, Augustine the Bishop p. 519 n. 84.

16. Cf. L. B. Paton, A Critical and Exegetical Commentary on the Book of Esther, ICC (1916) pp. 84ff.

17. TB Megillah 7b; Shulhan Aruk 695:2.

18. Van der Meer, Augustine the Bishop p. 517.

19. Cf. M. Pope, Studies Stinespring pp. 183-89, and A. Hennrichs, "Pagan Ritual and the Alleged Crimes of the Early Christians," in Kyriakon: Festschrift J. Quasten 1, ed. P. Greenfield and J. A. Jungemann (1970) 18-35.

20. Cf. J. Bauer, "Zum Totenkult im altsumerischen Lagasch," ZDMG Supplements I: XVII. Deutscher Orientalistentag. Teil I (1969) 107-114, and in particular p. 110 n. 8.

DORGZM, "god of the nuts." In the Nikkal Poem (24[77].43) the KṮRT, patronesses of birth, are hymned as "going down to the nuts," YRDT BORGZM. This recalls the Nut Garden of Song of Songs 6:11. The argument is presented elsewhere[21] in detail that the nut garden and valley of the Canticle is none other than that southwest of Jerusalem which is still called Wādī Jôz, "Nut Valley." This area, often mentioned in the Bible simply as "the valley" (HaHnaḤaL), is laden with cosmic, cultic and mythological import. There the populace of ancient Judah persisted in burning[22] their sons and daughters to Molek (cf. Lev. 18:21; 20:2-5; II Kings 23:10, Jer. 32:35). The valley is variously called Qidron, the Valley of (the Son[s] of) Hinnom (II Kings 23:10; Jer. 7:30f., 32:35), the Valley of Corpses (Jer. 31:40), the Valley of the Rephaim (Jos. 15:8; 18:16). It was also called the Valley of Jehoshaphat, the Valley of Decision (Joel 3:2, 12, 14) where the mobs of the dead of generations past will rise for judgment on the Day of the Lord. Here Jewish, Christian and Muslim tradition locate the entrance to the netherworld and the scene of the resurrection and final judgment, opposite the Mount of Olives (cf. Zech. 14:4), before the blocked-up Golden Gate of the present Old City walls. Below in Gethsemane the Christ reached the agonizing decision to confront Death. Nearby in the Church of the Holy Sepulchre a gold-coated cross of walnut wood preserves something of the cosmic symbolism of the Nut Garden which echoes in Adam of St. Victor's hymn *Nux est Christus*.[23]

The Valley of Hinnom will be discussed again below, but its mention here in connection with Danel and the Rephaim gives occasion to propose an explanation of the long-standing enigma presented by the regular epithet of the heroic figure Danel as "man of RPI" and "man of HRNMY," DNIL MT RPI // ÓZR MT HRNMY. W. F. Albright[24] already in 1939 compared the variant (?) biblical names Methusael and Methuselah (Gen. 4:18; 5:21-27) with Danel's epithets and related HRNMY to a place name HRNM in Syria mentioned in the Egyptian account of the battle of Qadesh fought by Ramses II, equating it with Hermel[25] of modern Lebanon. In light of the insight that the element ŠLḤ in the name MTūŠelaḤ designates the conduit to the netherworld,[26] it may be that the corresponding element in the variant MT(W)ŠAL represents the regular biblical term for the netherworld, Sheol. The Ugaritic parallelism of RPU and HRNM in Danel's title suggests that HRNM like RPU relates to the netherworld. The connection of HRNM with the biblical name Hinnom thus appears quite plausible. This equation was suggested by R. Good in an unpublished paper. There is another similar name Harmon mentioned once in Amos 4:3 in a context favoring connection with Hinnom, either as a variant with consonant metathesis, or as a corruption. The "cows of Bashan" who are on Mount Samaria (read Zion[?]), are to be taken with hooks through the breaches of the city wall, and cast to "the Harmon," HaHaRMōWNāH, a word that has remained unexplained. If we transfer the scene from Samaria to Jerusalem, as Amos flits between the two cities in 6:1, we find a ready explanation of Harmon in the equation HRMN / HRNM / HiNnōWM as variant names of the netherworld to which the infamous valley of Jerusalem was the entry. The biblical "son(s) of Hinnom" thus are the defunct denizens of the netherworld. Danel, man of RPI and HRNM, like the nonacentenarian antediluvian Methuselah, MT-ŠLḤ, "man of the netherworld," belongs to the legendary heroes of the distant past long resident in man's eternal infernal home, like his associates Noah and Job (Ezek. 14:14, 20). If one seeks for a "root" with which HRNM may be connected, the closest possibility appears to be Arabic *harim*, "be very old, weak, decrepit," which comports with the mixed conception of the dead as weak and torpid shades as well as mighty heroes. The latter type of designation may be antiphrastic euphemism. It is also interesting to note in connection with Albright's association of Ugaritic HRNM with Hermel of Lebanon that *harmal, hirmil* in Arabic is related to old age and decrepitude.

In column B of text 20[121] the Rephaim harness and hitch horses, mount their chariots and travel for two days, arriving on the third day at a threshing floor (GRNT) and plantation (MṬOT) where they are addressed by Danel who speaks of eating. Similarly in 21[122] someone, presumably Danel, invites the Rephaim into his house or palace, to a [M]RZO, a variant of MRZḤ, which we gather from a number of clues to be a sodality devoted to feasts for the dead. Since Danel's son Aqhat was murdered by the goddess Anat's henchman Yṭpn, it is a fair guess that this MRZḤ feast is for Aqhat. The mention of horses and chariots has

21. Song of Songs, Anchor Bible 7c (Garden City, N.Y., Doubleday, scheduled to appear in the fall of 1977).

22. Cf. M. Smith, "A Note on Burning Babies," JAOS 95 (1975) 477-79, in response to M. Weinfeld's attempt (UF 4 [1972] 133ff.) to explain away OT references to child sacrifice.

23. Cf. R. F. Littledale, A Commentary on the Song of Songs from Ancient and Mediaeval Sources (London, 1869) p. 293.

24. JBL 58 (1939) 97.

25. W. F. Albright, "The Traditional Name of the Syrian Daniel," BASOR 130 (1953) 27f.; and Yahweh and the Gods of Canaan (New York, Doubleday, 1968) p. 117.

26. Cf. Job, 3rd ed., Anchor Bible 15 (Garden City, N.Y., Doubleday, 1973) on Job 33:18b.

been taken by C. L'Heureux[27] as a crucial part of the evidence for the view that the divine Rephaim had their earthly human counterparts, the Rephaim of earth. This notion has its genesis in misapprehension of the divine blessing of King Krt, MID RM KRT / BTK RPI ARṢ (15[128].3.2-3,13-14), "greatly exalted be Krt among the Rephaim of earth." L'Heureux[28] argues that the Rephaim of earth here are not the shades, since the context is a blessing of Krt at the height of his success before the possibility of his death had been raised. The crucial point missed is that ARṢ "earth" here, as in numerous other passages, designates the netherworld.[29] The blessing bestowed by the gods is the gift of fertility:

Greatly exalted be Krt
Mid the Rephaim of Earth,
In the assembly of DTN
With their little ones will I bless him.
The gods bless, they go,
The gods go to their tents,
The family of El to their dwellings.
Then she conceived and bore him a son
She conceived and bore him children.

The Rephaim, the deified ancestors, were considered the source of fertility, as life eventually returns to earth whence it came. The connection of the root RPA with fertility is confirmed by the explanation of the name Hammurapi as meaning "extensive family" (*ᵈḪa-am-mu-ra-pi* : *ᵈKim-ta-ra-pa-aš-tum*).[30] The old Arabic blessing for newlyweds, *biʾr-rifāʾi waʾl-banīna*, "with health (?) and children," also shows the connection with fertility. On DTN see below.

L'Heureux's[31] argument that the chariot riders of the Rephaim Texts are human because "the mythological texts generally picture the gods as travelling on foot, flying, or riding on donkeys," is scarcely compelling since the gods surely were free to use whatever mode of locomotion they pleased. A fiery chariot and horses swung low to take the prophet Elijah up and out of this world (II Kings 2:11). Horses and chariots dedicated to the sun are mentioned in association with child sacrifice to MLK in the valley of (the sons of) Hinnom, II Kings 23:10f. Ezekiel's vision of the fantastic composite animal-machine on which the God of Israel rode (Ezek. 1 and 10) should discourage the effort to limit modes of divine transport. On one occasion, the Holy One of Israel rode a mare in order to deliver his people at the Reed Sea.[32]

The connection of horses with funeral rites is ancient, widespread, and persistent, and a motif worthy of separate investigation.

We look now at text 22.2[124] to see what we may learn and unlearn from it.

(2) HN BNK HN [ ]	Lo, your sons, lo [ ]
[ ] (3) BN BN AṮRK	[ ] sons' sons of your place
HN [ ] (4) YDK	Lo ' your hand
ṢÓR TNŠQ ŠPTK	The little one your lips will kiss.
ṮM (5) ṮKM BM ṮKM	There shoulder to shoulder
AḪM QYN IL (6) BLSMT	Brothers spill the holy balsams.
ṮM YṮBŠ ŠM IL MTM	There they register the name of the divine dead,
(7) YṮ/OBŠ BRKN ŠM IL ÓZRM	Register in reverence the name of the divine heroes.
(8) ṮM ṮMQ RPU BOL	There assemble Baal's Heroes,
MHR BOL (9) WMHR ONT	Baal's Soldiers and Anat's Soldiers.
ṮM YḤPN ḤYL (10) Y	There comes the Mighty One,
ZBL MLK OLLMY	Prince MLK the Wise.
KM TDD (11) ONT ṢD	Then rises Anat to hunt,
TŠTR OPT ŠMM	Propels herself, wings heavenward.

27. C. L'Heureux, "The Ugaritic and Biblical Rephaim," HTR 67 (1974) 265-74.

28. HTR 67 (1974) 271ff.

29. N. J. Tromp, Primitive Conceptions of Death and the Netherworld in the Old Testament (Rome, Pontifical Biblical Institute, 1969) pp. 23-46.

30. CAD K 377b s.v. *kimtu*.

31. HTR 67 (1974) 271f.

32. Cf. M. Pope, "A Mare in the Chariotry of Pharaoh," BASOR 200 (1970) 56-61.

(12) ṮBḪ ALPM AP ṢIN	They slaughter oxen, yea sheep,
ŠQL ṮRM (13) WMRI ILM	Fell bulls and fatling rams,
OGLM DT ŠNT	Calves a year old,
(14) IMR QMṢ LLIM	Sheep, frisky lambs.
KKSP (15) LOBRM ZT	Like silver to the departed (as) pay,
ḪRṢ LOBRM KŠ	Gold to the departed (as) fee.
(16) DPR ṮLḤN BQOL	Redolent the table with fig cake,
BQOL (17) MLKM	With fig cake royal.
HN YN YṢQ YN	Daylong they pour the wine,
ṮMK (18) MRṮ YN SRNM	Spill must, *lordly* wine,
YN BLD (19) ÓLL	Wine with bliss inebriant,
YN IŠRYT ONQ	Wine that limbers(?) the neck(?)
SMD (20) LBNN ṮL	Nectar of Lebanon, sack,
MRṮ YḤRṮ IL	Must divinely tilled.
(21) HN YM WṮN	Lo, a day and a second,
TLḤMN RPUM (22) TŠTYN	The Heroes eat, they drink.
ṮLṮ RBO YM	A third, a fourth day,
ḪMS (23) ṮDṮ YM	A fifth, a sixth day,
TLḤMN RPUM (24) TŠTYN	The Heroes eat, they drink.
BT IKL BPRO	In the banquet house at the summit,
(25) [YṢ]Q BIRT LBNN	They pour in the heart of Lebanon.
MK BŠBO [YMM]	Lo, on the seventh day]
[ ]ALIYN BOL	[ ] Mighty Baal

Line 3. *BN BN*: It is uncertain whether this is to be read as "among the sons of," or "son's sons." The concern for plenteous progeny is crucial in patriarchal religion. Cf. Gen. 13:14-16; 17:4-6. Among expressions of concern for progeny, Ps. 45:16 may be clarified on the basis of the Ugaritic use of TḤT in the sense of "among," as in 17[2 AQHT].5.7 YTŠU YṮB BAP ṮÓR/TḤT ADRM DBGRN, "He up and sat in the entrance of the gate // Among the nobles at the threshing floor." In this light the strange expression "instead of thy fathers" becomes "among thy fathers." The royal wedding is blessed with continuity of progeny.

"your place": The term AṮR, "place," occurs several times in the Rephaim Texts as the designation of the spot where the divine heroes gather, apparently within the house or palace of the host; cf. 20[121].2.1.2; 21[122].1.3,11,12; 22[123].5,11,21. The host extends the invitation LK BTY AṢḤKM//IQRAKM HKLY, "Come, to my house I call you // I summon you to my palace." The heroes respond with immediate action, AṮRH RPUM TDD // AṮRH LTDD ILNYM, "To his place the heroes rise // To his place rise the gods." Whether the final H of AṮRH is the possessive or the directive suffix is unclear, and immaterial. The verb here is the Nifᶜal of Ḏ(W)Ḏ,[33] like Akkadian *nazāzu*, and a synonym of Q(W)M, "rise." The divine heroes rise from their infernal abode to the house and "place" of their host.

The opportunity presents itself here to recant and repent a grievous error in interpretation of this passage, cited out of context in another article[34] wherein I construed ṢÓR as an adjective modifying YDK, "your little hand," and rendered what follows as "she/they will kiss your lips there, shoulder to shoulder." G. Tuttle in an unpublished paper proposed better stichometry based on the quadruple repetition of ṮM, "there," at the beginning of successive bicola. The crucial importance of stichometry is again illustrated.[35] Tuttle also observed that M. Dahood[36] in search of parallel pairs cited the ṮM // ṮM in lines 8-9 of this text, but ignored the preceding pair in lines 4-6 and also neglected to note the fourfold repetition of ŠāM in Ezek. 20:28. Here, as elsewhere,[37] "there" is apparently a circumlocution for the netherworld.

Efforts to penetrate the sense of this couplet have so far lacked conviction. The crux lies in the last three words. Beginning with the last word, BLSMT is just what it seems. Balsam, spices, and perfumes continued

33. Cf. M. Pope, "A Note on Ugaritic *ndd-ydd*, JCS 1 (1947) 337-41.
34. M. Pope, Studies Stinespring p. 193.
35. Cf. JSS 11 (1966) 231.
36. RSP 1 380, 603d.
37. Cf. M. Pope, Job p. 16 on Job 1:21, and p. 326 on Job 40:20b.

to be lavished on the dead into Christian times. A couplet cited by F. Van Der Meer,[38] descriptive of The Feasts of the Dead in Augustine's day will suffice:

> See how they fix their lips with a kiss on the glittering silver
> Pouring the balsam down—tears running down from their eyes.

The element IL, "god," before the balsam has been the impediment to the understanding of the line. The holy balsam apparently rates the divine determinative, though it was scarcely intended to suggest that the balsam itself was the object rather than the means of worship.

The troublesome word QYM must be the verb of which "brothers" is the subject and the holy balsam the object. A D-form of Q-M, like Aramaic and late Hebrew QaYyēM, is unlikely. Derivation from QWY presents phonological problems. The root QYY/A "vomit," seems semantically inappropriate, but might pass in the sense of "spill, pour, discharge," or the like.

Explanation of ṮBŠ is difficult. Akkadian *šabāšu* does not appear entirely fitting either in sense or sound. Resort to Arabic *ṯbt* seems most helpful, since this verb in the D-stem has the meaning "register," confirm (in the religious sense). The object of confirmation here is the name of the deified dead. As in the preceding line, IL before MTM is determinative, as it is before the name of Baal's holy mountain IL ṢPN, which does not mean "god of Ṣapān" but "divine Ṣapān."[39] The expression ṮBŠ ŠM thus would be equivalent to Akkadian *zakāru šuma* and Hebrew QāRāA ŠēM. Invocation of the name of the deceased was an important part of mortuary rites. The recurring use of *šumu* in Akkadian omens, blessing and curses is an index of the concern to preserve the name of the dead. The designations "caller of the name" (*zākir šumi*) and "power of water" (*nāq mē*) for progeny refer to primary duties of the son and heir as caretaker (*pāqid*) for his defunct progenitor.[40] This concern persisted in Christian feasts of the dead, especially during All Soul's month (February), when the annual commemoration of departed members of the family was celebrated at an evening meal where the dead were called by name and invited to join in the refreshment (*refrigerium*).[41]

No viable explanation for OBŠ has been offered and it seems best, despite the risk, to assume that it is an error for ṮBŠ, the scribe having neglected the wedge that distinguishes Ṯ and O. It may be that BRKN means "blessings" here, but it seems preferable to take the B as the preposition and connect RKN either with the Aramaic sense of bowing, resignation, or the Arabic connotation of calm perseverance. "Reverence" appears a fair guess for the present context.

Lines 8ff. The word ṮMQ, presumably a verb, has remained bothersome. A connection with Arabic *smq/k*, "be very high," is phonologically possible but the sense seems unsuitable in the present context. Arabic *qṯm*, "give the best part of one's own to another," was suggested by R. Good in an unpublished paper. Other expedients are possible with resort to metathesis and assimilation or dissimilation of consonants. One might appeal to Arabic *ṯbq*, "flow fast with masses of water," "shed copious tears," since weeping is a universal response to death. The form ṮMK occurs below in parallelism with YṢQ, "pour," which suggests that ṮMQ and ṮMK may be variants of ṮBQ. Without an assured etymology, one may look for help from the verb of the following couplet, which may or may not be an approximate synonym. Unfortunately this word also has received a variety of dubious explanations, variously relating it to Arabic *ḥfw/y*, "go barefoot," "be honored," *ḥ(w)f*, "surround," *ḥafana*, "scoop up with both hands," "grasp," *ḥff*, "surround, "rumble," "rustle." The more likely connection with Arabic *wḥf*, "approach, come, hasten, hurry," appears to have been overlooked. This general sense we conjecture also for the preceding ṮMQ. The subjects of ṮMQ are patently RPU BOL and the soldiers of Baal and Anat. These and other titles and epithets of lines 8-10 will be considered ensemble.

The notion that RPU is an epithet of El[42] has no basis in the Ugaritic texts, and it may be worthwhile to offer a corrective to that misconception here. The primary prooftext for the identification of El and RPU is UG 5.2 (RS 14.252).

YŠT RPU MLK OLM	Let drink RPU King Eternal,
WYŠT GṮR WYQR	Drink the Mighty and Glorious One

38. Van der Meer, Augustine the Bishop p. 514. Even in the graves of the poor, according to Van der Meer, p. 503, were pipes for the dried balsam.

39. Cf. UF 3 (1971) 118, 123, 376.

40. Cf. M. Bayliss, "The Cult of the Dead Kin in Assyria and in Babylonia," Iraq 35 (1973) 115-25, particularly 116f. on the duty of the caretaker (*pāqidu*/LÚ.SAG.ÈN.TAR) to call the name and pour water.

41. Cf. van der Meer, Augustine the Bishop pp. 500, 504, 505, 506, 508, and bibliography on the *refrigerium* p. 652 n. 7.

42. So F. M. Cross, Jr., Canaanite Myth and Hebrew Epic (Cambridge, Mass., Harvard University Press, 1973) 20f.

IL YṮB BOṮTRT	The god who dwells in Ashtaroth
IL ṮPṬ BHDROY	The god who rules in Edrei.

There is no warrant for taking IL here as the proper name of the head of the pantheon. It is the merit of B. Margulis[43] to have recognized that OṮTRT and HDROY here are the place names Ashtaroth and Edrei mentioned as the dwelling of "Og, King of Bashan, of the remnant of the Rephaim, who dwelt in Ashtaroth and in Edrei" (Josh. 12:4; 13:12, 31; cf. Num. 21:33; Deut. 1:4; 3:1, 10). The couplet IL YṮB BOṮTRT // IL ṮPṬ HDROY cannot mean "El (who) sits with Ashtart // El (who judges with Hadd the Shepherd," in view of the fact that Ugaritic YṮB B- and biblical YŠB B- always mean either "sit" or "dwell in," and never occur in the sense "sit with someone."[44] Moreover, HDROY cannot be a cognomen of Baal, since the element HD occurs in Ugaritic poetry only following mention of BOL in the preceding stich. This observation, for which I am indebted to G. Tuttle, is easily confirmed by a glance at Whitaker's Concordance. The restoration of HDR[OY] in UG 5.3.1.1, however, is wrong, despite the fact that it is preceded by BOL, because HDROY is a place name to be identified with the biblical Edrei. The spelling with initial H, if not a scribal error for the similar sign I, cannot undermine the identification in view of the biblical collocations of Edrei and Ashtaroth.[45] A further indication that IL in the passage under consideration is not the proper name El is patent in the succeeding lines:

IL YṮB BOṮTRT	The god who dwells in Ashtaroth,
IL ṮPṬ BHDROY	The god who rules in Edrei,
DYŠR WYḎMR	Who sings and chants
BKNR WBṮLB	To lute and flute,
BTP WBMṢLTM	To timbrel and cymbals,
BMRQDM DŠN	To castanets of ivory.

There is nothing to suggest that this divine virtuoso is El.

As indicated by the translation, it is assumed that RPU BOL, "Baal's Heroes," and MHR BOL, "Baal's Soldiers," are virtually synonymous and so also "Anat's Soldiers," since Baal and Anat as brother and sister consorts are closely allied. The precise identity of these heroic soldiers is not clear, but presumably they belong to the category of Rephaim, the deified dead. The military term recalls the zealot circumcellions of North Africa who were called, among other things, "soldiers of Christ,"[46] in their struggle to maintain the old-time religion against the Roman Church's effort to eliminate or reform certain features of their funeral feasts. In biblical references to orgiastic fertility and funerary rites, Baal and his consort Asherah or Ashtart (Anat has been almost completely expurgated) are frequently associated with MLK.

Lines 9ff. The parallel words ḤYLY and OLLMY, both with the *nisba-t* ending, are construed as titles of ZBL MLK, Prince MLK. The form ḤYLY cannot be equated with Hebrew ḤaY(i)L which in Ugaritic would be written ḤL, for *ḥêl*. Here the nominal pattern is probably that of the *nomen professionis*: ḤaYyāL. Similarly OLLMY is to be vocalized OaLLāMa/iYyu, the doubling of the L indicated in the orthography, as with Aramaic OaMMaYyāA. Arabic *ʿallāmiyy*, "(very) wise," corresponds exactly to the Ugaritic form.

The identity of this mighty and wise Prince MLK is not far to seek. There can be little doubt that he is to be equated with the biblical MōLeK whose infamous cult persisted for centuries in the Valley of Hinnom southwest of Jerusalem. The first Christian martyr in his last peroration recalled Israel's affair with MōLeK, Acts 7:43, quoting Amos 5:26 (after the LXX):

> you took up the tent of Moloch,
> the star of the god Rephan.

Both the Massoretic text and the LXX are obviously garbled in Amos 5:26. The LXX Raiphan is assumed to be a corruption of KiYyūN (Akkadian *kajamānu* with the ŠiQqūṢ vowels), but the collocation of MLK and RP-- is significant in light of the Ugaritic association of RPU and MLK. The Snake Text, UG 5.7 and 8 (RS 24.244 and RS 24.251), provides evidence which, correlated with UG 5.2.1-5, gives grounds for identifying RPU

43. JBL 89 (1970) 293f.

44. A. Rainey (JAOS 94 [1974] 187b) was justifiably dubious of Virolleaud's interpretation of YṮB B- as "sits beside."

45. The concluding sentence of M. Gorg ("Noch Einmal: Edrei in Ugarit?" UF 6 [1974] 474f.), "Ein lautlicher Vergleich mit dem biblischen Edrei kann also nicht geführt werden," is based on highly uncertain Egyptian data and the question whether we should expect the Ugaritic form to be spelled UDROY has no crucial bearing on the identification. Interchange of prosthetic A and H is no serious impediment seeing that it takes place in other instances, such as the prefix of the causative verbal stem.

46. Van der Meer, Augustine the Bishop p. 83.

MLK OLM with MLK. In the Snake Text the gods are invoked in hierarchical order (El, Baal, Dagan, Anat, Yar(i)ḫ, Resheph, Chemosh, MLK, Kothar-and-Ḫasis, Shaḥr-and-Shalim, Ḥoron) and the abode of each deity directly follows the god's name, the residence being either in the adverbial accusative or supplied with the directive suffix -H. Of the dozen deities summoned at and from their place of residence, MLK is in eighth place and his abode is Ashtaroth, TQRU . . . OM MLK OṮTRTH, "She calls . . . toward MLK at Ashtaroth," UG 5.7.41. Again, in the second tablet of the Snake Text, UG 5.8.1.17, MLK is placed *in* Ashtaroth, YISP ḤMT MLK BOṮTRT, "MLK-in-Ashtaroth collects the venom." Thus RPU MLK OLM, "the Hero, King Eternal," dwells and rules in/at Ashtaroth and Edrei while MLK resides in/at Ashtaroth. Both RPU MLK OLM and just plain MLK have the same address: Ashtaroth. The dual-address of RPU MLK OLM, Ashtaroth and Edrei, is also shared by the biblical "Og, King of Bashan, of the remnant of the Heroes (Rephaim), who dwelt at Ashtaroth and at Edrei." This same Og ruled over Mount Hermon and Salecah and all Bashan (Deut. 3:8, 10; Josh. 12:4, 5; 13:12). The assocation with fertility and strength is prominent in the poetic allusions to Bashan in the Bible. Bashan stands as a parallel to Lebanon in Jer. 22:20 and in collocation with Carmel in Jer. 50:19. The superlative trees of Bashan and Lebanon are mentioned in Isa. 2:13 and Zech. 11:2. The cows of Bashan are famous from Amos' strictures against the luxurious ladies of Samaria (Jerusalem?) who say to their uxorious husbands, "Bring and let's drink" (Amos 4:1), but the bulls (Ps. 22:12), rams and he-goats (Deut. 32:14; Ezek. 39:18) and the connections with slaughter, feasting and blood-drinking have not received due attention and to this we will return below. The cosmic and mythological connections of Bashan are attested in Ps. 68:15-23. Bashan is the mountain envied by other peaked mountains because it was there that Yahweh chose to dwell, there he conquered his enemies, took captives, there he will finally defeat Death and bring back (the redeemed?) from Bashan and from the depths of the Sea (MiBbāŠāN // MiMmĕṢûLôWT YāM, Ps. 68:23), and feet will wade in blood and dogs' tongues lap the gore of God's enemies. This much studied Psalm needs further study but this is too much to assay here.

The mythical character of Og, King of Bashan, the last of the Rephaim, is indicated by a Phoenician tomb inscription which invokes the Might Og[47] to visit the grave robber. Jewish folklore[48] about Moses leaping high in the air in order to hack at Og's ankles and thus destroy him appears as reliable historically as the account of Numbers 21:33-35.[49] That the biblical Og has the same address as RPU MLK OLM, does not mean that they *must* be identical. Og appears to be a minor figure among the Rephaim, while RPU and/or MLK are ranking deities. That RPU and MLK also are both located at Ashtaroth, does not necessarily mean that they are one and the same deity, but it seems likely that this is the case.

A brief but important article by J. F. Healey[50] has significantly advanced the case for the connection of the Akkadian *malikū* and *malkū* of Mari texts concerning funerary offerings for the dead, *kispum*, with the spirits of the dead or the underworld gods, as previously suggested by J. Aro.[51] Healey's new clue is line 32 of the list of gods in syllabic script which reads ᵈMA.LIK.MEŠ, for which the entry in the corresponding alphabetic list is MLKM. It is clear from the plural determinative of the syllabic entry that the words are plural and thus the alphabetic entry does not represent MilKōM. The divine determinative also confirms that we are dealing with deities. Healey[52] suggests equation of these MALKŪ/MLKM with the Mesopotamian Anunnaki since the title *ilū*(DINGIR.MEŠ-*u*) *ma-al-ku*, "counsellor gods" or "divine princes" is several times applied to the Anunnaki, especially in contexts relating to the netherworld. Kienast[53] argued that it was only in later periods that Anunnaki, the title of all the great gods, was specialized to refer in some texts to the gods of the netherworld in particular, but Kienast[54] also observed that *malkū* was a special title of the Anunnaki as infernal gods. The Anunnaki eat and drink and receive the *kispum* offerings for the dead, as do the *malikū* in the Mari texts. The *malkū* of the Old Babylonian omen texts are demonic and associated with ghosts (as in the phrase *qāti ma-al-ki u eṭemmim*) and Healey appropriately raises the question of further possible links with the Ugaritic RPUM. Healey noted that the "close parallel of the Ugaritic Šapšu's rule over the *rp'um* in the

47. Cf. J. Starcky, MUSJ 45 (1969) 262. Line 2, . . . LPTḤ O[LT ARN ZN LRGZ OṢMY HOG YTBQŠN HADR . . ., is translated by Starcky ". . . pour ouvrir] ce sarcophage et pour troubler mes os, le ʿOg me cherchera, le Puissant."

48. Cf. L. Ginzberg, The Legends of the Jews 3 346.

49. If Og should appear in the documents from Ebla as a historical monarch ruling Bashan from dual capitals at Ashtaroth and Edrei, I would, of course, be surprised and abashed. Meanwhile, we may count Og among the heroes of the dim past, and, to judge from the Phoenician tomb reference above, a sort of bogy to frighten grave robbers.

50. J. F. Healey, "*Malkū* : *mlkm* : Anunnaki," UF 7 (1975) 235-38.

51. OLZ 54 (1961) col. 604.

52. UF 7 (1975) 237.

53. B. Kienast, Studies Landsberger pp. 141-58.

54. Studies Landsberger p. 156f. Cf. J. F. Healey, UF 7 (1975) 237 nn. 40, 41.

Šapšu Hymn" (6.6[62.2].40ff.) "to Šamaš' rule over the *malkū*/Anunnaki in the Babylonian Šamaš Hymn suggests such a linking of *rpʾum* and *malkū*/Anunnaki."[55]

It is appropriate in this connection to consider the Ugaritic passages to which Healey refers. It is also important to note the context which is the preceding description of Anat's violent mourning for her defunct brother Baal and the burial and funerary sacrifices for him (6.6[62].2-29). On the reverse of the tablet after a break of several lines follows direct address, and we may reasonably assume that the addressant is Anat and the addressee her departed brother (6.6[62].42-52):

AP LTLḤM [L]ḤM TRMMT	Yea, may you eat meat of offerings
LTŠT YN TÓẒYT	Drink the wine of entreaty
ŠPŠ RPIM TḤTK	May Šapš rule the Heroes
ŠPŠ TḤTK ILNYM	May Šapš rule the deities
ODK ILM HN MTM ODK	Your comrades the gods, the dead your comrades.
KṮRM ḪBRK WḪSS DOTK	Koṯar your colleague, Ḫasis your companion.
BYM ARŠ WTNN	On the day of laceration and mourning,
KṮR WḪSS YD	May Koṯar and Ḫasis gash,
YTS KṮR WḪSS	Rip Koṯar and Ḫasis.

A minimum of comment, philological and otherwise, is proffered. The word TRMMT is *napax* thus far in Ugaritic, but very frequent as a biblical and rabbinic term for offering or sacrifice. The root ÓẒY is used several times in the sense of "entreat, beseech." The "wine of entreaty" may be that offered in necromancy to entreat the dead for guidance or help. The full import of Šapš' ruling the Rephaim is unclear, despite the Mesopotamian parallel noted above. The puzzling cliché used three times in contexts relating to Baal's demise at the hands of Mot (3[ONT.VI].5.26; 6[49].2.25; 4[51].8.22) may be germane to the problem of the relation of the solar deity and the infernal gods:

NRT ILM ŠPŠ	The lamp of the gods Šapš,
ṢḤRRT LA ŠMM	The glowing *orb* of heaven,
BYD BN ILM MT	Is in the power of divine Mot.

The period when Šapš is in Mot's power is the sterile interlude while Baal is in the netherworld. Whether the time that Šapš rules the Rephaim is when Baal is in the netherworld or out, or whether Baal's vicissitudes have any bearing on the relation, is unclear.

The cue to the meanings of OD and DOT is the presumably synonymous ḪBR "companion." Of possible "roots" for OD, O(w)D, "do (something) repeatedly," seems most likely. For DOT a plausible cognate is Arabic DOW, as in *daʿwat*, "call," *diʿwat* "claim of kinship." It is assumed that OD and DOT are virtual synonyms of ḪBR, designating participants in the rites.

For ARŠ we turn to the Arabic verb meaning "scratch one's face in sign of mourning." TNN as "dragon," makes little sense here, and the guess is that the word here is a T prefix noun of a "weak" root, perhaps WNN.

YD is construed as an apocopate form of WḌY, "scratch with the nails," a common mode of expressing grief. For YTR Arabic TRR, "cut," or NTR, "tear with hands or teeth," offers suitable parallels to WḌY, "lacerate."

Healey[56] notes finally that RPUM may be translated "princes," on the basis of Aistleitner's comparison with Akkadian *rubû/rubāʾum*. Quite apart from that dubious comparison, the title ZBL, usually rendered "prince," is applied to MLK in 22.2[123].12; 22.2]124].10 and also in 13[6].26.

Of interest is Healey's[57] reference to P. Jensen's notice that in the Qurʾān (43:77) the angel of hell to whom the damned cry for relief is named MāLiKun.

Lines 10ff. The verb Ṣ(w)D is used of Anat's roaming the mountains, hills and fields in search of her consort's corpse (5[67].6.26), and similarly of Mot's scouting the countryside to note the impact of Baal's demise (6[49].2.15). Baal also goes and hunts (YTLK WYṢD) in the steppe where he encounters the bovine monsters with horns like bulls, humps like buffalo, and faces like his own, 12[75].34. The noun MṢD is parallel to DBḤ, "sacrifice," in 14[KRT].2.79; 4.171. El also provided game for a sacrifice to which he invited the gods, IL DBḤ BBTH // MṢD ṢD BQRB HKLH, "El sacrificed in his house // Provided game in the midst of his palace" (UG 5.1.1.1). Esau went hunting and procured game to prepare the tasty dish for his father's

55. UF 7 (1975) 238 n. 44.
56. UF 7 (1975) 238 n. 44.
57. UF 7 (1975) 236 n. 15.

last meal (Gen. 27:3-6). Game or venison (ṢûWDNı̂YTāA) as the viand of the Jewish mourning meal was so relished that some were accused of unnecessary mourning just to be fed the savory dish (TB Šabbat 136a, Moed Qatan 20b).

It is uncertain whether TŠTR is a ŠT form of WRY > YRY, "throw," or a simple stem cognate with Arabic ŠTR, "wound, mangle." In the first instance OPT might mean either "she wings/flies," or "on wing," while in the second case OPT would mean "birds." Since OP is never used for "bird" in Ugaritic, but always OṢR (from OṢPR), we take the first choice.

Lines 12-14 are stereotype, occurring also in 4[51].6.40f., 1[ONT X].4.30f.

Lines 14ff. The next couplet presents complete synonymous parallelism. Silver and gold are a regular parallel pair, the middle word OBRM is the same in both lines, and it is therefore patent that ZT and KŠ must by synonyms. Starting with the assumption that ZT here means "olive(s)," all efforts to find a reasonable meaning for KŠ have proved fruitless. The cue offered by KSP and ḪRṢ, "silver" and "gold," leads to Akkadian *zittu* and *kaššu*, both meaning "payment," or the like.

It remains now to discover the meaning of OBRM. One may think of the commercial expression KeSeP OôBēR LaSsôḤēR (Gen. 23:16), apparently with reference to monetary weights current among merchants. This, however, would be a false lead. The connection of OBRM with the Rephaim and the cult of the dead has already been made by J. Ratosh,[58] who correctly divined that the term means "ancestors passed away." The biblical place name Iye Ha-Abarim (Num. 21:11, 33:43), and the mountain(s) of Abarim (Num. 27:12; 33:47-48), Ratosh refers to the dolmens in Transjordan, which have been generally assumed to be burial places and shrines for worship of the dead. This association illuminates the connection between successive encampments during Israel's wilderness wandering, when they camped at Oboth "ghosts" and moved thence to camp at Iye Ha-Abarim "ruins of the departed" on the border of Moab, both places being sites of dolmen concentrations. Ratosh goes on to develop the connection between the OăBāRı̂(Y)M and the Rephaim, relating them to the worship of the ancient fathers, the heroes and giants, men of renown, of Gen. 6:4. Ratosh, according to B. Halevi,[59] cited the Ugaritic Rephaim texts and even alleged that OBRM there stands in parallelism with RPUM, which is not exactly the case. Apparently overlooked by both Ratosh and Halevi, the passage Ezek. 39:11-21 confirms the meaning ascribed by Ratosh to OBRM. A translation of that passage follows, with notes on crucial points.

11. "And it shall be on that day
That I will give Gog a place-there,
A grave in Israel,
The Vale of the Departed facing the Sea,
Packed with the Departed.
There they shall bury Gog
And all his mob.
They will call it 'Vale of Gog's Mob,'
12. For the House of Israel will bury them
In order to purify the Land.
Seven (long) months
13. Will all people of the land bury.
And it will be their renown
On the day I get me glory,"
Says the Lord God.
14. Constant workers will separate
The Departed in the Land,
Burying the Departed
Left on the face of the Land—to purify it.
Seven months long will they search
15. And remove the Departed in the Land.
If one sees a human bone,
He will build a sign beside it
Until the buriers bury it
In the Vale of Gog's Mob,
16. Alias Crowd-Town.
So shall they purify the Land.
17. "And you, mere man,"
So says the Lord God,
"Tell the birds, every winged one,
Every beast of the field,
'Assemble yourselves, and come,
Gather yourselves round about,
Around the banquet I am providing you,
A great banquet on the mountains of Israel.
Then eat flesh and drink blood.
18. Flesh of the mighty you shall eat,
Blood of earth's princes you shall drink,
Bucks, rams, he-goats,
Bullocks, Bashan fatlings all.
19. So eat fat to satiety
And drink blood to drunkenness,

58. "On OēBeR in Scripture or ARṢ HOBRYM" (in Hebrew), Beth Mikra 47. This article is not accessible to me and the reference and summary are taken from B. Halevi, "Additional Notes on Ancestor Worship" (in Hebrew), Beth Mikra 64 (1975) 101-117; sketch of Ratosh's argument pp. 110ff. and English summary p. 172.

59. Beth Mikra 64 (1975) 110.

At my banquet I am providing you.
20. You will be sated at my table
With horses, chariots, warriors,
All men of war'," says the Lord God.

21. "So will I set my glory among the nations
And all nations will see my judgment
Which I execute,
And my hand which I lay on them."

v. 11. Place-there. The binding of MāQôWm-ŠāM is striking in the light of the use of both words with reference to the grave and the netherworld. On ŠāM, see above, and for MāQôWM, cf. Job 16:18, "O earth cover not my blood, let there not be a MāQôWM for my cry."

Departed. The destination of these "passengers," so KJ, or "travelers," RSV, is the Valley burial ground, a point that appears to have escaped interpreters generally.

Facing. It depends on the viewer as well as on the geographical situation whether QiDMāH means east or west. The Sea here is certainly not the Mediterranean. It would be quite unnecessary to characterize a Palestinian locale as east of the (Mediterranean) Sea, seeing that the whole country is so disposed. The guess that the Sea in question is that of Galilee also misses the mark. The Sea here must refer to the Dead Sea with which the Valley connects. The Good News Bible renders "east of the Dead Sea," correctly identifying the sea in question, but putting the valley on the wrong side of it.

The (Qidron) Valley, known today as Lady Mary's Vale, Wādī Sitti Maryam, lies between the eastern walls of the Old City and the Mount of Olives, beginning a little more than a mile north of the northwest corner of the city and running southeast for about a mile and a half under the name Wādī el-Jôz, "Nut Vale"; it turns sharply south and continues in that direction past the city, bending southeastward in its tortuous course to the Dead Sea. On the south side of the city it was called the Valley of the son(s) of Hinnom, being the north end of the Valley of Rephaim; cf. Josh. 15:8; 18:16; Jer. 19:2. The connection with the Rephaim is important for the mythological associations of the demise of Gog's mob.[60]

Packed. The basic sense of ḤSM appears to be "stop up, muzzle," as in Deut. 25:4, and the noun MaḤSôWM, Ps. 39:2. The subject of ḤōSeMeT, "it" (HîYA), refers obviously to the valley. KJ conjectured that the congestion was nasal, presumably from the stench of the corpses, "and it shall stop the *noses* of the passengers." RSV renders "it will block the travelers." The cause of the congestion is surely the crush of the "travelers" whose destination is the Valley, called in Jer. 31:40 "Valley of Corpses." The word ḤSMT is vocalized as an active participle, but the sense from our point of view is passival. The valley packs in and is packed with the passengers to the terminal depot.

v 14. This verse has vexed translators from of old. The difficulty derives from failure to appreciate that it is the travelers, those who have passed on, who receive burial. LXX and Syr simply ignored the troublesome travelers and RSV followed that lead, "They will set men apart to pass through the land continually and bury those remaining upon the face of the land," with a note on *bury* indicating that the Hebrew says *bury the travelers*. KJ followed the Targum, construing AT as the preposition "with" rather than the *nota objecti*. This reading of AT in the sense of OM is the basis of the supposition that there was division of labor between the OBRYM who went through the land locating and marking the corpses to be buried by the MQBRYM.

v. 15. remove: Reading WOBRW as Piʿel rather than Qal. The D-stem of OBR is found only twice in the OT, I Kings 6:21 and Job 21:10, in quite different contexts, yet each with the appropriate factitive-causative sense, "make to pass." The choice of the verb with cognate accusative here was probably dictated by desire to play on the term OôBěRîYM.

v. 16. Crowd-Town: The netherworld as a city is common motif in ancient Near Eastern literature.[61] It was a populous place, its denizens far outnumbering the measly minority of the quick. This concept of the "silent majority," the realization that the millions who tread the globe are but a handful to the tribes that slumber in its bosom, must be as old as human thought. Striking literary expression of the idea is voiced in Ishtar's threat:

> "I will raise up the dead, eating the living, so that the dead will outnumber the living."
> (Gilgamesh Epic VI 99-100, Ishtar's Descent 19-20)

The crowds (and) crowds that will gather in the Valley of Decision on the Day of the Lord, Joel 3:14, are the citizens of the infernal metropolis Crowd-Town, Mother-Earth from whose womb we come and to which we return; cf. Job 1:21, Gen. 3:19. Ps. 139:15 alludes to the idea that man is first fabricated and produced in

60. On the historical Gog, cf. M. C. Astour, "Ezekiel's Prophecy of Gog and the Cuthean Legend of Naram-Sin," JBL 95 (1976) 567-79.

61. Cf. N. J. Tromp, Primitive Conceptions of Death p. 152ff.

the depths of Earth—before entrance into this world by way of his earthly mother's womb.

v. 17. Under the figure of scavenger birds and beasts gorging on myriads of corpses, the ancient practice of eating and drinking the flesh and juices of the dead is evoked. In a Ugaritic mythological fragment (RS 22.225)[62] on the back of a lexical text we are told that the goddess Anat, going berserk at her brother's beauty, "ate his flesh without a knife and drank his blood without a cup." We are not informed whether her brother (Baal) was alive or dead, but we may assume that he was defunct and that she acted from what anthropologists of the past century called "morbid affection."

v 18 c, d. The powerful animals here represent ruling classes and military nobility, such as King KRT invited to his banquet as "his bulls" (ṮRH) and "his roebucks" (ẒBYH) 15[128].4.19. The tribal chiefs of Edom bore the title ALlûWP, related to AaLP, a horned bovine (Gen. 36:15-40). Isa. 34:6-7 presents the nobles of Edom as rams, he-goats, bulls whose blood and gore will soak the land on the banquet/sacrifice day of the Lord.

v. 19. Eating to satiety and drinking to drunkenness was proper form and literary cliché, whether one drank real blood or substituted wine. At El's funeral feast (MRZḤ) "the gods ate and drank // drank wine till sated // must till inebriated," in terms virtually identical with the present biblical verse.

Line 15. *Silver // gold, payment // fee.* Money for the dead to cover travel, subsistence and incidental expenses, is a venerable and persistent custom, surviving still in China where quantities of paper money, "Hell Bank Notes," are printed for the purpose. Primitive as well as advanced societies have preserved such customs, e.g., aboriginals of Australia and Bulgarians of Europe, the latter tossing money into the grave[63] before it is filled. The ancient Greeks placed a coin, the obol of Charon, in the corpse's mouth as fare (*naûlon*) for the ferry, and supplied also some honey cakes (*melitoutta*) as a sop for Cerberus. The gold stopper or muzzle (MḤSM, the same term as in Ps. 39:2) in/on the mouth of the Phoenician queen BaT NuOM[64] was apparently to keep her mouth shut rather than to pay her fare. This is of a piece with such devices as wiring the jaw to keep the mouth closed, putting weights on the eyelids (the traditional penny on the dead man's eye), binding the feet, or tying the big toes together, to keep the dead quiet and immobile.

Line 16. *Redolent*: DPR in Arabic relates to repulsive stench, putrid odor, an appropriate characterization of the pungent odor of fermented fruit.

Table: Still in Christian times the covers of the graves of the saints were called *mensae*.[65] Some were shaped like a dining-table, straight on one side and rounded on the other in the form of a C. The Greek term for the funeral feast was *perideipnon*, "round-the-table."[66] Older pagan graves were often elaborately equipped with tables and couches and even culinary set-up with ovens, water-supply and drainage. In tombs of the wealthy the celebrants reclined in cool comfort on sofas in the *cella* or in a room over the tomb with holes in the floor and pipes through which they shared their drinks with the guest of honor below.[67] Piping drink to the dead was an old custom, as attested by the Akkadian term *arūtu*,[68] designating a pipe for that purpose. In Syria-Palestine provision was made for liquid refreshment of the dead by access holes through the ground into the tomb, with bottomless jars to receive the libations. Channels were also carved in the rock as conduits for the liquid.[69] At Ras Shamra[70] a funeral vault was uncovered which had apertures in the walls and a large jar was set at an angle inside one of these openings, presumably for receiving liquid offerings. Also uncovered was a pipe with holes in the side to let the liquid flow into the soil. H. A. Hoffner, Jr.[71] has proposed a connection of the Hebrew term AôWB with Ugaritic ILIB and the deified personification of the sacral pits, ^{d}*a-a-bi* in Hittite rituals, corresponding to the Latin *mundus*, into and through which offerings were made to the dead. This *a-a-bi* preceded by the divine determinative seems, at times, according to

62. CRAIBL 1960 (Paris, 1961) 180-86. Cf. M. Astour, Hellenosemitica (1965) p. 180.

63. Cf. E. S. Hartland, on Death and Disposal of the Dead, ERE 4 430a.

64. H. Donner - W. Röllig, KAI 2.

65. Cf. van der Meer, Augustine the Bishop pp. 498, 509.

66. Van der Meer, Augustine the Bishop p. 500.

67. Van der Meer, Augustine the Bishop p. 500.

68. Cf. CAD A/2 324b s.v. *arūtu.*

69. Cf. F. L. Sukenik, "Installations for the Cult of the Dead in Canaanite Ugarit and Israelite Samaria" (in Hebrew), Qedem 2 (1945) 42-47; A. Parrot, Le Refrigerium dans l'au-delà (Paris, 1937) 69ff.

70. Cf. C. F. A. Schaeffer, "The Cuneiform Texts of Rash Shamra - Ugarit, 1939," pl. xxxviii fig. 1; Ugaritica 1 72 pl. xvii and 89.

71. H. A. Hoffner, Jr., "Second Millennium Antecedents to the Hebrew ʾ*ôb*," JBL 86 (1967) 385-401; references in English and Scottish ballads to tossing silver and gold around for the sake of the dead at wakes and funerals refer to doles for the poor or gifts to the church to insure prayers for the deceased: cf. L. C. Wimberly, Death and Burial Lore in the English and Scottish Popular Ballads, University of Nebraska Studies in Language, Literature, and Criticism 8 (1927) 96ff.

Hoffner,[72] to designate a personal deity related to the netherworld deity or chthonic spirit designated by the Hittite term *tarpiš*. In UG 5.13 (RS 24.253), a list of offerings to various gods, we read in line 19 WBURBT.ILIB Š, "and in the window of ILIB a sheep." The term "window" would apply very well to the sort of aperture found in the vaulted tomb at Ugarit. An Ugaritic expression for burial is to put one "in the hole of the earth gods" ŠT . . . BḪRT ILM ARṢ (5[67]5.5; 6[62].1.17; 19[AQHT].3.112,126,141). There is, of course, a difference between a hole as a grave and a window as an aperture leading into the grave, but the connection is still rather close and it is not too daring to assume that the terms ILIB and ILM ARṢ are virtually synonymous, and that the ILIB are the deified ancestors who can be reached by pipe-line into the earth. There are still problems to be solved in connection with Hoffner's suggestion about the relation of Ugaritic ILIB and the ^{d}*a-a-bi*, holy *mundus* of the Hittite texts, but the association is unquestionably very close.

Fig cake: For QOL one may look to Arabic *quᶜâl*, "blossoms" or *qaᶜl*, "poles to prop vines or dry dates." The rabbinic connection of QĕOîYLîYT, supposedly derived from the Judean town of Keilah, with dried or pressed figs, DĕBêYLāH, which are intoxicating,[73] combined with the Arabic association of the root QOL with drying of fruit, suggests that the original sense of the root was related to fruit and the drying or pressing of figs or dates which would certainly be pungent, as suggested by DPR.

Line 17. *Royal*: The assocation of MLKM with the gods of the netherworld, the deified dead, noted above in connection with the study by J. F. Healey,[74] suggests that the term here may be freighted with multiple entente. Whether the kings are human or divine, the term here functions as a superlative.

Spill: ṮMK apparently parallel to YṢQ, "pour," evokes Arabic ṮBQ which is used of pouring abundantly water, tears, or words, and presumably could also be used of wine.

Must: MRṮ, used twice in this text, lines 18 and 20, and once in 2009.3.1, occurs in Aramaic as MēYRaT and is cognate with Ugaritic TRṮ and Hebrew TîYRôWŠ, "must," fresh, new wine. Whether the word is connected with the root WRṮ is moot. Emendation of MēYŠāRîYM in Song of Songs 1:4 and 7:10 to MēYRaŠ, on the basis of the parallelism with YaYiN, "wine," is questionable.

Lordly wine: It may be that YN SRNM is in indirect parallelism with QOL MLKM, which would enhance the equation of SRNM with the biblical term applied only to the rulers of the Philistines and presumed to be of Anatolian origin, cognate with Greek *tyrannos*.

Bliss inebriant: It is tempting to take YN BLD as "domestic wine," relating Arabic *balad*, "district, province, country." It is intriguing to note among other bizarre meanings of Arabic BLD, such as "have the eye-brows separated" or "turn the palms (of the hand) outside," senses suggesting the influence of alcohol such as "not care for anything," "fall to the ground," "be confused." Thus it would not be necessary to divide BLD either as B-LD or BL-D. In a Ugaritic letter to the queen mother, 2009 [PRU 5.9].3.1, there is a marginal line which reads HN MRṮ DŠTT AŠLD BLDTK, which suggests that the B of BLD and BLDTK is the preposition. The clause AŠLD BLDTK, however, can hardly mean "I will cause to give birth to your giving birth." G. Tuttle in an unpublished paper has related LDT to Arabic *ladda*, "be sweet, delicious, pleasant," and the derived noun *ladda-t*, "joy, rapture, bliss, enjoyment." Accordingly the passage in the letter would mean something like "lo, the wine which you drink would I make delicious to your enjoyment." The present line YN BLD ÓLL Tuttle rendered "wine from the most delicious yield," connecting ÓLL with one of its Arabic meanings, "yield crops."

Line 19. This line YN IŠRYT ONQ remains enigmatic. The word IŠRYT occurs in 18[3 AQHT].2.28 in a broken context — MT IŠRYT —. Since MT with the meaning "man" occurs elsewhere in Ugaritic only in Danel's titles MT HRNMY // MT RPI, "man of H—" // 'man of R—," it has been generally supposed that IŠRYT is a place name. Mindful of the ill-fated Negebite hypothesis of the early days of Ugaritic studies, it seems prudent to resist the temptation to make any unknown word a proper name unless there is some basis other than desperation. It is a highly tentative guess, but it may be that IŠRYT is from the root ŠRY, "let loose." Another possibility is to relate it to AŠR, "blessed, happy." The word ONQ, usually taken with what follows, ONQ SMD LBNN, is troublesome, and previous efforts at translation are all unsatisfactory. On the assumption that wine is here characterized with respect to its effects, there are several possibilities also for ONQ. Connection with the noun meaning "neck" allows for speculation that in addition to the "stiff neck" of biblical parlance there may have been an opposite term "loose neck" which could be applied both to the physical and the emotional relaxation induced by alcohol. In Arabic ONQ in the second stem is connected

72. S.v. ʾôb in TDOT 1 (Grand Rapids, Eerdmans, 1974) 132.

73. Cf. M. Jastrow, Dictionary, s.v. DBYLH p. 279a, and QOYLH p. 1397b.

74. See above, n. 48.

with delusion, and in the third stem has the sense "take by the neck and draw toward one's self," i.e., "embrace." Either of these possibilities would serve the present context.

Nectar: SMD has been variously related to *samidu*, "fine flour," attested in Akkadian and Arabic, to Arabic *samada*, "lift the head with pride," to the Akkadian plant name *asmidu*, and to Aramaic SeMiDTuW, "bud"; it has also been divided into SM-D, ONQ SM DLBNN, "the purple necklace of Lebanon." Again, in view of the obvious fact that wine is still the subject, we invoke the famous SĕMāDāR of the Song of Songs 2:13, 15; 7:13, on the assumption that the final R is an afformative.

Line 20. *Sack*: ṬL here has usually been assumed to be the general term for "dew." D. Wortman, in an unpublished paper, has related the present use to rabbinic references to an austere wine called Ṭi(Y)LāA or Ṭi(Y(LYāA, mentioned, significantly, in the Talmudic tractate on heathen worship (TB Avodah Zarah 28a, 30a). In the latter passage Rabbi Joshua bar Levi opined that there are three kinds of wine to which the rule against uncovered liquids does not apply; one of these was *ṭilā*, which was so strong that it would break the wineskin. Rashi in commenting on *ṭilā* characterized it as so strong a snake wouldn't drink it. This same wine is mentioned in Giṭṭin 70a as being bad enough to cause a disease that could preclude divorce, the giving of a GēṬ. Arabic *ṭalla-t*, however, denotes a delicious wine or perfume, or a handsome woman. It is also interesting to note apropos of Rashi's remark that Arabic *ṭall/ṭill* designates a snake, and *ṭull* a drink (of milk).

The divine cultivation here is one of many poetic praises of wine as the gift of the gods.

The remainder of the text presents a variation on the common motif of the seven day cycle.

Line 24. *Summit*: The dozen occurrences of PRO in Ugaritic are all in broken or enigmatic contexts. As usual, there are multiple possibilities here. If BPRO is in synonymous parallelism with BIRT LBNN, "in the heart of Lebanon," then Arabic *firaᶜ*, "mountain summit" offers a perfect parallel. The biblical and rabbinic uses of PRO suggest wild abandon, neglecting the hair and ripping clothes in mourning, according to which one might render "with fervor," or the like.

A new and provocative Rephaim text discovered in the 1973 excavations, RS 34.126, has been treated briefly by A. Caquot[75] on the basis of photographs and copies made from molds. The autograph, however, was not included in Caquot's treatment. The text is of such interest as to compel comment and an effort to correlate some items with details discussed above. The lines, with a few exceptions, correspond to the stichometry. Where this appears not to be the case, the number of the line precedes the first word of the line. The translation below differs in several places from that offered by Caquot, and in some instances it will be expedient to try to show cause for the differences.

SPR DBḪ QLM	Order of intonation sacrifice(s):
QRITM RPI A[RṢ]	You invoke the Heroes of Earth.
QBITM QBṢ D[DN]	You invoke the gathering of Di[dān],
QRA BLKN RP[IM]	Invoke BLKN(?) of the Her[oes],
5. QRA TRMN RP[IM]	Invoke TRMN(?) of the Her[oes],
QRA BDN W RD[N]	Invoke BDN alias RDN,
QRA ṮR OLLMN[ ]	Invoke the Bull, Savant,
QRA RPIM QDMYM	Invoke the ancient Heroes,
QRITM RPI ARṢ	You invoke the Heroes of Earth,
10. QBITM QBṢ DD[N]	You invoke the gathering of Did[ān],
QRA OMṮTMR M[L]K	Invoke Ammištamru the k[i]ng,
QRA U NQM[D ML]K	Invoke king Niqmad,
KSI NQMD O[ ]TY	Throne of Niqmad . . .
WYDMO TDM ONH LPNH	Then let him weep, let his eye flow before him,
15. YBKY ṮLḪN ML[A]	Let him weep a table fu[ll],
WYBLO UDMOTH ODMT	And swallow his violent tears,
ODMT WODMT ṮDMT	Violent, violent, stammering.
18. IŠḪN ŠPŠ	Burn, O Šapš,
WIŠḪN (19) NYR ṬBT	Burn, O goodly luminary.

75. "Resumé des Cours de 1974-75," in L'Annuaire du Collège de France, 75 Année pp. 426-29. Professors Schaeffer and Caquot of the Collège de France have both kindly given permission to discuss the text on the basis of the preliminary publication.

OLN ŠPŠ TṢḤ	On high let Šapš cry:
20. AṮR BOLK LKSH	"After your lord, to his cup,
AṮR (21) BOLK ARṢ RD	After your Baal descend to Earth.
ARṢ (22) RD WŠPL OPR	To Earth descend, be low in the Dust,
TḤT (23) BDN W RDN	With BDN alias RDN,
TḤT ṮR (24) OLLMN	With the Bull Savant,
TḤT RPIM QD<MYM>	With the an<cient> Heroes,
25. TḤT OMṮTMR MLK	With king Ammištamru,
TḤT U NQ[MD] MLK	With king Niqmad."
OŠTY WṮ[OY ṮN W]ṮO[Y]	One and an offer[ing, two and] an offering,
ṮLṮ [W]ṮOY [ARBO] WṮO[Y]	Three [and] an offering, [four] and an offer[ing],
ḪMŠ WṮOY [ṮṮ W]ṮOY	Five and an offering, [six and] an offering,
30. ŠBO WṮOY	Seven and an offering.
TQ[RY] OṢR (31) ŠLM	P[resent] a bird as peace offering.
ŠLM OMR[PI]	Health (to) Ammura[pi],
32. WŠLM BNH ŠLM ARYH	Health (to) his sons, health (to) his progeny,
ŠLM BTH ŠLM UGRT	Peace (to) his house, peace (to) Ugarit,
ŠLM ṮÓRH	Peace to its gates.

Intonation: The reading is uncertain and Caquot did not venture a translation, but suggested that the reading of the initial letter as Q might connect the word with QL, "fall" while the reading Ẓ might connect it with "darkness," or, less likely, with "statue." The reading ẒLM might be favored in consideration of the fact that the funeral feast was regularly a nocturnal affair. At evening the dead man's name was called and he was invited to come and partake of the sacrificial meal. The invocation of the name of the dead suggests the possibility that QL-M/T may be connected with Q(w)L, voice. An inscription of Šamši-Adad commemorating the construction at Terqa of a *bīt kispi*, "funeral-feast house," dedicated to "Dagan," mentions in line 7 a building described as É KU-*ul-ti-šu*. Finkelstein[76] proposed to read this as "*bīt qūltišu* "the house of his 'intonation'," i.e., the building where the living king (or his representative) intones the names of his dead ancestors in an atmosphere of hushed reverent attention. Upon being thus invoked—conjured up in an atmosphere approaching that of a seance—the ancestral spirits, and any additional spectral guests invited to participate in the occasion, were then tendered the *kispu*-offering." There may be difficulty in connecting QLM with Q(w)L, namely that the -M plural ending is apparently not otherwise attested with this noun. But it is not unusual for a noun to have different plural forms in various Semitic dialects or within a single dialect. Ten consecutive lines of our text begin with the order to call or invoke the departed by title or name, so that "intonation" seems a likely guess.

Line 3. This is the first attestation of QBA in Ugaritic and Caquot's remark that it appears to correspond to Akkadian *qabû* is certainly true.

DD[N]: QBṢ DD[N] here and in line 10 is manifestly a variant of QBṢ DTN of 15[128].3.4,15; cf. above p.

Before attempting to divine the sense of DTN/DDN we should look at a text in which DTN plays a significant role, UG 5.6 (RS 24.274):

KYMÓY ADN	When comes the Lord
ILM RBM OM DTN	of the great gods to DTN
WYŠAL MṮPṬ YLD	and asks a child verdict
WYONY.NN [ ]	Then he answers [. . .]
5. TONY.N[N]TQ	She/they answer [. . .]
WŠP [ ]	[ ]
ḤDṮ[ ]Ḥ[ ]	New [. . .]
BBT [ ] LBNT [ ]	In the house [. . .] incense
WŠT BBT Ṯ[N]P [ ]	And put in the house [. . .]
10. HY YD/LH WYM[ÓY]	[. . .] and comes

76. JCS 20 (1966) 116a.

MLAKK OM DT[N]	Your messenger to DT[N]
LQḤ MṮPṬ	receives the verdict.
WYONY.NN	Then answers him
DTN BTN MḤ[ ]	DTN as he gives MḤ[ ]
LDG W[A]KL	to drink and eat
WAṮR IN MR[Ṣ]	and then no mal[ady]

comes . . . to: As pointed out by Virolleaud,[77] the verb MǴY, "arrive," employs the preposition L with the destination, as MǴY ḤRN LBTH, "Horon came to his house." It may also be used with a preposition, as PONH LTMǴYN HDM // RIŠH LYMǴY APSH, "his feet did not reach the footstool // his head did not reach the top." One might think, Virolleaud conceded, that the preposition L is here replaced by OM which is always the one used with the verb LAK, "send," but one can see from what follows in lines 11 and 13, according to Virolleaud, that OM can only be a substantive, doubtless "people," Hebrew OaM. But a look at Virolleaud's autograph and transcription will show that line 13 is irrelevant since OM does not occur there. As for line 11, it has to be connected with the remnant of the verb at the end of the preceding line, to be restored as WYM[ǴY], and then it presents exactly the same problem as line 1-2, the otherwise unattested use of the preposition OM with the verb MǴY. There is, however, also a difficulty with taking OM as the noun "people," in construct with DTN, and that is the fact that there is no certain example of OM in Ugaritic as a noun meaning "people." The apparent exception is in the expression ZTR OM-H/Y/K (17[2 AQHT].1.28,-46;2), on which see above. One might propose that OMDTN be taken as the royal name Ammiditana, but this seems to be excluded by the clear reading of lines 13-14, WYONY.NN DTN, without OM. Thus it appears that OM is not bound to DTN which is presumably the same DTN as in the phrase QBṢ DTN/DDN. Now in the Genealogy of the Hammurapi Dynasty,[78] Ditānu is the sixth name of the list which corresponds with Didānu, the ninth name of the Assyrian King List, and confirms the equation of Ugaritic DTN/DDN and the compound QBṢ DTN/DDN. Ditānu/Didānu is thus an early ancestor of the West Semitic kings who has long since joined the infernal heroes, BTK RPI ARṢ. It appears, moreover, that Ditānu, or Didānu, is *primus inter pares* among the assembly of the deified dead who are collectively called PḪR QBṢ DTN, "the plenary gathering of (descendants of) Ditān." As a descendant of the hero Ditān, Krt now has merit among the patrons and dispensers of fertility, his deified progenitors, because he is now blessed with progeny to take the place of his lost family.

This title ADN ILM RBM, "Lord of the Great Gods," is so far unique in the Ugaritic texts, although "the house of the Great Gods," BT ILM RBM, occurs first in a list (1090.2) of recipients of wine for various guilds and foreign personnel, as well as for the house of IL ANN (1090.17). The identity of these great gods, as well as that of their Lord, remains unclear. At any rate, this Lord of the Great Gods comes to Ditān to request a MṮPṬ YLD, an expression very close to that used by Manoah when he questioned the angel (MLAK), who had promised his barren wife a son, as to the future of this promised child, "what will be the MIŠPaṬ of the boy (HaNnaOaR)" (Jud. 13:12). This angel with shiny face like a god was doubtless of the order of Rephaim who convey the blessing of fertility and to whom one also resorts for information about the future. Thus the Sitz im Leben of UG 5.6 is illuminated by Jud. 13:12.

From the last lines, 13-16, it appears that DiTāN gives someone something to drink (LDG manifestly cognate with Arabic *laḏaja*, "sip") and [e]at ([A]KL), after which there is no MR[Ṣ], "sickness." Thus it seems that the query about a child, perhaps the absence of one, and/or his future (note that Manoah asked about the destiny of the promised heir before he was sure of the realization) is connected with a mal[ady] (MR[Ṣ]), presumably impotence, sterility and/or barrenness, which disappears with the sipping and [e]ating of something.

Line 6. BDN *alias* RDN: BDN may be a near synonym of ṮR, "bull," in the following line. Again Arabic offers clues, with *badan*, "dignity," or "old mountain goat," and *budun*, "animal sacrificed at Mecca according to a vow." For RDN one may invoke the cosmic bull Ridyā mentioned in the Talmud (TB Taᶜnit 25b, Yoma 21a), with elision of the Y before the aN afformative by a process analogous to that which produced LTN as the Ugaritic equivalent of Hebrew LiWYāTāN, "Leviathan."

Line 7. *Savant*: The form OLLMN occurs in 1[ONT X].4.5, but with lacunae before and after. It must be related to OLLMY of 22.1[123].12 and 22.2]124].10, the one form with suffix -āN, the other with the *nisba-t* -a/iY, both presumably meaning "wise," "knowing," or the like. This recalls the biblical term

77. Ugaritica 5 564.

78. Cf. Finkelstein, JCS 20 (1966) 95b.

YiDdĕOôWNîY, "knowing one," with both N and Y afformatives. The exact mode(s) of the communication between the medium and the spirit, the dead, is not entirely clear from the several biblical allusions (Lev. 19:31; 20:6, 27; Deut. 18:11; I Sam. 28:3, 9; II Kings 21:6; 23:24; Isa. 8:19; 19:3; II Chron. 33:6), but it is patent that the ghost is the source of the knowledge however obtained by the medium for the client.

Line 8. *Ancient Heroes*: This is the only occurrence thus far of QDM with the *nisba-t* ending in Ugaritic. The biblical adjective QaDMôWNîY has both the -ôN and the îY afformative, like YiDdĕOôWNîY. In Job 18:20 it now seems likely that the QaDMôWNîYM are, as Budde suggested, the former generations who are now in Sheol, which is just where one would expect them to be. Another change for future revision of the Anchor Bible Job.

Lines 11-12. With Ammištamru and Niqmad we come down to the two generations of kings of Ugarit immediately preceding the king who must be reigning at the time this text was composed. The spelling of Ammištamru's name here in the Ugaritic alphabet makes it transparent the etymology of the second component of OM-ṮTMR, which is to be connected with Arabic *ṯamar*, both verb and noun fraught with connotations of fertility, "bear fruit, increase, prosper" and the like.

Line 13. *Throne of Niqmad*: The invocation of Niqmad's chair or throne is of special interest in view of the widespread custom of setting up a chair for the dead. Among the Ashanti in Africa, for example, there is the report that in the worship of the ancestral spirits carried out by a queen-mother, seven stools belonging to dead queen-mothers have offerings placed upon them.[79] The ghost-chair (GIŠ.GU.ZA GIDIM=*kussu eṭimmi*) is several times mentioned in Mesopotamian documents. To the references given by M. Bayliss[80] add the prescription[81] *ana eṭemmi kimtišu* GIŠ.GU.ZA *tanaddi*, "you set up a chair for the ghosts (of the deceased) of his family." This custom persisted down to Christian times[82] with the *cathedra*, an empty chair for the ghost of the guest of honor at the funeral meal. Chairs of carved stone were built-in beside the sarcophagus in early Christian burials. The Roman church as far back as the end of the third century attempted to supplant the ancient ancestor worship, the *parentalia*, feasts for the dead celebrated for nine days following the Ides of February. (It is scarcely accidental that the supposed date of martyrdom of a shadowy Saint Valentine coincides with an old celebration of love which still gets more popular attention than the good saint whose name has been attached to the date.) The Roman clergy made the last day of the old *parentalia*, February 22, an ecclesiastical commemoration service for departed bishops, paying honor to spiritual predecessors rather than ancestors according to the flesh, and the chair for the departed progenitor became the throne of the bishop of bishops, Saint Peter. February 22 had long been known in Greek as *kathedra* and it became in Christian Rome *cathedra Petri*. The date was used to celebrate the installation of the bishop of the day and as the *natale episcoporum* in order to divert attention of the faithful in their family feasts from the ghost's chair to Saint Peter's throne.[83] It is not unlikely that the explanations of Elijah's Chair and Cup in Jewish ritual go back to a similar effort to rid a persistent practice of its pagan associations.[84]

Line 15. A table full of tears is not strange, seeing that the table in question was probably a cover over the grave, like the *mensa* of Christian burials.

Line 16. *Swallow*: Anat when she wept for her dead brother, "drank tears like wine" (6[62].1.10).

Lines 16-17. *Violent*: ODM is presumably cognate with Arabic ʿ*aḏam*, "seize with the teeth, bite, chew violently, blame, rebuke, refuse, reject," actions and feelings that comport with violent weeping in reaction to death in the family. The choice of ODM was probably in the interest of paronomasia, DMO/ODM.

Stammering: Arabic *ṯadm*, "stammerer," seems not too remote from violent weeping. Metathesis leads to Arabic *ṯamad*, associated with the finding and preserving and exhausting of water, but for purposes of drinking rather than weeping.

Line 18. Caquot[85] rendered "Chauffe, Shapash, chauffe Luminaire," making ṮBT the beginning of the following line, ṮBT OLN ŠPŠ TṢḤ, "Sois-nous favorable, Shapash," and leaving TṢḤ to begin the following

79. Cf. Encyclopaedia Britannica s.v. "Ancestor Worship."

80. Iraq 35 (1973) 119 n. 33.

81. CAD K 589b s.v. *kussû*.

82. Cf. T. Klauser, Die Cathedra im Totenkult der heidnischen und christlichen Antike, Liturgiegeschichtliche Forschungen 9 (1927). Cf. van der Meer, Augustine the Bishop p. 503.

83. Van der Meer, Augustine the Bishop p. 508.

84. Cf. G. Margoliouth, on Ancestor Worship (Jewish), ERE 1 459b. The open door for Elijah and the custom of stepping into the street to invite the hungry and needy to join the Passover meal suggest that this may be a survival and reinterpretation of the ancient invitation to All Souls, particularly the neglected dead. The custom of wearing the *kittel*, a long, white robe, while conducting the Seder, as a reminder of the grave shroud, tends to reinforce this suggestion despite evidence and argument that festive clothing was white from ancient times. Cf. H. Schauss, Guide to Jewish Holy Days: History and Observance (First Schocken Paperback Edition, 1962) 83 and 294 n. 89.

85. Annuaire 75 Année p. 427.

line. TṢḤ Caquot connected with ṢḤḤ, "gleam," and rendered, hesitatingly, "Tu luiras(?) à la suite de ton Baal, sur sa coupe." It is clear, however, from 6[49].6.22f., OLN ŠPŠ TṢḤ LMT, "On high Šapaš cried to Mot," followed by direct address, "Hear, O divine Mot," etc., that TṢḤ is from Ṣ(w)Ḥ, "shout," which is used more than seventy times in the Ugaritic texts. ṬBT then is not a verb, but an adjective modifying NYR, like RBT in NYR RBT, "great luminary," in 16.1[125].37.

Line 20. What Šapš cries in a variant of the expression of grief which Anat and El voiced at the news of Baal's demise, AṮR BOL A/NRD BARṢ, "after Baal I/we will descend into Earth" (5[67].6.24; 6[62].1.7), and Jacob's anguish when he though Joseph was dead, "I will go down mourning to my son in Sheol."[86]

Your lord: BOLK refers, presumably, to king Niqmad, the latest among the deceased named.

His cup: Cup, KS, is here used, as in Ps. 11:6, in the sense of "fate," i.e., death; cf. Mark 14:36; Luke 22:42; John 18:11. The mourner is exhorted to follow his lord in grief and share his fate in the netherworld among his sainted ancestors, heroes ancient and recent. The "cup of consolation" which one drinks for his dead parents, Jer. 16:7, may symbolize the common human destiny.

Lines 21-25. *With*: The preposition TḤT here has the meaning "with/among" as in 17[2 AQHT].5.6 and 19[1 AQHT].1.22 where Danel sits "*among* the nobles" TḤT ADRM, hardly "at the feet of (?)."[87]

As usual with Ugaritic celebrations, the sacrifices continue for seven days, as in Jewish tradition (Gen. 50:10; Ecclus. 22:130.

The seven days of sacrifice invoking the defunct ancestors, far and near, the ancient heroes (RPUM QDMYM), as well as the most recently departed kings, Ammištamru and Niqmadu, are carried out to assure both the welfare of the dead and the consequent peace and prosperity of the reigning King Ammurapi, his family and his city-state of Ugarit and its citizens. The sequence of kings, Ammištamru-Niqmadu-Ammurapi, indicates Ammištamru II, Niqmadu III and the first(?) and last Ammurapi of Ugarit, who presumably perished with his city. The omission of Ibiranu, father of Niqmadu III, is puzzling.[88]

The prayer for peace on behalf of the last ruler of Ugarit provokes rueful rumination on the frailty of human hopes, and it recalls the similar expression of faith in divine providence at the end of UG 5.2 (RS 24.252). Some lines at the beginning of that text were cited above depicting the god RPU, King Eternal, in a convivial scene with drinking, singing and music, along with the high-flying goddess of love and war, the violent Virgin Anat. The middle of the text is largely lost, but the last several lines are nearly complete and merit our attention. Stichometry is crucial in the interpretation of Ugaritic poetry, and the following arrangement, which differs notably from other treatments, is based on a study by G. Tuttle.[89]

(6) [ ] RPI MLK OLM	[ ] of RPU, King Eternal,
BOZ (7) [RPI M]LK OLM	By the strength of [RPU, K]ing Eternal.
BḌMRH BL (8) [ANH]	By his power, by [his] mi[ght],
BḤTKH BNMRTH	By his rule, by his goodness,
LR (9) [MM B]ARḤ OZK	To ex[alt in] the land your strength,
ḌMRK.L[A] (10) NK	Your power, your m[ig]ht,
ḤTKK NMRTK	Your role, your goodness
BTK (11) UGRT	In the midst of Ugarit
LYMT ŠPŠ WYRH	For the days of Sun and Moon
(12) WNOMT ŠNT IL	And the pleasant years of El.

The conjectural restoration of a verb[90] at the beginning of line 6 is ill-considered because RPI has the genitive

86. Cf. N. J. Tromp, Primitive Conceptions of Death pp. 85-91.

87. So D. Pardee, UF 7 (1975) 353, with appropriate question mark.

88. Cf. M. Liverani, Storia di Ugarit (1962) pp. 125-28 on Ibiranu; p. 129 on Niqmadu III; pp. 131-35 on Ammurapi and the destruction of Ugarit; Tavola I on synchronism of kings of Ugarit with those of Hatti, Mitanni, Assyria, Karkemish, Amurru and Egypt.

89. An unpublished paper on RS 24.252; cf. G. Tuttle, "Case Vowels on Masculine Singular Nouns in Construct in Ugaritic," in Biblical and Ancient Near Eastern Studies in Honor of William Sanford LaSor (Grand Rapids, Mich., Eerdmans, to appear in fall 1977), the last three paragraphs of Section II.

90. F. M. Cross, Jr., Canaanite Myth p. 21 restored [*yaṯputu* ?] at the beginning of both of the first two lines, and arranged and rendered the lines thus:

[yaṯpuṭu ?] rapiʾ malk ʿôlami baʿuzzi[hu]
[yaṯpuṭu ?] malk ʿôlami ba-ḏimrihu
bal [yamluk] ba-ḥatkihu ba-namirtihu
larā[mim ba]ʾarṣi ʿuzzaka
ḏimrika la [panē]nu (?) ḥatkika
namirtuka ba-tôk ʾUgarīti
la-yāmāt šapši wa-yariḫi
wa-naʿimtu šanāti ʾili

Let Rapiʾ the eternal king [judge ?] in might

singular or oblique plural ending and thus cannot be the subject of a finite verb. The series of five roughly synonymous terms for pwoer and authority (OZ, ḌRM, L[A]N, ḤTK and NMRT) ascribed by means of the third-person possessive suffix to the god RPU, King Eternal, is besought to be bestowed on someone who is then addressed directly, as shown by the second-person possessive suffixes in the repeated nominal series. The person addressed would be the reigning king of Ugarit for whom the prayer is offered that RPU King Eternal may endue him (the king) with his (the god's) divine gifts of authority and power as long as Sun and Moon shall last, rivalling the years of the venerable El. The mention of El here is no argument for his identification with RPU King Eternal in view of the evidence that the latter deity dwells in Ashtaroth and/or Edrei (UG 5.2.1.3) and in light of the Snake Text (UG 5.7), which shows that El and his abode (UG 5.7.3) are separate and distinct from that of MLK at Ashtaroth (UG 5.7.41).

Time and circumstance prevent revision of these random notes in the light of recent studies. An article by the leading Dutch Ugaritologist J. C. de Moor came to hand too late to be used.[91] The treatment of RS 34.126 by T. H. Gaster in a privately printed Festschrift has not yet been seen by the writer.[92] These studies and others to come will add to our understanding of the Rephaim of the Bible and other ancient Semitic texts and to our appreciation of the antiquity of concern for all souls and belief in the communion of saints. The memory of Jack Finkelstein, admiration of his erudition, gratitude for his contributions to scholarship, and affection for him as a faithful colleague and friend, strengthen the bonds of that communion. ZēKeR ṢaDdīYQīYM LiBRāKāH.

Let [the eter]nal king [judge ?] in strength.
Verily let him [rule] his offspring in his grace.
To ex[alt (?)] thy might in the earth
Thy strength be[fore] us (?) thy offspring,
Thy grace in the midst of Ugarit
As long as the years of Sun and Moon
and the pleasance of the years of ʾEl

There are several questionable grammatical features and incongruities in Cross' treatment, beginning with the restoration of the verb [yaṯpuṭu ?] with indicative modal ending but rendered as jussive, and continuing with the subject of the verb in the genitive case. The addition of the possessive suffix to BOZ at the end of line 6 is unwarranted, for Virolleaud's copy shows no room at the end of the line and nothing written on the edge. The suffix mistakenly added to BOZ is then ignored in translation, as is the plainly preserved suffix of BḌMRH, "by/in his strength." As divined by G. Tuttle, the cue to the syntax is the two series of five identical nouns with different possessive suffixes. The first noun OZ lacks the suffix in the first series because it is in construct relation with what follows: BOZ [RPI M]LK OLM. In place of Cross' conjectured *bal* [*yamluk*] at the end of line 7 and the beginning of line 8 we prefer Tuttle's restoration BL[ANH] "with his might," and similarly at the end of line 9 and the beginning of line 10 L[A]NK instead of Cross' *la*[*pani*]*nu* (?), which ignores the following clear K of Virolleaud's copy, as well as the testimony of L. Fisher (HTR 63 [1970] 489-90 n. 20). The restoration LR[MM B]ARṢ OZK, however, seems quite acceptable. The meaning "offspring" for ḤTK, appropriate in other contexts, seems unsuitable here and the sense "rule," as in the verbal use ŠPŠ RPIM TḤTK // ŠPŠ TḤTK ILNYM (6.6[62.2].46) appears to fill the bill. The basic sense of ḤTK is "cut," the active participle ḤāTiK being used in the sense of "progenitor, sire" (6.[49].4.35) and the passive participle, presumably, in the sense of "progeny, scion" (10[76].3.35). The form of the noun here meaning "rule, governance, decision-making," or the like, is conjectural and it may be that Cross' vocalization *ḥatk* is right for the wrong reason. For all its merit as a pedagogical device (see Cross, Canaanite Myth p. 21 n. 50), the vocalization of Ugaritic is a risk which the present writer prefers to avoid in print. It is certainly easier to find fault with the efforts of others' vocalizations than to proffer impeccable specimens of one's own. The value of vocalization for prosody is patent, but the "fudge factor" in the interest of syllabic symmetry should be reduced by consistent policy with respect to case and modal endings (with respect to the former see Tuttle's study [above, n. 89], and in particular the catalogue of errors and inconsistencies in Cross' vocalizations detailed in n. 5). Syllable counting thus far has not produced wholly satisfactory results. Note that in the few lines cited above with Cross' vocalization the count varies between 9 and 13 syllables. Before counting the syllables of a conjectural vocalization, utmost care should be given to stichometry since a single misplaced word can wreck every hope of correct analysis of sense or prosody.

91. J. C. de Moor, "Rapi'uma-Rephaim," ZAW 88 (1976) 323-45.

92. T. H. Gaster, "An Ugaritic Feast of All Souls," in Concepts, Critiques and Comments: A Festschrift in Honor of David Rose (privately printed, New York, 1976) pp. 97-106.

NEBUCHADNEZZAR I'S ELAMITE CRISIS IN THEOLOGICAL PERSPECTIVE

J. J. M. Roberts
The John Hopkins University

In an earlier paper I have argued that an adequate comparative study of biblical and Mesopotamian views of history "must examine the theological interpretations of historical events across the whole spectrum of literary genres native to the cultures being compared."[1] I suggested that one way of doing this "is to take a typical event such as the fall of a royal cult center and then to trace the theological reflections on that event through the literature of both cultures."[2] This paper will make a beginning toward that larger project by examining the Babylonian reflections on one particular sequence of events. Since J. J. Finkelstein, though his main research was concentrated elsewhere, always maintained an interest in the nature of Mesopotamian historical thought[3] and the light Mesopotamian studies could shed on biblical material,[4] it is with genuine pleasure that I dedicate this preliminary study to his memory.

The crisis brought on by the Elamite sack of Babylon, the plunder of its gods—particularly the removal of the statue of Marduk—and the ultimate resolution of this crisis by Nebuchadnezzar I's conquest of Elam and subsequent return of Marduk was widely celebrated in Babylonian literature.[5] It is referred to in two contemporary inscriptions of Nebuchadnezzar I[6]; it is the occasion of a "prophecy" of Marduk[7]; it is the subject of at least one and probably two epics of uncertain date[8]; and it may be celebrated in an unusual historical hymn to Marduk.[9] Despite Brinkman's doubts, two bilingual poems—or two fragments of the same larger work—probably refer to the same events.[10] The so-called Kedorlaomer texts also seem to deal with this historical era,[11] and, finally, there are additional references to it in omen texts.[12] In short, thanks to the abundance and diverse genres of our sources, we are able to see this sequence of events from several different viewpoints. Thus it provides us with a model example of the ways in which the Babylonians interpreted the fall and subsequent restoration of a royal cult center involving the removal and return of its divine images. Even if some of the sources used actually refer to a later conflict with the Elamites, it will not significantly affect the results, since this concrete historical sequence is chosen merely as an example of the typical interpretation.

The two contemporary inscriptions are perhaps the least theological in their treatment of the events. One simply states that Nebuchadnezzar went to Elam, smote it, took the hand of Marduk, and returned this god together with the goddess Eriya to Babylon.[13] The second, however, is not without theological interest. According to it, Marduk, the king of the gods, gave Nebuchadnezzar the command, and he took up arms to *avenge* Akkad.[14] The historical background for such vengeance is not given—the contemporaries of

1. J. J. M. Roberts, "Myth Versus History: Relaying the Comparative Foundations," CBQ 38 (1976) 1-13.
2. CBQ 38 (1976) 1-13.
3. See, for instance, his important article, "Mesopotamian Historiography," PAPS 107 (1963).
4. See, for an example, his article "An Old Babylonian Herding Contract and Genesis 31:38f.," JAOS 88 (1968) 30-36.
5. For the history, see J. A. Brinkman, A Political History of Post-Kassite Babylonia, AnOr 43 (Rome, Pontifical Biblical Institute, 1968) 104-110.
6. L. W. King, Babylonian Boundary-Stones (London, British Museum, 1912) nos. 6 and 24.
7. Rykle Borger, "Gott Marduk und Gott-König Šulgi als Propheten: Zwei prophetische Texte," BiOr 28 (1971) 3-24.
8. K.3426 and K.2660. For bibliography on these texts see Brinkman, Political History p. 328, nos. 4.3.8 and 4.3.9. K.3426 (=CT 13 48) mentions Nebuchadnezzar by name, but K.2660 (=3 R 38 no. 2) may be about a somewhat later king, though Nebuchadnezzar still appears the most likely candidate.
9. DT 71; copy in BA 5 386-87. Manfred Weippert wants to connect it to Assurbanipal's defeat of the Elamites, and he points out that the name of the deity praised does not occur on the preserved part of the text (ZAW 84 [1972] 482 nn. 108-109), but the hymn's resemblance to the other texts celebrating the success of Nebuchadnezzar I argues for the earlier date.
10. K.344+BM 99067 (=4R[2] 20 no. 1+AJSL 35 [1918] 139) is accepted by Brinkman and listed with bibliography in Political History p. 329 no. 4.3.10. His reservations about the second text (ibid. p. 19 n. 81) may well have been dispelled by W. G. Lambert's masterful edition of the text which utilized additional pieces not known to Brinkman at the time ("Enmeduranki and Related Matters," JCS 21 [1967] 126-31). If both these texts deal with Nebuchadnezzar I's Elamite war, as they probably do, it is hard to dissociate DT 71, discussed above, from the same event.
11. A. Jeremias, "Die sogenannten Kedorlaomer-Texte," MVAG 21 (1916) 69-97. Pinches' copies in JTVI 29 (1897) 43-90 were not available to me.
12. See Brinkman, Political History p. 328 no. 4.3.6 and p. 329 no 4.3.11.
13. BBSt. 24 obv. 7-12.
14. BBSt. 6 i 12-13: *ūtaʾʾiršuma šar ilāni Marduk ana turri gimilli māt Akkadî ušatbâ kakkêšu.*

Ancient Near Eastern Studies in Memory of J. J. Finkelstein
Connecticut Academy of Arts and Sciences, Memoir 19

Nebuchadnezzar hardly needed an explanation—but it clearly implies that the Elamites had sinned against Marduk and his land in the past. After its report of Marduk's command, the text then describes the ensuing campaign. Its primary concern is to glorify Nebuchadnezzar and his servant LAK-ti-Marduk, for whose benefit the *kudurru* containing the inscription was set up, by relating their endurance and courage in the face of great adversity. Two further theological statements are made, however. The difficult march is achieved because "the gods carry" Nebuchadnezzar.[15] Moreover, the outcome of the battle was decided by the command of Ishtar and Adad; thus Nebuchadnezzar routed Ḫulteludish, king of Elam, who then disappeared permanently.[16]

Far more interesting theologically is the prophecy text recently re-edited by Borger.[17] This text has Marduk narrate past history in autobiographical form down to the time just prior to Nebuchadnezzar's Elamite campaign. As far as the often fragmentary text allows one to judge, the emphasis is on the earlier "trips" of Marduk's statue. Muršilis' capture and removal of Marduk's statue becomes a business trip ordered by Marduk himself to establish trade connections between Babylon and Ḫatti[18]:

> I gave the command. I went to the land of Ḫatti. I questioned Ḫatti. The throne of my Anu-ship I set up within it. I dwelt within it for 24 years, and I established within it the caravan trade of the Babylonians.

A sojourn in Assyria, no doubt reflecting Tukulti-Ninurta's removal of the Marduk statue following his victory over Kashtiliash, is also mentioned, but the reason for this trip is obscured by a break.[19] Marduk's favorable treatment of Assyria, however, suggests it was presented as a peaceful visit.[20]

Nevertheless, Marduk makes it clear that he was in charge of the situation; he may have gone away on trips, but he always returned[21]:

> I am Marduk the great lord. I alone am lord of destinies and decisions. Who has taken this road? Wherever I went, from there I returned.

This strong affirmation of Marduk's control of history following the recitation of past events involving the removal of Marduk's statue from Babylon prepares the stage for the god's interpretation of a more recent disaster, one apparently still too disquieting to be easily dismissed as a business trip—the Elamite conquest of Babylon and plunder of Marduk's statue. Marduk does not refer to the event as a defeat. Indeed Marduk asserts he himself gave the command for his departure from Babylon as well as for Babylon's subsequent misfortunes[22]:

> I myself gave the command. I went to the land of Elam, and all the gods went with me—I alone gave the command. The food offerings of the temples I alone cut off.

Marduk's very insistence on this point, however, suggests there were those who questioned this interpretation of history. Perhaps this doubt took concrete form as less than enthusiastic support by the nobility, army, or populace for Nebuchadnezzar's proposed Elamite campaign.[23] The campaign appears to have suffered initial setbacks which one of the later texts attributed to the baleful opposition of the rebellious god Erra.[24] Whether Nebuchadnezzar's contemporaries, like the later writer, interpreted this setback as a thwarting of Marduk's will by a rival god is uncertain, but it certainly could have raised questions about Marduk's control of history.[25]

15. BBSt. 6 i 22: *illak šarru nasqu ilāni našûšu.*

16. BBSt. 6 i 40-41: *ina pi Ištar u Adad ilāni bēlī tāḫāzi ulteshir Ḫulteludiš šar māt Elamti ītemid šadâšu.* Adad's help in this victory is also alluded to in another inscription of Nebuchadnezzar. See BiOr 7 (1950) 42-46 and plates I-III, and the additional references listed in Brinkman, Political History pp. 325-26 no. 4.2.1.

17. BiOr 28 (1971) 3-24.

18. BiOr 28 (1971) 5:13-19.

19. BiOr 28 (1971) 6, the beginning lines of K.7065.

20. BiOr 28 (1971) 7:12′.

21. BiOr 28 (1971) 7:18′-21′a.

22. BiOr 28 (1971) 7:21′b-24′.

23. CT 13 48:1-3 speaks of Nebuchadnezzar terrifying his nobles by his rage over Babylon's predicament, and though the text does not have that in mind, they were probably frightened by what Nebuchadnezzar intended to do about the situation. At any rate, 3R 38 no. 2 rev. 6′-8′ pictures the panic and despair which gripped even the Babylonian king prior to the first engagement.

24. 3R 38 no. 2 rev. 9′-11′:

[*itt*]*i sitāt nišī ina rēš Uknê ūqīšuma*
[*ul itū*]*ramma kī la libbi ilī Erra gašri ilī*
[*qur*]*ādīya unappiṣ*

[wit]h the rest of the people I waited for him alongside the Kerkha river.
[. . . did not] turn back, but Erra, strongest of the gods, against the will of the gods
shattered my [war]riors.

The text goes on to describe the effects of the plague and the fear which caused Nebuchadnezzar to withdraw, first to Kar-Dur-Apil-Sin, and subsequently from there as well (lines 12′-16′).

25. A unique biblical passage which contains a remark bearing some resemblance to this interference by a rival deity is the peculiar notice at the end of 2 Kings 3. Following Yahweh's oracle promising victory (3:18-19), the Israelites and their allies

According to Marduk, however, the time of his sojourn outside Babylon was over, he longed for his city, and he summoned the gods to once more bring their tribute to Babylon.[26] At this point, then, the actual prophecy begins[27]: a king will arise in Babylon who will renew the sanctuaries, and bring Marduk back. Happy conditions will once again exist in Babylon. In the process, this king, with whom Marduk and all the gods are in covenant, will thoroughly destroy Elam.[28] One could question whether this prophecy is not in fact a *vaticinium ex eventu*, particularly since it exists only in late copies, but the tone of the document argues for dating the original prior to Nebuchadnezzar I's Elamite victories.[29] Otherwise it is difficult to explain the great concern to underscore Marduk's control of history; after Nebuchadnezzar's successful execution of Marduk's orders such concern would have had little point. Thus the text would appear to be a genuine "prophecy of salvation" seeking credence by an appeal to past history.[30] As such, it would, of course, antedate Nebuchadnezzar's own inscriptions and perhaps provide part of the background for his statement that Marduk ordered him to avenge Akkad.

The other treatments of these historical events are neither identical to one another, nor do they all represent the same literary genres, but for the sake of convenience, they may all be discussed together without serious distortion of the evidence. Taken together, they provide us with a kind of schema for the interpretation of the various moments in the sequence from cause to disaster to resolution.

Several of the texts, at least as far as they are preserved, ignore the origin of the problem,[31] but one which traces its development through the reigns of several kings appears to place the blame on the "wicked Elamites,"[32] a motif that finds numerous echoes in the other texts.[33] Another text, however, while it holds no

---

relentlessly annihilate the Moabites (verses 20-26) until, in a final act of desperation, the Moabite king sacrifices his eldest son and successor to his throne on the city wall (verse 27a). The result of that offering, presumably made to his own god, is then stated in a peculiarly succinct manner (verse 27b):

wyhy qṣp gdwl ʿl yśrʾl wysʿw mʿlyw wyšbw lʾrṣ

And great wrath fell upon Israel, so they withdrew from him and returned home.

Yahweh is not mentioned as the agent of this wrath, and this raises some suspicion that the deuteronomic historian's source blamed Israel's discomfiture, not on Yahweh, but on the intervention of a Moabite deity well known in Israel.

If the Bible provides only the vaguest parallel to Erra's interference with the divine assembly's will, it provides very clear parallels to Marduk's insistent claim that he was the author of Babylon's defeat by Elam. A very instructive text in this regard is Ezek. 8:1-11:23. Yahweh was irritated because the Israelites left in Jerusalem were saying "Yahweh does not see; Yahweh has left the country" (8:12; 9:9). This view may have been based partly on the Babylonians' plundering of the temple treasures, presumably including the ark, in 597 B.C. (2 Kings 24:13). There is certainly evidence for a belief that equated the loss of the ark with the loss of Yahweh's presence (1 Sam. 4:21-22), and it may have been to counter this popular view that the importance of the ark was discounted in the oracle preserved in Jer. 3:16. At any rate, the saying that offended Yahweh, whatever its origin, denied Yahweh's control of history. He was no longer in charge of Jerusalem's fate. In response to this challenge Ezekiel asserts that Yahweh himself was planning the city's destruction (8:18ff.). This point is underscored with graphic symbolism when the fire that is to fall on the city is taken from between the cherubim, that is, from the fiery glory of the divine presence itself (10:2, 6).

Whether Ezekiel's prophecy convinced many of his contemporaries that the final destruction of Jerusalem was Yahweh's own work, perfectly compatible with his control of history, may be doubted, particularly in view of the unbelief confronted by the later Second Isaiah. (It must have been easier for the Babylonians to believe Marduk's happier prophecy with its similar claims, at least following Elam's defeat.) Ezekiel's oracle did, however, catch the imagination of later writers struggling to explain subsequent disasters in a way consonant with God's sovereignty. The author of the Syriac Apocalypse of Baruch, for instance, has Yahweh reassure Baruch that "the enemy will not overthrow Zion, nor shall they burn Jerusalem" (5:3). In fulfillment of that promise God first sends an angel who removes the most holy objects—the veil, the ark, its cover, the two tablets, the holy raiment of the priests, the altar of incense, the forty-eight precious stones of the high priest's adornment, and all the holy vessels—from the temple and commits them to the earth's keeping (6:5-10). Then four angels with burning lamps who have been standing at the four corners of Jerusalem overthrew its wall and burned the temple (6:4; 7:1-8:1). Only then are the human enemies of Jerusalem permitted to enter the city; its destruction is really the work of God alone (8:2-5).

26. BiOr 28 (1971) 8:12-17.

27. BiOr 28 (1971) 8:19ff.

28. BiOr 28 (1971) 11:21′-23′.

29. Borger leaves open both possibilities, BiOr 28 (1971) 21. There is certainly no valid *a priori* reason for rejecting this text as a genuine prophecy. Genuine prophecies promising victory to the king are well known from Mari and the later Assyrian oracles, and they often contain elements which function to allay doubts or fear in the king's mind. Marduk's insistence on his control of history may have had the same function in our text, particularly if it were composed in an attempt to get Nebuchadnezzar to move against Elam. Moreover, the promises made do not read like a description after the fact. Where they rise above vague traditional *topoi*, they read more like a priestly program than historical reality.

30. Yahweh argues in much the same way in Second Isaiah (41:2-4; 42:24-25; 46:9-13; 51:12-16; 52:4-12; 54:7-17).

31. CT 13 48; $4R^2$ 20 no. 1 and duplicates; and DT 71.

32. 3R 38 no. 2, especially obv. 4′-5′:

[*ša*] *eli abbēšu arna*<*šu*> *šūturu šurbû ḫīṭušu kabtu*

[*lemn*]*ēti ukappida ana māt Akkadî ibtani teqītu*

[(Kudur-naḫḫunti) . . . who]se sin was far greater than that of his forefathers, whose heavy crime exceeded theirs,

[. . .] planned wicked things against the land of Akkad, plotted insolence.

33. $4R^2$ 20 no. 1:12-13; DT 71:14-17, 10-12; JCS 21 (1967) 129:23; MVAG 21 (1916) 86:33; 90:33.

higher opinion of the Elamites, finds the cause in the Babylonians' own sins which provoked Marduk to anger and led him to command the gods to desert the land.[34] As a result, the people were incited to sin, became godless, and evil multiplied.[35] At this stage the Elamites entered to devastate the land, destroy the cult centers, and carry off the gods.[36] According to another text this evil took place according to the plan of Marduk.[37]

The removal of Marduk's statue, however, created some problems for this view. The text that places the blame on the Elamites uses language so similar to the Erra epic in describing Marduk's departure from the seat of his dominion that one must doubt that its author attributed the event to Marduk's own planning.[38] At worst he was taken into exile by force; at best, like the hapless victim of Erra's duplicity in the Erra epic, he was tricked. Even the text which traces the cause of the disaster to the Babylonians' sin leaves the impression that the Elamites carried the destruction further than Marduk intended, though Marduk remained in control of the situation.[39] After describing the behavior of the wicked Elamites, it significantly adds the comment, "Marduk . . . observed everything."[40] Such a motif could be merged with the interpretation that attributed the disaster to the god's planning,[41] but the text that actually talks about Marduk's planning underscores Marduk's control in a different, but highly effective manner. According to it, the wicked Elamite, when he entered the sanctuary to work his design on Marduk, was so terrified by the divine statue's splendor that he withdrew and tried to force a third party, the native priest, to do his dirty work.[42] Though this stands in marked contradiction to another text's statement that the Elamite did not fear Marduk's great divinity,[43] it effectively conveys the impression that the Elamites' removal of the statue was possible only by Marduk's acquiescence, and even then was not accomplished without considerable trepidation.

As a result of these disasters there was great lamentation in Babylon.[44] In his lament, king Nebuchadnezzar describes the pitiful situation in Babylon.[45] "How long," he asks Marduk, "will you live in an enemy land?"[46] He implores Marduk, "Remember Babylon the well-favored, turn your face to Esagil which you love."[47] The royal epic that mentions the initial disaster speaks of the people looking for Marduk's sign,[48] and after that setback, lamentation is renewed.[49] The end of this particular text is not preserved, so we can only guess at the outcome, but in the other texts, Nebuchadnezzar's prayer was heard.[50] The other epic relates that Marduk gave a favorable response, commanded Nebuchadnezzar to bring him back to Babylon, and promised him Elam as his reward.[51]

The description of Marduk's revenge on Elam is most detailed in the hymn to Marduk, perhaps because

34. JCS 21 (1967) 128:15-18a.

35. JCS 21 (1967) 128:18b-22.

36. JCS 21 (1967) 129:23-24.

37. MVAG 21 (1916) 88:4-5: *nakru Elamû urriḫ lemnētu u Bēl ana Bābili ušakpidu lemuttu*, "The Elamite enemy hastened his evil work, and Bel instigated evil against Babylon."

38. 3R 38 no. 2 obv. 10′: [*Marduk bē*]*la rabâ iddeki ina šubat* [*šarrūtīšu*], "The great lord [Marduk] he made rise from the throne of [his majesty]." This points more to a forcible removal than the passage in the Erra epic, where Erra tricks Marduk into leaving by promising him that he would mind the world while Marduk was away, see L. Cagni, L'Epopea di Erra, Studi Semitici 34 (Rome: Istituto di Studi del Vicino Oriente, 1969) 76-79, I 168-92. Both texts, however, speak of Erra acting against the will of the gods. See note 24 above, and compare Erra I 102: *bēlum Erra minsu ana ilāni* [*lemut*]*tim tak*[*pud*], "Lord Erra, why have you planned evil against the gods?"

39. JCS 21 (1967) 129:25.

40. JCS 21 (1967) 129:25. One may compare this with Isaiah's oracle against Assyria in Isa. 10:5-19.

41. As is true of the Isaiah passage mentioned above and in Nabonidus' very similar treatment of Sennacherib's desecration of Babylon (MVAG 1/1 [1896] 73ff. i 18-41; translated in ANET^2 [1955] 309). See my discussion in CBQ 38 (1976) 1-13.

42. MVAG 21 (1916) 86:20-29. The statue in question is actually referred to as that of En-nun-dagal-la, one of the lesser members of Marduk's divine entourage (CT 24 28:64; 15:9), but A. Jeremias suggested that this name may be used here as simply another name for Marduk (MVAG 21 [1916] 87 n. 3).

43. DT 71:15-16.

44. 4R^2 20 no. 1:5-10; CT 13 48:5-7.

45. CT 13 48:6-7: *aḫulap ina mātīya šaknū bakê u sapādu / aḫulap ina nišīya šaknū numbê u bakê*, "Be merciful! In my land there is weeping and mourning. Be merciful! Among my people there is wailing and weeping."

46. CT 13 48:8: *adi mati bēl Bābili ina māti nakiri ašbāti*? Cf. the similar "how long" formulations found in Israelite public laments (Psalms 74:10; 79:5; 80:5).

47. CT 13 48:9-10: [*li*]*b*?-*bal*-[*k*]*it ina libbīka Bābili banûmma* / [*an*]*a Esagil ša tarammu šusḫira panīka*. Compare this to the following biblical passages: *zkr ʿdtk qnyt qdm / gʾlt šbṭ nḥltk / hr ṣywn zh šknt bw*, "Remember your congregation which you acquired long ago, the tribe of your possession which you redeemed, Mount Zion in which you dwelt" (Ps. 74:2); *ʾlhym ṣbʾwt šwb nʾ / hbṭ mšmym wrʾh / wpqd gpn zʾt*, "God of hosts, turn back. Look from heaven and visit this vine" (Ps. 80:15).

48. 3R 38 no. 2 rev. 5′:*išteniʾū dīn Mar*[*duk*]. For the reading of the divine name as Marduk, see Brinkman, Political History p. 106 n. 575. What the Babylonians sought was an omen that the period of Marduk's wrath was over, but apparently they were disappointed. Compare Ps. 74:9: *ʾtwtynw lʾ rʾynw / ʾyn ʿwd nbyʾ / wlʾ ʾtnw ywdʿ ʿd mh*, "We have not seen our signs, there is no longer a prophet, and there is no one with us who knows, 'How long'."

49. 3R 38 no. 2 rev. 17′-24′.

50. 4R^2 20 no. 1:9-11; DT 71:10-12; and CT 13 48:11.

51. CT 13 48:12-18. The oracle is also mentioned in BBSt. 6 i 12-13 (see n. 14 above), and in BiOr 7 (1950) pl. III 16 (see Brinkman, Political History p. 106 n. 575).

the other texts are broken in precisely the places where this material would have been recorded.[52] It is striking that the hymn, in contrast to Nebuchadnezzar's inscriptions, ignores the king's role in the defeat of Elam, and attributes the whole victory to the deity.[53] The Elamite did not reverence Marduk's great divinity, but blasphemed.[54] He became haughty, trusted in himself, forgot Marduk's divinity, and broke his oath.[55] Thus the devastation wrought on Elam was a just punishment for the Elamite's sin. As a result of the victory, of course, Marduk returned in triumph and splendor to his own city and temple.[56]

Though the omen texts add little to the preceding sketch, one should perhaps note the temporal element mentioned in the apodosis of one[57]:

> . . . , the Umman-manda will arise and rule the land. The gods will depart from their daises, and Bel will go to Elam. It is said that after 30 years vengeance will be exercised, and the gods will return to their place.

This calls to mind the statement in the prophetic text, "I fulfilled my years"[58]; it speaks to the lamenting question, "How long?"[59]; and it has an analogue in the later tradition of Marduk's decision to leave Babylon for 70 years,[60] which in turn may be compared to Jeremiah's famous prophecy of the 70 year captivity.[61]

The preceding discussion is by no means a sufficient foundation upon which to base wide ranging comparative judgements on the theological significance of history in Mesopotamia and Israel. I have dealt with only one example of one typical event in Mesopotamia, and I have limited my discussion of the comparative biblical material, giving only the briefest hints as to where I think one should turn for the most relevant parallels. In my judgement, however, it is this kind of detailed examination of individual episodes which must be extended further, both on the Mesopotamian and biblical sides, before comparative judgements can be either significant or meaningful, much less serve as fundamental elements of interpretive constructs.[62] If the discussion has persuaded anyone to take a fresh look at the way history was theologically interpreted in Mesopotamia or Israel, it has accomplished its modest goal.

52. 4R^{2} 20 no. 1, while it contains the king's lament and Marduk's positive response, has no picture of the devastation of Elam. It moves immediately from positive response to a description of Marduk's return. This is surprising, and it may suggest that the description of devastation (lines 1-4) found before the lament (lines 5ff.) actually pictures Marduk's treatment of Elam. If so, the lament would be for a positive oracle to return the divine statue rather than for victory over the Elamites. Note that after Agum-kakrime received divine orders to return Marduk on an earlier occasion, he still went to the trouble of consulting Šamaš (5R 33 i 44-ii 8), and we actually have several inquiry texts in which Assurbanipal seeks divine approval for his plans to return Marduk to Babylon (J. A. Knudtzon, Assyrische Gebete an den Sonnengott [Leipzig, 1893] nos. 104, 105, and 149).

53. It might be well to rethink Israel's hymnic celebration of the deliverance at the Reed Sea in that light.

54. DT 71 obv. 14-15: [*Elam*]*û ša la pitluḫu rabītu ilūssu* [*eli*] *ilūtīšu ṣīrtu iqbû mēriḫtu*.

55. DT 71 rev. 10-12: [. . .] *ušarriḫa ramānšu* [. . .] *ittaklu emūqu* [. . . *l*]*a iḫsusa ilūtka*; rev. 19-20: [. . .] *zikirka kabtu* [. . .] *ḫu la*? *aṣ-ṣu-ru ma-mit-su*.

56. 4R^{2} 20 no. 1:12f.

57. 3R 61 no. 2:21′-22′: *Umman-manda itebbīma māta ibēl parakkī ilū itebbûma Bēl ana Elamti illak iqqabbi ina* 30 *šanāti tuqtû uttarru ilū rabūtu* <*ana*> *ašrīšunu iturrū*. See Brinkman, Political History p. 108 n. 585.

58. BiOr 28 (1971) 8:12: *ūmīya umallīma šanātīya umallīma*. The idea that there were predetermined limits to the periods of divine wrath which could be discovered through omens or oracles (see n. 48 above) was widespread. Cf. Nabonidus' statement: 21 *šanāti qirib Aššur irtame šubassu imlû ūmū ikšuda adannu inūḫma uzzašu libbi šar ilī bēl bēli Esagil u Bābili iḫsus šubat bēlūtīšu*, "For 21 years he (Marduk) established his seat in Assur, but when the days were fulfilled and the set time arrived, his anger abated, and the heart of the king of the gods, the lord of lords, remembered Esagil and Babylon, the seat of his lordship" (MVAG 1/1 [1896] 73ff. i 23-24).

59. This was a crucial question during times of tribulation, whether those tribulations affected a group (see notes 46 and 48, above), or only a single individual. As an example of the latter, see the lament of the sufferer in Ludlul, *u adanna siliʾtīya bārû ul iddin*, "Nor has the diviner put a time limit on my illness," BWL 44-45:111. When a time limit was given, and it passed without the hoped-for change, that was the source of even greater discouragement: *akšudma ana balāṭ adanna īteq*, "I survived to the next year; the appointed time passed" BWL 38-39:1.

This may be another part of the background to the Israelites' discouraging assessment, "Yahweh has left the country," discussed in note 25 above. Ezekiel's oracle in which this sentiment is expressed is dated to the sixth month of the sixth year (Ezek. 8:1), or exactly two years and one month after Hananiah gave his famous oracle in which Yahweh promised, "Within two years I will bring back to this place all the vessels of Yahweh's house, which Nebuchadnezzar king of Babylon took away from this place and carried to Babylon . . . ." (Jer. 28:1-4; LXX preserves the original date formula in verse 1). With the failure of so much of the favorable prophecies of that period (Jer. 27:16ff.), it is no wonder that the psalmist could say, "We have not seen our signs, there is no longer a prophet, and there is no one with us who knows 'How long'" (Ps. 74:9). It was not so much that there were no prophets, it is simply that their words had failed, and they had lost credibility.

60. R. Borger, Die Inschriften Asarhaddons, Königs von Assyrien, AfO Beiheft 9 (Graz, 1956) 14-15 Episodes 6-10.

61. Jer. 29:10.

62. See my critical remarks on one such construct in CBQ 38 (1976) 1-13. For the application of this approach to biblical material see the forthcoming monograph jointly authored by P. D. Miller, Jr. and this writer, The Hand of the Lord: A Study of 1 Sam. 2:12-17, 22-25, 27-36, 4:1b-7:1.

A BLESSING OF KING URNINURTA

Åke W. Sjöberg
The University Museum
University of Pennsylvania

CT 36 28-30 (BM 96697) is a balag hymn to the goddess Inanna, concerned with the blessing of King Urninurta of Isin by the gods An and Enlil. This composition was treated by A. Falkenstein in ZA 49 (1950) 106-112 (transliteration and translation) and pp. 122-137 (philological commentary); see also S. Langdon, JRAS (1925) 487ff., and also A. Falkenstein's translation of this composition in SAHG pp. 105-109 (No. 21). S. N. Kramer has published his collations of CT 6 28-30 in Iraq 36 (In Honour of Sir Max Mallowan, 1974) 93-97, with some improvements of Falkenstein's treatment. In this article, dedicated to the memory of Professor Jacob J. Finkelstein, I publish for the first time CBS 8088, a duplicate of BM. No. 96697. The tablet contains four columns (obv. i-ii; rev. i-ii), unfortunately with many breaks. It measures: length 15 cms., width 9 cms., and thickness 2.7 cms. The text was found in Nippur; it was catalogued in the University Museum on April 23, 1917.

The subscript is not preserved in the London text, cf. Falkenstein, ZA 49 (1950) 84. My restorations of the end of the composition as [ki-šú]-bi-im "it is its [finale]" followed by [balag]-^{d}inanna-kam depend on CT 36 38 end: ki-šú-bi-im balag-^{d}inanna-kam; this balag composition contains 28 ki-ru-gú's; further RA 17 (1920) 50: ki-šú-bi-im balag-dingir-maḫ; it contains 9 ki-ru-gú's. For these two balag compositions, see H. Hartmann, Die Musik der sumerischen Kultur pp. 210f.; see further J. Krecher, Sumerische Kultlyrik p. 30 (b. Balag).

Text A: CBS 8088
Obv. and Rev.

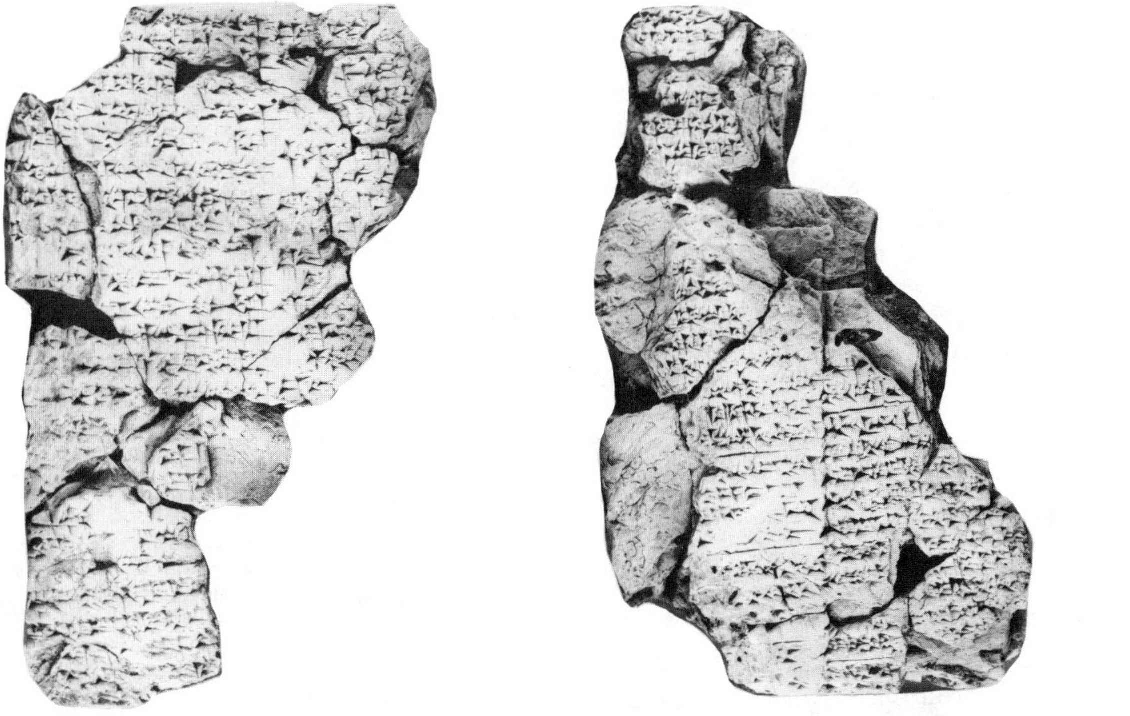

CBS 8088 (text A), i=1-20; ii=21-29; iii (rev. i)=55-69; iv=70-end (A has an extra line following 71). Note that in text B (BM 96697=CT 36 29-30) the first line of the composition is broken away.

Ancient Near Eastern Studies in Memory of J. J. Finkelstein
Connecticut Academy of Arts and Sciences, Memoir 19

[x x x x (x)]-ru? maḫ?-a-ni zà nu-sá[1]
[x x x x (x)] x x gi₆-ù-na kár-kár
[   ]-a ní me-lám [gùr]-ru
[x x]-gá-ni-šè dingir-gal-gal-e-ne ḫu-luḫ-ḫa im-⌜du₈-du₈⌝

5. [x]x-du₁₁[1]-ga-ni an-gin$_x$ maḫ ᵈen-líl-gin$_x$ u$_x$-ru
   ⌜ᵈinanna⌝ sag-kal me-nì[1]-nam-ma zà-dib-nin-e-ne
   [g]iš-ḫur-nam-lugal-la šu-du₇-du₇ ki[1]-bi gi₄-gi₄-dè
   [sag]-gi₆ si-sá-sá-e-dè[1] ús-gi-na dab₅-bé-dè
   geštú-ga-ni[1] [n]am-gub[2] šà-ga-né[3] zi-dè-eš-e nam-túm[4]

10. [ᵈ]ur-ᵈnin-urta nam-sipa-zi-gál-la-šè un-šár-ra mi-ni-in-pà[1]
    [x] nàm-tar-ra[1] me-zi ḫal-ḫa-dingir-gal-gal-e-ne-šè[2]
    é-kur ki-tuš-kù-an-ᵈen-líl-lá ní su-zi gùr-ru-šè[1]
    lugal-ra šu-ni im-ma-an-dab₅ sun$_x$(BÚR)-na-bi mi-ni-in-ku₄
    in-nin e-ne-da-nu [a]n*[1]-ki-a nam nu-tar-re-dè

15. an ᵈen-líl-da bára-ge₄-si-a-na ad mu-un-na-ni-ib-gi₄*-gi₄[1]
       ki-ru-gú-diš-a-kam
    an-gal du₁₁-ga-zu nì-maḫ-àm a-ba-a šu mi-ni-ib[1]-bal-e
    a-a ᵈen-líl nam-gal tar-ra-zu ság-di nu-zu-a
    ᵈur-ᵈnin-urta šul á-ág-gá-ne-ne DI-DI mu-un-zu-a-ar[1]

20. nam-sipa-zi-gál-un-šár-ra du-rí-šè sag-e-eš rig₇-ga-na-ab-z[é]-en[1]
    é uru.ki dù-dù[1] kalam gi-né šà-kù-ta mu-u₈-túm
    kur-kur-re á-ág-gá-bi mu-un-zu á-gal ḫé-ág-e[1]
    U.ENKARA[1]-a-né ki-bal ḫé-en-GAM-e ús-gi ḫé-bí-ib-dab₅-bé[2]
    sig-ta igi-nim-šè kalam-ma rab$_x$(LUGAL)-gin$_x$ šu ḫé-em-ri-ri-e[1]

25. ka-ta-è-a-ni [. . .]/[1]
    udu-gin$_x$ ka ú-kú ḫa-ba-kin*-kin* gú a-nag ḫa-ba-gá-gá[1]
       ki-ru-gú-min-kam-ma-àm
    ᵈur-ᵈnin-urta mu-sud-rá-šè un-gá ᵈutu-gin$_x$ dalla ḫé-ni-in-è*[1]
    giš-gi-gál-bi-im

30. dingir numun-è a-a-nì-nam-šár-ra-ke₄
    lugal-ra gù-zi mu-na-an-dé nam mu-ni-ib-tar-re
    giš-eren-suḫ me-te-kisal-é-kur-ra
    ᵈur-ᵈnin-urta kalam-ma gizzu-zu ní ḫé-eb-ši-te-en-te-en
    kur-kur-re sipa-zi-bi ḫé-me-en

35. ᵈutu-gin$_x$ di-si-sá ku₅-ru-zu-uš igi-bi ḫé-em-ši-gál-e
    bára-nam-lugal-la suḫuš-gi-na-ba
    ᵈur-ᵈnin-urta dúr-gar-ra-zu-dè sag an-šè ḫé-ni-in-íl
    aga*-zi-dè me-te ḫé-em-mi-in-gál
    ní su-zi ur-maḫ-nam-lugal-la túg-ma₆-šè ḫé-em-mu₄

40.   ki-ru-gú-èš-kam-ma-àm
    é-ana$_x$(AN)-ka me-bi ḫa-ba-gub-bé

Notes to the transliteration:

1. 1: line broken away in text B.
5. 1: sign collated by S. N. Kramer, text B; text A has clearly KA = du₁₁-.
6. 1: text A has -nì-, cf. Kramer on text B.
7. 1: text B has ki- (coll.), so also text A.
8. 1: B: si-sá-e-dè; A: si-sá-sá-[e]-dè.
9. 1: A: GIŠ.T[ÚG].PI-ni; B: [GIŠ].TÚG.PI-ga-ni. — 2: [n]am-gub; B: na-an-gu[b]. — 3: text A has two partially erased signs (šà ni) before šà-ga-ni. — 4: B: one line; A: last part indented.
10. 1: B: one line; A: last part indented.
11. 1: B: nam-tar-re. — 2: A: me-⌜zi⌝ ḫal-ḫa-dingir-gal-e-ne-šè; B: me-zi ḫa[l- x]-dingir-gal-gal-e-ne-šè.
12. 1: A: gùr-ru-šè; B (coll.): KÁRA-šè.

14. 1: no traces of sign in copy (text B), coll.
15. 1: last part of line indented in text A.
17. 1: -íb- in A where last part of the line is indented.
19. 1: last part of line indented in text A.
20. 1: last part of line indented in text A.
21. 1: A has é uru.ki dù-dù; text B: ? uru dù-dù (see S. N. Kramer's collation of this line).
22. 1: last part of line indented in text A.
23. 1: text A may have ENKARA instead of U.ENKARA in text B. — 2: last part of line indented in text A.
24. 1: last part of line indented in text A.
25. 1: this line is omitted in text B.
26. 1: last part of line indented in text A.
28. 1: dalla ḫ[é . . . .] indented in text A.

^{d}ur-^{d}nin-urta bàd-gal-zu gá-e-me-en u$_4$-ul-du-rí-šè
g̃iš-gi$_4$-gál-bi-im
erím-gál-za u$_4$-gin$_x$ gù bí-ra
me-lám-zu muru$_x$(IM.DUGUD)-dugud-da-gin$_x$ kur nu-še-ga-zu ḫé-em-dul
[bár]a-bára-gal-gal ní-G̃ÌR-e-ne
[x x x] x x gi-dili-dù-a-gin$_x$ kìlib-ba-bi sag ḫé-em-da-sìg-ge-ne
[x x]x-ra LI NE [. . . .][1]
[im-u$_x$]-lu-gin$_x$ zi-zi-da-zu-dè
[k]ur-ki-bal-zu sì-ge*[1] ù-mu-e-AK
un-bi LÚ×GÁNA-a um-mu-DU.DU
ì-si-in.ki uru-me-gal-gal-la-za
^{d}ur-^{d}nin-urta g̃iš-⌈šudun⌉ gú-ba gar-ni
an-gal a-[a]-dingir-re-e-ne-ke$_4$
^{d}ur-^{d}nin-urta sipa-g̃iš-tuku-ni-ir nam ul-šè nu-kúr-ru mu-ni-in-tar[1]
ki-ru-gú-limmu-kam-ma-àm[1]
en eš[1]-bar-an-ki šu-na gál kur-gal ^{d}en-líl-le
lugal-ra mu-ni an-zà-šè pa-è im-ma-an-ak/a$_5$
^{d}ur-^{d}nin-urta nam-nir nam-šul-la am-gin$_x$ gú ḫé-ni-peš
^{d}ir$_9$-ra ur-sag-gin$_x$ me x [x]-an-TUK-TUK
^{d}nin-urta en u$_4$-ḫuš-erím-ma dumu-šu-gar-gi$_4$-mu
ki-mè-ka KA[1]-tab-zu ḫé-a[2] giskim ḫé-mu-e-ti-le
kur-gú-erím gú-bi-da [x]?-zu zar-re-eš ḫa-ma-ab-sal-e
šu-luḫ-kù-é-kur-ra ba-an-ši-i[b-   ]-en u$_4$-šú-uš-e gub-ba[1]
nindaba*-zu banšur-maḫ unú*-gal*-gá sud-rá-šè ḫé-em-mi-in-gál[1]
sag ḫé-e-íl[1] g[ú a]n-šè ḫé-e-zi[2] ti nu-kúr-ru za-a-àm
ki-ru-gú-iá-kam-ma-àm[1]
nam-tar[1]-ra an-gal [^{d}n]u-nam-nir en-nì-zi-gál-la-šè
^{d}a-nun-na dingir-gal-gal-e-ne ḫè-ám ba-ni-in-ne-eš
sag-gi$_6$ ki-tuš-ba ge-en-ge-né kur-kur ús-a sì-ke[1]
un[x]x[x]x ka-téš gá-gá g̃ìri-ni-šè GAM-e[1]
^{d}inanna dumu-gal-⌈^{d}⌉su[e]n-na nitadam-ki-ág-gá-né[1]
sag-kešda* me-nì-nam-ma mu-un-ur$_4$-ur$_4$ šu-ni-šè mu-u$_8$-gar
mìn-na-ne-ne ki-^{d}en-líl-lá-ta ḫúl-la nam-[ta]-è
é*?-gal*? ki-tuš làl* nì-du$_{10}$-ba dúr ki ba-ni-in-gál-le-eš[1]
[x]x x-e lugal-la-ni nu-til-e zi-dè-eš na-mu-un-e
ki-ru-gú-àš-[kam]-ma-àm
[š]ul me-dím-sa$_6$-sa$_7$ x [š]e-er-[še]-er-ra sag*-íl*-i*-dè*
ḫi-li ul gùr-ru me-te-na-ám-ù-mu-un-na bára*-kù-ge du$_7$-re$_6$
^{d}ur-^{d}nin-urta me-kal-kal-la-zu šà-ab-mu im-mi-ir
i-bí-zi-íl-la-za mi-ni-in-pà-dè mu-pà-da-mu-me-en
an*-gal-e kur-zà-til-la-ba sù-ud-šè bí-in-diri-ge

48. 1: text B rev. 1.

50. 1: "probably GI rather than BI" (Kramer).

55. 1: based on text B; two full lines in text A. Text A rev. i 1′: (^{d}ur-^{d}n[in-. . . . .]).

56. 1: omitted in text A which however has a dividing line after this line.

57. 1: preserved in text A.

62. 1: text B rev. 15 KA (copy, no coll. by Kramer); text A may have s[ag-. — 2: text A: ḫé-em.

64. 1: A: [. . . . .-n]a ba-ši-íb-NE-⌈NE⌉ x[. . . .]; B: ba-ši-i[b-]-en.

65. 1: text A: ⌈PAD.^{d}INANNA⌉-zu banšur?-maḫ unú(TE.UNU)-gal-x x; A: nindaba*-zu ban[šur-x] unú*-gal*-gá.

66. 1: A: sag ḫè-e-íl; B: sag ḫe-íl. — 2: AL ḫé-é-[; B: ḫé-zi.

67. 1: omitted in text A which however has a dividing line after this line.

68. 1: also text B has -tar- (Kramer).

70. 1: text A rev. ii 1.

71. 1: Falkenstein restores the first part of this line (text B) ukù-[kur-nu-š]e-[ga] ka-téš . . .; text A seems to have]-re ka-téš gá-gá.

72. 1: text A has an extra line following line 71 (only few traces preserved); it cannot be an indented line 71b g̃íri-ni-šè GAM-e since there was enough space for the second part of this line in text A following ka-téš gá-gá.

75. 1: Kramer collated text B as follows: é*?-gal*? ki-tuš làl*-níg-dùg-kalam-ma but text A has nì-du$_{10}$-ba dúr ki ba-ni-[. A: l]àl.

úr*-kù-nam-ti-la SI.A-mu u$_4$-zu sù-sù-dè[1]
šul* ^{d}en-líl-le é-kur-ta á![1]-bi mu-un-da-an-ág[2]
x x* [bá]ra mí-zi-dè-eš-du$_{11}$-ga-mu / mù̌š nam-bí-ga-ga-an[1 2]
^{d}nanna* an-kù-ga pa-è-a ka-na-ág-e u$_6$*-di-gin$_x$[1]
[^{d}u]r-^{d}nin-urta-mu kur-kur-re ḫi-li ḫu-mu-u$_8$-ši-ak-e[1]
  ki-ru-gú-imin-kam-ma-àm[1]
^{d}ur-^{d}nin-urta-mu ^{d}mu-ul-líl-le /nam-sipa-ka-na-ág-gá-kam zi-dè-eš mu-un-p[à-d]è-en[1]
giš-[g]i$_4$-gá[l]-bi-im
[. . .]x KA-kù eš-bar-zi du$_{11}$-ga nu-kúr-ru-mu-uš[1]
[. . . . . .] á-nun ḫé-em-te-gál[1]
[. . . . .]-an-TUK-TUK x[1]

[ki-šú]-bi-im
[balag]-^{d}inanna-kam

[. . . . .] . . , when she appears great, no one can keep pace with her,
[. . . . . . .] . . . in the night glowing,
[. . . . .]. . . who is garbed in awe-inspiring sheen,
By her [ord]ers the great gods are filled with fear,
Her . . . utterance is great like (that of) An, mighty(?) like (that of) Enlil,
Inanna, (she is) foremost, with all me's, surpassing among the divine Ladies,
She makes perfect the rules of kingship; to 'restore' it
(And) to provide justice for the black-headed people and to let them have a stable governance,
She has set her mind and truly yearned for;
Among the numerous people, she has called Urninurta to be the shepherd for the living beings.
Into [the house] where destiny is determined, where the (divine) me's are distributed to the great gods,
Into the Ekur, the holy seat of An (and) Enlil, that is garbed in awe and fear,
She made the king whom she took by the hand, humbly enter,
(There) the Lady without whom no destiny is determined in heaven (and) earth,
Is sitting with An (and) Enlil on the dais, taking counsel with them.
  It is the first kirugu.
(She says:)
"Great An, your command is great, who can revoke it?
Father Enlil, the great destiny you determine, no (one) knows (how) to 'scatter' it,
To Urninurta, the youthful man who knows (how) to carry out your(!) order,
Bestow upon him the 'shepherdship' over the living beings, the numerous people!
(How) to build houses and cities, (how) to 'make firm' the land he has brought (with him) from the pure womb,
He knows (how) to give orders to all countries, he may give a great order!
May his sibir(-staff) subdue the hostile country, may he let it have a stable governance,
From below to above may he *clamp down* upon the land like a neck-stock(?),
[May] his utterance [. . .] . . . [. . .],
As for sheep, may he search for food (for them) to eat, may he let them have water to drink!"
  It is the second kirugu.

83. 1: line read according to text B; text A: [. . . .]-mu? e ki ⌜x x u$_4$⌝-zu x [x x].
84. 1: text B copy has DA. text A á-bi. — 2: A: mu-da-an-ág.
85. 1: text A: nam-bi(for bí)-ga-ga-an. — 2: mù̌š nam- etc. indented in B but not in A.
86. 1: A: kalam-e u$_6$-di-dè.
87. 1: text A: ḫu-mu-ši-ak-e.
88. 1: omitted in text A which however has a dividing line following line 87.
89. 1: text A: [. . . . nam-sipa]-kalam-ma-šè [. . . . mu]-un-p[a-d]è-en (two lines).
91. 1: text A: [. . . .]-kù eš-bar-zi du$_{11}$-ga nu-kúr-ru-mu-uš (one line); text B: [. . . .]-x-kù KA-kù eš-[. . . .] / nu-kúr-[. . . .].
92. 1: A: [. . . . á]-⌜nun⌝ ḫ[é-. . . .].
93. 1: only in text A: last x may be an erasure.

May Urninurta come forth among the people like Utu during the 'long year'!
It is its antiphon.
The god who lets the seed grow, the father of everything,
Said truly to the king, determining his destiny:
"Chosen cedar, the befitting one for the courtyard of the Ekur,
Oh Urninurta, may the land refresh itself in your shadow,
May you be the shepherd of all lands,
May they look upon you when you, like Utu, make a just verdict,
When you take your seat upon the royal dais with its firm foundation,
May you, Urninurta, proudly raise (your) head towards the sky,
May the legitimate crown be the befitting one,
May you dress in the robe, (full of) awe (and) fear, the 'lion of kingship'!"
It is the third kirugu.
"In the Eanna may you place its (divine) me's!
Oh Urninurta, I am your great wall for ever!"
It is its antiphon.
"Down upon your enemy you scream like a stormwind,
May your sheen like a heavy raincloud cover the land which is disobedient to you,
The great sovereigns, the powerful ones(?),
Because of you[r clamor] may tremble like a solitary reed,
[. . .] . . . [. . .]
You rise like the Sou[th wind],
(And) when you have plotted against the hostile land,
When you have taken its people prisoners,
In Isin, your city of the great (divine) me's,
Place on their neck, Urninurta, the yoke!"
The great An, the father of the gods,
Determined (it) as a destiny, everlasting (and) unchangeable, for Urninurta, his obedient shepherd.
It is the fourth kirugu.
The En, who has in his hand the decision of heaven (and) earth, the Great Mountain Enlil,
Let for the king his name come forth (reaching) the outer limit of heaven:
"Urninurta! In authority (and) youthfulness may you 'make fat' your neck like a wild bull!
Like Irra, the heroic warrior, . . . [. . .] . . . ,
Ninurta, the En, the furious storm for the enemy, the son, my avenger,
May be your *helper* on the battlefield, may you put your trust in him,
The enemy land . . . may he spread out in heaps for me!
The holy šuluḫ-rite of the Ekur . . . , serving daily,
Your offerings may be everlasting on the lofty altar in my Unugal!
May you raise (your) head, may you lift (your) neck towards the sky, life, unchangeable, is yours!"
It is the fifth kirugu.
The destiny determined by the great An (and) Nunamnir, the En of all living beings,
The anunna, the great gods, say "So it may be!" (to it).
To 'make firm' the black-headed people in their dwelling-place, to guide all lands,
To put . . . people in unison, to bow them down to his foot,
Inanna, the great daughter of Suen, his beloved spouse,
Gathered . . . all (divine) me's and placed them in his hand:
Both, in joy, went out from the place of Enlil,
In the Palace, the dwelling-place (full of) sweet honey, they took their seats,
. . . her king . . . does not cease, she truly speaks to him.
It is the sixth kirugu.
"Youthful man with beautiful (and) well-formed limbs, . . . in radiance proudly lifting (his) head,
Full of charm and beauty, fit for the lordship, worthy of the pure dais,
Urninurta, I have determined (to give you) your precious (divine) me's,

When(?) you truly lifted your eye, I called you, you are the one I called,
The great An has made you surpassing forever in the outer limit of the 'mountain',
The pure lap of life . . . to make your days long,
Has Enlil in the Ekur commanded, youthful man,
. . . the dais I care for, you shall not cease (to sit on it),
Like at Nanna, when he appears in the pure sky, admired by the land,
May all lands rejoice at you, Urninurta.
It is the seventh kirugu.
Urninurta, Mullil has truly called you to be the shepherd of the land."
It is its antiphon.
"[. . .]. my holy word(?) (and) decision which cannot be changed,
[. . .] may lordly strength be with(?) you,
[. . . . .] . . . ."

It is its [finale].
It is a [balag] for Inanna.

Notes to Text

1. maḫ-a-ni zà nu-sá also occurs in TCS 3 43:443 (referring to Ninazu) and BE 29 1 rev. iii 37 (TCS 3 133:443; see now Å. W. Sjöberg, Kramer Anniversary Volume, p. 418 line 117).

2. gi$_6$-ù-na kár-kár referring to Inanna also occurs in ZA 52 (1957) 59, VAT 9205:26 (cf. Falkenstein's commentary ZA 52 [1957] 72).

4. In text A there is space enough for [á-ág]-gá-ni-šè before dingir-gal-gal-e-ne.

11. A. Falkenstein: [nin] nam-tar-re; S. N. Kramer, Iraq 36 (1974) 96 fn. 12:11. "Into the house that decrees the fates": [é] nam-tar-re, cf. UET 6/1 118 rev. i (col. iii) 12-16 (cf. K. Oberhuber, ArOr 35 [1967] 263 f.) = dupl. CBS 10512 rev. 5′-6′ (cf. OrSuec 23-24 [1974-75] 159 n. 1): èš-bi èš-za-gin èš nam-tar-re-dam é-kur é-za-gìn é nam-tar-re-dam.

13. While text A has gùr-ru (at the end), text B has KÁRA=guru$_6$=*našû* (AHw 1 762 s.v. *našû* II: guru$_9$).

21. I read kalam gi-né (Falkenstein: ukù gi-né) because of giš-gidri-nì-si-sá kalam ge-en-ge-en = *ḫaṭṭi mīšarim mu-ki-na-at mātim*, RA 39 (1942-1944) 10:112ff.

23. For ENKARA and U.ENKARA, cf. J. van Dijk, MIO 12 (1966) 70.

33. We expect kalam-e (subject) instead of kalam-ma. For ní te-en(-te-en) "to refresh oneself, to cool off," see TCS 3 132.

39. A reading téš-maḫ-nam-lugal-la instead of ur-maḫ-man-lugal-la (téš = *baštu* "dignity; pride") may be preferable; cf. ZA 49 (1950) 116:15 su-zi me-te-nam-dingir-ra ur-maḫ-nam-lugal-la where also a reading téš-maḫ-nam-lugal-la seems preferable; see finally Nisaba Hymn, line 76 á-ág-gá-nam-lugal-la mu-e-gá-gá ur-maḫ (one text omits -maḫ) mu-dul-e-en (var. mu-du$_7$-du$_7$-e) which D. Reisman, S. N. Kramer Anniversary Volume p. 342, translates as follows: "He performs the duties of kingship for you, you overcome a lion (for him)" where téš-maḫ mu-dul-e-en "you cover him with great pride" might be preferable. See also UET 6/2 104:48 UR-maḫ-en-[na]-bi-šè: H. Steible, Rīmsîn, mein König, Freiburger Altorientalische Studien 1 (1975) 37, "Löwen des en-tums" (ur-maḫ-).

46. Falkenstein reads ní-ḫuš-e-ne "die schrecklichen"; a reading ní-gìr or ní-ir$_9$ (corresponding to Akk. *mugdašru*) is also a possibility, cf. Å. W. Sjöberg, OrNS 35 (1966) 300, where I quote our line and translate "die grossen (Herren, die) auf den Hochsitzen (thronen), die überlegene Kraft besitzen"; cf. also ZA 63 (1973) 11 commentary to line 40.

47. For gi-dili-dù-a and gi-dili-dù-a-gin$_x$ sag-sìg(-sìg), see B. Alster, Dumuzi's Dream, pp. 91ff. where our line (p. 92) has been restored as [za-pa-ág-z]u-šè gi-dili-.

50. For sì-ga ak (sì-ki ak) "to plot, pursue, strive for," see Å. W. Sjöberg, ZA 65 (1975) 221 commentary to line 69 where this passage is quoted.

51. For DU.DU.=laḫ$_x$(=**šalālu*), cf. Sjöberg, OrSuec. 23-24 (1974-75) 174 commentary to No. 3, text A rev. i = B obv. i line 15′.

73. References for sag-kešda (some of them in connection with me = *parṣu*) have been collected by A. Falkenstein in ZA 47 (1942) 215. Falkenstein interprets sag-kešda (in agreement with H. Zimmern, Lipitištar p. 29) as = sag-kešda-ak = *naʾādu* ("aufmerken, aufpassen, beachten"); in ZA 49 (1950) 139, he preferred a translation "(be)hüten"; cf. Hallo-van Dijk, YNER 3 88 sag-kešda "watch, guard" (= *itʾudu*). Add: A. Falkenstein, ZA 52 (1957) 59:9 (Inanna) nam-lugal sag-kešda me-nì-nam-ma šu-zu la-ba-ra-è (line read according to Falkenstein's copy ZA 52 [1957] 57); SRT 36:50 sag-kešda-me-zi-za, see G. R. Castellino, RSO 32 (1957) 19, where he translates (in agreement with Falkenstein) "L'attento al tuo fedele decreto." A translation of sag-kešda in our line as "to guard" or "guard" (s.) is highly doubtful; also ZA 52 (1957) 59:9 remains difficult. Cf. MSL 13 235 Kagal Tabl. B i 46-47 sag-kéš = [. . .], sag-kéš = [. . .].

83. Cf. S. N. Kramer, Iraq 36 (1974) 97 fn. 23.

92. For the expression á-nun ḫé-em-te-gál, cf. Å. W. Sjöberg, ZA 63 (1973) 36 No. 5:51.

TWO OLD-BABYLONIAN ROYAL INSCRIPTIONS

Edmond Sollberger
Department of Western Asiatic Antiquities
The British Museum

The Old-Babylonian royal inscriptions published here are known only from my French translations in IRSA.[1] Since the planned companion volume of transliterations is not likely to appear in the very near future, I offer here a full edition of these two texts as a modest tribute to the memory of a very close friend and fellow Old Babylonian.

1.   BM 64265 = 82-9-18,4241 (=IRSA IVC6l). Fragment from top of tablet, reverse completely destroyed, maximum dimensions 82×69 mm., provenance Sippar. Neo-Babylonian copy of royal inscription[2] of Ḥammu-rāpī.

    ḫa-am-mu-ra-pí diğir kalam-[ma-na]
    lú an-né me-lám nam-lugal-la mu-u[n-dul₅-la]
    ᵈen-líl-le nam-a-ni gal-le-eš bí-i[n-tar-ra]
    ní-tuku ka sì-sì-ke diğir gal-gal-e-ne
5.   [šà-ba]l-bal su-mu-la-DIĜIR dumu-nita kala-ga ᵈEN.ZU-mu-ba-[l]í-iṭ
    [num]un da-ri-a nam-lugal-la
    [luga]l kala-ga lugal KÁ.DIĜIR.RA.ki
    [lug]al da-ga-an kur mar-tu [me-en]
    du₁₁-ga gu-la an ᵈen-líl-bi-da-g[é]
10.   giskim-ti ᵈutu ᵈiškur-bi-da-gé
    [usu] maḫ ᵈAMAR.UTU-a-ta
    [me-lám ᵈz]a-ba₄-ba₄ ᵈinana-e-ne-bi-t[a]
    [zà zi-da] gin-na-ğu₁₀
    [   ] NI x [   ]
15.   [   ]UD? x [·   ]
    [   ] x [   ]
    . . . . .

    I, Ḥammu-rāpī, the god of his country,
    whom An has covered with royal splendour,
    whose great fate Enlil has decreed,
    who reveres, who fervently prays to the great gods,
5.   the scion of Sumu-la-Ilum, the mighty heir of Sîn-muballiṭ,
    of very ancient royal lineage,
    the mighty king, the king of Babylon,
    the king of the entire Martu-land:—
    (by) the great command of An and Enlil,
10.   (by) the omen of Utu and Iškur,
    by the supreme power of Marduk,
    by the splendour of Zababa and Inana
    who walk at my right side,
    . . . . .

1. The epithet, which is applied to kings of the Ur and Isin dynasties (references in Seux, Epithètes p. 389), is nowhere else used for Ḥammu-rāpī. It shows that, although they never spelt their names with the divine

---

1. Sollberger and Kupper, Inscriptions royales sumériennes et akkadiennes (Paris 1971), IVC6l and IVC8a. Both texts are quoted, without reference, by W. G. Lambert in Garelli ed., Le Palais p. 429.

2. It is described by Lambert, Le Palais p. 429, as a "hymn to Ḥammurabi." The preserved portion of the text does not, however, differ in wording and style from the Old-Babylonian royal inscriptions.

Ancient Near Eastern Studies in Memory of J. J. Finkelstein
Connecticut Academy of Arts and Sciences, Memoir 19
© Connecticut Academy of Arts and Sciences, 1977

indicator, the kings of the first dynasty, or at any rate Ḫammu-rāpī, did claim divine status. This, however, does not in my view (against Finet, Code p. 37 note a) invalidate E. Reiner's re-interpretation of *i-lu* LUGAL-*rí* in CH iii 16 (RA 64 [1970] 73).

2. Cf. CH r. xxvi 45ff.

3. Literally, "whose fate Enlil has in great manner decreed."

4. ka sì-sì-ke is probably a "syllabic" spelling of ka sa$_6$-sa$_6$-ge = *muštēmiqum.*

4-7. The whole passage, from ka sì-sì-ke on, except for the use of "king" instead of "sun" of Babylon, is an exact translation of CH iv 65ff: *muštēmiqum ana ilī rabiūtim, liblibbi ša Sumu-la-Ilum, aplum dannum ša Sīn-muballiṭ, zērum dārium ša šarrūtim, šarrum dannum, šamšu Babilim.* — For the title "sun of GN," see Seux, Epithètes pp. 283 and 460.

6. Literally, "everlasting seed of kingship"; on this phrase, see Lambert, Le Palais p. 427ff.

8. Ḫammu-rāpī is given this title only twice: here and in IRSA IVC6i (in IVC6o he is simply called "king of the Martu"). It is also given to Ammī-ditāna in IVC9a.

12f. Cf. Ḫammu-rāpī's 36th year-name: . . . me-lám ^{d}za-ba$_4$-ba$_4$ ^{d}inana-e-ne-bi-ta zà zi-da gal-bi bí-in-diri-ga. Cf. also CH r. xxvii 88f: *Zababa . . . āliku imnīya.*

2. BM 55472 = 82-7-4,45 (= IRSA IVC8a). Fragment from centre of tablet, reverse completely destroyed, maximum dimensions 77×70 mm., precise provenance unknown.[3] Bilingual inscription of Abī-ešuḫ. Although written in an Old-Babylonian hand, it is not a contemporary inscription but a later school-copy. This is made clear by the unfinished state of the Akkadian translation and also by the very fact that we have here a bilingual text in the narrow sense of the phrase. In all the so-called bilingual inscriptions of the First Dynasty the two versions are written each on a separate monument.[4]

The Sumerian column is more damaged than the Akkadian but it can be restored from King, LIH 68[5] and from the usual phraseology of royal inscriptions.

. . . . .	. . . . .
(šà-[bal]-b[al])	*[li-ib-li-ib-bi]*
(su-mu-l)a-DIĜIR-[gé]	⌜*ša*⌝ [*s*]*u*[*mu-la*]D[IĜIR]
(dumu-nita) nir-ĝ[al]	DUMU.NITA *e-te-el-lu*[*m*]
([s]a-am-su)-i-lu-na-gé	*ša sa-am-su-i-lu-n*[*a*]
([num]un) [d]a-rí	NUMUN *da-rí-um*
([na]m-lugal)-la-gé	*ša šar-ru-tim*
[lugal kal]a-ga	LUGAL *da-núm*
[lugal KÁ]DIĜIR.RA.ki-a	LUGAL KÁ.DIĜIR.RA[.KI]
[lugal ki-e]n-gi ki-uri-gé	LUGAL KALAM *šu-*[*me-ri-im*]
	ù ak-k[*a-di-im*]
[lugal ^{d}uba]-da 4-ba-gé	LUGAL *mu-u*[*š-te-eš-mi*]
[ka teš-a] íb-sì-ga[6]	*ki-ib-ra-*[*at ar-ba-im*]
[lu-ḫa-i]a.ki	*in* GÚ I$_7$ *a-ra-aḫ-t*[*im*]
[ki-tuš s]ù-ga-gé	*lu-ḫa-i*[*a*]
(gú i$_7$ a-ra-aḫ)-tum-(ka)-ta	*šu-ba-at re-ša-a-tim*
(ḫa-am-mu-ra)-pí	
(ad-da)-[n]i	
([b]í-in-dù)-⌜a⌝	
([na]m-sumun-bi-[ta])	
([ba]-gul-[la])	
([gib]i[l-bi] mu-n[i-in-dù])	

3. The tablet was purchased from Spartoli in 1882. Its provenance is registered as "Babylon" but this should not be taken at face-value as in early acquisition registers it is often used for "Babylonia."

4. With the apparent exception of King, CT 21 40ff. = LIH 60 and Gadd and Legrain, UET 1 146 + Stephens, YOS 9 39-61 (both Ḫammu-rāpī).

5. Restorations from this text are in ordinary brackets.

6. Lines 11′-12′ written as one line in the Sumerian column.

[Abī-ešuḫ, ...],

1′-12′ the scion of Sumu-la-Ilum, the princely heir of Samsu-ilūna, of very ancient royal lineage, the mighty king, the king of Babylon, the king who compels obedience from the Four Quarters,

13′-21′ has built anew Luḫaya, the country seat which his (grand)father, Ḫammu-rāpī, had built on the bank of the Araḫtum (and) which, because of its oldness, had fallen in disrepair.

The (re)building of Luḫaya is commemorated in one of Abī-ešuḫ's year-names[7] though Ḫammu-rāpī himself apparently never bothered to record the original building. The Araḫtum seems to have been rather popular for siting riverside country houses: Ammī-ditāna too built one for himself and recorded the fact in his 20th year-name.[8] For the translation "country seat" (French "maison de plaisance") of ki-tuš sù-ga (or šà du_{10}-ga in Ammi-ditana's year-name) = *šubat rēšātim*, see IRSA p. 228 n. 1. On the *name* Luḫaya, see Goetze apud Bottéro, ed., Problème des Ḫabiru p. 201 ad p. 22.

7. Year-name "v": see Ungnad, RLA 2 186b; Goetze, JCS 5 (1951) 102a. Luḫaya is there described as an uru and the crucial ki-tuš sù-ga is missing.

8. Ungnad, RLA 2 188b. A longer form appears in Finkelstein, YOS 13 245.

1. BM 64265

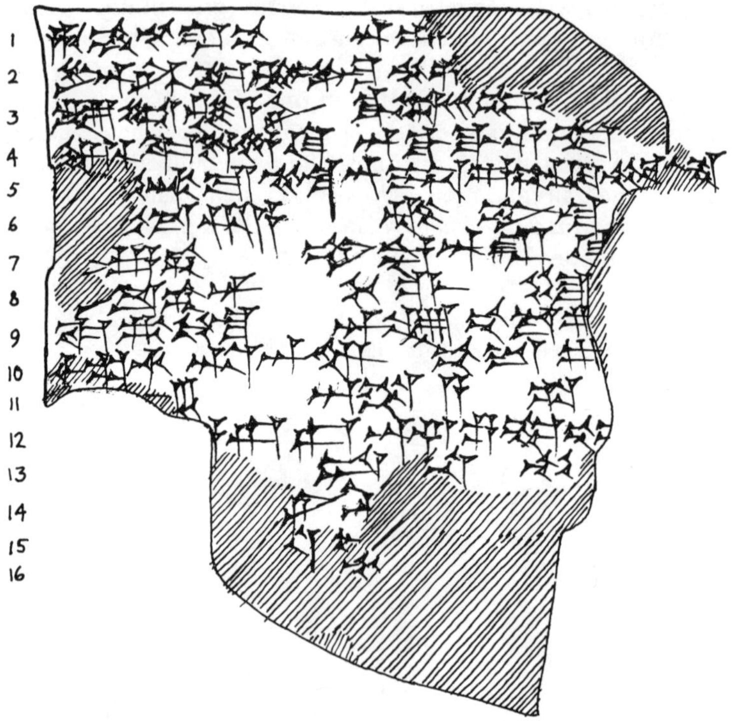

2. BM 55472

EXTISPICY REPORTS FROM THE OLD BABYLONIAN AND SARGONID PERIODS

Ivan Starr
Wayne State University

It is a privilege to dedicate this study[1] of three unpublished extispicy reports to the memory of Professor J. J. Finkelstein, who first aroused my interest in the omen literature. The reports in question are YBC 16148 (Old Babylonian); K.109 (Sargonid); K.4300 (Sargonid). YBC 16148 was purchased for the Yale Babylonian Collection from the Banks estate in 1971 and was identified by the late Professor J. J. Finkelstein and by Professor W. W. Hallo. I wish to thank the latter for permission to publish it. The two major studies of Old Babylonian and Kassite extispicy reports are those of Goetze, JCS 11 (1957) 89-105, and Nougayrol, JCS 21 (1969) 219-235. The reader will find in these studies information concerning previously published material. The Sargonid reports are grouped in Klauber, PRT 102ff. The two reports published here are from the Kuyunjik collection. I wish to thank the Trustees of the British Museum for permission to publish them.

YBC 16148

1 UDU.NITÁ *li-pí-it qá-ti* [*a-na*(?)] ^{d}GÌR.RA.GAL
a-na šu-lum ÌR MA GAL MAḪ
[UZ]U *te-er-tum* KI.GUB TUK
[GÌR TUK][2] KAL TUK SILIM-*ma* TUK
[ZÉ ZA]G[3] GI.NA
i-[*na*] GÙB ZÉ *ti-bu* GAR[4]
i-[*n*]*a* GÙB ZÉ U ŠUB
ŠU.SI *ki-ma pi la-bi*
GÙB ŠU.SI [. . .] GAB
ḪAR ZAG *t*[*a*(?)-*li*(?)]-*il*
ŠU.SI ḪAR MÚRU-*tum*
i-na re-ši-ša GÙB GAB
DAL ŠÀ 2 14 *ti-ra-nu*
a-na šu-ul-mi-ka ša-al-ma-at
d[*a-b*]*a-ba-am* TUK
ITI AB.È U_4-22-KAM
MU *Am-mi-ṣa-du-qá* LUGAL-*e*
ÍD *Am-mi-ṣa-du-qá nu-ḫu-uš ni-ši*

"One sheep for the extispicy [to] GÌR.RA.GAL, for the well-being of Warad-?. Extispicy: it had a 'station'; [it had a 'path']; it had a 'reinforcement'; it had an 'appeasement'[5]; [the right side of the gall bladder] was firm; on the left side of the gall bladder there was an elevation; on the left side of the gall bladder there was a perforation; the 'finger' was like the mouth of a lion; the left side of the 'finger' was severed . . . The lung was suspended(?) on the right; the middle 'finger' of the lung was severed in its head on the left; there were two diaphragms; the number of the coils of the colon was 14. It was favorable for your well-being, (but) it had debatable(?) features. Ammiṣadūqa 16."

Commentary

Line 1. The introductory formula, of which several variations are attested, specifies the number and

1. Research for this study was made possible by a Faculty Research Grant from Wayne State University.
2. The restoration seems certain in the light of the usual order of parts in Old Babylonian and Kassite extispicy reports. Cf., e.g., KI.GUB GÌR KAL SILIM TUK, JCS 21 (1967) 225 K 2.
3. The restoration is suggested by numerous examples, e.g., JCS 21 (1967) 220ff. passim; JCS 11 (1957) 100 9:5; BE 14 4:4b, etc.
4. For occurrences of this protasis in Old Babylonian and Kassite extispicy reports, cf. JAOS 38 (1918) 85:52b; JCS 21 (1967) 221 E 5.
5. The translation of these and related terms is purely conventional.

Ancient Near Eastern Studies in Memory of J. J. Finkelstein
Connecticut Academy of Arts and Sciences, Memoir 19

gender of the sheep used for the ritual; the type of ritual involved; the name of the deity to which the sacrificial animal was dedicated.[6] The deity invoked here, GÌR.RA.GAL, is attested to date only once, in an Aššur text, KAV 65 ii 21. It is absent from the Old Babylonian god list VAT 7759, which was used by Weidner, together with related texts, to form a composite god list.[7] The group where GÌR.RA.GAL appears is identified with Nergal,[8] who is not, to my knowledge, one of the gods commonly invoked in Old Babylonian extispicies.[9]

Line 2. The opening formula is usually followed by statement of purpose (of the extispicy), the most common one being *ana šulmim*, "for well-being," or *ana šulum* X.[10] Extispicies, however, were performed not only for well-being, but for sundry other purposes, such as the success of an enterprise (*ana epēš ṣibūtim*[11]), the safe arrival of a boat (*ana šulum eleppim*[12]), a profitable day at the market,[13] etc.

Line 3. The extispicy report proper begins with the four organs which normally head the list of observations in Old Babylonian and Kassite reports: *naplastu/mazzazu, padānu, danānu, šulmu*.[14] Of the four, the first two organs, the 'station' and the 'path,' are represented in Hittite liver models by two perpendicular creases or fissures on the ventral lobe of the liver. The identification of the 'station' with the reticular impression on the liver had been suggested by Biggs.[15] In the "orientation liver"[16] the NA (i.e., 'station') does indeed occupy an area corresponding to that of the reticular impression. The extent of that area, however, may have varied with time and place. To the Neo-Assyrian diviner the NA may have signified the area of the entire reticular impression; in the Hittite models, however (where the usual designation of the 'station' is KI.GUB), it may have signified only a part thereof.

Line 4. Actual livers of sheep disclose a fissure located close to the border of the ventral lobe of the sheep which may represent the 'path' (*padānu*).[17] Note also the location of the 'path' in the "orientation liver." The *danānu* (KAL) and the *šulmu* (SILIM) are harder to identify, although both the Hittite models and the "orientation liver" place the former in the area of the umbilical fissure (*bāb ekallim*). In the Hittite models[18] it seems to grow out of the walls of the umbilical fissure.[19] The *šulmu* appears in the "orientation liver" between the *danānu* and the *martu* (i.e., the gall bladder), which is also its location in the canonical order of parts of the liver. Note also the elongated crease with the accompanying protasis in the Hittite liver model KBo 7 no. 7 BE SILIM-*ma a-na* SAG ZÉ *im-qut-ma*, "if the *šulmu* descends towards the head of the gall bladder," where the *šulmu*, located between the umbilical fissure and the gall bladder, points towards the latter.[20]

Line 8. For the identical protasis, with a favorable apodosis, cf. Boissier, Choix 45:3, BE ŠU.SI GIM *pi la-bi-ma* NUN GABA.RI NU TUK-*ši*, "if the 'finger' is like the mouth of a lion: the ruler will have no rival."

Line 10. Although *ḫašû talil/la talil* is a standard observation in Old Babylonian and Kassite reports,[21] it is not attested, to my knowledge, in the omen texts. A rare exception is K.4121:12 BE ḪAR 15 *ta-lil ri-ṣú-ut*

6. For a discussion of the opening statement in Old Babylonian and Kassite extispicy reports, cf. Goetze, JCS 11 (1957) 94. *Lipit qāti* is the commonest of the variants of the opening statement. On *lipit qāti* cf. now CAD L 202a sub *liptu*.

7. Cf. "Altbabylonische Götterlisten," AfK 2 (1924-25) 1ff.

8. Cf. the composite list, AfK 2 (1924-25) 16 iii 11-17a.

9. For the names of deities commonly invoked in Old Babylonian and Kassite reports, cf. Goetze, JCS 11 (1957) 94b.

10. Cf. Renger, ZA 59 (1969) 211. I am unable to explain ÌR MA GAL MAḪ.

11. Babyloniaca 2 (1908) pl. 6:2.

11. JCS 11 (1957) 93 CUA 101:13; cf. also p. 95 n. 37.

13. If the translation of YBC 11056:1-4 (=JCS 11 [1957] 91), offered below, is valid: 1 SILA$_4$ *ne-pé-eš-ti* MÁŠ.ŠU.GÌD.GÌD *a-na sa-ḫi-ir-ti ša i-ša-mu i-na sú-qí ši-ma-ti a-na ne-me-li in-na-ad-di-in*, "one lamb for the ritual of the diviner to determine whether merchandise he (the owner of the sheep?) buys in the market will be sold at a profit." (One is tempted to see the last part of the passage as a query, i.e., "will the merchandise (bought) be sold at a profit?"). For a different translation, cf. Goetze, JCS 11 (1957) 94 n. 21.

14. For the ominous significance of the presence or absence of these organs, cf. I. Starr, HUCA 45 (1974) 22.

15. Cf. RA 63 (1969) 160 (drawing of a sheep's liver) and 165; JNES 33 (1974) 353.

16. Cf. Nougayrol, RA 62 (1968) 50 (the drawings must be viewed upside down).

17. Note the crease on the ventral lobe of the sheep's liver in the illustration from Sisson's The Anatomy of the Domestic Animals, reproduced by Biggs, RA 63 (1969) 160; cf. also 165 n. 2.

18. E.g., KBo 7:7, 8:8, etc.

19. Is one to assume that *abullu* in *danānum ša abullim* in the Mari liver model RA 35 (1938) 59 13 F II (to be distinguished from another *abullu* on the liver) is to be identified with the *bāb ekallim*? and is *danānu*, therefore, the "reinforcement" of the umbilical fissure? Cf. Nougayrol, RA 40 (1946) 66.

20. Contra Landsberger and Tadmor, IEJ 14 (1964) 204 n. 12 and 212 n. 30, who argue that the *šulmu* is not attested in the Hittite liver models. Furthermore, I would identify the large X between the umbilical fissure and the gall bladder in the reconstruction of the Hazor liver model (IEJ 14 [1964] 209 fig. 4; cf. 206 fig. 1) with the *šulmu* rather than with the *danānu*. The configuration may be that of two *šulmu*'s lying crosswise.

21. On *talālu*, cf. von Soden, Or. NS 22 (1953) 260f.; Nougayrol, JCS 21 (1967) 222 n. 31. The meaning of the verb remains uncertain, due mostly to the paucity of information. Both Goetze and Nougayrol translated: "suspended." Von Soden suggests a meaning "ist vorgeschoben" in the omen texts. Nougayrol

ERIM NUN DINGIR DU-[*aq*], "if the lung is suspended(?) on the right: the god will go to the aid of the ruler's army."[22]

Line 11. The *ubān ḫaši qablītum* is clearly marked on the lung model Rm 620.[23] Its distinctive shape (cf. CT 31 40 ii) leaves no doubt that it is to be identified with the intermediate lobe, i.e., the *lobe azygos* of the right lung.[24]

Line 13a. DAL ŠÀ, i.e., *tallu libbi* (or *tallu ša libbi*) had been identified with the diaphragm, the thick, leaf-shaped muscle which separates the thoracic and abdominal cavities.[25] It is one of the less frequently occuring observations in Old Babylonian extispicy reports.[26] An extensive collection of omens dealing with the diaphragm is YOS 10 42 ii 48-iii 49. Note, e.g., ii 48 [*šumma* (MAŠ) 2(?)] *ta-al-lu* [*t*]*a-aš-ni-in-tum*, "if there are two (?) diaphragms . . . strife."

Line 13b. Old Babylonian and Kassite reports usually complete their observations by noting the number of the coils of the colon. The numbers attested are invariably 10, 12, 14.[27]

Line 14. Old Babylonian and Kassite extispicy reports do not always record the result of an extispicy (i.e., whether it was favorable or unfavorable). Where they do, the most common formula is *šalmat*, "(the extispicy is) favorable," or *ana šulmim/šulmika šalmat*, "it is favorable for (your) well-being."[28]

Line 15. The (favorable) result of an extispicy is sometimes followed by an additional statement (aside from the common *piqittu*, "check-up"), of which several variants are attested, e.g.: *aḫītam išū; aḫīssa tallat*; and (once) *aḫīssa ša warkatim parāsi*.[29] These statements seem to tell us that while the extispicy turned out to be favorable for the purpose for which it was undertaken, not all its protases were favorable.[30] This, perhaps, is what *dabābam išū* in the present report refers to. It is so far unique among the closing statements in the Old Babylonian and Kassite reports, and may signify something like: "it (the extispicy) had a debatable feature (or features)."

K.109

Obverse

[ ] *u* GIŠ.TUKUL [ ]
[EDI]N(?) U MÚRU GAB 2 *šá* [ ]

[BE NA *u* G]ÌR(?) GAR.MEŠ[31] SILIM BAL-*ma* [ZÉ IGI]
[IZI].GAR BIR-*aḫ* É [LÚ][32]
[BE IG]I KAR-*ti pa-šiṭ*[33] ZÉ *ina* SIG-*šá e*-[*liš dak-šat*]
šá NUN UGU GAL.MEŠ-*šú* INIM.MEŠ-*šú* GIG.[MEŠ-*ṣa*][34]
BE ŠU.SI *kaṣ-ṣa-at* ŠUB-*ti* ERIM-*ni*
BE *ina* DAGAL 2.30 U GÌR RA-*at*

assumed it to be related to *alālu* (i.e., hang, suspend), as it well may be. When the thoracic cavity is opened, the lung collapses immediately to a fraction of its original size and loses its normal shape (cf. Sisson, The Anatomy of the Domestic Animals [4th ed., 1953] p. 540f.; May, The Anatomy of the Sheep [2nd. ed., 1964] p. 44). This is, perhaps, what *talil* in the extispicy reports tries to convey about the condition of the lungs.

22. The prediction for the following line, involving the left side of the lung, is, unfortunately, broken off (BE ḪAR 2.30 *ta-lil* SUḪUŠ [. . .]), but it would normally be the opposite of that of the right side (i.e., unfavorable), in keeping with the basic principle of prognostication.

23. Boissier, Choix pls. A and B (between pp. 76 and 77).

24. Cf. Nougayrol, RA 40 (1946) 93; Hussey, JCS 2 (1948) 25; Landsberger and Tadmor, IEJ 14 (1964) 203 n. 5.

25. Cf. Hussey, JCS 2 (1948) 25.

26. E.g., JCS 11 (1957) 101 12:19-20; 30-31; Babyloniaca 2 (1908) pl. 6:9; 24.

27. On the ominous significance of the number of the coils of the colon, cf. I. Starr, HUCA 45 (1974) 23.

28. For a discussion of the closing statements in Old Babylonian and Kassite reports, cf. Goetze, JCS 11 (1957) 95. Goetze translated *ana šulmim* in these contexts (cf. the introductory statement) "for a favorable omen." It seems to me, however, that the closing formula is simply a reaffirmation of the purpose of the extispicy as recorded in the introductory statement, i.e., "(for) well-being," (similarly Nougayrol, "bien-être").

29. Cf. Goetze, JCS 11 (1957) 95f.; Nougayrol, JCS 21 (1967) 222f. (G, H).

30. For *aḫītu*, "adverse feature," cf. CAD A/1 192.

31. For this restoration, cf. Knudtzon, Gebete 30 r. 8; possibly also 97 r. 11.

32. The apodosis is restored from TCL 6 3 r. 15.

33. Cf. PRT 126:3.

34. The notable thing about this omen is that according to TCL 6 2:21 and 22 (and its duplicate CT 28 43:11-12) the apodosis here should have been a favorable one: (21) BE ZÉ *ina* SIG-*šá* AN.TA *dak-šat* LÚ ḪAL MU SAL.SIG$_5$ TI-*qí* (22) BE ZÉ *ina* MURÚ-*šá* AN.TA *dak-šat šá* NUN UGU GAL.MEŠ INIM.MEŠ-*šú* GIG.MEŠ-*ṣa*. The scribe for some reason reversed the order of apodoses, a rare occurrence in the omen literature. It is impossible, at present, to account for the source of the confusion.

GÌR LÚ GUB.BA *šá* KUR KÚR[35]
BE *ina* UGU MÁŠ KAM-*tum* ŠUB-*at*
mim-ma NÍG.GÁ LÚ DINGIR APIN-*eš*
BE AN.TA-*tum* EDIN ḪAR *šá* 15 *i-bir*
KAM-*tum* EDIN ZI.GA *bu-lim*

Reverse

BE *ina* 15 U+SAG ḪAR GIŠ.TUKUL GAR-*ma* AN.TA IGI
ERIM-*ni* DINGIR.MEŠ-*šá* TAG$_4$.MEŠ-*ši*
BE U ḪAR MÚRU ŠUḪUŠ-*šá* BAR KAK.ZAG.GA *e-bi*
BE ŠÁ.NIGIN 12 ŠÀ UDU SILIM SI.LAL

BE SILIM BAL-*ma* ZÉ IGI ZÉ *ina* SIG-*šá e-liš dak-šat*
BE ŠU.SI *kaṣ-ṣa-at ina* DAGAL 2.30 U GÌR RA-*at*
BE *ina* UGU MÁŠ KAM-*tum* ŠUB-*at*
BE AN.TA-*tum* EDIN ḪAR *šá* 15 *i-bir*
BE *ina* 15 U+SAG ḪAR GIŠ.TUKUL GAR-*ma* AN.TA IGI
7 TAG.MEŠ GAR

---

di-ib-bi šá ina ŠÀ IM.GÍD.DA *an-na-[a*]
[*šá p*]*i*(?) DINGIR-*ti-ka* GAL-*ti* x [ ]
[*i*]*n-ni-ip-pu-šu u i-šal-l*[*i-mu*(?)]
[. . .].MEŠ *ma-a-la in-ni-ip-*[*pu-šu*(?)]

Obverse

". . . and a 'weapon'-mark . . . the back of the 'finger' is severed in the middle . . . [if the 'station' and the 'pa]th' are present; (if) the 'appeasement' is overturned [and faces the gall bladder]: [the fro]nt of the atrophied part(?)[36] is effaced; (if) the gall bladder has a swelling(?) upward[37] in its narrow part: the orders of the ruler will be disagreeable[38] to his officials; if the 'finger' is severed: downfall of the army; if on the left of the 'finger in (its) wide part there is a 'foot'-mark: it is the 'foot'-mark of the ecstatic of the enemy country; if above the 'increment' there is an *erištu*-mark: the man will request[39] . . . from the god; if the top part hangs over the right ridge of the lung: request of the steppe, loss of cattle."

Reverse

"If there is a 'weapon'-mark on the right side of the 'turban' of the lung and it faces upward: the gods of my army will abandon it; if the base of the middle 'finger' of the lung is loose; the breastbone is thick; if the number of the coils of the colon is 12; the inside of the sheep is sound. Check-up. (Lines 5-9 are a repetition of the unfavorable protases.) There are 7 unfavorable (omens). The words which are in this "oblong" tablet . . . In accordance with the command of your great godship . . . will be performed and completed . . ."

Commentary

The Sargonid texts (both queries and reports) maintain on the whole the canonical order of the parts of the liver as we know it from the Old Babylonian and Kassite reports.[40] The two differ, however, in their

35. For the syllabic writing of *rupšu* for DAGAL, cf. now Nougayrol, JCS 21 (1967) 225 K 4 and n. 49.

36. In protases of omen texts, KAR-*tu* is normally read *nēkemtu*, one of the fortuitous marks (Nougayrol's term) on the exta. It is uncertain whether this is what IGI KAR-*ti* here stands for.

37. *dakāšu* and *dikšu* in omen texts are almost exclusively associated with the gall bladder. The meanings offered for these terms in extispicy by the CAD, "to become severed," and the like, have been called into question. For a detailed discussion of the problems involved, cf. Riemschneider, ZA 57 (1965) 134f. and n. 19.

38. Cf. AHw 1 610a sub *marāṣu* 5b.

39. I have been unable to determine the meaning of NÍG.GÁ.

40. For a list of parts of the exta as they appear in the Sargonid texts, cf. Aro in La Divination en Mésopotamie ancienne p. 115. For a list of parts in the Old Babylonian reports, cf. Nougayrol, JCS 21 (1967) 232. The latter, however, includes terms which are limited to reports from Mari.

choice of protases. Aside from those known to us from the Old Babylonian reports and common to both traditions (i.e., the Old Babylonian and Sargonid), the protases of the Sargonid texts favor certain conditions rarely or never attested in the earlier periods. For example, aside from reporting that the 'station' (NA) and the 'path' (GÍR) are present on the liver (cf. line 4), the Sargonid texts show a predilection for the protasis MÚRU NA/GÍR *pašṭa*, "the middle of the 'station'/'path' is effaced." Other protases favored by these texts involve the presence of two 'paths' in various positions with respect to each other.[41] Where the *danānu* (KAL) is concerned, its absence is more often noted than its presence.[42] The Sargonid texts also lay much more stress than do the Old Babylonian and Kassite reports on the parts of the 'finger' (i.e., the caudate lobe). Some of the commonest protases in the Sargonid texts concern the *ṣēr ubāni* and the *rupuš ubāni* (cf. line 9).[43] Another organ which makes a more frequent appearance in the Sargonid texts than it does in the earlier period is the *ṣibtu* ('increment,' cf. line 11), whose suggested identification with the papillary lobe (or process)[44] is supported by the "orientation liver." With the *ṣibtu* (occasionally the *nīru*, 'yoke'), the inspection of the liver usually comes to an end. Turning to other parts of the exta, we note some protases very common in the Sargonid texts, but rare or unattested in the Old Babylonian reports.

Line 13. *elītu/šaplītu*, the "upper/lower" part is first attested in Kassite reports.[45] The only thing that can be said about this obscure pair with reasonable certainty is that in the canonical order of parts of the exta it occurs where the inspection of the liver ends and that of the lungs begins. The order of parts of the lungs in the Sargonid texts is somewhat less rigid than that of the liver, so that *elītu/šaplītu* are occasionally preceded by other parts of the lung (e.g., *kutal ḫašî*),[46] an indication that the location of the pair is to be sought among parts of the exta other than the liver.[47] This pair is associated in omen texts almost exclusively with two protases[48]: 1. *elītu/šaplītu alik* (or *illik*, usually written DU-*ik*); 2. *elītu/šaplītu ṣēr ḫašî ša imitti ibir*. Of the two, the first protasis is the more common. Aside from the ubiquitous *elītu/šaplītu*, the Sargonid queries (it is not attested in the reports)[49] display a *qablītu* (written MÚRU-*tum*). This seems to me, however, to be nothing more than an abbreviation of ŠU.SI ḪAR MÚRU-*tum* rather than an independent part.[50] Note that aside from the fact that *ubān ḫašî qablītum* and *qablītum* (MÚRU-*tum*) occupy an identical place in the canonical order of parts of the exta, the verbs associated with the former (*uššur/rakis*) are the very same which are associated with the latter.

Reverse, line 3a. *ubān ḫašî qablītum*, the middle 'finger' of the lung (i.e., the intermediate lobe) is well represented in extispicy reports of all periods. In the Old Babylonian reports the verb most commonly associated with it is *paṭāru*.[51] In the Sargonid reports the protases most commonly associated with it are *ubān ḫašî qablītum išissa uššur* (BAR)/*rakis* (ŠÈR-*is*), "the base of the middle 'finger' of the lung is loose/bound."[52]

Line 3b. *kaskasu*, the breast-bone, appears occasionally in Old Babylonian reports. It is a standard feature in the Sargonid texts, the most common observation being *kaskasu ebi* (for a different protasis cf. K.4300:6).

Line 4. The Sargonid texts normally note, as do the Old Babylonian and Kassite reports, the number of the coils of the colon (*tirānu*). The number most common in the Sargonid texts is 12, 14, 16.[53] An observation not attested in the earlier periods is *libbi šuʾi šalim*, with which the Sargonid texts invariably complete the extispicy reports. Occasionally the condition of the vertebrae (KIŠIB.MEŠ, *kunukkū*) or the rib cage (KAK.TI, *sikkat ṣēli*) is also noted.[54]

A protasis attested in Kassite reports, and quite common in the Sargonid texts is *kubšu eli kīdīti rakib*

41. Cf. Klauber, PRT index 173f.

42. For the ominous significance of this fact, cf. I. Starr, HUCA 45 (1974) 22.

43. Cf. Klauber, PRT index 168.

44. For the identification of *ṣibtu*, cf. Hussey, JCS 2 (1948) 29; Biggs, RA 63 (1969) 166.

45. JCS 11 (1957) 104a 22:8; r. 7. Also BE 14 4:6. A rare occurrence in an Old Babylonian report may be YOS 10 10:1, *e-li-a-tum ša-pa-la*.

46. Cf. PRT 105, 122. Note also the order of parts in 116.

47. A difficult passage which refers to the location of *elītu* without, however, clarifying the matter, is Boissier, DA 11:19ff. For a translation, cf. CAD E 99a sub *elītu*.

48. For references to these protases in omen texts, cf. CAD E 98b sub *elītu*.

49. Cf. Aro, in La Divination en Mésopotamie p. 115.

50. I.e., *elītum, qablītum, šaplītum* as assumed by Aro, La Divination en Mésopotamie p. 115.

51. E.g., passim in the works of Goetze and Nougayrol cited above.

52. This is attested already in Kassite reports, cf. JCS 11 (1957) 101 18:9; BE 14 4:8. For occurrences in the Sargonid texts, cf. PRT index 168.

53. Cf. note 27 above.

54. Cf. Aro, La Divination en Mésopotamie p. 115.

(and its opposite *kīdītu eli kubšu rakib*), "the 'turban' straddles the 'outside,' or the 'outside' straddles the 'turban'."[55] A very obscure organ attested only in the Sargonid texts is *ḫasīsu* (always written *ha-si-si*).[56] From its place in the order of parts it may be associated with the lungs. By the same token, some protases common in the Old Babylonian and Kassite reports, such as *ḫašû talil/la talil* are not attested in the Sargonid texts.

K.4300

Obverse

B[E . . .
BE [. . .
BE [. . .
BE MÁS [. . .
BE AN.TA D[U-*ik*
BE KAK.ZAG.GA *ina* SAL.[LA-*šú* GAM-*iš* ZI.GA(?)][57]
BE ŠÀ.NIGIN 2.30 GUR.MEŠ 16 [ŠID.MEŠ-*šú-nu*][58]
ERIM-*ni* DINGIR.MEŠ-*šá ina* IZI.GAR[.MEŠ UŠ.MEŠ-*ši*]

Bottom Edge

3-*tum* 6 TAG.ME[Š GAR]

Reverse

ki-i LÚ ERIM.MEŠ LÚ[. . .
šá ᵐ*Aššur-bani*(DÙ)-*apli*(A) LUGAL [. . .
a-na UGU [. . .
a-na MU[L . . .
TA U_4 20 [+x
EN U_4 2[0+
šá M[U(?) . . .
in[*a*(?) . . .

"If the 'increment' . . . If the upper part is mov[able(?)] . . . If the breast-bone is perforated in its *ruq*[*qu*: defection]. If the coils of the colon are turned (and) their number is 16: the gods of my army will [lead it] into strife(?). Third (extispicy); there are 6 unfavorable (omens)."

Commentary

Line 7. This is the only omen in this report which is in a fairly complete state of preservation. As is the case with omens in the other reports, this one too is taken from the extensive body of canonical omens. The text in question is K.3832+ reverse 4, and its opposite ibid. obverse 23.

Line 9. This practice of examining more than one set of entrails (in this case 3) was evidently more common in this group than was previously assumed.[59]

Reverse. Of the reverse, hardly anything of note, with the exception of the name of the king, Aššurbanipal, is preserved. We do know that the reports were actually concerned with the affairs of this king, notably his war against his brother, Šamaš-šum-ukin of Babylon.[60]

To sum up: in their present state of preservation (K.4300 is no more than a fragment) the two Sargonid reports published here shed no light whatsoever on the political history of the later Sargonid kings. Their sole significance is in the context of extispicy reports of the Sargonid period. As such, they represent but one of the two traditions of extispicy attested in that period. The other is the so-called queries, in which the immediate royal concern which was placed as a query before the god Šamaš forms the bulk of these texts. Where extispicy reports are embedded in these queries, they follow, rather than precede, the latter. In the

55. For references, cf. CAD K 345 sub *kīdītu*.
56. Cf. PRT index 170b.
57. The restoration is uncertain. It is suggested by Klauber, PRT 138:13.
58. Cf. PRT 44 r. 14.
59. Cf. Aro, La Divination en Mésopotamie p. 110f.
60. Cf. Aro, La Divination en Mésopotamie p. 109.

reports, the opposite is the case. The extispicy report is the major concern of the text, with the subject of the query and related matters following.[61] The reports differ from the queries also in the fact that they usually, if not always, provide unfavorable protases with suitable apodoses and then enumerate the former again at the end of the report, and finally list the sum total of these, e.g., x TAG.MEŠ.[62] The last detail, which is characteristic of the reports only, is helpful in identifying reports among unpublished fragmentary Sargonid texts.

The three extispicy reports published here represent the two periods in which the practice of recording extispicies is attested in Mesopotamia. A major difference between the Old Babylonian and Sargonid practices is that, in the former case, the extispicies were performed, according to the evidence of the reports, for private individuals.[63] For this purpose, a short introductory statement, such as *ana šulum* PN or the like in the Old Babylon reports was quite adequate. On the other hand, the queries on behalf of the Sargonid kings, embracing, as they did, a multiplicity of royal concerns, called for a much more elaborate format. There is some reason to believe that extending the scope of extispicy to embrace the multitude of concerns reflected in the Sargonid texts was an innovation of Esarhaddon.[64]

61. Cf. Aro, La Divination en Mésopotamie p. 111.

62. Aro, La Divination en Mésopotamie p. 110.

63. This statement must be qualified. There is little doubt that extispicies were performed for the kings of the first dynasty of Babylon, to whose reign (notably that of Ammiṣaduqa) most of the published extispicy reports belong. Note, for example, the statements of Samsuiluna (VAS 16 165) and Ammiditana (LIH 56). However, where the name of the person for whom the extispicy was performed is recorded, it is that of a private individual. E.g., *ana šulum Kubburum*; *ša Kubburum*, described as UGULA DAM.GÀR.MEŠ, "overseer of the merchants," an important position in the Old Babylonian period. Cf. Nougayrol, JCS 21 (1967) 220 B 2; C 10. Note also *ša Appā*, p. 225 K 1; *ana šulum Bēltani*, JCS 11 (1957) 94b, etc.

64. Cf. Aro, La Divination en Mésopotamie p. 112.

YBC 16148

obv.

rev.

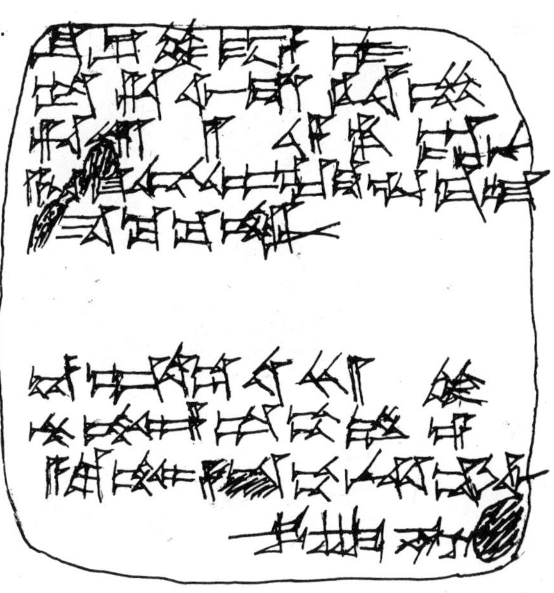

K.109

obv.

rev.

K.4300

obv.

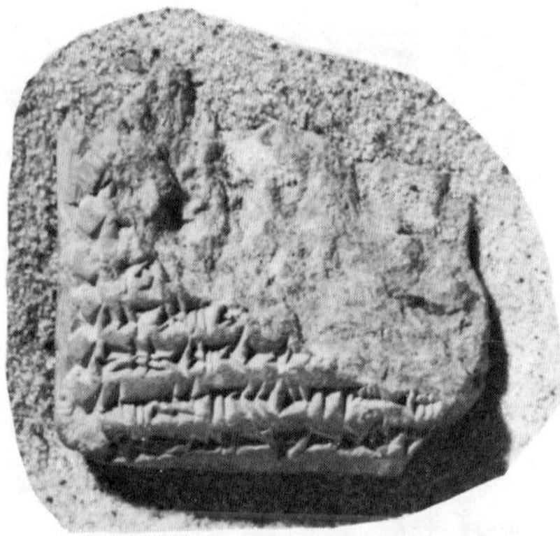

rev.

OBSERVATIONS ON ASSYRIAN HISTORIOGRAPHY

Hayim Tadmor
The Hebrew University

Two categories of historical writing in Ancient Mesopotamia are clearly distinguished from the rest: the Annals in Assyria and the Chronicles in Babylonia. In the early days of Assyriology, the term "annals" was applied rather indiscriminately to a variety of historical compositions. Subsequently, "annals" were defined more precisely as official royal texts that describe the events of each year, written in the first person, as if reported by the king himself. Such inscriptions begin with a list of the king's attributes and end with a building inscription or dedication. In contrast, "chronicles" are non-royal historical inscriptions that record events in chronological order; they are written in the third person. Such records were not intended to serve as building inscriptions or as dedicatory inscriptions to the gods. Until recently, only the Babylonian—or more exactly the Neo-Babylonian—Chronicles were known. So little has survived from the Assyrian Chronicles that the existence of this category was not noticed until Ernest Weidner, who published several chronicle fragments dating to the Middle Assyrian period, drew the attention of scholars to the existence of the text-genre. In the present inquiry, I shall consider some principles of editorial procedure in the development of the Annals, the relation of the Annals to the Chronicles, and the antiquity of the chronistic genre in Assyria.[1] Moreover, I believe that the annalistic form of royal history-writing developed in Assyria under the influence of the chronicles rather than under that of the Hittite annalistic prototypes.[2]

I. The historical category known as "annals" first appears in the late Middle Assyrian period, during the reign of Tiglath-Pileser I. The Aššur prism of that king reveals this new literary genre in all its complexity: metaphorical language, poetic comparisons, epic hyperbolae, as well as specific *topoi* such as the royal hunt of lions, his putting draft animals to the plow, and his having stored more barley than his fathers.[3] These features, arranged in a chronological narrative, are combined here for the first time in a high style that was imitated by Tiglath-Pileser's immediate successors, but was not used again until the historical inscriptions of the Sargonids.

In the Aššur prism of Tiglath-Pileser I which records the events of the first five years of his reign, the entry for each year is separated from that of the next by a laudatory passage that becomes a kind of doxology. At the end of the historical narrative a summary states: "These are the lands which I conquered from the beginning of my reign until my fifth *palû*," (AKA p. 83 44-45).

Clearly, the arrangement is chronological though the events of each year are not designated by a *palû*, i.e., a term of office, or by an eponym year, as in the annals of later kings.[4] In another recension of the Annals of Tiglath-Pileser, dating, it is suggested, to his eleventh year (Borger, Thontafel A),[5] only a dividing line separates the entry of one year from that of the next; the last statement again lists the countries conquered, this time during the king's tenth *palû*. The next recension (Borger, Thontafel B, C and the second Aššur prism, KAH 2 63)[6] follows the same pattern; it was composed, I believe, in the twentieth or twenty-first year of the king's reign.

Two characteristics of the Annals of Tiglath-Pileser I call for comment. The first—a well-known

1. These topics were first dealt with in two papers: "The Beginnings of Assyrian Historiography" read at the Fourth World Congress of Jewish Studies, Jerusalem 1965, and "The Origin and Growth of the Assyrian Royal Annals" presented before the Annual Meeting of the American Oriental Society, Cambridge, Mass. 1971. (See provisionally: Tadmor, "Chronology of the Ancient Near East in the Second Millennium B.C.E.," The World History of the Jewish People 2/1 [ed. B. Mazar; Tel Aviv, 1970] 67 and 261 n. 15). Meanwhile, several scholars have independently arrived at somewhat similar conclusions: J. M. Munn-Rankin, "Assyrian Military Power, 1300-1200 B.C.," CAH² (rev. ed. Chapter 25 [=fasc. 49] 1967) 25; W. Röllig, "Zur Typologie und Entstehung der babylonischen und Assyrischen Königslisten," *lišān mitḫurti*: Festschrift W. von Soden, AOAT 1 (Neukirchen-Vluyn, 1969) 274-75; and A. K. Grayson, Assyrian and Babylonian Chronicles, TCS 5 (Locust Valley, N.Y., 1975) 101. I am grateful to Professor Grayson for putting at my disposal the galley proofs of this corpus prior to its publication.

2. The notion that the Annals genre in Assyria owes its form and style to the Hittite prototypes has never been properly investigated. It originated with a very cautious suggestion of H. G. Güterbock (ZA 44 [1938] 98) and was restated, with more confidence, by A. Goetze (Kleinasien [2nd. ed.; München, 1957] p. 175).

3. AKA p. 88 lines 100-104; Borger, Einleitung 1 129.

4. H. Tadmor, JCS 12 (1958) 22-33.

5. Borger, Einleitung 1 109, 114-16 (=E. Weidner, AfO 18 [1957] 343-46).

6. Borger, Einleitung 1 109, 116-20 (=Weidner, AfO 18 [1957] 347-53).

Ancient Near Eastern Studies in Memory of J. J. Finkelstein
Connecticut Academy of Arts and Sciences, Memoir 19

phenomenon—is the periodic rewriting of the Annals: in each recension the scribes abbreviated, deleted, interpolated, and often completely rewrote the earlier accounts before adding the current information in greater detail. The scribes of almost every Assyrian king of the first millennium, especially those of Aššurbanipal, employed similar techniques, often perfecting them.

The second phenomenon—unnoticed so far—is the existence of a pattern of five and ten year recension periods in the Annals of Assyrian kings of the eleventh, tenth, and perhaps even the ninth centuries: recensions of royal annals tended to be composed periodically during the king's second year, then shortly after his fifth year, after his tenth year, and again at about his twentieth year. This practice is not uniform. For example, in a recension of the Annals of Adad-nirari II, apparently from his nineteenth year,[7] the narrative, commences only with the events of the eleventh year,[8] which suggests the existence of a previous recension of the first ten years.

This principle of compiling a new recension of annals every five or ten years can be followed in the inscriptions of several Assyrian kings of the ninth century, especially in those of Aššurnasirpal II. An account of this king's fifth regnal year appears on a commemorative stela—a monolith—set up at Kurkh on the Upper Tigris,[9] and a recension comprising his first five years is represented by the inscription on the votive stela set up in the Ninurta Temple in Calah.[10] A longer version of the Annals was copied on the pavement slabs at the Ninurta Temple.[11] At first, the arrangement of the material in that version appears rather anomalous, but it becomes understandable in the light of the five/ten-year recension pattern. The scribe first copied the complete recension of five years, identical to that on the monolith from the Ninurta Temple, culminating in a self-laudatory summary and a short building account.[12] The text on the pavement slabs, composed sometime after year eighteen, then continues with the events from various years: year six, a number of undated years (according to Brinkman,[13] at least four years), and probably an account of the year preceding the composition of the text. Such potpourri can hardly be referred to as "the final edition of the Annals."[14]

Traces of the same recension pattern can be detected in the inscriptions of the later kings of the ninth century: Šalmaneser III[15] and Šamši-Adad V. The latter's Calah Monolith, and the Aššur stela covering the events of the first four and six campaigns, respectively,[16] were produced shortly after his tenth year, 814. The same pattern may also account for the strange fact that the Sabaʾa stele of Adad-nirari III begins with year five, the year in which he marched against Hatti, and not with year six, the year in which he encamped against Arpad.[17]

II. In order to consider the relation of the Annals to the Chronicles, we have to return to the Annals of Tiglath-Pileser I. The recension that we have assigned to his twentieth year contains an intrusive passage. The text states, "in the eponym-year (*ina līmi*) of Aššur-šuma-ereš, and for the second time in the eponym-year of Ninuaya, I encountered Marduk-nadin-aḫḫe (King of Babylon) in a chariot-battle, defeating him."[18] This dating by the *limmu* is notable: no other event in the inscriptions of Tiglath-Pileser I is dated in that fashion. How can we account for this exceptional practice? It seems very probable that the editor of the Annals of Tiglath-Pileser copied or paraphrased a passage from a chronicle, which recorded the Babylonian wars of Tiglath-Pileser and dated them—as an Assyrian chronicle of that period would naturally do—in terms of the *limmu* years. Indeed, the compiler of the so-called Synchronistic History[19] must have drawn his information from the same source. In describing the relations between Assyria and Babylonia at the time of Tiglath-Pileser I, he even employs the same wording: *šanûtēšu sidirtu ša narkabāti . . . iškun.*[20] The only

7. The text (KAH 2 84) is dated to the *limmu* of Ili-napišta-uṣur, the eponym for the year 893. This *limmu* would correspond to Adad-nirari's 19th regnal year on the assumption that he came to the throne in 912 and his own eponym year was 910, his second full year (see A. Poebel, JNES 2 [1943] 74).

8. That is, in the *limmu* of Dur-mati-Aššur, the eponym for the year 901.

9. AKA pp. 222ff.

10. AKA pp. 242ff. and Y. de Gac, Les inscriptions d'Assur-naṣir-aplu III (Paris, 1907) pp. 129ff.

11. AKA pp. 254ff.

12. Col. ii 124-35=AKA pp. 343-46; Luckenbill ARAB 1 §§467-68.

13. Brinkman, Political History pp. 390-94.

14. Luckenbill, ARAB 1 138. The complex interrelation between the various versions of the Ashurnaṣirpal Annals was discussed by Schramm, Einleitung 2; cf. also W. de Filippi, RA 68 (1974) 141ff. (in response to B. W. W. Dombrowski, RA 67 [1973] 131ff.), and, more recently, Samuel M. Paley, King of the World: Ashur-nasirpal II of Assyria 883-859 (New York, 1976) pp. 145-58.

15. The extant recensions of the Annals of Shalmaneser III were composed shortly after his 6th, 9th, 16th, 18th, 20th and 31st years. See Schramm, Einleitung 2 102-10.

16. Schramm, Einleitung 2 106-109. Cf. Brinkman, Political History pp. 207-208 nn. 1290-91; Grayson, Chronicles p. 244.

17. Tadmor, Iraq 35 (1973) 144ff.

18. E. Weidner, AfO 18 (1957) 351 lines 49-51.

19. Grayson, Chronicles pp. 50-59.

20. Grayson, Chronicles p. 164 lines 14′-16′; pp. 247-48.

difference is the use of the first person in the Annals as against the third person in the Synchronistic History, and also the omission in the Synchronistic History of the *limmu* year, since it does not employ specific dating.

The assumption that the compiler of Tiglath-Pileser's Annals had access to the chronicles that described the relations between Assyria and Babylonia is further supported by the fact that three out of four extant fragments of Middle Assyrian chronicles—VAT 10281[21], VAT 10453+10465,[22] and VAT 13056 (formerly 13049)[23]—are concerned with the Assyro-Babylonian encounters, though written from a partisan—Assyrian—point of view. One would also expect that the dating system in these Assyrian chronicles would be in terms of the *limmu* years, but as it happens, in all of the extant fragments, the left side of the column is broken off. A possible occurrence of a date is that of [*ina limi*] *Ṣilli-Adad* in VAT 13056:3, at the heading of a new section describing an encounter of Enlil-nirari with Kurigalzu (II) of Babylonia (last quarter of the fourteenth century).[24]

The fact that a royal inscription incorporates texts couched in a dry chronistic style is even more evident in the "Broken Obelisk" of Aššur-bel-kala, son of Tiglath-Pileser I.[25] The first four columns of this document are explicitly formulated in the third person; the subject of the recital is a king whose name is not mentioned. The fifth column uses the first person. The events are recorded tersely and laconically, e.g.: in a certain year, in MN, he waged war against GN; in that year, in MN_2, in the course of an expedition against GN_2, he waged war, etc.; in MN_3, in the *limmu* of PN, at the time of the expedition against a certain city, he waged war, etc. Event pursues closely upon event in colorless language, which lacks the vigorous embellishments of annalistic writing.

Actually, this text is an entirely unusual creation. It blends neither with the style of the Annals of Tiglath-Pileser nor with that of Aššur-bel-kala, and represents an attempt to create a new style which compares poorly with that of the royal inscriptions of the eleventh century. The scribe lifts passages verbatim from insipid, colorless chronicles or war reports which record in the third person the military engagements of the king. This material fills the first three columns; immediately after, the scribe starts to write quite differently, using the first person and that metaphorical style whose form was firmly cast in the time of Tiglath-Pileser I. He even includes the well-known *topos* of the royal hunt, describing the king's fight with wild beasts and exotic feats of royal bravery.[26] Finally, in the fifth column, he continues the building inscription with the usual detail that concludes an annal-text.

The literary experiment embodied in the "Broken Obelisk" informs us of the quest for style in historical writing in the royal court. The admirable blending of styles does not come about until the time of Adad-nirari II. From then on, the classic form of the annals is clearly delineated. Although it follows the history of the king year by year, it does not force the description of the events into a literary uniformity, rather, it gives literary imagination and stylistic innovation a free hand. Gradually, this new form of the annals made the older sequential forms, especially the colorless chronicle, obsolete. However, the coexistence of chronicles with annals is still attested, though indirectly, as late as the early eighth century. The author of the Synchronistic History,[27] composed in the days of Adad-nirari III or his successor Shalmaneser IV, must have had at his disposal a contemporary Assyrian chronicle when he described the relations between Assyria and Babylonia in the days of Adad-nirari II, Shalmaneser III, Šamši-Adad V, and Adad-nirari III.[28] Moreover, the inscriptions of Shalmaneser III contain a passage about the relations between Shalmaneser and Marduk-zakir-šumi of Babylonia, the wording of which is very close to, if not identical with the parallel passage in the Synchronistic History.[29] It is, therefore, very likely that all of the sources concerned are, in fact, drawing the Babylonian *topos* from a contemporary chronicle[30] concerned with Assyrian-Babylonian relations.

21. E. Weidner, AfO 4 (1943) 213ff.; Grayson, Chronicles pp. 187f.

22. E. Weidner, AfO 17 (1956) 384; Tadmor, JNES 17 (1958) 133ff.; and Grayson, Chronicles p. 189.

23. E. Weidner, AfO 20 (1959) 115ff. (=Grayson, Chronicles p. 189).

24. Weidner, AfO 20 (1959) 115.

25. Borger, Einleitung 1 135ff.; Brinkman, Political History, Appendix D.

26. AKA pp. 128ff.

27. Cf. Grayson, Chronicles p. 53.

28. I differ from Grayson (Chronicles p. 54) in regard to the sources of the Synchronistic History, though the passage about Shamsi-Adad's visit to the cultic centers of Babylonia (iv 9-12) derives ultimately from an official royal account (Grayson, Chronicles p. 245).

29. iii 27-36; Grayson, Chronicles pp. 167, 240-42.

30. Of special interest is the passage on the throne-base inscription from Calah, inscribed as an architectural space-filler: P. Hulin, Iraq 25 (1963) 56. This appears to be a quotation from a chronicle. It is also not unlikely that the court scribe of Shalmaneser has substituted here the original date with a more general *ina tarṣi* formula. (For use of that formula in the Chronicles, see Grayson, Chronicles p. 51 n. 5).

III. As noted above, the earliest king mentioned in the extant Middle Assyrian chronicle fragment is Enlil-nirari I. In the Synchronistic History, which ultimately derives from chronicles, the earliest entry is about Puzur-Aššur III and Burnaburiaš I of Babylonia—late sixteenth or early fifteenth century. (In the extant copy of the Synchronistic History it is misplaced and comes after the entry about Aššur-bel-nišešu and Kara-indaš of Babylonia who reigned in the last quarter of the fifteenth century.)[31] There is, however, some evidence that the chronistic genre existed long before the Middle Assyrian period. A well-known document, the Assyrian King List, has preserved a typical chronistic statement regarding Šamši-Adad I:

> Šamši-Adad, the son of Ila-kabkabi, went away to Babylonia in the time of Naram-Sin: in the eponym-year of Ibni-Adad, Šamši-Adad came back from Babylonia (Karduniaš); he seized Ekallate and he stayed in Ekallate for three years. In the eponym-year of Atamar-Ištar, Šamši-Adad came up from Ekallate, and removed Erišu, son of Naram-Sin, from the throne, seized the throne and reigned for thirty-three years.[32]

Only in the time of Šamši-Adad, or in the days of his immediate successor, would it have been possible to list the exact dates for the events of his life: the precise year of his journey to Babylonia, his residence in Ekallate, and his seizure of power in Assyria, all dated by *limmu*. After that time, the royal throne was taken away from the heirs of Šamši-Adad, and his grandson was called "foreign seed" by the new king.[33] Not much later the "period of darkness" descended upon Assyria. We must therefore assume that in the days of Šamši-Adad I or of his son Išme-Dagan there existed, as Landsberger has shown, a contemporary Assyrian chronicle from which the early compiler of the Assyrian King List, working at that time, quoted the dates and details of Šamši-Adad's ascension to the throne of Assyria.[34]

It can hardly be accidental that it is also in the age of Šamši-Adad that we find the earliest example of the narrative style common in later Assyrian historical inscriptions. The text in question, inscribed on a broken commemorative stele now in the Louvre (AO 2776) was published some sixty years ago by de Genouillac, and has rightly been attributed to Šamši-Adad I.[35] Since the text is fragmentary and anonymous, it has not yet been considered in relation to the problem of the beginnings of historical writing in Assyria. It reads:

col. ii	col. iii
ana kerḫisu ērub	*ana māt*
šēp(a)(!) *Adad bēliya*	*Qabrā*
aššiqma	*aḫḫabitma*
mātam šâti	*mātam šâti*
utaqqin(!)[36]	*ebūrša*
šakniya	*amḫaṣma*
aštakkama	*alāni dannāti*(!)
isin Ḫumṭim[37]	*ša māt Urbēl*
ana Šamaš u Adad	*kalāšunu*
ina Arrapḫimma	*ina waraḫ Magrānim*
lū aqqi	*uṣabbitma*
waraḫ Addarim	*birātiya*
ina ûmim 20-*šu*	*lū aštakkan*
Zaʾibam	
[*lū*] *ēbirma*	

31. Grayson, Chronicles pp. 158, 286.

32. I. J. Gelb, JNES 13 (1954) 212.

33. B. Landsberger, JCS 8 (1954) 32; Grayson, Royal Inscriptions 1 30.

34. Landsberger, JCS 8 (1954) 33-34; 109-110; and cf. F. R. Kraus, "Könige, die in Zelten wohnten," Mededelingen der Koninklijke Nederlandse Akademie van Wetenschappen, Afd. Letterkunde N.R. 28/2 (1965) 16-18; W. Röllig in Festschrift W. von Soden pp. 274-75. Landsberger also noted that the use of "Karduniash" for Babylon points to the Middle Assyrian period, when the Assyrian King List was edited. See also J. A. Brinkman, Or. NS 42 (1973) 315-16.

35. H. de Genouillac, RA 7 (1910) 151-56. A. Goetze drew attention to this document and suggested that it was composed for Dadusha, King of Eshnunna, RA 46 (1952) 155-59, but E. Forrer, RLA 1 243, W. von Soden, Or. NS 22 (1953) 256, J. R. Kupper, Or. NS 27 (1958) 442, and J. Laessøe, The Shemshara Tablets (København, 1959) p. 74, have given ample reasons for considering it as a text belonging to Shamshi-Adad I. Grayson has included it in his Royal Inscriptions under that king's historical inscriptions (p. 26).

36. For *šēp(a) Adad* (Sandhi writing!) and *ú-táq(!)-qí-in*, see W. von Soden, Or. NS 22 (1953) 257.

37. *ḫu*(!)-*um*(!)-*ṭim*, following von Soden's reading, Or. NS 22 (1953) 256-58.

> I entered its fortress. I kissed the feet of Adad my lord, and I reestablished that land (i.e., reorganized it politically). I appointed my governors over them, and I sacrificed the offering of the summer festival to Šamaš and Adad, in Arrapḫa proper. In the month of Adar, on the 20th of the month, I crossed the river Zab, and I raided the land of Qabra. As to that country, its yield I ruined. Moreover, in the month of Magranum, I captured all of the fortified cities of the land of Urbel (= Arbela), and I established fortresses of my own.

The entire text is formulated in the first person; it reveals several elements, well-known from the historical documents from the Middle Assyrian period onwards: war waged in the name of a god, the taking of spoils, the conquest of a region and its annexation to Assyria, the appointing of a governor and the establishing of fortresses. Since the stele is fragmentary, we cannot know whether the text contained events of more than one year.

From what was this "annalistic" style derived? Here one can offer only guesses. A similar style, already found in the foundation inscription of Yaḫdun-Lim of Mari,[38] describes in colorful stock phrases and within the formula of a single year, the downfall of the confederation of *Marū-Iamīna* (*Mar-mi-im* in the text).[39] Not dissimilar narration is also found in a recently published historical inscription of Zimri-Lim of Mari[40] (a draft for a commemorative stele) and in the inscriptions of Samsu-iluna of Babylon.[41]

Significantly, this new form of historical narration appears in what we might call the "Amorite Age." It may have been either older Sumerian forms of narration adopted by the scribes in the courts of the Amorite kings, or, more likely, they may be a specifically North Mesopotamian contribution to the art of history-writing. This conclusion raises the possibility that the Old Hittite historical documents, especially the Annals of Hattušili I,[42] owe their inspiration to earlier North Mesopotamian or even North Syrian prototypes, transmitted perhaps through Aleppo or some other intermediary, together with the cuneiform writing. However, the conservative scribes of Babylonia (with whom the form of the chronicle might have originated) continued to write in the old style. They kept the chronicle form almost until the very end of the Babylonian civilization, but never blended it with that of the official royal building inscription, and never produced historical narration in the form of annals that remained endemic to Assyria. The latter, the contribution of the Assyrian scribes, is a product of a complex literary process, which it is not the purpose of this paper to unravel. It was our object to draw attention to several new factors in the elucidation of that process, one to which Jack Finkelstein has contributed in his masterly study on Mesopotamian historiography.

38. A. L. Oppenheim, ANET³ (Supplement) p. 556, and G. Dossin, Syria 32 (1955) 14-15 iii 3-27.

39. iii 17, 21. The same name is written *Ma-ar Mi-i* or DUMU.MEŠ *Mi-i* in ARMT 11 18, 19, 43; see Burke's discussion, ARMT 11 p. 124, and especially M. Weippert, The Settlement of the Israelite Tribes in Palestine (London, 1971) p. 111 n. 41.

40. G. Dossin, Syria 48 (1971) 1-6.

41. E. Sollberger, RA 61 (1967) 41 lines 39-54; RA 63 (1969) 35 lines 101-112.

42. H. Otten, MDOG 91 (1958) 73-84; F. Imparati, Studi Classici e Orientali 14 (1965) 40ff.; and C. Saporetti, ibid. pp. 77ff.

WAS THERE AN INTEGRATED GILGAMESH EPIC IN THE OLD BABYLONIAN PERIOD?

Jeffrey H. Tigay
University of Pennsylvania

Although it is generally agreed that the "canonical" version of the Gilgamesh Epic (henceforth GE) was composed in the last half or quarter of the second millennium, probably in the Kassite period,[1] it is widely assumed that the integrated Akkadian epic, with its plot and unifying themes, is a product of the Old Babylonian period. In the past two decades a number of scholars have noted that this assumption has never been substantiated.[2] They ask, in effect: is there any evidence against an assumption that the Akkadian Gilgamesh texts of the Old Babylonian period are simply independent, disconnected episodes, like the Sumerian Gilgamesh compositions? The purpose of this paper is to adduce evidence in support of the view that the integrated epic existed in the Old Babylonian period.

I

Since the adventures of Gilgamesh first became known to modern scholars in the form of GE, it is not surprising that the subsequently discovered Sumerian forerunners of the epic were also first taken to be parts of a single integrated epic.[3] This view was rejected by Kramer in 1944.[4] Kramer argued, on the basis of the varying lengths of the six Sumerian tales then known and their character as "individual, disconnected tales,"[5] that the Sumerian tales comprised independent narratives which had not been united into a single epic, and that the composition of the epic, with an unfolding plot linking the episodes, was a Babylonian contribution. Some years later further evidence for this position was adduced by L. Matouš.[6] He noted that GEN and the Sumerian account of the flood began with mythological introductions, a feature which typically appears at

1. W. von Soden, MDOG 85 (1953) 23; ZA 40 (1931) 187; 41 (1933) 129f.; W. G. Lambert, JCS 11 (1957) 1-14; F. Böhl, Het Gilgamesj-Epos² (1952) p. 16; RLA 3/5 (1968) 364; cf. W. W. Hallo, IEJ 12 (1962) 15f. B. Landsberger dates the Gilgamesh Epic about 1250 B.C. (Garelli, Gilg. p. 34), and L. Matouš dates it about 1100 (Garelli, Gilg. p. 93f.).

This article is dedicated to the memory of J. J. Finkelstein, in appreciation for the privilege of being among his students.

I am indebted to my colleagues, Barry L. Eichler, Erle Leichty, and Åke W. Sjöberg, for calling to my attention and putting at my disposal the unpublished tablets cited in n. 30, and for helpful comments on an earlier version of this article.

Special abbreviations:

DG	The Death of Gilgamesh, ed. Kramer, BASOR 94 (1944) 2-12; ANET³ pp. 50-52
GA	Gilgamesh and Agga, ed. Kramer, AJA 53 (1949) 1-18; ANET³ pp. 44-47
GBH	Gilgamesh and the Bull of Heaven (cf. P. M. Witzel, AnOr 6 [1933] 45-68)
GE	The late ("canonical") version of the Gilgamesh Epic, cited according to Thompson, Gilg.
GEN	Gilgamesh, Enkidu, and the Netherworld, ed. Shaffer, as below
Gilg. Bo.	KUB 4 12: Thompson, Gilg. pp. 43f.; ANET³ p. 82 (obv.)
Gilg. Har. B	van Dijk, Sumer 13 (1957) 66 and 91, ed. van Dijk, Sumer 14 (1958) 114-21; ANET³ p. 504
Gilg. Me.	Meissner, MVAG 7 (1902); ANET³ 89f.
Gilg. Meg.	Goetze and Levy, Atiqot 2 (1959) 121-28 pl. XVIII
Gilg. Mi	CT 46 16, ed. Millard, Iraq 26 (1964) 99-105; ANET³ p. 507
Gilg. O.I.	Bauer, JNES 16 (1957) 254-62; ANET³ pp. 504f.
Gilg. P	Langdon, PBS 10/3 (1917); ed. Jastrow and Clay, YOR 4/3 (1920) 62-86; Thompson, Gilg. pp. 20-24; ANET³ pp. 76-78
Gilg. Ur	UET 6 394, ed. Gadd, Iraq 28 (1966) 105-121
Gilg. Y	Jastrow and Clay, YOR 4/3 (1920) 87-102; Thompson, Gilg. pp. 25-29; ANET³ pp. 78-81
GLL	Gilgamesh and the Land of the Living, ed. Kramer, JCS 1 (1947) 3-46; van Dijk in Garelli, Gilg. pp. 69-81
Hit. Gilg.	The Hittite version(s); Tablet I cited from ed. Otten, Ist.Mitt. 8 (1958) 93-125; other fragments from ed. Friedrich, ZA 39 (1929) 1-82 (cf. Laroche, RHA 82 [1967] 121-38); for no. 8, see ANET³ pp. 85f.
Shaffer, Sources	A. Shaffer, Sumerian Sources of Tablet XII of the Epic of Gilgameš (unpubl. Ph.D. diss., University of Pennsylvania, 1963)

2. C. J. Gadd, Teachers (1956) p. 7f.; D. O. Edzard, in H. W. Haussig (ed.), Wörterbuch der Mythologie 1 (1965) 72; T. Jacobsen and W. W. Hallo apud H. N. Wolff, JAOS 89 (1969) 393 n. 2. Cf. the doubt about Gilg Me implied by von Soden, MDOG 85 (1953) 21.

3. S. Langdon, JRAS 1932 912; Shaffer (Sources, p. 4) also cites SRT 35.

4. S. N. Kramer, "The Epic of Gilgameš and its Sumerian Sources: A Study in Literary Evolution," JAOS 64 (1944) 7-23, 83.

5. Kramer, JAOS 64 (1944) 18. Cf. Jack M. Sasson, "Some Literary Motifs in the Composition of the Gilgamesh Epic," Studies in Philology 69 (1972) 264. For a possible seventh Sumerian episode see Kramer in UET 6/1 p. 7 no. 60.

6. Garelli, Gilg. p. 87f.

Ancient Near Eastern Studies in Memory of J. J. Finkelstein
Connecticut Academy of Arts and Sciences, Memoir 19

the beginning of a composition,[7] and that GLL (version A),[8] GA, and GEN were listed as separate entries in Sumerian literary catalogues.[9] These facts show that none of these tales was preceded by another.[10] That GLL A, GA, GEN, and fragment B of DG were not followed by any other episode is shown by the doxological formula (DN) zà-mí(-zu du_{10}-ga-àm) with which they end, since this formula typically appears at the end of a composition.[11]

The demonstration of the separateness of the Sumerian tales at first had no effect upon general opinion concerning the Old Babylonian tablets and fragments of the Akkadian version. They were still taken to be parts of an already unified epic, rather than independent tales like the Sumerian ones. This assumption is still widely taken for granted.[12]

The direct textual evidence in favor of such an assumption is not extensive. The Old Babylonian Gilg P is identified in its colophon as tablet two of its series and Gilg Y, its sequel, is, to judge from its appearance and script, from the same edition.[13] This edition thus contained at least four tablets, the first not extant, the second dealing with the advent of Enkidu, and the third with preparations for the journey to the Cedar Mountain; the latter implies at least one more tablet describing the journey itself. While this evidence points to a composition which contains more than a single episode, it hardly adds up to the full, integrated epic known from GE. None of the other Old Babylonian texts demonstrably belongs to this edition and most, with their different appearance, number of columns, and find-sites, clearly do not. Their mere existence in itself implies nothing about the possible integration of the epic in this period.

Recently H. N. Wolff attempted briefly to adduce some evidence which might overcome doubts about the epic's early unification.[14] She noted the use of a "week-long suspension" followed by a "change of the character and outlook of the person concerned"[15] twice, at strategic points, in the Old Babylonian version, and inferred that this indicates "the work of an author pursuing a specific line of thought." She concluded, however, that this implies at most a single author (not necessarily a single composition) and is, in addition, subjective.

II

The earliest direct evidence for a fuller Gilgamesh epic comes from the 14th-13th century Gilgamesh texts unearthed at Boghozköi. The Akkadian fragment Gilg Bo, which is not part of the "canonical" version[16] covers part of the journey to the Cedar Mountain on its obverse, while its reverse contains part of the Bull of Heaven episode.[17] These two episodes were therefore connected by the time of this fragment, the 14th-13th centuries,[18] and the connection is not limited to the "canonical" version.[19]

In the Hittite version[20] a number of tablets likewise cover several episodes each. The first tablet covers in abbreviated form the events narrated in GE I-V. The events of GE VI (as well as III-V) are presupposed by Hit. Gilg No. 8 and its partially overlapping duplicate No. 9, which include episodes found in GE VII-X, from Enkidu's dream in which the gods condemn him for his part in killing Huwawa and the Bull of Heaven,

7. See G. Castellino, VT Supplements 4 (1957) 117f. for a list of texts, and compare the comment of E. A. Speiser, Genesis (1964) p. lvii.

8. The same is true of GLL version B (ì(NI)-a-lum-lum): see catalogues B:16, L:39, P:14, and UET 6/1 123:10 (see the next note for bibliography).

9. Kramer, BASOR 88 (1942) 10-19 (catalogues P and L). Further catalogues listing Gilgamesh texts have since come to light: UET 5 86 (catalogue B; see I. Bernhardt and S. N. Kramer in WZJ 6 [1956-57] 393 n. 4); UET 6/1 123 (see Kramer, RA 55 [1961] 169-76).

10. This type of argument is challenged by C. Wilcke, Lugalbanda (1969) p. 8.

11. Cf. also UET 6/1 60:17.

12. A. Heidel, The Gilgamesh Epic² (1949) p. 15; T. Jacobsen, in H. and H. A. Frankfort (ed.), Before Philosophy (1949) p. 223; E. A. Speiser, ANET³ p. 73; T. Bauer, JNES 16 (1957) 261; B. Landsberger, in Garelli, Gilg. pp. 33f.; J. R. Kupper, Garelli, Gilg. p. 102; H. W. F. Saggs, The Greatness That Was Babylon² (1968) p. 370; J. J. Stamm, Asiatische Studien 6 (1952) 12; J. Laessøe in Studia Orientalia Pedersen (1953) p. 211.

13. Jastrow and Clay, YOR 4/3 (1920) 17f. A. Shaffer has now confirmed that *šūtur eli* [ ] in the colophon of Gilg P was the Old Babylonian incipit and hence the title of the epic; see his note apud D. J. Wiseman, "A Gilgamesh Epic Fragment from Nimrud," Iraq 37 (1975) 158 n. 22. For the position of the incipit in the colophon cf. the Old Babylonian colophons in Lambert and Millard, Atra-ḫasīs (1969) p. 32.

14. JAOS 89 (1969) 393 n. 2.

15. Cf. Sasson, Studies in Philology 69 (1972) 272.

16. Von Soden, MDOG 85 (1953) 22.

17. The reverse apparently skips from Gilgamesh's toilet (=GE VI 1ff.) to Ishtar's indignation (=GE VI 80ff.), omitting, with the possible exception of rev. 8f., Ishtar's proposal and Gilgamesh's rejection. Cf. J. R. Kupper in Garelli, Gilg. p. 100 and von Soden in ZA 59 (1959) 221.

18. H. Otten, in Garelli, Gilg. p. 139; cf. B. Landsberger and H. Tadmor, IEJ 14 (1964) 214.

19. See n. 16.

20. See the works cited in the list of abbreviations s.v. Hit. Gilg., and A. Kammenhuber, Münchner Studien zur Sprachwissenschaft 21 (1967) 45-58.

through Gilgamesh's mourning over Enkidu and his meeting with Siduri. These tablets clearly bespeak an integrated epic. According to A. Kammenhuber the Hittite Gilgamesh fragments date from the second half of the fourteenth century,[21] giving a *terminus ad quem* for the integration of the epic.

Whether the Akkadian fragment and the Hittite tablets point to the state of affairs in the Old Babylonian period cannot be determined, since the derivation of the Boghazköi Akkadian texts[22] and the Hittite versions of Babylonian literature[23] is still an open question.

III

Despite the paucity of direct evidence for the integration of the epic in the Old Babylonian period, there is ample indirect evidence to this effect. A comparison of GE with its Sumerian forerunners reveals certain features which are either unique to the Akkadian epic or play a unique role in it and constitute the cement unifying its episodes. These features are all attested in the Old Babylonian version.

The theme which unifies the epic's several episodes is, as is well known, Gilgamesh's quest to overcome death in some fashion, a quest also recognized in a collection of omens about Gilgamesh where he is said to have "sought life like Ziusudra."[24] Dossin has noted that "the unity [of the epic] is assured for it as much, if not more, by the role given to Enkidu as by that of Gilgamesh."[25] It is Enkidu's death, which gave Gilgamesh a first-hand experience of death, which became the turning point from Gilgamesh's pursuit of lasting fame to his literal quest for immortality. In order for Enkidu's death to have such a decisive effect on Gilgamesh, Enkidu should be more than a servant. In the Sumerian episodes Enkidu was once or twice affectionately termed Gilgamesh's friend (ku-li),[26] though his status as servant (ìr, šubur) and Gilgamesh's as king/master (lugal) predominated.[27] The epic seized upon these sporadic hints of a loftier status for Enkidu and applied them across the board, consistently terming Enkidu Gilgamesh's friend and companion (*ibru, tappu*), brother (*aḫu*), and equal (*mašlu, kima*).[28] Already in GEN Gilgamesh had grieved over Enkidu's capture by the netherworld; he truly cared for Enkidu, servant though he was,[29] and tried to recover him. But there Gilgamesh's emotional response was not one of distraction, and did not issue in an attempt to escape death himself. Finally, it is only Enkidu's status as a friend and equal which creates a need to account for his origins.

All these developments in the character and role of Enkidu, which constitute decisive integrating factors in the epic, are already present in the Old Babylonian fragments and tablets.[30] An unpublished Nippur fragment[31] describes the creation of Enkidu to contend with Gilgamesh and bring relief to Uruk, a role which

21. Kammenhuber, Münchner Studien 21 (1967) 46.

22. Cf. A. L. Oppenheim, AnBib. 12 (1959) 292.

23. H. G. Güterbock in S. N. Kramer (ed.), Mythologies of the Ancient World (1961) p. 154; Otten, in Garelli, Gilg. p. 139; Kammenhuber, Münchner Studien 21 (1967) 46, 55; Otten (Garelli, Gilg. p. 140) and Kammenhuber (Münchner Studien 21 47) have raised the possibility that the Hurrian Gilgamesh material still consisted of separate episodes. However, the reference to Enkidu as Gilgamesh's brother (cf. Kammenhuber) implies the integrated epic, as we shall see below.

24. Lambert in Garelli, Gilg. pp. 44f.; see also GE I i 39 (Wiseman, Iraq 37 [1975] 160). Cf. the Sumerian text quoted by M. Civil, JNES 28 (1969) 72 no. 18.

25. ". . . cette unité lui est assurée autant, sinon davantage, par le rôle prête à Enkidou que par celui de Gilgameš." Academie Royale de Belgique: Bulletin de la Classe des Lettres, 5e serie, 42 (1956) 588; cf. Shaffer, Sources pp. 19, 21-25; Kramer, JAOS 64 (1944) 18-19.

26. GBH: VAS 10 196 r. "ii" 11; GEN 247 (237 in C. Wilcke's citation of the passage, ZA 59 [1959] 71; Wilcke's restoration of ku-li in the previous line seems ruled out in Shaffer's edition, Sources p. 86). GEN is the Sumerian original of GE XII, and although the Akkadian translation is hardly the work of the creator of the integrated epic, its treatment of Enkidu's status is the same. Where the Sumerian text terms Enkidu Gilgamesh's servant (ìr or šubur), the Akkadian either drops the word or reads otherwise (GEN 177, 241, 243=GE XII 6, 80, 84); the Akkadian also adds two lines, with no counterpart in the known Sumerian manuscripts, calling Enkidu Gilgamesh's brother (*aḫu*) and friend (*ibru*) (GE XII 81 and 87, added after the translations of GEN 241 and 245). On the other hand, GE XII 54 adds to the translation of GEN 222 a clause which calls Enkidu Gilgamesh's servant (ÌR); perhaps the clause is based on an unknown Sumerian *Vorlage*.

Jastrow's references to Enkidu as Gilgamesh's brother in Sumerian texts are erroneous (YOR 4/3 33): the first involves Ishtar, not Enkidu, and in the second the sign is lugal, not šeš.

27. E.g., GLL 3, 8, 9, 95, 96, 103, 153; GBH r. "ii" 17; GEN 177, 178, 206, 241; GA 42. Note, however, the similarity of GEN 250=GE XII 93, 95 to Gilg P i 20, 32-34.

28. For Old Babylonian examples of friend, equal, and like, see below, nn. 35 and 36. For friend in the later versions see Gilg Bo obv. 8, 10, 13, 21; Gilg Meg r. 2, 7, 17; Gilg Ur obv. 5, r. 60 (all Middle Babylonian); GE I iv 41; vi 1, 21; II vi 3, 6, 9; etc. For brother, see Hit. Gilg. no. 8:19, 22 (on the Hurrian version, see above. n. 23). On GE XII, see above, n. 26.

29. Cf. Shaffer, Sources pp. 22f.

30. Most of the Old Babylonian material is translated in ANET[3] pp. 76-81, 504-505, 89-90, and 507 (see above, n. 1, s.v. Gilg Har B, Me, Mi, O.I., P, and Y). Two unpublished fragments are UM 29-13-570 and 2 N-T 79 (partially quoted by Shaffer, Sources p. 23 n. 3, from a copy by J. J. Finkelstein). Dr. Aage Westenholz has kindly shown me the copies he has made of both; they are to be published by W. G. Lambert.

31. 2 N-T 79:4: [*li-iš*]*-ta-an-na-an-ma* UNUG.KI *li-iš-tap-ši-iḫ*, "Let them contend, that Uruk may have peace" =GE I ii 32 (the passage is quoted by Shaffer, Sources p. 23 n. 3).

he plays in the Old Babylonian Gilg P as well.[32] This role presupposes an account of Gilgamesh's tyranny over Uruk, which is also mentioned in Gilg P.[33] Enkidu's introduction to civilization is partly narrated in the same tablet.[34] Throughout the Old Babylonian material Enkidu is called Gilgamesh's friend[35] and "like" him.[36] The Old Babylonian version of Gilgamesh's journey to Utnapishtim has the journey motivated by grief over Enkidu.[37] (Presumably Gilgamesh reached Utnapishtim in this version; there is no way to know whether the account of their meeting included a full rehearsal of the flood story, as it does in GE.[38])

Given their absence from the Sumerian episodes, each of these developments makes sense only in the context of the integrated epic,[39] the existence of which in the Old Babylonian period is thus confirmed.[40]

32. Gilg P. cols. v-vi.
33. Col. iv.
34. Cols. ii-iii.
35. Gilg Y ii 40; iii 14; iv 5, 26; v 21f; vi 27; Gilg Har B 3, 10; Gilg O.I. obv. 14; r. 5 (cf. 1); Gilg Me ii 7; Gilg Mi iii 4′.
36. Gilg P i 17; v 15.
37. Gilg Me ii; Gilg Mi iii.
38. Cf. the opposing views of Landsberger and Matouš in Garelli, Gilg. pp. 34 and 90.
39. Cf. also Bauer, JNES 16 (1957) 261f.
40. That some of these developments took place in Sumerian forerunners which are not available to us is ruled out by Kramer, JAOS 64 (1944) 16 n. 60. More recently discovered variant recensions of the Sumerian compositions show no greater similarity to the Akkadian epic in matters which touch upon the essence of that epic.

THE OLD BABYLONIAN TEXTS FROM KISH: A FIRST REPORT*

N. Yoffee
University of Arizona

The city of Kish bears a unique reputation in the Mesopotamian historical tradition, a reputation that far exceeds any direct textual evidence from Kish and which is not associated with any kings or princes who extended political hegemony from their home city. The references to Kish in the "Sumerian King List," accompanying arguments of a putative amphictyony centered in Kish (based on the use of a royal title that may incorporate the name of the city), and the association of Sargon of Agade with Kish, are all familiar issues to the student of early Mesopotamian history.[1] During the Akkadian and Ur III periods there are no indications of any political strength centered in Kish. In the absence of power following the collapse of Ur III, kings from Kish interacted with many of their neighbors in the twin struggles for independence and dominion. With the establishment of the primacy of a long-lived dynasty in Babylon, however, Kish became only a part of the larger Babylonian state, albeit an important part. Although texts and archaeological materials indicate that Kish was at times an important and prosperous community well into the Sassanian period,[2] its proximity to its more important neighbor, only eight miles to the west, reduced Kish to the status of practically a suburb of Babylon.[3]

While reviewing some recent publications of Old Babylonian texts,[4] I was struck by the considerable number of documents that apparently originated in Kish and which date to the time of the last kings of the "First Dynasty of Babylon." These texts are important, on the one hand, because the terminal part of the Old Babylonian period has been only meagerly attested. On the other hand, compared to texts from earlier times, these documents show marked differences in economic and religious activities during the time of the extreme weakness of the last kings of Babylon.

In an effort to construct a model that would account for these changes in *late* Old Babylonian society, I recently took advantage of the chance to study the texts recovered from the site of Kish by French and British excavation teams, which are now conserved in museums in Istanbul and Oxford respectively.[5] The nature of those documents, however, makes it necessary to examine more closely the history, and sources for that history, of the *earliest* part of the Old Babylonian period (in the area around Kish). In this paper I will initially review, briefly, the standard literature concerning the political history of this area, as some reconsideration

*The substance of this paper was read at the 184th meeting of the American Oriental Society, Santa Barbara, Cal., March 27, 1974.

1. W. W. Hallo's discussion of the titles lugal kiš.ki and lugal kiš (only the latter supposedly equivalent to *šar kiššatim*) in Early Mesopotamian Royal Titles (1957) 21-28, concludes that kiš and kiš.ki were not distinct designations, but rather both referred only to the "king of Kish." A suggestion that the veneration of the title "King of Kish" was due to a political organization centered around Kish paralleling Jacobsen's notion of a "Kengir league" ("Early Political Development in Mesopotamia," ZA 52 [1957] 91ff., reprinted in Toward the Image of Tammuz, ed. W. Moran [1970] pp. 140-41; cf. also Image of Tammuz pp. 150ff. for a discussion of the kings of Kish) was made by Gelb, in "Sumerians and Akkadians in their Ethno-Linguistic Relationship, Genava 8 266-67. In the same volume, in "Sumerer und Semiten in der frühen Geschichte Mesopotamiens," pp. 241-58, Edzard discussed the Semitic names in the Kish dynasty, first to rule after the flood according to the "Sumerian King List," and the opposition between northern and southern dynasties first mentioned by Kraus, ZA 50 (1952) 45ff. The most famous of the early Kish kings is Etana, central figure of the myth usually called by his name. (For the last textual additions to "Etana," see J. Kinnier-Wilson, "Some Contributions to the Legend of Etana," Iraq 31 (1969) 8-17, and for the most recent discussion, H. Freydank, "Die Tiertafel im Etana-Mythos: Ein Deutungsversuch," MIO 17 [1971] 1-13.) Some kings of Kish not in the Sumerian King List are noted by A. Goetze, "Early Kings of Kish," JCS 15 (1961) 105-111.

2. McGuire Gibson, City and Area of Kish (1972) p. 3, and Langdon in H. Field's Arabs of Central Iraq, Field Museum Memoirs, Anthropology 4 (1935) 81.

3. Langdon, Ecavations at Kish 1 (1924) 31. See there, pp. 43-44, for references to the overgenerous estimates of classical writers who seemed to have thought that the ruins of Kish were actually a part of Greater Babylon. Brief accounts of early European explorers to the area can be found in Langdon, Exc. Kish 1 Chapter 4, and Gibson, Kish p. 67. P. R. S. Moorey will present evaluations of these early accounts and a detailed catalogue of the material finds arranged by provenience at the site of Kish in his forthcoming monograph on Kish.

4. In the course of preparing a dissertation on aspects of the Crown's administration and bureaucracy in the latter part of the Old Babylonian period: "The Economic Role of the Crown in the Old Babylonian Period (unpubl. Ph.D. dissertation, Yale University, 1973; revised edition in press, to appear in Bibliotheca Mesopotamica, Undena Publications).

5. This research was made possible by a grant from the American Schools of Oriental Research, and I am pleased to be able to express my appreciation to ASOR for this grant and to all those instrumental in its award.

Ancient Near Eastern Studies in Memory of J. J. Finkelstein
Connecticut Academy of Arts and Sciences, Memoir 19

of the historical sources is now in order. Then, I will present a progress report on the research accomplished in connection with my proposed publication of the as yet unpublished and/or unedited texts from Kish. Finally, I will discuss, albeit in abbreviated form, a few thoughts on social change in the Old Babylonian period, particularly as some of these thoughts were generated by the study of texts from Kish.

The first notice of Old Babylonian tablets said to have come from Kish was announced in a few brief paragraphs by the Rev. Johns in 1910.[6] Johns had been given access to a fairly large collection of tablets, of which he summarized the dates and contents of only twenty-five. There was immediate interest in the tablets due to the appearance, together with the second and third kings of the "First Dynasty of Babylon," of two new and at least partly contemporary kings, Mananâ and Yawium. Most of the tablets, according to Johns, concerned the business activities of one Šumšunu-watar. In 1911 Johns published a few of the dates from this collection[7]; in the same year he allowed Stephen Langdon to publish thirty-one tablets, all of which were later acquired by the Royal Scottish Museum in Edinburgh.[8] The remainder of the collection was dispersed, and the majority of the texts mentioned in Johns' articles have not turned up to this day.

Also in 1911, Thureau-Dangin published seven tablets with dates or references to kings Mananâ and Yawium and another new king, Ḫalium.[9] These tablets also concerned transactions of Šumšunu-watar. He also published an inscription of Ašduni-e/arim, an independent king of Kish in the Old Babylonian period, from whose reign there are still no dated tablets. According to the seller of these texts, their provenience was Uhaimir, and in two of the tablets the oath was sworn in the name of Zababa, patron deity of Kish. Thureau-Dangin therefore concluded that all of the texts of Johns and Langdon, also said to come from Uhaimir, as well as his own, came from Kish.

In 1912, intrigued by the Thureau-Dangin tablets which he himself had obtained,[10] and by the possibilities of excavating Kish, H. de Genouillac carried out operations there lasting three months.[11] Over 1400 tablets and fragments were unearthed by this expedition, mainly from an area near the ziggurat in Uhaimir. It was already heavily pitted, and in Genouillac's opinion it was the place of origin of the published Mananâ-Yawium tablets.[12] The excavated tablets were "duly divided"[13] between the Royal Ottoman Museum in Istanbul and the Louvre, with Istanbul receiving the lion's share, but Paris obtaining the best preserved ones. These latter include the Old Babylonian letters later edited by Kupper,[14] and most of the Sumerian literary materials. Because of the Great War and ensuing inconstancies, Genouillac was unable to return to Istanbul for over a decade, but selected texts, together with a brief catalogue, finally appeared under the title Premières recherches archéologiques à Kich in 1924. The second volume, containing the copies of all the texts in Paris, came out the following year.

Prior to the publication of Genouillac's campaign, the Field Museum of Chicago and the Ashmolean Museum of Oxford, under the general leadership of Stephen Langdon, decided to excavate at Kish.[15] This expedition, lasting ten years beginning in 1923, turned up hundreds of tablets and fragments. Of these, Gelb has published a volume of Old Akkadian texts,[16] van der Meer one of lexical texts,[17] and Gurney[18] and Langdon[19] many selected, interesting pieces. To this date, however, only three Old Babylonian documents have been published[20] (excluding lexical or literary materials that may be Old Babylonian).

6. "A New King of Kish?," PSBA 32 (Dec. 1910) 279-81.

7. "The Mananâ-Iapium Dynasty at Kish," PSBA 33 (Mar. 1911) 98-103.

8. "Tablets from Kish," PSBA 33 (Nov. 1911) 185-92 with 7 plates, and (Dec. 1911) 232-42 with 7 plates.

9. "Ašduni-erim roi de Kiš," RA 8 (1911) 65-79. In Santa Barbara, Prof. A. L. Oppenheim informed me that another unpublished tablet with an incomplete date of Ḫalium is in the Oriental Institute.

10. Genouillac, Kich 1 10.

11. Genouillac, Kich 1 15ff.; Gibson, Kish p. 69 gives a brief description and review of these excavations.

12. Genouillac, Kich 1 19-20.

13. The "division" seems to have been carried out under dubious auspices; cf. Genouillac, Kich 1 20 and n. 1 (this was kindly pointed out to me by Prof. F. R. Kraus).

14. "Lettres de Kiš," RA 53 (1959) 19-38; 177-82.

15. Exc. Kish 1 (1924) is the first volume of Langdon's report. Gibson, Kish pp. 70ff., gives a good description of the excavations. A convenient bibliography for the various publications concerning the Kish excavations is to be found in R. S. Ellis, A Bibliography of Mesopotamian Archaeological Sites (Wiesbaden, 1972) 47-48.

16. Sargonic Texts in the Ashmolean Museum, Oxford, MAD 5 (1970).

17. Syllabaries A, B[1] and B, OECT 4 (1938); also, many texts from Kish were published by P. van der Meer in "Tablets of the ḪAR-ra=*ḫubullu* Series in the Ashmolean Museum," Iraq 6 (1939) 144ff.

18. "A List of Copper Objects," Iraq 31 (1969) 3-7; "The Fifth Tablet of the Topography of Babylon," Iraq 36 (1974) 39-52.

19. In OECT 6 (1927); the fragments of *enūma eliš* are from Kish.

20. These were published in "Tablets Found in Mound Z at Ḫarsagkalamma (Kish)," RA 24 (1927) 89-93; cf. Gibson, Kish p. 107 n. 182. Today, however, these tablets are not in the Ashmolean's collections.

Other texts dating to Mananâ, Yawium and related kings—altogether more than a dozen kings—were published by Lutz in 1932,[21] and in the late 1950's by Rutten[22] and Simmons.[23] From the discussions of Kraus,[24] Edzard,[25] Kupper,[26] Simmons,[27] and Reiner,[28] it is generally conceded that most of these monarchs were not local kings of Kish but had ruled over it for a time. Some of the texts referring to these kings, consequently, may not come from Kish at all, but rather from the home cities of those kings. As Zababa, patron deity of Kish, only appears in the oaths of the tablets mentioning king Yawium, the search for the home cities of the other rulers generally reduces itself to an analysis of the gods mentioned in oaths with those rulers.

Examination of all the Istanbul tablets and of the texts in Paris published in Genouillac, Kich 2, as well as a survey of the Old Babylonian documents in the Ashmolean Museum, has failed to yield so much as one tablet dated to the "Mananâ-Yawium" group of kings. Langdon, Excavations at Kish 1,[29] recorded finding a tablet of Yawium, but this tablet does not exist in Oxford. The sole exception is Genouillac, Kich 2 D 6, which has an unplaced ús-sa date and an oath by one of the kings who presumably ruled in Kish, Sumu-ditan and by the divinity Lugalmarad.[30] The parties in this text also occur in a contract published by Simmons with a different date but with the same king and god in the oath.[31] A third text, one published by Langdon, refers to Sumu-ditan, but with the god Numušda in the oath.[32] Further discussion of these early Old Babylonian kings will be incorporated in a monograph on the early history of Kish and must be deferred at this time. Genouillac's notion, however, that the texts published in 1911 came from the same pitted area from which he removed most of his texts seems fallacious. No texts of Mananâ or Yawium or of the Šumšunu-watar archive have been identified in Istanbul or Paris.[33]

On present knowledge we may group the Old Babylonian texts from Kish into three categories, roughly corresponding to the means of their acquisition[34] and in chronological sequence: First, there is the "Mananâ-Yawium" group, dating to the earliest part of the Old Babylonian period, including those tablets published by Langdon and Thureau-Dangin and a few of the texts published by Simmons. Added to these are five unpublished texts belonging to the Šumšunu-watar and related archives now conserved in the Bodleian Library at Oxford.[35] Texts that need to be considered along with these groups include those published by Lutz, Rutten, and the majority of those Simmons' texts (which belong to the YBC and NBC collections at Yale) though few of these may actually be from Kish. Second, there are texts excavated at Kish from the Genouillac and Langdon expeditions. These texts date from the reign of Sumula'el to the time of Ammi-ditana and include (in Oxford) the complete (long-form) date of year Ammi-ditana 14 in Sumerian on the

21. Real Estate Transactions from Kish, UCP 10/3 (1932).

22. "Un lot de tablettes de Mananâ," RA 52 (1958) 208-235; RA 53 (1959) 77-96; RA 54 (1960) 19-40; 147-52.

23. JCS 14 (1960) 117-25; JCS 15 (1961) 49-58.

24. "Kazallu und andere nordbabylonische Kleinstaaten vor der Zeit des Ḫammurabi," AfO 16 (1952-53) 319-23.

25. Zwischenzeit (1957) pp. 130-35, chapter on Kish. Other sections are also relevant to discussions of the early rulers of cities near Kish in the early part of the Old Babylonian period.

26. J. Kupper, Les nomades en Mésopotamie au temps des rois de Mari (1957), esp. pp. 197-203.

27. JCS 14 (1960) 75-87. This is still the most important and most comprehensive analysis of the early kings and texts from Kish.

28. "The Year Dates of Sumu-jamūtbāl," JCS 15 (1961) 121-24. Goetze's article "Sumu-yamūtbāl, a Local Ruler of the Old Babylonian Period," JCS 4 (1950) 65-72, must also be utilized in connection with the study of the history of early Old Babylonian Kish.

29. Langdon, Exc. Kish 1 13-14. This is also mentioned by Gibson in Kish p. 74 and n. 79. In this note Gibson does not give the Ashmolean number of the tablet, and, as he has since informed me, he was unable to locate it in the Ashmolean Museum. From Gibson's notes (of Langdon's notes) it is impossible to say whether this "Yawium" appears in the text itself, or was part of a date formula.

30. mu-ús-sa giš.má-gur$_8$-maḫ ^{d}nin-šubur ba-dù.

31. JCS 14 (1960) 84-85 no. 126.

32. PSBA 33 (1911) text no. 1.

33. Gibson, in Iraq 34 (1972) 119, seems to have thought that Genouillac discovered texts of the "Ḫalium, Yawium type."

34. By this I mean to imply that most of the "Mananâ-Yawium" texts were apparently obtained at about the same time (and possibly from the same dealer?); compare the articles published by Johns, Langdon, and Thureau-Dangin, and the remarks of Rutten, RA 52 (1958) 208. The texts presently in the Bodleian Library in Oxford (see n. 35 below), which were acquired by Langdon, were also purchased at about this time. I have no information concerning the tablets at Berkeley published by Lutz, or the group of texts at Yale published by Simmons, but the latter was not obtained through the same intermediaries who supplied the Kish texts at Yale that date to the end of the Old Babylonian period (texts from Kish published in YOS 13 are in the MLC collection; those edited by Simmons are in the YBC and NBC collections; see below).

35. These tablets have an "AB" signature in the Bodleian catalogue; they are now housed in the Ashmolean Museum. I must thank Dr. Moorey for his kind help in making these texts available to me. The will be published together with the Old Babylonian texts excavated at Kish and other Old Babylonian materials in Oxford. The possibility of their existence in the Bodleian Library was determined from Langdon, Exc. Kish p. 12 n. 4.

obverse and Akkadian on the reverse.[36] Third, there are texts in disparate publications which on internal criteria (references to officials of Kish, the cult of Zababa, etc. and cross-referencing), come from Kish and generally date to the end of the Old Babylonian period. Foremost among these are more than one-hundred texts published in YOS 13, all from the MLC collection at Yale, and twenty-one texts in Manchester, published in Szlechter, TJA.[37] Also in this group, but not dating to such a late period, are texts in TCL 1 of Thureau-Dangin and in Speleers, Reçueil.[38] A few of the texts recently published by Klengel in VAS 18 also belong in this third category.[39]

The Old Babylonian texts from Kish will be published duly in several installments. The Istanbul documents, including some recopies of Genouillac's texts and some copies of tablets only summarized in his catalogue, will be edited by Mr. Veysel Donbaz of the Istanbul Archaeological Museums and myself. The editions will be accompanied by commentaries on some of the more interesting materials. These include an adoption contract, wherein the parents formalize their marriage only after the adoption,[40] and an archive of sixteen texts all dated in one month in the 11th year of king Sin-muballiṭ, which refer to the production of bricks.[41] These latter documents are especially interesting for the tasks specified and the resulting reconstruction of the administrative bureau responsible for the production of the bricks in Kish. Another, and as far as I am aware, unique text is an involved account of rations. These rations are allocated according to a family-estate (*bītum*), first listing the head of the estate, this individual then followed by a list of various family members, including infants, mothers-in-law and servants. Some of the families are related, and thus the text is thought to be an example of the presence of a family-compound living unit in a Mesopotamian city.[42]

The Old Babylonian texts from Kish now in Oxford, including tablets acquired by the Kish expedition from other sites and a number of materials conserved in the Bodleian Library, will be published at a later date.[43]

One other task involved in the study of the Kish texts in Oxford will be to correlate the information in these texts with their listed proveniences, thus attempting to delineate certain living areas in Kish from both archaeological and philological perspectives. McGuire Gibson has already done much of the initial work on the proveniences and his article in Iraq 34 on the archaeological uses of cuneiform texts will point the way for future research on this part of the Kish textual project.[44]

The philological analysis of the Old Babylonian texts from Kish, however, is planned to extend beyond the examination of the contents of the excavated texts in Istanbul and Oxford. Texts from Kish date from the earliest part of the Old Babylonian period to the very end of the period. Internal investigations of the "Mananâ-Yawium" group of texts and diachronic comparisons with the excavated texts dating to the middle of the period and those purchased texts dating to its last days, will hopefully highlight some of the institutional changes occurring during an almost four-hundred year span of time.

The general model of the Old Babylonian period has heretofore tended to portray the entire block of time

36. The full Sumerian formula for this year is not found in Ungnad's article "Datenlisten" in RLA 2, nor in Morgan's lists in MCS 2.

37. Remarks on these texts by Finkelstein may be found in his "Introduction" to YOS 13 (1972) pp. 7ff. and n. 25.

38. Speleers notes in Reçueil (1925) p. i, that many of these texts were acquired for the Musée Cinquantenaire in Brussels by Genouillac; cf. Genouillac, Kich 1 10. Along with some texts from Kish, Speleers published an important collection of documents from Marad; cf. Edzard, Zwischenzeit pp. 127-29. There are also a few texts from Marad in the Ashmolean's collections.

39. VAS 18 (1973); he edited a few of the texts in JCS 23 (1970) 124ff.

40. This text is a combination of Genouillac, Kich 1, catalogue "B 17" (see also pl. 6), which is the reverse(!) and "B 28," its envelope, which preserves most of the obverse. A new copy of "B 17," now Ki 607, and a copy of Ki 618 (=B 28), plus a discussion of the text will be published in V. Donbaz and N. Yoffee, Old Babylonian Texts from Kish Conserved in the Istanbul Archaeological Museums.

41. These texts were mentioned by Kupper in RA 53 (1959) 20 and n. 3, as many persons mentioned in these tablets also occur in the letters he edited. Full editions and commentaries will appear in the monograph dealing with the Kish texts in Istanbul. Remarks on the administrative hierarchy as exemplified in these tablets will include information such as may be culled from Kupper's letters, and from those edited by Kraus in AbB 5 (1972).

42. Gelb and Diakonoff have long been interested in the social organization of the "community" in Mesopotamia, possible extended-families and lineages. For Gelb's notion (in brief) of the meaning and function of *bītum* as a socio-economic unit, see "Approaches to the Study of Ancient Society," in JAOS 87 (1967), esp. p. 6. Compare also the views of Gelb and Diakonoff in Edzard (ed.), Gesellschaftsklassen im Alten Zweistromland (1972).

43. I must thank Prof. O. R. Gurney for his kind permission to examine these texts.

44. "The Archaeological Uses of Cuneiform Documents: Patterns of Occupation at the City of Kish," Iraq 34 (1972) 113-23. Moorey's articles in Iraq 26, 28, and 30 elucidating the excavations are also invaluable in this attempt to reconstruct lifeways in Old Babylonian Kish.

after the downfall of Ur and before the fall of Babylon as an undifferentiated period of private enterprise par excellence, with especially little awareness of the socio-political structure at the end of the period. It is my contention that the economic and social influence of the crown in the Old Babylonian period was more pervasive than is often considered to be the case. The long, drawn-out time of weakness at the end of the period was marked by the diminishing amount of land controlled by the Crown and the increasing reliance of the Crown on community manpower to cultivate its land and to staff its administration. New ranks within the bureaucratic structure were created and filled by men who were probably community leaders. As these ranks became hereditary, the power of the Crown further decreased.[45]

It has been argued by Harris that toward the time of Hammurapi there was a secularizing tendency, especially insofar as court decisions were removed from temple to palace auspices.[46] From an early inspection of the continuum of texts from Kish, it is the suggestion here that toward the latter part of the Old Babylonian period the pendulum began to swing in the opposite direction. As traditional social values were breaking down in conjunction with the decrease in the Crown's influence, the socio-economic role of the temple grew increasingly. The *balṭu-šalmu* texts studied by Harris, which date predominantly to the latter stages of the period, reflect the growing economic (and perhaps emotional) importance of the temple.[47] Documents from Kish in the late Old Babylonian period associate a great many officials with the cult of Zababa and other deities venerated in Kish, and in many instances these officials assume some economic functions previously maintained by the Crown. At present, every aspect of the late Old Babylonian period is in need of research, as only recently has a sufficiently large corpus of texts become available for study. The dynamics of social and cultural change in Mesopotamia, moreover, are not very well understood in any period, and are usually attributed to shifts in ethnic populations.

It will be assumed in further analysis of the Kish texts that the political organization did not exist in a closed system, but was embedded in an environment by which it was effected and in turn reacted. Resource inputs from the community were matched by outputs of authoritative policies—most dramatically by *mīšarum*-acts—designed to channel those inputs.[48] As royal correspondence indicates, the tightly controlled political organization of Hammurapi bypassed lower-order community controls to form a powerful military and efficient economic machine.[49] This policy of centralization, however, contained the seeds of its own destruction. As the amount of territory controlled by the later Old Babylonian kings diminished, the policies of intensified centralization and proliferating bureaucracy to manage decreasing agricultural resources did not optimize the potentialities of these resources. Community leaders with their own local power bases began to assume more of the Crown's normative functions and temples became important credit institutions.

In broad terms, these seem to be some of the socio-political changes occurring in the latter part of the Old Babylonian period. It is intended that the project of analyzing the excavated and acquired texts from Kish will further test these explanatory hypotheses within a deductive framework. From this research on the Old Babylonian texts from Kish, along with the Old Babylonian materials assembled and analyzed by the Sippar and Larsa projects,[50] it is hoped that some new reflections of the developmental aspects of Mesopotamian cultural institutions in the Old Babylonian period may be gained and new methodologies for their study may be generated.

45. Arguments for this position, which cannot be adumbrated here, are discussed in the study cited in note 4, above.

46. "On the Process of Secularization under Ḫammurapi," JCS 15 (1961) 117-20. In "Some Aspects of the Centralization of the Realm under Ḫammurapi and his Successors," JAOS 88 (1968) 727-32, Harris considers that this process went unabated also under the last rulers of the dynasty.

47. "Old Babylonian Temple Loans," JCS 14 (1960) 126-37.

48. It is considered that any social system (including Mesopotamian society) "functions as a whole by virtue of the interdependence of its parts": A. Rapoport, Modern Systems Research for the Behavioral Scientist: A Sourcebook (ed. W. Buckley, Chicago, 1968) p. xvii.

49. For a recent discussion of Ḫammurapi taking a personal interest in minute affairs of his empire, see W. Leemans, "King Ḫammurapi as Judge," Symbolae David (1968) 107-29, and the review of same by Finkelstein, JAOS 90 (1970) 255-56. Ḫammurapi and a limited number of high officials with very direct loyalties to him closely administered his newly conquered territory (in the south), apparently with little recourse to local officials and community leaders. The southern part of the "empire" quickly broke away from this centralized control in Babylon during the reign of Samsu-iluna.

50. R. Harris, Ancient Sippar: A Demographic Study of an Old Babylonian City 1894-1595 B.C., Uitgaven van het Nederlands Historisch-archaeologisch Instituut te Istanbul 36 (1975). I am unaware of the current status of the Leningrad Larsa Project.

JACK FINKELSTEIN

Leon Lipson
Yale University Law School

As we meet[1] to build what raft we can out of the wreck of mortality by reminding ourselves of the force and meaning of a life that was, it may be of some use to recall briefly Jack Finkelstein's recent venture into the analysis of certain contemporary legal problems, from a perspective that others considered rather special. It was an enterprise to which, as even lawyers could see, he brought wide erudition and an ardent curiosity; but other qualities emerged as well.

Law-school friends had known of his legal interests before, though at a distance. Some of us, testing the upper layers of the deeps of Ancient Jewish Law, had had occasion to consult Jack about sources, topics, and people. He had been unsparing, both of his time and in his appraisals; he had put us on the track of many good ideas and derailed us from some bad ones. Others, from social acquaintance, knew already how in casual conversation (which his very intensity prevented from being ever wholly casual) he would take up current politics in Washington or the Hall of Graduate Studies, or the fine points of Oriental carpets or French wines, with as much zeal and zest as he bestowed on his life's work. . . .

A few years ago, Jack began to talk to us about his research project on the Goring Ox, which is only partially to be described as an investigation of the ancient origins of certain modern norms and standards in Western law—in particular, those that had to do with pecuniary composition for injuries to the person. We had first of all, of course, to get used to his time-frame and -scale. Sometimes, for example, one would seek to place in perspective his hearty approval or disapproval of a fifteenth-century English case by suggesting to him that those old materials carried little weight now, after all the years that had gone by. Later one came to see that though the fifteenth century might seem ancient to an American jurist, the fifteenth century seemed pretty recent to Jack. Still later one began to understand that, as often as not, the fifteenth century that Jack considered late was three thousand years *prior* to the fifteenth century that we considered early. To Jack, a case or decree or inscription might preserve its freshness and importance by its contemporary moment, by the principle that it illustrated, or (especially) by the place it occupied in the great chain of becoming, whose links he never tired of trying to puzzle out.

Jack had an ambitious plan, a multi-level problem in the history of ideas, a lot of history to fit together, a great deal of evidence to organize and explain; miles to go, and promises to keep. If experts or judges got in his way, he gave them attentive hearing and limited mercy. He swung his vast learning lightly, without malice. In conversation as in his written work, his exposition was dramatic. He used bold colors and long strokes on a canvas that was large enough to make room for the cosmological presuppositions of the Hittites and the ecological imperatives of Spaceship Earth. He would marshal the smallest of details in order to throw light on the broadest of categories, legal and philosophical: fault, rights, justice, community, humanity, being itself.

Though Jack was professionally aware of the assumptions and mindsets built into his own intellectual make-up by his Jewish training, he also remained within that very Jewish tradition in that in the end he always tied the intellectual substance of ideas to their possible ethical import. As a Jew, also, he may have felt obliged to use his scholarly authority to insist on due recognition for ancient Mesopotamian culture in a modern world that had been—perhaps too much, he believed—affected by the culture of his own forebears: he seems, that is, to have designed and then undertaken a mission of historical atonement and redress across the millennia.

When, at last, Jack led the Goring Ox into the courtroom, he had committed himself to the exploration of fields to which he had been something of a stranger. Nothing daunted, he had plunged eagerly into the mysteries of English precedent, American social insurance, Soviet penology, foundations of tort liability, sovereign immunity, and other pockets of law each one of which takes up the full time of many a specialist. To us he sometimes seemed to be approaching the new subjects as a *naïf*; that was not wholly wrong, but we may have erred in demanding subtlety when we ought simply to have respected profundity. Because he had

1. The text of this address was delivered at the memorial service held in Dwight Chapel, Yale University, on December 19, 1974. For other memorial notices, see William W. Hallo, Assur 1/4 (1975) 1-2, and Harry A. Hoffner, Jr., JAOS 95/4 (1975) 589-91. [*ed.*]

Ancient Near Eastern Studies in Memory of J. J. Finkelstein
Connecticut Academy of Arts and Sciences, Memoir 19

not yet practiced the convenient moves by which the prudent adept slides basic questions out of the way, he produced an original and challenging structure of first principles, historic development, and doctrinal confrontation. No specialist would accept that structure without demur; none would mistake it for the product of another specialist in the same pocket; but none could ignore it safely. Thus he swiftly made himself a welcome intruder, one who caused far less trouble than he was worth. Advocates and courts were quick to recognize his contribution; he has been cited by the highest of judicial authority even while, to his perplexity, the academic resonance seemed flat or muffled. Word will reach the legal scholars before long; it is a pity Jack could not stay round to watch it happen. In this field, his work is a monument on which construction has been halted, at least for the time being: a monument that even in its unfinished state dominates its countryside.

BIBLIOGRAPHY OF JACOB J. FINKELSTEIN

compiled by

Peter Machinist and Norman Yoffee

1952 "The Middle Assyrian *šulmānu*-texts," *Journal of the American Oriental Society* 72 77-80.

1953 "Cuneiform Texts from Tell Billa," *Journal of Cuneiform Studies* 7 111-176.

1954 "An Old Babylonian SA.GAZ List," in J. Bottéro (ed.), *Le Problème des Ḫabiru*, Cahiers de la Société Asiatique 12 177-181.

"Subartu and the Old Babylonian Sources," *Proceedings of the 23rd International Congress of Orientalists, Cambridge, 21st-28th August 1954* 134-135.

1955 "Subartu and Subarians in Old Babylonian Sources," *Journal of Cuneiform Studies* 9 1-7.

1956 "Hebrew חבר and Semitic °ḪBR," *Journal of Biblical Literature* 75 328-331.

"A Hittite *mandattu*-text," Journal of Cuneiform Studies 10 101-105.

"The Akkadian Religious Texts from Sultantepe in the Archaeological Museum, Ankara, Turkey," *Yearbook of the American Philosophical Society* 340-41.

1957· with O. R. Gurney, *The Sultantepe Tablets* 1, British Institute of Archaeology at Ankara, Occasional Publications, 3. London.

"Assyrian Contracts from Sultantepe," *Anatolian Studies* 7 137-44.

"The So-called 'Old Babylonian Kutha Legend," *Journal of Cuneiform Studies* 11 83-88 and 1 pl.

1958 "Bible and Babel," *Commentary* 26 431-44.

Review of Franz Köcher, *Keilschrifttexte zur assyrisch-babylonischen Drogen- und Pflanzenkunde: Texte der Serien* uru.an.na=*maltakal*, ḪAR-*ra:ḫubullu und* Ú GAR-*šú, in Orientalistische Literaturzeitung* 53 230-33.

1959 "The Bible, Archaeology, and History," *Commentary* 27 341-49.

"The Year Dates of Samsuditana," *Journal of Cuneiform Studies* 13 39-49.

Review of E. R. Lacheman, *Economic and Social Documents*, Excavations at Nuzi, 7, in *American Journal of Archaeology* 63 290-91.

1960 Review of R. Jestin, *Nouvelles Tablettes sumériennes de Šuruppak au Musée d'Istanbul*, in *American Journal of Archaeology* 64 191-92.

1961 "Ammiṣaduqa's Edict and the Babylonian 'Law Codes'," review article of F. R. Kraus, *Ein Edikt des Königs Ammi-ṣaduqa von Babylon*, in *Journal of Cuneiform Studies* 15 91-104.

Critical reviews of: J. Bottéro, *Archives royales de Mari*, 7 (Textes cunéiformes); J. Bottéro, *Archives royales de Mari*, 7 (Transcription et Traduction); M. Birot, *Archives royales de Mari*, 9 (Textes cunéiformes); E. Szlechter, *Tablettes juridiques de la 1re Dynastie de Babylone conservées au Musée d'Art et d'Histoire de Genève*, in *Journal of Cuneiform Studies* 15 128-31.

1962 "'Mesopotamia' in Cuneiform Sources," *Actes du XXV Congrès internationale des Orientalistes* 1 (Moscow) 219-225.

"Mesopotamia," *Journal of Near Eastern Studies* 21 73-92 and pl. X.

1963 "The Antediluvian Kings: A University of California Tablet," *Journal of Cuneiform Studies* 17 39-51.

"Mesopotamian Historiography," *Proceedings of the American Philosophical Society* 107 461-72.

1965 "Some New *Misharum* Material and Its Implications," *Studies in Honor of Benno Landsberger on His Seventy-fifth Birthday April 21, 1965*, Assyriological Studies 16 233-46.

1966 "Sex Offenses in Sumerian Laws," *Journal of the American Oriental Society* 86 355-72.

Ancient Near Eastern Studies in Memory of J. J. Finkelstein
Connecticut Academy of Arts and Sciences, Memoir 19

"The Genealogy of the Ḫammurapi Dynasty," *Journal of Cuneiform Studies* 29 95-118 and pls.

"Ancient Near Eastern Religion," *Darthmouth College Comparative Studies Center, Report of the 1965-66 Seminar on Religion in Antiquity*, ed. J. Neusner (in private circ., 1966) 92-103.

1967 co-editor with Moshe Greenberg of *Oriental and Biblical Studies: Collected Writings of E. A. Speiser*, Philadelphia, University of Pennsylvania Press.

"E. A. Speiser: An Appreciation," *ibid.*, 605-16.

"A Late Old Babylonian Copy of the Laws of Ḫammurapi," *Journal of Cuneiform Studies* 21 (Albrecht Goetze Anniversary Volume) 39-48 and pl.

"*Ana bīt emim šasû*," *Revue d'Assyriologie* 61 127-36.

1968 *Cuneiform Texts from Babylonian Tablets in the British Museum*, 48: *Old Babylonian Legal Documents*, London, British Museum.

"Mishpaṭ: Ha-Mishpaṭ ba-Mizraḥ ha-qadmon (=Law: Law in the Ancient Near East)," in *Encyclopaedia Miqraʾit* 5 588-614.

"An Old Babylonian Herding Contract and Genesis 31:38f.," *Journal of the American Oriental Society* 88/1 (Essays in Memory of E. A. Speiser=American Oriental Series 53) 30-36.

1969 Contributions to J. B. Pritchard (ed.), *Ancient Near Eastern Texts Relating to the Old Testament* (3rd edition), Princeton, Princeton University Press, 523-28 (Collections of Laws from Mesopotamia and Asia Minor), 542-49 (Additional Mesopotamian Legal Documents).

"Three Amarna Notes," *Eretz Israel* 9 (W. F. Albright Volume) 33-34.

"The Laws of Ur-Nammu," *Journal of Cuneiform Studies* 22 66-82.

"The Ḫammurapi Law Tablet BE XXXI 22," *Revue d'Assyriologie* 63 11-27 and pl.

"The Edict of Ammiṣaduqa: A New Text," *Revue d'Assyriologie* 63 45-64, 189-90.

Review of W. G. Lambert and A. R. Millard, *Atra-ḫasīs: The Babylonian Story of the Flood*, in *Journal of Biblical Literature* 88 477-78, 480.

1970 "On Some Recent Studies in Cuneiform Law," review article of *Symbolae Iuridicae et Historicae Martino David Dedicatae, 2: Iuris Orientis Antiqui*, in *Journal of the American Oriental Society* 90 243-56.

1971 Review notice of S. Parpola, *Neo-Assyrian Toponyms*, in *Bulletin of the American Schools of Oriental Research* 202 30.

1972 *Old Babylonian Letters and Documents*, Yale Oriental Series, 13, New Haven, Yale University Press.

"Albrecht Goetze," *Journal of the American Oriental Society* 92 197-203.

"Albrecht Goetze," *Yearbook of the American Philosophical Society* 174-78.

1973 "Mesopotamia: Cuneiform Law," *Encyclopaedia Judaica* 16 (2nd printing) 1505f-1505k.

"The Name of Ḫammurapi's Sixth Year," *Revue d'Assyriologie* 67 111-18.

"The Goring Ox: Some Historical Perspectives on Deodands, Forfeitures, Wrongful Death and the Western Notion of Sovereignty," *Temple Law Quarterly* 46 169-290.

1974 "Bibliography of Albrecht Goetze (1897-1971)," *Journal of Cuneiform Studies* 26 2-15.

"The West, the Bible and the Ancient Near East: Apperceptions and Categorisations," *Man* 9 591-608.

"ʿOlam ve-Adam ba-Kosmologiyah shel ha-Mizraḥ ha-qadmon ve-ha-Miqra (=The Universe and Man in the Cosmology of the Ancient Near East and of the Bible)," *Molad* NF 6 122-33 (translation of preceding entry).

1976 "*Šilip rēmim* and Related Matters," *Cuneiform Studies in Honor of Samuel Noah Kramer*, Alter Orient und Altes Testament 25 187-94.

"Cutting the *sissiktu* in Divorce Proceedings," *Die Welt des Orients* 8 236-40.

TO APPEAR

"Mesopotamia 2500-1000 B.C.," in *Communication and Propaganda.*

The Ox That Gores.

INDEX

The index is limited to lexical items, and then only to those terms whose inclusion in the index was indicated by the authors of the various contributions. After some thought it was decided to print the index entries in the forms in which they were cited in the body of the volume, rather than attempt to superimpose a uniform citation system. The only exception to this rule is that if a word is cited by two different authors in two different transcription systems, all page numbers referring to that word are grouped together under the form of its first occurrence.

AKKADIAN

tamgurtu, 124 n. 47
tâmtu, 22
tašmû, 19
te-eḫ-ri, 123 n. 35
te-er-ḫi, 123 n. 35
tebû, 21
têdištu, 19
têliltu, 15 n. 34; 20
tirānu, 205
tuāru, 125 n. 53
ṭābiḫ kārī, 127 n. 69
ṭâbiḫu, 24 n. 55
ṭābtu, 127 n. 67
ṭâbu, 20
ṭêmu, 20; 22
ṭīṭu, 22
ṭuppi aḫātūti, 45
ṭuppi mārtūti u kallatūti, 45
ṭuppi riksi, 45 and nn. 1, 2
u, 19
ú-qu-u, 19
û, 152
ubān ḫaṣî qablītum, 203
ugbabtum, 148
-u(m), 19
um-mu, 12 n. 20
umma, 122
ummi eqli, 122 n. 28
ummu, 153
ummum, 152; 153
ûmu, 20
umum, 153
uppu, 129ff.
uppi aḫi, 131
uqqû, 21
urqîtu, 20; 23
uššur, 205
uṭṭurū, 126
uznu, 21; 22
zakāru šuma, 169
zateru, 164
zibbatu, 15 n. 34
zikru, 23
zīm labbi, 73
zittu, 173
zūzu, 123

SUMERIAN AND LOGOGRAMS

A, 16; 18; 20; 21
A.AB.BA, 22
A.RÁ, 16; 20; 22
AB, 16; 22
AN, 20; 22; 23
AN.KI.A, 25
ALIM, 16; 21
apen, 153
araguba, 152
ASARI, 16
AŠ UGU, 124 n. 51
bad, 149
bař$_4$, 149
BÍ, 16; 17; 21
B[ÍR], 16; 18
BU, 16; 21
BUR, 18
DA, 16; 18; 19 and n. 42
DAGAL, 204 n. 35
DAL ŠÀ, 203
dele, 153
DINGIR, 15 n. 34; 16; 18; 19; 20; 21; 22; 23; 25 and n. 58
DIRI, 12 n. 21; 20; 22
DU, 17 and n. 40
DÙ, 15 n. 34; 17; 20; 21; 22; 25
[DU$_6$.D]U, 16
DU$_8$, 16; 17; 20; 22
DU$_{10}$, 17; 20
DÚR, 16; 19; 20; 21
É, 17; 20; 21 n. 48
È, 17; 20
[È?], 21
E$_{11}$, 17
EN, 25
EN.GI$_6$.DU.DU, 24 n. 55
EN.KUR.KUR, 16; 18; 21
ÈŠ/ŠÈ, 20
GA, 17
gag, 149
GAL, 16; 20; 22
[GAL?], 15 n. 34
gàr, 153
gaza-da, 160
[GE$_{14}$?], 17; 21; 22
GI, 16; 20; 21; 22; 23
[GI?], 17
GIB, 124
GIL, 16
GILIM, 16
GIL(IM), 21; 23 and n. 50
GIN, 17 n. 40
GÌR, 24 n. 55; 205
GIŠ.TÚG, 109
GIŠ-TUKUL, 149
GÚ, 17; 18
GÙ, 20
GU[R$_8$]/[GU]R$_8$/[GUR]$_8$, 17; 20; 21
ḪA, 17
ḫal, 147
ḪAR, 17
ḪI, 17
I, 24 n. 55
ÌB, 20
idim, 147
IGI, 20
ÌL, 16; 18; 21
ÌL, 18
IM, 16; 17; 21; 22
IM.DIRI, 12 n. 21
IR, 17; 19 n. 42; 21; 22; 24 n. 51
IR/IR$_5$, 18
IR$_5$17; 21; 22
ka, 154
ka-aš—bar, 148
KA×LI, 17 n. 40
kab, 153
kag$_x$, 154
KAK, 17; 22
KAK.TI, 205
KAL, 205
kas, 148
ga.kas—bar, 148
kaskal, 148
kaskas, 148f.
kaš, 148
KI.GUB, 205
KIB, 17
kisal, 153
KIŠIB.MEŠ, 205
kižal, 153
KU, 16; 17; 20
KÙ, 15 n. 34; 20; 21
KU$_6$, 17; 22
KUL, 22
KUN, 15 n. 34
KUN.SAG.GA, 15 n. 34
kur, 152
KUR, 17
kur$_4$, 152
LÁ, 25
lá, 154
LAGAB, 20
lagab, 153
lagal$_x$, 153
lagar, 153
LI, 18; 23
LI.LI, 23
LU, 25
LÚ, 16; 18; 19; 20
LUGAL, 16; 20; 25
LUGAL.DÚR, 16
MA, 17; 18; 19; 20; 21; 22; 23
MA$_4$, 17; 20
MAḪ, 16; 20; 21; 22; 23
MAR, 22; 25
MÂR, 15 n. 32
maš, 152
ME, 17 n. 40
MER, 25
mèš, 153
mež, 153
MIN, 17
MU, 17 n. 40; 18; 21
MU.BÍ, 21 n. 47
MU$_6$, 17 n. 40
MU$_9$, 17; 21
MUN, 127 n. 67
NA, 21; 202
nagal$_x$, 153
NE, 17
NÉ.BI.RU, 20
NIGIN, 23
nin$_x$, 153
NU, 19; 20
NUN, 20; 21; 22
nun, 153
PA$_4$, 21
pab, 148
pap, 148
RA, 15 n. 34; 17; 18; 19 and nn. 42, 43; 23
RA/RÁ, 17
RA(<RI), 22
RÁ, 16; 17 and n. 40

PROPER NAMES